Facets of Qing Daoism

Daoism series

Facets of Qing Daoism

Monica Esposito

UniversityMedia
2016

Copyright © 2016 UniversityMedia, Wil / Paris
www.universitymedia.org
All rights reserved.

Printed on acid-free and lignin-free paper

Library of Congress Cataloging-in-Publication Data
Esposito, Monica 1962–2011
    Facets of Qing Daoism. / Monica Esposito
    p. cm. — (UniversityMedia, East-West Discovery)
    Includes bibliographical references and index
    ISBN 978-3-906000-07-7 (acid-free paper)
    1. China—Religion—17th century—18th century—19th century.
    2. Daoism—Taoism—Quanzhen—Longmen—History.
    3. China—Intellectual life—Qing dynasty.
    4. Religion—Daoism—Buddhism.
    5. China—History—17th century—18th century—19th century.
I. Title.

ISBN 978-3-906000-06-0 (hardcover, 2014)
ISBN 978-3-906000-07-7 (paperback, 2016)

Dr. Monica Esposito (1962–2011)

Contents

List of Tables and Figures V
List of Abbreviations VI
List of Publications by Monica Esposito VIII
Preface by the Editor 1

1. DAOISM IN THE QING (1644–1911) 5

History 9
    The Zhengyi School 9
    The Quanzhen School 12
    The Western School 18
    The Jingming School 19
Texts 21
    Canons 21
    Inner Alchemical Collections 22
    Ritual Texts 30
    Gazetteers 30
Worldview 33
    Syncretism of the Three Teachings 33
    Cultural Integration: State Ritual and Standardization of Local Cults ... 34
    Morality Books (*Shanshu* 善書) 36
    Cultural Diversity: Sectarian Religion and Precious Scrolls ... 36
Practice 39
    Spirit Writing 39
    Inner Alchemy Simplified 41
References 43

2. THE LONGMEN SCHOOL AND ITS CONTROVERSIAL HISTORY DURING THE QING DYNASTY 55

Preface 55
Introduction: Origins of the Longmen lineage in the *Mind-Lamp* ... 57
The Foundation: The role of Baiyun guan in the Orthodox Longmen lineage. Brief analysis of Epigraphic Sources 63
The Pillars: Patriarchs and their Lineage 67
    The Orthodox Longmen lineage at Baiyun guan and Zhao Daojian ... 67
    The Longmen lineage at Huashan. Ma Zhenyi and Wang Qingzheng ... 71
    Foundation of the Longmen lineage in Huashan by Jiang Shanxin ... 73
    The Second Patriarch: Zhang Dechun 75

The Third Patriarch: Chen Tongwei 76
The Longmen lineage at Laoshan: Sun Xuanqing 80
The Orthodox Longmen lineage from the 4th to the 7th Generation 82
The Fourth Patriarch: Zhou Xuanpu 82
The Fifth Patriarch: Zhang Jingding 86
The Sixth Patriarch: Zhao Zhensong 88
The Seventh Patriarch: Wang Changyue 90
A proof of the a posteriori creation of the Orthodox Longmen lineage:
The case of Wu Shouyang 100
THE ANCESTORS 108
The specificity of the Longmen lineage: the figure of Donghua Dijun ... 108
Donghua Dijun as Xiaotong jun or Li Babai 111
Donghua Dijun as Li Tieguai and Li Ya 114
The messianic power of the Perfected Li 121
CONCLUSION 126
ABBREVIATIONS 130
PRIMARY & SECONDARY SOURCES 131

3. LONGMEN DAOISM IN QING CHINA: DOCTRINAL IDEAL AND LOCAL REALITY 143

Wang Changyue (d. 1680), the Longmen reformer 147
The precepts as means to attain Immortality 149
Allusion to Chan Buddhism in Wang's soteriological doctrine 151
Confucian self-education and Buddhist soteriology 153
The creation of Longmen branches after Wang Changyue 155
The local Jingaishan tradition and its founding patriarchs 156
Min Yide, the main compiler of Longmen texts 160
Min Yide's works at Mt. Jingai, sanctuary of Longmen Yunchao branch 162
The Secret of the Golden Flower and Min Yide's Longmen doctrine 165
The esoteric ordination in the Longmen branch of Mt. Jingai 169
The joint cultivation of Nature and Vital Force 171
The ambiguous figure of Perfected Yin and his doctrine of Central Path 173
Min Yide's "Path of Men" and "Path of Immortals" 177
The doctrine of Healing the World and its corpus of texts 179
The efficacy of the Celestial Immortals in the world 183
CONCLUSION 187
APPENDIX: Annotated list of texts in the *Daozang Xubian* 道藏續編 191
ABBREVIATIONS 212
SOURCES 213

4. BEHEADING THE RED DRAGON: THE HEART OF FEMININE INNER ALCHEMY 225

    Woman, the moon, and menstrual blood 225
    Chujing 初經, the "Primal Instant" of Realization in feminine alchemy
    and the role of Celestial Water (Tiangui 天癸) 229
    Woman as inverted mirror of man 234
    CONCLUSION 236

5. AN EXAMPLE OF DAOIST AND TANTRIC INTERACTION DURING THE QING DYNASTY: THE LONGMEN XIZHU XINZONG 240

    Esoteric Teachings (Mijiao) during the Qing 240
    Daoism during the Qing: Longmen—the gate of Daoist ordinations 242
    Fundamental sources for Longmen history and doctrine: Min Yide's
        Jingai xindeng and Gu Shuyinlou cangshu 248
    Biographies of Min Yide 256
    Biographies of Jizu Daozhe 269
    The Figure of Jizu Daozhe and his role 277
        The foreign origin of Jizu daozhe 277
        Jizu daozhe as specialist of doufa, recipient of the Chishi Tuoluoni Jing .. 283
        Jizu daozhe as disciple of Wang Changyue and recipient of the Yishi
            Shuoshu 287
    CONCLUSION 291
    ABBREVIATIONS 293
    PRIMARY SOURCES 294
    SELECTIVE THEMATIC BIBLIOGRAPHY 298

COMPREHENSIVE BIBLIOGRAPHY
    PRIMARY SOURCES 307
    SECONDARY SOURCES 319
INDEX 345

List of Tables and Figures

Table 1: List of Emperors and Reigns of the Qing Dynasty.................................8
Fig. 1: Lineage Chart of Early Daoist Longmen Traditions...............................62
Fig. 2: Geographical Distribution of Early Longmen Traditions........................66
Fig. 3: Vinaya and Doctrinal Lines of the Longmen Tradition.........................146
Fig. 4: The three-faced and six-armed Vajravārāhī..227
Fig. 5: The immortal foetus...237
Fig. 6: Three-tiered altar...245
Fig. 7: Overall view of Mt. Jingai..250
Fig. 8: Old Plum Blossom Abbey on Mt. Jingai..250
Fig. 9: Mt. Jingai Abbey & Daoist priests...251
Fig. 10: Lü Dongbin (from Jindan dayao)...251
Fig. 11: Longmen genealogical chart in Min Yide's Jingai xindeng..................253
Fig. 12: Min Yide (Gu Shuyinlou cangshu)..254
Fig. 13: Tongbai abbey (Tiantai mountain range)...258
Fig. 14: Tongbai gong abbess Ye Gaoxing and the author...............................259
Fig. 15: Daoyin postures from a Mawangdui manuscript................................260
Fig. 16: The Three Sages (Confucius, Buddha, and Laozi)..............................270
Fig. 17: Pavilion of Qingyang gong in Chengdu...275
Fig. 18: Taizi hermitage on Mount Jizu..276
Fig. 19: Emperor Qianlong as the bodhisattva Mañjuśrī.................................281
Fig. 20: Genealogical chart of Longmen and Jizu daozhe................................292

List of Abbreviations

BYGZ	*Baiyun guan zhi (Hakuunkan shi)* 白雲觀志 [Gazetteer of the White Clouds Abbey] by Oyanagi Shigeta 小柳司氣太. Tokyo: Tōhō bunka gakuin Tōkyō kenkyūjo, 1934.
DJYL	*Changchun daojiao yuanliu* 長春道教源流 [Origins and Development of the Daoist Teachings of (Qiu) Changchun]. 1879. By Chen Minggui 陳銘珪 (1824–1881). In *Zangwai daoshu* 藏外道書 31:1–157.
DTYL	*Daotong yuanliu* 道統源流 [Origins and Development of Orthodox Daoism] by Yan Liuqian 嚴六謙 (*hao*: Zhuangyan jushi 莊嚴居士). Wuxi: Zhonghua yinshuju, 1929.
DZ	*Daozang* 道藏 [The Daoist Canon]. Text numbers are given according to Kristofer Schipper and Franciscus Verellen (eds.), *The Taoist Canon*, Chicago: Chicago University Press, 2004).
DZJH	*Daozang jinghua* 道藏精華 [Essential Blossoms of the Daoist Canon]. Ed. by Xiao Tianshi 蕭天石. Taipei: Ziyou 自由, 1982.
DZJHL	*Daozang jinghua lu* 道藏精華錄 [Record of Essential Blossoms of the Daoist Canon] by Ding Fubao 丁福保 (*zi*: Shouyi zi 守一子, 1874–1952). Reprint in 2 vols. (*shang / xia*). Zhejiang guji chubanshe, 1989.
DZJY	*Chongkan Daozang jiyao* 重刊道藏輯要 [Reedited Epitome of the Daoist Canon] by Yan Yonghe 閻永和, Peng Hanran 彭瀚然 and He Longxiang 賀龍驤. Chengdu: Erxian an 二仙庵, 1906. Repr. 25 vols. Taipei: Xinwenfeng, 1977.
DZXB	*Daozang xubian* 道藏續編 [Supplementary Collection of the Daoist Canon], 4 vols., by Min Yide 閔一得 (1758–1836). Wuxing: Jingai cangban, 1834. Photolithographic edition by Ding Fubao 丁福保 (*zi*: Shou yi zi 守一子, 1874–1952) entitled *Daozang xubian chuji* 道藏續編初集. Shanghai: Yixue shuju. Repr. Beijing: Haiyang 1989.

JGXD	*(Chongkan) Jingai xindeng* (重刊)金蓋心燈 [Re-edition of the Transmission of the Lamp of Mind from Mt. Jingai], 10 vols., by Min Yide (1758–1836). Wuxing: Yunchao, Gu Shuyinlou cangban, 1876 (1st ed. 1821). Repr. in *Zangwai daoshu* 藏外道書 31.
SKQS	*Wenyuan ge Siku quanshu* 文淵閣四庫全書 [Complete Texts in Four Repositories]. 1773–1782. 1500 vols. By Yong Rong 永瑢 et al. Edited by Zhu Jianmin 朱建民. Taiwan: Shangwu yinshuguan, 1986.
T	*Taishō shinshū daizōkyō* 大正新修大藏經 [Newly edited Buddhist Canon of the Taishō period], 85 vols., edited by J. Takakusu and K. Watanabe. Tokyo: Taishō issaikyō kankōkai, 1924–32.
YLCS	*Gu Shuyinlou cangshu* 古書隱樓藏書 [Collection from the Ancient Hidden Pavilion of Books], 14 vols., by Min Yide (1758–1836). Wuxing: Jingai Chunyang gong cangban, 1904. Repr. in *Zangwai daoshu* 藏外道書 10:150–721.
ZHDZ	*Zhonghua Daozang* 中華道藏 [China's Daoist Canon], 49 vols. Beijing: Huaxia, 2004.
ZWDS	*Zangwai daoshu* 藏外道書 [Daoist Texts Outside the Daoist Canon], edited by Hu Daojing 胡道靜 et al. Chengdu: Bashu shushe, 1992 (vol: 1–20); 1994 (vol. 21–36).
ZZ	*Shinsan Dainihon Zokuzōkyō* 新纂大日本續藏經 [New Great Japanese compilation of Additions to the Buddhist Canon]. 90 vols. Tokyo: Kokusho Kankōkai, 1975–1989.

List of Publications by Monica Esposito

MONOGRAPHS

1987 *La pratica del Qigong in Cina. Introduzione ad una scuola contemporanea e ai suoi testi (con una traduzione del Wuxi chanwei, breve studio sulle cinque respirazioni)* [Qigong Practice in China. Introduction to a Contemporary School and its Texts (with a translation of the *Wuxi chanwei*, Succinct Presentation of the Five Respirations)]. M.A. thesis. Venice: Università degli Studi di Venezia, Facoltà di Lingue e Letterature Straniere.

1993 *La Porte du Dragon. L'école Longmen du Mont Jin'gai et ses pratiques alchimiques d'après le Daozang xubian (Suite au Canon Taoïste)* [The Dragon Gate. The Longmen School of Mt. Jingai and its Alchemical Practices according to the *Daozang xubian* (Supplementary Collection of the Daoist Canon)]. Ph. D. thesis (under the direction of Isabelle Robinet). Paris: University of Paris VII. (For emended PDF version of 2012 see below.)

1995 *Il Qigong, la nuova scuola taoista delle cinque respirazioni* [Qigong, the New Daoist School of Five Breaths]. Padova: Muzzio. ISBN 978-8-876694-74-5

1997 *L'alchimia del soffio: La pratica della visione interiore nell'alchimia taoista* [The Alchemy of Breath: The Practice of Inner Vision in Daoist Alchemy]. Rome: Astrolabio–Ubaldini. ISBN 978-8-834012-30-7.

2012 *La Porte du Dragon—L'école Longmen du Mont Jin'gai et ses pratiques alchimiques d'après le Daozang xubian (Suite au canon taoïste)*. 2 vols. Ph. D. thesis, University Paris VII, 1993. Indexed PDF version with emendations and handwritten comments by the author and with English bookmarks for all chapters and subsections: Rorschach / Kyoto: UniversityMedia, 2012. Free download of both volumes at the address www.universitymedia.org/Esposito_PhD.html.
Vol. 1: ISBN 978-3-906000-15-2, PDF, 86 MB
Vol. 2: ISBN 978-3-906000-16-9, PDF, 54 MB

2013 *Creative Daoism*. Wil / Paris: UniversityMedia. ISBN 978-3-906000-04-6 (hardcover).

2013 *The Zen of Tantra*. Wil / Paris: UniversityMedia. ISBN 978-3-906000-25-1.

2014 *Facets of Qing Daoism*. Wil / Paris: UniversityMedia. ISBN 978-3-906000-06-0 (hardcover).

2016 *Creative Daoism*. Wil / Paris: UniversityMedia. ISBN 978-3-906000-05-3 (paperback).

2016 *Facets of Qing Daoism*. Wil / Paris: UniversityMedia. ISBN 978-3-906000-07-7 (paperback).

Editions

1998 Editor in chief of all articles on Chinese religion (Daoism) and Inner Alchemy (Daoism) in Jean Servier (ed.), *Dictionnaire critique de l'ésotérisme* [Critical Dictionary of Esoterism]. Paris: Presses Universitaires de France.

2004 (In collaboration with Hubert Durt). Special volume of *Cahiers d'Extrême-Asie* (no. 14) in memory of Isabelle Robinet: Pensée taoïste, alchimie et cosmologie [Daoist Thought, Alchemy and Cosmology].

2006~ Guidelines for project collaborators and edition of articles submitted by specialists for the *International Daozang jiyao Project*, founded and directed by Monica Esposito.

2008 *Images of Tibet in the 19th and 20th Centuries* (2 volumes). Collection "Études thématiques" (no 22). Paris: École française d'Extrême-Orient.

Articles

1988 Review of "Shen Hongxun, Taiji wuxigong–La pratica delle cinque respirazioni del Polo Supremo" [Taiji wuxigong–The Practice of the Five Breaths of the Supreme Ultimate] publ. Shanghai: Taiji wuxigong yanjiuhui, 1986. In *Biologica* (Journal of the philosophy department, Università Ca'Foscari, Venice), 1/1988, pp. 225-226.

1992 "Il Daozang xubian, raccolta di testi alchemici della scuola Longmen" [The Daozang xubian, a Collection of Alchemical Texts of the Longmen School]. Venice: *Annali dell'Istituto Universitario Orientale*, LII / 4, pp. 429-449.

1993 "Journey to the Temple of the Celestial-Eye", in David W. Reed (ed.), *Spirit of Enterprise, The 1993 Rolex Awards*. Bern: Buri, pp. 275-277.

1995 "Il Ritorno alle fonti– per la costituzione di un dizionario di alchimia interiore all'epoca Ming e Qing" [Return to the Sources. Preparation of a Dictionary of Inner Alchemy of the Ming and Qing]. In Maurizio Scarpari (ed.), *Le fonti per lo studio della civiltà cinese* [Sources for the Study of Chinese Civilization]. Venice: Libreria Editrice Cafoscarina, pp. 101-117.

1996 "Il Segreto del Fiore d'Oro e la tradizione Longmen del Monte Jin'gai" [The Secret of the Golden Flower and the Longmen Tradition of Mt. Jin'gai]. In Piero Corradini (ed.), *Conoscenza e interpretazione della civiltà cinese* [Knowledge and Interpretation of Chinese Civilization]. Venice: Libreria Editrice Cafoscarina, pp. 151-169.

1998 (In collaboration with Chen Yaoting 陳耀庭) "Yidali daojiao de yanjiu 意大利道教的研究" [Research on Daoism in Italy]. *Dangdai zongjiao yanjiu 當代宗教研究* No. 1, pp. 44-48.

1998 A dozen articles in the *Dictionnaire critique de l'ésotérisme* [Critical Dictionary of Esoterism], ed. by Jean Servier (Paris: Presses Universitaires de France): "Absorption des effluves cosmiques" [Absorption of Cosmic Essences], pp. 5-6; "Alchimie féminine" [Feminine Alchemy], pp. 51-52; "Alchimie intérieure" [Inner Alchemy] (in collaboration with Isabelle Robinet), pp. 55-58; "Art de l'alcôve" [Arts of the Bedroom], pp. 58-60; "Corps subtil" [Subtle Body], pp. 343-345; "Daoyin" [Daoyin Gymnastics], pp. 365-367; "Délivrance du cadavre" [Deliverance of the corpse], pp. 377-378; "Exorcisme" [Exorcism], pp. 500-502; "Géographie sacrée" [Sacred Geography], pp. 532-534; "Immortalité et Taoïsme" [Immortality and Daoism], pp. 642-645; "Souffle et respiration embryonnaire" [Breath and embryonic respiration], pp. 1216-1218; "Tao" [Dao], pp. 1262-1263.

1998 "Longmen pai yu *Jinhua zongzhi* banben laiyuan" 龍門派與金華宗旨版本來源 [The Longmen School and the Origin of the Different Editions of the *Secret of the Golden Flower*]. Paper presented at the Dōkyō bunka kenkyūkai 道教文化研究会 at Waseda University, Tokyo (March 1998).

1998 "The different versions of the Secret of the Golden Flower and their relationship with the Longmen school." *Transactions of the International Conference of Eastern Studies*, XLIII, pp. 90-109.

1998 "Italia no kangaku to dōkyō kenkyū" イタリアの漢学と道教研究 [Italian Sinology and Daoist Studies], in Nakamura Shōhachi 中村璋八 (ed.), *Chūgokujin to dōkyō* 中国人と道教. Tokyo: Kyūko shoin 汲古書院, pp. 83-104.

1998 (In collaboration with Jean-Luc Achard) "Una tradizione di rDzogs-chen in Cina. Una nota sul Monastero delle Montagne dell'Occhio Celeste" [A Tradition of rDzogs chen in China: A Note on the Celestial Eye Monastery]. *Asiatica Venetiana* 3, pp. 221-224.

1999 "Orakel in China" [Oracles in China]. In A. Langer and A. Lutz (eds.), Orakel – Der Blick in die Zukunft [Oracles—Visions of the Future]. Zürich: Museum Rietberg, pp. 304-314.

2000 "Daoism in the Qing (1644-1911)", in L. Kohn (ed.), *Daoism Handbook*. Leiden: Brill, pp. 623-658. (Revised edition: Chapter 1 of M. Esposito, *Facets of Qing Daoism*. Wil / Paris: UniversityMedia, 2014, pp. 5-53).

2001 "Longmen Taoism in Qing China–Doctrinal Ideal and Local Reality", *Journal of Chinese Religions* 29 (special volume on Quanzhen edited by Vincent Goossaert and Paul Katz), pp. 191-231. (Revised and enlarged edition: Chapter 3 of M. Esposito, *Facets of Qing Daoism*. Wil / Paris: UniversityMedia, 2014, pp. 143-221).

2001 "In Memoriam Isabelle Robinet (1932-2000) –A Thematic and Annotated Bibliography". *Monumenta Serica* XLIX, pp. 595-624.

2001 Articles on Daoism and Inner Alchemy in *Le grand dictionnaire Ricci de la langue chinoise* (six volumes). Paris: Desclée de Brouwer.

2004 "The Longmen School and its Controversial History during the Qing Dynasty." In John Lagerwey (ed.), *Religion and Chinese Society: The Transformation of a Field*, pp. 621–698. Hong Kong: École française d'Extrême-Orient & Chinese University of Hong Kong. (Revised edition: Chapter 2 of *Facets of Qing Daoism*. Wil / Paris: UniversityMedia, 2014, pp. 55-142).

2004 "A Thematic and Annotated Bibliography of Isabelle Robinet (revised and enlarged edition)". *Cahiers d'Extrême-Asie* 14, pp. 1-42.

2004 "Sun-worship in China–The Roots of Shangqing Taoist Practices of Light". *Cahiers d'Extrême-Asie* 14, pp. 345-402.

2004 "Gyakuten shita zō—Jotan no shintai kan" 逆転した像–女丹の身体觀 [The Inverted Mirror: The Vision of the Body in Feminine Inner Alchemy], tr. by Umekawa Sumiyo 梅川純代. In Sakade Yoshinobu sensei taikyū kinen ronshū kankō kai 坂祥伸先生退休記念論集刊行会 (ed.), *Chūgoku shisō ni okeru shintai, shizen, shinkō* 中国思想における身体・自然・信仰 [Body, Nature, and Faith in Chinese Thought]. Tokyo: Tōhō shoten 東方書店, pp. 113-129. (English version entitled "Beheading the Red Dragon: The Heart of Feminine Inner Alchemy" in Chapter 4 of M. Esposito, *Facets of Qing Daoism*. Wil / Paris: UniversityMedia, 2014, pp. 223-237).

2004 "Shindai ni okeru Kingai-zan no seiritsu to Kinka shūshi" 清代における金蓋山龍門派の成立と『金華宗旨』 [The Secret of the Golden Flower and the Establishment of the Longmen Tradition on Mt. Jingai in the Qing Era], in Takata Tokio 高田時雄 (ed.), *Chūgoku shūkyō bunken kenkyū kokusai shinpojiumu hōkokusho* 中国宗教文献研究国際シンポジウム報告書. Kyoto: Kyoto daigaku Jinbun kagaku kenkyūjo 京都大学人文科学研究所, pp. 259-268. (See below for the annotated version of 2007 and for the enlarged English version in Part IV of M. Esposito, *Creative Daoism*).

2005 "Shindai dōkyō to mikkyō: Ryūmon seijiku shinshū" 清代道教と密教：龍門西竺心宗 [An Example of Daoist and Tantric Interaction during the Qing: The Tantric Lineage of Xizhu xinzong]. In Mugitani Kunio 麦谷邦夫 (ed.), *Sankyō kōshō ronsō* 三教交渉論叢 [Studies on the Interaction between the Three Teachings]. Kyoto: Kyoto daigaku Jinbun kagaku kenkyūjo 京都大学人文科学研究所, pp. 287-338. (Revised English version in Chapter 5 of M. Esposito, *Facets of Qing Daoism*. Wil / Paris: UniversityMedia, 2014, pp. 239-304).

2007 "Shindai ni okeru Kingai-zan no seiritsu to Kinka shūshi" 清代における金蓋山龍門派の成立と『金華宗旨』 [The Secret of the Golden Flower and the Establishment of the Longmen Tradition on Mt. Jingai in the Qing Era], in Kyoto: Kyoto daigaku Jinbun kagaku kenkyūjo 京都大学人文科学研究所 (ed.), *Chūgoku shūkyō bunken kenkyū* 中国宗教文献研究, Kyoto: Rinsen shoten 臨川書店, pp. 239-264. (Enlarged and revised English version in Part IV of Monica Esposito, *Creative Daoism*. Wil / Paris: UniversityMedia, 2013, pp. 263-315).

2007 "The Discovery of Jiang Yuanting's Daozang jiyao in Jiangnan—A Presentation of the Daoist Canon of the Qing Dynasty", in Mugitani Kunio 麦谷邦夫 (ed.), *Kōnan dōkyō no kenkyū* 江南道教の研究 [Research on Jiangnan Daoism]. Kyoto: Kyoto daigaku Jinbun kagaku kenkyūjo 京都大学人文科学研究所, p. 79-110. Chinese translation published in *Xueshu Zhongguo* 學術中國, 2007.11, pp. 25-48. (Revised and augmented version in Part III of Monica Esposito, *Creative Daoism*. Wil / Paris: UniversityMedia, 2013).

2008 Twenty-one articles for *The Encyclopedia of Taoism* (edited by Fabrizio Pregadio), London, Routledge. 1. Collected Works of the Perfected Lü of Pure Yang (Chunyang Lü zhenren wenji 純陽呂真人文集) (vol. 1, p. 280-281); 2. "exteriorization of the spirits"; "egress of the Spirit" (chushen 出神) in inner alchemy (vol. 1, p. 282-284); 3. Sequel to the Taoist Canon (Daozang xubian 道藏續編) (vol. 1, p. 347-350); 4. Mother of the Dipper (Doumu 斗母 / 斗姆) (vol.1, p. 382-383); 5. Spirit of the Valley (gushen 谷神) (vol. 1, p. 466); 6. Scripture of Wisdom and Life (Huiming jing 慧命經) (vol. 1, p. 520-521); 7. "fire times"; fire phasing (huohou 火候) in inner alchemy (vol.1, p. 530-531); 8. Gate of the Dragon (Longmen 龍門) (vol. 1, p. 704-706); 9. Complete Writings of Ancestor Lü [Dongbin] (Lüzu quanshu 呂祖全書) (vol. 1, p. 726-728); 10. Min Yide 閔一得 (vol. 2, p. 747-748); 11. Gate of the Vital Force (mingmen 命門) (vol. 2, p. 750); 12. Bathing; ablutions (muyu 沐浴) in inner alchemy (vol. 2, p. 753-754); 13. Muddy Pellet (niwan 泥丸) (vol. 2, p. 775-777); 14. Inner alchemy for women (nüdan 女丹) (vol. 2, p. 778-780); 15. Three Passes (sanguan 三關) (vol. 2, p. 835-836); 16. Joint cultivation (shuangxiu 雙修) (vol. 2, p. 906-907); 17. The Ultimate Purport of the Golden Flower of the Great One (Taiyi jinhua zongzhi 太一金華宗旨) (vol. 2, p. 961-962); 18. Heart of Heaven; Celestial Heart (tianxin 天心) (vol. 2, p. 988); 19. Wang Changyue 王常月 (vol. 2, p. 1008-1010); 20. Mysterious Pass (xuanguan 玄關) (vol. 2, p. 1131-2); 21. Intention (yi 意) (vol. 2, p. 1158-9)

2008 "rDzogs chen in China: From Chan to Tibetan Tantrism in Fahai Lama's (1921-1991) footsteps", in Monica Esposito (ed.), *Images of Tibet in the 19th and 20th Centuries*. Collection Thématiques no 22, Paris: École française d'Extrême-Orient, vol. 2, p. 473-548. (Revised and augmented version in Monica Esposito, *The Zen of Tantra*. Wil / Paris: UniversityMedia, 2013).

2009 "Yibu Quanzhen Daozang de faming: *Daozang jiyao* ji Qingdai Quanzhen rentong 一部全真道藏的發明：道藏輯要及清代全真認同 [The Invention of a Quanzhen Canon: The Daozang Jiyao and Qing-era Quanzhen Identity]. In *Wendao Kunyushan* 问道昆崳山, edited by Zhao Weidong 趙衛東. Jinan: Qilu shushe: 303–343. (Revised and much augmented English version in Xun Liu and Vincent Goossaert [eds.]. *Quanzhen Daoism in Modern Chinese History and Society*. Berkeley: Institute of East Asian Studies, 2014, pp. 44-77).

2009 "The Daozang Jiyao Project: Mutation of a Canon". *Daoism: Religion, History and Society*, 2009.1, pp. 95-153.

2010 "Qingdai daozang—Jiangnan Jiang Yuanting ben Daozang jiyao zhi yanjiu 清代道藏—江南蒋元庭本《道藏輯要》之研究 [The Daoist Canon of the Qing — A Study of the Daozang jiyao version by Jiang Yuanting]. *Zongjiao xue yanjiu* 宗教学研究 3, pp. 17-27.

2011 "Shindai dōkyō ni okeru sankyō no hōko to shite no Dōzō shuyō—Zaike shinto to seishokusha no ken'i no taiji 清代における三教の寶庫としての《道藏輯要》—在家信徒と聖職の權威の對峙." [Daozang jiyao – The Last Qing Daoist Canon as Receptacle of the Three Teachings: Lay and Clerical Authorities Face to Face], in Kunio Mugitani 麥谷邦夫, *Sankyō kōshō ronsō zokuhen* 三教交涉叢論續編. Kyoto: Kyoto daigaku jinbun kagaku kenkyūjo, pp. 431–469. Revised English version in Monica Esposito, *Creative Daoism*, Part 3, chapters 3–5 (pp. 219-260).

2011 "Qingdai quanzhen santan dajie yishi de chuangli" 清代全真三壇大戒儀式的創立, Zhao Weidong 趙衛東 (ed.)., *Quanzhendao yanjiu* 全真道研究 II. Jinan: Qilu shushe, pp. 204-220. (See the substantially augmented argument in Monica Esposito, *Creative Daoism*. Wil / Paris: UniversityMedia, 2013, pp. 91-173).

2014 "The Invention of a Quanzhen Canon: The Wondrous Fate of the Daozang jiyao." In Xun Liu and Vincent Goossaert (eds.), *Quanzhen Daoism in Modern Chinese History and Society*. Berkeley: Institute of East Asia Studies, pp. 44-77.

Forthcoming: "The Daozang Jiyao and the Future of Daoist Studies", in Lai Chi Tim and Cheung Neky Tak-ching (eds.), *New Approaches to the Study of Daoism in Chinese Culture and Society*. Hong Kong: Chinese University Press.

Translations

1991 (from French) Catherine Despeux, *Le immortali dell' antica Cina. Taoismo e Alchimia femminile*. Rome: Ubaldini.

2008 (from Japanese) Onoda Shunzō 小野田俊蔵, "The Meiji Suppression of Buddhism and Its Impact on the Spirit of Exploration and Academism of Buddhist Monks", in *Images of Tibet in the 19th and 20th Centuries*, collection "Études thématiques" no 22. Paris: École française d'Extrême-Orient, vol. 2, pp. 225-242.

2008 (from Chinese) Chen Bing 陳兵, "The Tantric Revival and Its Reception in Modern China", in *Images of Tibet in the 19th and 20th Centuries*, collection "Études thématiques" no 22. Paris: École française d'Extrême-Orient, vol. 2, pp. 387-427.

Conference Papers

2002 "A Sino-Tibetan Tradition in China at the Southern Celestial Eye Mountains: A First Comparison between Great Perfection (rDzogs chen) and Taoist Techniques of Light." Paper presented at the Conference "Tantra and Daoism: The Globalization of Religion and its Experience." Boston University, April 19-21, 2002.

2003 "How Neidan has developed: A View on Inner Alchemy in Late Imperial China." Paper presented at the conference "The Roots of Taoist Inner Alchemy", Stanford University, May 30-31, 2003. (The distributed list of texts contained in the *Daozang xubian* forms in revised and completed form the Appendix to Chapter 3 in M. Esposito, *Facets of Qing Daoism*. Wil / Paris: UniversityMedia, pp. 191-211).

2006 "Daozang jiyao yanjiu jihua-Cong zhushushi bianmu dao shuweihua diancang." 道藏輯要研究計畫—從註疏式編目到數位化典藏 [The Daozang Jiyao Research Project—From an Annotated Catalog to the Digitization of its Scriptures]. Paper presented at the Conference of Exchange of Experiences in the Work of Digitizing Religious Scriptures 數位寶典—宗教文獻數位化工作經驗交流會, Academia Sinica Institute of History and Philology, March 7, 2006.

2006 "Daozang jiyao ji qi bianzuan de lishi—Shijie Qingdai Daozang suoshou daojing shumu wenti 道藏輯要及其編纂的歷史—試解清代道藏所收道經書目問題" [The History of the Compilation of the *Daozang jiyao*—Solving its Numbering Problem]. Paper presented at the *First International Academic Symposium of Taoist Literature and its Path to Immortality* 第

一屆道教仙道文化國際學術研討會. Gaoxiong, Zhongshan University, November 10–12, 2006.

2008 "Yibu Quanzhen Daozang de faming: Daozang jiyao ji Qingdai Quanzhen rentong" 一部全真道藏的發明：道藏輯要及清代全真認同. Paper presented at the Quanzhen conference in Shandong Moping, October 9-12, 2008.

2009 "The Daozang Jiyao and the Future of Daoist Studies." Paper presented at the international conference "New Approaches to the Study of Daoism in Chinese Culture and Society", Chinese University of Hong Kong, November 26-28, 2008.

2010 "Qingdai Quanzhen jiao zhi chonggou: Min Yide ji qi jianli Longmen zhengtong de yiyuan" 清代全真教之重構：閔一得及其建立龍門正統的意願 [The Reinvention of Quanzhen during the Qing Dynasty: Min Yide and his Will to Orthodoxy]. Paper presented at the International Quanzhen conference 探古鑑今－全真道的昨天,今天與明天, Hong Kong, January 6-8, 2010.

Documentaries

1993 Journey to the Temple of the Celestial-Eye Mountains. 10-minute video, Rolex Awards for Enterprise, Selected Projects.

1995 Voyage dans le Khams et l'Amdo méridionale [Voyage in the Khams and Southern Amdo]. 10-minute video, CNRS European Project.

2000 (In collaboration with Urs App) *Oracles in China*. 11-minute video for the millennial "Oracle" exhibition at the Museum Rietberg, Zürich.

2000 (In collaboration with Urs App) *Oracles in Japan*. 10-minute video for the millennial "Oracle" exhibition at the Museum Rietberg, Zürich.

2000 (In collaboration with Urs App) *Dangki: Chinese Oracle Kids*. 11-minute video for the millennial "Oracle" exhibition at the Museum Rietberg, Zürich.

2001 (In collaboration with Urs App) *Dangki – Les chamanes de la Chine* [Dangki: Shamans of China]. 51-minute video, broadcast in 2001 and 2002 on the France 2 TV channel.

2002 (In collaboration with Urs App) *On the Way to Tōhaku's Pine Forest*. 20-minute video for the exposition on the art of painter Hasegawa Tōhaku at the Museum Rietberg, Zürich.

2003 (In collaboration with Urs App) *Der Teebesen* [Chasen—The Tea Whisk]. 20-minute video shown at the "Bamboo" exposition at the Ethnological Museum of Zurich University in 2003 and at the Völkerkundemuseum München in 2006.

Preface by the Editor

Some years before her sudden passing due to pulmonary emboly on March 10, 2011 (one day before the terrible Tōhoku earthquake), my wife Monica Esposito envisaged publishing a volume entitled *Facets of Qing Daoism* and for this purpose began correcting several of her published articles on the general history of Qing Daoism, the institutional and doctrinal history of the Longmen 龍門 ("Dragon Gate") tradition, and inner alchemy (*neidan* 內丹).

Her interest in these topics dated from the mid-1980s when, during several prolonged stays in China as a sinology student, she had become fascinated by *Qi* 氣-related practices such as Taijiquan 太極拳 and Qigong 氣功 which form the subject of her M.A. thesis (University of Venice, 1987) and her first book in Italian.[1] Her enthusiasm for Qigong and Taijiquan not only led to intensive practice—as described by the friends who knew her as a student, and as recorded in a Youtube video[2]—but also to the purchase and shipping of dozens of boxes full of Chinese books and journals: a rich collection of materials documenting China's "Qigong fever" of the 1980s and early 1990s that will be made accessible, along with the rest of her large library, at her alma mater in Venice.

The lineage claims of some of her Chinese teachers and the assertion of most Daoist priests to belong to the Longmen 龍門 lineage of Daoism led to growing curiosity about such lineages and a thirst for broader knowledge of Ming and Qing Daoism, both of which found expression in her subsequent research and publications. After her move to Paris she obtained in 1988 the DEA (Diplôme d'études appliquées) at the University of Paris VII with a thesis on texts contained in the *Daozang xubian* 道藏續編 (Supplementary Collection of the Daoist Canon) and went on working, under the direction of Isabelle Robinet, on her Ph.D. thesis containing a pioneering

---

[1] *La pratica del Qigong in Cina. Introduzione ad una scuola contemporanea e ai suoi testi (con una traduzione del Wuxi chanwei, breve studio sulle cinque respirazioni)* [Qigong Practice in China. Introduction to a Contemporary School and its Texts (with a translation of the *Wuxi chanwei*, Succinct Presentation of the Five Respirations)]. M.A. thesis. Venice: Università degli Studi di Venezia, Facoltà di Lingue e Letterature Straniere, 1987.

[2] See the descriptions by Tiziana Lippiello, Alain Arrault, and Catherine Despeux in "In Memoriam Monica Esposito (1962–2011)", *Cahiers d'Extrême-Asie* 20 (2011), pp. vii–xii. A UniversityMedia video of her Taijiquan practice is found on Youtube.

presentation of Longmen doctrine and deconstruction of premodern Daoist history. In 1993 she presented this thesis (see p. VIII) and passed her Ph.D. exams at the University of Paris VII with the highest distinction.

During her frequent stays in China she visited many Daoist sites to collect data and copy inscriptions. Near an ancient Daoist cave on Southern Mt. Tianmu 南天目山 (Zhejiang province) she discovered a Tantric Buddhist nunnery founded by Fahai 法海 Lama. While living at this monastery for several months at a time between 1988 and 1991, and again between 1994 and 1996, Monica not only engaged with the Chinese nuns in all religious practices but also recorded and copied the Sino-Tibetan Lama's daily teachings, filmed rituals and scenes of the nunnery's daily life, and collected scriptures that she later used in her publications on Chinese Tantric Buddhism, rDzogs-chen, and Daoism. In the early 1990s she also engaged in the study and practice of rDzogs-chen in Europe, and all these endeavors bore fruit during her Kyoto years (1997–2011) in form of a conference paper on practices of light in China and Tibet,[3] a long article entitled "Sun-worship in China—The Roots of Shangqing Taoist Practices of Light",[4] two magnificent *Images of Tibet* volumes that she conceived and edited,[5] and the posthumously published book *The Zen of Tantra*,[6] a pioneering monograph on rDzogs-chen in China that contains her account of the practices at Fahai Lama's monastery and a presentation of his life and teachings.

After several years dedicated to field work in China and Japan, the production of several documentaries about shamanic practices and oracles (see p. XV), and the publication of seminal articles on Qing Daoism in general and the Longmen tradition in particular,[7] Monica was in 2003 nominated Associate professor at the Institute for Humanistic Studies of Kyoto University (Kyōto daigaku Jinbun kagaku kenkyūjo 京都大学人文科学研究

---

[3] "A Sino-Tibetan Tradition in China at the Southern Celestial Eye Mountains: A First Comparison between Great Perfection (rDzogs chen) and Taoist Techniques of Light." Paper presented at the Conference "Tantra and Daoism: The Globalization of Religion and its Experience." Boston University, April 19-21, 2002.

[4] "Sun-worship in China–The Roots of Shangqing Taoist Practices of Light". *Cahiers d'Extrême-Asie* 14 (2004), pp. 345-402.

[5] *Images of Tibet in the 19th and 20th Centuries* (2 volumes). Collection "Études thématiques" (no 22). Paris: École française d'Extrême-Orient, 2008.

[6] *The Zen of Tantra*. Wil / Paris: UniversityMedia, 2013.

[7] The articles featured in Chapters 1, 2, and 3 of the present book were all written before she became professor.

所). Her field work on present-day religious phenomena such as spirit-writing tied seamlessly into her research on Daoist texts that had been revealed at altars dedicated to this practice. Of particular interest to her was the *Daozang jiyao* 道藏輯要 or "Essence of the Daoist Canon." This collection of about 300 texts was, so its preface claims, compiled following the order of the immortal Lü Dongbin that was communicated via spirit-writing. In 2005 Monica successfully applied for funds from the Chiang Ching-kuo Foundation, and in 2006 the computer input of the first batch of the canon's texts began while she recruited sixty international collaborators for the International Daozang Jiyao Project that she founded and directed. Its aim is the establishment of a comprehensive catalog of all editions and versions of this Qing-era Daoist canon, a detailed description of the history and content of each text by the best specialists in the field, and the publication in both Chinese and English of a comprehensive catalog, articles on all texts, and related studies. In 2007 Monica received an additional four-year grant from the Japan Society for the Promotion of Science (Nihon gakujutsu shinkōkai 日本学術振興会) for the team of specialists working under her direction at Kyoto University, in Taiwan, and in mainland China. From 2007 she published a series of groundbreaking articles in English, Chinese, and Japanese on this Qing Daoist canon's different versions, history, and connection to various traditions of Daoism and Buddhism (see the list on pp. XI–XIII above).

While contributions by project collaborators in various languages began to be submitted, Monica established collaboration with the Centre for Daoist Studies at the Chinese University of Hong Kong (Xianggang zhongwen daxue Daojiao wenhua yanjiu zhongxin 香港中文大學道教文化中心) where the publication of three English and three Chinese volumes was envisaged. Her position as project director has now been assumed by that center's director, Prof. Lai Chi Tim 黎志添, and several international editing committees are reviewing the work of fifty-nine contributors in order to prepare it for publication. Monica would be elated to see her cherished project in such able hands.

My task here consisted in serving as her copy editor. Since she had made a variety of changes in her computer files and also added corrections on printouts, I incorporated these to the best of my abilities. Given that the chapters were written as articles, I left their individual bibliographies and references intact; but to facilitate reference I added a comprehensive bibliography and an index at the end. My remarks are marked by curly brackets. What follows is a list of the five chapters' original publication data and major changes.

1. *Daoism in the Qing (1644–1911)*

    First published in: L. Kohn (ed.), *Daoism Handbook*, 623–658. Leiden: Brill, 2000: 623–658.

2. *The Longmen School and its Controversial History during the Qing Dynasty*

    First published in: John Lagerwey (ed.), *Religion and Chinese Society: The Transformation of a Field*, vol. 2, pp. 621–698. Paris: EFEO & Chinese University of Hong Kong, 2004.

3. *Longmen Taoism in Qing China: Doctrinal Ideal and Local Reality*

    First published in the *Journal of Chinese Religions* 29 (2001): 191–231 (Special Number on Quanzhen ed. by Vincent Goossaert and Paul Katz).

    The author incorporated a section from her conference paper "Qingdai Quanzhen jiao zhi chonggou: Min Yide ji qi jianli Longmen zhengtong de yiyuan 清代全真教之重構：閔一得及其建立龍門正統得意願" "[Reinventing Quanzhen during the Qing: Min Yide and his will to Longmen Orthodoxy] presented at the International Quanzhen conference, Hong Kong: January 6–8, 2010. The Appendix is based on her unpublished contribution to "The Roots of Neidan" Conference, Stanford University, May 30–31, 2003.

4. *Beheading the Red Dragon: The Heart of Feminine Alchemy*

    Only a Japanese translation of this paper has hitherto been published: "Gyakuten shita zō—jotan no shintai kan 逆転した像－女丹の身体觀." In Sakade Yoshinobu sensei taikyū kinen ronshū kankō kai 坂出祥伸先生退休記念論集刊行会 (ed.), *Chūgoku shisō ni okeru shintai, shizen, shinkō* 中国思想における身体・自然・信仰. Tokyo: Tōhō shoten 東方書店, 2004, pp. 113–129.

5. *An Example of Daoist and Tantric Interaction during the Qing Dynasty: The Longmen Xizhu xinzong*

    Only a Japanese translation of this paper has hitherto been published: "Shindai dōkyō to mikkyō: Ryūmon seijiku shinshū 清代道教と密教：龍門西竺心宗." In Mugitani Kunio 麦谷邦夫 (ed.), *Sankyō kōshō ronsō* 三教交渉論叢. Kyoto: Jinbun kagaku kenkyūjo 人文科学研究所, 2005, pp. 287–338.

In her stead I wish to express profound gratitude to all who supported Monica's work: to her dear family; Professors Isabelle Robinet, Yoshinobu Sakade and Kunio Mugitani; all members of her research team and collaborators; and her many friends and colleagues in East and West.

The editor   Urs App

Daoism in the Qing (1644–1911)

Daoism in the Qing dynasty displays three characteristics: strong state control, an increase in lay activities, and a tendency toward unification and standardization among the Daoist schools.

Following their Ming predecessors, Qing rulers strove to establish **tight state control over all religious organizations**. To this end they imposed numerous legal limits on the size of the clergy, restricted the number of sanctioned monasteries and temples, and controlled the scope of all religious activities. Thus "abbots, priest and nuns were always subject to indirect state supervision and remained at the beck and call of the emperor and his agents" (Smith 1990:293). As in the Ming era (1368–1644), religious administration was a function of the Ministry of Rites (*libu* 禮部), one of the six boards of the central administration. Within it, Daoism was particularly governed by the Daolu si 道錄司 (Central Daoist Registry), "a central government agency responsible for certifying and disciplining Daoist religious practitioners throughout the empire" (Hucker 1985:489), which had control over appropriate boards and officers on the provincial, departmental, prefectural, and county levels (*Daqing huidian* 大清會典 248.16a). These official committees tended to be more concerned with upholding laws and rules than with the spiritual guidance or religious activities of the people (Yang 1961).

The Qing rulers personally venerated Tibetan Buddhism, and under emperor Qianlong 乾隆 (re. 1736–1795) the Gelugpa school became the state religion. As official doctrine they adopted the *Neo-Confucianism* of the Cheng-Zhu school, using it both for imperially endorsed rituals and as the basis of the examination system (Liu 1993: 298). Daoists were progressively marginalized by their lack of moral authority and decreasing numbers, and priests lived in isolated monasteries and came in contact with secular society only during the performance of religious services for individuals or groups. Even in these, however, they were often replaced by trade guilds, local elites, or other groups. Like Buddhists they had local associations, but they lacked a strong religious structure, had inadequate financial support and, incapable of controlling resources, did not participate in charitable works.

As a result, Daoists were not prominent in society and suffered from the generally low status of the clergy which, exonerated from taxes, was considered unproductive and a burden to state coffers. This low status "deterred many intellectuals from taking the vow, depriving institutional religion of a supply of educated leadership" (Yang 1961). It also weakened the structural position of clerical religions and promoted the organization of a laity outside these religious channels. Many functions once filled by clerics were now taken over by the local magistrates in cooperation with the gentry and merchants—as described especially in local gazetteers (see Taylor 1995). Large numbers of people who felt the need for a religious life became secular devotees or joined new forms of sectarian groups (Yang 1961).

This leads us to the second characteristic of Qing Daoism: *the growth of lay organizations and practices.* Apart from the low status of clergy, this growth was also encouraged by the imperial Confucianism, established by the Qing emperors on the model of their Ming predecessors, which was accompanied by bringing certain sections of the clergy into civil service (Berling 1980:47–48). It is interesting to note that one of the most celebrated laymen of the Manchu dynasty was Emperor Yongzheng 雍正 (re. 1722–1735) who showed how one could combine official functions associated with Confucian doctrine with a personal belief in Buddhism and Daoism. His support of the unity of the three teachings (*sanjiao heyi* 三教合一) encouraged increased lay practice and promoted lay religious life. Overall, during the Qing, then, the increase in the number of laymen was inversely proportional to the decline of religious vocation (see Bardol 1992).

At the same time, however, this increased lay activity also encouraged new forms of popular and lay Daoism that found expression in morality books, the revelation of precious scrolls, and spirit writing cults—all predominantly lay-centered, oriented toward popular religion, and strongly inspired by Daoist beliefs and practices. There were local Daoist schools, spirit writing groups, and sectarian associations following Daoist teachings that were outside the range of imperial control and also beyond the reach of the official arm of the clergy. They paved the way for the form Daoist popular practice still takes in China today.

Nonetheless, the Manchu emperors of the Qing dynasty (1644–1911) did create a state-controlled and well-indoctrinated clergy, and this provided a certain uniformity of Daoism and countered plurality and spontaneity among Daoist schools. This *movement toward unity* is the third characteristic of Qing Daoism. It was of capital importance for the formation of modern official Daoism, distinguished by "standardization of schools." According to official sources the Qing, as had the Ming, recognized only two main Daoist schools: Zhengyi 正一 (Orthodox Unity) and Quanzhen 全真 (Complete Perfection; see *Daqing huidian* 大清會典 248. 16a). The latter, particularly under its Longmen 龍門 branch, standardized the northern and southern schools of inner alchemy (*neidan* 內丹) and integrated so many aspects of Zhengyi doctrine that it became difficult to tell them apart (see Esposito 1993). However, in order to understand the specific character of Chinese religion, it is necessary to take into account the difference between the official version of events and what really happened. Under what can be called a "Longmen standardization," a variety of Daoist schools continued to exist at the local level, but in order to survive they were sometimes obliged to claim descent from the Longmen lineage. This was the case with some minor schools of inner alchemy such as the Wu-Liu 伍柳 School, an eclectic group under the umbrella of Longmen that mixed inner alchemy with Huayan 華嚴 Buddhism, and the Jingming 淨明 (Pure Brightness) school which was linked to the immortal Lü Dongbin 呂洞賓 and incorporated certain aspects of Confucian doctrine.

In the following, I shall first present an outline of the history and major figures of some important Daoist schools of the Qing, then discuss new forms of doctrine and the impact of state control under the heading "Worldview," and finally turn to spirit writing and inner alchemy under the heading "Practice."

Reign Name	"Temple" Name	Posthumous name	Reign Period
Shunzhi 順治	Shizu 世祖	Zhangdi 章帝	1644–1661
Kangxi 康熙	Shengzu 聖祖	Rendi 仁帝	1662–1722
Yongzheng 雍正	Shizong 世宗	Xiandi 憲帝	1722–1735
Qianlong 乾隆	Gaozong 高宗	Chundi 純帝	1735–1796
Jiaqing 嘉慶	Renzong 仁宗	Ruidi 睿帝	1796–1820
Daoguang 道光	Xuanzong 宣宗	Chengdi 成帝	1820–1850
Xianfeng 咸豐	Wenzong 文宗	Xiandi 顯帝	1850–1861
Tongzhi 同治	Muzong 穆宗	Yidi 毅帝	1861–1875
Guangxu 光緒	Dezong 德宗	Jingdi 景帝	1875–1908
Xuantong 宣統	Gongzong 恭宗	Xundi 遜帝	1908–1911

Table 1: List of Emperors and Reigns of the Qing Dynasty (1644–1911)

HISTORY

The Zhengyi School

The Zhengyi school of the Celestial Masters was the most officially recognized among Qing Daoist schools. It continued to exert significant religious influence on the Daolu si 道錄司 (Central Daoist registry) through its leader, the Celestial Master with headquarters on Mount Longhu 龍虎山 in Jiangxi. To perform this government function, he was given a staff of twenty-seven priests by the Board of Rites.[1]

In 1651, during the SHUNZHI ERA (1644–1661), the 52nd Celestial Master Zhang Yingjing 張應京 was officially ordered to manage the Daoist religion. He was appointed specifically to prevent heretic religious influences. He was given the formal title "Great Perfected of the Lineage of Orthodox Unity" (Zhengyi sijiao da zhenren 正一嗣教大真人) and was equipped with a seal of the first rank.[2] In 1655, the 53rd Celestial Master Zhang Hongren 張洪仁 (1624–1667) was invited to court and lived at the Lingyou gong 靈右宮 (Numinous Palace to the Right) in Beijing together with the highest officials.[3]

Emperor Shengzu of the KANGXI ERA (1662–1722) showed a even more positive attitude toward Daoism. In 1675 he invited the 54th Celestial Master Zhang Jizong 張繼宗 (1666–1715) to court and gave him a plaque with his Daoist name Bicheng 碧城 written in the emperor's own hand. Zhang was frequently asked to perform rainmaking and flood-control rites, and in 1703 received the prestigious title "Grand Master of Splendid Happiness" (Guanglu dafu 光祿大夫). In 1713, he obtained imperial funds for the reconstruction of the halls on Mount Longhu.[4] After his death, he was succeeded by Zhang Xilin 張錫麟 (hao: Longhu zhuren 龍虎主人).

---

[1] See *Qingshi gao* 情史稿 115.3331.

[2] *Qingshi gao* 情史稿 115.3331; *Bu Han tianshi shijia* 補漢天師世家, in Oyanagi, Shigeta 小柳司氣太, *Hakuunkan shi* 白雲觀志 [Gazetteer of the Abbey of the White Clouds]. Tokyo: Tōhō bunka gakuin Tōkyō kenkyūjo 東方文化學院東京研究所 1934:349.

[3] *Bu Han tianshi shijia* 補漢天師世家, in Oyanagi 1934:350.

[4] *Bu Han tianshi shijia* 補漢天師世家, in Oyanagi 1934:350–1.

Emperor Shizong of the **YONGZHENG ERA** (1722–1735) proposed the unity of the three teachings and, in the literary inquisition of 1772–1788, attempted to purge the country of all heterodox ideas. He was a firm believer in exorcism and the efficacy of rituals and showed particular respect for the Celestial Masters while also offering lands to other religious groups. He gave Zhang Xilin the title "Grand Master of Splendid Happiness" and, in 1731, furnished funds for the reconstruction of the Shangqing gong 上清宮 (Great Clarity Palace) on Mount Longhu (*Bu Han tianshi shijia*, in Oyanagi 1934:351).

This construction project occurred under the leadership of Lou Jinyuan 婁近垣 (1689–1776).[5] Born into a family of Daoist priests, he joined the religion on Mount Longhu where he studied with Zhou Dajing 周大經 and received both thunder rites (*leifa* 雷法) and talismans. In 1727, Lou joined Zhang Xilin on his journey to the capital; and after the latter's death in Hangzhou, Lou complied with Zhang's last wishes that he serve the emperor with loyalty.[6] In 1730 he successfully cured the emperor and obtained his favor, becoming abbot of the Qin'an dian 欽安殿 in the imperial palace and chief administrator of Mount Longhu with the rank 4A (*Qingshi gao* 情史稿 115.3332). As Grand Minister (*dachen* 大臣), he was put in charge of the reconstruction of the mountain sanctuaries.[7]

Later Lou was also accepted in an elect circle of disciples to whom the emperor taught Buddhist sūtras (see Chen 1993). In 1733 he was formally installed in the Da guangming dian 大光明殿 (Palace of the Great Light; *Daqing huidian* 248.16b), a Daoist imperial office, and received the title "Perfected of Mysterious Orthodoxy" (Miaozheng zhenren 妙正真人; *Qingshi gao* 115.3332). Lou retained a high position at court even after the emperor's death and, in 1736, received the title "Grand Master of Thorough Counsel" (Tongyi dafu 通議大夫) from the subsequent emperor, Qianlong 乾隆 (re. 1735–96). He also became supervisor of the Daoist registry and abbot of Beijing's Dongyue miao 東嶽廟 (Temple of the Eastern Peak; see Chen 1993).

Lou's main work focused on the restoration of temples on Mount Longhu 龍虎山, about which he also compiled the *Chongxiu longhu shanzhi* 重修

---

[5] Zi Sanchen 三臣, *hao* Langzhai 朗齋, Shangqing waishi 上情外史 or "Inofficial Historian of Highest Clarity," from Lou 婁 district near Shanghai.

[6] *Bu Han tianshi shijia* 補漢天師世家, Oyanagi 1934:351; *Chongxiu longhu shanzhi* 重修龍虎山志 6.42a.

[7] *Chongxiu longhu shanzhi* 1.6b-7a, 6.42b.

龍虎山志 (Gazetteer of the Reconstruction of Mount Longhu, 16 j.). He also wrote a commentary to the *Zhuangzi* called *Nanhua jingzhu* 南華經注 and the *Yuxuan miaozheng zhenren yulu* 御選妙正真人語錄 (Imperially Selected Recorded Sayings of the Perfected of Mysterious Orthodoxy, in *Chongxiu longhu shanzhi*, j. 11) — the only Daoist work included in emperor Shizong's collection *Yuxuan yulu* 御選語錄 (Imperially Selected Recorded Sayings). In his *Recorded Sayings*, Lou emphasizes the importance of the three teachings, into which he integrates Buddhist materials that he studied with emperor Shizong 世宗 (re. 1722–1735). Finally, he compiled an important collection of Daoist rituals entitled *Huanglu keyi* 黃籙科儀 (Yellow Register Liturgies, 12 j.).

Emperor Gaozong 高宗 of the QIANLONG ERA (1735–1796) supported Neo-Confucianism, encouraged the production of great encyclopedic literary works, and sponsored the compilation of the gigantic *Siku quanshu* 四庫全書 (Complete Books in Four Repositories). He promoted neither Chinese Buddhism nor Daoism but proclaimed the Gelugpa teaching as the state religion. His lack of interest in Daoism is reflected in the *Siku quanshu* which contains only 430 scrolls of Daoist works (Liu 1993:301).

The two practitioners of inner alchemy that had been established previously at court, Zhang Taixu 張太虛 and Wang Dingqian 王定乾, were banished (Liu 1993:301), and the Celestial Masters were no longer allowed to come to audience. Moreover, in 1752, as "Perfected of Orthodox Unity" (Zhengyi zhenren 正一真人), they were demoted to nominal Rank five from Rank three and were no longer allowed to apply for honorary titles. (*Qingshi gao* 115.3332). The Celestial Masters thereafter had authority only over Mount Longhu, no longer served as general administrators of Daoism, and lost their supreme authority in Jiangnan. Furthermore, in 1742, the emperor stopped appointing Daoists to the position of Music Master (Taichang leyuan 太常樂員) at the Court of Imperial Sacrifices (taichang si 太常寺) and instead gave it to Confucian officials.[8]

Under the SUCCEEDING EMPERORS, however, Celestial Masters such as Zhang Qilong 張起隆 and Zhang Yu 張鈺 (58th and 59th generation) were allowed back to court and again received prestigious titles.[9] Nevertheless, the influence of Daoism continued to decline until, in the Daoguang period

---

[8] See *Qingshi gao* 情史稿 114.3285.
[9] See *Bu Han tianshi shijia* 補漢天師世家, in Oyanagi 1934:352–53.

(1820–1850), the title "Perfected of Orthodox Unity" disappeared altogether and the relationship between the court and the Celestial Masters came to an end (Liu 1993:302).

The Quanzhen School

During the Qing dynasty the Quanzhen 全真 school enjoyed a renaissance, albeit one that would sputter out with the fall of the dynasty. The first upsurge began right at the end of Ming, when many Confucians and literati joined Quanzhen to show their loyalty to the Ming and their disappointment with the Manchu conquest. Although the Qing rulers gave all formal ritual and talismanic privileges to the Zhengyi school, they liked Quanzhen because of the strong discipline and moral rules that form the basis of its official doctrine. As its followers lived in monasteries and followed an ascetic and well-regulated conduct, the school conformed to government rules and regained some of the official and literati prestige it had once enjoyed under the Jin and Yuan. Its Longmen branch emerged as the leading group (Chen 1988).

This LONGMEN BRANCH traces itself to a place called Longmen 龍門 in Longzhou 隴州 Prefecture of Western Shaanxi where Qiu Chuji 邱處機 (1148–1227) underwent his ascetic training. According to the *Jingai xindeng* 金蓋心燈 (see below), although traditionally linked with Qiu, the Longmen school appeared much later, probably during the Ming (see Esposito 1993). It represents a late school of inner alchemy that cannot be traced back to northern Quanzhen alone; rather, it combines the traditions of several local Daoist movements in south China. Although the purported historical origin and lineage of the school are full of contradictions (Esposito 1993; Mori 1994), it is nonetheless important because it was the most influential vehicle in the handing down of theories of inner alchemy. Even today, most Daoist temples in both north and south China claim to belong to this branch.

The established lineage of Longmen goes back to Wang Changyue 王常月 (?-1680), abbot of the BAIYUN GUAN 白雲觀 (White Cloud Abbey) in Beijing since 1656. Even under the Ming, the Baiyun guan was often visited by emperors in celebration of Qiu Chuji's birth, while the common people came to worship at his grave.[10] In the Qing, the Baiyun guan had a dual role

---

[10] See Hu Ying's Stele of 1444, in Oyanagi 1934:124–28.

as a public monastery with an altar platform for formal ordinations and as the headquarters of the Longmen branch (see Yoshioka 1970 & 1979).

Regarding the first role, the abbot of a public monastery was also the Master of Discipline who transmitted the precepts (*chuanjie lüshi* 傳戒律師). Under Wang Changyue's supervision, that is, under the direction of the Longmen school, the Baiyun guan became a major training center for all kinds of Daoist schools, promoting a "standardization" of religious rules in conformity with the ruling Confucian ethics. The *Zhuzhen zongpai zongbu* 諸真宗派總簿 (Comprehensive Register of all Genuine Lineages; in Oyanagi 1934:91) reveals that many schools accredited at the Baiyun guan differed in terms of their "lineage verse" (*paishi* 派詩). This was commonly used as a form of "ideogram genealogy" (*zipu* 字譜), with every Daoist belonging to a particular school receiving one of the verse's characters as part of his or her religious name (Yoshioka 1979). The official appointment of the Baiyun guan as agency overseeing the spiritual formation of all ordained Daoist priests (*shoujie zhe* 受戒者), independent of their various schools, was crucial to its widespread influence under the Qing.

The second role of the Baiyun guan was as headquarters of the Longmen school. Longmen first claimed supremacy over the Daoist priesthood in the north (just as the Celestial Masters did in the south) . Then, helped by the Baiyun guan's official position as ordination monastery, the school extended its influence throughout China, creating a *de facto* "Longmen standardization" of Daoism. Many Daoist schools continued to exist in their diversity, but they were compelled to subsume themselves to Longmen, at least officially, to ensure their survival.

The first Qing abbot of the Baiyun guan was WANG CHANGYUE 王常月 (?-1680).[11] In his early years, he travelled around famous mountains and, in 1628, met Zhao Fuyang 趙復陽 on Mount Wangwu 王屋山 (Shanxi). Zhao, a sixth-generation Longmen patriarch, gave Wang the Longmen precepts as well as the ordination name of Changyue ("Constant Through the Months)", making him seventh Longmen patriarch. For nine years, Wang studied the classics of the three teachings and visited many masters until he met Zhao once again, on Mount Jiugong 九宮山 (Hubei). Zhao predicted that Wang would become the main representative of Longmen at the Baiyun guan. In 1655, Wang went to live in the Lingyou gong in the capital, and one year later he indeed became abbot of the Baiyun guan. All this is

---

[11] Originally Wang Ping 王平, *hao* Kunyang 昆陽 from Lu'an 潞安 in Shanxi.

reported in the *Jingai xindeng* 金蓋心燈 (1.15a-17b) by Min Yide 閔一得, a major source on Longmen history (see below).

As abbot, Wang reorganized Daoist religious precepts in accordance with Neo-Confucian ethics as supported by the Qing court. He divided them into three stages: (1) precepts of initial perfection (*chuzhen jie* 初真戒); (2) intermediate precepts (*zhongji jie* 中極戒); and (3) precepts of celestial immortality (*tianxian jie* 天仙戒). According to him, the precepts were an indispensable means to enlightenment and an important element in the education of the Daoist clergy. They represented a compromise between the aim of becoming a monk, inherited from Quanzhen Daoism, and the necessity of living in the world following the social rules of Confucianism. This compromise constitutes the core of Longmen doctrine, as Wang explained in his *Biyuan tanjing* 碧苑壇經 (Platform Sūtra of the Jade Garden), a work influenced by the *Platform sūtra* of the sixth Chan patriarch Huineng 慧能. It consists of discourses given by Wang during an ordination ceremony held at the Biyuan guan 碧苑觀 in Nanjng and is contained in Min Yide's *Gu shuyinlou cangshu* 古書隱樓藏書 (see below) as well as in the modern collection *Zangwai daoshu* 藏外道書[12] under the title *Longmen xinfa* 龍門心法 (Core Teachings of Longmen). The court approved of this concept because it encouraged Confucian morality and also because it drew on Chan Buddhist doctrines that were supported by the early Qing emperors (Bardol 1992) as well as by many officials and men of culture (see Esposito 1993).

Wang also is said to have authored a history of Quanzhen transmission entitled *Bojian* 缽鑑 (Examination of the Bowl)[13] and the *Chuzhen jielü* 初真戒律 (Precepts of Initial Perfection).[14] The latter includes the *Nüzhen jiujie* 女眞九戒 (Nine Precepts for Women Perfected; see Despeux 1990). After Wang's death, the Kangxi Emperor gave him the posthumous title "Eminent Master who Embraces the One" (Baoyi gaoshi 抱一高師), and ordered a sacrifice hall built with his portrait and a dispatch of officers to be present at a ceremony in his honor.

With Wang Changyue, the Longmen lineage was established and Longmen teachings began to spread throughout China. He ordained thousands

---

[12] *Daoist Texts Outside the Canon*; abbr. ZWDS; 6:729–85.

[13] This text is either lost or never existed; see Esposito 1993; Mori 1994.

[14] *Daozang jiyao* [DZJY] *zhangji* 7; Chongkan ed. 24.10469–87; ZWDS 12.

of disciples in Beijing, Nanjing, Hangzhou and elsewhere.[15] Through him, Longmen became a key Daoist school of the Qing, one that remains active to the present day.

Another key patriarch of the school was MIN YIDE 閔一得 (1748/58–1836).[16] Min was the eleventh patriarch of the Longmen school on Mount Jingai 金蓋山 and the founder of a group called Fangbian pai 方便派 (Skillful Means) in Shanghai. He came from a distinguished family and his father Min Genfu 閔艮甫 had passed the provincial examination in Henan (*Jingai xindeng* 8.1a).

In his early years, Min was very weak, and his father brought him to the Tongbai gong 桐柏宮 (Cypress Temple) on Mount Tiantai 天台山 (Zhejiang), where Gao Dongli 高東籬 (?-1768), the tenth Longmen patriarch, cured him with Daoist gymnastics (*Jingai xindeng* 8.1a, 6a). Gao's disciple Shen Yibing 沈一炳 (1708–1786)[17] then became Min's master and taught him the basic Longmen principles. Min later recovered his health, finished his studies, and followed his father's wishes by becoming a departmental vice magistrate (*Zhou sima* 州司馬) in Yunnan. While there, in 1790, he allegedly encountered Jizu daozhe 雞足道者 (Daoist of Chicken Foot Mountain), a semi-legendary figure who, himself a recipient of Longmen ordination, came to play an important role in Min's spiritual development (*Jingai xindeng* 6.1a-2b).[18] Jizu daozhe was later credited with having established in Yunnan a Longmen branch called Xizhu xinzong 西竺心宗 (Mind School of India), a kind of Tantric-Daoist branch. Min claimed to have received two texts from him: the *Lüzu sanni yishi shuoshu* 呂祖三尼醫世說述 (Explanations of the Three Sages' Doctrine of Healing the World [revealed via spirit writing] by Patriarch Lü) and the *Foshuo chishi tuoluoni jing* 佛說持世陀羅尼經 (*Vasu[n]dhārā-dhāraṇī*), both included in his *Gu shuyinlou cangshu* 古書隱樓藏書 (Collection from the Ancient Hidden Pavilion of Books; see below). According to other biographies, Min also received a Dipper method which included the recitation of mantras based on their Sanskrit pronunciation.

---

[15] *Jingai xindeng* 1.15a-17b; Esposito 1993.

[16] Originally Min Tiaofu 閔笤尃, *hao* Buzhi 補之, Xiaogen 小艮, *daohao* Lanyunzi 懶雲子 or "Master of the Lazy Clouds," from Wuxing 吳興 (modern Huzhou 湖州) in Zhejiang province. {For Min's biographies see below, pp. 160 ff and 256 ff.}

[17] *Hao*: Qingyun 輕雲; Taixu weng 太虛翁.

[18] {See here below, Chapter 5}.

Having become the eleventh patriarch of Longmen and an initiate of the "India" branch, Min withdrew to Mount Jingai and devoted himself to writing the history of Longmen patriarchs and branches, paying particular attention to the local tradition. This work is the *Jingai xindeng* 金蓋心燈 (Transmission of the Mind-Lamp from Mount Jingai, 10 j.), an important source for Longmen history. In addition, Min collected Longmen texts on inner alchemy in his *Gu shuyinlou cangshu* 古書隱樓藏書, which is central to our understanding of Qing inner alchemical ideas and practices.

A contemporary of Min Yide was yet another eleventh-generation Longmen patriarch who is associated with Mount Qiyun 栖雲 (Gansu) and was named Liu Yiming 劉一明 (1734–1821).[19] What little we know about his life is gleaned from biographical notes in his extensive writings. Liu was apparently born into a rich family and studied the Confucian classics in his youth. However, as he tells us in the preface to the *Wugen shujie* 無根樹解 (Explanation of "The Tree Without Roots"[20]), he soon developed a strong interest in inner alchemical poetry, especially that of Zhang Sanfeng 張三丰, and dedicated himself to the study of perfection and the elucidation of inner alchemy. In his *Huixin waiji* 會心外集 (Outer Collection of the Encounters with the Mind), Liu recalls that he left his family and wife at the age of eighteen. In the prefaces to his *Wudao lu* 悟道錄 (Record of Awakening to the Path) he writes that sometime before turning twenty he was stricken with a terrible illness that no medicine could cure. Then, on his way to Nan'an 南安 (Gansu), he met Pengtou laoweng 蓬頭老翁 (Old Man of the Tousled Head) who gave him a powerful recipe that restored his health. This story is interesting because it follows a stereotyped paradigm. The seed of the quest for immortality is instilled in the adept during a long illness which seems incurable until, nearly desperate, he meets a superb master who gives him a miraculous drug. Liu writes that he was awakened to the Dao through his disease.

After his recovery, in 1760, Liu met Kangu laoren 龕谷老人 (Old Man of the Recessed Cavern) in Yuzhong 榆中 (Gansu). The latter, dressed in Confucian garb, unexpectedly transmitted to him the secret formulas of inner alchemy. Nevertheless, he still felt a need to look for further enlightened masters and deepen his quest for truth, and so he "roamed with the clouds,"

---

[19] *Hao* Wuyuan zi 悟元子 or "Master Awakening to the Prime," Supu sanren 素樸散人 or "The Simple Unemployed," Beihe sanren 被褐散人 or "The Unkempt Unemployed," from Pingyang 平陽 in Shanxi.

[20] Poems by Zhang Sanfeng.

visiting Buddhist and Daoist masters north and south. During these years Liu acquired a deep knowledge of the three teachings and a thorough understanding of the significance of their classics. His efforts eventually led him to his longed-for encounter with a genuine master. In 1772, at the age of thirty-nine, Liu met Xianliu zhangren 仙留丈人 (Elder Remaining Immortal) who freed him from all of his doubts.

During the later part of his life, he withdrew to Mount Qiyun 栖雲 (Gansu, Yuzhong district), where for twenty years he lived in the Chaoyuan guan 朝元觀 (Abbey of Worshiping the Prime), writing in a lodge called Zizai wo 自在窩 (Nest of Freedom). Here he also engaged in further self-cultivation and transmitted Daoist teachings to selected disciples. As a result, his fame spread far and wide throughout northwest China (modern Shaanxi, Shanxi, Gansu, Ningxia). Liu wrote numerous books, mostly edited in a collection called *Daoshu shier zhong* 道書十二種 (Twelve Daoist Books; see below).

An earlier Daoist who claimed to be a Longmen adherent but is better known for his association with the so-called Wu-Liu school was WU SHOUYANG 伍守陽 (ab. 1552–1641).[21] According to his biography by Shen Zhaoding 申兆定 (fl. 1764), Wu Shouyang took up the life of a recluse and attained realization only at the age of seventy after his mother's death. He thought of himself as a disciple of the Longmen branch (Boltz 1987:198), but this has not been undisputed. In his works he claims a lineage connection to Cao Changhua 曹常化 (1562–1622),[22] a disciple of Li Zhenyuan 李真元 (1525–1573?),[23] who in turn studied with Zhang Jingxu 張靜虛 (b. 1432),[24] a Longmen master associated with Mount Wudang 武當山.[25]

According to another biography by Min Yide (*Jingai xindeng* 2.1a-2b), Wu was linked to the eighth Longmen generation through Zhao Fuyang 趙復陽 who persuaded him to seek instruction from Wang Changyue on Mount Wangwu (Shanxi). All of this suggests that Wu Shouyang's original affiliation to a local Longmen branch was obscured by the official, stan-

---

[21] *Zi* Duanyang 端陽, *hao* Chongxu zi 沖虛子; from Nanchang.

[22] *Hao* Huanyang 還陽.

[23] *Hao* Xu'an 虛庵.

[24] *Hao* Hupi 虎皮.

[25] *Xianfo hezong yulu* 仙佛合宗語錄, DZJY *biji* 1.85a-86a; see Liu 1984:186; Mori 1994:193–95, 211.

dardized Longmen claim that linked him with Wang Changyue (Esposito 1993; Mori 1994). Also, even though Min Yide's biography mentions Cao Changhua as Wu's master, it places the encounter several decades earlier, at the time when he fled to Mount Lu on the northern border of Jiangxi. Wu at this time received instruction in inner alchemy from Cao Changhua and Li Niwan 李泥丸, alleged master of the five thunder rites (*wu leifa* 五雷法) who was linked with Mount Jingai (see Esposito 1993). What Wu learned from Cao he then put into his *Tianxian zhengli* 天仙正理 (Proper Principles of Celestial Immortality, DZJY *biji* 4–5), after which he also wrote the *Wu zhenren dandao jiupian* 伍真人丹道九篇 (Nine Chapters on the Alchemical Path by the Perfected Wu).[26] This latter work contains the instructions he gave while serving as tutor of the Prince of Ji, sometimes identified as Zhu Youlian 朱由練 (d. 1635; Boltz 1987:200), Zhu Changchun 朱常淳 or Zhu Cikui 朱慈燡 (Mori 1994:191, 201).

Wu's name was later linked with that of Liu Huayang 柳華陽 (1735–1799), a Chan monk and author of the *Huiming jing* 慧命經 (Book of Wisdom and Life).[27] Some of their works were published together under the title *Wu Liu xianzong* 伍柳仙宗 (Immortality Teachings of Wu and Liu), creating a lineage called the Wu-Liu school. Eclectic in character, this work drew on the inner alchemical traditions of the Song and Yuan, joining them with Chan and Huayan Buddhism, and presenting them in a readily comprehensible language inspired by Confucian, Daoist, and Buddhist teachings as well as medical theories.

The Western School

Another Qing school of inner alchemy was the Western School, also known as the Yinxian pai 隱仙派 or "Hidden Immortal School," or again as the Youlong pai 猶龍派 or "Like Unto a Dragon School" (see Wong 1988a). It flourished in Leshan 樂山 district (Sichuan) in the nineteenth century, and its main representative was Li Xiyue 李西月 (fl. 1796–1850).[28] Li says

---

[26] DZJY *biji* 6; Chongkan ed. 17.7630–39.

[27] Dated 1794; translations Wilhelm 1929 and Wong 1998. {See M. Esposito, *Creative Daoism*, Part 4}.

[28] Orig. Yuanzhi 元植, *zi* Pingquan 平泉, *hao* Changyi shanren 長乙山人 or "Hermit of Changyi," Zixia dong zhuren 紫霞洞主人 or "Master of Purple Clouds Cavern," Shibenzi 食本子 or "Devourer of Books," Tuanyangzi 團陽子 or "Master of Round Yang;" see Wong 1988a:1–62; Yokote 1994:70.

that he received the name Xiyue from the immortal Lü Dongbin 呂洞賓 when he met him on Mount Emei 峨眉山 (Sichuan) together with Zhang Sanfeng (*Daozang jinghua* 道藏精華, abbr. DZJH 2-2). He regarded himself as a disciple of both masters and particularly devoted himself to the transmission and collection of Zhang's alchemical teachings, compiling also the *Zhang Sanfeng quanji* 張三丰全集 (Complete Works of Zhang Sanfeng).

Among his works are also a commentary to the *Wugen shu* 無根樹 (Tree Without Roots), a collection of poems attributed to Zhang Sanfeng (*Daoshu qizhong* 道書七種, DZJH 8), and a collection of exegeses to the *Taishang shisanjing* 太上十三經 (Thirteen Supreme Classics; see below). Li further explains his alchemical theories in the *Daoqiao tan* 道竅談 (Discussion of the Opening of the Path) and the *Sandong bizhi* 三洞秘旨 (Secret Principles of the Three Vehicles), both edited by Chen Yingning 陳攖寧 in the twentieth century (DZJH 2-2). In the latter text in particular, Li divides the alchemical firing process into three stages called the "three vehicles." The first is employed to transport vital energy (*qi* 氣) and corresponds to the microcosmic orbit (*xiao zhoutian* 小周天); the second transports essence (*jing* 精) and corresponds to the circulation of the jade liquid (*yuye* 玉液); the third transports both essence and vital energy and corresponds to the macrocosmic orbit (*da zhoutian* 大周天; see Yokote 1994). The three vehicles clearly recall the Buddhist parable of the three carts, mentioned in the *Lotus Sūtra* (Yokote 1994).

Overall, Li's alchemical theories reflect the tendency of the time to join the three teachings and clarify alchemical practices from a physiological viewpoint. His work is important because it sheds light on the teachings and history of the Western School associated with Zhang Sanfeng and other schools similarly linked with this immortal.

THE JINGMING SCHOOL

The Jingming school (Jingming pai 淨明派), prominent under the Song and Yuan, continued under the Qing as part of the Longmen and the official Zhengyi legacy;[29] it was particularly associated with the well-known *Jinhua zongzhi* 金華宗旨 (Secret of the Golden Flower).[30] Having lost some lin-

---

[29] See Akizuki 1978; Chen 1990 & 1991; Qing 1996:126–29.
[30] Translations Wilhelm 1929; Cleary 1992. {See M. Esposito, *Creative Daoism*, Part 4}

eage continuity, the school attempted to reconstruct itself with the help of spirit writing, calling particularly upon the immortal Lü Dongbin.[31] A different perspective is found in the *Xiaoyao shan wanshou gong zhi* 逍遙山萬壽宮志 (Gazetteer of the Palace of Longevity on Mount Xiaoyao).[32] It says that Xu Shouchen 徐守誠 (1632-1692) was the major patriarch of the school. He belonged to Longmen in the eighth generation and withdrew to Xishan (Jiangxi) to devote his life to the restoration of the local Jingming temple and the renewal of Jingming doctrine (Qing 1996:127-28).

Another important representative of the school was Fu Jinquan 傅金銓 (b. 1765)[33] whose work contributed greatly to the diffusion of Jingming teachings (Qing 1996:194-208). Information about Fu's life is scarce. He was born into a wealthy family and received a classical education, excelling in painting, music, calligraphy, and other subjects (*Beixi lu* 杯溪錄, ZWDS 11.1). He travelled in Jiangxi, Jiangsu and Hunan and, in 1817, moved to Sichuan where he transmitted his teachings (Qing 1994, 1: 399). Fu claimed to have obtained some teachings from Lü Dongbin, but he also placed high emphasis on Confucian values of filial piety and loyalty. His doctrines are reflected in his *Daoshu shiqi zhong* 道書十七種 (Seventeen Daoist Books, see below), in which he collected the dialogues of Liu Yu 劉玉, the original founder of the Jingming school, emphasized Confucian ethics, and argued for the necessity of living in the world in accordance with moral and social rules. Fu is also the author of certain texts on women's inner alchemy (see Despeux 1990; Wile 1992) and of several commentaries on alchemical classics (ZWDS 11: 745-861).

---

[31] Esposito 1998a, 1998b; Mori 1998a, 1998b.

[32] J. 13; *Zangwai daoshu* 臧外道書 20:819-21.

[33] *Zi* Dingyun 鼎雲, *hao* Jiyizi 濟一子 or "Master Saving the One," Zuihua laoren 醉華老人 or "Old Man Drunk on Flowers," from Jinxi 金溪 in Jiangxi.

TEXTS

Canons

Daozang jiyao 道藏輯要 (Essence of the Daoist Canon), dat. 19th c.

Depending on edition and exemplar up to almost 340 texts.
Editions: The main edition of this text collection in use today is the *Chongkan daozang jiyao* 重刊道藏輯要 (Reedited Essence of the Daoist Canon) which was compiled in 1906 under the supervision of the abbot Yan Yonghe 閻永和 and with the help of Peng Hanran 彭瀚然 and He Longxiang 賀龍驤. It is based on the early 19th-century original canon of Erxian'an 二仙庵 (Hermitage of the Two Immortals) in Chengdu whose plates had been destroyed in a 1892 fire. Repr. Taipei: Kaozheng, 1971 (25 vols.); Taipei: Xinwenfeng, 1977; Chengdu: Erxian'an, 1986 (see Chen 1987; Ding 1996).

This canon contains Daoist texts not only from the *Daozang* but also from private collections, libraries, and temples of the Ming and Qing. Its origins are somewhat obscure. According to the introduction of the Erxian'an edition, Peng Dingqiu 彭定求 (1645-1719) first compiled it during the Kangxi era (1662-1722; see Wong 1982:3-4), but this seems historically unlikely (Liu 1973:107-8). Another account is found in a gloss to the list of contents of the collection, the *Daozang jiyao zongmu* 道藏輯要總目 as contained in the *Daozang jinghua lu* 道藏精華錄 (repr. 1989, 1:1a-8a), where the compilation is attributed to Jiang Yupu 蔣予蒲 (1755-1819, *zi* Yuanting 元庭) and dated to the Jiaqing era (1796-1820). According to this gloss, Jiang had the printing blocks engraved in Beijing and then delivered them back to the south. However, soon after his return north, he died in Beijing, and for this reason only a few copies of this original edition circulated.[34] One copy, the property of Yan Yanfeng 嚴雁峰 (1855-1918), was preserved in the Sichuan provincial library in Chengdu and formed the basis for carving the plates of the new Erxian'an edition (Ding 1996:216).

The collection has various prefaces gained through spirit writing at the Awakening Altar (*juetan* 覺壇) where Jiang Yupu and his companions worshiped. These prefaces include clear instructions by Lü Dongbin to these

---

[34] Wong 1982:5-6; Yoshioka 1955:176; Liu 1973:108; Ding 1996:216-18.

Daoists that they should edit and publish the compilation.[35] The fact that they date from the Jiaqing era, matching the time when Jiang Yupu supposedly compiled it, supports his being the original editor. The contents of the *Daozang jiyao* are, apart from scriptures from the Ming Daoist canon, mostly texts on inner alchemy that were allegedly received through spirit writing. They shed light on the popularity of the practice as well as on the cult of the immortals, especially that of Lü Dongbin (see Katz 1996). It is a fundamental source on the cults, schools, doctrines and practices of Ming and Qing Daoism.

Daozang jinghua lu 道藏精華錄 (Record of Essential Blossoms of the Daoist Canon)

100 texts, 10 sections, by Ding Fubao 丁福保 (1874–1952, *zi* Shouyi zi 守一子), ed. Shanghai: Yixue, 1922; Zhejiang guji, 1989.

This collection consists mostly of works from the *Daozang* and the *Daozang jiyao* on inner alchemy and nourishing life, but it also contains some biographical notes, doctrinal statements, and ritual texts. It continues earlier encyclopedias, such as the *Yunji qiqian* 雲笈七籤 (Seven Tablets in a Cloudy Satchel) and the *Xiuzhen shishu* 修真十書 (Ten Books on the Cultivation of Perfection) and includes important Ming-Qing inner alchemical texts. Each of these texts features after the title a brief abstract and some notes on its origin.

Inner Alchemical Collections

Wu Liu xianzong 伍柳仙宗 (Immortality Teachings of Wu and Liu)

4 texts. Edited by Deng Huiji 鄧徽績, dat. 1897.

This collection begins with two texts by Wu Shouyang 伍守陽 (1574–1634). The first text, the *Tianxian zhengli* 天仙正理 (Proper Principles of Celestial Immortality)[36] has two sections called "Simple Explanations" (*qianshu* 淺說) and "Forthright Discourses" (*zhilun* 旨論). The first con-

---

[35] Ding 1996:216–17; Esposito 1998a:11–12 & 1998b; Mori 1998b:18–19.
[36] Also in DZJY *biji* 4–5; Chongkan ed. 17.7541–95.

tains the alchemical teachings Wu received from Cao Changhua 曹常化 (1562–1622), with a commentary by his disciple Wu Shouxu 伍守虛 (zi Zhenyang 真陽). The second section consists of nine essays dealing with vital energy Before and After Heaven, basic medicines, the alchemical cauldron, the firing process, refining the self, laying the foundations, refining the medicine, controlling the energy, and embryo respiration. Each essay contains a saying by master Wu Shouyang with extensive annotation by his disciple Wu Shouxu, and the second section concludes with a note on the origin of the nine essays and a more general postface.

The second text of this collection is the *Xianfo hezong yulu* 仙佛合宗語錄 (Recorded Sayings on the Common Tradition of Daoism and Buddhism)[37] which contains questions and answers of Wu's disciples with a critical commentary by Wu Shouxu. The main theme of this text is the pursuit of transcendence as analogous to the attainment of Buddhahood, a theme probably also central in an earlier text, the *Xianfo tongyuan* 仙佛同源 (Common Origins of Daoism and Buddhism; lost) by Zhao Youqin 趙友欽 (fl. 1329; see Boltz 1987:201). Wu's text is interesting because it provides a concrete explanation on how to distinguish reality from illusion, how to realize instantaneousness in the regulation of the firing process and how to understand key terms such as *zhenyi* 真意 (true intention) and *shouzhong* 守中 (guarding the center).

The third and fourth texts of the *Wu Liu xianzong* are by Liu Huayang 柳華陽 (1735–1799). The third is the *Huiming jing* 慧命經 (Book of Wisdom and Life),[38] dated 1794, with a preface containing some biographical notes on the author. The first part includes a series of eight illustrations on inner alchemical practice with explanations, while the remainder presents various related theories.

The fourth and final text is the *Jinxian zhenglun* 金仙証論 (A Testimony to Golden Immortality, dat. 1799), written at the Renshousi 仁壽寺 (Temple of Humane Life) in Beijing. It is divided into eighteen sections, the first six of which concern the practice of the microcosmic orbit and the refinement of *jing* 精 and *qi* 氣. Section 7 focuses on the moment of production of the small medicine, i.e. the experience of instantaneousness in the firing process, which is the starting point of the second stage of refining *qi* and *shen*. Later sections discuss the foundation of real practice and

---

[37] Also DZJY *biji* 6; 1; 2.1a-25a;3.31b-39b; Chongkan ed. 17.7403–7540.
[38] Translations Wilhelm 1929; Wong 1998.

the difference between the different orbits (sect. 11). The last third of the text deals with the right vision of discernment and the path leading to the third stage, culminating in a section entitled "Resolving Doubts" (*jueyi* 決疑) containing questions posed by Liu's disciples with answers. The text ends with a supplement called "On Dangers" (*weixian shuo* 危險說) that explains obstacles to practice such as the incursion of discursive thoughts, the erroneous understanding of the principles, and the fall into heterodox paths.

Daoshu shiqi zhong 道書十七種 (Seventeen Daoist Books)

17 texts. By Fu Jinquan 傅金銓 of the Daoguang era (1796–1850), ed. Shudong shancheng tang, 1825 (see Needham et al. 1983, 5:5, 231, 240–43); Guangling guji, 1993; ZWDS 11).

These seventeen texts can be divided into three groups: 1. exegeses by Fu Jinquan; 2. texts written by Fu Jinquan; 3. texts written by other authors.

The first group contains Fu's commentaries on texts associated with Lü Dongbin, such as the *Lüzu wupian* 呂祖五篇 (Five Compositions of Patriarch Lü) and the *Duren haijing* 度人頦經 (The Path of Universal Salvation), dat. 1815

The second group contains works by Fu Jinquan 傅金銓:

1. *Xingtian zhenggu* 性天正鵠 (Striking the Center of Celestial Nature's Target), on Jingming practice;
2. *Daohai jinliang* 道海津梁 (Bridge of the Sea of the Path), on Jingming practice;
3. *Chishui yin* 赤水音 (Songs on the Red Water), poetry on alchemy;
4. *Yiguan zhenji yijian lu* 一貫真機易簡錄 (Simple Notes on the Mechanism that Unifies All), prose on alchemy;
5. *Xinxue* 心學 (Study of the Heart-Mind), syncretistic teachings;
6. *Beixi ji* 杯溪集 (Collection from Bei Mountain Stream), collection of poems;
7. *Ziti suohua* 自題所畫 (Painting Inscriptions), poems and art inscriptions.

The third group consists of works by various Daoist masters and schools, including texts such as:

Qiaoyang jing 樵陽經 (Classic of Qiaoyang) which includes the *Qiaoyang zi yulu* 樵陽子語錄 (Records of the Master Qiaoyang [sobriquet of Liu Yu 劉玉]) and other early texts related to the Jingming 淨明 school;

Sanfeng danjue 三丰丹訣 (Sanfeng's Alchemical Formulas) which includes various texts attributed to Zhang Sanfeng;

Qiuzu quanshu 邱祖全書 (Complete Works of the Patriarch Qiu [Chuji]) containing the recorded sayings of Qiu Chuji (see Mori 1998c). According to Pan Jingguan 潘靜觀, a Longmen disciple, this text was preserved by Zhang Bixu 張碧虛, a disciple of Qiu Chuji.[39]

The collection also presents the *Tianxian zhilun* 天仙值論 (Forthright Discourses on Celestial Immortality) by Wu Shouyang of the Wu-Liu school under the title *Nei jindan* 內金丹 (Inner Golden Elixir), and it contains under the heading *Wai jindan* 外金丹 (Outer Golden Elixir) a number of texts on operative alchemy that are attributed to Guangchengzi 廣成子, Ge Xuan 葛玄, Liu An 劉安 and others. As a whole, it is useful for the study of late Jingming thought, of the Longmen school, and of inner alchemical theory in the Ming and Qing.

Gu shuyinlou cangshu 古書隱樓藏書 (Library of the Ancient Pavilion of Hidden Books)

35 texts, 14 vols., by Min Yide 閔一得, collected in the Chunyang gong 純陽宮 (Palace of Master Chunyang [Lü Dongbin]) on Mount Jingai and first edited in 1834. It was reedited variously (see Qing 1996:116). The 1904 edition was reprinted by Guangling guji 廣陵古籍 in 1993). Twenty-three texts of the collection, mostly inner alchemical texts and commentaries, also appear in the *Daozang xubian* 道藏續編 (Supplementary Collection of the Daoist Canon), first edited on Mount Jingai in 1834 and since then reprinted variously.[40]

The texts contained in the *Gu shuyinlou cangshu* can be divided into three groups: 1. commentaries or texts revised by Min Yide 閔一得 and other masters; 2. texts written by Min himself; 3. texts written by other masters.

---

[39] See Pan Jingguan 潘靜觀. 1815. "Yulu houxu 語錄後序 (Postface to the Record)." In Fu Jinquan, *Jiyi zi Daoshu shiqi zhong*. 濟一子道書十七種 (Seventeen Books by Master Who Saves the One). ZWDS 11:289–90.

[40] Shanghai: Yixue shuju 1952; Beijing: Haiyang, 1989; Beijing: Shumu wenxian, 1993. See Esposito 1992, 1993.

The first group contains Min's notes on a number of established texts, including the *Xiuzhen biannan* 修真辯難 (Debate on the Cultivation of Perfection) by Liu Yiming 劉一明; the *Yinfujing* 陰符經 (Scripture on Joining with Obscurity) by Li Quan 李筌; the *Jindan sibaizi* 金丹四百字 (Four-hundred Words on the Golden Elixir) by Zhang Boduan 張伯端, with commentary by Peng Haogu 彭好古 and revised by Min Yanglin 閔陽林 (Min Yide comments only the preface by Zhang Boduan); and Min's full notes on the *Xiuxian bianhuo lun* 修仙辨惑論 (On Doubts Concerning the Cultivation of Immortality) by Bai Yuchan 白玉蟾, under the title *Guankui bian* 管窺編 (A Personal View).

Also included are Min's annotations and revisions of hitherto unpublished manuscripts that had been stored in different temples. These include the *Huangji hepi zhengdao xianjing* 皇極闔闢證道仙經 (Immortals' Scripture Testifying to the Path of Opening and Closing the Sovereign Ultimate) and the *Liaoyang dian wenda bian* 寥陽殿問答編 (Questions and Answers from the Liaoyang Hall). Both are manuscripts from the Qingyang gong 青羊宮 (Black Sheep Temple) in Chengdu that were transmitted by the semi-legendary Yin Pengtou 尹蓬頭 (*Daozang xubian* 1.7b; Esposito 1993). There is, in addition, a version of the *Taiyi jinhua zongzhi* 太一金華宗旨 (Secret of the Golden Flower) revised by Longmen masters from Mount Jingai (Esposito 1993 & 1996; Mori 1998a). Min also included a cycle of texts on the doctrine of healing the world (*yishi* 醫世), which he claimed to have received from Jizu daozhe and from his master Shen Yibing, and wrote a commentary on this subject under the title *Du Lü zushi sanni yishi shuoshu guankui* 讀呂祖師三尼醫世說述管窺 (A Personal Reading of the Explanations of the Three Sages' Doctrine of Healing the World by Patriarch Lü). The first part of the collection contains towards its end a cycle of texts on precepts, transmitted by Shen Yibing and compiled by Min Yide in the context of the cultivation of celestial immortality. Here also are two texts on feminine inner alchemy and related moral rules (Despeux 1991; Wile 1992; Esposito 1993).

The second group contains a number of Min's own works, such as the *Suoyan xu* 瑣言續 (Sequel to an Ignored Transmission), *Erlan xinhua* 二懶心話 (Heart-to-Heart Dialogue Between the Two Leisurely [Masters]),[41] and *Tianxian xinchuan* 天仙心傳 (Heart Transmission of Celestial Immortality).

---

[41] Italian translation in Esposito 1997.

The third group contains works (1) of Confucian background, (2) materials associated with Zhang Sanfeng, and (3) several Tantric or Buddhism-inspired works. Among the first, Confucian works, there are the *Jiuzheng lu* 就正錄 (Record of the Realization of Rectitude), *Yu Lin Fenqian xiansheng shu* 與林奮千先生書 (Letter to Master Lin Fenqian), both by the Confucian Lu Shichen 陸世忱. Second, works associated with Zhang Sanfeng include the *Sanfeng zhenren xuantan quanji* 三丰真人玄譚全集 (Complete Collection of the Mysterious Words by the Perfected Sanfeng), attributed to Zhang Sanfeng. In the third sub-group there is a Tantric work, the *Foshuo chishi tuoluoni jing* 佛說持世陀羅尼經 (*Vasu[n]dhārā-dhāraṇī*), which also appears to exist in a Tibetan version (see Esposito 1993), and the *Biyuan tanjing* 碧苑壇經 (Platform Sūtra of the Jade Garden), a lecture by Wang Changyue on Longmen principles for the ordained.

Daoshu shier zhong 道書十二種 (Twelve Daoist Books)

> By Liu Yiming 劉一明. Editions: Changde (Hunan): Huguo'an, 1819; Shanghai: Yihua tang 1880; Shanghai: Jiangdong shuju 1925; Taipei: Xinwenfeng 1983; Beijing: Zhongguo zhongyiyao 1990; ZWDS 8.

This collection's materials can be divided into three groups: 1. Liu's commentaries on the *Yijing* 易經; 2. Liu's commentaries on alchemical classics; 3. Liu's own writings.

The first group contains two texts, beginning with the *Zhouyi chanzhen* 周易闡真 (True Explanation of the "Changes," 4 j., pref. 1798, trl. Cleary 1986a). *Chanzhen* here means an "authentic exegesis," and it concerns the explanation of truth inherent in the investigation of principles, the truth of the fulfillment of inner nature and understanding of the meaning of destiny. The first chapter has thirty diagrams on the *Yijing*, transmitted from the Song and Yuan, some of which are traditionally attributed to Chen Tuan 陳摶. The remaining three chapters contain a commentary on the sixty-four hexagrams as well as their individual lines. The second text of this group is the *Kongyi chanzhen* 孔易闡真 (True Explanation of the Confucian "Changes," two sections, no pref., trl. Cleary 1986a: 239–323). It contains an exegesis of the *Daxiang zhuan* 大象傳 (Commentary of General Images) and of the *Zagua zhuan* 雜卦傳 (Commentary on Miscellaneous Hexagrams).

The second group of texts in this collection presents Liu's commentaries on alchemical classics. Here we have his *Cantongqi zhizhi* 參同契直指 (Direct Pointers to "The Triplex Agreement," pref. 1799, Pregadio 1996:83); *Wuzhen zhizhi* 悟真直指 (Direct Pointers to "Awakening to Perfection," pref. 1794, trl. Cleary 1987; see Miyakawa 1954); *Yinfujing zhu* 陰符經註 (Commentary on the Scripture on Joining with the Hidden, pref. 1779, trl. Cleary 1991:220–38); *Huangting jingjie* 黃庭經解 (Explanations of the Yellow Court Scripture) and *Jindan sibaizi jie* 金丹四百字解 (Explanations of the Four Hundred Words on the Golden Elixir, pref. 1807, trl. Cleary 1986b). Liu compares the various classics, and with the help of the teachings he received from his Daoist masters, explains the meaning of their symbolic language and sheds light on their abstruse alchemical terminology. He thus offers an exegesis that cleverly mixes his knowledge of the three teachings with that from his alchemical and spiritual experiences.

The third group of texts in the *Daoshu shier zong* contains eight texts from Liu's own hand. They begin with the *Xiyou yuanzhi* 西遊原旨 (The Original Meaning of the "Journey to the West," pref. 1778, 1798, trl. Yu 1991; Cleary 1991), a work midway between an alchemical exegesis and an independent work. It is an alchemical explanation of the novel *Xiyouji* 西遊記 (Journey to the West). Some Ming and Qing scholars, including Liu, erroneously attributed this work to Qiu Chuji and confused it with the record of his journey to Chinggis Khan, also entitled *Xiyouji* (DZ 1429). In his comments, Liu links the one-hundred chapters of the novel to secret alchemical practices and shows how they represent the true alchemical quest, a journey to perfection that takes place in the adept's body (Despeux 1985: 65–66, 70–72).

Next in this group is the *Xiangyan poyi* 象言破疑 (Resolving Symbolic Language, 2 sections, pref. 1811, trl. Cleary 1986a: 51–118). Liu here presents seven diagrams to illustrate the natural process of human creation, which he divides into three stages: gestation, childhood, and adulthood (see Li 1988:554–58; Liu 1991:237–39). A third text is the *Tongguan wen* 通關文 (Treatise on Going through the Passes, 2 sections, pref. 1812). It is related to the *Xiuzhen jiuyao* (see below) and its first section on "Seeing Through Things of the World." Liu here presents a list of fifty passes to prevent adepts from sinking into the ocean of worldly sufferings. Passes that must be overcome include the pass of desire, the pass of affection, and the pass of honors. The list represents a series of stages of progressive awareness (see Li 1988:559–60).

Fourth in this group is the *Xiuzhen biannan* 修真辯難 (Debate on the Cultivation of Perfection, 2 sections, preface dated 1798). This is a dialogue between master and disciples on various ways of attaining perfection. The fact that it is also contained in Min Yide's *Gu shuyinlou cangshu* demonstrates the importance of Liu's ideas in Longmen teachings.

Liu's fifth work contained here is the *Shenshi bafa* 神室八法 (Eight Elements of the Spiritual Abode, pref. 1798). The "spiritual abode" is a metaphor for the nature of the mind and thus for the basis of true alchemical cultivation. Liu presents a list of eight spiritual qualities needed as the basic materials for building one's spiritual abode: firmness, flexibility, sincerity, trustfulness, temperance, peacefulness, emptiness and spiritual clarity (see Li 1988:563–67).

The sixth text is the *Xiuzhen jiuyao* 修真九要 (Nine Principles in the Cultivation of Perfection, pref. 1798) which presents a list of nine principles matching nine stages of spiritual cultivation. They begin with "Seeing Through Things of the World" and continue on to "Realizing Destiny Through the Outer Medicine" and "Realizing Inner Nature Through the Inner Medicine" (see Li 1988:559–63).

This text is followed by the *Wudao lu* 悟道錄 (Record of Awakening to the Path, two sections, prefaces dated 1810, 1811, trl. Cleary 1988). This text contains Liu's cosmological theories. The text especially points out the indissoluble bond between macrocosm and microcosm and emphasizes the fundamental balance between yin and yang (see Li 1988:559–63).

The eighth and last text here is the *Huixin ji* 會心集 (Collection of Encounters of the Mind, 2 parts, 2 sections, pref. 1801). The first section of the inner part consists of poems in five- and seven-character verse, compositions of irregular verses, and songs illustrating the alchemical path. The second section includes ten treatises, such as "Discussion of the Great Dao Going back to the One," "Gathering the Medicine," and "The Firing Process." All are devoted to the explanation of alchemical practices. The first section of the outer part has poems, inscriptions and eulogies, while the second section consists of songs and miscellaneous prose, including songs on "Women's Alchemy" and the "Debate on the Three Teachings."

Ritual Texts

Guangcheng yizhi 廣成儀制 (Ritual Systematization of Master Guangcheng)

> 270 texts, ed. by Chen Chongyuan 陳仲遠 (*hao* Yunfeng yuke 雲峰羽客 or "Feathered Host of the Cloudy Peak"); see Qing 1996:139, 465).
> Editions: Chengdu: Erxian'an, 1911, reprinted 1913; ZWDS 13–15.

This work represents the most complete collection of liturgical Quanzhen texts. It includes texts used in Quanzhen temples, works on popular and regional cults (Yangzi valley, Sichuan), and materials on the rituals of other Daoist schools such as the Lingbao and Qingwei as they were standardized under to the Quanzhen model. The book is a valuable resource concerning the development and progressive standardization of Daoist ritual under Quanzhen canonization.

Gazetteers

Chongxiu Longhu shanzhi 重修龍虎山志 (Gazetteer of the Reconstructions of Mt. Longhu)

> 16 juan, preface dated 1740. By Lou Jinyuan 婁近垣 (1689–1776).
> Editions: Xylographic version in Shangqing gong on Mount Longhu; ZWDS 19: 419–636; *Daojiao wenxian* 2 (Taipei: Danqing tushu, 1983); Taipei: Guangwen shuju yinxing, 1989; *Zhonghua xu daozang* 中華續道藏 [Supplement to the Daoist Canon], vol. 3 (Taipei: Shinwenfeng, 1999).

The text describes the history of Mount Longhu and its temples, drawing upon an earlier record by Yuan Mingshan 元明善 (1269–1322, *Daojiao wenxian* 1) and following "what remained of a 10-ch. topography by the 43rd Celestial Master Zhang Yuchu (1361–1410)" (Boltz 1987:276, note 157). It begins in *juan* 1 with imperial decrees regarding the mountain, the rebuilding of its temples, and the titles granted to its Celestial Masters as well as certain biographical notes on its author.

Juan 2 describes the landscape surrounding Mount Longhu; *juan* 3–4 present its temples and hermitages; *juan* 5 cites relics of the past and gives information on its Buddhist temples; *juan* 6 contains biographies of Celestial Masters from Zhang Daoling to Zhang Xilin (55th); *juan* 7 has those of other local Zhengyi masters; *juan* 8 provides an account of imperial honorific titles conferred on the Celestial Masters and the transmission of seals since the early Ming; *juan* 9 deals with land donations made to the mountain; *juan* 10 through 16, finally, contain artistic and literary works, recorded sayings, epigraphic sources, elegies, and miscellanea. The gazetteer is an important resource for the history of the Celestial Masters and their relationship to Mount Longhu. It is of particular interest for the study of their development under the Ming and Qing dynasties.

Several other gazetteers were compiled during the Qing:

Maoshan quanji 茅山全志 (Complete Gazetteer of Mount Mao)

> 14 *juan*, preface dated 1878, by Da Changuang 笪蟾光, ed. ZWDS 20: 697–964.

This text contains drawings of the mountain, reprints of epigraphic records such as stelae and temple inscriptions, relics of the past and biographies of local patriarchs and Maoshan masters from Wei Huacun 魏華存 to Liu Dabin 劉大彬 (fl. 1317–1328), 45th Shangqing patriarch and author of the earlier *Maoshan zhi* 茅山志 (Record of Maoshan, DZ 304; see Boltz 1987:103; Schafer 1980). The collection contains important materials for the study of the Daoism associated with the mountain, including also a survey of overall historical and religious development from the Song to the late Ming.

Huayue zhi 華嶽志 (Gazetteer of Sacred Mount Hua) also known as *Huashan zhi* 華山志 (Gazetteer of Mount Hua)

> 8 *juan*, preface dated 1821, 1831, by Li Rong 李榕, ed. ZWDS 20: 3–185.

The compiler Li Rong lived on the mountain for twenty years and presents a comprehensive collection of relevant drawings, relics, biographies, epigraphic sources, literary works, and more. He relies heavily on earlier compilations, such as Wang Chuyi's 王處一 *Xiyue huashan zhi* 西嶽華山志 (Gazetteer of Mount Hua, the Western Peak, DZ 307; see Boltz 1987:107–9) and Li Shifang's 李時芳 *Huayue quanji* 華嶽全集 (Complete Collection on Mount Hua, 13 j.), supplemented by Ma Mingqing 馬明卿. All of these use epigraphic sources and various other materials concerning the mountain, but the Qing-dynasty *Huayue zhi* constitutes the a final product combining the information from all previous gazetteers.

Xiaoyao shan wanshou gong zhi 逍遙山萬壽宮志 (Gazetteer of the Palace of Longevity on Mount Xiaoyao)

> 15 *juan*, preface dated 1878, by Jin Guixin 金桂馨 and Qi Fengyuan 漆逢源 (eds.), ZWDS 20: 653–977.

This collection of materials about the Longevity Temple on Xishan (Jiangxi) contains important sources on the Xu Xun 許遜 cult and the Jingming school (see Akizuki 1978:63–86).

Jingu dong zhi 金鼓洞志 (Gazetteer of the Golden Drum Cavern)

> 8 *juan*, dated 1796–1820, by Zhu Wenzao 朱文藻 upon request of Zhang Fuchun 張復純, the 14th patriarch of Longmen at the Helin Gong 鶴林宮 (Crane Forest Temple) of the Jingu dong.
> Editions: *Wulin zhanggu congbian* by Ding Bing 丁丙, dat. 1833 (Taipei: Jinghua shuju, 1967); ZWDS 20:189–299.

The Helin Temple still exists as a Longmen center at the foot of Mount Zilong north of Qixia Peak in modern Hangzhou. It has been a Longmen temple since Zhou Mingyang 周明陽 (1628-1711).

The text begins in *juan* 1 with a portrait of Lü Dongbin and four characters allegedly written in his own hand. *Juan* 2–3 contain a description of the local landscape and surrounding places, including travel notes and eulogies (also in *juan* 5). *Juan* 4 is devoted to, among other things, the history and development of the temple, descriptions of its sanctuaries, halls, layout, and other features. *Juan* 7 lists the names of related Longmen patriarchs from the 5th to the 14th generations, while *juan* 8 contains supplementary notes, epitaphs and biographies of ancient sages and eminent personages who had sojourned there.

WORLDVIEW

Syncretism of the Three Teachings

Late imperial China generally was characterized by unity and integration. This is evident in the thought of many philosophers who developed theories and methods of self-cultivation that mixed Confucianism with Buddhism and Daoism. The unity of the three teachings shaped Ming and Qing society and was acclaimed by religious schools, sects and lay associations in the wider populace, the intellectual elite of the time, and even the emperors. Syncretism as a means to reconcile different elements of different religious traditions was and still is central to Chinese religious life. Despite its flexibility, it tended to establish further levels of orthodoxy and thus, paradoxically, paved the way for more pronounced sectarian activities (see Berling 1980). Generally, Ming and Qing rulers and their representatives were suspicious of any organized religious elements that did not support the "kingly way" and persecuted all forms of religious and intellectual heterodoxy. The organized religions, therefore, had to adopt their own values to Confucian cultural norms. These norms were completely accepted not only by them (see Smith 1983) but also by various heterodox associations—the White Lotus 白蓮, for example, adopted the six Confucian maxims of the first Ming emperor into its popular chant (see Naquin 1985).

Still, the two dynasties were not entirely alike. The Ming government saw the three teachings as a source of official legitimacy; the Qing, as a foreign dynasty, used them to emphasize the role of Neo-Confucianism in contrast to Buddhism and Daoism. The Qing pursued complete control over all religious organizations and attempted to concentrate them around certain well-defined and well-controlled schools that were faithful to official policy. At the end of the Ming, the Confucian elite (e.g., Wang Yangming 王陽明, Lin Zhaoen 林兆恩, Wang Fuzhi 王夫之) supported the syncretic movement and contributed to the propagation of the religious and intellectual theories of the three teachings. By contrast many Qing scholars, shocked by the disastrous consequences of Ming despotism, felt it necessary to go back to the source of the "original" Confucian spirit. They traced the Ming collapse and its cataclysm of 1644 to the empty speculations regarding the inner quest of sanctity that had begun in Song times. Accordingly, they adopted a pragmatic policy and strongly rejected Buddhist and Daoist doctrines (see Cheng 1997).

Thus, like the Ming dynasty, the Qing period was open to syncretic impulses, but in a more covert way. The Ming witnessed the spread of lay syncretistic associations, supported even by the ruling elite, and also the production of many religious and morality books that focused on meeting the needs of laymen and narrowing the gap between common people and the elite. The Qing, by contrast, cut all links with these associations and their publications because they were too independent of government control; instead, they used morality pamphlets to propagate models of social behavior and ethics consistent with Confucian doctrines. Obsessed with ensuring subject-monarch loyalty on the basis of filial piety, the Qing court employed morality books and so-called "Sacred Edicts" as instruments of indoctrination. For example, the Kangxi emperor's "Sacred Edict" of 1670 was expected to be read aloud by officials and village elders in public meetings in all rural localities. Even more publicized was the *Shengyu guangxun* 聖語廣訓 (Extensive Explanation of the "Sacred Edict"), an amplification of Kangxi's edict produced by his son, the Yongzheng emperor. It was published in a number of popularized versions, some of them written in local dialects (see Chang 1967; Mair 1985).

This phenomenon of widespread Confucian propaganda facilitated cultural integration and greater uniformity of norms. However, cultural integration was concomitant with cultural heterogeneity, and the late imperial period was characterized not only by uniformity and consensus but also by diversity and dissidence (Rawski 1985).

Cultural Integration: State Ritual and the Standardization of Local Cults

The Qing dynasty placed great emphasis on imperial ritual (*li* 禮), in a manner compatible with Neo-Confucianism (see Zito 1997). They "copied the Ming system down to the smallest detail, often exceeding its dynastic predecessor in ceremonial exuberance" (Smith 1990:285). The Qing emperors paid unprecedented homage to Confucius, and in the waning years of the dynasty, elevated his worship to the first level of state sacrifice, assuming that "the moral transformation of the people is the dynasty's first task and the regulations of ritual constitute the great item of moral transformation" (Smith 1990:288). Important and distinctive ritual compilations were produced under imperial patronage, while ritual handbooks of various sorts circulated widely throughout the empire. Some of them were written for officials and scholars; others for literate commoners, including ritual specialists (Hayes 1985:100–3).

Even though institutional Buddhism and Daoism had their own separate structures and sets of rituals, they—like all members of Chinese society—were expected to adhere at least to the basic elements of ceremonial behavior. Parallel to imperial ritual, Buddhist and Daoist priests, as well as various other ritual specialists, played a major role in local festivals and other rites that remained virtually independent of the state. Community leaders also acted as officiating priests and often replaced them, taking part in charitable works and assisting actively in the construction of approved temples. "Eager to cooperate with state authorities in the standardization of cults," local elites with interest in land and commerce saw their participation in such events as a way to "gentrify" themselves and their home communities (Watson 1985:293). The process of cultural integration in late imperial China, then, also brought about greater religious uniformity. Unsanctioned local deities, although never completely eradicated, gradually disappeared, while new, officially recognized ones were installed. "The promotion of state-approved cults in south China was so successful that, by the mid-Qing, local gods had been effectively superseded by a handful of approved deities" (Watson 1985:293). Different local cults could be joined under a single deity, thus serving the needs of various social classes yet participating in the standardization of cults. Such is the case of Mazu 媽祖 to whom the Qing founder gave the title Tianshang shengmu 天上聖母 (Heavenly Saintly Mother), and who rose to the position of Tianhou 天后 (Empress of Heaven) in 1737 (see Wädow 1992). The literati elite thus played an important role "by ensuring that religious cults conformed to nationally accepted models" (Watson 1985:322).

Morality Books (Shanshu 善書)

Parallel to the acceptance of more uniform religious symbols and deities, late imperial China also saw a remarkable multiplication of religious books written for non-elite groups. Their content was believed to have been revealed by deities in charge of rewards and punishments, and they were based on Confucian ethics mixed with the popular Buddhist concept of karma and Daoist beliefs in longevity and immortality. Their first forerunner was the twelfth-century *Taishang ganyin pian* 太上感應篇 (Treatise on Retribution of the Most High, DZ 1167). The text was first printed in 1164 and distributed by a Song emperor to convey the message that good and bad fortune do not come without reason, and the text was reprinted many times (see Bell 1996). However, while this text and its early successors still focused on the workings of karma and other Buddhist values such as compassion and piety, texts published since the Ming placed a higher emphasis on practical moral teachings (see Yau 1999). One form of moral practice appeared in the so-called Ledgers of Merit and Demerit (*Gongguo ge* 功過格; see Brokaw 1991), which measured each good or bad deed in assigned points and allowed a person to save accumulated good deeds to earn good fortune. 3,000 good deeds were believed to grant one a son, while 10,000 would allow one to pass the examination for the *jinshi* 進士 degree (see Berling 1985). Anyone, not just the educated elite, could become a virtuous sage if he or she could follow this practical science of moral cultivation. While for individuals these morality books were a concrete way of clarifying moral obligations and of calculating progress in moral cultivation, for the court printing them they served not only to accumulate merits but also to reinforce values that maintained societal stability under Qing rule.

Cultural Diversity: Sectarian Religion and Precious Scrolls

Moral cultivation was also central to the practice of sectarian groups, but in their case the government saw it as a source of dissidence because it was propagated outside of orthodox vehicles of transmission. Early modern forms of sectarian activity appeared first in the Yuan in the form of lay Buddhist groups, which gradually integrated Daoist concepts and practices such as healing, divination, and exorcism into their system (see Overmyer

1976; 1985). At the end of the Yuan, some of these groups became more militant, as can be seen in the case of the White Lotus, which changed from a passive devotional group to a millenarian movement (see ter Haar 1992).

Similarly, a new type of vernacular literature called *baojuan* 寶卷 (precious scrolls) appeared among sectarian groups under the Ming and Qing. Early examples contain vernacular discussions of orthodox Buddhist teachings composed by Buddhist monks; later works were authored by charismatic leaders and their movements, for example Luo Menghong's 羅蒙紅 Luojiao 羅教 (Teaching of Luo) or Wuwei jiao 無為教 (Nonaction Religion), who used precious scrolls to express their doctrines (see Overmyer 1985). The phenomenon grew in tandem with economic progress, population increase, and the country's confrontation with Western traders — all social and economic changes which, by the mid-sixteenth century, had ushered in a new phase in China's history.

The new religious groups were a social alternative to the institutionalized religions of the ruling monastic institutions and their temple-cults, which were controlled by the established elite. They drew their inspiration from Buddhism, Daoism, and local oral traditions and spread widely, so that by the late Ming some were supported by court eunuchs, officials, and their wives (see Sawada 1957). The court at that time helped in the printing of *baojuan*, but under the Qing this form of support was cut off and the groups were forced underground (see Naquin 1976). The Qing elite and government despised popular practices performed by Buddhist monks, Daoist priests, and village spirit mediums, although they participated in the state cult and often patronized local temples, hiring Buddhist and Daoist professionals. The movements, then, found adherents less among the ruling elite than among the wider populace. By the eighteenth century they had become part of popular religion, absorbing deities like Guanyin, Confucius and Laozi into their pantheons. Popular deities thus became increasingly dominant, in contrast with earlier movements where they played only a secondary role.

The term "White Lotus sectarianism" has been proposed to subsume all mid-Qing religious groups that share a new mythological framework and incorporate the Maitreyist goddess Wusheng laomu 無生老母 (Eternal Venerable Mother; see Naquin 1985). These groups usually focused either on sūtra-recitation or on meditation. Groups of the sūtra-recitation type adopted the ideal of Buddhist monkhood and developed an organizational structure concordant with congregational and devotional institutions; their main activity consisted of sūtra-recitation, *baojuan* (precious scrolls), morality books, and other texts. Mid-Qing examples of such groups, which also had literati followers, included the above-mentioned Luojiao and the Hongyang jiao 紅楊教 (Religion of Expansive Yang).[42] Groups of the meditation type focused on contemplative practices, healing, and martial arts; their organization consisted of personal networks and lacked any fixed structure.[43]

The different orientation of these groups may have been the product of continuing conflict between elite lay Buddhists, observant of traditional forms, and religious groups outside the traditional monastic framework (see ter Haar 1992). Many sūtra-recitation groups, moreover, incorporated beliefs in Maitreya's coming and Wusheng laomu 無生老母, the Eternal Venerable Mother, so that a schism developed between them and the elite attached to lay Buddhism. Social changes further increased the difference since, after the mid-Ming, families belonging to non-elite religious groups sometimes had members participating in examinations or in the educational system. This frightened the defenders of Confucian morality who, though they tolerated the monasteries, felt threatened by the non-elite religious groups.

By the late Ming, "the literati's practice of lay Buddhism became a difficult undertaking" (ter Haar 1992), a situation exacerbated by increased persecutions under the Qing. This governmental hostility, far from preventing the emergence of religious groups, contributed to their involvement in millenarian uprisings (see Naquin 1981). In another line of development, by the mid-nineteenth century, religious groups merged with community structures, and entire villages adopted White Lotus leadership and techniques of self-defense. Ming and Qing editions of *baojuan* then came to be supplemented by spirit writing scriptures as the basis of new sects.

---

[42] See Overmyer 1978; Kelley 1982; Sawada 1957.
[43] See Naquin 1976; Overmyer 1976.

PRACTICE

Spirit Writing

Spirit writing or planchette writing (*fuji* 扶乩) was a form of divination analogous to consultation of the *Yijing*, geomancy, astrology, *fengshui* 風水, physiognomy, and dream interpretation. The practice began in Tang times, with a cult in honor of Magu (see Chao 1942) and was structurally organized under the Song, but its origins go back to shamanic spirit possession. It centers on receiving automatically written messages transmitted by the spirits of gods, immortals, or culture heroes who "take possession of a writing implement to compose what they will" (Jordan and Overmyer 1986). Spirit writing was embraced by many literati not only as a means of predicting their lifespan, fortune, and examination topics, but also to cure illness, bring rain, and procure other necessities of life. Spirit writing specialists or mediums appeared everywhere and in all social classes. Like professional fortune-tellers, they could predict disasters and provide medical advice in the form of charms or prescriptions (see Smith 1991).

Spirit writing required several devices, beginning with an altar (*jitan* 乩壇) which, during the Ming and Qing, could be found in every prefectural and county capital (see Xu 1941). It was often located in religious temples, usually Daoist but sometimes also Buddhist, or also in association halls, domestic residences, and aristocratic or imperial palaces. A special hall devoted to the practice (*luantang* 鸞堂) typically contained a square table (*xiang'an* 香案), on which there was a tray, known as planchette (*jipan* 乩盤, *shapan* 砂盤), covered with sand or incense ashes. The writing instrument had a T-shaped form (*jijia* 乩架) and was made of peachwood or willow, which are believed to have demon-dispelling qualities. To its end, a sharp tip (*jibi* 乩筆) was attached, cut from the southeastern side of a tree exposed to the yang influence of the rising sun on a day and at a time deemed auspicious (De Groot 1892–1910:1321–22; Gōyama 1994:470). During the procedure, two mediums held (*fu* 扶) the two extremities of the instrument's handle, hence the term *fuji* 扶乩 or "to support the divining instrument" (Smith 1991:226). This was the most common term used in the early Qing, but there were others: *fuji* 扶箕 (supporting the stick), *jiangluan* 降鸞 (descent of the phoenix), *fuluan* 扶鸞 (supporting the phoenix) and *feiluan* 飛鸞 (the flying phoenix).[44]

Before inviting the spirit to descend into the stick, devotees offered food or flowers, burned incense, drew talismans, recited incantations, and underwent ceremonies of purification. As the spirit entered the stick, it began to move automatically, tracing characters on the sand-covered planchette. One person was in charge of reciting the characters (*changluan* 唱鸞) while another noted them down (*luluan* 錄鸞).

Spirit writing was highly popular in late imperial China and was practiced by some very illustrious scholar-officials and literati.[45] They liked it not only because it could give advice on official examinations but also because it emphasized morality. By the early seventeenth century, then, morality books were frequently composed by means of the planchette, mostly revealed by Guandi 關帝 (see Duara 1988), Wenchang 文昌 (see Kleeman 1994), and Lü Dongbin 呂洞賓 (see Katz 1996). The values expressed in such texts were largely Confucian, but also included popular ideas inspired by Buddhism and Daoism. The presence of these elements did not dissuade Qing officials or the gentry from supporting their publication or writing colophons to them. Even scholars involved themselves in the practice, so that Jiang Yupu 蔣予蒲 (1755–1819), for example, presided over a spirit writing altar called *jueyuan* 覺源 or *juetan* 覺壇 which was at the root of the compilation of the *Daozang jiyao* 道藏輯要, the *Lüzu quanshu* 呂祖全書, and other Qing religious texts.[46]

Ming and Qing law officially prohibited the practice, but because it was ardently pursued by those very officials who were supposed to enforce that law, spirit writing survived and flourished throughout the empire. Still, it seems that, like many other shamanic activities, it was practiced more heavily in the south (Gōyama 1994:476). Moreover, non-elite local diviners and shamanic mediums were responsible for many of the spirit texts that circulated widely in Qing society (see Jordan and Overmyer 1986). The spirit writing activities of non-elite practitioners are important not only regarding the development of "sectarian" spirit-writing scriptures, but also as an indication of Ming-Qing cultural integration. Parallel to the elite use of spirit writing, independent religious associations formed around spirit

---

[44] See Gōyama 1994:473–74; Jordan and Overmyer 1986.

[45] See Xu 1941; Jordan and Overmyer 1986; Gōyama 1994.

[46] See Esposito 1998a, 1998b; Mori 1998a, 1998b; Yau 1999.

writing altars. Here morality books were composed in a simple classical style, resembling that used by literati spirit-writers and similarly supporting Confucian values. Only in the late nineteenth century did "sectarian scriptures" appear with mythological content inspired by the Eternal Venerable Mother, but even these retained the format of morality books (ibid.). Such texts can still be found in Taiwan and Hong Kong today, as can spirit writing groups, sometimes nowadays also called "spirit religions" (*shenjiao* 神教), "Confucian spirit religions" (*ruzong shenjiao* 儒宗神教) or "phoenix worship" (*bailuan* 拜鸞). The reference to Confucianism in names such as Rujiao 儒教 or Kongjiao 孔教 (Confucian religion) may well reflect their association with the educated art of writing (ibid.). Several Hong Kong groups are related more directly to Daoism and are generally called *daotan* 道壇 (Daoist altar) or *daotang* 道堂 (Daoist hall). They often hold spirit writing sessions devoted to Lü Dongbin and other Daoist divinities.[47] Indeed, most Daoist sects in Hong Kong began as spirit writing circles and only gradually developed into formal religious organizations, using the Daoist institutions and ritual system as their model. Contemporary Daoist movements can therefore be seen to have emerged from local religious centers rather than secret religious societies (Shiga 1995).

INNER ALCHEMY SIMPLIFIED

We can conclude by saying that moral cultivation was a key preoccupation of Ming-Qing society, propagated in a syncretistic formulation by thinkers such as Lin Zhaoen 林兆恩 (see Berling 1980), as well as by founders of new Daoist schools such as Lu Xixing, Wu Shouyang and Wang Changyue (see Tang 1995). The government strove for a simplified Confucian ethos to be adapted by the entire population, and so did the religious leaders with their doctrines. As a result, Daoist masters devoted themselves to clarifying obscure inner alchemical theories, leaving out their intricate alchemical symbols, and to simplify them in order to facilitate everybody's understanding of the essence of true cultivation (Esposito 1993).

Lin Zhaoen, for example, used Buddhist, Daoist and Neo-Confucian theories as the basis of his sixteenth-century popularization of meditation as a path to englightement (see Berling 1980). Wu Shouyang similarly formulated his alchemical theory on the basis of a mixture of Buddhist and

---

[47] See Tsui 1991; Shiga 1995, 1999.

Daoist doctrines and proposed the attainment of the Confucian humanist path as a first step (see Tang 1995). Wang Changyue of the Longmen school regarded the goal of immortality as attainable for anyone who followed the gradual path of precepts that included the cultivation of Confucian moral principles.[48]

The disclosure of inner-alchemical arcana and the transmission of religious beliefs were further facilitated by popular novels such as the *Fengshen yanyi* 封神演義 (Creation of the Gods; trl. Gu 1993) and the *Dongyou ji* 東遊記 (Journey to the North; see Liu 1962), as well as by the development of sectarian associations. The latter, in particular, integrated methods of meditation inspired by Buddhism and Daoism into their main practices. By the 1760s they were even proposing martial arts as a practical application of Daoist and medical theories of the circulation of energy (see Naquin 1981). Charismatic figures such as Zhang Sanfeng were not only regarded as celestial Daoist monks, but also became patriarchs of inner-alchemy schools[49] and founders of schools of martial arts.[50] Inner-alchemical theories, therefore, were no longer restricted to circles of initiates but became part of a popular culture. They can still be found in folk practices, for example in what is now called *qigong* 氣功.[51]

This was not the product of a simple "popularization." Rather, it resulted from a long process of social and intellectual change, from the increasingly shared values of a widely propagated written culture that emerged over the course of two dynasties.

---

[48] Chen 1988; Esposito 1993; Tang 1985; Qing 1996.
[49] See Wong 1982, 1988; Akioka 1994.
[50] See Despeux 1981; Engelhardt 1981; Vercammen 1989, 1991.
[51] See Engelhardt 1987; Despeux 1988; Miura 1989; Esposito 1995.

REFERENCES

Akioka, Hideyuki 秋岡英行. 1994. "Chō Sanhō to Shindai Dōkyō seiha 張三峰と清代道教西派" [Zhang Sanfeng and the Western school of Daoism in the Qing period]. *Tōhō Shūkyō* 東方宗教 83: 1–15.

Akizuki, Kan'ei 秋月觀. 1978. *Chūgoku kinsei dōkyō no keisei: Jōmyōdō no kisoteki kenkyū* 中国近世道教の形成：浄明道の基楚的研究 [The Structure of Premodern Daoism: Basic Studies on the Jingming Dao]. Tokyo: Sōbunsha 創文社.

Bardol, Philippe. 1992. "Le bouddhisme Chan sous la dynastie des Qing, à l'époque du *Xindeng Lu*," M.A. thesis, Paris: Institut National des Langues et Civilisations Orientales.

Barrett, Thomas. 1978. "Chinese Sectarian Religion." *Modern Asian Studies* 12: 333–352.

Bell, Catherine. 1996. "Stories from an Illustrated Explanation of the *Tract of the Most Exalted on Action and Response*." In *Religion of China in Practice*, edited by Donald S. Lopez, Jr, 437–445. Princeton: Princeton University Press.

Berling, Judith. 1980. *The Syncretic Religion of Lin Chao-en*. New York: Columbia University Press.

———. 1985. "Religion and Popular Culture: The Management of Moral Capital in *The Romance of the Three Teachings*. In *Popular Culture in Late Imperial China*, edited by David Johnson, Andrew J. Nathan and Evelyn S. Rawski, 188–218. Berkeley: University of California Press.

Boltz, Judith M. 1987. *A Survey of Taoist Literature, Tenth to Seventeenth Centuries*. Berkeley: University of California, Institute of East Asian Studies & Center for Chinese Studies.

Brokaw, Cynthia. 1991. *The Ledgers of Merit and Demerit: Social Change and Moral Order in Late Imperial China*. Princeton: Princeton University Press.

Chang, Chung-li. 1967. *The Chinese Gentry: Studies on Their Role in Nineteenth-Century Chinese Society*. Seattle: University of Washington Press.

Chen, Bing 陳兵. 1988. "Qingdai quanzhen longmen pai zhongxing 清代全真龍門派的中興神 [The Renewal of the Quanzhen Longmen

School during the Qing Dynasty]. *Shijie zongjiao yanjiu* 世界宗教研究 1988/2:84–96.

Chen, Bing 陳兵. 1990. "Ming-Qing daojiao liang dapai 明清道教兩大派" [The Two Great Schools of Ming-Qing Daoism]. In *Zhongguo daojiao shi* 中國道教史, edited by Ren Jiyu 任繼愈, 672–82. Shanghai: Shanghai wenwu.

———. 1991. "Ming Qing daojiao" 明清道教 [Ming-Qing Daoism]. In Mou Zhongjian 牟鐘鑑 (ed.), *Daojiao tonglun* 道教通論 [A General Discussion of Daoism], 551–579. Jinan: Wenlu.

———. 1992. "Ming-Qing Quanzhen dao 明清道教 [The Quanzhen of the Ming-Qing Dynasties]. *Shijie zongjiao shi* 世界宗教研究 1: 40–51.

Chen, Wenyi 陳兔宜. 1993. "Tan Miaozheng zhenren Lou Jinyuan you Qing Shizong de zhiyu zhi Gaozong de youli." *Daojiao xue tansuo* 7:295–313.

Chen, William. 1987. *A Guide to Tao-tsang chi yao*. New York: Stony Brook.

Cheng, Anne. 1997. *Histoire de la pensée chinoise*. Paris: Seuil.

Cleary, Thomas. 1986a. *The Taoist I Ching*. Boston and London: Shambhala.

———. 1986b. *The Inner Teachings of Taoism*. Boston and London: Shambhala.

———. 1987. *Understanding Reality*. Honolulu: University of Hawaii Press.

———. 1988. *Awakening to the Tao*. Boston and Shaftesbury: Shambala.

———. 1991. *Vitality, Energy, Spirit: A Taoist Sourcebook*. Boston and London: Shambhala.

———. 1992. *The Secret of the Golden Flower. The Classic Chinese Book of Life*. San Francisco: Harper.

Dean, Kenneth. 1993. *Taoist Rituals and Popular Cults of Southeast China*. Princeton: Princeton University Press.

de Bary, Wm Th., (ed.). 1975. *The Unfolding of Neo-Confucianism*. New York: Columbia University Press.

———. 1981. *Neo-Confucian Orthodoxy and the Learning of the Mind and Heart*. New York: Columbia University Press.

De Groot, J. J. M. 1892–1910. *The Religious System of China*. 6 vols. Leiden: E. Brill.

———. 1903–4. *Sectarianism and Religious Persecution in China*. Amsterdam.
Despeux, Catherine. 1981. *Taiji quan, art martial de longue vie*. Paris: Guy Trédaniel.
———. 1985. "Les lectures alchimiques du *Hsi-yu chi*." In Gert Naundorf et al. (eds.). *Religion und Philosophie in Ostasien: Festschrift für Hans Steininger*, 61–72. Würzburg: Könighausen und Neumann.
———. 1988. *La moelle du phénix rouge: santé et longue vie dans la Chine du XVI siècle*. Paris: Guy Trédaniel.
———. 1990. *Immortelles de la Chine Ancienne*. Puiseaux: Pardès.
Ding, Peiren 丁培仁. 1996. *Daojiao dianji baiwen* 道教典籍百問 [A Hundred Questions on the Daoist Sciptures]. Beijing: Jinri Zhongguo 今日中國.
Duara, Prasenjit. 1988. "Superscribing Symbols: The Myth of Guandi, Chinese God of War." *Journal of Asian Studies* 47, 4: 778–95.
Engelhardt, Ute. 1981. *Theorie und Technik des Taijiquan*. Schorndorf: WBV Biologisch-medizinische Verlagshandlung.
———. 1987. *Die klassische Tradition der Qi-Übungen: Eine Darstellung anhand des Tang-zeitilichen Textes Fuqi jingyi lun von Sima Chengzhen*. Wiesbaden: Franz Steiner.
Esposito, Monica 1992. "Il *Daozang xubian*, raccolta di testi alchemici della scuola Longmen." *Annali dell'Istituto Universitario Orientale* 4: 429–49.
———. 1993. *La Porte du Dragon—L'école Longmen du Mont Jin'gai et ses pratiques alchimiques d'après le Daozang xubian (Suite au canon taoïste)*. 2 vols. Ph. D. Université Paris VII.
———. 1995. *Il qigong—La nuova scuola taoista delle cinque respirazioni*. Padova: Muzzio.
———. 1996. "Il Segreto del Fiore d'Oro e la tradizione Longmen del Monte Jingai." In *Conoscenza e Interpretazione della Civiltà Cinese*. edited by P. Corradini, 151–169. Venezia: Ca' Foscarina.
———. 1997. *L'alchimia del soffio*. Roma: Ubaldini.
———. 1998a. "Longmen pai yu *Jinhua zongzhi* banben laiyuan 龍門派與「金華宗旨」版本來源" [The Longmen school and the origin of the different versions of the *Secret of the Golden Flower*]. Paper presented at the Dōkyō bunka kenkyūkai 道教文化研究会 at Waseda University in Tokyo.

———. 1998b. "The different versions of the *Secret of the Golden Flower* and their relationship with the Longmen school." *Transactions of the International Conference of Eastern Studies* 43: 90–109.

Feng, Youzhi 馮佑哲 and Li, Fuhua 李富華. 1994. *Zhongguo minjian zongjiao shi* 中國民間宗教史 [History of Chinese Popular Religions]. Taipei: Wenjin 文津.

Gōyama, Kiwamu 合山究. 1994. "Min Shin no bunjin to okaruto shumi 明清の文人とオカルト趣味 [The Occult Predilection of Ming and Qing Literati]." In *Chūka bunjin no seikatsu* 中華文人生活, edited by Ken Arai 荒井建, 469–502. Kyoto: Heibonsha 平凡社.

Gu, Zhizhong, trans. 1992. *Creation of the Gods*. 2 vols. Beijing: New World Press.

Hayes, James. 1985. "Specialists and Written Materials in the Village World." In *Popular Culture in Late Imperial China*, edited by David Johnson, Andrew J. Nathan and Evelyn S. Rawski, 75–111. Berkeley: University of California Press.

Hucker, Charles. 1985. *A Dictionary of Official Titles in Imperial China*. Stanford: Standford University Press..

Hummel, Arthur W. 1943–44. *Eminent Chinese of the Ch'ing Period (1644–1912)*. Washington: Library of Congress.

Isobe, Akira 磯部彰. 1980. "Chūgoku ni okeru 'Saiyūki' no juyō to ryūkō 中国における西遊記に受容と流行 [The Reception and Spread of *The Journey to the West* in China]. *Tōhō shūkyō* 東方宗教 55: 26–50.

Johnson, David. 1997. "Confucian Elements in the Great Temple Festivals of Southeastern Shansi in Late Imperial Times." *T'oung-pao* 83, 1–3: 126–161.

Jordan, David K. and Overmyer, Daniel. 1985. *The Flying Phoenix: Aspects of Chinese Sectarianism in Taiwan*. Princeton: Princeton University Press.

Katz, Paul. 1996. "Enlightened Alchemist or Immoral Immortal? The Growth of Lü Dongbin's Cult in Late Imperial China. In *Unruly Gods: Divinity and Society in China* edited by Meir Shahar and Robert P. Weller, 70–104. Honolulu: University of Hawai'i Press.

Kelley, David E. 1982. "Temples and Tribute Fleets: The Luo Sects and Boatmen's Associations in the Eighteenth Century." *Modern China* 8: 361–91.

Kleeman, Terry F. 1994. *A God's Own Tale: The Book of Transformations of Wenchang, the Divine Lord of Zitong*. Albany: State University Press.

Oyanagi, Shigeta 小柳司氣太. 1934. *Hakuunkan shi* 白雲觀志 [Gazetteer of the Abbey of the White Clouds]. Tokyo: Tōhō bunka gakuin Tōkyō kenkyūjo 東方文化學院東京研究所.

Li, Yangzheng 李養正. 1989 *Daojiao gaishuo* 道教概說 [An Outline of Daoism]. Beijing, Zhonghua shuju.

Li, Yuanguo 李遠國. 1985. "Daojiao qigong yu neidan shu yanjiu 道教與氣功與內丹術研究" [A Study on Inner Alchemy and Daoist Qigong]. In *Daojiao yanjiu wenji*, edited by Li Yuanguo. Chengdu: Bashu shushe.

———. 1987. *Qigong jinghua ji* 氣功精華集 [An Anthology of Qigong]. Chengdu: Bashu shushe.

———. 1988. *Daojiao qigong yangsheng xue* 道教氣功養生學 [A Study on the Daoist nurturing principle and Qigong]. Chengdu: Sichuan sheng shehui kexue yuan 四川省社會科學院.

Li, San-pao. 1993. "Ch'ing Cosmology and Popular Precepts." In *Cosmology, Ontology and Human Efficacy*, edited by R. Smith and D.W.Y. Kwok, 113–139. Honolulu: University of Hawai'i Press.

Liu, Guoliang 劉國梁. 1991. *Daojiao jingcui* 道教精萃 [The Essence of Daoism]. Changchun: Jilin wenshi 吉林文.

Liu, Kwang-Ching. 1990. "Orthodoxy in Chinese Society." In *Orthodoxy in Late Imperial China*, edited by Liu Kwang-Ching, 1–24. Berkeley: University of California Press.

Liu, Jingcheng 劉精誠. 1993. *Zhongguo daojiao shi* 中國道教史 (History of Chinese Daoism). Taipei: Wenjin 文津.

Liu, Ts'un-yan 劉存仁. 1962. *Buddhist and Taoist Influences on Chinese Novels*. Wiesbaden: Harrassowitz.

———. 1967. "Yanjiu Mingdai Daojiao sixiang zhongriwen shumu juyao 研究明代道教思想中日文書目舉要" [Research on Essential Chinese and Japanese Sources on Ming era Daoist Thought]. *Chongji xuebao* 崇基學報 6:2:107–130.

———. 1973. "The Compilation and Historical Value of the *Tao-tsang*." In *Essays on the Sources for Chinese History*, edited by Donald Leslie, 104–20. Canberra: Australian National University Press.

——— (ed.). 1984 "Wu Shou-yang: The Return to the Pure Essence." In *New Excursions from the Hall of Harmonious Wind*, 184–208. Leiden: Brill.

Ma, Xisha 馬西沙 and Han, Bingfang 韓秉方. 1992. *Zhongguo minjian zongjiao shi* 中國民間宗教史 [History of Chinese Popular Religion]. Shanghai: Renmin.

Mair, Victor. 1985. "Language and Ideology in the Written Popularizations of the *Sacred Edict*." In *Popular Culture in Late Imperial China*, edited by David Johnson, Andrew J. Nathan and Evelyn S. Rawski, 325–359. Berkeley: University of California Press.

Min, Zhiting 閔智亭. *Daojiao yifan* 道教儀範 [Patterns of Daoist Rites]. Zhongguo daojiao xueyuan bianyin.

Miura, Kunio. 1989. "The revival of *Qi*: Qigong in Contemporary China." In *Taoist Meditation and Longevity Techniques*, edited by L. Kohn, 331–362. Ann Arbor: The University of Michigan, Center for Chinese Studies.

Miyakawa, Hisayuki 宮川尚志.1954. "Ryū Ichimei no *Goshin chokushi* ni tsuite 劉一明の悟眞直指について" [A Study on the *Wuzhen zhizhi* by Liu Yiming]. *Okayama Daigaku Hōbungakubu gakujutsu kiyō* 岡山大学法文学部学術機要 3: 49–59.

Mori, Yuria 森由利亜. 1994. "Zenshinkyō Ryūmon-ha keifu kō 全眞教龍門派系譜考" [A Study on the Lineage of the Longmen School of Complete Perfection Heritage). In *Dōkyō bunka e no tenbō* 道教文化への展望 [Perspectives on Daoist Culture], edited by *Dōkyō bunka kenkyūkai* 道教文化研究会, 180–211. Tokyo: Hirakawa 平河.

———. 1998a. "Taiitsu kinka sōshi no seiritsu to hensen—Sho hanpon no jo, chū no kijutsu wo tegakari ni 太乙金華宗旨の成立と変遷—諸版本の序・注の記述を手がかりに—" [The Formation and Transformations of *Taiyi jinhua zongzhi*, based on the Prefaces and Notes of Different Versions]. *Tōyō no shisō to shūkyō* 東洋の思想と宗教, 15:43–64.

———. 1998b. "*Taiyi jinhua zongzhi* and the Spirit Writing Cult to the Patriarch Lü (Lü Dongbin) in Qing China." Paper presented at the Seminar for Research in Religion, Komazawa University, Tokyo.

———. 1998c. "Kyuso goroku ni tsuite 邱祖語錄について" [About the Records of Patriarch Qiu]. In *Dōkyō no rekishi to bunka* 道教の歴史と文化 [History and culture of Daoism], edited by Yamada Toshiaki

山田利明 and Tanaka Fumio 田中文雄, 257–273. Tokyo: Yūzan kaku 雄山閣.

Mou, Zhongjian 牟鍾鑒 et al. (eds.). 1991. *Daojiao tonglun* 道教通論 [A General Survey of Daoism]. Jinan: Wenlu.

Naquin, Susan. 1976. *Millenarian Rebellion in China: The Eight Trigrams Uprising of 1813*. New Haven: Yale University Press.

———. 1981. *Shantung Rebellion: The Wang Lun Uprising of 1774*. New Haven: Yale University Press.

———. 1982. "Connections Between Rebellions: Sect Family Networks in North China in Qing China." *Modern China* 8: 337–360.

———. 1985. "The Transmission of White Lotus Sectarianism in Late Imperial China." In *Popular Culture in Late Imperial China*, edited by David Johnson, Andrew J. Nathan and Evelyn S. Rawski, 255–291. University of California Press.

Needham, Joseph et al. 1983. *Science and Civilisation in China*, vol. V/5. Cambridge: Cambridge University Press.

Overmyer, Daniel L. 1976. *Folk Buddhist Religion: Dissenting Sects in Late Traditional China*. Cambridge, Mass: Harvard University Press.

———. 1978. "Boatmen and Buddhas: The Lo chiao in Ming Dynasty China." *History of Religion* 17.3–4:284–288.

———. 1981. "Alternatives: Popular Religious Sects in Chinese Society." *Modern China* 7.2:153–90.

———. 1985. " Values in Chinese Sectarian Literature: Ming and Ch'ing *pao-chüan*. " In *Popular Culture in Late Imperial China*, edited by David Johnson, Andrew J. Nathan and Evelyn S. Rawsky, 219–254. Berkeley: University of California Press.

Plaks, Andrew. 1987. *The Four Masterworks of the Ming Novel*. Princeton: Princeton University Press.

Pregadio, Fabrizio. 1996. *Zhouyi Cantong Qi: Dal Libro dei Mutamenti all'elisir d'oro*. Venezia: Ca' Foscarina.

Qing, Xitai 卿希泰 (ed.). 1994. *Zhongguo daojiao* 中國道教 [Chinese Daoism]. Shanghai: Zhishi 知識. 3 Vols.

———. 1996. *Zhongguo daojiaoshi* 中國道教史 [History of Chinese Daoism]. Vol. 4. Chengdu: Sichuan renmin 四川人民.

Rawski, Evelyn S. 1979. *Education and Popular Literacy in Ch'ing China*. Ann Arbor: University of Michigan, Center for Chinese Studies.

———. 1985. "Economic and Social Foundations of Late Imperial Culture." In *Popular Culture in Late Imperial China*, edited by David Johnson, Andrew J. Nathan and Evelyn S. Rawsky, 3–33. Berkeley: University of California Press.

Ren, Jiyu 任繼愈 (ed.). 1990. *Zhongguo daojiao shi* 中國道教史 [History of Chinese Daoism]. Shanghai: Shanghai renmin.

Sakai, Tadao 酒井忠夫. 1960. *Chūgoku zensho no kenkyū* 中国善書の研究 [Researches on Chinese Morality Books]. Tokyo:Kokusho kankōkai 国書刊行会.

———. 1970. "Confucianism and Popular Educational Works." In *Self and Society in Ming Thought*, edited by Wm. Th. de Bary, 331–66. New York: Columbia University Press.

Sawada, Mizuho 沢田瑞穂. 1957. "Kōyōkyō shitan 弘陽教試探 [Preliminary investigation of the Hung-yang Sect]. *Tenri daigaku gakuhō* 天理大学年宗報 24: 63–85.

Schafer, Edward H. 1980. *Mao Shan in T'ang Times*. Society for the Study of Chinese Religions Monograph no. 1. Boulder, Col: Society for the Study of Chinese Religions.

Seaman, Gary. 1987. *Journey to the North: An Ethnohistorical Analysis and Annotated Translation of the Chinese Folk Novel "Pei-you chi."* Berkeley: University of California Press.

Shahar, Meir. 1996. "Vernacular Fiction and the Transmission of Gods' Cults in Late Imperial China." In *Unruly Gods: Divinity and Society in China* edited by Meir Shahar and Robert P. Weller, 184–211. Hawaii: University of Hawai'i Press.

Shek, Richard. 1980. *Religion and Society in Late Ming: Sectarianism and Popular Thought in Sixteenth and Seventeenth Century China*. Ph. D. diss. University of California, Berkeley.

———. 1982. "Millenarianism Without Rebellion: The Huangtian Dao in North China." *Modern China* 8: 305–336.

Shiga, Ichiko 志賀市子. 1995. "Hong Kong no dōtan 香港の道壇" [Daoist Institutions in Hong Kong]. *Tōhō shūkyō* 東方宗教 85: 1–13.

Smith, Richard. 1983. *China's Cultural Heritage: The Ch'ing Dynasty, 1644–1912*. Boulder: Westview Press.

———. 1990. "Ritual in Ch'ing Culture." In *Orthodoxy in Late Imperial China*, edited by Liu Kwang-Ching, 281–310. Berkeley: University of California Press.

———. 1991. *Fortune-Tellers and Philosophers*. Boulder: Westview Press.

Tang, Dachao 唐大潮. 1985. "Ming–Qing zhi ji daojiao sanjiao heyi sixiang de lilun biaoxian luelun 明清之際道教三教合一思想的理論表現略論" [Brief Presentation of the Syncretic Theory of the Three Teachings in Ming–Qing Daoism]. *Shijie zongjiao yanjiu* 世界宗教研 3: 87–95.

Taylor, Romeyn. 1995. "Some Changes and Continuities in the Official Religion During Ming and Qing: A Survey of Gazetteers." (Paper presented at the Paris conference on State and Ritual in East Asia. Paris: Collège de France, June 1995).

———. 1997. "Official Altars, Temples and Shrines Mandated for All Counties in Ming and Qing." *T'oung pao* 88, 1–3: 93–125.

Ter Haar, B. J. 1992. *The White Lotus Teachings in Chinese Religious History*. Leiden: E. Brill.

Tsui, Bartholomew P. M. 1991. *Taoist Tradition and Change. The Story of the Complete Perfection Sect in Hong Kong*. Hong Kong: Christian Study Centre on Chinese Religion and Culture.

Vercammen, Dany. 1989. *Neijia wushu — The Internal School of Chinese Martial Arts: Its Written and Oral Tradition, History, and the Connection with Qigong* (3 vols). Ph.D. thesis, Ghent University, Belgium.

———. 1991. *The History of Taijiquan*. Antwerp: Belgian Taoist Association (Dao Association).

Wädow, Gerd. 1992. *Tien-fei hsien-sheng lu: Die Aufzeichnungen von der manifestierten Heiligkeit der Himmelsprinzessin. Einleitung, Übersetzung, Kommentar*. St. Augustin/Nettetal: Steyler Verlag, Monumenta Serica Monograph 29.

Wang, Zhizhong 王志忠. 1995a. "Lun Mingmo Qingchu Quanzhen jiao 'zhongxing' de chengyin" 論明末清初全真教中興的成因 [On Contributing Factors to the 'Revival' of Quanzhen between the End of Ming and the Beginning of Qing]. *Zongjiao xue yanjiu* 宗教學研究 3, 1995: 32–38.

———. 1995b. "Quanzhen jiao Longmen pai qiyuan lunkao" 全真教龍門派起源論 [A Study on the Origin of the Longmen branch of the Complete Perfection]. *Zongjiao xue yanjiu* 宗教學研, 1995/4: 9–13.

Watson, L. James. 1985. "Standardizing the Gods: The Promotion of T'ien Hou ("Empress of Heaven") Along the South China Coast, 960–1960." In *Popular Culture in Late Imperial China*, edited by David Johnson,

Andrew J. Nathan and Evelyn S. Rawski, 292–324. Berkeley: University of California Press.

Wile, Douglas. 1992. *Arts of the Bedchamber: The Chinese Sexual Yoga Classics Including Women's Solo Meditation Texts*. Albany: State University of New York Press.

Welch, Holmes H. 1967. *The Practice of Chinese Buddhism, 1900–1950*. Cambridge, Mass: Harvard University Press.

Welch, Holmes H., and Anna Seidel (eds.). 1979. *Facets of Taoism*. New Haven: Yale University Press.

Wilhelm, Richard. 1929. *Das Geheimnis der Goldenen Blüte: ein chinesisches Lebensbuch*. Zürich: Rascher.

Wong, Eva. 1998. *Cultivating the Energy of Life, A Translation of the Huiming ching and its Commentaries*. Boston: Shambhala.

Wong, Shiu Hon. 1982. *Investigation into the Authenticity of the Chang San-feng Ch'uan-chi*. Canberra: Australian National University Press.

———. 1988a. *Daojiao yanjiu lunwen ji* 道教研究論文集 (A Collection of Daoist studies). Hong Kong: Zhongwen wenxue.

———. 1988b. *Mingdai daoshi Zhang Sanfeng kao* 明代道士張三丰考 [On the Ming Daoist Zhang Sanfeng]. Taiwan, Xuesheng.

Xu, Dishan 許地山. 1941. *Fuji mixin di yanjiu* 扶箕迷信底研究 [A Study on the Foundation of the Superstition of Planchette-writing]. Shanghai. Shangwu yinshuguan.

Yang, C.K. 1961. *Religion in Chinese Society*. Berkeley: University of California Press.

Yao, Chi-on 遊子安. 1999. *Quanhua jinzhen—Qingdai shanshu yanjiu* 勸化金箴—清代善書研究 [The Quanhua jinzhen—Research on Qing era morality books]. Tianjin: Tianjin renmin.

Yokote, Hiroshi 横手裕. 1994 "Ri Kankyo shotan—aru dōkyōteki shugyōhō to chōetsu no michi 李涵虛初探 — ある道教的修行法と超越の道" [Preliminary studies on Li Hanxu—A particular Daoist Practice and the Way of Transcendence]. Kamata Shigeru 鎌田繁 and Mori Hideki 森秀樹. *Chōetsu to shinpi—Chūgoku, Indo, Isurāmu no shisō sekai* 超越と神秘 —中国・インド・イスラームの思想世界" [The Transcendence and the Mystics—The Worldview of Islam, India and China]. Tokyo: Daimeidō 大明堂.

Yoshioka, Yoshitoyo 吉岡義豐. 1955. *Dōkyō kyōten shiron* 道教経典史論" [On the History of Daoist Scriptures]. Tokyo: Dōkyō kankōkai 道教刊行会.

———. 1970. *Eisei e no negai: Dōkyō* 永生への願い：道教 [The Quest for Immortality: Daoism]. Tokyo: Tankōsha 淡交社.

———. 1979. "Taoistic Monastic Life." In *Facets of Taoism*, edited by H. Welch and A. Seidel, 229–252. New Haven, Conn.: Yale University Press.

Yu, Anthony C. 1991. "How to read *The Original Intent of the Journey to the West*." In *How to Read the Chinese Novel*, edited by David L. Rolston, 299–315. Princeton: Princeton University Press.

Yü, Chün-fang. 1981. *The Renewal of Buddhism in China: Chu-hung and the Late Ming Synthesis*. New York: Columbia University Press.

Zito, Angela. 1977. *Of Body and Brush: Grand Sacrifices as Text / Performance in Eighteenth-Century China*. Chicago: University of Chicago Press.

The Longmen School and its Controversial History during the Qing Dynasty

Preface[1]

If one were to visit Daoist temples in Southern and Northern China, one would be surprised to hear that most of them affirm one and the same lineage, i.e., the Longmen pai 龍門派. It seems that something like a "Longmen fashion" began to spread rapidly from the beginning of the Qing dynasty (1644–1911). This phenomenon of "standardized lineage" that seems to characterize Qing Daoism has its counterpart in Buddhism. Asked to which lineage a Buddhist monk belongs, most will even today answer "Linji"—just as Daoists answer "Longmen".[2] How come?

For Daoism, this trend can be traced back to the end of the Ming dynasty (1368–1644). Under the strong domination of the Zhengyi 正一 legacy at the court, the Quanzhen 全真 school began to be reevaluated. The first upsurge came in the waning years of the Ming when Confucians and lite-

---

[1] My thanks go to Professor Chen Yaoting 陳耀庭 of the Shanghai Academy of Social Science for his useful explanations on the *Jingai xindeng* 金蓋心燈 during my six-month fellowship at the Academy in 1989–90. I am also indebted to Prof. Yoshinobu Sakade 坂出祥伸 of Kansai University (Osaka) for having invited me to Japan to continue my research on the history of the Longmen in the framework of a post-doctorate fellowship of the Japanese Foundation for the Promotion of Science. I am also grateful to Prof. Kunio Mugitani 麥谷邦夫 of Kyoto University's Jinbun kagaku kenkyūjo for his kind support in freely and happily lending me books and articles from his private library, and to Urs App for innumerable discussions and other help.

[2] Holmes Welch, *The Practice of Chinese Buddhism* 1900–1950, 281 and 396, Cambridge, Massachusetts: Harvard University Press, 1967, and *Daojiao yuanliu* 道教源流 6.28b (hereafter cited in the notes as DJYL), *Zangwai daoshu* 藏外道書 (ZWDS) 31:113.

rati joined the Quanzhen parishes to show their loyalty and demonstrate their disappointment with the Manchu conquest.³ Paradoxically, the Quanzhen school experienced a "renaissance" under the name of Longmen 龍門 not under the Ming dynasty but the Qing conquerors. In contrast with the Ming court, the Qing emperors appreciated the strong discipline and moral rules of Quanzhen to such an extent that they chose it for conveying public ordinations. The motor of the court-approved reorganization of Daoist discipline was a Longmen master: Wang Changyue 王常月 (Wang Kunyang 王崑陽, ?-1680). As abbot of the public monastery of the White Clouds (Baiyun guan 白雲觀) in the Beijing capital, Wang began from 1656 to convey official ordinations and to supervise the religious training of the Daoist clergy independent of their original affiliation. Starting with Wang Changyue, the abbotship of the Baiyun guan was given to Longmen masters, and Longmen influence under the Qing became widespread — a fact that proved crucial for the creation of Longmen as an institutionalized school with its own lineage.⁴

But when did this Longmen lineage arise? This is difficult to pinpoint, but by way of analysis of epigraphic and hagiographic materials one can see that the Longmen patriarchal tradition was probably a construction of the end of the Ming and that in its "incubation" period it was linked with the Zhengyi. At the outset it was the product of hermits who, influenced by the ancient ideal of Quanzhen, devoted themselves to ascetic training without being necessarily affiliated with the Quanzhen order.

However, the emergence of the Longmen as a school complete with a well-defined patriarchal lineage seems to have come about only from the mid-seventeenth century and the advent of Wang Changyue at Baiyun guan. There was one compelling reason for this emergence: the necessity for the Longmen masters to establish a lineage relationship in order to ensure the hereditary Longmen abbotship and monopoly on performing ordination. The fundamental source of the early history and lineage of Longmen is the *Bojian* 缽鑑 (Examination of the Bowl), a lost or possibly fictitious work attributed to Wang Changyue.

---

[3] Chen Bing 陳兵, "Qingdai Quanzhen Longmen pai de zhongxing" 清代全真龍門派的中興, *Shijie zongjiao yanjiu* 世界宗教研究, 2, 1988: 84–96.

[4] See for example Yoshioka Yoshitoyo 吉岡義豊, *Eisei e no negai: Dōkyō* 永生への願い: 道教, 199, Kyoto: Tankōsha, 1970.

Introduction

The origins of the orthodox Longmen lineage according to the Transmission of the Mind-Lamp

It is interesting to note that the *Bojian* that can be regarded as "the foundation stone of the Longmen lineage" is only known through the quotations of the *Jingai xindeng* 金蓋心燈 ([Transmission of the] Mind-Lamp of Mount Jingai, 1821, repr. 1876; abbr. JGXD). Though the *Bojian* has been mentioned in recent scholarly studies, it seems that nobody has actually held this text in hand.[5] If one consults the existing sources on Longmen history, one can immediately see that most references to the Longmen patriarchal lineage stem from the early nineteenth-century *Jingai xindeng*. On the model of Chan 禪 Buddhist *Transmission of the Lamp* histories (*chuandeng lu* 傳燈錄), this text appears to have been written as a model for promoting Longmen "for the protection of the state."[6] Like its Chan counterparts, the *Jingai xindeng* established in explicit genealogical terms the origin and development of the Longmen lineage by mapping out a "family tree." Starting from the Ancestor of the Dao (Daozu 道祖, i.e., Laozi) and from the Lineage Master of the Dao (Daozong 道宗, i.e., Lü Dongbin 呂洞賓), this tree has conveyed a distinctive identity to Longmen Daoism until today.

Moreover, the *Jingai xindeng* transmitted detailed biographies of Longmen masters of South-eastern China which are a remarkable tool for shedding light on the still barely known Daoism of the Ming and Qing dynasties. This text has so far received scant scholarly attention. It was published

---

[5] See for example Chen Bing 陳兵, "Qingdai Quanzhen Longmen pai;" Mori Yuria 森由利亞, "Zenshinkyō ryūmonha keifu kō" 全真教龍門派系譜考, in Dōkyō bunka kenkyūkai (ed.), *Dōkyō bunka e no tenbō* 道教文化への展望, 189, Tokyo: Hirakawa, 1994; Qing Xitai 卿希泰 (ed.), *Zhongguo daojiao* 中國道教, vol. 3: 393, Shanghai: Zhishi, 1994, and *Zhongguo daojiao shi* 中國道教史, vol. 4: 81, Chengdu: Sichuan Renmin, 1996.

[6] For the role played by the Chan *Lamp Histories* see Theodore Griffith Foulk, "The Chan school and its place in the Buddhist Monastic Tradition," Ph. D. diss., University of Michigan, 1987: 42–44 and 50–52.

for the first time in 1821 by Min Yide 閔一得 (1758–1836),⁷ the eleventh Longmen master, at the library of the Ancient Hidden Pavilion of Books (Gu Shuyinlou cangshu 古書隱樓藏書) in the Yunchao temple of Mount Jingai (Huzhou, Zhejiang). The majority of the biographies of the *Jingai xindeng* include commentaries by the well-known scholar Bao Tingbo 鮑廷博 (1728–1814)⁸ and are revised by Bao Kun 鮑錕 (fl. 1814).⁹ For his commentaries, Bao Tingbo consulted fifty-two works which he listed at the beginning of the *Jingai xindeng* (1a-2b in ZWDS 31:161–162) under the title "Jingai xindeng zhengkao wenxian lu" 金蓋心燈徵考文獻錄 (Index of works used for the compilation of the *Mind-Lamp of Mount Jingai*).

In addition to the biographies of South-eastern masters, the *Jingai xindeng* is also the fundamental source for the presentation of the first seven generations of patriarchs who are recognized as the holders of the Longmen orthodox lineage (*Longmen zhengzong* 龍門正宗) at the Baiyun guan in Beijing, at its affiliated monasteries, and by subsequent Longmen branches and sub-branches. In fact, this lineage also appears in the *Hakuunkan shi / Baiyun guan zhi* 白雲觀志 (abbr. BYGZ), the monograph of the Baiyun abbey compiled in classical Chinese by Oyanagi Shigeta 小柳司氣太 (1870–1940), and in a similar work on the Taiqing gong 太清宮 (another important Longmen monastery in Shenyang 沈陽, Liaoning) by Igarashi Kenryū 五十嵐賢隆.¹⁰ From the Qing dynasty, the list of the first seven Longmen patriarchs came to represent for all ordained Daoist clergy the orthodox lineage of Longmen abbots of the Baiyun guan, a lineage that was

---

[7] On the life of Min Yide see Monica Esposito, "Daoism in the Qing (1644–1911)," in Livia Kohn (ed.), *Daoism Handbook*, 630–31, Leiden: Brill, 2000 {here above, pp. 15–16} and "Longmen Taoism in Qing China: Doctrinal Ideal and Local Reality," *Journal of Chinese Religion* 29, 2001, 199–203 {Chapter 3 here below, pp. 160–165}.

[8] Native of Xin'an 新安 (Anhui), style names Yiwen 以文 and Tongchun 通純. Bao was known as the Zhejiang erudite (*boshi* 博士) and during the Jiaqing era (1796–1820) passed the provincial examination. He was the editor of the *Zhibuzu zhai congshu* 知不足齋叢書 in 30 volumes (1776). In 1792 he came to Mount Jingai in order to take charge of the JGXD's compilation, and in 1811 he revised it along with Min Yide and other Longmen disciples (Nancy Lee Swan, "Pao T'ing-bo," in Arthur Hummel (ed.), *Eminent Chinese of the Ch'ing Period*, 612–13, Taipei: Ch'eng Wen Publishing Company, 1975, and "Zhibuzu zhai zhuren zhuan" 知不足齋主人傳 (JGXD 7. 31a-32a, in ZWDS 31:311–312).

[9] Bao Kun 鮑錕 was native of Yuhang 餘杭 (modern Hangzhou); see his preface of 1814 (JGXD 1a-2b, in ZWDS 31:159–60).

[10] BYGZ 32–35; Igarashi Kenryū 五十嵐賢隆, *Taiseikyū shi* 太清宮志 (Gazetteer of the Taiqing gong), 64–65, Tokyo: Kokushō kankōkai, 1938.

progressively adopted by other Longmen public monasteries. Moreover, this list was also accepted by Longmen sub-branches which, after the advent of Wang Changyue, allegedly spread throughout China.[11]

Here the biographies of the first seven Longmen patriarchs will either be translated in their entirety or summarized from the *Jingai xindeng*, their main source. According to the commentator Bao Tingbo 鮑廷博, these biographies of the *Jingai xindeng* are based on the following works:

(1) *Bojian* by Wang Changyue (?–1680)
(2) *Daopu yuanliu tu* 道譜源流圖 (Map of the Origins and Development of Daoist Genealogical Registers) compiled by the Eighth Longmen Vinaya Master Lü Yunyin 呂雲隱 (fl. 1710);[12]
(3) *Yangshi yilin* 揚氏逸林 (Circle of Recluses) by Yang Shen'an 揚慎菴, a compilation which is said to be mostly based on Wang Changyue's *Bojian*;
(4) *Bojian xu* 缽鑑續 (Supplement to the Examination of the Bowl) by the Ninth Longmen Doctrinal Master (*zongshi* 宗師) Fan Qingyun 范清雲 (Taiqing 太清, 1606–1748?!) who allegedly received the *Bojian* in 5 *juan* from Wang Changyue in 1667 and later expanded it to 9 *juan*;[13]
(5) *Dongyuan yulu* 東原語錄 (Recorded Sayings of Dongyuan) by Lü Quanyang 呂全陽.[14]

However, except for the *Daopu yuanliu tu*, all of these works seem to have survived only in the quotations of the *Jingai xindeng*.

Like in Chan *Lamp Histories*, the *Jingai xindeng* was given the vital task of conveying an official self-image of its lineage. The creation of its own ancestry—which was certainly modeled on that of the Quanzhen official hagiographies—, was designed to confirm not only the noble pedigree of the

---

[11] See for example the "Longmen zhengzong liuchuan zhipai tu" 龍門正宗流傳支派圖 (JGXD I: 1a-7b, in ZWDS 31:166–168), *Longmen zhengzong jueyun benzhi daotong xinchuan* 龍門正宗覺雲本支道統薪傳 (ZWDS 31: 427–446); *Jingudong zhi* 金鼓洞志 (ZWDS 20:189–299); DTYL; and Yoshioka Yoshitoyo, *Dōkyō no jittai* 道教の實態, 231–32, Kyoto: Hōyū shoten, 1975.

[12] "Daopu yuanliu tu" 道譜源流圖 by Lü Yunyin 呂雲隱 (JGXD 1a-7b in ZWDS 31:162–65; and DZJHL *shang* 1a-4b). For the biography of Lü see JGXD (2.27a-29a in ZWDS 31:198–99).

[13] "Fan Qingyun zongshi zhuan" 范青雲宗師專 JGXD (3.46b/4-5 in ZWDS 31: 231).

[14] For his biography see JGXD (3. 19a-20a, in ZWDS 31:217–18).

institutionalized Longmen order at the capital but even more to ensure the orthodoxy of the various affiliated Southern branches. A majestic edifice was built for that purpose with the help of scholars and Longmen disciples under the guidance of Min Yide 閔一得. A retired scholar of the mid-eighteenth and early nineteenth century, Min Yide was a key figure in the promotion of the self-image of the "orthodox" Longmen in Southern China. He portrayed the Longmen not only as the Longmen institutionalized order at the capital with a standardized ordination system and monastic rules, codes of behavior and liturgy, but also as an intellectual and doctrinal tradition capable of producing specific inner-alchemical theories on cosmology, self-cultivation, and ethics.

The focus here is on the early history of the Longmen. In spite of its importance as the key school of Qing Daoism, it has so far received very little scholarly attention. Instead of examining only the façade of this historical edifice like most previous studies, I will try to lay bare its structure and explore its interior.[15] This examination leaves out doctrinal aspects which are treated elsewhere.[16] Let us now take a look at this edifice. If, at first glance, its style appears influenced by the taste of the epoch and by those who commissioned it, a close look also reveals the design of its architects.[17] Once one enters the edifice, one is able to appreciate the models that inspired these

---

[15] Although there are some Chinese studies about Longmen history, they tend to simply accept the official version of this history; see for example Chen Bing, "Qingdai Quanzhen Longmen pai," 1988, and "Ming Qing daojiao" 明清道教, in Mou Zhongjian 牟鐘鑑 (ed.), *Daojiao tonglun* 道教通論, 551–579, Jinan, Wenlu, 1991; Qing Xitai (ed.), *Zhongguo daojiao*, vol. 1: 200–205, and *Zhongguo daojiao shi*, vol. 4: 77–181. For the first critical studies see (in chronological order) Monica Esposito, "La Porte du Dragon—L'école Longmen du Mont Jin'gai et ses pratiques alchimiques d'après le *Daozang xubian* (Suite au canon taoïste)," Ph.D. diss., Université de Paris VII, 1993 {PDF version 2012}; Mori Yuria, "Zenshinkyō ryūmonha keifu kō"; Wang Zhizhong 王志忠, "Quanzhen jiao Longmen pai qiyuan lunkao" 全真教龍門派起源論, *Zongjiao xue yanjiu* 宗教學研究, 4, 1995: 9–13 and "Lun Mingmo Qingchu Quanzhen jiao 'zhongxing' de chengyin" 論明末清初全真教中興的成因, *Zongjiao xue yanjiu* 宗教學研究, 3, 1995: 32–38 (thanks to Mori Yuria for sharing a copy of these two articles); and Zeng Zhaonan 曾召南, "Longmen pai" 龍門派, in Hu Fuchen 胡孚琛 (ed.), *Zhongguo daojiao dacidian* 中國道教大辭典, 66–67, Beijing: Zhongguo shehui kexue, 1995.

[16] M. Esposito, "La Porte du Dragon"; *L'alchimia del soffio*, Roma: Ubaldini, 1977, and "Longmen Taoism in Qing China: Doctrinal Ideal and Local Reality" {Chapter 3 here below}.

[17] These architects are, as mentioned above, Min Yide, Bao Tingbo and Min Yide's disciples or fellow practitioners; see the prefaces to JGXD I (ZWDS 31: 158–161).

architects and the ideals they aspired to. Like chambers which ultimately converge in a singular central hall, the biographies of the first Longmen patriarchs appear to have been constructed so as to apportion the guest of honor his central place. Although, on the surface, the edifice seems well built, as soon as one examines it with attention, its solidity is progressively reduced, and the walls crumble one by one leaving but a plan that reflects the intention of its architects. The seven patriarchs as portrayed in the *Jingai xindeng* form the pillars of the edifice which even today houses official Daoism—the Daoist Association of China—as represented by the Baiyun guan in Beijing. But what do these pillars consist of? What do they carry? Where are they anchored? What style do they exhibit?

Due to the dearth of previous research on this complicated topic and the abundance of sources, the present investigation should be regarded as a sort of architectural sketch of an edifice that is still largely unexplored. This edifice was built on the grave of the ideal founder Qiu Chuji 邱處機 (1148–1227), and its pillars are formed by the patriarchs, i.e., the seven principal masters of the ideal "Longmen orthodox lineage." In the compound of this ideal edifice, though obscured by the splendor of the main buildings, other lineage edifices can be discerned (see the "Lineage Chart" in Fig. 1). The main ideal edifice was designed to be occupied by the abbot Wang Changyue 王常月 (Wang Kunyang) and was established as the Baiyun guan of Beijing. From the Qing dynasty onward, the Baiyun guan became the headquarters of the orthodox Longmen lineage as the direct heir of the Quanzhen legacy. In order to support its claim of religious and historical affiliation with the ancient Quanzhen order, the Longmen attempted to anchor its genealogy in the famous early thirteenth-century figure of Qiu Chuji. An orthodox Longmen lineage was established based on the claim that its origin goes back to the "Quanzhen Beizong" (Quanzhen Northern Lineage). This was designed to link the Longmen patriarchs to the prestigious position which the Quanzhen order had enjoyed during the beginning of the Yuan dynasty as a Daoist school supported by the emperor.

After having presented the biographies of the first orthodox Longmen patriarchs along with those of some important Longmen figures connected with them, the list of Longmen Daoist Ancestors will be compared with that of the Quanzhen Five Ancestors (*wuzu* 五祖). This comparison will then shed more light on a fundamental discrepancy that characterizes the entire creation of the "orthodox" Longmen lineage.

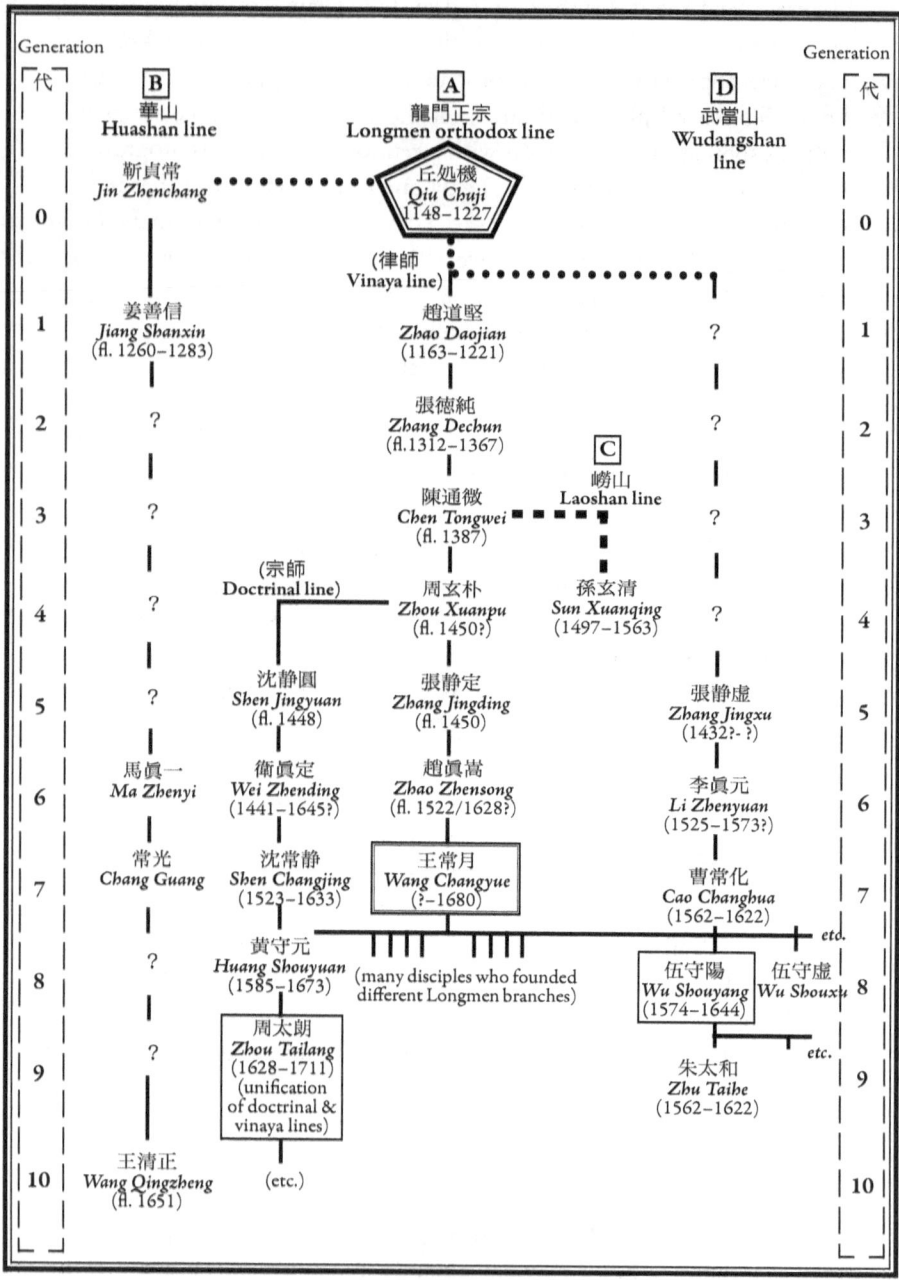

Fig. 1: Lineage chart of early Daoist Longmen traditions

The Foundation

The role of the Baiyun guan in the Orthodox Longmen lineage: Brief analysis of Epigraphic Sources

According to Min Yide's *Jingai xindeng* 金蓋心燈 of 1821, the "Longmen orthodox transmission" (*zhengzong liuchuan* 正宗流傳) starts with the transfer of the "Lamp of Mind" from Qiu Chuji 邱處機 (1148–1227) to his disciple Zhao Daojian 趙道堅 (1163–1221).[18] The foundation of the Longmen lineage is thus allegedly due to Qiu Chuji. The term Longmen refers to a place, the Longmen mountains 龍門山 in the Longzhou district 隴州 (Western Shaanxi) where Qiu underwent his ascetic training. As is well known, Qiu was the most famous among the Seven Perfected of the Quanzhen school.[19] Because of his important relationship with the ruler he was even granted a biography in the official history of the Yuan dynasty (*Yuanshi* j. 202). He was in particular celebrated for his long journey to Central Asia to meet Chinggis Khan.[20] Following this meeting, the Quanzhen school entered its Golden Age by obtaining an edict granting exemption from taxes and labor. Thus Qiu Chuji became the leader of all native religions in North China by taking charge of all "those who leave their families".[21] Once Qiu returned to Beijing in 1224, he took control of the Tianchang guan 天常觀

---

[18] The name *xindeng* 心燈 is said to originate from here; see "Zhao Xujing lüshi zhuan" 趙虛靜律師傳, JGXD I, 1b (ZWDS 31:167).

[19] According to most recent sources, every one of the Seven Perfected of Quanzhen founded his own school; see Judith M. Boltz, *A Survey of Taoist Literature*, 279–280 note 172, Berkeley: Institute of East Asian Studies & Center for Chinese Studies, University of California, 1987.

[20] This journey was reported in the *Changchun zhenren xiyouji* (DZ 1429 fasc. 1056) by Li Zhizhang, one of the eighteen disciples who took part in it; tr. Arthur Waley, *Travels of an Alchemist: The Journey of the Taoist Ch'ang-ch'un to the Hindukush at the Summons of Chingiz Khan*, London: George Routledge & Sons, Ltd 1931; see also J. Boltz, *A Survey of Taoist Literature*, 66–68 and 157–59.

[21] Yao Tao-chung, "Quanzhen: Complete Perfection," in Livia Kohn (ed.), *Daoism Handbook*, 572, Leiden: Brill, 2000.

(Abbey of Celestial Endurance). Soon afterwards, the abbey was renamed in Qiu's honor to Changchun gong 長春宮 (Palace of Perennial Spring). When Qiu passed away in 1227, his corpse was buried next to this Palace.[22] A subordinate temple was then built in its vicinity by Yin Zhiping 尹志平 (1169–1251), one of the main disciples of Qiu Chuji, and it was called Baiyun guan 白雲觀 (White Cloud Abbey).[23]

If during the Yuan dynasty (1279–1368) the Baiyun guan was the headquarter of the Quanzhen, and the Changchun gong was the center of Qiu Chuji's teachings, with the advent of the Ming only the Baiyun guan survived. However, a great change took place in this temple: the Baiyun guan now fell under the supervision of the Zhengyi 正一. After its destruction at the end of the Yuan, the Baiyun guan was rebuilt at the end of the fourteenth century by the Celestial Masters of the Zhengyi tradition. At that time, the Zhengyi had more influence at the Ming court than the Quanzhen order which appears to have lost its identity and power.[24] But since the temple was conceived as a memorial shrine built over Qiu Chuji's grave, the Baiyun guan's prestigious tradition survived independently from the original Quanzhen affiliation. The temple continued to enjoy strong devotion for the tomb of its saint Qiu Chuji by the people and imperial authorities alike. According to Hu Ying's stele of 1444, after a visit to Qiu Chuji's tomb by the crown prince on the occasion of Qiu's birthday (the 19th day of the first lunar month), the restoration of this temple began in 1394. Influential masters linked to the Zhengyi were successively in charge of carrying on the restoration work.[25] At the end of a long reconstruction, the Baiyun guan finally opened its doors as the center in charge of the spiritual training of Daoists and their ordination. Paradoxically, the Quanzhen monastic tradition at the Baiyun guan was at that time rehabilitated thanks to the Zhengyi masters who gradually integrated in their order all kinds of Daoist schools. Under a Zhengyi-approved reorganization, the important Qingwei

---

[22] J. Boltz, *A Survey of Taoist Literature*, 66–68 and 127–28, and P. Marsone, "Le Baiyun guan de Pékin: épigraphie et histoire," *Sanjiao wenxian* 3, 1999: 79–80.

[23] BYGZ 12–13. As Pierre Marsone ("Le Baiyun guan," 80) remarks, the name Baiyun guan in that period refers to buildings annex built by Yin Zhiping.

[24] Ishida Kenji 石田憲司, "Mingdai Dōkyō shijō no Zenshin to Seii" 明代道教史上の全真と正一, in Sakai Tadao 酒井忠夫 (ed.), *Taiwan no shūkyō to Chūgoku bunka* 台湾の宗教と中国文化, 145–185, Tokyo: Fukyūsha, 1992.

[25] "Baiyun guan chongxiu ji" 白雲觀重修記 (1444) by Hu Ying 胡濙 (BYGZ 4.124-28).

master (and patriarch of the Jingming zhongxiao dao) Liu Yuanran 劉淵然 (1351–1432) took the Daoist name of Changchun in honor of the Perfected Qiu Chuji and celebrated the beginning of a new era for the "Zhengyi Qingwei–Quanzhen."[26]

Nevertheless, at the end of the Ming dynasty the Quanzhen order appeared again in the Baiyun guan. However, only under the official guidance of Wang Changyue did the Quanzhen order gain its independence as the new "Longmen orthodox lineage."[27] As abbot of the Baiyun guan, Wang Changyue was recognized as belonging to the seventh Longmen patriarchal generation affiliated with the Quanzhen Northern tradition. But how was this patriarchal line transmitted to Wang Changyue, and from where did it originate?

On the basis of the Ming epigraphic sources it appears difficult to trace the Quanzhen Northern tradition of Longmen back to the Baiyun guan. Although the grave of its founding patriarch was situated in this abbey, the supervision of the Baiyun guan was throughout the Ming not in the hands of Quanzhen or Longmen masters.[28]

---

[26] I refer here to a new era for the "Zhengyi Qingwei-Quanzhen" since one can see in Liu Yuanran its founding patriarch. Liu Yuanran (1351–1432) received from Emperor Renzong the name of "Changchun zhenren" along with a position of the second rang equalling that of the Zhengyi zhenren 正一真人. He transmitted his Daoist methods to the 43rd Celestial Master Zhang Yuchu 張宇初 (*Mingshi*, j. 299, 7654/12-13 and 7656/9-12). He was the disciple of Zhao Yizhen 趙宜真 (d. 1382; see K. Schipper, "Master Chao I-chen and the Ch'ing-wei School of Taoism," in Akizuki Kan'ei 秋月觀暎 (ed.), *Dōkyō to shūkyō bunka* 道教と宗教文化, 715–734, Tokyo: Hirakawa, 1987) and received from him the heritage of the Golden Elixir of the Northern Lineage (北派金丹之傳); see "Shao Yizheng chongjian Baiyun guan Changchun dian beilüe" 邵以正重建白雲觀長春殿碑略 (1457) in *Rixia jiuwen kao* 日下舊聞考 (1774/1882, j. 94, SKQS vol. 498). See also Ishida Kenji 石田憲司, "Mingdai Dōkyō shijō no Zenshin to Seii," 157, and P. Marsone, "Le Baiyun guan," 85 & 98. *Added remark by the author*: In addition, see Akizuki Kan'ei (*Chūgoku kinsei*, 150–160) on Liu Yuanran's role as patriarch of the Jingming zhongxiao dao in the early Ming era and as head of the highest agency in the central government in charge of Daoist affairs, the Daolu si 道籙司, during the reigns of Taizu (1368–1398) and Chengzu (1403–1424). Liu also held the title of *zhenren* 真人 (Perfect Master) which put him on equal footing with the Celestial Master upon whom the same title was conferred by the Ming court. Quoted by Richard Shek, "Daoism and Orthodoxy," 2004, p. 152.

[27] BYGZ: 24.141–42, 162–63; JGXD (I, 1.15a-16b, in ZWDS 31:183–84).

[28] In fact, in the different stelae of the Ming dynasty we found only references to Daoist figures close to the Zhengyi order such as Li Shizhong 李時中, Ni Zhengdao 倪

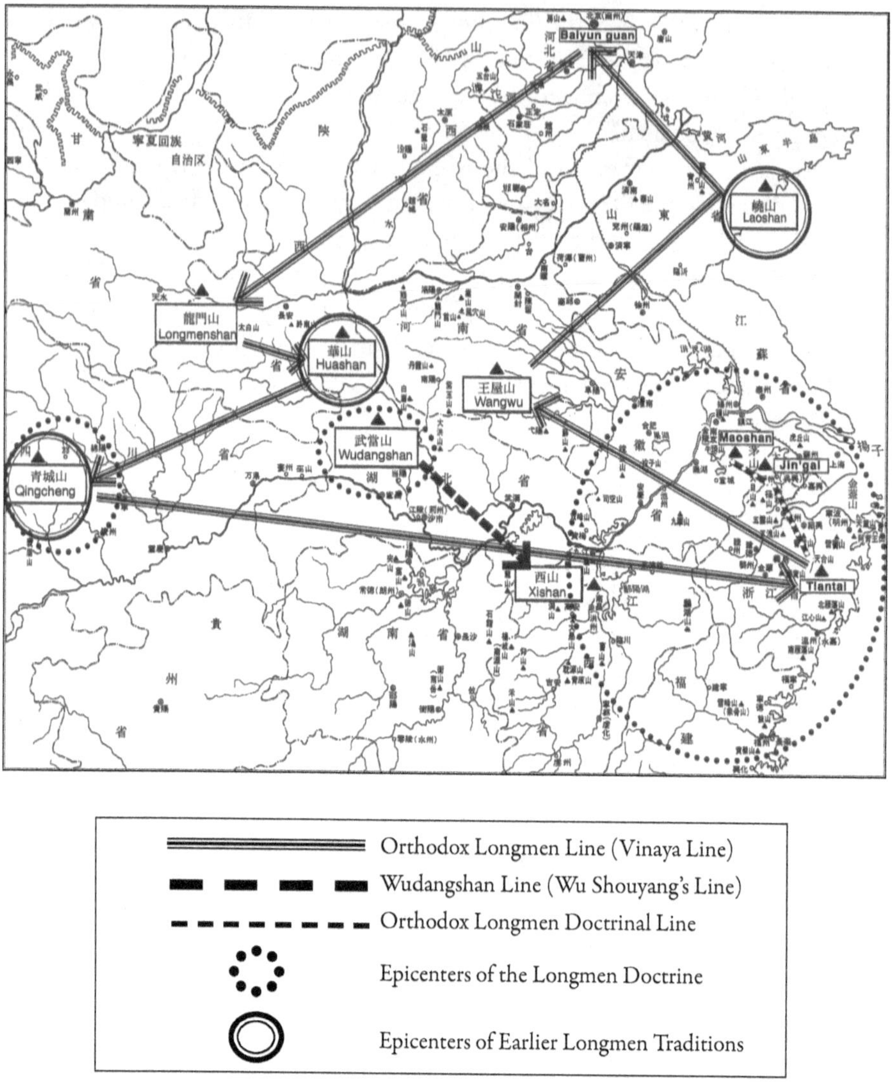

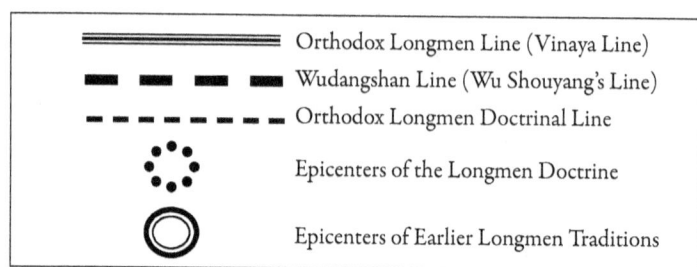

Fig. 2: Geographical Distribution of Early Longmen Traditions

正道, Shao Yizheng 邵以正, etc., but none to masters linked with the Quanzhen or with the Longmen lineage; see "Baiyun guan chongxiu ji" 白雲觀重修記 (BYGZ 4.125), *Rixia jiuwen kao* (1774/1882 j. 94 in SKQS vol. 498: 463–472), Ishida Kenji, "Mingdai Dōkyō shijō no Zenshin to Seii," 155, and P. Marsone, "Le Baiyun guan," 83–86.

THE PILLARS:
PATRIARCHS AND THEIR LINEAGE

THE ORTHODOX LONGMEN LINEAGE AT THE BAIYUN GUAN WITH ITS FIRST PATRIARCH ZHAO DAOJIAN [LINE A, NO.1][29]

According to the *Jingai xindeng* 金蓋心燈, the Longmen lineage was nevertheless related to the Baiyun guan, and its continuity was ensured by Qiu Chuji's disciple Zhao Daojian 趙道堅 (1163–1221).[30] The text stages a fateful meeting between Zhao Daojian and Qiu Chuji who greets Zhao on his arrival in the following way:

> "Here is the pillar of the Mysterious Teaching (*xuanmen* 玄門), the guide of Celestial Immortals. Some day, the charge of carrying on the Lamp of Mind (*xindeng* 心燈) by transmitting the method of precepts (*jiefa* 戒法) will be in your hands."
>
> 此元門柱石。天仙領袖也。他日續心燈而流傳戒法者。必此子矣。

The tale continues:

> Afterwards, Zhao followed the Patriarch [Qiu] to Yan [Beijing] for spreading the teaching. He acted in the world in spontaneous harmony and without talking. At times he attended [Patriarch Qiu] throughout the night without uttering a word. The Patriarch thus transmitted to him the secret of spontaneity and pure emptiness, upon which Zhao withdrew to Mount Longmen for many years.
>
> After having come out [from this retreat], he stayed with the Patriarch [Qiu] at the Baiyun guan and gathered a great number [of disciples]. The fifteenth day of the first month of the *bingchen* year of the Zhiyuan era (1280), Zhao received the Initial Precepts of Perfection (*chuzhen*

---

[29] Such references point to the lineage chart in Figure 1 (p. 62).
[30] From the "Zhao Xujing lüshi zhuan" (JGXD 1. 1a-2b in ZWDS 31:176) we learn very little about Zhao's life except that his original name was Jiugu 九古 (Daoist surname: Xujing 虛靜 and lineage name: Daojian). He was born in Xinye 新野 (Hebei) and was a disciple of Qiu Chuji. In 1312 he is said to have transmitted the Longmen precepts to Zhang Dechun 張德純, the second Longmen Patriarch. Neither the date of birth nor the date of death of Zhao are mentioned; see also notes 32 and 39.

jie 初真戒) as well as the Intermediate Precepts (*zhongji jie* 中極戒).³¹ After having practiced in accordance with the rules without losing his sublime virtue, the Patriarch personally transmitted the "seal of mind" (*xinyin* 心印) to Zhao and entrusted him with robe and bowl. Zhao received the Precepts of Celestial Immortals (*tianxian jie* 天仙戒) along with a four-verse *gatha* amounting to twenty characters that forms the Longmen lineage poem: "Dao de tong yuan jing, zhen chang shou tai qing, yi yang lai fu ben, he jiao yong yuan ming" (道德通元靜。真常守太清。一陽來復本。合教永圓明).³²

遂侍祖遊燕闡教。凡有作為不言自合。或侍終夜不發一語。祖乃傳以清虛自然之秘。棲隱龍門者多載。復出侍祖於白雲觀。統大眾。師於至元庚辰。正月望日。受初真戒、中極戒。如法行持。無漏妙德。祖乃親傳心印。付衣缽。受天仙戒。贈偈四句。以為龍門派計二十字。

This biography portrays the figure of the first Patriarch according to the model of a genuine Quanzhen master who has made liminal experiences.³³ In the case of Zhao, this is underlined by the mention of his voluntary silence that brought about the reception of the ideal Longmen teaching defined as "the secret of spontaneity and pure emptiness," a transmission that enabled him to undergo the necessary period of ascetic training. Only after this could he be recognized as a master capable of teaching and able to receive the initial Longmen investiture. This preliminary investiture here consists of two stages of precepts: the Initial Precepts of Perfection, and the Intermediate Precepts which were destined to become part of the Longmen standardized ordination system conveyed to the entire Daoist clergy. However, according to the *Jingai xindeng*, the final investiture that makes Zhao Daojian the first Longmen Vinaya Master capable of ensuring the

---

[31] On these precepts see M. Esposito, "Longmen Taoism in Qing China: Doctrinal Ideal and Local Reality," 194–196. {See Chapter 3 here below, pp. 149–153, and the much more detailed discussion in Monica Esposito, *Creative Daoism*, Wil/Paris: UniversityMedia, 2013, pp. 91–173}.

[32] "Zhao Xujing lüshi zhuan" (JGXD I, 1.1a-2b); see M. Esposito "La Porte du Dragon," 103. The fourth character of the poem is here *yuan* 元, but as is known, this was a substitution for the taboo character *xuan* 玄 during the Kangxi era (1662–1722).

[33] Stephen Eskildsen, "Asceticism in Ch'üan-chen Taoism," *British Columbia Asian Review* 3/4, 1990: 153–91, and Vincent Goossaert, "The Invention of an Order: Collective Identity in 13th-century Quanzhen," *Journal of Chinese Religion* 29, 2001, 111–138.

continuity of the orthodox Longmen lineage was to take place only in 1280 at the Baiyun guan through a "direct transmission" of the Patriarch Qiu. In this "direct transmission," the last stage of precepts, that of the Celestial Immortals (*tianxian jie* 天仙戒), was conveyed to Zhao, and as in the Chan tradition he received "robe and bowl" along with a lineage poem. Ever since, this poem was seen as the means of orthodox Longmen integration; its characters were used for naming every generation of Longmen patriarchs. After ordination, each future Longmen patriarch received a lineage name (*paiming* 派名 or *ming* 名) composed of two characters, the first of which was taken from the verse.³⁴ Zhao, for example, has as lineage name *Daojian* 道堅: this indicates that he belongs to the first generation of Longmen orthodoxy, while the second generation features the character *De* 德, and so on.

According to the glosses by Bao Tingbo, this poem was officially conferred by the Emperor Shizu (Qubilai; r. 1260–1293) as a legal proof of the foundation of the Longmen school.³⁵ Later, it was expanded from twenty to one hundred characters. Although we still do not know the exact provenance of this poem, it is certain that it was transmitted neither by Qiu Chuji nor by the Mongol emperor Qubilai. As Goossaert has pointed out, the Quanzhen system of transmitting religious names was very similar to that used by lay Buddhist movements such as the White Lotus.³⁶ It was not based, as in the case of the Longmen, on the principle of generational names, but rather in opposition to it. The names of Qiu Chuji's disciples were in fact limited to a three-character system (Dao 道, De 德 and Zhi 志) which gave all "Quanzhen clerics a concrete sense of belonging to the same timeless and universal community."³⁷ Conversely, the generational principle embodied in the Longmen poem was to lead to another kind of phenomenon where various branches and sub-branches split from the "standardized unique lineage" trunk and manifested their own local and creative identities thanks to their symbolic link with the certified orthodoxy of the correct Longmen lineage.

---

34 H. Welch, *The Practice of Chinese Buddhism*, 279–285 and Yoshioka Yoshitoyo, "Taoist Monastic Life," in Holmes Welch & Anna Seidel (eds.), *Facets of Taoism*, 231, New Haven and London: Yale University Press, 1979.

35 Bao attributes this information to the *Yangshi yilin* 楊氏逸林 and the *Quanzhen lu* 全真錄 (see "Zhao Xujing lüshi zhuan" [JGXD 1. 2a/7 in ZWDS 31:176]).

36 V. Goossaert, "The Invention of an Order," 131 and Barend ter Haar, *The White Lotus Teachings in Chinese Religious History*, 39–40, Leiden: Brill, 1992.

37 V. Goossaert, "The Invention of an Order," 132.

Returning to Zhao: the fact that, before becoming the first Longmen patriarch, he withdrew to the place where Qiu Chuji had undergone his ascetic training, was supposed to confirm that the Longmen lineage was originally related to Mount Longmen in Shaanxi. Now, if we analyze other sources regarding Zhao Daojian, we discover another version of the story. According to these sources, Zhao died in Saram on the fifth day of the eleventh month of 1221 while accompanying Qiu Chuji to meet Chinggis Khan.[38] Qiu Chuji also died some years later, in 1227, after having returned from Central Asia and resided in his Palace in Beijing. The date of 1280 for the direct transmission that supposedly took place at the Baiyun guan thus appears quite wondrous or maybe macabre if we conceive it as a meeting of two living dead persons for the purpose of conveying the perfect Longmen transmission. But why would Qiu Chuji have chosen a disciple who died before him to ensure the continuity of the "Lamp of Mind"? It may have been due to the fact that Zhao was the only one of the eighteen disciples of Qiu Chuji who was related in some way to Mount Longmen. According to the biographer Li Daoqian 李道謙 (1219–1296), Ma Danyang 馬丹陽 (1123–1183)—one of the Seven Perfected of Quanzhen—ordered Zhao in 1180 to contact Qiu Chuji at Longmen in order to receive his teachings. When they met, Qiu Chuji is said to have given the name *Dao*jian to Zhao.[39] The fact that Qiu is said to have designated Zhao as the first Longmen Patriarch, regardless of the inconsistencies of a such choice, shows the iron will of the Longmen lineage to be affiliated with the Baiyun guan as well as with the place where the Patriarch Qiu himself had undergone his ascetic training: Mount Longmen in Shaanxi. This obstinacy may point to a controversy among different groups about establishing the right sanctuary of the nascent Longmen lineage.

---

[38] *Zhongnan shan zuting xianzhen neizhuan* (DZ 604 fasc. 955 *zhong* 10b-12b); *Changchun zhenren xiyouji* (DZ 1429 fasc. 1056 *shang*: 22b, [tr. A. Waley, *Travels of an Alchemist*, 73–74, 125, 131]); BYGZ 34; M. Esposito, "La Porte du Dragon," 102; Mori Yuria "Zenshinkyō ryūmonha keifu kō," 184–87; Wang Zhizhong, "Quanzhen jiao Longmen pai qiyuan lunkao," 9.

[39] *Zhongnan shan zuting xianzhen neizhuan* (DZ 604, fasc. 955 *zhong* 11a-b). From this biography we know that the name of Zhao was Jiugu 九古. He was born in Tanzhou 檀州 (the modern Miyun 密雲 in Beijing) in 1163. In 1179 he became a disciple of Ma Danyang. After having met Qiu Chuji at Longmen and received the lineage name *Dao*jian, he followed Qiu's teachings. In 1219 he was chosen to accompany Qiu Chuji to meet Chinggis Khan, but he died in 1221 before arriving in Samarkand.

The Longmen Lineage at Huashan

The movement of hermits at Huashan: Ma Zhenyi and Wang Qingzheng (fl. 1651) [Line B, Nos 6, 10]

According to the *Guangyang zaji* 廣陽雜記 (Miscellaneous Records of Guangyang), a certain Sun Zongwu 孫宗武 (fl. 1651)[40] claimed that the Longmen lineage was originally affiliated with Mount Wangdiao 王刁 of Huashan 華山 (Shaanxi), a sanctuary that Qiu Chuji was once in charge of. The name of this mountain harks back to two masters Wang Yao 王遙 and Diao Ziran 刁自然, two immortals of the beginning of the Song dynasty.[41]

This place was also related to a Longmen master of the sixth generation called Ma **Zhen**yi 馬真一 whose disciple of the tenth generation, Wang Laiyang 王萊陽 (lineage name: **Qing**zheng 清正) restored the Baiyun guan in Beijing.[42] Thanks to Wang, the Baiyun guan was renovated from top to bottom and the Longmen lineage established itself in this monastery.[43]

However, the names of these two Longmen masters do not have any place in the Longmen "orthodox lineage" as reported by the *Jingai xindeng*. Even in the epigraphic sources concerning the rebuilding of the Baiyun guan at

---

[40] Sun Zongwu (*wei*: Yunjin 雲錦; *zi*: Changfa 長發) was born in Chengdu and was a Ceremonial Companion (*yibin* 儀賓) of Shu Prefecture (Sichuan). After having fled from the disorders of the invaders, he escaped to the dynastic capital and its environs. Afterwards, he had his home temporarily in Shuntian 順天 (Beijing). In 1651 he was provincial graduate (*juren*); see *Guangyang zaji* by Liu Xianting (1957:3.130). When he was in Huashan, he had as friend the Longmen master Wang Laiyang from whom he heard the history of the Longmen lineage; see DJYL 7.32b (ZWDS 31:134).

[41] *Guangyang zaji* by Liu Xianting (1957:3.130), and DJYL 6.28b-29a (ZWDS 31:113-14).

[42] According to the Longmen poem of twenty characters, Ma Zhenyi is recognized as belonging to the sixth Longmen generation; see *Guangyang zaji* by Liu Xianting (1957: 3.130).

[43] *Guangyang zaji* by Liu Xianting (1957: 3.130) and DJYL 7.32b (ZWDS 31:134). The "Baiyunguan juanchan beiji" 白雲觀捐產碑記 (stele by Cai Yongqing 蔡永清, 1811, in BYGZ 145) mentions a certain charitable person Wang (王善人), contemporary of Wang Changyue 王常月 (alias Kunyang), who built the Sanqing ge 三清閣 in the Baiyun guan; see P. Marsone, "Le Baiyun guan de Pékin," 88 and 100.

the beginning of the Qing, nobody mentions the name of its purported restorer Wang Qingzheng. Fortunately, one finds a brief mention of these two Daoists in the work of the Longmen master Chen Minggui 陳銘珪 (1824–1881). In his *Changchun daojiao yuanliu* 長春道教源流 (Origins and development of the Daoist Teachings of [Qiu] Changchun, 1879, abbr. DJYL, 7.31a-32a), Chen relates that Ma Zhenyi (nickname: Fengdian 峰巔 or Fengdian 瘋顛) lived in the Wangdiao dong 王刁洞 of Huashan with three Daoists:

> [In this grotto] they had only rocks as beds. There were not any books or writings, nor alchemical furnaces or ingredients [for the preparation of the elixir]. With his disciple Changguang and others, like the ignorant and dull, they did not discuss alchemical processes and did not perform any purification rites or offerings or use any talismans or registers. Their teachings were simply based on complete perfection as well as on purity and tranquillity. During the winter, they would bathe themselves, and hot vapors steamed up like in summer.[44] When they were invited by functionaries to deal with drought, they did not erect any altar nor burn any incense but went on simply drinking a lot of wine without any further consideration. While they were drinking, rain fell in a downpour. When they were asked to tell a fortune, they answered in a snap, and they were always marvellously accurate.

> 無榻几因石為床。無經書文字。無藥物丹爐。其弟子常光等。椎魯無知。不談燒煉黃白等法。不為齋醮符籙等事。清靜全真以為教。能冬月以雪為沐浴。氣蒸蒸如暑。值旱官迎之署。不立壇不焚香。但索酒大飲。飲間雨下如注。或問吉凶矢口而答。無不奇中。

One day Ma Zhenyi suddenly left the grotto and nobody knew where he had gone. People thought that he was still living in Liaodong 遼東.[45]

---

[44] This reminds one of the powers of magicians and medicine men to produce heat (see Mircea Eliade, *Le chamanisme et les techniques archaïques de l'extase*, 104 & 369 ff., Paris: Payot, 1983), and more particularly of the well-known Tibetan practices of inner heat or *gtum-mo* (Geshe Kelzang Gyatso, *Clear Light of Bliss*, London: Wisdom, 1982).

[45] DJYL 7.31a-32a (ZWDS 31:134). This biography stems from Li Jie's 李楷 *Hebin wenji* 河濱文集 (*Huayue zhi*, j. 2, 36b-37b, in ZWDS 20: 68–69); see Qing Xitai (ed.), *Zhongguo daojiao shi*, vol. 4: 151.

According to the *Shengjing tongzhi* 盛京通志, Ma Zhenyi came from Henan. During the Ming he lived at the Beizhen miao 北鎮廟 of Liaoning before going to Huashan.[46] He had many disciples, but only one is mentioned under the lineage name of *Chang*guang 常光. On the basis of the Longmen poem we can thus assume that this disciple of Ma Zhenyi belongs to the seventh generation of Longmen.[47]

With regard to Wang Laiyang, the text of Chen Minggui mentions nothing about his life except that his lineage name was *Qing*zheng (i.e. 10th Longmen generation) and that, as the heir of Ma Zhenyi's tradition, he was celebrated for having established the Longmen lineage at Baiyun guan.[48]

The Foundation of the Longmen lineage in Huashan by Jiang Shanxin (1196-1274) [Line B, No. 1]

Chen Minggui (DJYL 6.27b-29a in ZWDS 31:113–14) also relates that Wang Laiyang (Qingzheng) heard from Ma Zhenyi that Qiu Chuji once was in charge of Huashan and had at that time a certain Jin Zhenchang 靳貞常 as disciple. Jin transmitted Qiu's teaching to Jiang Shanxin 姜善信. Native of Zhaocheng 趙城 (Henan), the 19-year-old Jiang met master Jin and withdrew to the Wangdiao grotto at Huashan. Later, following Jin's will, Jiang underwent his training at Mount Longmen in another grotto of Wangdiao. In fact, it seems that there were two grottoes in honor of Wang and Diao: at Huashan and Longmen. Afterwards, Jiang received the favors of the Yuan court and was officially named Jingying zhenren 靜應真人 (Perfected in Resonance with Tranquillity) by emperor Shizu (r. 1260-1293). At Mount Longmen he then built the Jianji gong 建極宮 (Palace of Ascending the Throne) on the ruins of the Dayu miao 大禹廟 (Temple of the Great Yu); to this Palace, an official plaque written by the Minister of Revenue (*Da sinong* 大司農) Yao Shu 姚樞 was granted. Jiang appointed five of his disciples as caretakers of this Palace; they are reported to have been far and near called Tianshi 天師 (Celestial Masters).[49]

---

[46] Qing Xitai (ed.), *Zhongguo daojiao shi*, vol. 4: 152–53.

[47] DJYL 7.31b (ZWDS 31:134); Li Jie's 李楷 *Hebin wenji* 河濱文集 (*Huayue zhi* j. 2, 37a/4, in ZWDS 20: 69); and Qing Xitai (ed.), *Zhongguo daojiao shi*, vol. 4:153.

[48] DJYL 7.32b (ZWDS 31:134).

[49] DJYL 6. 27b-29a (ZWDS 31:113–14); Wang Zhizhong, "Quanzhen jiao Longmen pai" 1995: 10–11; and *Huayue zhi* j. 2.33a (ZWDS 20: 67).

Based on Jiang's biography and notes by Chen Minggui one can thus see that the Longmen lineage of Jiang Shanxin was affiliated with the Jianji gong at Mount Longmen (Shaanxi) where there was a grotto devoted to two Song immortals: Wang Yao and Diao Ziran. These locations were closely related to the eremitic tradition of the Wangdiao dong of Huashan (Shaanxi) which came to be well known through the sixth Longmen master Ma *Zhen*yi. Furthermore, Jiang's Jianji Palace is said to have been officially recognized by Emperor Shizu through the donation of a plaque. The state-approved position of this Palace under the reign of Qubilai Khan may be shown by the fact that its administrators were known as Celestial Masters. This may fit with the period when, after capturing Lin'an, the Mongols turned to the Celestial Masters.[50]

One can thus suppose that in Huashan there were groups of hermits that, by claiming their link to Qiu Chuji, were also connected with the Wangdiao grotto of Mount Longmen. Their Wangdiao grottos at Huashan and Mt. Longmen as well the officially recognized Jianji Palace of Mt. Longmen could be the earlier "physical sanctuaries" of the early Longmen tradition. As we are going to see, a trace of this Huashan affiliation in the early Longmen tradition can be detected even in the orthodox Longmen lineage [Line A] through the figures of the second and the third Longmen patriarchs.[51]

---

[50] In fact, Qubilai made the 36th Celestial master Zhang Zongyan 張宗演 (1244–1291) and his successors supervisors of Daoism in the Jiangnan region. "Zhang set a precedent for the regime by delegating administration in the Yuan capital Yanjing (Beijing) to literati surrogates, whom Mongols called patriarchs of the Teachings of Mysteries (Xuanjiao 玄教)"; see Lowell Skar, "Ritual movements, deity cults and the transformation of Daoism in Song and Yuan times," in Livia Kohn (ed.), *Daoism Handbook*, 427, Leiden: Brill, 2000; and Qing Xitai (ed.), *Zhongguo daojiao shi*, vol. 3: 281–320.

[51] BYGZ 34.

The Orthodox lineage of the Longmen from the Second to the Third Patriarch [Line A, Nos 2–3]

The Second Patriarch: Zhang Dechun (fl. 1312–1367)

Lineage name (*ming*): **Dechun** 德純 (Pure Virtue)
Original name (*benming*): Heng 珩
Daoist surname (*hao*): Bizhi 碧芝 (Magic Mushroom of Jade)
Birth-place: Kaifeng 開封 or Luoyang 洛陽 (Henan).

According to the "Biography of the Vinaya Master Zhang Bizhi" ("Zhang Bizhi lüshi zhuan" 張碧芝律師傳 in JGXD 1:3a-b; ZWDS 31:176), Zhang was born into a wealthy family of Luoyang. He was tall, courageous, and dauntless. Instead of taking care of his family he preferred to visit alchemists and experts of occult techniques. Only after having ruined his family and while ravaged by diseases did he realize the futility of his original interests and decided to become a Daoist priest. For more than thirty years he thus devoted himself completely to Daoism in order to eradicate his past habits. One day, after having heard that "the Longmen robe and bowl" were already conveyed to the Patriarch Zhao Daojian, he decided to serve him and persisted for more than eighteen years. During that time, although he did not receive any teachings, he never lost his faith and respect for his master. Zhao thus realized that Zhang was indeed a Vessel of the Dao (*daoqi* 道器) and, foreseeing his imminent death, called Zhang to his side and said:

> "In bygone days, my master Qiu [Chuji] has widely spread the Wondrous Spirit [of Daoism]; he extensively put it in action and converted the people. How could it be that those who [at that time] obtained the Dao and took charge of the lineage remained so few? At any rate, it was only to me that he transmitted the Supreme Dao (*wushang zhi dao* 無上之道), and since then already thirty years have passed. In order to prevent the Orthodox Lineage of the Most High from being disgraced, I never dared to transmit it to incapable men. Having obtained you as successor, my task is now achieved."

> 昔我子邱子。大闡元風。廣行教化。其間得道承宗者。豈為鮮少。乃獨以無上之道。傳付於我。今又三十年矣。不敢輕授匪人。以辱太上正宗。得子以承。我事畢矣。

As second Patriarch, "Zhang withdrew to Huashan (Shaanxi) and shouldered the Vinaya teaching for years" (*jianhe lüjiao younian* 肩荷律教有年) until 1367 when he transmitted it to Chen *Tongwei* 陳通微 before disappearing.

By their portrayal of Zhang Dechun's behavior at the beginning of this biography, the compilers may have intended a more general critique against those people who, instead of taking charge of social duties, preferred to devote themselves to researching occult and illusory arts and techniques. This critique matches the official attitude also shared by Quanzhen's "purist and ideal vision" which promoted the respect of Confucian morality and advised against the vain search for techniques of immortality.[52] The compilers seem also to allude to a symbolic master-disciple transmission of the "Supreme Dao" which follows the Chan Buddhist model. The first and the second patriarchs are in fact portrayed like Chan masters who made a great effort to find a "vessel" worthy of taking over the lineage.[53] The orthodox Longmen lineage is referred to as "Taishang zhengzong" 太上正宗 (the orthodox lineage of the Most High) and consists of Vinaya regulations.

The Third Patriarch: Chen Tongwei (fl. 1387)

Lineage name: *Tongwei* 通微 (Penetrating the Subtle)
Original name: Zhizhong 致中
Daoist name: Chongyi zi 沖夷子 (Master Filled with the Invisible)
Birth-place: Dongchang 東昌 (Shandong)

As the "Chen Chongyi lüshi zhuan" 陳沖夷律師傳 (JGXD j. 1:4a-b) points out, Chen first learned "the Zhengyi's method of prayers and exorcism" (*Zhengyi quxie qidao zhi fa* 正一驅邪祈禱之法) from some Daoists and exhibited such extraordinary abilities that the people competed to have

---

[52] See V. Goossaert, "The Invention of an Order: Collective Identity in 13th Century Quanzhen"; and M. Esposito, "Longmen Taoism in Qing China: Doctrinal Ideal and Local Reality" {Chapter 3 here below}. One must also add that some emperors were attracted to alchemical arts and died after having absorbed the drugs of immortality; see, for example, Pierre-Henry de Bruyn, "Daoism in the Ming (1368–1644)," in Livia Kohn (ed.), *Daoism Handbook*, 594–622, Leiden: Brill, 2000.

[53] Dale S. Wright, "Les récits de transmission du bouddhisme Ch'an et l'historiographie moderne," *Cahiers d'Extrême-Asie* 7, 1993–94: 108.

him as teacher. However, Chen suffered from these distractions and, wanting to liberate himself from this attention, fled to Huashan 華山 (Shaanxi). Passing by the hermitage of Master Zhang Dechun, he discovered him completely absorbed in the recitation of the *Daodejing*. Impressed by his calm and peaceful appearance, he knelt down before him and begged him for his instruction. As the master did not react, he decided to stay with him to cultivate the humility needed to be accepted as his disciple. This happened only after many years, when he received from him the lineage name *Tongwei* 通微 (Penetrating the Subtle) and the "three-stage precepts" (the full Longmen ordination). Subsequently, he was in accord with the marvelous virtue of the Way and dedicated himself entirely to Daoist practice. He propagated his teachings widely in the Shaanxi and Shanxi regions and passed them on to the Daoists who had previously taught him the Zhengyi method. Still, he kept wandering for years without encountering any disciple worthy of his instruction. He retired to Mt. Qingcheng 青城山 (Sichuan), and it is only in 1387 that he accorded the transmission to Zhou *Xuan*pu 周玄朴.

As portrayed in this biography, one could at first put Chen in the category of wonder-workers inside the Zhengyi order, but he preferred asceticism. Although he became popular on account of his extraordinary powers, he abandoned such distractions in favor of a purist ideal of self-cultivation. This shows, depending on one's perspective, the intention of the compilers of this biography or of its protagonist to claim "Quanzhen identity."[54] This identity, which purportedly was transmitted from the Yuan dynasty on, here takes shape in the pure and tranquil methods of meditation and recitation of the *Daodejing*, as well as in the transmission of the "three-stage precepts." It thus seems that the compilers of this biography have the intention of investing the Longmen lineage and the figure of its third Patriarch with a specific "Quanzhen identity," an identity that was to be completely actualized in the figure of the seventh Patriarch Wang Changyue. It is in fact to the latter that the Longmen tradition will attribute the reform of the "three-stage precepts," although these precepts were already cited in the first biographies of the Longmen patriarchs. Her we are thus probably dealing with a dream — a dream by the compilers who tried to trace the lineage claim of Wang Changyue and successors back to the ideal disciples of Qiu Chuji — and at the same time a dream of the subject of this biography. The latter also embodies the aspiration of unifying the Quanzhen teachings with those of the dominant Zhengyi order in charge of Daoist Southern legacies.

---

[54] On this identity see V. Goossaert, "The Invention of an Order."

In reality, this aspiration was actualized not under the guidance of the Quanzhen or Longmen patriarchy but rather thanks to the Zhengyi integration put forward by the 43rd Celestial Master Zhang Yuchu 張宇初 (1361–1410) who, during the Ming, promoted Quanzhen as the ideal movement of ascetics devoted to self-cultivation.[55] As the biography of the third Longmen patriarch Chen Tongwei shows, this ideal was also adopted by the Longmen, which is often portrayed as a specific Daoist lineage primarily based on the cultivation of purity and tranquillity that deals neither with alchemical and life-prolonging techniques nor with rituals or talismans.[56] However, this characterization remains a simple ideal and neither matches historical reality nor the complex history of the Longmen lineage.

Furthermore, by alluding to the presence of the Zhengyi in Chen's biography, the compilers may also show that the "Longmen tradition" was going to take the road to the South (see the "Geographical Distribution" in Figure 2). This is pointed at by the statement that Chen, after having spread his teachings in the regions of Shaanxi and Shanxi, withdrew to Mt. Qingcheng (Sichuan). Although they were natives of Northern China, Chen Tongwei and his disciple Zhou Xuanpu are said to have fled to Sichuan, the place of origin of the Celestial Masters as well as the location where the Southern legacy was established.[57]

As this biography underlines through the ideal transmission of teachings between Chen Tongwei and the Zhengyi Daoists, the Quanzhen ideal of ascetic tradition had to come to grips with the effective liturgical power of the Zhengyi in the South and ended up being integrated into it. According to the *Daotong yuanliu* 道統源流 (Origins and Development of Orthodox Daoism; *xia* 1), from Chen Tongwei (3rd generation, fl. 1387) until Shen Jingyuan 沈靜圓 (5th generation, fl. 1448), the Longmen transmission also included that of the Lingbao registers. This may indicate that the "northern identity" of the Quanzhen was lost inside the Zhengyi. In fact, during the Yuan, after the unification of China, a new "Quanzhen identity" was reformulated by Southern adepts who promoted a theory of unification between Northern (Quanzhen) and Southern Lineages. At the beginning

---

[55] See Florian Reiter, *Grundelemente und Tendenzen des religiösen Taoismus*, Stuttgart: Franz Steiner, 1988; and M. Esposito, "La Porte du Dragon," 11–18.

[56] See for example the Preface by Chen Minggui 陳銘珪 and his presentation of the teaching of the Quanzhen [DJYL 1b and 1.4a-20a in ZWDS 31: 1 & 2-10]).

[57] Fabrizio Pregadio & Lowell Skar, "Inner alchemy (*Neidan*)," in Livia Kohn (ed.), *Daoism Handbook*, 470–71, Leiden: Brill, 2000.

of the Ming dynasty (1368–1644), Northern and Southern *neidan* 內丹 traditions were then progressively regrouped under the label of Quanzhen, while old and new liturgical movements were absorbed into the Zhengyi.[58] Further integrations of Southern legacies under the Zhengyi occurred during the Ming when a liturgical integration seems to have "caused all Daoists of this order to call themselves Qingwei Lingbao."[59] This may explain why the *Daotong yuanliu* 道統源流 states that the Longmen patriarchs who were necessarily connected with the Zhengyi legacy also transmitted the Lingbao registers.[60]

Furthermore, according to the *Daotong yuanliu* (*xia* 1), before leaving the North, Chen Tongwei (fl. 1387) conferred his transmission also on a Quanzhen Daoist named Sun Xuanqing 孫玄清 (1497–1569).[61] With such claims, we come face to face with contradictions that characterize the orthodox lineage of the Longmen. Its first patriarch, Zhao Daojian, died before Qiu Chuji, the purported founder of Longmen, and now the third-generation patriarch Chen Tongwei is said to have transmitted the Longmen legacy to the fourth-generation disciple Sun Xuanqing who appears to have been living around one century later. If the *Jingai xindeng* omitted to record this transmission, other Longmen sources mention Sun Xuanqing 孫玄清 (1497–1569) as an important Quanzhen master of the end of the Ming dynasty who came to be affiliated with Longmen. The importance of such a figure has surely been taken into account by later sources which felt the need to link the Longmen lineage to that of Sun Xuanqing. Before returning to our "orthodox lineage," we will thus have a brief look at this figure.

---

[58] As is well known, from the late Tang the Zhengyi established itself at Mt. Longhu and superseded the other two major Daoist centers of the southeast: the Lingbao and Shangqing schools, respectively at the Gezao shan 閤皂山 (Jiangxi) and Maoshan 茅山 (Jiangsu); see L. Skar, "Ritual movements," 415–16, 420, 427–29, 453; and F. Pregadio & L. Skar, "Inner alchemy (*Neidan*)," 469–72, 479–81.

[59] See V. Goossaert, "The Quanzhen Clergy, 1700–1950." In *Religion and Chinese Society*, ed. by John Lagerwey, vol. 2, 701. Hong Kong: École française d'Extrême-Orient & Chinese University of Hong Kong, 2004.

[60] In fact, after 1352, when the Lingbao headquarter on Gezao shan was destroyed by rebels, it never regained its glory. This was probably due to the "greater authority laid upon Celestial Masters on nearby Longhu shan," who inherited its registers and transmitted them to other schools; see L. Skar, "Ritual movements," 428.

[61] I have calculated his date of birth based on the biography of the DTYL (7. 26a-b in ZWDS 31: 131); but Qing Xitai (*Zhongguo daojiao shi*, vol. 3: 483) gives the date 1517 without mentioning his source.

The Longmen lineage at Laoshan: Sun Xuanqing (1497–1569) [Line C No. 4]

Besides the short biographical note of the *Changchun daojiao yuanliu* 長春道教源流 (*xia*, 1), Sun has a longer biography in the *Daotong yuanliu* 道統源流 (j. 7: 26a-b, ZWDS 31:131). According to the latter, Sun Xuanqing 孫玄清 (1497–1569, *zi*: Jinshan 金山, *hao*: Haiyue shanren 海岳山人) was an important Daoist affiliated with Laoshan 嶗山. He was later recognized as the fourth-generation Longmen patriarch who in Laoshan started his own school under the name of Jinshan 金山 or Laoshan.

Sun Xuanqing was born in Qingzhou Prefecture 青州府 (Shouguang district 壽光縣, Shandong). In his early years, he became priest at Mingxia dong 明霞洞 of Laoshan 嶗山 (Shandong) and honored a certain Li Xiantuo 李顯陀 as master. Afterwards, he travelled to Tiecha shan 鐵查山 (Shandong), and at the Yunguang dong 雲光洞[62] he met another master called Tongyuan zi 通源子, who transmitted to him "the method for mapping out a strategy for going up and down from Heaven's Door" (*shengjiang tianmen yunchou zhi fa* 昇降天門運籌之法).[63] When he was nineteen years old, he was brought by Perfected Taihe (Taihe zhenren 太和真人)[64] of the Mo district (Mo xian 墨縣, Shandong) to the Huangshi gong 黃石宮. There Sun underwent his ascetic training for more than twenty years.[65] Later, after having met Zhang Pengtou 張蓬頭 and discussed with him the oral teachings concerning the cultivation of Perfection, he experienced enlightenment.[66] In 1558, he stayed at the Zuobo tang 坐缽堂 (Hall of Sitting

---

[62] This is the place where Wang Chuyi 王處一 (1142–1217) and Hao Dadong 郝大通 (1140–1212), two of the Seven Quanzhen Perfected, underwent their ascetic training and claimed to have experienced enlightenment; see J. Boltz, *A Survey of Taoist Literature*, 164, 165.

[63] I have found no other trace of this method which may be connected to a divinatory art of calculating the moment for transcending ordinary time.

[64] A master called Taihe zi is quoted in the *Laoshan zhi* j. 5, but he is supposed to have died at the beginning of the Ming dynasty; see Qing Xitai (ed.), *Zhongguo daojiao*, vol. 4: 19.

[65] This Palace is one of the many temples of Laoshan. It is located north of Hualou shan 華樓山 and was built in the Yuan dynasty (*Laoshan zhi* j. 3); see Qing Xitai (ed.), *Zhongguo daojiao*, vol. 4: 19

[66] A certain Zhang Pengtou is quoted in the JGXD (VI, 6 *shang* 15a-b, in ZWDS 31: 284) as the tenth master of the Longmen Tantric branch Xizhu xinzong. The same

around the Bowl-clepsydra) of Beijing's Baiyun guan for one year.[67] He became so expert and skillful that he was asked by the court to perform rain-making rituals for a drought that ravaged the area around the capital. After his success, he received the official title of "Huguo Tianshi Zuozan Jiaozhu Ziyang Zhenren" 護國天師左讚教主紫陽真人 (Perfected of Purple Yang, Auxiliary Bishop of Left Celestial Master, Protector of the Country). He died in 1569 at the age of 73. He was later recognized as belonging to the fourth Longmen generation. He was also reputed to have founded his own school under the name of Jinshan 金山 or Laoshan 嶗山.[68]

From this biographical note in the *Daotong yuanliu*, we can see that Sun was a Daoist affiliated with Laoshan. As is known, this mountain was associated during the Yuan dynasty with the Quanzhen tradition of Qiu Chuji and Liu Chuxuan 劉處玄 (1147–1203). During the Ming and Qing dynasties it was a sanctuary frequented by many Daoists.[69] So far I have not found any other mention of the masters Sun came into contact with; the Laoshan lineage needs to be further studied. Here, I limit myself to the hypothesis that one of Sun's masters, *Tong*yuan zi 通源子, may belong to the third generation of Longmen if we take "Tong" as his lineage name based on the Longmen poem in twenty characters. This may indicate that a Longmen lineage already existed in Laoshan but was different from that recorded in the *Jingai xindeng*. However, contradicting this hypothesis, the *Daotong yuanliu* claims that Sun was a disciple of Chen *Tong*wei 陳通微 (fl. 1367). As mentioned above, this affiliation seems improbable not only because of

---

Zhang is also said to be the son of the Ming loyalist Qu Shisi 瞿式耜 (JGXD VI, 6 *shang*: 6b/1–2, in ZWDS 31: 280; *Jinhua zongzhi* 金華宗旨, chap. 3, DZXB I:4a/4). However, the dates of Zhang Pengtou do not correspond to the period when Sun would have met him, but since Zhang is regarded as *shenren* 神人 who appeared one hundred years after his death to a master of the seventeenth century (JGXD VI. 6 *shang*: 15a-b in ZWDS 31:284; *Jinhua zongzhi*, chap.3 DZXB I:4a/3–4), he could be the kind of saint capable of living different lives in different epochs. It is important to note that the master of Zhang Pengtou, Da Jiaoxian 大腳仙, reportedly withdrew to Laoshan during the end of the Ming dynasty ("Da Jiaoxian zhuan" JGXD VI. 6 *shang*: 5a-6a in ZWDS 31:279–80). He was a contemporary of Wu Shouyang (1574–1644).

[67] The hall was devoted to a collective meditation with a bowl used as clepsydra which was a particularity of Quanzhen communities; see J. Boltz, *A Survey of Taoist Literature*, 239 and note 679.

[68] This biography stems from a Qing work by Liang Jiaowu 梁教無 entitled *Xuanmen bidu* 玄門必讀; see DJYL 7: 26a-b in ZWDS 31:131.

[69] Qing Xitai (ed.), *Zhongguo daojiao*, vol. 4: 197–200.

the gap of more than one hundred years between Chen and Sun but also because of the evident will to create a link with the Laoshan line by claiming the ideal figure of Chen Tongwei as master of an important historical figure such as Sun Xuanqing.

From this biography it also appears that the Quanzhen practice was still alive since Sun actually engaged in the "cultivation of Perfection" and took part in the Quanzhen collective meditation (*zuobo* 坐缽) at the Baiyun guan. However, one does not find any mention of the presence of Longmen masters inside that monastery, and even what is here designated as "Quanzhen meditation" (*zuobo*) at the Baiyun guan was at that time supervised by the Zhengyi masters. The latter were responsible of state-supporting rituals, and it was under their control that Sun received the official title of "Celestial Master Protector of the Country."

Before returning to the orthodox line of Longmen masters, we can thus conclude that the Longmen order seems to have not yet been established at Baiyun guan when Sun Xuanqing settled there, and that it did not yet possess a genuine doctrinal center. Although Sun was affiliated with the Laoshan Quanzhen tradition of the Seven Perfected, this tradition was in fact integrated into the Zhengyi tradition with which Sun shared Quanzhen collective meditation and the official title of Celestial Master.

The orthodox Longmen lineage from the Fourth to the Seventh Generation [Line A, Nos. 4–7]

The Fourth Patriarch: Zhou Xuanpu (?-1450?)

Lineage name: *Xuan*pu 玄朴 (Mysterious Simplicity)
Original name: Zhisheng 知生
Daoist surname: Dazhuo 大拙 (Great Ignorant)
Birth-place: Xi'an 西安 (Shaanxi)

In the "Zhou Dazhuo lüshi zhuan" 周大拙律師傳 (JGXD j. 1.5a-b, in ZWDS 31:178) Zhou is portrayed as a man out of the ordinary. While immersing himself in Daoist teachings, he was content even working as a peasant. However, close to the end of the Yuan dynasty, the region around the capital was engulfed in such anarchy that nobody was spared. Zhou decided to retire to the Zhongnan region (Shaanxi), but even there he was bothered by brigands. At that time, the Yuan court launched an appeal to get the help of men of extraordinary abilities and experts in occult techniques. To that end, it sent envoys on an emergency quest throughout the land. Zhou thus left his family and took refuge in Mt. Qingcheng where he became a disciple of Chen Chongyi 陳沖夷—i.e., third Longmen patriarch Chen Tongwei 陳通微 who is said to have "shouldered the precept doctrine"—and obtained from him the method of precepts (*jiefa* 戒法).

The compilers of this biography then point out that the vast majority of Daoist masters preferred living in the mountains in order to devote themselves to ascetic practices, and that they refrained from involvement in society to such an extent that they did not even consider propagating their teachings.

> At that time, the Mysterious Teaching [of Daoism] was in shambles. "Men of good will" all wanted to save their skin and avoid blame. Zhou hid in Mt. Qingcheng, and for more than fifty years he did not set foot in the dust of the world. He faced the wall and engaged in introspection so as to avoid bothering his mind by teachings and worldly matters. His disciples were numerous, yet all of them refrained from occupying themselves with the propagation of the teaching. The Vinaya Teaching was facing extinction.
> 是時元門零落。有志之士。皆全身避咎。師隱青城。不履塵市。五十餘年。面壁內觀。不以教。相有為之事累心。弟子數人。皆不以闡教為事。律門幾致湮歿。

It seems that only toward the end of his life, at the age of 150 years (!), he found two disciples capable of receiving his teachings. Once this transmission was accomplished, he took leave in 1450, whereupon his trace is lost.

Portrayed as a simple man linked with field labor but endowed with "monastic qualities," Zhou Xuanpu embodies a key moment for the Longmen transmission. On the one hand, this is reflected in the upheaval and economic hardship of the ending dynasty, and on the other in the loss of spiritual integrity of the Vinaya transmission. The "transmission of the Lamp" no more takes place, as in Chan's ideal line, from one master to one disciple, but it now splits into two lines. Two disciples are thus said to have received Zhou's teachings:

(a) Zhang *Jing*ding 張靜定 (fl. 1450), the holder of the Vinaya Line represented by "Vinaya Masters who after having received the precepts are firmly able to respect the regulations of the Vinaya" (*fan cheng shoujie fa hou queneng zunshou jielü zhe cheng lüshi* 凡承受戒法後確能遵守戒律者稱律師);[70] and

(b) Shen *Jing*yuan 沈靜圓 (fl. 1448), the holder of the Doctrinal Line (i.e. Line of the Teachings of the Lineage) represented by "Doctrinal masters who excel in morality and learning and are in charge of the lineage and the transmission of the dharma" (*fan chengzong chuandao pinxuejianyou zhe cheng zongshi* 凡承宗傳道品學兼優者稱宗師).[71]

The Vinaya transmission, which represented the driving force of the ideal Longmen line from its purported founder Qiu Chuji to the fourth patriarch, is now described as something almost extinguished. However, in contrast with the two previous biographies, the compilers mention that Zhou had many disciples. By this claim they may want to show that Longmen had already begun to organize itself in groups of masters who had, as their fundamental prerequisite, ascetic training yet left aside the pure rules of the original Quanzhen order. This may allude to the end of Quanzhen as an institutional order that conveys ordinations, and to the survival of Quanzhen as a symbol of asceticism among groups of hermits, itinerant monks or Confucian recluses. In contrast with the Chan-modeled earlier patriarchs, the Confucian recluses seem now to be the protagonists of a new phase of Longmen transmission, provided that one thus interprets the compilers' reference to "men of good will" who did not collaborate any more with the government.[72] This change is underlined in the biographies of the subsequent masters by their length and by variations in literary style as well as by the superimposition of the scholar-priest ideal. This ideal replaces that of the simple and uncultivated men of the first period who were more akin to the aspirations of the Chan and Quanzhen eremitic traditions.

Furthermore, this biography sheds light on something which seems to characterize Chinese history. During the periods of division which often

---

[70] "Fanlie 凡列" in DTYL.

[71] "Fanlie 凡列" in DTYL.

[72] Chen Bing, "Qingdai Quanzhen Longmen pai de zhongxing"; Wang Zhizhong, "Lun Mingmo Qingchu Quanzhen jiao 'zhongxing' de chengyin"; and Zeng Zhaonan, "Longmen pai." As Qing Xitai (*Zhongguo daojiao shi*, vol. 3: 481) points out, this may fit with the exclusion of the Quanzhen school from the government that took place at the beginning of the Ming; see also note 76 below.

characterize the end of dynasties, the South was often seen as the cradle of "loyalists" who fled the foreign invaders and harbored dreams of a reunified China under the government of a Sage-emperor. This "loyalist line" is here incarnated in the "Doctrinal Line" (*zongshi* 宗師) which, according to the *Jingai xindeng*, spread with the fifth patriarch Shen Jingyuan in the Jiangsu and Zhejiang regions and achieved reunification with the Vinaya Line (*lüshi* 律師) thanks to Wang Changyue (see the "Geographical Distribution," Fig. 2, p. 66). Likewise, one may also compare the division of these two lines — Vinaya and Doctrine — with that between the Northern and Southern Lineages which were unified during the Yuan dynasty in a "Quanzhen Northern and Southern tradition." With the advent of the Ming and their policy of reunification, the Quanzhen Northern Lineage allowed its original denomination to be integrated into the all-inclusive, state-approved Southern Lineage, "which was used in the cultural politics of the Ming reunification by Southerners to promote southern (Chinese) over northern traditions (in particular the Quanzhen order) which many felt had been too much under the sway of Mongolian rulers."[73] During the Qing, the situation was exactly reversed. The Southern traditions, which were at the basis of the nascent constitution of the Longmen, were this time labeled "Quanzhen's Longmen Northern lineage" in the hope of greater acceptance by the Qing foreign dynasty.

In the following, only the Vinaya line will be discussed; it can be regarded as the Qing ideal extension of the Northern Quanzhen tradition which, although promoted by Southerners during the Ming, embodied the Daoist orthodoxy at the state-approved Baiyun guan through the figure of its reformer and abbot Wang Changyue.[74]

---

[73] See Lowell Skar, "Alchemy, Local Cults, and Daoism: A Perspective on the Formation of the Southern Lineage from Tang to Ming," Paper presented at the Conference "Religion and Chinese Society: The Transformation of a Field," Hong Kong, May 29–June 2, 2000.

[74] For a presentation and analysis of the Longmen Doctrinal Line see M. Esposito, "La Porte du Dragon," 110–125.

The Fifth Patriarch: Zhang Jingding (fl. 1450) [Line A, No. 5]

Lineage name: *Jing*ding 靜定 (Serene Concentration)
Original name: Zongren 宗仁
Daoist surname: Wuwo 無我 (Egoless)
Birth-place: Yuhang 餘杭 (modern Hangzhou, Zhejiang)

According to the "Zhang Wuwo lüshi zhuan" 張無我律師傳 (JGXD j. 1:6a-7a, ZWDS 31:178–179), Zhang hailed from a family of officials and excelled in Confucian studies. During the Yongle era (1403–1424) he was admitted to the official exams organized by the state. It seems that he did not manage to get to the examination locale in time and thus lost the chance of getting his degree. He thus decided to leave public life and refrain from engaging in any official function, becoming a private instructor in Tiaoxi 苕溪 (Zhejiang). After the death of his parents he fell into such despair that he felt the need to leave all worldly affairs. Once this decision was made, he summoned his sons and said to them:

> I have fulfilled my great obligations to you and shall not tire myself anymore. Though heaven and earth are immense, I must set out to roam about. How could I be attached until old age to learning and sit around waiting for death?

> 了此一件人子大事。吾此形骸。不復累爾矣。天地雖闊。我當逍遙其間。安能拘拘于老學究。坐以待死耶。

Thus he visited the famous mountains and called on eminent and accomplished men. Had he had the chance of meeting a patriarch like Chen Chongyi, he used to say, he would not have hesitated to revere him as his teacher. He was glad to finally arrive at Tiantai 天臺 (Zhejiang) where he stayed with three or four Daoists of the Yellow-Hats (*huangguan jia yushi* 黃冠家羽士, lit. Feathery masters of the Yellow-hatted family). Considering them as masters, he served them and did not even refuse to chant and participate in their liturgy. He was initiated into the classics of Daoism and alchemical formulae which he understood at a glance.

> For more than ten years he lingered [on Tiantai]. He embodied Yanzi's "sitting and forgetting [oneself]" and Ziqi's "losing the other" and then changed his name to "Egoless." His disciples increased in

number; nevertheless, he set his mind to look [for a true master]. One day a Daoist beggar told him: "The Tiantai scenery is no match for that of Qingcheng. Why don't you once go there?"

盤桓十餘年。體顏子之坐忘。子綦之喪耦也。更號無我。弟子益眾。然猶志在訪求。一日有乞食道者曰。天台景致。不如青城。師何不一遊。

It seems that this encounter led to his voyage to Mt. Qingcheng. After a journey with many hazards, he finally arrived and met Zhou Dazhuo 周大拙 (fourth patriarch Zhou Xuanpu) whom he immediately recognized as his true master. Zhou confirmed Zhang's understanding of the Dao by saying:

"Since the Dao is as you say, I charge you with the all-important matter." Holding up the fly-whisk, Vinaya regulations and [registers of] the masters' lineage, he [master Zhou] handed them over and said: "Though the present age obliges us to hide our traces, the unique line of the former saints cannot but continue. In the future, you must choose the most capable disciple and confer it on him, and he in turn must transmit it and put it in action.

道雖如是。有一大事託子。乃舉如意、戒律、師派。授之，曰。雖時當晦蹟。先聖一脈。不可不續。後當擇一至士授之。再傳而行矣。

Thereupon Zhang again retired to Tiantai and in 1522 gave the transmission to Zhao Zhensong 趙真嵩.

Starting from this biography, one notes a change: the ideal of the Daoist is now close to that of the Confucian recluse who chose self-cultivation after having fulfilled his social duties. He also represents one who can harmoniously integrate other teachings and ways of practicing; for example, Zhang "did not even refuse to perform liturgy with the Yellow Hats" since he had already transcended the apparent contradictions between Daoist schools. He achieved "the equanimity of things" of Ziqi while attaining simultaneously the self-realization of Yanzi.

Furthermore, the Longmen Vinaya transmission which hitherto had been limited to recording the passing of "the Lamp of Mind" from master to disciple in order to ensure the continuity of an endangered lineage, now includes something else: for the first time, the compilers refer to the regalia of the Daoist not from the point of view of one who received it (robe and bowl, symbol of a secret ordination based on the Chan model), but from the point of view of the Vinaya Master who transmits his own ritual instruments of investiture that are necessary for succession (fly-whisk, vinaya regulations, and the registers of masters' lineage) at a public ordination platform. The power of the Longmen as the Daoist school responsible for performing court-approved public ordinations is thus becoming apparent and, although the time is still not ripe, the "unique line of the former sages" is bound to culminate in the figure of its abbot Wang Changyue. He will embody the ideals of the Saint who will be able to exercise his religious activity while assisting a good emperor.

The compilers may also want to indicate in this biography that the geographical sanctuary of a new Longmen tradition is going to be transferred to Mt. Tiantai (Zhejiang) from its original place, Mt. Qingcheng. It is of interest to note that in all the biographies that we have analyzed so far, the sanctuary of Mt. Qingcheng played a fundamental role in the Longmen transmission. Was it indeed one of the early centers responsible for the creation of an orthodox lineage of this kind, or is this only what the hagiographers and compilers want to make us believe? This question may find a preliminary answer when we analyze the Longmen line of Daoist ancestors.

The Sixth Patriarch: Zhao Zhensong (fl. 1522–1628) [Line A, No. 6]

Lineage name: *Zhen*song 真嵩 (Genuine Peak)
Original name: Deyuan 得源
Daoist surname: Fuyang zi 復揚子 (Master Returning to Yang)
Birth-place: Langya 瑯研 (Shandong)

According to the "Zhao Fuyang lüshi zhuan" 趙復陽律師傳 (JGXD j. 1. 11a-12b, in ZWDS 31:181), Zhao was born under the protection of the constellation of the Dipper to which his parents are said to have prayed for a descendant.

From his youth, Zhao showed aversion to celebrity; yet at 20 years of age, he was already known as a specialist of the classics and of history as well as of Buddhism and Daoism. Both of his parents died when he was 25, and their loss opened up an abyss of suffering in his heart which was filled with the desire to repay in filial gratitude all that they had given to him. He thus journeyed to Mt. Wudang (Hubei) before going to the Maoshan (Jiangsu). There he withdrew to devote himself to the study of Daoist works. Subsequently, he traversed southern Jiangsu and northern Zhejiang in the hope of finally encountering a genuine master. But this hope was not fulfilled until, four years later, he arrived at Mt. Tongbai 桐柏山 (Tiantai, Zhejiang) where he met (fifth Longmen patriarch) Zhang Jingding 張靜定. After having noticed Zhao's abilities to perceive the permanency of Dao in every thing, master Zhang conferred the lineage name *Zhen*song (Genuine Peak) on him. However, Zhao had to wait some more years for the transmission by Zhang of the quintessence of the Vinaya (*jiezhi* 戒旨). Zhang instructed him to retire to the "Celestial Grotto of Pure Emptiness" situated at the heart of the Wangwu mountains (Henan).

Complying with the wishes of his master, he went into ascetic retreat, and though "a white monkey offered him fruits," he persisted in his wall-gazing meditation to such extent that "a sparrow could build its nest in his top-knot." But only when, one day, he heard voices resembling those of his parents in the mountains, were his eyes finally opened. Appropriately, this happened exactly at the end of the traditional three-year period of ascetic training. Thus, at the end of this retreat, he knew the satisfaction of having fulfilled his filial obligations toward his parents who appeared to him and confirmed this.

Tradition also reports that after returning to Mt. Tiantai, Zhao once more withdrew to Mt. Wangwu where he gave the transmission to Wang Changyue (?-1680) in the year 1628.

At first sight, one notes that the biography of the sixth patriarch is rich in details and fabulous elements known from the traditional hagiographies of China's Eminent Monks. Ideals of asceticism mix themselves with prophecies and the image of the perfect scholar-priest who renounces celebrity and official career in favor of ascetic ideals. Furthermore, in contrast with earlier masters, the figure of Zhao appears to be fixated on repaying his debt of gratitude to his parents. It is the force of his filial piety that makes him undergo ascetic training. The ascetic period is also for the first time described by stereotyped metaphors while showing literary links with traditional Buddhist hagiographies.[75] These references may reflect the dominant role

---

[75] The biography of the Buddhist monk Yongming Yanshou 永明延壽 (904–975), for example, mentions that when he did the ninety-day meditation at Mt. Tiantai, birds built nests in the folds of his robes (see Albert Welter, "The Contextual Study of Chinese Buddhist Biographies: The Example of Yung-Ming Yen-Shou [904–975],"

that a Confucian elite, well instructed in the Three Teachings, played in the elaboration of an official image of the Longmen lineage more in accord with the taste of the Ming court.[76]

Furthermore, if we analyze this biography from a geographical point of view, we find that the transmission from Mt. Qingcheng is moved to Zhejiang and Henan while other important mountain centers like Wudang and Maoshan are also mentioned. If we compare this information with that of earlier biographies adduced above, we may arrive at the conclusion that at the end of the Ming the Longmen tradition had probably already spread to different places. The compilers have for example pointed to Mt. Hua and Mt. Qingcheng as early sanctuaries, followed by Tiantai and Wangwu, and they made passing references to Wudangshan and Maoshan. Conversely, in other sources we found that early sanctuaries of the Longmen were located in Huashan and Laoshan (see the "Geographical Distribution" in Figure 2). But before drawing some conclusions, I will present a tentative translation of the biography of Wang Changyue, the figure for whom the architects of these early Longmen biographies have built their hagiographical edifice.

THE SEVENTH PATRIARCH: WANG CHANGYUE (?-1680), STATE-APPROVED REFORMER OF THE LONGMEN LINEAGE AT THE BAIYUN GUAN [LINE A, NO. 7]

Lineage name: *Changyue* 常月 (Perseverance for Months)
Original name: Ping 平
Daoist name: Kunyang 崑陽
Birth-place: Lu'an 潞安 (Shanxi).

---

in Phyllis Granoff & Shinohara Kōichi (eds.), *Monks and Magicians: Religious Biographies in Asia*, 247–268, Oakville: Mosaic Press, 1988). The story of monkeys providing food is also known from earlier biographies of Eminent Monks (Shinohara Kōichi, "Passages and Transmission in Tianhuang Daowu's Biographies," in Phyllis Granoff & Shinohara Kōichi (eds.), *Other Selves. Autobiography & Biography in Cross-Cultural Perspective*, 140, Oakville: Mosaic Press, 1994).

[76] During the Ming dynasty, the Quanzhen school was largely excluded from the official religion and depreciated by the Ming court for its teachings based on the cultivation of the self, while the Zhengyi was more appreciated for focusing on salvation and placing special emphasis on filial piety; see John Lagerwey, *Taoist Ritual in Chinese Society and History*, 260, New York: Macmillan Publishing Company, 1987; and M. Esposito, "La Porte du Dragon," 10–15.

In contrast with the previous six patriarchs, the life of Wang Changyue is recorded in a variety of sources. The main ones are:

(1) "Wang Kunyang lüshi zhuan" 王崑陽律師傳 (*Jingai xindeng*, j. 1:15a–17b) reportedly based on: Fan Taiqing's 范太清 *Bojian xu* 缽鑑續; Lü Yunyin's 呂雲隱 "Wang Kunyang zhuan" 王崑陽傳; Tao Shi'an's 陶石庵 *Jingai yunjian* 金蓋雲箋; Zhao Zhensong's *Fuyang de daoji* 復陽得道記 (stemming from the *Bojian* attributed to Wang Changyue);
(2) *Daotong yuanliu* 道統源流, xia 2;
(3) "Kunyang Wang zhenren daoxing bei" 崑陽王真人道行碑 (Stele on the Virtuous Behavior of the Perfected Wang Kunyang) by Wanyan Chongshi 完顏崇實 (1886, in *Baiyun guan zhi* 白雲觀志 j. 4:162–63 with a short biographical note in *Baiyun guan zhi* j. 2:35; and in *Baiyun xianbiao* 1848, 52a–53b, ZWDS 31:400);
(4) *Changchun daojiao yuanliu* 長春道教源流 j. 7:31b (ZWDS 31:134).

The *Jingai xindeng* reports the following about Wang Changyue's life:

> During his childhood, a Daoist told him after having observed him: "Qiaoyang has been reborn" and, having made this prophecy, was no more seen.[77]
>
> Although his parents respected Daoism and revered Zhang Mayi, [Wang] at the outset hardly showed any interest. After Zhang Mayi had passed by and given a great demonstration of his spiritual powers by healing him of a grave illness, Wang left his home to visit him. Though still adolescent, his mind which was devoted to the Dao was already tranquil. He traveled widely, visiting the famous mountains, and braved dangers and obstacles, wind and frost; thus he was on his way for months and years, cold season after hot. Before he noticed it, more than 80 years had passed. When he reached Mt. Wangwu, his heart fluttered in premonition as if he were to meet a perfect being. This turned out to be the Perfected Zhao Fuyang [Zhensong] who had lived there in seclusion for a long time. [Wang] implored him to instruct him, but the Perfected one did not respond for months. Nourishing himself from pine branches and pure sources, Wang prostrated and requested [Zhao's teaching] with increasing insistence.

---

[77] The gloss adds that this Daoist is probably Zhang Mayi 張麻衣 who belongs to Zhao Zhensong's lineage.

Mayi came by especially to support Wang's demand. [So Wang] obtained the [lineage] name Changyue (Persevering for Months) and learned that Zhang [Mayi] and the Perfected [Zhao] were friends. Furthermore, [Mayi] requested that the precepts be given [to Wang], and they were handed to him in two volumes. The Perfected [Zhao] gave him the following injunction: "Achieving the Way is extremely easy and at the same time extremely difficult. Ascetic practices are a definite prerequisite since the various external affairs must be gotten rid of once and for all. Adhere to the rules and keep them with care while immersing yourself in the classics. Realize the original hidden intent of the *Daode[jing]*'s "self-so" and search for the true knack of the *Nanhua[jing]*'s "vitality," and you will be stable; 'a great vessel is complete only in the evening [i.e., late in life].'"[78]

Prostrating himself again, Wang received [Zhao's] teaching. Making the rounds of the mountains, he tasted all kinds of sweetness and bitterness. Without a moment's rest he sought to peruse the classics of all Three Teachings. He came by an old Daoist monastery with countless Daoist scriptures and examined them day and night. Whenever his lamp was on the verge of going out he lighted it anew with incense; in its radiance he read for eight or nine years. He went to question masters in more than twenty places and received the seal of approval of more than fifty people.

幼有道士顧之曰。樵陽再生矣。言訖不見。然初無好尚。父兄皆留心元門。尊事張麻衣。麻衣為師治危疾。大顯神力而去。師棄家訪之。時年弱冠。而向道之心已篤。遍遊名山。踰越險阻。風霜道途。歲月寒暑。幾於相忘者。八十餘年。至王屋山。得得心動。遂遇至人。至人者。復陽趙真人也。隱居久。就懇指示。真人不答者月餘。師食松枝飲清泉。拜求更切。麻衣特至為之請。命名常月。始知張與真人友也。又為求戒。授以二冊。真人囑曰。成道甚易。然亦甚難。必以苦行為先。種種外務。切須掃除。依律精持。潛心教典。體道德自然之元奧。探南華活潑之真機。方為穩當汝。大器當晚成。師再拜受教。周流諸山間。甘苦備嘗。搜覽三教經書。孜孜不怠。過一古觀中。道籍頗多。晝夜檢閱。每乏燈。以香續火。光照而讀。八九年間。參師二十餘處。印證五十餘人。

---

[78] This last sentence, 大器晚成, stems from the *Daodejing* (chap. 41).

Confronted with the troubles at the end of the Ming dynasty, Wang went to Jiugong mountains 九宮 mountains in Hubei where he met again Zhao Fuyang 趙復陽 (lineage name: Zhensong 真嵩) who asked him about his spiritual progress. When Wang told him of the decline of Daoism, the rise of heterodoxy, and the political troubles, Zhao said to him:

> "(...) If one acts against one's time, one acts erroneously. How could one avoid the injustices of the world and the envy of the mob? I entrust to you the matter of which I alone was in charge for three hundred years. Treasure it and keep it secret, and when the time is ripe it will flourish and it will be upon you to propagate the Wondrous Spirit [of the teaching]."

He then in turn transmitted to him the Precepts of the Celestial Immortals.

He added: "Formerly, during the era of Emperor Shizu of Yuan, Perfected Lord [Qiu] Changchun widely promoted the teaching of precepts. He propagated the treasure of the pure and serene rules of the Most High. As [his disciples] approved of each other from mind to mind and transmitted from patriarch to patriarch while keeping pure silence and refraining from action, the singular transmission was conferred in secret and could not be widely promulgated. For this reason the feathered vagabonds and companions of the Way rarely observed the rules of comportment and were thus hardly in a position to know that the arcane Way has its precepts. Now the chance has presented itself to entrust you with this important matter; if it is not you, who else could it be?" Then he transmitted robe and bowl. But Wang said that, slow-witted as he was, he had to decline. The Perfected one said, "If one finds a person and transmits, it is not a matter of being forced. When in twenty years you travel to Beijing and visit [the grave of] Patriarch Qiu at the Baiyun guan, the time will be ripe to put the Way into action."

Wang was born on the 22nd day of the fifth month of the year *renwu* in the Jiajing era (1522). In the autumn of the year *yiwei* of the Shunzhi era (1655) he arrived at the capital and settled in the Lingyou palace. On the fifteenth day of the third month of the year *bingshen* (1656) he conveyed the precepts at Baiyun guan. The chance to protect the teaching had fallen into place naturally, and it all was in accord with the words of the Perfected one.

若違時妄行。安能免世俗之謗議。匪類之妒忌哉。吾有三百年來獨任之事。當付於子。寶而秘之。時至而興。大闡元風。是在子矣。遂轉授天仙戒。又云。昔我長春真君於元世祖時。廣行戒法。流演太上清靜律寶。心心相印。祖祖相傳。皆守靜默而厭有為。單傳秘授。不能廣行。是以羽流道侶。鮮睹威儀。幾不知元門有戒矣。今因緣將到。任大事者。非子而誰。乃傳衣缽。師辭謝不敏。真人曰。得人而傳。非勉強也。子于二十年後。遊燕京。謁邱祖於白雲觀。是道行之時也。師生嘉靖壬午。五月二十二日。於順治乙未。秋遊京師。掛單靈佑宮。歲丙申。三月望日。說戒於白雲觀。因緣護法。天然會合。皆符真人語。

Following the intention of the compilers of this biography, one may divide their record into five parts. The first one starts with a prophecy which is only found in the version of the *Jingai xindeng* and is used as symbol of a new beginning for the Longmen school through the "rebirth of Master Qiaoyang 樵陽." According to the *Qiaoyang jing*, 樵陽經—a text included in Fu Jinquan's 傅金銓 *Daoshu shiqi zhong* 道書十七種 (1835, ZWDS 11)—Qiaoyang was the surname of the well-known Liu Yu 劉玉 (style name: Yizhen, 1257–1308), the codifier of the liturgical Jingming zhongxiao dao 淨明忠孝道 which had developed around the 13th century in the Jiangxi region. However, in the commentary of the *Huangji hepi xianjing* 皇極闔闢仙經 (j. *xia*, chap. 10 in DZXB 1: 5b/1–2) it is said:

> Qiaoyang is the surname of an ancient Perfected man whose family name was Wang. No one knows when he lived. At the exact moment when the Vinaya Master Wang Kunyang of Luzhou was born, an immortal passing by his house said: "Qiaoyang is reborn!" The Vinaya lineage of the Most High (Lord Lao) will prosper again from now on.

> 樵陽者。古真人之號。姓王。不知何代人。王崑陽律祖。潞洲人。相傳生時。有仙人過其門曰。樵陽再生矣。太上律宗。從此復振矣。

According to this, Wang Kunyang (lineage name **Chang**yue) was the new manifestation of a Perfected man called Wang Qiaoyang 王樵陽. I have not been able to find any master with such a name but I think that, since we are in a prophetic context, this name may refer to a new appearance of a figure such as Liu Yu, i.e., a founder of a new school who, by endorsing the moral codes identified with Confucius, was as though supported by the emperor. This supposition may be confirmed by an important substitution that the Longmen school adopted in the lineage of its Daoist Ancestors. We will return to this later.

The second part marks Wang's spiritual career, which starts with a reference to an extraordinary Daoist healer called Zhang Mayi 張麻衣. As is well known, Mayi daozhe 麻衣道者 was one of the different nicknames adopted by the immortal Lü Dongbin for converting the people; but it also was the nickname of the master who allegedly transmitted the *Taiji tu* 太極圖 to Chen Tuan 陳摶.[79] In contrast with the other biographies, Mayi appears only in the *Jingai xindeng*. He plays the role of mediator between Wang Changyue and the sixth Longmen patriarch Zhao Zhensong; only thanks to him could Wang receive the ordination and his lineage name. Mayi, then, functions as a kind of seal through which Wang entered into the orthodox Longmen lineage and became the seventh patriarch.

The meeting between Wang and Zhao at Mt. Wangwu and the deprivations and pains of Wang while waiting for Zhao Fuyang's transmission are similarly recorded in the text of the *Baiyun guan zhi*'s stele (BYGZ, j. 2:163). However, this stele and the *Jingai xindeng* texts differ in their portrayal of the intervention of Mayi. The stele makes no mention of the transmission of precepts in two volumes. The compilers of the *Jingai xindeng* may have wanted to point out that now the Longmen possessed written texts for ordination. Wang Changyue is said to be the author of one of the main Longmen ordination texts known under the title *Chuzhen jielü* 初真戒律 (The Regulation of the Initial Precepts of Perfection, 1656, DZJY 24 *zhangji* 7 and ZWDS 12: 13–31). The compilers also add that, after the official investiture, Wang realized that Mayi belonged to the same lineage as his master Zhao Zhensong—which may mean that Wang finally understood that Mayi was in reality a manifestation of the immortal Lü Dongbin 呂洞賓, the Founding Patriarch of the Quanzhen Northern and Southern Lineages and Lineage Master of the Dao (道宗).

The third part introduces Wang's ascetic training including the period of isolation, the importance of travelling far in search of enlightened masters, the necessity of receiving confirmation of one's spiritual realization through debates while still possessing broad knowledge of the Three Teachings, etc.

---

[79] Isabelle Ang, "Le culte de Lü Dongbin des origines jusqu'au début du XIVème siècle. Caractéristiques et transformations d'un Saint Immortel dans la Chine pré-moderne," Ph. D. diss., Université de Paris VII, 1993.

This is also recorded in a similar way in the *Baiyun guan zhi*'s stele (BYGZ, j. 2: 163).

The fourth part confirms through an encounter dialogue between Zhao and Wang that the orthodox Longmen transmission has been passed on. On this occasion Zhao Zhensong claims that it was "three-hundred years that he was in charge of it," which means that Zhao is now presented by the compilers as a simple link (the alter ego of Mayi / Lü Dongbin) between the purported founder Qiu Chuji and Wang Changyue. The compilers then show the intention of setting apart the previous line of Longmen Vinaya Masters by saying that theirs was only a secret transmission which proved unable to promulgate the pure and serene rules of the Most High (Lord Lao), with the result that Daoist discipline was on the verge of disappearing. The initial prophecy which opened this biography is now concretized by presenting Wang Changyue as the direct heir of Qiu Chuji.[80] Wang Changyue seems thus to be promoted in Qiu Chuji's wake as the founder of the Longmen institutionalized lineage which achieved sponsorship by the emperor who gave him the official title Guoshi 國師 (State Instructor).[81] This seems to me to be the inner meaning of the prediction of Zhao that concludes this encounter dialogue.[82]

The fifth part ends with the realization of this prediction and the investiture of Wang Changyue as abbot of the Baiyun guan. According to the stele in *Baiyun guan zhi* (BYGZ 4.163), Wang received a similar prediction not from his master Zhao but from the Dipper Mother (Doumu 斗母) when he lived on Huashan. The text of the stele adds that after his death in 1680 he was buried in the western hall of the Baiyun guan. The Kangxi emperor gave him the posthumous title Baoyi gaoshi 抱一高師 (Eminent Master who Embraces the One) and ordered a memorial hall built for his mortal remains with his portrait. This hall still exists in the western part of the Baiyun guan under the name Citang 祠堂 (Hall of Ancestral Worship).

---

[80] Wang is in fact regarded by his disciples as the one who has revitalized "l'esprit de famille" of the Perfected Qiu Chuji (*Qiu Changchun zhenren zhi jiafeng* 邱長春真人之家風); see the postface to the *Longmen xinfa* 龍門心法 by Shao Shoushan and Zhan Shouchun (ZWDS 6:785). On the term *jiafeng* see Dale S. Wright, "Les récits de transmission du bouddhisme Ch'an et l'historiographie moderne," *Cahiers d'Extrême-Asie* 7, 1993–94: 109.

[81] JGXD (1. 17b; j. 2:4a).

[82] Similar predictions attributing the future success of a religion to a relationship with political rulers were also a characteristic of the Buddhist Fayan school; see for example A. Welter, "The Contextual Study of Chinese Buddhist Biographies," 258.

If we now take a look of Chen Minggui's *Changchun daojiao yuanliu* 長春道教源流 (DJYL 7.32b), we note that Wang Changyue's biography contrasts with the official version elaborated in the *Jingai xindeng* and in the Baiyun guan stele. There are only a few lines devoted to him, just after Wang Qingzheng, the purported restorer of the Baiyun guan from Huashan. At first glance, Wang Changyue does not appear as a figure of great importance, and his biographical note is somehow affiliated with the Huashan hermits, Ma Zhenyi and Wang Qingzheng. Chen Minggui gives only the following information about Wang Changyue:

> Wang Changyue, style name: Kunyang. He restored the Yinxian an (Hermitage of the Recluse Immortal) of the Huju guan in Jiangning (Jiangsu). This hermitage was built of grass by Gao Xuanli, a Daoist of Laoshan in 1526, and named Zhulin daoyuan. In 1630 its name was changed to Yinxian an. Wang Kunyang had the behavior of a Daoist and lived for a while at the capital's Baiyun guan. After his death in this hermitage, Li Gao made an inscription for him.[83]

> 王常月字崑陽。嘗恢復江甯虎踞關之隱仙菴。菴為嘉靖五年嶗山道人高玄禮結草。名竹林道院。崇禎三年易今名。崑陽有道行。曾寓京都白雲觀。後化於菴中。李皋為之銘。

Here it is mentioned that Wang rebuilt a hermitage affiliated with a Laoshan master Gao *Xuan*li 高玄禮 who, according to the Longmen poem, might be linked with the fourth generation of Longmen by the character *xuan* 玄. In contrast with other biographies, what seems emphasized here is that Wang may belong to an eremitic tradition which, like the Huashan tradition of Ma Zhenyi and Wang Qingzheng, was transmitted at Laoshan. We may find further support for the possible affiliation of Wang Changyue with Laoshan in a short passage quoted by Wang himself in the *Biyuan tanjing* 碧

---

[83] This short biographical note stems from the *Jinling shizheng* 金陵詩徵 by Zhu Xu 朱緒 (DTYL 7.31b). At the end of the biographical note on Wang Changyue, a gloss is added to the effect that according to the *Jiangning fuzhi* 江寧府志 the name of Yinxian an 隱仙庵 was given in honor of Tao Hongjing 陶宏景. During the Ming the Yinxian an was visited by Leng Tiejiao 冷鐵腳 and Yin Pengtou 尹蓬頭 (DJYL 7.31b). Yin Pengtou was famous for having allegedly written two alchemical scriptures inserted in the DZXB; see M. Esposito, "La Porte du Dragon," 154–55, 184–226. The hermitage of Yinxian an is also mentioned by Long Qiqian 龍起潛 (a disciple of Wang Changyue) in his preface (1674) to Wang Changyue's *Chuzhen jielü* 初真戒律 (DZJY *zhangji* 7: 27b).

苑壇經 (Platform Sūtra of the Jade Garden, 1663, j. *zhong*: 14; ZWDS 10: 186):

> There was a Daoist who in the middle of his life left his family. He roamed with the clouds to call upon [masters] and met some companions [of the Way]. Together they made a vow to build a hermitage at Laoshan in Shandong in order to practice. Afterwards, because of war troubles, they left the mountains and reached the foot of Mount Wangwu in Henan, where six of them settled to meditate in the same place.

> 有一道人半路出家。參訪雲遊。遇見幾箇侶伴。同發下願。結菴在山東牢山修行。後因兵亂。便同相下山。到河南王屋山下。住單打坐。六人一處。

If Wang refers to his own eremitic life, why do the biographical notes included in the *Jingai xindeng* and in the stele mention neither Wang's connection with Laoshan nor his affiliation with a hermitage in Jiangsu? According to the biography of the *Jingai xindeng*, Wang was connected with the Wangwu (Henan) and Jiugong mountains (Hubei) while the stele also mentions Huashan. Internal evidence suggests that we are dealing here with the creation of an ideal biography where the figure of Wang Changyue is given the role of unique heir of the genuine Quanzhen tradition of Qiu Chuji who transcends all local affiliations. However, from the sources analyzed above, we know that an earlier movement of the Longmen was active at Huashan and that, at the end of the Ming, another Longmen lineage was present at Laoshan in the figure of the fourth-generation master Sun Xuanqing 孫玄清 (1497–1569). The mention of the affiliation of Wang Changyue with Laoshan may reflect the supremacy of this line that the orthodox lineage wants to set aside.

The biographies of the first seven patriarchs representative of the Longmen orthodox lineage of the Baiyun guan (the lineage that was to be accepted in all the Longmen affiliated monasteries) allow some preliminary conclusions concerning the intentions of the architects of the Longmen hagiographical edifice:

(1) The biographies exhibit the editors' desire to link the name of Longmen with the mountains in Shaanxi where its purported founder Qiu Chuji underwent his ascetic training;

(2) They also show the intent of establishing as its headquarters Beijing's Baiyun guan, the memorial shrine of its ideal founder Qiu Chuji and early

sanctuary where the first Longmen Patriarch Zhao Daojian supposedly received the Longmen transmission directly from Qiu Chuji;

(3) They portray the ancient Longmen transmission as mainly consisting in passing on "the robe and the bowl" along with the sacred poem. These represent the regalia of the Daoist who has formally received the Longmen ordination.[84] Only after having received the full three-stage precepts can a Daoist priest become a genuine Longmen Vinaya Master;

(4) They affirm the investiture of Wang Changyue as the reviver of the original discipline of Qiu Chuji. Wang Changyue presides over the public ordination platform by holding the rank of abbot at the Baiyun guan. He does not exhibit any local affiliation since he is the unifier of the Southern and Northern traditions, the State Instructor who assists a good emperor.

But the Longmen portrayal also exhibits many discrepancies. These discrepancies show another current of Longmen history which also becomes evident when one reads the official biographies. One of the early Longmen sanctuaries was probably linked to the eremitic tradition of the Wangdiao grotto of Huashan whose Wang Qingzheng was the purported restorer of the Baiyun guan at the beginning of the Qing dynasty. However, the orthodox Longmen lineage, which was certainly established *a posteriori* at the Baiyun guan, neither mentions the name of Wang Qingzheng nor his affiliation with Huashan.[85] The obvious reason is that it wanted to promote the figure of Wang Changyue since Wang received the official support of the Kangxi emperor. Through him, the Longmen could be accepted and protected by the Qing court.

---

[84] Yoshioka Yoshitoyo, "Taoist Monastic Life," 236–38.

[85] A further proof of the *a posteriori* creation of the orthodox Longmen lineage lies in the fact that, around the end of the Ming dynasty, there were already other Longmen lineages at Wudang (Hubei), Maoshan (Jiangsu) or Xishan (Jiangxi) which were omitted by the Longmen hagiography or allegedly integrated into the orthodox lineage; see for example the earlier lineage of Maoshan at the end of the Ming dynasty with Yan Xiyan 閻希言 (?-1588), the lineage of Kong Changgui 孔常圭 and his disciples at Xishan, or even the other lineage at Wudang with the fourth Longmen generation master Bai Xuanfu 白玄福 (fl. 1656) which was later integrated into that of Wang Changyue (Wang Kunyang); see Qing Xitai (ed.), *Zhongguo daojiao shi*, vol. 4:100–104, 126–131. I am sure that through analysis of local gazetteers, etc. we will find other groups who, without having been integrated into the orthodox Longmen lineage, can nevertheless be affiliated with Longmen. This must be a part of future research necessary for deepening our understanding of the early history of Longmen and of Ming-Qing Daoism as a whole.

It is thus evident that a Longmen official lineage was created in order to establish Wang Changyue as the unique Vinaya Master who spread the orthodox Daoist discipline of Qiu Chuji throughout China, and that this was achieved by linking him to various Longmen local lineages that existed before him. Fortunately, one can still detect the signs of this superimposition in the works of Wu Shouyang 伍守陽 (1574–1644), an important Longmen Daoist of the end of the Ming dynasty.[86]

A Proof of the *A Posteriori* Creation of the Orthodox Longmen Lineage: the Case of Wu Shouyang [Line D, Nos. 5–8]

In the *Jingai xindeng*, Wu Chongxu 伍沖虛 (lineage name: *Shou*yang 守陽; style name: Duanyang 端陽, original name: Yang 陽) is presented as the eighth Longmen master and disciple of Wang Changyue.[87] According to the *Jingai xindeng*, Wu came from Ji'an 吉安 (Jiangxi). At the age of twenty he was offered official appointment but refused the official career and fled to Mt. Lu 廬山 (Jiangxi) where he honored as masters Cao Changhua 曹常化 (Daoist surname: Huanyang 還陽) and Li Niwan 李泥丸. Master Cao transmitted to him the secrets of the Great Elixir, and Li Niwan conveyed to him the "Testament of Shen Donglao" (*Donglao yishu* 東老遺書).[88] After 57 years, Wu had not yet accomplished the elixir and thus made another visit to Li Niwan at Mt. He 何山 (north-west slopes of Mt. Jingai 金蓋山 in Huzhou, Zhejiang). After having received from Li the method of the Five Thunders (*wulei fa* 五雷法), Wu could finally make the elixir. However, when he was on the verge of absorbing it, Li Niwan appeared and

---

[86] On this problem see the fundamental study by Mori Yuria, "Zenshinkyō ryūmonha."

[87] "Wu Chongxu lüshi zhuan" 伍沖虛律詩傳 (Biography of the Vinaya Master Wu who ascended to Heaven), JGXD 2. 1a-2a (ZWDS 31: 185–86).

[88] Shen Donglao 沈東老 of Wuxing (Huzhou, Zhejiang) was recorded as the producer of the excellent "white wine of the eighteen immortals" after having received a visit from the immortal Lü Dongbin (see Farzeen Baldrian-Hussein, "Lü Tung-pin in Northern Sung Literature," *Cahiers d'Extrême-Asie*, 2, 1986:147 and I. Ang, "Le culte de Lü Dongbin des origines," 25). In the JGXD (7.13b) it is said that Shen Donglao received from Mei Zichun 梅子春 the method of the White and Yellow (alchemy).

warned him that he was still not ready for such an experience and needed more spiritual training.

Meanwhile, Wu was appointed tutor of Prince Ji 吉王; but feeling that he was also not yet ready for that task he fled to the Tiantai mountains. According to the *Jingai xindeng*, Wu's full realization was only possible once he met Zhao Zhensong (Fuyang, fl. 1522) at Tiantai who introduced him to Wang Changyue on Mt. Wangwu. Wu then received the three stage precepts from Wang Changyue along with the lineage name *Shou*yang, whereupon he could finally absorb the elixir and transcend worldly matters. He was thus called "Master who ascended to Heaven" (Chongxu zi 沖虛子). He wrote the *Xianfo hezong* 仙佛合宗 (Merged Tradition of Buddhism and Daoism) and the *Tianxian zhengli* 天仙正理 (Correct Principles of Celestial Immortality) and died in Wuling 武陵 (Hangzhou) in 1644.

If we now compare this summarized *Jingai xindeng* biography with the biographical notes quoted in the works of Wu Shouyang, we remark many discrepancies. According to details provided by Wu Shouyang himself in his *Xianfo hezong yulu* 仙佛合宗語錄 (Recorded Sayings on the Merged Tradition of Buddhism and Daoism, DZJY biji 3.45a-59b) and comments by his cousin Wu Shouxu 伍守虛, he was born in 1574 from a family of officials. His father Wu Xide 伍希德 was appointed to various high posts and in 1578, when Wu was five years old, became prefect of Weimo 維摩 in Yunnan. Around the age of ten, Wu started receiving a classical education and reading the work of Wang Chongyang 王重陽 (1113–1170) until at age 13 he felt the first calling to his future Daoist vocation. In 1593, at the beginning of his twenties, he met his master Cao Changhua who transmitted to him teachings on the common heritage of Buddhism and Daoism as well as alchemical procedures. Wu drew a portrait of this period in his "Wu zhenren xiuxian ge" 伍真人修仙歌 (*Xianfo hezong yulu*, DZJY biji 3. 48b-56a). From 1593 until 1612 he underwent ascetic training at Xishan (Jiangxi) and finally realized the alchemical teachings of his master. Between 1612 and 1618, he was appointed tutor of Prince Ji in Changsha (Hunan). Prince Ji (Zhu Cikui 朱慈煃) became one of his main disciples (lineage name: Taihe 太和) and granted him the title of Guoshi 國師 (State Instructor).[89] Later, Wu returned to his native region and devoted himself to teaching and writing. In 1622 when his master Cao died, Wu finished his *Tianxian zhengli* and transmitted its secret teaching to Prince Ji.

---

[89] Mori Yuria, "Zenshinkyō ryūmonha," 191, 201, and 208 note 59.

Other important teachings were again transmitted to Prince Ji in 1629 and in 1632, when Wu gave him the entire transmission of the *Xianfo hezong*. In 1639 Wu added his preface to the commentary of the *Tianxian zhengli*, and in 1640 to his other work entitled *Wu zhenren dandao jiupian* 伍真人丹道九篇 (Nine Chapters on the Elixir Path by the Perfected Wu). In his later years, Wu abandoned all his activities in order to be by his mother's side. He waited for her to pass away (1641) before dying himself in 1644 at the age of 70.

We note that in his works, Wu Shouyang never mentions the name of Wang Changyue, although in his preface to the *Tianxian zhengli zhilun* 天仙正理直論 (Forthright Discourses on the Correct Principles of Celestial Immortality, 1639) he signed as "the disciple who received the second half of a seal (as a warrant of belonging to) the eighth generation of the Perfected Qiu's school" (*Qiu zhenren menxia diba pai fenfu lingjie dizi* 邱真人門下第八派分符領節弟子).[90] In the Preface by Shen Zhaoding 申兆定 entitled "Wu zhenren shishi ji shoushou yuanliu lüe" 伍真人事實及授受源流略 (A survey of the entire transmission and biographical facts of the Perfected Wu, 1764), one finds mention also of the line of transmission of Wu Shouyang's masters from the fifth generation until his own eighth generation (Fig. 1, p. 62, D5-D8):

(5) Fifth Longmen master Zhang *Jing*xu 張靜虛 (1432?-?)
(6) Sixth Longmen master Li *Zhen*yuan 李真元 (1525–1573?)
(7) Seventh Longmen master Cao *Chang*hua 曹常化 (1562–1622)
(8) Eighth Longmen master Wu *Shou*yang 伍守陽 (1574–1644)

In this text's preface, Shen claims that, according to the Longmen poem, Wu Shouyang belongs to the eighth generation under the character *Shou* 守.[91] We can then see that there is no mention of Wang Changyue as Wu's master. In the exegesis to the *Tianxian zhengli zhilun*, Wu Shouxu comments on the reference to "the eighth generation of the Perfected Qiu Changchun's school" (Qiu Changchun zhenren menxia diba pai 邱長春真人門下第八派) by saying that this lineage was based on the poem in twenty characters. This poem is the same that was allegedly transmitted by

---

[90] DZJY biji 4.11a. On the meaning of *fujie* 符節 see Wu Shouxu's explanations to Wu Shouyang's "Wu zhenren xiuxian ge" 伍真人修仙歌 (*Xianfo hezong yulu*, DZJY biji 3:53a-b; see Mori Yuria, "Zenshinkyō ryūmonha," 192–93 and Qing Xitai (ed.), *Zhongguo daojiao shi*, vol. 4: 40).

[91] *Tianxian zhengli* (DZJY biji 4. 3a-b).

Qiu Chuji to Zhao Daojian.[92] However, Wu Shouxu did not mention this hypothetical transmission but says that the poem was written by Qiu Chuji at Mount Longmen, east of Beijing, when Qiu supervised his teaching in order to establish his own school that was later called Longmen.[93]

What can thus be remarked is that Wu Shouyang mentions neither the name of Wang Changyue nor that of Longmen in his works; he only claimed that he was officially recognized as disciple of Qiu Chuji. The name Longmen was known only later, at the earliest when Wu Shouxu added his commentary to Wu Shouyang's work (1639?). Before that time, there probably were only some masters who claimed to be "disciples of Qiu Chuji." They already have a lineage name based on the poem that was credited to Qiu Chuji and transmitted generation by generation. The existence of this transmission based on the poem can be historically documented, in the case of Wu Shouyang's lineage, at least from the fifth Longmen master Zhang *Jing*xu 張靜虛 (1432? -?). A short biographical note of this master is included in Wu Shouyang's *Xianfo hezong yulu* 仙佛合宗語錄 (DZJY *biji* 1:85a-b) under the nickname Pihu zuo Zhang zhenren 皮虎坐張真人 (Perfected Zhang Sitting on the Tiger's Pelt), who withdrew to Mount Wudang.

In the commentary of the *Xianfo hezong yulu* (1630–33), Wu Shouxu adds that Zhang 張 (lineage name: *Jing*xu 靜虛) was born in 1432 at Pizhou (Jiangsu) and belongs to the Northern Lineage of Longmen (Beizong Longmen 北宗龍門); the character Jing in his name indicates that he belongs to Longmen's fifth generation. He obtained the Dao in the Biyang dong 碧陽洞 of Sichuan "by receiving from the master the tenet of immortality" (*shou shi xianzhi* 受師仙旨). In order to spread the teachings of his school (*jiaomen* 教門), he travelled throughout China and refused the summons of the Jiajing 嘉靖 emperor (re. 1522–1566).[94] Since he often used a tiger's pelt for sitting in meditation he was known as Zhang Pihu 張皮虎. He withdrew to Mount Wudang in the cave of the Tiger's Ear Cliff (*Hu'er ya shiqiao* 虎耳崖石竅), well away from the world, and transmitted his secret method

---

[92] See the biography of Zhao Daojian above.

[93] *Tianxian zhengli zhilun* (DZJY *biji* 4. 52a); see Mori Yuria "Zenshinkyō ryūmonha," 192.

[94] Liu Ts'un-yan (*New Excursions from the Hall of Harmonious Wind*, 186, Leiden: Brill, 1984) doubts the validity of Zhang's birth date because Zhang was said to have refused a summons from Emperor Shizong of the Jiajing reign (1522–1566); see J. Boltz, *A Survey of Taoist Literature*, 324 note 551.

(*wulong pengsheng* 五龍捧聖, the Five Dragons supporting the Saint) only to his disciple Li Xu'an 李虛庵 from Lujiang 廬江 (Anhui).[95]

Concerning Li Xu'an (lineage name: **Zhen**yuan 真元), Wu Shouxu added in the commentary that he was born in Lujiang in 1525. After having "benefited the world through the medicine" (*yi yi jishi* 以醫濟世), he built a hermitage and paid visits to the immortal master (Zhang Jingxu) from his nineteenth to fifty-fifth year. At that time, in 1579, after having obtained Zhang's complete transmission of the Great Dao of Celestial Immortality (*tianxian dadao* 天仙大道) as well as the inner and outer Golden Elixir (*neiwai jindan* 內外金丹), Li transcended worldliness and attained sanctity by being borne aloft by the Five Dragons (*pengsheng chao* 捧聖超).[96]

Li Xu'an in turn transmitted his teaching to Cao Huanyang 曹還陽 (lineage name: **Chang**hua 常化) who was born in Wuyang 武陽, south of Nanchang prefecture 南昌 (Jiangxi) in 1562. After having undergone ascetic training, "he obtained the method of the Five Dragons bearing aloft the Saint and transformed his Spirit in samādhi by giving birth to the [immortality] embryo" (*de wulong pengsheng zhuanshen ruding wei huaitai* 得五龍捧聖轉神入定為懷胎). In 1622, "during wall-meditation, his Yang Spirit left [his body] and reached Mount Xishan, east to Xinjian district (Jiangxi), before returning to Emptiness as the great retirement" (*chu yangshen ru Xinjian xian xi zhi Xishan, mianbi huanxu wei dayin* 出陽神入新建縣西之西山面壁還虛為大隱).[97] He had many disciples, the most famous of which is Wu Shouyang.

From these short biographical notes one can conclude that the legacy of Wu Shouyang started with Zhang Jingxu 張靜虛 [Line D No. 5] when Zhang received the transmission of immortality from an unknown master in Sichuan around the middle of the Ming dynasty. As we see, this may be in accord with the information that the third and the fourth Longmen Vinaya Masters of the Longmen orthodox lineage were active in Sichuan during the first part of the Ming dynasty. However, if we are to believe Wu Shouxu's commentary, Zhang Jingxu was responsible for spreading Longmen teachings throughout China yet reserved the secret transmission only to a single disciple. This may indicate that a more systematic tradition resembling a "school" (*jiaomen* 教門) could at that time (1400–1500) have begun to

---

[95] *Xianfo hezong yulu* (DZJY biji 1. 85a-b).

[96] *Ibid* (DZJY biji 1. 85b).

[97] *Ibid* (DZJY biji 1. 86a).

spread in different regions of China. However, the original status of an esoteric tradition of hermits living in caves, isolated from the world without any contact with social and political affairs, remains a characteristic of Zhang's life. The essence of the secret transmission that Zhang gave to a unique disciple is closely related to Mount Wudang through the method called "the Five Dragons bearing aloft the saint" (*wulong pengshen*). The name of this method reminds of the mythological event that marked at Mount Wudang the ascension to Heaven of the Dark Emperor (Xuandi) on the backs of five dragons.[98] It is also connected with the construction of one of the main temples of Wudang, the Wulong guan 五龍觀,[99] as well as with the Wulong pai 五龍派, a local school of Wudang represented during the Yuan dynasty by Cao Guanmiao 曹觀妙 (?-1236).[100]

According to de Bruyn, the Wulong school developed from the ancient cult of the five dragons which existed at Mount Wudang since the Tang dynasty but did not survive after 1275 when the Quanzhen school came to restore the Wulong guan.[101] The Quanzhen school at Mount Wudang was soon supplanted by the Qingwei school under the supervision of the Zhengyi. One can surmise that the secret method transmitted by Zhang Jingxu and related to the local tradition of Mount Wudang survived the interference of the great schools like the Quanzhen and Zhengyi-Qingwei among local hermits in an underground way, or that it may have been integrated and progressively combined with the teachings of these schools.

But what does the method of the Five Dragons of Zhang Jingxu consist of? According to the explanations of Wu Shouxu, this method refers to a specific inner alchemical practice. It represents the moment in the macrocosmic circulation (*da zhoutian* 大周天) for collecting the great medicine

---

[98] *Wudang fudi zong zhenji* (1291; DZ 609 fasc. 962, j. 3) by Liu Daoming; see Pierre-Henry de Bruyn, "Le Wudang shan: Histoire des récits fondateurs," Ph.D. diss., Université de Paris VII, 1997: 76. The ascension to Heaven astride five dragons is also mentioned in the biography of Chen Tuan, who also withdrew for a while to Mount Wudang; de Bruyn, "Le Wudang shan," 90.

[99] *Wudang fudi zong zhenji* (1291; DZ 609 fasc. 962, j. 3.10/7–9); see Mori Yuria, "Zenshinkyō ryūmonha," 194.

[100] On this school and its representative Cao Guanmiao see de Bruyn, "Le Wudang shan," 95–96, 98–99, 100.

[101] 1275 is the date when Wang Zhenchang 汪真常, a Quanzhen Daoist, came to Mount Wudang with his six disciples to rebuild the monastery of Wulong; see de Bruyn "Le Wudang shan," 98–99 and 111.

and having it rise to the crown of the head through the Three Passes.[102] The ascension to heaven of the Dark Emperor is thus compared with the ascension of the Great Medicine of True Yang to the sinciput.[103] According to Despeux, the mention of the Dark Emperor in explicit alchemical terms seems to stem from the thunder methods of the Qingwei school. This would indicate that the method of Five Dragons of Zhang Jingxu, which refers to Xuandi by way of inner alchemical metaphors, was probably elaborated inside the Qingwei school during the Ming dynasty.[104] It thus appears sensible that the Longmen transmission of Wu Shouyang was in some way related to the Qingwei since this school enjoyed at that time a prestigious position at Mount Wudang. One may also adduce the fact that to Liu Yuanran 劉淵然 (1351–1432), one of the main Qingwei masters active at the Baiyun guan, was granted the surname Changchun 長春 in honor of Qiu Chuji, as a supplementary hint of the Quanzhen integration inside the Zhengyi-Qingwei legacy.[105] The Longmen transmission of Zhang Jingxu may have had close links with the Qingwei school by claiming its own identity as an eremitic tradition affiliated with Qiu Chuji. Zhang's disciple, Li Xu'an (lineage name *Zhen*yuan) was also reputed for his successful rainmaking and therapeutic powers which were probably related to Qingwei thunder rituals. The mention in his biographical note that "at the beginning he benefited the world through the medicine" may allude to Li's original affiliation with thunder rituals which were codified during the Ming under Zhengyi-Qingwei supervision. According to the *Luzhou fuzhi* 盧州府志, Li Xu'an was in fact also surnamed Li Niwan 李泥丸, a name of one of Wu Shouyang's masters who, according to the biography of the *Jingai xindeng*, conveyed to him alchemical texts as well as the Five Thunder method. It is then clear that the Longmen lineage as recorded in the *Jingai xindeng* built another version of facts and grafted its own ideal patriarchs on earlier historical figures. In

---

[102] For some explanations on this practice see M. Esposito, "La Porte du Dragon," 60–84; Isabelle Robinet, *Introduction à l'alchimie intérieure taoïste*, 120–31, Paris: Le Cerf, 1995; and M. Esposito, *L'alchimia del soffio*.

[103] *Tianxian zhengli qianshuo* (DZJY biji 5:18a-b). According to Mori Yuria ("Zenshinkyō ryūmonha," 194), this method represents the micro-cosmic orbit, but I think that it refers to the macro-cosmic orbit since the text speaks of the Great and not of the Small Medicine.

[104] Catherine Despeux, *Taoïsme et corps humain*, 140–42, Paris: Guy Trédaniel, 1994 and de Bruyn, "Le Wudang shan," 62–63 and note 226.

[105] Ishida Kenji, "Mingdai Dōkyō shijō no Zenshin to Seii," 157; and notes 26 and 28 above.

the *Jingai xindeng*, Li Niwan is not at all linked with the historical master Li Xu'an but appears as a semi-divine figure endowed with alchemical and therapeutic powers. As we will see, these powers are at the source of earlier cults associated with his surname Niwan (Mud Ball). We will find further support for this process of integration of local traditions and figures (like that of Li Niwan) inside the Longmen orthodox lineage by examining its Ancestors.

Returning now to the masters of Wu Shouyang, we can see that with Li Xu'an (Zhenyuan) [Table 1, p. 62, D 6] and his disciple Cao Changhua [D 7], the hitherto secret and eremitic Longmen tradition begins opening to a wider public. This has been indicated by the statement that Cao transmitted his teaching to many disciples.

From the analysis of Wu Shouyang's lineage one may then deduce a certain evolution of the Longmen transmission which has also been indicated in the post-facto creation of the orthodox Longmen lineage. From an initial period characterized by strong isolation of Longmen masters during which the transmission took place only from a single master to a single disciple inside circles of hermits, one detects the traces that lead to a successive period of wider diffusion. This diffusion occurred probably around the end of the Ming dynasty and involved, in the case of Wu Shouyang's lineage, the spread from Mount Wudang (Hubei) to Xishan and its Jiangxi region—both famous places under the control of the Zhengyi.

With regard to Wu Shouyang's legacy, one can thus conclude by saying that although the native sanctuary of Longmen was ideally located in the North and associated with Mount Longmen of Qiu Chuji, the center of its teachings was established during the waning years of the Ming dynasty between Mount Wudang and Xishan. In the Jiangxi region, the Longmen doctrine found its systematization thanks to Wu Shouyang's works. Additional study on the Longmen doctrine of Wu Shouyang will be of utmost importance for defining the role that the Quanzhen and Zhengyi-Qingwei schools played in the elaboration of this doctrine, as well as for understanding the influence that the local tradition of Mount Wudang exercised on it. This doctrine reflects the variety of Longmen local traditions that arose beyond the standardized transmission of Longmen precepts on which the Longmen identity was officially based. In fact, another Longmen identity shines through the orthodox version: an identity whose traces appear in the adoption of its Daoist ancestors.

The Ancestors

The Specificity of the Longmen Lineage: The Figure of Donghua Dijun

If we compare now one of the lists of the Quanzhen Five Ancestors (*wuzu* 五祖) with that of the first five Longmen Daoist Ancestors (*daozu* 道祖), we discover another fundamental discrepancy. At first sight the names of the first five Longmen Ancestors are more or less congruent with those of the Quanzhen. The latest Quanzhen list presented in the *Jinlian zhengzong xianyuan xiangzhuan* 金蓮正宗仙源像傳 (Illustrated Biographies of the Immortal Origins of the Orthodox Lineage of the Golden Lotus, 1327, DZ 174 fasc. 76) gives for example:

(1) Hunyuan Laozi 混元老子;
(2) Donghua dijun 東華帝君;
(3) Zhengyang zi 正陽子 (Zhongli Quan 鍾離權);
(4) Chunyang zi 純陽子 (Lü Dongbin 呂洞濱);
(5) Haichan zi 海蟾子 (Liu Haichan 劉海蟾).[106]

In the Longmen list of the *Daopu yuanliu tu* 道譜源流圖 (JGXD 1a, in ZWDS 31:162) we find:

(1) Xuanxuan Huangdi 玄玄皇帝 (Laozi 老子);
(2) Jinque dijun 金闕帝君 (Yin Xi 尹喜);
(3) Donghua dijun 東華帝君;
(4) Zhengyang dijun 正陽帝君 (Zhongli Quan 鍾離權);
(5) Chunyang dijun 純陽帝君 (Lü Dongbin 呂洞濱).

The only changes appear to consist in the addition of Jinque dijun (Yin Xi) and the omission of Liu Haichan.

However, in the most "authoritative" Quanzhen list based on the *Jinlian zhengzong ji* 金蓮正宗記 (Account of the Orthodox Lineage of the Golden Lotus, 1241 [DZ 173, fasc. 75–76]) Laozi is omitted and the five ancestors are given as:

(1) Donghua dijun; (2) Zhongli Quan; (3) Lü Dongbin; (4) Liu Haichan; (5) Wang Chongyang.[107]

---

[106] J. Boltz, *A Survey of Taoist Literature*, 64.

[107] Yao Tao-chung, "Quanzhen Complete Perfection," 579.

Although the list of the five Quanzhen ancestors presents some variants, the "orthodox line" of Quanzhen ancestors in the Quanzhen hagiographies features Donghua dijun as Wang Xuanfu 王玄甫.[108] By contrast, when one reads the gloss of the *Daopu yuanliu tu* 道譜源流圖 (JGXD 1a, in ZWDS 31:162) concerning Donghua dijun 東華帝君 in the Longmen list, one discovers that his name is Li Ya 李亞 and no more Wang Xuanfu. Furthermore, in the Longmen list (JGXD 2a, in ZWDS 31:163), Wang Xuanfu has not disappeared but has simply found a less prominent place under the name Xihua dijun 西華帝君. He has become the Sovereign Lord of the Western Florescence and master of Zhang Guolao 張果老, one of the Eight Immortals. It is certain that the Longmen wanted to reserve Donghua dijun's place for another figure. Why? What is the role of Donghua dijun inside Daoism?

Donghua dijun was originally one of the great Shangqing deities better known as Qingtong jun 青童君 (Lord Azure Lad) to whom the Quanzhen order gave a new role.[109] The preface (1241) of the *Jinlian zhengzong ji* states

---

[108] *Jinlian zhenzong ji* (DZ 173, fasc. 75–76, j. 1.1a-2b) while the *Jinlian zhengzong xianyuan xiangzhuan* (DZ 174 fasc. 76, 13a-14a) gives only the family name Wang. For the latest Quanzhen sources, see for example the *Baiyun xianbiao* 白雲仙籙 (1848, ZWDS 31:375). On the figure of Wang Xuanfu as Donghua dijun see Florian Reiter, "Der Name Tung-hua ti-chün und sein Umfeld in der taoistischen Tradition," in *Religion und Philosophie in Ostasien. Festschrift für Hans Steininger*, edited by Gert Naundorf et al., 95–99, Würzburg: Königshausen & Neumann, 1985 (thanks to Vincent Goossaert for the reference); and Pierre Marsone, "Wang Chongyang (1113–1170) et la fondation du Quanzhen," 461–63, Ph. D. diss., Paris: École Pratique des Hautes Études, section des Sciences Religieuses, 2001.

[109] Florian Reiter, "Der Name Tung-hua ti-chün, " 87–101. The image of Qingtong jun has roots in the ancient legend of the Royal Sire of the East (Dongwang gong 東王公), a solar deity who is also a male counterpart of the goddess Xiwangmu 西王母. As recorded in the fifth century by Tao Hongjing (456-536), his full title is Jiuwei taizhen yubao wang, Jinjue shangxiang, Da siming, Gaochen shi, Donghai wang, Qinghua xiaotong jun 九微太真玉保王金闕上相大司命高晨師東海王青華小童君 (Lord Little Lad of Azure Florescence, King of the Eastern Sea, Master of the Lofty Down, Great Supervisor of Destinies, Supreme Minister of the Golden Tower, Jade Conservator King of the Greatest Realization of Ninefold Tenuity; see W. Paul Kroll, "In the Halls of the Azure Lad," *Journal of the American Oriental Society* 105/ 1, 1985: 75–94; and Kamitsuka Yoshiko 神塚淑子, "Hōshō Seidō kun o megutte 方諸青童君をめぐって," *Tōhō shūkyō* 東方宗教 76, 1990: 1–23). He played an important role in the Shangqing texts as a mediator figure, notably involved in the revelation of the *Purple Texts* (see Isabelle Robinet, *La révélation du Shangqing dans l'histoire du taoïsme*, 2: 109–120, Paris: E.F.E.O, 1984 and R. Stephen Bokenkamp, *Early Daoist Scriptures*, 281–372, Berkeley: University of Cali-

in fact that the heritage of Quanzhen originated with Donghua dijun.[110] This claim seems to survive in the latest Longmen order which also traces its origins to him. In his work on "Taoist Monastic Life" (based on observations from 1940 to 1946 at the Baiyun guan in Beijing) Yoshioka Yoshitoyo records:

> The tao-shi's robes are usually blue (*ch'ing-lan* 青籃). In Five Elements thought, *ch'ing* signifies the "vital spirit of the blue (or green) dragon." It is the color of the East and of the element wood. The use of this color is explained as indicating descent from Lord Tung-hua 東華帝君, the founder of the Daoist religion.[111]

This means that the figure of Donghua dijun continued to enjoy great importance in the institutionalized Longmen order at the Baiyun guan, as he was regarded as the founder of the Daoist religion from whom the blue color of the Daoist clergy's robes stems. As father of the Daoist clergy, Donghua dijun became for the Longmen the central figure for a new organization of the monastic code which allegedly took place at the beginning of the Qing dynasty under the purported guidance of Wang Changyue. But why did the Longmen (which claims its heritage from the Northern Quanzhen lineage through its most influential disciple Qiu Chuji) substitute the Quanzhen figure of Donghua dijun (Wang Xuanfu) by Li Ya?

---

fornia Press, 1997). Lord Azure Lad was associated with the paradise domain of the Eastern Florescence (Donghua 東華) or Azure Florescence (Qinghua 青華) and, as Great Supervisor of destinies, with the Huayang celestial grotto (Huayang dongtian 華陽洞天) of the Terrestrial Immortals (Kamitsuka Yoshiko, "Hōshō Seido kun o megutte," 13–15). As we will see, these original associations given to Qingtong jun will be later found in the figure of Donghua dijun as the patriarch of the Quanzhen and Longmen. With regard to the new role of Donghua dijun in the Quanzhen see F. Reiter, "Der Name Tung-hua ti-chün," 95–99; Hachiya Kunio 蜂屋邦夫, *Kingen jidai no dōkyō—shichi shin kenkyū* 金元時代の道教—七眞研究, 247–250, 319–24 and 450, Tokyo: Tōkyō daigaku Tōyō bunka kenkyūjo hōkoku, Kyūko shoin, 1998; and Pierre Marsone, "Wang Chongyang (1113–1170) et la fondation du Quanzhen," 279–280 and 461–63. {ME note: For Donghua dijun and associated figures see in addition my more recent study: Monica Esposito, "Sun-worship in China–The Roots of Shangqing Taoist Practices of Light," *Cahiers d'Extrême-Asie* 14, 2004: 345–402.}

[110] J. Boltz, *A Survey of Taoist Literature* 278, note 164.

[111] I refer here to the translation of Yoshioka Yoshitoyo, "Taoist Monastic Life," 237; see also Yoshioka Yoshitoyo, *Eisei e no negai*, 207.

Donghua Dijun as Xiaotong Jun or Li Babai

If we analyze the figure of Donghua dijun as presented in the *Jingai xindeng* we may find some answers to this question. The gloss of the *Daopu yuanliu tu* 道譜源流圖 (JGXD 1a, in ZWDS 31:162) says:

> Donghua dijun, family name Li, name Ya, style name (*zi*): Yuanyang; surname (*hao*) Xiaotong jun. He was a man of the Spring and Autumn period. He received official titles by the Yuan court as Quanzhen daojiao zhu Donghua zifu Fuyuan liji Shaoyang dijun (Sovereign Lord of the Young Yang, Assistant of the Origin for establishing the Poles, Eastern Efflorescence of the Purple Court, Founder of Quanzhen Daoism). In the ritual registers he is called Tieshi Yuanyang shangdi (Supreme Sovereign of the Original Yang Master Iron), and by the people Tieguai Li zushi (Patriarch Li Iron Crutch).
>
> 姓李名亞字元陽號小童君。春秋時人。元朝敕封全真大教主東華紫府輔元立極少陽帝君。法錄稱鐵師元陽上帝。世稱鐵拐李祖師。

While the official titles, which were reportedly conveyed by the Yuan court, correspond for the most part to those quoted in Quanzhen hagiographies in honor of Donghua dijun Wang Xuanfu,[112] Donghua dijun's surname Xiaotong jun 小童君 harks back directly to the Shangqing deity Qinghua Xiaotong jun 青華小童君 (Lord Little Lad of Azure Florescence), who is also known simply as Qingtong 青童 (Azure Lad).[113] Now the same appellation Xiaotong jun is also found in the "Li Niwan zhenren zhuan 李泥丸真人專" (Biography of the Perfected Li Niwan, [JGXD 8.48a-49b in ZWDS 31:362-63]), a divine immortal (*shenxian*) who played a preeminent role in the transmission of Longmen's alchemical methods.[114] In fact,

---

[112] The *Jinlian zhengzong xianyuan xiangzhuan* (DZ 174 fasc. 76, 13b) mentions for example Donghua Zifu Shaoyang dijun 東華紫府少陽帝君 as the title conferred by Emperor Shizu (r. 1281-1293) of the Yuan dynasty, while Emperor Wuzong (r. 1307-1319) is said to have honored him with the additional title Donghua Zifu Fuyuan liji Dadi jun 東華紫府輔元立極大帝君. On the different titles, and in particular on the figure of Wang Xuanfu, see F. Reiter, "Der Name Tung-hua ti-chün," 95-97.

[113] See note 109 above.

[114] M. Esposito, "La Porte du Dragon," 144-154, 246-79 and 348-374; and M. Esposito, "Longmen Taoism in Qing China" {here below, Chapter 3}. For a discussion of the category of *shenxian* in relation with Donghua dijun see F. Reiter, "Der Name

this biography records two transformations of Li Niwan under the names of Li Babai 李八百 and Xiaotong jun. To the latter, a gloss adds that Xiaotong jun was also known under the title Shaoyang dijun 少陽帝君 or Donghua qingtong 東華青童.[115] As the Xiaotong jun who is mentioned here is thus doubtless Donghua dijun (the ancient Qingtong jun), he shares in the *Jingai xindeng* also some links with the figure of Li Niwan and his transformation under the guise of Li Babai.

Let us then have a brief look at the two transformations of Li Niwan. According to the first story, Li Babai appeared in 1069 in Suzhou. After having resuscitated the mother of a certain Wu 吳 by using mud and hot water, he became known as Immortal Mud Ball (Niwan xian 泥丸仙). In the second story, a beggar of Songjiang 松江 (Zhejiang) in 1615 offered incense to a picture of Xiaotong jun and prayed for his mother's health and family fortune. One day, Xiaotong jun appeared to the beggar under the guise of a Daoist expert in alchemical arts. After having displayed his wonderful alchemical abilities, he gave the beggar a basin full of gold and revealed to him his new identity as Li Niwan.[116]

From these two stories one can gather the dual identity of the divine immortal Li Niwan and the close relationship between the figure of Xiaotong jun—Li Niwan / Babai—Li Niwan. Furthermore, in these two stories Li Niwan is said to be native of Sichuan. He exhibits great talents as healer and alchemist to reward people who are animated by profound filial piety. His magical powers clearly hail from his association with Li Babai, the expert alchemist of the Han dynasty who, according to the *Taiping guangji* 太平廣記 (7.49–50), transmitted the secret formula for saving the world (*dushi zhi jue* 度世之訣) to Tang Gongfang 唐公昉.[117] This also reminds of Li

---

Tung-hua ti-chün," 87–90.

[115] JGXD 8.48a/2–3 (ZWDS 31: 362). While the title Shaoyang is shared with the Quanzhen Donghua dijun, the title Donghua Qingtong harks back to the original Shangqing deity; see note 109 above.

[116] For a brief account of these two transformations see M. Esposito, "La Porte du Dragon," 147 and 149–151.

[117] The same story is also found in the *Shenxian zhuan* 神仙傳 (tr. Gertrud Güntsch, *Das Shen-hsien chuan und das Erscheinungsbild eines Hsien*, Frankfurt: Verlag Peter Lang, 1988) and is also briefly mentioned in the biography of Tang Gongfang (*Lishi zhenxian tidao tongjian* 歷世真仙體道通鑑, DZ 296, fasc. 138–48, 11.3b–4a). On the figure of Li Baibai see the study of Yamada Toshiaki 山田利明, "Shinsen Ri Happyaku den kō 神仙李八百伝考," in Yoshioka Yoshitoyo hakase kanreki kinen kenkyū ronshū kankōkai 吉岡義豊博士還暦記念研究論集刊行会 (ed.), *Yoshioka*

Xu'an 李盧庵 (Zhenyuan 真元, Fig. 1, p. 62, Line D, No. 6), one of Wu Shouyang's masters who was also called Li Niwan, probably because he was known, in Li Babai's wake, for his therapeutic powers (as one who "benefited the world through medicine" *yi yi jishi* 以醫濟世).

It is known that the name Li Babai was very popular in Sichuan during the third century and also appears in an early list of the "Eight Immortals of Sichuan" which was quoted by Qiao Xiu 譙秀 in the *Jinshu* 晉書.[118] According to Qiao Xiu, Li Babai was a hermit who lived in the Longmen grotto 龍門洞 in the Xindu 新都 district of Chengdu.

In the present context, it is of interest to point out that Donghua dijun, the purported Ancestor from whom "the heritage of Quanzhen originated," exhibits in the *Jingai xindeng* the signs of another transformation which now takes place in the context of the Longmen lineage. As one of the main Longmen ancestors he is no more associated with Shandong (or with places linked to the Seven Perfected), as was the case with the Quanzhen Ancestor Donghua dijun (Wang Xuanfu). Rather, in the Longmen lineage he now shows a clear connection with Sichuan. This may indicate that the name of Longmen has not only ties—as the tradition claims—to the place where Qiu Chuji underwent his ascetic training or to the eremitic tradition of Huashan, but also to the Longmen grotto of the Xindu district where Li Babai, one of the various transformations of Donghua dijun, withdrew. This link can only be understood if one goes back to the origin of the divinity Donghua dijun who, in the guise of the Azure Lad (Qinghua xiaotong jun), played a prominent role in the revealed scriptures of the Shangqing school.[119] Before arriving at some conclusions, we will now have a look at-

Yoshitoyo hakase kanreki kinen dōkyō kenkyū ronshū 吉岡義豊博士還暦記念道教研究論集, 145–163, Tokyo: Kokusho Kankōkai, 1977.

[118] The list of the Eight Immortals features: Rongcheng gong 容成公, Li Er 李耳, Dong Zhongshu 董仲舒, Zhang Daoling 張道陵, Zhuang Junping 莊君平, Li Babai 李八百, Fan Changsheng 范長生 and Er Zhu xiansheng 爾朱先生; see Perceval W. Yetts, "More Notes on the Eight Immortals," *Journal of the Royal Asiatic Society*, 1992: 403 and Pu Jiangqing, "Baxian kao" 八仙考, *Qinghua xuebao*, 1, 1931: 92. However, Pu Jiangqing doubts the authenticity of this source and presents variants of this list (92–94); see also Evelyne Mesnil, "Zhang Suqing et la peinture taoïste à Shu," *Cahiers d'Extrême-Asie*, 9, 1996–97: 145–147 and note 37.

[119] For his association with other Daoist schools and movements see W. Paul Kroll, "In the Halls of the Azure Lad," and Kamitsuka Yoshiko, "Hōsho Seidō kun o megutte." Kamitsuka (8–13) in particular points out that the figure of Xiaotong developed from ancient cults (also incorporated by the nascent Celestial Master legacy) which were probably connected with the coastal regions of China and more particularly

Donghua dijun's other names as mentioned in the *Daopu yuanliu tu* 道譜源流圖.

The Integration of Different Traditions in the Longmen Lineage: Donghua Dijun as Li Tieguai and Li Ya

If some different associations of the figure of Donghua dijun are partially explained by the biography of Li Niwan, we do not find any mention of Donghua dijun's connection with Li Tieguai 李鐵拐 and Li Ya 李亞. As is well known, Li Tieguai is one of the Eight Immortals, represented by a lame beggar leaning on his iron crutch. He is said to be a disciple of Xiwangmu 西王母, the Queen Mother of the West, from whom he obtained immortality after having been cured of an ulcer in his leg. He had a hard childhood. In his youth he lost his parents and was ill-treated by a shrewish sister-in-law. Taking refuge in the hills, his soul left his body to visit Huashan.[120] This is the introduction to the famous story of soul-wandering which characterizes the figure of the immortal Li Tieguai. This story is inspired by that of an ascetic named Li Ningyang 李凝陽. This ascetic, who was instructed by Laozi himself, was recognized as an expert of ecstatic flights. One day, before his soul left his body to meet Laozi at Huashan, he told his disciple to keep his body for one week and to burn it at the end of the seventh day if he did not return. The disciple, knowing that his mother was on the verge of dying and aware of his great filial wish to be at his mother's side, burned the body of his master Li ahead of time. On his return Li, who was deprived of his original bodily shell, was obliged to take over the only body available, that of a crippled beggar. His emblems are thus his famous iron crutch, a gold fillet for his hair that Laozi gave him as a consolation, and a pilgrim's gourd.

---

with the Jiangnan region. This may furnish a proof for the association of Longmen's Donghua dijun not only with Sichuan but also with the Jiangnan region where activities of the multiple manifestations of Li Babai took place.

[120] V. Rodolphe Burkhardt, *Chinese Creeds and Customs*, 158, Hong Kong: South China Morning Post, 1919; Perceval W. Yetts, "The Eight Immortals," *Journal of the Royal Asiatic Society*, 1916: 773–807; Yetts, "More Notes on the Eight Immortals;" Richard F.S. Yang, "A Study in the Origin of the Eight Immortals," *Oriens Extremus* 5, 1958: 1–22; T.C. Lai, *The Eight Immortals*, Hong Kong: Swindon Book Co, 1974.

Li thus became the patron of pharmacists and of exorcists who use their art for curative purposes.[121]

From this brief account of Li Tieguai's "life," we gather that different themes and figures have converged in this immortal: (a) the association with Xiwangmu and her ancient exorcist and healing powers;[122] (b) the extraordinary power of soul-flights coming from his association with the ascetic Li Ningyang;[123] (c) the recurrent theme of filial piety which we have already remarked in the stories of Li Niwan; and (d) Li Tieguai's association with beggars, pharmacists, and exorcists that shows some connection with the previous figure of Li Niwan / Li Babai.

Furthermore, it is important to note that the figure of Li Tieguai / Li Ningyang also has different origins. According to the *Lidai shenxian tongjian* 歷代神仙通鑑 (1.4a) by Xu Dao 徐道 of the Ming dynasty, the expert of soul-flights Li Ningyang was recognized by the Master of Rain Chisong zi 赤松子 as the incarnation of a mythical emperor of antiquity called Jushen shi 駏神氏 who was capable of "walking with the rapidity of the thunderclap." After having received Laozi's teachings, Li Ningyang became Li Tieguai.[124] This may explain why, as recorded in the *Daopu yuanliu tu* 道譜源流圖, he is said to have lived, like his master Laozi, during the Spring and Autumn Period. Moreover, the name of Li Ningyang was also associated with a grotto in the Zhongnan mountains where, according to the *Jinlian zhengzong xianyuan xiangzhuan* (DZ 174, fasc. 76; 13b/3–4),

---

[121] *Lidai shenxian tongjian* (j. 5), *Liexian quanzhuan* 列仙全傳 (j. 1), *Qianque leishu* 潛確類書, and *Baxian chuchu dongyouji* 八仙出處東遊記; see Ma Shutian 馬書田, *Huaxia zhushen* 華夏諸神, 160–63, Beijing: Yanshan, 1991.

[122] The association with Xiwangmu was primarily a characteristic of Qingtong jun, the original Shangqing deity; see for example F. Reiter, "Der Name Tung-hua ti-chün," 91.

[123] Furthermore, one can also remark that the name Li Ningyang 李凝陽 shows some homophony with the name Li Niwan whose curative abilities were certainly drawn from his links with the famous Han alchemist Li Babai, as well as with Li Lingyang 李靈陽, one of Wang Chongyang's companions (see Hachiya Kunio, *Kingen jidai no dōkyō*, 8–9). It is interesting to note that even in Ren Jiyu 任繼愈 (ed.), *Zhongguo daojiao shi* 中國道教史, Shanghai: Shanghai renmin, 1990, 520 and in Qing Xitai (ed.), *Zhongguo daojiao shi*, vol. 3: 33, the name Li Lingyang has been written as Li Ningyang. This confusion may have some relationship with the name of the grotto located in the Zhongnan mountains; see below.

[124] *Lidai shenxian tongjian* (5. 1b, 2a-3b), Ma Shutian, *Huaxia. zhushen*, 160 and Zong Li 宗力 & Liu Qun 劉群, *Zhongguo minjian zhushen* 中國民間諸神, 783, Shijiazhuang: Hebei renmin, 1987.

Donghua dijun *Wang* appeared before conferring his transmission to the immortal Zhongli Quan. It is thus clear that the figure of Li Ningyang was in some way mixed up with that of Donghua dijun (Wang Xuanfu) of the Quanzhen order, the recipient of Laozi's teachings and master of Zhongli Quan.[125] However, this same Li Ningyang was also, during the Ming, associated with Li Tieguai.[126]

With regard to the figure of Li Ya 李亞, one finds his name as master of Zhongli Quan in the list of the Southern Lineage (Nanzong 南宗). In the "Ti Zhang Ziyang Xue Zixian zhenren xiang" 題張紫陽薛紫賢真人像, Bai Yuchan 白玉蟾 (1194–ca. 1227) reports that "Li Ya transmitted the formulae of the firing process (*huofu* 火符), alchemical measuring (*daogui* 刀圭), and Mercury and Metal (*jin'gong* 金汞) to Zhongli Quan"[127] and draws the following line of transmission: Li Ya → Zhongli Quan 鍾離權 → Lü Yan (Lü Dongbin) → Liu Haichan 劉海蟾 → Zhang Boduan 張佰端 (ca. 983-ca. 1082) → Shi Tai 石泰 (d. 1158) → Chen Nan 陳楠 (d. 1175/91) → Bai Yuchan. Conversely, Bai Yuchan's second-generation disciple Xiao Tingzhi 蕭廷芝 in the "Dadao zhengtong" 大道正統 (1260) starts his list with Fuli Yuanshi tianzun 浮黎元始天尊, and after a long succession arrives at Huayang zhenren Li Ya 華陽真人李亞, who is presented as master of Zhongli Quan and disciple of Lutai zhenren Zhao Sheng 鹿

---

[125] I refer here to his biography in the *Jinlian zhengzong xianyuan xiangzhuan* (DZ 174 fasc. 76, 13b) where it is stated that he obtained the Dao of the Most High (*Taishang zhi dao* 太上之道) before withdrawing to Mount Kunyu 崑嵛 (Shandong). In the *Jinlian zhengzong ji* (1. 1a-2b) it is explained that the transmission from the Most High that he received consisted in a set of scriptures obtained from Baiyun shangzhen 白雲上真. Baiyun shangzhen in turn had received it from Jinmu 金母 (Xiwangmu), and Jinmu from Taishang (Laozi); see also F. Reiter, "Der Name Tung-hua ti-chün," 95–96; and P. Marsone, "Wang Chongyang (1113–1170) et la fondation du Quanzhen," 461–63.

[126] During the Song, the figure of Li Tieguai was probably inspired by that of a certain "Limping Liu" (Liu Bozi 劉跛子) or even by a crippled immortal (*boxian* 跛仙) who obtained Lü Dongbin's teaching at Mount Jun. In a theatrical piece of the Yuan dynasty ("Lü Dongbin du Tieguai Li Yue" 呂洞賓度鐵拐李岳 by Yue Baichuan 岳百川), Li Tieguai was presented as one of the disciples of Lü Dongbin; see Ma Shutian, *Huaxia zhushen*, 161.

[127] *Qiongguan Bai zhenren ji* 瓊琯白真人集 (4.12a in DZJY *louji* 婁集 4, vol. 14: 6287); cf. Yokote Yutaka 橫手裕, "Zenshinkyō to nanshū hokushū 全眞教と南宗北宗," in Tetsurō Noguro 鉄郎野口 et al., *Dōkyō no seimeikan to shintai ron* 道教の生命觀と身体論, 193, Tokyo: Yūyama kaku, 2000.

臺真人趙昇.¹²⁸ As is known, Zhao Sheng was one of Zhang Daoling's disciples. He was also said to have initiated the Shenxiao master Lin Lingsu 林靈素 (1076–1120) in the Five Thunder rites and informed him about the worldly manifestation of Donghua dijun in the figure of emperor Huizong (r. 1102–1125).¹²⁹

This means that Li Ya is a figure connected with the Southern liturgical movements of the Song era and necessarily with the Celestial Masters' legacy.¹³⁰ In fact, the name Li Ya is featured in the list of the patriarchs of the Thunder ritual of the Shenxiao 神霄 legacy (as Qinghua dijun Li Ya 青華帝君李亞), where it is followed by the names of Wang Shouzhen 王守真 (714–789), Wang Wenqing 王文卿 (1093–1153), and Bai Yuchan 白玉蟾 (1194–1227?).¹³¹ As it is not my purpose here to examine the origin of Li Ya and his link with the above-mentioned Shenxiao Thunder ritual legacy, I will limit myself to pointing out that Li Ya's integration in the Longmen lineage must be the fruit of a long process of incorporation of older schools

---

¹²⁸ *Daode zhenjing sanjie* (DZ 687, fasc. 370–71, 6a-b). Huayang zhenren, one of the titles for Donghua dijun, is also mentioned in the *Lishi zhenxian tongjian* (DZ 296, fasc. 138–48, 2.15b) as master of Zhongli Quan but under the name of Wang Xuanfu.

¹²⁹ *Lishi zhenxian tidao zhenjian* (DZ 296, fasc. 138–48.53.2b); see F. Reiter, "Der Name Tung-hua ti-chün," 94–95; and Qing Xitai (ed.), *Zhongguo daojiao shi*, vol. 2: 601. For the identification of Qinghua dijun as Lin Lingsu see L. Skar, "Ritual movements, deity cults," 436. On the contrary, Reiter ("Der Name Tung-hua ti-chün," 94–95 and note 45) identifies Qinghua dijun as the wordly manifestation of the emperor Huizong himself. On Lin Lingsu's 林靈素 relationship with the emperor Huizong, see M. Strickmann, "The Longest Taoist Scripture," *History of Religions* 17, 3–4, 1978, 331–354; Qing Xitai (ed.), *Zhongguo daojiao shi*, vol. 2: 599–601; and E. Davis, *Society and the Supernatural in Song China*, 2001, 27 and 34–38. As is known, Huizong had a strong inclination for the *fangshi* 方士 (Masters of Recipes). Among them, a very famous one was Wei Hanjin 魏漢津 who is said to have been the disciple of Li Liang 李良, a Tang immortal known also as Li Babai (Qing Xitai [ed.], *Zhongguo daojiao shi*, vol. 2: 593).

¹³⁰ Longhu shan 龍虎山 (the headquarters of the Celestial Masters in Jiangxi) "became the authoritative center of many of the new cults and movements, at first unofficially and then through official decrees (by early Yuan and Ming emperors)." L. Skar, "Ritual movements, deity cults," 415–16.

¹³¹ *Xiantian leijin yinshu* 先天雷晶隱書 (8. 1a in *Daofa huiyuan*, DZ 1220, fasc. 884–945), a thunder method in honor of Shenxiao Yuqing zhenwang Changsheng dadi 神霄玉清真王長生大帝 and Ziguang tianhou Molizhi 紫光天后摩利支 (Doumu 斗母). L. Skar ("Ritual movements, deity cults," 436) points out that Qinghua dijun 青華帝君 would be Lin Lingsu 林靈素 himself who got the task of divulging the divine mandate for a theocratic age and of transmitting the main Shenxiao scripture.

and movements.¹³² In this process, the Southern legacy and its therapeutic thunder rites certainly played a prominent role and left their mark in the Longmen lineage in the choice of the name Li Ya for the Longmen Founding Ancestor Donghua dijun. This long process of incorporation of earlier traditions into the Longmen lineage may be observed in its adoption and transformation of different ancestral lists which, from the middle of the Yuan dynasty on, have been erected in order to establish a common source for the Southern and Northern Lineages. It is then important to remark that the list presented by Ke Daochong 柯道沖, the disciple of the renowned Daoist priest Li Daochun 李道純 (fl. 1288–90), presents an extraordinary similarity with the above list of the Longmen ancestors:

Taishang Hunyuan Laozu 太上混元老祖 → Guanling Yin Xi 關令尹子 → Jinque dijun 金闕帝君 → Donghua dijun → Zhongli Quan → Lü Dongbin → Liu Haichan.¹³³

Apart from Liu Haichan, who in Ke Daochong's list is regarded as the common source for the transmission of the Southern and Northern lineages, the names of the first ancestors coincide with those of the *Jingai xindeng*'s list of Longmen ancestors. The only difference is that, in the *Jingai xindeng*, Jinque dijun seems to have absorbed the name of the preceding ancestor Yin Xi, while Donghua dijun carries the name of Li Ya. Conversely, in Ke Daochong's list, Jinque dijun and Donghua dijun do not have any worldly names. Furthermore, the similarity between Ke Daochong's list and that of the *Jingai xindeng* may show how the creation of the Longmen lineage can be seen as the prolonged effort to unify Southern and Northern traditions in a central movement or Central Branch (the original aspiration of Li

---

¹³² For a study on the Thunder rites see Lowell Skar, "Administering Thunder: A Thirteenth-century Memorial deliberating the Thunder Rites," *Cahiers d'Extrême-Asie* 9, 1996–97: 159–202.

¹³³ Ke Daochong's preface to the *Xuanjiao da gong'an* 玄教大公案 (1324, DZ 1065, fasc. 734, 1a-b), by presenting Lü Dongbin as the common source for the transmission of the Southern and Northern Lineages, draws the line of Huayang 華陽 — [Wang] Xuanfu 玄甫 —Zhongli Quan—Lü Dongbin. Conversely, in the preface (1325) of the *Shangyang zi jindan dayao* 上陽子金丹大要 (DZ 1068, fasc. 736–38, 1.1a-b), Chen Zhixu 陳致虛 (1298–after 1335) presents Lü Dongbin as the common source for the transmission of the Southern and Northern Lineages and thus draws the line Huayang 華陽 — [Wang] Xuanfu 玄甫 —Zhongli Quan—Lü Dongbin. See also J. Boltz, *A Survey of Taoist Literature*, 179–186; Qing Xitai (ed.), *Zhongguo daojiao shi*, vol. 3: 374–82; Yokote Yutaka, "Zenshinkyō to nanshū hokushū"; and F. Pregadio & L. Skar, "Inner alchemy (*Neidan*)," 471–72 and 479–81.

Daochun's movement inherited now by the Longmen) which would transcend any apparent contradictions.[134] However, in the "central unification" of the Longmen, this new school did not forget to heap renewed honors and veneration on its own patriarchs and ancestors. Just as the Quanzhen school had previously done with the figure of Donghua dijun *Wang*, the Longmen tried to legitimize itself as a new orthodox legacy by incorporating and transforming again the figure of Donghua dijun into a deity that, in the end, was rather different from what was earlier established by the Quanzhen patriarchy. Instead of accepting the Quanzhen Northern tradition of Donghua dijun (Wang Xuanfu),[135] the Longmen preferred to recuperate the Shangqing origins of Donghua dijun and its original links with southern cults. Prior to further canonization in the Longmen lineage thanks to the *Jingai xindeng*, this southern heritage of Donghua dijun had already taken on specific contours in the therapeutic thunder rituals of the Song and Yuan dynasties under the name of *Li* or *Li Ya*.[136]

In the Longmen context as provided by the *Jingai xindeng*, an association of Li Ya with the above-mentioned Li Tieguai–Li Ningyang is possible because of Li Ningyang's link with the ancient mythical emperor able to "walk with the rapidity of the thunderclap." Furthermore, the name Li Ya resembles that of the famous diviner and beggar Li A 李阿, whose biography in the *Taiping guangji* (j. 7) follows just after the alchemist Li Babai with whom he shares the nickname Babai sui gong 八百歲公 (Sir Eight-Hundred-Years).[137] If Li Ya really had some connection with Li A — which

---

[134] The famous Jiangsu Daoist Li Daochun was among the first to revere both the Southern legacy of Zhang Boduan and the Northern Quanzhen patriarchy. His *Zhonghe ji* (Anthology of the Harmony of the Middle) became in the doctrinal domain the symbol of this unification which was later defined by scholars as *zhongpai* (Central Branch) in symmetry with the Southern and Northern Lineages; see F. Pregadio & L. Skar "Inner alchemy (*Neidan*)," 480. On the role that this "Central Branch" played in the doctrinal elaboration of the Longmen see M. Esposito, "Longmen Taoism in Qing China" {see here below, Chapter 3}.

[135] In fact the figure of Donghua dijun (Wang Xuanfu) was also linked with the Northern tradition and its cults as well as with the individual sphere of the Quanzhen Seven Perfected; see F. Reiter, "Der Name Tung-hua ti-chün," 95–99 and P. Marsone, "Wang Chongyang (1113–1170) et la fondation du Quanzhen," 461–63.

[136] In the lineage of masters (*shipai* 師派) allegedly transmitted by Bai Yuchan (*Fahai yizhu* 法海遺珠, DZ 1166 fasc. 825–33, 14.4a), Qinghua dijun carries the name of Li Zhe 李矗.

[137] Yamada Toshiaki, "Shinsen Ri Happyaku," 147 and Qing Xitai, ed. *Zhongguo daojiao shi*, vol. 1: 261–284. For his successive manifestations in the world see also Qing

has yet to be proved—could he then also be linked to the Lijia dao 李家道 (the Way of the Li family)?

As is well known, according to the *Baopuzi* 抱朴子, a diviner called Li A was regarded as the founder of the Lijia dao in Sichuan around the beginning of the third century.[138] Similarly to the above-mentioned Li Babai, a certain Li A was also recognized as one of the "Twelve Immortals of Sichuan" depicted by the Daoist priest and painter Zhang Suqing 張素卿 (ca. 845-ca. 957).[139] According to Pu Jiangqing (1958:93–94), Zhang Suqing would have substituted the name of Li Babai of the earlier list of the "Eight Immortals of Sichuan" with that of Li A. It was probably not by chance that the beggar Li A of the Han dynasty, who withdrew to the Qingcheng 青城 mountains, was preferred by Zhang Suqing to Li Babai; after all, Zhang himself was living in Qingcheng as a religious official restoring its different temples.[140]

In conclusion, the *Jingai xindeng*'s portrayal of the figure of Donghua dijun incorporates different traditions: (a) local cults associated with Sichuan and Jiangnan through the figures of Xiaotong jun, Li Babai—Li A, Li Niwan; (b) various lists of immortals with Li Babai, Li A, Li Tieguai; (c) various genealogical lists of the Quanzhen Northern tradition of Donghua dijun (Wang Xuanfu) with the affirmation of Southern traditions featuring Li Ningyang—Li Tieguai—Li Ya; and (d) a new elaboration of the healing and exorcist powers of Li Babai through the integration of the Shenxiao therapeutic thunder rituals of the figure of Qinghua dijun Li Ya. This last point was certainly present in the figure of Li Niwan (Li Zhenyuan), the master who had allegedly transmitted the Five Thunder rites to Wu Shouyang and was later integrated in the Longmen "orthodox line."[141]

Finally, the integration of Li Tieguai (Li Ningyang)— Li Ya (Li A?)—Li Niwan—Li Babai in the figure of Donghua dijun points to one more aspect that must not be ignored.

Xitai ed. *Zhongguo daojiao shi*, vol. 2:459 and 593

[138] James Ware, *Alchemy, Medicine and Religion in the China of A.D. 320: The Nei P'ien of Ko Hung (Pao-pu-tzu).*, 158–60, Cambridge (Mass.): M.I.T. Press, 1966, and Anna Seidel "The Image of the Perfected Ruler in Early Taoist Messianism: Lao-tzu and Li Hung," *History of Religions*, 9, 1969–70: 231.

[139] On this list see E. Mesnil, "Zhang Suqing et la peinture taoïste à Shu,"146–47.

[140] On Zhang's activities, see E. Mesnil, "Zhang Suqing et la peinture taoïste à Shu."

[141] Li Niwan played an important role in transmitting Longmen scriptures; see M. Esposito, "La Porte du Dragon."

The Messianic Power of the Perfected Li

It was mentioned above that the figure of Li Babai was also known as one of the ancient "Eight Immortals of Sichuan" who was affiliated with the Longmen grotto in Sichuan. This figure was later (probably in the list of the "Twelve Immortals" of the painter Zhang Suqing when he was active in the Qingcheng mountains) superimposed on Li A. We have also noted that a confusion between the alchemist Li Babai and the diviner Li A, founder of the Lijia dao, existed already in the third century and that the exploitation of the nickname Babai was already considerable at the time of Ge Hong 葛洪 (283–343). Li A was in fact said to have appeared later, in the fourth century, in the region of Wu 吳 (Jiangsu and part of Zhejiang) under the guise of a certain Li Kuan 李寬. Like Li A, Li Kuan was a diviner of Sichuanese origin who gained so much fame through his healing rituals using talismans and holy water that he got the same nickname Li Babai. According to Ge Hong, Li's tradition had "filled the land south of the Yangzi" with many prophets named Li whom Ge denounced as charlatans.[142]

Nevertheless, prophets named Li 李 continued to arise in south China during the Six Dynasties, among them figures like the well-known Li Hong 李弘 who became the symbol of Laozi's appellation as messiah. Thereafter, the name Li—the family name of Laozi—was invoked both by "heterodox" movements and "orthodox" authorities. As is well known, this name was also adopted by many emperors who claimed to be incarnations of the divine Lord in order to justify their dynastic mandate. The figure of Li was thus not limited to persecuted rebels or charlatans but also embodied the imperial messiah. His dangerous powers were thus channeled and his abilities of Sage, Perfect Ruler, and savior of the people put to the service of ruling dynasties.[143]

---

[142] Anna Seidel, "The Image of the Perfected Ruler," 231–32.

[143] Anna Seidel "The Image of the Perfected Ruler"; Anna Seidel, "Taoist Messianism," *Numen* XXXI, 2, 1984: 161–174; Christine Mollier, *Une apocalypse taoïste du Ve siècle: Le Livre des Incantations Divines des Grottes Abyssales*, Paris: Collège de France, Institut des Hautes Études Chinoises, 1990; Livia Kohn, "The Beginnings and Cultural Characteristics of East Asian Millenarianism," *Japanese Religions* 23, 1–2, 1998: 29–51; and Christine Mollier, "Messianism and millenarianism," in F. Pregadio (ed.), *The Encyclopedia of Taoism*, vol. 1, 94–96, London: Routledge, 2008.

We can find a similar framework in the records of the *Jingai xindeng* where the popular figure of the alchemist/healer/exorcist Li Babai—Li A—Li Niwan—Li Tieguai—Li Ya fluctuates between orthodoxy (list of immortals, list of southern legacies) and heterodoxy (Lijia dao) until it finds permanent status and recognition in the "orthodox line" of Daoist Ancestors of the Longmen in the form of Donghua dijun *Li Ya*. The stories recorded in the *Jingai xindeng* about the transformation of Li Babai into Li Niwan—who had resuscitated the mother of a certain Wu of Suzhou using water and mud—certainly remind us of the Li family's tradition of cures with holy water and talismans. During the Ming, when he is said to have reappeared, he also displayed the original abilities of the Han alchemist Li Babai. In addition to these elements, Li Babai/Li Niwan offered his recompenses only to people animated by strong filial piety. This Confucian virtue was thus put in evidence in all the stories recorded by the *Jingai xindeng* and portrayed as the "official prerequisite" for obtaining Li's grace.[144] This theme reappears in the figure of the immortal Li Tieguai who was also recognized as patron of exorcists and honored as Qinghua dijun Li Ya in the therapeutic thunder rituals of the Shenxiao legacy.

What seems now clear is that the figure of the Longmen Ancestor Donghua dijun, *Li* 李, integrates and allows to resurface the ambivalencies and contradictions that have characterized Chinese religion since its beginnings: its eternal struggle between "orthodox" and "heterodox" forms, between messianic beliefs (shared by imperial dynasties and organized Daoist religious structures) and dangerous beliefs adopted by heterodox rebellious movements. Therapeutic abilities, which are stressed in the figure of Li Babai-Li Niwan in the *Jingai xindeng*, were in fact also the prerogative of institutionalized Daoist schools like the Celestial Masters which claimed to have obtained its mandate and hereditary title directly from Laozi in order to integrate the chaotic and dangerous cults into a well-administered church. The priests of this Most High Lord Lao's church were not to oppose but to assist the secular government. But in times of crisis, this same church could not avoid the upsurge of messianic beliefs which formed part of its original constitution (as well as that of Daoism in general) by looking forward to the return of Lord Li and the reestablishment of his reign of peace.[145]

---

[144] This was also one of the fundamental "Quanzhen values" which was propagated by Quanzhen Southern masters like Miao Shanshi 苗善時 (fl. 1288–1324); see I. Ang, "Le culte de Lü Dongbin des origines."

[145] A. Seidel, "The Image of the Perfected Ruler," 240.

Qingtong jun 青童君 (Lord Azure Lad), the original Shangqing deity who later became the Quanzhen Patriarch Donghua dijun (Wang), was also directly related to the Celestial Masters' founding figure Zhang Daoling 張道陵 (34–156 CE). According to the biography of Zhang Daoling in the *Shenxian zhuan* 神仙傳 (4.16a/b) and in *Han Tianshi shijia* 漢天師世家 (DZ 1463, fasc. 1066, j. 2), Donghai Xiaotong 東海小童 (one of the names of Qingtong jun) appeared to Zhang Daoling as the manifestation of Laozi in the world in order to bestow on him "the Way of the Orthodox Unity."[146] Conversely, in the Shangqing texts, Qingtong jun is mainly regarded as the Supreme Minister of Jinque Housheng dijun 金闕後聖帝君, the savior of the world who, under the appellation of Li Hong 李弘, "will come forth from the Qingcheng mountains."[147]

Thus it is hardly by chance that the Longmen list of Daoist Ancestors, in contrast with the earlier Quanzhen Northern lists, has reinserted the name of Jinque dijun 金闕帝君 before that of Donghua dijun. Heir to the long process of unification between the Northern and Southern Lineages that took place from the Yuan dynasty on, the Longmen lineage shows itself as the product of southern legacies and the elaboration by southern literati. Although in the gloss of the *Daopu yuanliu tu* 道譜源流圖, Jinque dijun is identified with Yin Xi 尹喜 instead of Li Hong, this does not mean that its Shangqing origins had been forgotten. He is the holder of Laozi's teachings but also one of its various manifestations and a possible apparition of Lord Li in the world.[148] Both of his functions are now in the hands of his disciple Donghua dijun who, as he appeared in the past to Zhang Daoling for inaugurating the Way of the Celestial Masters, presently conveys the new mandate to the Longmen patriarchs. He may reappear by "coming forth again from the Qingcheng mountains" (one of the earlier Longmen sanctuaries) as the Perfect Ruler in order to reestablish a realm of peace.

The fact of having substituted the Quanzhen ancestor Donghua dijun *Wang* (King) with Donghua dijun *Li* (Perfect Ruler) may also be explained

---

[146] P. W. Kroll, "In the Halls of the Azure Lad," 75, note 3 and Yoshiko Kamitsuka, "Hōshō Seidō kun," 9.

[147] A. Seidel, "The Image of the Perfected Ruler," 243; see also Yoshiko Kamitsuka, "Hōshō Seidō kun," 1–2 and 13–19.

[148] The absorption of Yin Xi here may show not only the previous integration of the Louguan group into the Quanzhen but also a transmission of its functions as "the archetypal disciple and ordinand of the Tao" to Donghua dijun. On the figure of Yin Xi see Livia Kohn, "Yin Xi: the Master at the Beginning of the Scripture," *Journal of Chinese Religion*, 25, 1997:83–139.

by a hidden allusion to the ancient and well-known prophecy according to which "Li Hong will be King." Although the Shangqing masters (or now the Longmen masters) inserted Lord Li into their list of Daoist ancestors, the hope of the advent of Li as Perfect Ruler lived on among common people as well as literati.[149] It is thus interesting that the compilers of the hagiographies of the seven official Longmen Patriarchs in the *Jingai xindeng* added a prophecy concerning the future abbot of the Baiyun guan, referring to his manifestation under the guise of a certain master Qiaoyang (Liu Yu). In master Qiaoyang's wake, they now regard Wang Changyue as the restorer of the Northern lineage of Qiu Chuji which carries imperial support for the Baiyun guan. At the end of Wang Changyue's biography they added Wang's own statement that he "truly is the Superior of Daoist Priesthood and the State Instructor" (*guoshi weiyi de shi wo* 國師威儀的是我).[150]

Purportedly, Wang was officially invested by the court to convey public ordinations at the Baiyun guan, and in particular he is known to have received the support of the Kangxi emperor (re. 1662–1722) for reforming the Daoist Vinaya. He was honored by official grants and inscriptions. However, the prophecy by the compilers of Wang's biography in the *Jingai xindeng* that "Qiaoyang was going to be reborn" and was to reinvigorate the "Vinaya lineage of the Most High (Lord Lao)," and also the above-mentioned statement about Wang as Guoshi 國師 (State Instructor), may carry a hidden message. This may be understood in the political context of the time when these biographies were compiled. After the Jiaqing era (1796–1819), Daoism enjoyed reduced official control and was freer to elaborate its own messianic dreams and its hope for the return of a Perfect Ruler. With this in mind, another look at Wang Changyue's biography yields supplementary information:

(1) A hidden reference to the Liu family under the allusion to Wang Changyue's reincarnation as Qiaoyang (Liu Yu), which may refer to the origin of the prophecy as a reminiscence of the special relation between the Li and Liu families under the Han ("The Liu family will rise again, and the Li family will be their coadjutors" 劉氏復興，李氏為輔)[151] — "a stereotyped phrase expressing the belief that a good (Daoist) rule is about to be

---

[149] A. Seidel, "The Image of the Perfected Ruler," 231 and 244–247.
[150] "Wang Kunyang lüshi zhuan" (JGXD 1.17b in ZWDS 31:184).
[151] A. Seidel, "The Image of the Perfected Ruler," 218.

established and that at such a propitious moment Li Hong cannot be far away."[152]

(2) The reference to Wang Changyue as *guoshi* 國師 (National Instructor) at the end of the *Jingai xindeng* biography may also recall the ancient distinction made inside the school of the Celestial Masters between *guoshi* and *tianshi* 天師 (Celestial Master): the first "was the title assumed by the spiritual leader at the time when he exercised only his religious authority while assisting a good emperor," whereas the second "was the title of the politico-religious leader in times when there was no able emperor."[153] A dual message may then be conveyed by this controversial Longmen lineage whose creation was more connected with the Celestial Masters' Zhengyi legacy than with the Quanzhen Northern patriarchy. If the emperor recognizes the position of Daoism, as he did with Wang Changyue, there will be a realm of peace in China with the support of Lord Li; but if this support were lacking, Lord Li would come again to be King himself.

The Longmen was in fact not only the official Vinaya school which produced the abbots and lived in Baiyun guan under the ideal founding Patriarch Qiu Chuji: it was also an authentic movement that had developed during the Ming dynasty inside and outside the Zhengyi-Qingwei legacy as the symbol of the asceticism and eremitic lineage inspired by the saint Qiu Chuji. This same nascent lineage was, at the end of the Ming dynasty, the potential hotbed of loyalists hoping to see China reunified and ruled by sage emperors. Messianic and millenarian dreams bred by southern traditions were probably at the source of the constitution of a Longmen "orthodox lineage" and left their marks on it under the convenient name of "Quanzhen Northern heritage."

---

[152] A. Seidel, "The Image of the Perfected Ruler," 238.
[153] A. Seidel, "The Image of the Perfected Ruler," 234.

Conclusion

As we have seen, the Longmen "orthodox lineage" was certainly created to promote the figure of abbot Wang Changyue as genuine heir of the Longmen Vinaya teaching, while the ideal founding patriarch of the Longmen lineage remained Qiu Chuji. The return to the Baiyun guan, the locale of the memorial shrine of the saint Qiu Chuji, became possible through an ideal edifice of "seven generations of masters" which constituted the beginning of the new phase of "institutionalization" for the Longmen. From Wang Changyue on, the abbots responsible for conveying public ordinations to the entire Daoist clergy were for the most part chosen from the Longmen lineage. An ideal line of Ancestors and Patriarchs was thus designed to ensure the prestigious position of the Longmen lineage over other schools; and its "family tree" was apparently modeled on that of the Quanzhen in order to portray itself as the official institutionalized order. However, since the Longmen lineage was progressively elaborated inside southern literati circles, it was the product of a long southern integration of the Quanzhen Northern tradition. This integration, which started under the Yuan dynasty with the propagation of Quanzhen teachings in Jiangnan, found a new expression during the Ming in the drive to unify and standardize southern and northern traditions under the supervision of the Zhengyi legacy. The creation of the Longmen lineage with its multiple sub-branches linked by a system of ramifying generational names seems in the final analysis to be more akin to the spirit of the Zhengyi legacy than to that of an "ideal" Quanzhen patriarchy.

Through analysis of the biographies of the Longmen patriarchs and the presentation of other Longmen lines, we have tried to discover blue-prints that show alternative designs of the seemingly streamlined Longmen lineage edifice. Although the biographies of the first seven Longmen patriarchs provide, as we have tried to show, elements for building an "orthodox line" of Longmen transmission, we cannot but notice some interesting coincidences. The creation of the Longmen "orthodox line" and the substitution of Quanzhen figures with Longmen "new ancestors" bears various signs of connection with Sichuan, the breeding ground of messianic movements as well as the original sanctuary of the Celestial Masters. A focus of this strange coincidence is the figure of Donghua dijun *Li* who, as founder of the "Quanzhen Longmen Daoism," also embodied one of the different manifestations of Li Babai, the hermit of the Longmen grotto of Sichuan. Could this indicate a link of the "Longmen" name with that of the grotto of Li Babai in Sichuan instead of the mountain in Shaanxi where the ideal founder Qiu Chuji withdrew? Could this link show that the actual foundation of the Longmen was at the outset associated with the Celestial Masters and not with the Quanzhen? Or does it simply exhibit the constant ambivalence of the Longmen Lineage and the multiplicity of its nascent sanctuaries?

Li Ya / Li A, the substitute of Li Babai, may also allude to the close link of the nascent Longmen with the Qingcheng mountains. One will recall that Qingcheng was the same sanctuary where the future incarnation of the messiah Li Hong—Jinque dijun, the master and precursor of Donghua dijun—was supposed to appear. This Sichuan presence and the mention of Qingcheng mountains were also stressed in the biographies of the first Longmen Patriarchs. The third Longmen Patriarch Chen Tongwei allegedly left Huashan to withdraw to Qingcheng in the latter part of his life. In his wake, the center of the Longmen transmission settled at the Qingcheng mountains until the fifth patriarch Zhang Dechun (fl. 1450) brought it from Sichuan to the Tiantai mountains in Zhejiang. From there, the Longmen transmission allegedly spread throughout southern China. Moreover, the propagation of Longmen teachings in the fictitious biographies of its patriarchs follows a line of propagation similar to that of the "Li cults" whose messianic traditions, as Seidel pointed out, seem all to have come from the common region of Shu (Sichuan).[154] The Longmen may thus also show, through the biographies of its own patriarchs, a genuine identity as a "southern heritage" which, due to its will to orthodoxy during the Qing, called itself "Quanzhen Northern lineage."

Although we know that the *Jingai xindeng* was compiled under the supervision of Min Yide, a Longmen master active in Zhejiang and thus certainly heir of southern local traditions, we cannot but remark that what he has reported in his work was, during the Qing dynasty, already adopted in the Baiyun guan, the official monastery of the Quanzhen Northern legacy. As paradoxical as this might seem: this "orthodox line" of the Quanzhen-Longmen Northern lineage, which formed the official pedigree of the Baiyun guan's Longmen abbots, was in reality elaborated among southern lineages' groups. Under the name of "Northern lineage," these groups were finally more linked with the Zhengyi legacy than the Quanzhen patriarchy.

---

[154] A. Seidel, "The Image of the Perfected Ruler," 232–33.

But there may be a logic to this paradox. After all, the Longmen movement developed during the Ming dynasty in a period when the Zhengyi order was the main supervisor of Daoist schools and when even the Quanzhen was integrated as symbol of self-cultivation and eremitic asceticism. The Longmen nascent edifice was thus probably erected under Zhengyi supervision and even more under the Qingwei influence, since the Qingwei master Liu Yuanran was a "new manifestation" of Qiu Chuji at the Baiyun guan. It is certain that in that period a wider integration of Quanzhen teachings, cults, and saints took shape among the Zhengyi-Qingwei, which was the major repository of all important southern legacies. These southern legacies left their mark on what was later recognized as the Longmen "Northern Lineage." Just as during the Ming the Quanzhen Northern Lineage, symbol of the Mongols, was abandoned in favor of the Southern Lineage, at the end of the Ming and during the Qing the "Northern Lineage" was reborn to become again the symbol of the orthodoxy which established itself at the Baiyun guan, the seat of today's Daoist Association.

It is just the discrepancy between what was later defined as the official version of events and what really happened that characterizes Chinese religion. If one accepts that there was a "Quanzhen renaissance" under the name of Longmen pai which occurred during the Qing dynasty, then one can also not ignore the fact that this was the result of a long integration process of different and older Daoist traditions. Studying the construction of the Longmen lineage edifice and its elaboration thus necessitates a deconstruction of the lineage by and from its purported "historical sources;" here, the *Jingai xindeng* or *Transmission of the Mind-Lamp from Mount Jingai* served this purpose.[155] It seems no coincidence that we have found in Daoism a similar process to that which characterized the birth of the patriarchal lineage in Chan Buddhism. That was also the fruit of a controversial pseudo-historical construction involving a curious intermingling of "Northern" and "Southern" schools. Moreover, it does not appear to be by chance that Longmen's historical artifice was, like that of Chan in the early Song era, set in stone through the compilation of a *Lamp History*. Played in a Daoist key, this endeavor was even less encumbered by history; but in the immortal tunes of these biographies one can, behind the strident melody of Wang Changyue's

---

[155] The works of Yanagida Seizan and Bernard Faure have been the models of such deconstruction for Chan history and help to better understand the formation process of the Longmen lineage.

lineage, also detect distinct echoes of the Longmen of the first period and its caves on Huashan, Laoshan, Qingcheng shan or Wudang shan.

However, the genuine story of the Longmen lineage still remains much of a mystery and is in dire need of detailed studies which could reveal the complex process of integration of many other local traditions that played a fundamental role in its constitution. Typical of nascent Daoist lineages, the Longmen, beyond its self-image of institutionalized order, still embodied the hopes of earlier or marginal groups who saw in it the dream of realizing a celestial realm of Great Peace right in this world with the help of an enlightened emperor. This hope has been central for the elaboration of a specific Longmen doctrine which claimed its independence from the stereotyped Longmen teaching at the Baiyun guan and its standardized ordinations and monastic rules by infiltrating another model inside the orthodoxy.[156] Signs of this can already be detected, at the end of the Ming dynasty, in the mention of two Longmen lines: Doctrinal 宗師 and Vinaya 律師.[157] These two lines are one more symptom of the fundamental difference between Southern and Northern traditions, of the eternal struggle between official and marginal movements, and of the will to orthodoxy that underlies both.

---

[156] On the meaning of Longmen public and private ordinations see M. Esposito, "Longmen Taoism in Qing China" (in particular p. 201, note 55, and pp. 219–221) {here below Chapter 3: note 63 (pp. 162–162), and pp. 187–190}. For a portrait of Longmen doctrine see Monica Esposito, "La Porte du Dragon" and "Longmen Taoism in Qing China" {here below, Chapter 3; and now also M. Esposito, *Creative Daoism*. Wil / Paris: Universitymedia, 2013}.

[157] {For a detailed discussion of the Vinaya line of Longmen Daoism, see Parts One & Two of Monica Esposito, *Creative Daoism*. Wil / Paris: Universitymedia, 2013.}

ABBREVIATIONS

BYGZ — *Baiyun guan zhi (Hakuunkan shi)* 白雲觀志 (Gazetteer of the White Clouds Abbey) by Oyanagi Shigeta 小柳司氣太. Tokyo: Tōhō bunka gakuin Tōkyō kenkyūjo, 1934.

DJYL — *Changchun daojiao yuanliu* 長春道教源流 (Origins and Development of the Daoist Teachings of [Qiu] Changchun 1879), by Chen Minggui 陳銘珪 (1824–1881). Reprint in ZWDS 31:1–157.

DTYL — *Daotong yuanliu zhi* 道統源流志 (Gazetteer on the Origins and Development of Orthodox Daoism) by Yan Liuqian 嚴六謙 (*hao*: Zhuangyan jushi 莊嚴居士). Wuxi: Zhonghua yinshuju, 1929.

DZ — *Daozang* 道藏 (the numbers are given according to Kristofer Schipper and Franciscus Verellen (eds.), *The Taoist Canon*, Chicago: Chicago University Press, 2004).

DZJHL — *Daozang jinghua lu* 道藏精華錄 (Record of Essential Blossoms of the Daoist Canon) by Ding Fubao 丁福保 (*zi*: Shouyi zi 守一子, 1874–1952). Reprint in 2 vols. (*shang / xia*). Zhejiang guji chubanshe, 1989.

DZJY — *Chongkan Daozang jiyao* 重刊道藏輯要 (Reedited Epitome of the Daoist Canon) by Yan Yonghe 閻永和, Peng Hanran 彭瀚然 and He Longxiang 賀龍驤. Chengdu: Erxian an 二仙庵, 1906. Reprint in 25 vols. Taipei: Xinwenfeng, 1977.

DZXB — *Daozang xubian* 道藏續編 (Supplementary Collection of the Daoist Canon), 4 vols., by Min Yide 閔一得 (1758–1836). Wuxing: Jingai cangban, 1834. Photolithographic edition by Ding Fubao 丁福保 (*zi*: Shou yi zi 守一子, 1874–1952). Shanghai: Yixue shuju. Reprint Beijing: Haiyang 1989.

JGXD — (*Chongkan*) *Jingai xindeng* 金蓋心燈 ([Re-edition of the] Transmission of the Mind-Lamp of Mt. Jingai), 10 vols., by Min Yide (1758–1836). Wuxing: Yunchao, Gu Shuyinlou cangban, 1876 (1st ed. 1821). Reprint in *Zangwai daoshu* 藏外道書 31.

SKQS   *Wenyuan ge Siku quanshu* 文淵閣四庫全書 (Complete Texts in Four Repositories, 1773–1782), 1500 vols. by Yong Rong 永瑢 et al. Edited by Zhu Jianmin 朱建民. Taipei: Shangwu yinshuguan, 1986.

YLCS   *Gu Shuyinlou cangshu* 古書隱樓藏書(Collection from the Ancient Hidden Pavilion of Books), 14 vols., by Min Yide 閔一得 (1758-1836). Wuxing: Jingai Chunyang gong cangban, 1904. Reprint in *Zangwai daoshu* 藏外道書 10:150-721.

ZWDS   *Zangwai daoshu* 藏外道書 (Daoist Texts not included in the Daoist Canon) edited by Hu Daojing 胡道靜 et al. Chengdu: Bashu shushe, 1992 (vol: 1–20); 1994 (vol. 21–36).

PRIMARY SOURCES

Baiyun xianbiao 白雲仙表 (A Chart of the Immortals of Baiyun Abbey). 1848. Meng Huoyi 孟豁一. ZWDS 31: 373 ff.

Biyuan tanjing 碧苑壇經 (Platform Sūtra of the Jade Garden). Transmitted by Wang Changyue 王常月 (?-1680), compiled by Shi Shouping 施守平 and revised by Min Yide. YLCS edition (reprinted in ZWDS 10: 158-217).

Changchun zhenren xiyouji 長春真人西遊記 (The Journey to the West of the Perfected [Qiu] Changchun). Li Zhichang 李志常 (1193-1256). DZ 1429 fasc. 1056.

Daode zhenjing sanjie 道德真經三解 (A Threefold Explication of the Daodejing). 1298. Deng Qi 鄧錡. DZ 687, fasc. 370-71.

Daofa huiyuan 道法會元 (Collected Sources on Daoist Ritual). 1356. DZ 1220, fasc. 884-941.

Fahai yizhu 法海遺珠 (Bequeathed Pearls from the Sea of Ritual). 1344. DZ 1166 fasc. 825-33.

Guangyang zaji 廣陽雜記 (Miscellaneous Records of Guangyang). Liu Xianting 劉獻廷. Beijing: Zhonghua shuju, 1957.

Han Tianshi shijia 漢天師世家 (DZ 1463, fasc. 1066).

Huangji hepi xianjing 皇極闔闢仙經, abbr. for *Yin zhenren Donghua zhengmai huangji hepi zhengdao xianjing*.

Huayue zhi 華嶽志 (Monography of the Peak of Hua). Compiled by Li Rong 李榕 (fl. 1821). Edited by Yang Xiwu 楊翼武 (fl. 1831). ZWDS 20: 3–185.

Jingudong zhi 金鼓洞志 (Monograph on the Jingu Grotto). 1807. Zhu Wenzao 朱文藻 (1736–1806). ZWDS 20: 189–299.

Jinhua zongzhi 金華宗旨 (The Secret of the Golden Flower). Edited by Jiang Yuanting 蔣元庭 (1755–1819) and revised by Min Yide 閔一得 (1758–1836). DZXB I: 1a-15b.

Jinlian zhengzong ji 金蓮正宗記 (Record of the Orthodox Lineage of the Golden Lotus). 1241. Qin Zhian 秦志安 (1188–1244). DZ 173, fasc. 75–76.

Jinlian zhengzong xianyuan xiangzhuan 金蓮正宗仙源像傳 (Illustrated Hagiographies of the Immortal Origins of the Orthodox Lineage of the Golden Lotus). 1326. Liu Tiansu 劉天素 & Xie Xichan 謝西蟾. DZ 174 fasc. 76.

Lishi zhenxian tidao tongjian 歷世真仙體道通鑒 (Comprehensive Mirror of the Perfected and Immortals who embodied the Dao through the Ages). Zhao Daoyi 趙道一 (late 13th century). DZ 296, fasc. 138-48.

Longmen xinfa 龍門心法 (Core Teachings of the Longmen). 1663. Transmitted by Wang Changyue 王常月 (?-1680) and compiled by Zhan Tailin 詹太林 and Tang Qingshan 唐清善. ZWDS 6: 727–785.

Longmen zhengzong jueyun benzhi daotong xinchuan 龍門正宗覺雲本支道統薪傳 (Uninterrupted Transmission of the Orthodox Teaching in the Right Lineage of the Longmen Jueyun Branch). 1927. Lu Yongming 陸永銘. ZWDS 31: 427–446.

Qiongguan Bai zhenren ji 瓊琯白真人集 (Anthology of Perfected Bai of Haiqiong). DZJY *louji* 婁集 4, vol. 14.

Rixia jiuwen kao 日下舊聞考 (Investigation of Peking's Antiquities). 1774/1882. SKQS vol. 497–99.

Shangyang zi jindan dayao 上陽子金丹大要 (Great Essentials on the Golden Elixir of Shangyang zi). Chen Zhixu 陳致虛 (1298-after 1335). DZ 1067, fasc. 736–38.

Tianxian zhengli 天仙正理 (Correct Principles of Celestial Immortality). Wu Shouyang 伍守陽 (1574–1634). DZJY *biji* 4, vol. 17.

Tianxian zhengli qianshuo 天仙正理淺說 (Simple explanations of the Correct Principles of Celestial Immortality). Wu Shouyang. DZJY *biji* 5, vol. 17.

Tianxian zhengli zhilun 天仙正理直論 (Forthright Discourses on the Correct Principles of Celestial Immortality). 1639. Wu Shouyang. DZJY *biji* 4, vol. 17.

Wudang fudi zongzhen ji 武當富地總真集 (Collection of the Assembled Perfected of Mount Wudang). 1291. Compiled by Liu Daoming 劉道明. DZ962 fasc. 609

Xianfo hezong yulu 仙佛合宗語錄 (Recorded Sayings on the Merged Tradition of Buddhism and Daoism). Wu Shouyang and annotated by Wu Shouxu 伍守虛. DZJY *biji* 1, vol. 17.

Xuanjiao da gong'an 玄教大公案 (The Great Case of the Teachings of the Mysteries). 1324. Wang Zhidao 王志道. DZ 1065, fasc. 734.

Yin zhenren Donghua zhengmai huangji hepi zhengdao xianjing 尹真人東華正脈皇極闔闢證道仙經. 1831. Attributed to Yin Pengtou 尹蓬頭, edited by Min Yide.

Zhongnan shan zuting xianzhen neizhuan 終南山祖庭仙真內傳 (Inner Biographies of the Immortals and Perfected at [Wang Chongyang's] Ancestral Hall in Zhongnan Mountains). Li Daoqian 李道謙 (1219–1296). DZ 955 fasc. 604.

SECONDARY SOURCES

Ang, Isabelle. 1993. "Le culte de Lü Dongbin des origines jusqu'au début du XIVème siècle. Caractéristiques et transformations d'un Saint Immortel dans la Chine pré-moderne." Ph. D. diss., Université de Paris VII.

———. 1997. "Le culte de Lü Dongbin sous les Song du Sud." *Journal Asiatique* 285, 2, 1997: 473–507.

Baldrian-Hussein, Farzeen. 1986. "Lü Tung-pin in Northern Sung Literature." *Cahiers d'Extrême-Asie* 2, 1986: 133–169.

———. 1996–97. "Taoist Beliefs in Literary Circles of the Song

Dynasty—Su Shi (1037–1101) and his Technique of Survival." *Cahiers d'Extrême-Asie* 9, 1996–97: 15–53.

Bertuccioli, Giuliano. 1953. "Note taoiste II. A proposito di un recente caso di applicazione del rogo nel convento taoista del Pai-yun Kuan." *Rivista degli studi orientali* XXVIII, 1953: 185–186.

———. 1957. "Il Taoismo nella Cina contemporanea." *Cina* 2, 1957: 67–77.

Bokenkamp, R. Stephen. 1997. *Early Daoist Scriptures*. Berkeley: University of California Press.

Boltz, Judith M. 1987. *A Survey of Taoist Literature Tenth to Seventeenth Centuries*. Berkeley: University of California, Institute of East Asian Studies & Center for Chinese Studies.

———. 1993. "Not by the Seal of Office alone: New Weapons in Battles with the Supernatural." In *Religion and Society in T'ang and Sung China*, edited by Patricia Buckley Ebrey and Peter Gregory, 241–305. Honolulu:University of Hawaii Press.

Burkhardt, V. Rodolphe. 1919. *Chinese Creeds and Customs*. Hong Kong: South China Morning Post.

Chen, Bing 陳兵. 1985. "Jindan pai Nanzong qiantan" 金丹派南宗淺探 (A Brief Study of the Southern lineage of the Golden Elixir school). *Shijie zongjiao yanjiu* 世界宗教研究 4, 1985: 35–49.

———. 1988. "Qingdai Quanzhen Longmen pai de zhongxing" 清代全真龍門派的中興 (The Qing dynasty's renewal of the Quanzhen Longmen school). *Shijie zongjiao yanjiu* 世界宗教研究 2, 1988: 84–96.

———. 1991. "Ming Qing daojiao" 明清道教 [Ming-Qing Daoism]. In Mou Zhongjian 牟鐘鑑 (ed.), *Daojiao tonglun* 道教通論 [A General Discussion of Daoism], 551–579. Jinan: Wenlu.

———. 1992. "Mingdai Quanzhen dao" 明代全真道(Quanzhen in Ming Times). *Shijie zongjiao yanjiu* 世界宗教研究 1, 1992:40–51.

Davis, Edward L. 2001. *Society and the Supernatural in Song China*. Honolulu: University of Hawai'i Press.

de Bary, William Theodore. 1970. "Individualism and Humanitarianism in Late Ming Thought." In *Self and Society in Ming Thought*, edited by Wm Theodore de Bary, 145–225. New York: Columbia University Press.

———. 1975. "Neo-Confucian Cultivation and the Seventeenth-Century

'Enlightenment.'" In *The Unfolding of Neo-Confucianism*, edited by Wm Theodore de Bary, 141–216. New York: Columbia University Press.

de Bruyn, Pierre-Henry. 1997. "Le Wudang shan: Histoire des récits fondateurs." Ph.D. diss., Université de Paris VII.

———. 2000. "Daoism in the Ming (1368–1644)." In *Daoism Handbook*, edited by Livia Kohn, 594–622. Leiden: Brill.

Despeux, Catherine. 1979. *Traité d'Alchimie et de Physiologie taoïste*. Paris: Les Deux Océans.

———. 1994. *Taoïsme et corps humain*. Paris: Trédaniel.

Dong, Zhongji 董中基. 1987. *Daojiao Quanzhen zuting Beijing Baiyun guan* 道教全真祖庭北京白雲觀 (The Abbey of the White Clouds, ancestral seat of the Daoism of Quanzhen). Beijing: Zhongguo daojiao xiehui.

Eliade, Mircea. 1983. *Le chamanisme et les techniques archaïques de l'extase*. Paris: Payot.

Erdberg-Consten, Eleanor. 1942. "A Statue of Lao-tzu in the Pö-yun-kuan." *Monumenta Serica* VII, 1942: 235–241.

Eskildsen, Stephen. 1989. "The Beliefs and Practices of Early Ch'üan-chen Taoism." M. A. Thesis, University of British Columbia.

———. 1990. "Asceticism in Ch'üan-chen Taoism." *British Columbia Asian Review* 3/4, 1990:153–91.

Esposito, Monica. 1993. "La Porte du Dragon—L'école Longmen du Mont Jin'gai et ses pratiques alchimiques d'après le *Daozang xubian* (Suite au canon taoïste)." Ph.D. diss., Université de Paris VII.

———. 1997. *L'alchimia del soffio*. Roma:Ubaldini.

———. 2000. "Daoism in the Qing (1644–1911)." In *Daoism Handbook*, edited by Livia Kohn, 623–658. Leiden: Brill. {Revised edition here above, Chapter 1}

———. 2001. "Longmen Taoism in Qing China: Doctrinal Ideal and Local Reality." *Journal of Chinese Religion* 29, 2001. {Revised edition here below, Chapter 3}

Faure, Bernard. 1984. "La volonté d'orthodoxie." 3 vols. Thèse d'État, École Pratique des Hautes Études, Section des Sciences Religieuses.

———. 1989. *Le Bouddhisme Ch'an en mal d'histoire: Genèse d'une tradition religieuse dans la Chine des T'ang*. Paris: École Française d'Extrême-Orient.

Foulk, Theodore Griffith. 1987. "The Chan school and its Place in the Buddhist Monastic Tradition." Ph. D. diss., University of Michigan.

Girardot, Norman J. 1983. *Myth and Meaning in Early Taoism: The Theme of Chaos (hun-tun)*. Berkeley: University of California Press.

Goossaert, Vincent. 2001. "The Invention of an Order: Collective Identity in 13th Century Quanzhen." *Journal of Chinese Religion* 29, 2001: 111–138.

———. 2004. "The Quanzhen Clergy, 1700–1950." In *Religion and Chinese Society*, edited by John Lagerwey, vol. 2, 699–771. Hong Kong: École française d'Extrême-Orient & Chinese University of Hong Kong, 2004.

Groner, Paul. 1989. "The Ordination Ritual in the Platform Sūtra within the context of the East Asian Buddhist Vinaya Tradition." In *The Sixth Patriarch Platform Sūtra in Religious and Cultural Perspective*, edited by Fo Kuang shan, 220–250. Taichong: Fo Kuang shan.

Güntsch, Gertrud. 1988. *Das Shen-hsien chuan und das Erscheinungsbild eines Hsien*. Frankfurt: Peter Lang.

Gyatso, Geshe Kelzang. 1982. *Clear Light of Bliss*. London: Wisdom.

Hachiya Kunio 蜂屋邦夫. 1998. *Kingen jidai no dōkyō—shichi shin kenkyū* 金元時代の道教—七眞研究 (The Daoism of the Jin and Yuan Dynasties—Research on the Seven Perfected). Tokyo: Tōkyō daigaku Tōyō bunka kenkyūjo hōkoku, Kyūko shoin.

Hawkes, David. 1981. "Quanzhen Plays and Quanzhen Masters." *Bulletin de l'Ecole Française d'Extrême Orient* 69, 1981: 153–170.

Hummel, Arthur, ed. 1975. *Eminent Chinese of the Ch'ing Period*. Taipei: Ch'eng Wen Publishing Company.

Huters, Theodore et al. 1997. *Culture and State in Chinese History*. Stanford: Stanford University Press.

Igarashi, Kenryū 五十嵐賢隆. 1938. *Taiseikyū shi* 太清宮志 (Gazetteer of the Palace of Great Purity). Tokyo: Kokushō kankōkai.

Ishida, Kenji 石田憲司. 1992. "Mingdai Dōkyō shijō no Zenshin to Seii" 明代道教史上の全真と正一 (The Quanzhen and Zhengyi in Ming Daoism). In Sakai Tadao 酒井忠夫 (ed.), *Taiwan no shūkyō to Chūgoku bunka* 湾の宗教と中国文化 (Taiwanese Religion and Chinese Culture), 145–185. Tokyo: Fukyūsha.

Katz, Paul. 1996. "Enlightened Alchemist or Immoral Immortal? The

Growth of Lü Dongbin's Cult in Late Imperial China." In *Unruly Gods: Divinity and Society in China*, edited by Meir Shahar and Robert P. Weller, 70–104. Honolulu: University of Hawaii Press.

Kaltenmark, Max. *Le Lie-sien tchouan*. Paris: Collège de France, 1987.

Kamitsuka, Yoshiko 神塚淑子. "Hōsho Seidō kun o megutte 方諸青童君をめぐって" (On Fangzhu Qingtong jun). *Tōhō shūkyō* 東方宗教 76, 1990: 1–23.

Kieschnick, John. *The Eminent Monk Buddhist Ideals in Medieval Chinese Hagiography*. Honolulu: University of Hawaii, 1997.

Kohn, Livia. "Yin Xi: the Master at the Beginning of the Scripture." *Journal of Chinese Religion*, 25, 1997:83–139.

———. "The Beginnings and Cultural Characteristics of East Asian Millenarianism." *Japanese Religions* 23, 1–2, 1998: 29–51.

Kroll, W. Paul. "In the Halls of the Azure Lad." *Journal of the American Oriental Society* 105/1, 1985: 75–94.

Lagerwey, John. *Taoist Ritual in Chinese Society and History*. New York: Macmillan Publishing Company, 1987.

Lai, T.C. *The Eight Immortals*. Hong Kong: Swindon Book Co., 1974.

Liu Ts'un-yan. 1970. "Taoist Self-Cultivation in Ming Thought." In *Self and Society in Ming Thought*, edited by Wm. T. de Bary, 291–326. New York: Columbia University Press.

———. 1984. *New Excursions from the Hall of Harmonious Wind*. Leiden: Brill.

Ma, Xiaohong 馬曉宏. 1986. "Lü Dongbin shenxian xinyang suyuan" 呂洞賓神仙信仰溯源 (Tracing the source of the cult of the Divine Immortal Lü Dongbin). *Shijie zongjiao yanjiu* 世界宗教研究 XXV, 3, 1986: 79–95.

Ma, Shutian 馬書田. 1991. *Huaxia zhushen* 華夏諸神 (Chinese divinities). Beijing: Yanshan CBS.

Marsone, Pierre. 1999. "Le Baiyun guan de Pékin: épigraphie et histoire." *Sanjiao wenxian* 3, 1999:73–136.

———. 2001. "Wang Chongyang (1113–1170) et la fondation du Quanzhen." Ph.D. diss., Paris: Ecole Pratique des Hautes Études, section des Sciences Religieuses.

McRae, John R. 1993. "Yanagida Seizan's Landmark Works on Chinese Ch'an." *Cahiers d'Extrême-Asie* 7, 1993–94: 51–103.

Mesnil, Evelyne. 1996–97. "Zhang Suqing et la peinture taoïste à Shu." *Cahiers d'Extrême-Asie* 9, 1996–97: 131–158.

Min, Zhiting 閔智亭. 1990. *Daojiao yifan* 道教儀範 (Patterns of Daoist rites). Beijing: Zhongguo daojiao xueyuan.

Mollier, Christine. 1990. *Une apocalypse taoïste du Ve siècle: Le Livre des Incantations Divines des Grottes Abissales*. Paris: Collège de France, Institut des Hautes Études Chinoises.

———. 2008. "Messianism and millenarianism." In *The Encyclopedia of Taoism*, edited by Fabrizio Pregadio, vol. 1, 94–96. London: Routledge.

Mori, Yuria 森由利亞. 1990. "Sōdai ni okeru Ryo Dōhin setsuwa ni kansuru ichi shiron" 宋代における呂洞賓説話にかんする一試論 (A Preliminary Study on Lü Dongbin-related Stories of the Song Dynasty). *Bungaku kenkyūka kiyō, bessatsu* 文學研究科紀要, 別冊 17, 1990: 55–65.

———. 1994. "Zenshinkyō ryūmonha keifu kō" 全真教龍門派系譜考 (A Study on the Lineage of the Longmen School of Complete Perfection Heritage). In *Dōkyō bunka e no tenbō* 道教文化への展望 (Observations on Chinese Culture), edited by Dōkyō bunka kenkyūkai, 181–211. Tokyo, Hirakawa.

Ōfuchi, Ninji 大淵忍爾. 1964. *Dōkyō shi no kenkyū* 道教史の研究 (Research on the history of Daoism). Okayama: Okayama Daigaku Kyōsaikai Shosekibu.

Pregadio, Fabrizio & Skar, Lowell. 2000. "Inner alchemy (*Neidan*)." In *Daoism Handbook*, edited by Livia Kohn, 464–497. Leiden: Brill.

Pu, Jiangqing 浦江清. 1931. "Baxian kao" 八仙考 (A Study on the Eight Immortals). *Qinghua xuebao* 1, 1931: 89–136.

Qing, Xitai. 卿希泰 ed. 1994. *Zhongguo daojiao shi* 中國道教 (Chinese Daoism), 4 vols. Shanghai: Zhishi.

———, ed. 1996. *Zhongguo daojiao shi* 中國道教史 (History of Chinese Daoism). 4 vols. Chengdu: Sichuan Renmin.

Reiter, Florian. 1983. "Some Observations concerning Taoist Foundations in Traditional China." *Zeitschrift der Deutschen Morgenländischen Gesellschaft* 133, 1983: 363–376.

———. 1985. "Der Name Tung-hua ti-chün und sein Umfeld in der taoistischen Tradition." In *Religion und Philosophie in Ostasien. Festschrift für Hans Steininger*, edited by Gert Naundorf et al., 87–101. Würzburg: Königshausen & Neumann.

———. 1988. *Grundelemente und Tendenzen des religiösen Taoismus*. Stuttgart: Franz Steiner.

Ren, Jiyu 任繼愈 ed. 1990. *Zhongguo daojiao shi* 中國道教史 (History of Chinese Daoism). Shanghai: Shanghai renmin.

Robinet, Isabelle. 1984. *La révélation du Shangqing dans l'histoire du taoïsme*, 2 vols. Paris: École Française d'Extrême-Orient.

———. 1984. "Notes préliminaires sur quelques antinomies fondamentales entre le bouddhisme et le taoïsme." In *Incontro di Religioni in Asia tra il III e il IV secolo d. C.*, edited by Lionello Lanciotti, 217–242. Firenze: Leo S. Olschki.

———. 1995. *Introduction à l'alchimie intérieure taoïste*. Paris: Le Cerf.

Sawada, Mizuhō 澤田瑞穗. 1981. "Ishū Hakuunkan jinbōki 維修白雲觀尋訪記 (Report of a Visit to the Restored Abbey of White Clouds)." *Tōhō shūkyō* 東方宗教 57, 1981: 71–77.

Schipper, Kristofer. 1987. "Master Chao I-chen and the Ch'ing-wei School of Taoism." In *Dōkyō to shūkyō bunka*, edited by Akizuki Kan'ei, 715–734. Tokyo: Hirakawa.

———. 1991. "Temples et liturgie de Pékin." *Annuaire de l'EPHE* (Vème Section) 100, 1991–92: 91–96.

Seidel, Anna. 1969. "The Image of the Perfected Ruler in Early Taoist Messianism: Lao-tzu and Li Hung." *History of Religions* 9, 1969–70: 216–247.

———. 1983. "Imperial Treasures and Taoist Sacraments: Taoist Roots in the Apocrypha." In *Tantric and Taoist Studies in Honour of R.A. Stein*, edited by Michel Strickmann, 291–371. Bruxelles: Institut Belge des Hautes Études Chinoises.

———. 1984. "Taoist Messianism." *Numen* XXXI, 2, 1984: 161–174.

Shinohara, Kōichi. 1994. "Passages and Transmission in Tianhuang Daowu's Biographies." In *Other Selves Autobiography & Biography in Cross-Cultural Perspective*, edited by Phyllis Granoff and Shinohara Kōichi, 132–149. Oakville, Buffalo: Mosaic Press.

Skar, Lowell. 1996–97 "Administering Thunder: A Thirteenth-Century Memorial Deliberating the Thunder Rites." *Cahiers d'Extrême-Asie* 9, 1996–97: 159–202.

———. 2000. "Ritual movements, deity cults and the transformation of

Daoism in Song and Yuan times." In *Daoism Handbook*, edited by Livia Kohn, 413–463. Leiden: Brill.

———. 2000. "Alchemy, Local Cults, and Daoism: A Perspective on the Formation of the Southern Lineage from Tang to Ming." Paper presented at the Conference "Religion and Chinese Society: The Transformation of a Field," Hong Kong, May 29–June 2, 2000.

Strickmann, Michel. 1978. "The Longest Taoist Scripture." *History of Religion*, 17, 3–4, 1978:331–354.

Swan, Nancy Lee. 1975. "Pao T'ing-bo." In *Eminent Chinese of the Ch'ing Period*, edited by Arthur Hummel, 612–13. Taipei: Ch'eng Wen Publishing Company.

ter Haar, Barend. 1992. *The White Lotus Teachings in Chinese Religious History*. Leiden: Brill.

Waley, Arthur. 1931. *Travels of an Alchemist: The Journey of the Taoist Ch'ang-ch'un to the Hindukush at the Summons of Chingiz Khan*. London: George Routledge & Sons, Ltd.

Wang, Zhizhong 王志忠. 1995. "Quanzhen jiao Longmen pai qiyuan lunkao" 全真教龍門派起源論考 (A Study on the Origin of the Longmen Branch of the Quanzhen School). *Zongjiao xue yanjiu* 宗教學研究 4, 1995: 9–13.

———. 1995. "Lun Mingmo Qingchu Quanzhen jiao 'zhongxing' de chengyin" 論明末清初全真教中興的成因 (On Contributing Factors to the 'Revival' of Quanzhen between the End of Ming and the Beginning of Qing). *Zongjiao xue yanjiu* 宗教學研究 3, 1995: 32–38

Ware, James. 1966. *Alchemy, Medicine and Religion in the China of A.D. 320: The Nei P'ien of Ko Hung (Pao-pu-tzu)*. Cambridge (Mass.): M.I.T. Press.

Welch, Holmes. 1967. *The Practice of Chinese Buddhism 1900–1950*. Cambridge, Massachusetts: Harvard University Press.

Welter, Albert. 1988. "The Contextual Study of Chinese Buddhist Biographies: the Example of Yung-Ming Yen-Shou (904–975)." In *Monks and Magicians Religious Biographies in Asia*, edited by Phyllis Granoff and Shinohara Koichi, 247–268. Oakville: Mosaic Press.

Wright, Dale S. 1993–94. "Les récits de transmission du bouddhisme Ch'an et l'historiographie moderne." *Cahiers d'Extrême-Asie* 7, 1993–94: 105–114.

Yanagida, Seizan 柳田聖山. 1967. *Shoki zenshū shisho no kenkyū* 初期

禪宗史書の研究 (Studies on the Historical Sources of Early Chan). Kyoto: Hōzōkan 法藏館.

Yamada, Toshiaki 山田利明. 1977. "Shinsen Ri Happyaku den kō" 神仙李八百伝考 (Observations on the Biography of Li Babai). In *Yoshioka Yoshitoyo hakase kanreki kinen kenkyū ronshū kankōkai* 吉岡義豊博士還暦記念研究論集刊行会, edited by *Yoshioka Yoshitoyo hakase kanreki kinen dōkyō kenkyū ronshū* 吉岡義豊博士還暦記念道教研究論集 (Collected Studies on Daoism Offered to Dr. Yoshioka Yoshitoyo on his Sixtieth Birthday), 145–163. Tokyo: Kokusho Kankōkai.

Yang, Richard F.S. 1958. "A Study in the Origin of the Eight Immortals." *Oriens Extremus* 5, 1958: 1–22.

Yao, Tao-chung. 1980. "Chuan-chen: A New Taoist Sect in North China During the 12th and 13th centuries." Ph. D. diss., University of Arizona.

———. 2000. "Quanzhen: Complete Perfection." In *Daoism Handbook*, edited by Livia Kohn, 567–593. Leiden: Brill.

Yetts, Perceval W. 1916. "The Eight Immortals." *Journal of the Royal Asiatic Society*, 1916: 773–807.

———. 1922. "More Notes on the Eight Immortals." *Journal of the Royal Asiatic Society* 1922: 397–426.

Yokote, Yutaka 横手裕. 2000. "Zenshinkyō to nanshū hokushū" 全眞教と南宗北宗 (The Quanzhen school and the Northern and Southern Lineages), in Tetsurō Noguro 鉄郎野口 et al., *Dōkyō no seimeikan to shintai ron* 道教の生命観身体論 (The Daoist View of Life and Body), 180–196. Tokyo: Yūyama kaku.

Yoshioka, Yoshitoyo 吉岡義豊. 1970. *Eisei e no negai: Dōkyō* 永生への願い：道教 (The Quest for Eternal Life: Daoism). Kyoto: Tankōsha.

———. 1975. *Dōkyō no jittai* 道教の実体 (Daoism Today). Kyoto: Hōyū shoten.

———. 1979. "Taoist Monastic Life." In *Facets of Taoism*, edited by Holmes Welch & Anna Seidel, 229–252. New Haven and London: Yale University Press.

Yü, Chun-fang. 1981. *The Renewal of Buddhism in China: Chu-hung and the Late Ming Synthesis*. New York: Columbia University Press.

Zeng, Zhaonan 曾召南. 1995. "Longmen pai" 龍門派. In *Zhongguo*

daojiao dacidian 中國道教大辭典, edited by Hu Fuchen 胡孚琛, 66–67. Beijing: Zhongguo shehui kexue.

Zong, Li 宗力 and Liu Qun 劉群. 1987. *Zhongguo minjian zhushen* 中國民間諸神 (China's Popular Pantheon). Shijiazhuang: Hebei renmin.

Longmen Daoism in Qing China—
Doctrinal Ideal and Local Reality*

The Quanzhen 全真 school of Daoism was founded around 1170 and enjoyed great success during the Yuan dynasty (1281–1367). It seems to have been in eclipse during the Ming dynasty (1368–1644). However, at the end of that dynasty, the Quanzhen school experienced a "renaissance" under the name of "Longmen" 龍門, which is none other than the key Daoist school of the Qing period (1644–1911). Since this school was in charge of public ordinations, it represented by far the most common lineage shared by Daoist priests from the Qing until the present.[1] Thus, if one asks Daoists to which lineage they belong, most will even today answer "Longmen"— just as Buddhist monks are likely to answer "Linji."[2] In spite of its obvious importance, this school of Daoism has so far received scant scholarly attention, and its history as well as its doctrine are still barely known. Having

---

* My thanks go to Fabrizio Pregadio for his proof-reading and useful corrections; and to Urs App for having turned my "English-French" into English and for discussions that let me better understand the deep parallels between Chan and Longmen lineage creation.

[1] Public ordination refers to a collective ceremony of "taking the vows" or "accepting the precepts" (*shoujie* 受戒) which takes place in an authorized monastery at whose ordination platform the cleric is fully recognized as a member of the clergy. See Yoshioka Yoshitoyo, "Taoist Monastic Life," in Holmes Welch & Anna Seidel (eds.), *Facets of Taoism*, 235–236, New Haven and London: Yale University Press, 1979; and Holmes Welch, *The Practice of Chinese Buddhism 1900–1950*, 285–296, Cambridge, Massachusetts: Harvard University Press, 1967.

[2] Welch, *The Practice of Chinese Buddhism*, 281 & 396; Yoshioka, "Taoist Monastic Life," 233, 235–236. For the question concerning the creation of the Longmen lineage see Monica Esposito, "The Longmen School and its Controversial History during the Qing Dynasty." In *Religion and Chinese Society: The Transformation of a Field*, ed. by John Lagerwey. 2 vols. Hong Kong: École française d'Extrême-Orient & Chinese University of Hong Kong, 2004, vol. 2: 621–698 {see here above, Chapter 2}.

examined the history of the Longmen and its lineage,[3] I will here focus on a number of central questions about its doctrine.

The foundation of the Longmen lineage allegedly goes back to Qiu Chuji 邱處機 (1148-1227);[4] but only under the guidance of Wang Changyue 王常月 (d. 1680; also called Wang Kunyang 王崑陽) did it constitute itself as a genuine school with an official lineage and organized temples. In 1656, as abbot of the Baiyun guan 白雲觀 in Beijing, Wang was in fact the principal driving force behind a court-approved reorganization of Daoist discipline. Through public ordinations sponsored by the government, he established a precepts program centered on rules of proper behavior which included also spiritual teachings and exhibited signs of inspiration by Chan 禪 Buddhism. Wang's teaching was combined with strong Confucian ethics and Buddhist soteriology; it represented a kind of "ordination manual" for all Daoist priests independent of their original affiliation. Under Wang, Longmen acquired the monopoly of ordination. This promoted widespread "Longmen standardization" of Daoist doctrine throughout China, which still persists today.[5] However, if one analyzes the works by Wang Changyue and his Longmen disciples, one immediately notes something different behind the veil of Longmen indoctrination. In the different mountains and monasteries of North and South that are affiliated with Longmen, Wang's Longmen teaching was thoroughly mixed with older local traditions, their cults, and their saints. The Daoism of the Qing and modern times is thus characterized both by an apparent uniformity of doctrine and by a large variety of teachings independent from Wang Changyue's school. Deeply linked to specific regions and temples, these teachings established their identity through the foundation of local branches.

---

[3] Esposito, "The Longmen School" {here above, Chapter Two}.

[4] The name "Longmen" traditionally refers to the place in the Longzhou 隴州 district (Western Shaanxi) where Qiu Chuji underwent his ascetic training. According to other hypotheses, the name of Longmen may be traced back to a place in Huashan 華山 (Shaanxi) or even to a grotto located in Sichuan. See Monica Esposito, *La Porte du Dragon—L'école Longmen du Mont Jin'gai et ses pratiques alchimiques d'après le Daozang xubian (Suite au canon taoïste)*, 144–54, Ph.D diss., Université de Paris VII, 1993 {PDF version 2012}; Wang Zhizhong 王志忠, "Quanzhen jiao Longmen pai qiyuan lunkao" 全真教龍門派起源論考 [A study on the origin of the Longmen lineage of the Quanzhen school]," *Zongjiao xue yanjiu* 宗教學研究 4 (1995): 9–13; and Esposito, "The Longmen School" {here above, Chapter Two}.

[5] Esposito, "Daoism in the Qing," 631–634 {here above, Chapter One, pp. 16–20. For the history and characteristics of the ordination system see Part Two of Monica Esposito, *Creative Daoism*. Wil / Paris: UniversityMedia, 2013}.

In what sense can one thus speak of a genuine Longmen teaching ? And if it exists, does it have fundamental characteristics that transcend the regional variety of Longmen local branches? By way of a brief presentation of the important seventeenth-century figure of Wang Changyue and his work, I will first describe what can be regarded as the official teachings of the Longmen school. For that purpose, instead of presenting those texts where he gave a simple list of rules and interdictions to be observed by the Daoist ordinands, I will examine the doctrinal aspects of Wang Changyue's teachings as explained in the *Biyuan tanjing* 碧苑壇經 (Platform Sūtra of the Jade Garden). Then, I will try to shed light on some peculiarities of Longmen doctrine through a comparison of Wang Changyue's teachings with the works of a specific branch of Longmen, namely, the branch of Mount Jingai 金蓋山 (Zhejiang). This local branch is important since it claims to be the receptacle of Longmen orthodox teaching after the death of Wang Changyue by virtue of its appropriation of the famous *Secret of the Golden Flower* and the possession of a corpus of texts collected in the *Daozang xubian* 道藏續編 (Supplementary Collection of the Daoist Canon). The history of this branch will be thus unfolded through the presentation of its founding patriarch, Tao Jing'an 陶靖菴 (1612–1673), and particularly through the life and works of Min Yide 閔一得 (1758–1836), the compiler of the *Daozang xubian*. A brief examination of the *Daozang xubian* will conclude this chapter.[6]

---

[6] The *Daozang xubian* 道藏續編 (hereafter abbreviated as DZXB) forms a kind of canon of the Longmen inner alchemical doctrine. {For a description of the contents see the Appendix to the present chapter.} For some fundamental studies of inner alchemical theories, see for example: Farzeen Baldrian-Hussein. *Procédés secrets du joyau magique—Traité d'alchimie taoïste du XIe siècle*, Paris: Les Deux Océans, 1984; Catherine Despeux. *Traité d'alchimie et de physiologie taoïste*, Paris: Les Deux Océans, 1979; Joseph Needham & Lu Gui-djen. *Science and Civilisation in China*, vol. V-5, Cambridge: Cambridge University Press, 1983; Fabrizio Pregadio & Lowell Skar. "Inner Alchemy (Neidan)," in *Daoism Handbook*, ed. by L. Kohn, 464–497, Leiden: Brill, 2000; Isabelle Robinet. "Original Contributions of Neidan to Taoism and Chinese Thought," in *Taoist Meditation and Longevity Techniques*, ed. by L. Kohn & Y. Sakade, 297–330, Ann Arbor: The University of Michigan, 1989; I. Robinet. "Recherche sur l'alchimie intérieure (neidan): l'école Zhenyuan," *Cahiers d'Extrême-Asie* 5 (1989–90): 141–62; I. Robinet, *Introduction à l'alchimie intérieure taoïste*, Paris: Le Cerf, 1995; and Douglas Wile. *Arts of the Bedchamber: The Chinese Sexual Yoga Classics Including Women's Solo Meditation Texts*. Albany: State University of New York Press, 1992.

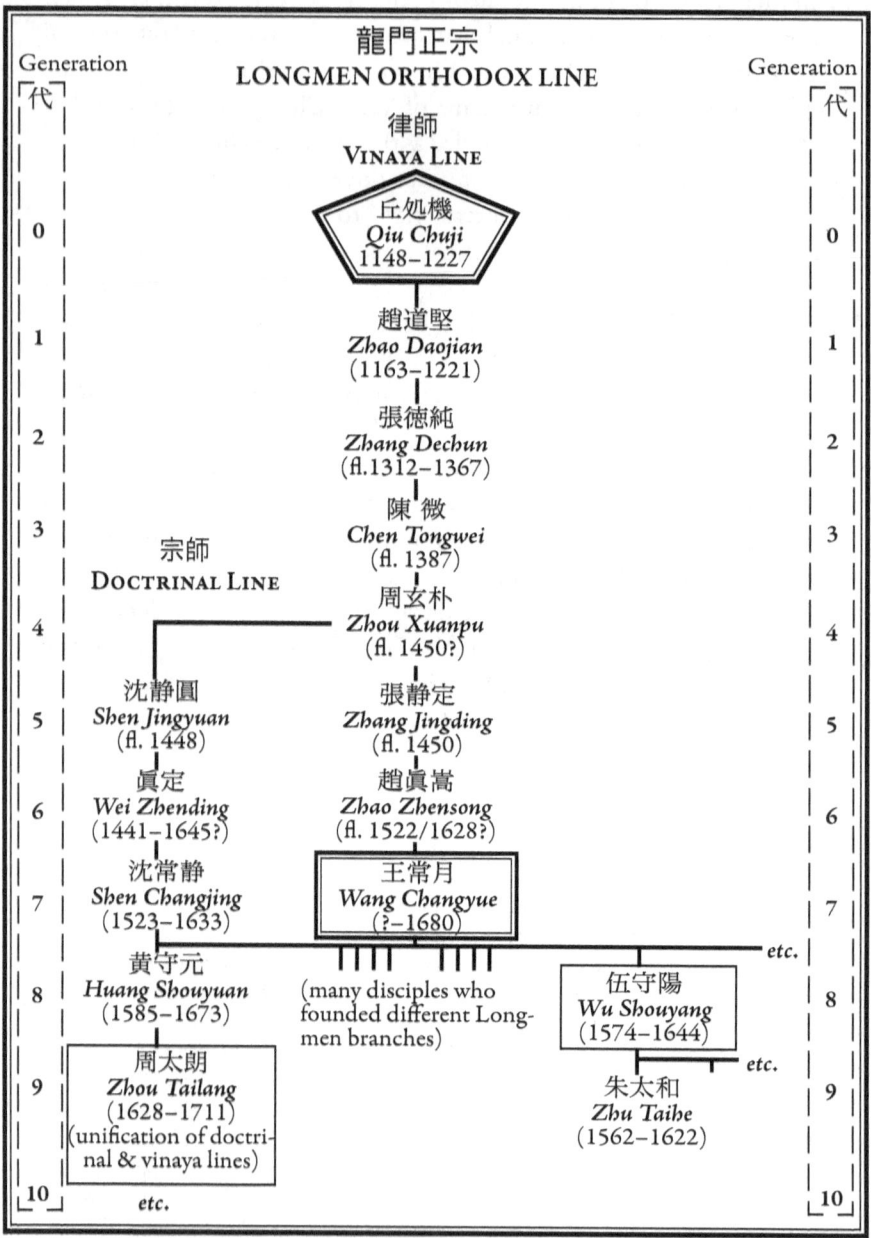

Fig. 3: Vinaya and Doctrinal Lines of the Longmen Tradition

Wang Changyue (d. 1680), the Longmen Reformer

Wang Changyue 王常月, the seventh Longmen patriarch (Fig. 3, 7th generation of the Vinaya line), is considered to be the main reformer of this school but can actually be regarded as its founder. He is said to have revived the ancient tradition of Qiu Chuji 邱處機 (1148–1227) and restored the Vinaya Line (*lüzong* 律宗) of the Most High Laozi by recovering the Daoist discipline and establishing an organized Longmen lineage.[7] According to his biographers, he was born in the prefecture of Lu'an 潞安 (Shanxi) in a family of Daoist practitioners.[8] His attraction to this religion was boosted by a miraculous cure from a serious disease.[9] He then left his family and went travelling around famous mountains to search for enlightened masters. Finally, in 1628, he met Zhao Zhensong 趙眞嵩 (Fuyang 復陽) on Mount Wangwu 王屋 (Henan).[10] Zhao was the sixth Longmen patriarch and heir

---

[7] Postface [1663] to the *Longmen xinfa* 龍門心法 by Shao Shoushan 邵守善 and Zhan Shouchun 詹守椿, *Zangwai daoshu* 藏外道書 6: 785 (hereafter abbreviated as ZWDS); and *Biyuan tanjing* 碧苑壇經, j. *shang*, chap. 1 (ZWDS 10:159). See also *Yin zhenren Donghua zhengmai huangji hepi zhengdao xianjing* 尹真人東華正脈皇極闔闢證道仙經, j. *xia*, chap. 10 (DZXB 1: 5b/2).

[8] Some biographers claim he was born in 1522, while others mention 1594 (see *Jingai xinden* 金蓋心燈 1: 1.16b; hereafter abbreviated as JGXD). For his life see JGXD 1: 1.15a–17b; *Daotong yuanliu zhi* 道統源流志 *xia* 2 (hereafter abbreviated as DTYL); "Kunyang Wang zhenren daoxing bei 崑陽王真人道行碑," in Oyanagi Shigeta 小柳司氣太, *Baiyun guan zhi* (jap. Hakuunkan shi) 白雲觀志 4.162–163, Tokyo: Tōhō bunka gakuin Tōkyō kenkyūjo, 1934 (hereafter abbreviated as BYGZ); *Changchun daojiao yuanliu* 長春道教源流 7.163 (hereafter abbreviated as DJYL). See also Esposito, "La Porte du Dragon," 91–101 and "The Longmen School" {here above, Chapter Two}; Qing Xitai 卿希泰 (ed.), *Zhongguo daojiao* 中國道教, 4 Vols. Shanghai: Zhishi 知識, 1994, vol. 1:392–93; and Qing Xitai 卿希泰 (ed.), *Zhongguo daojiao shi* 中國道教史, 4 vols, Chengdu: Sichuan Renmin, 1996, vol. 4: 79–100.

[9] This story is only reported by Min Yide who, as representative of the Longmen branch of Mount Jingai, intends to show that the reformer Wang Changyue also strongly appreciated Daoist healing techniques. See JGXD 1: 1.15. Wang Changyue is in fact supposed to have been attracted, in particular, by the divine healing powers of Zhang Mayi 張麻衣. Mayi daozhe 麻衣道者 was a nickname of the immortal Lü Dongbin 呂洞賓, as well as of the purported master who transmitted the Taiji diagram 太極圖 to Chen Tuan 陳摶 (ca. 906–989). {See also p. 95 above.}

[10] *Biyuan tanjing* 碧苑壇經 (Platform Sūtra of the Jade Garden), transmitted by Wang Changyue 王常月, compiled by Shi Shouping 施守平 and revised by Min Yide. Reprinted in ZWDS 10, here 186.

of the Longmen Vinaya line[11] which he transmitted to Wang along with the lineage name of Changyue 常月 (Constant Through the Months).[12] As seventh Longmen Vinaya Master (lüshi 律師), Wang kept on roaming with the clouds, studying the classics of the Three Teachings (sanjiao 三教) and visiting other masters until he met Zhao once again at Mount Jiugong 九宮 (Hubei). This time Zhao prophesied that Wang was going to become the main reformer of Daoist discipline at the capital. In 1655, this prophecy was confirmed: Wang was in fact appointed abbot of the dominant Quanzhen abbey, the Baiyun guan 白雲觀 in Beijing. In 1656 he began to perform public ordinations for Daoist novices. The content of these ordinations was established by Wang Changyue in the 1656 work entitled *Chuzhen jielü* 初真戒律 (Code of Precepts of Initial Perfection)[13] as well as in a later compilation by Wang's disciples that is known under the title of *Biyuan tanjing* 碧苑壇經 (Platform Sūtra of the Jade Garden), an allusion to the famous *Platform Sūtra* of the Sixth Chan Patriarch Huineng 慧能.[14]

---

[11] For Zhao's life see JGXD 1: 1.11a-12b; BYGZ 1.35; DTYL xia 1. According to JGXD, the Longmen lineage (see Fig. 3) was divided from the fourth Patriarch Zhou Xuanpu 周玄朴 (Zhou Dazhuo 周大拙, d. ca. 1450) into two lines: the line of the Vinaya Masters (lüshi 律師) led by Zhang Jingding 張靜定 (Zhang Wuwo 張無我, fl. 1450) and the line of the Doctrinal or Founding Masters (zongshi 宗師) led by Shen Jingyuan 沈靜圓 (Shen Dunkong 沈頓空); see Esposito, "La Porte du Dragon," 106–111 and "The Longmen School" {here above, Chapter Two}.

[12] The lineage name (paiming 派名 or ming 名) marks the entry for a Buddhist monk or a Daoist adept into an ancestral line of masters and is also regarded as the symbol of his separation from his original lay-life. In the Longmen school, the lineage name was composed of two characters, the first of which was taken from a Longmen poem that was used character by character to name Longmen patriarchs generation by generation; see Yoshioka, "Taoist Monastic Life," 231. For the Buddhist counterpart see Welch, *The Practice of Chinese Buddhism*, 279–285.

[13] This text is found in the *Chongkan Daozang jiyao* 重刊道藏輯要 (hereafter abbreviated as DZJY) vol. 24 (zhangji 張集 7: 25a-61b); and ZWDS 12:13–31. For a brief survey of this text's content see Catherine Despeux, "Chuzhen jielü," in *The Encyclopedia of Taoism*, ed. by Fabrizio Pregadio, vol. 1:284–85. London: Routledge, 2008. {See also Monica Esposito, *Creative Daoism*, Part Two.}

[14] This text is found in the first volume of Min Yide 閔一得, *Gu Shuyinlou cangshu* 古書隱樓藏書, Wuxing: Jingai Chunyang gong cangban, 1904 (hereafter abbreviated as YLCS). I use here the reprint in ZWDS (10:158–217). Another version of this text is also known under the title *Longmen xinfa* 龍門心法 [Core Teachings of the Longmen], ZWDS 6:727–785. It shows some differences with the *Biyuan tanjing* 碧苑壇經 that would be worthy of further study. For the influence of the *Platform Sūtra* of Chan's Sixth Patriarch Huineng from different perspectives see Fo Kuang shan (ed.), *The Sixth Patriarch Platform Sūtra in Religious and Cultural Perspec-*

The *Biyuan tanjing* consists of discourses by Wang Changyue held during an ordination in 1663 at the Biyuan abbey in Nanjing. The focus of the ceremony lies on inculcating a strong desire to realize enlightenment. This is said to be achieved through the progressive path of the so-called "ordination of the threefold altar" (*santan dajie* 三壇大戒).[15] As we will see, it was intended for both lay and monastic believers and tailored by Wang to meet the needs of the ruling class.

The Precepts as the Means to Attain Immortality

The key word of Wang's teaching is *jie* 戒 (precepts), which represents "the staff for subduing the demons" (*xiangmo zhi chu* 降魔之杵), "the talisman for protecting life" (*huming zhi fu* 護命之符), "the ladder for ascending to Heaven" (*shengtian zhi ti* 昇天之梯), "the lamp for illuminating the way" (*yinlu zhi deng* 引路之燈), etc.[16] According to Wang, the meaning of *jie* 戒 lies in the daily practice of "subduing the discursive mind and following the Path." In its truest sense it addresses neither monastic precepts nor external behavior but the genuine mind (*zhenxin* 真心): "Keep the precepts in your mind, as you would keep something in your hand; once you let go of it, it gets lost. Likewise, once the precepts in your mind are abandoned, they are broken."[17] By making use of this mind for keeping the precepts, "one can

---

tive (Report of the International Conference on Ch'an Buddhism). Taichong: Fo Kuang shan, 1989. On the meaning of the term *tan* 壇 as referring to a precepts or ordination platform (*jietan* 戒壇), see Paul Groner, "The Ordination Ritual in the Platform Sūtra within the Context of the East Asian Buddhist Vinaya Tradition," in the same volume, 220–250 (here 220–222).

[15] This term refers in the Buddhist context to an ordination conferred in three stages or acts: (1) the novice ordination, (2) the *bhiksu/bhiksuni* ordination or complete ordination, and (3) the Bodhisattva ordination. See Karl Ludwig Reichelt, *Truth and Tradition in Chinese Buddhism*, 229–240. Taipei: SMC. Publishing Inc. 1990 (1st ed. 1927). I follow here the more literal translation given by Bianchi: "Generally in China the precepts of novitiate, complete ordination and the Bodhisattva precepts are conferred in one unique session during the period called 'ordination of the threefold altar'" (Ester Bianchi, *The Iron Statue Monastery*, 90. Firenze: Leo S. Olschki, 2001.) {For more information see Monica Esposito, *Creative Daoism*, Part Two.}

[16] *Biyuan tanjing* 碧苑壇經, ZWDS 10:168.

[17] *Biyuan tanjing* 碧苑壇經, ZWDS 10:169. Unless otherwise indicated all translations are mine.

attain immortality and realize the Path."[18] In fact, the respect for precepts is thus portrayed in a systematic way as a process of gradual practice corresponding to different levels of control of body (*shen* 身), mind (*xin* 心) and intention (*yi* 意)[19] that leads to the realization of the Highest Vehicle (*zuishang cheng* 最上乘) of the Celestial Immortality (*tianxian* 天仙). According to Wang, this necessitates three stages of ordination :

(1) The Initial Precepts of Perfection (*chuzhen jie* 初真戒) which are intended for male and female novices, as well as laymen and laywomen. They consist of:

    (a) Taking Refuge in the Three Jewels (Dao, sacred scriptures, and master);[20]

    (b) Five cardinal lay precepts;[21]

    (c) Ten precepts for novices;[22]

    (d) Nine precepts for women.[23]

---

[18] *Biyuan tanjing* 碧苑壇經, ZWDS 10:161. In fact, for Wang the "attaining of immortality" is a synonym of "enlightenment" since "Immortal and Buddha are of the same mind." See ZWDS 10:208.

[19] On these three concepts see Robinet, *Introduction à l'alchimie intérieure*, 193–195. It is interesting to note that Wang Changyue calls them *sanbao* 三寶 (three jewels) and puts them in connection with the refuge in the Three Jewels (Dao, sacred scriptures, and master). See *Biyuan tanjing* 碧苑壇經, ZWDS 10:160. The term *sanbao* is also used in inner alchemy for designating the three alchemical ingredients: *jing* 精, *qi* 氣, and *shen* 神.

[20] *Biyuan tanjing* 碧苑壇經, ZWDS 10:159–162; and *Chuzhen jielü* 初真戒律, DZJY 24 *zhangji* 7:34a-b and ZWDS 12:17.

[21] For the Five Precepts that are quoted in the *Chuzhen jielü* 初真戒律 under the section "Taishang Laojun suoming zhigong guigen wujie" 太上老君所命积功歸根五戒 (DZJY 24 *zhangji* 7: 34b-35a and ZWDS 12:18), see the *Taishang Laojun jiejing* 太上老君戒經 (DZ 784, fasc. 562). They consist of the five precepts of Buddhism: to abstain from killing, intoxication, lying, sexual misconduct, and stealing.

[22] The list of the Ten Precepts is given in the *Chuzhen jielü* under the section "Xuhuang tianzun suoming chuzhen shijie" 虛皇天尊所命初真十戒 (DZJY 24 *zhangji* 7: 35a-35b; ZWDS 12:17) which corresponds to *Xuhuang tianzun shijie wen* 虛皇天尊十戒文 (DZ 180, fasc. 77). See Mori Yuria 森由利亞, "Zenshinkyō ryūmonha keifu kō" 全真教龍門派系譜考, in Dōkyō bunka kenkyūkai (ed.), *Dōkyō bunka e no tenbō* 道教文化への展望, 197–198, Tokyo: Hirakawa, 1994. During the Tang, they constituted the Precepts of Initial Perfection that were intended for those who "leave the family" (Kristofer Schipper. "Taoist Ordination Ranks in the Tunhuang Manuscripts," in *Religion und Philosophie in Ostasien. Festschrift für Hans Steininger*, ed. by Gert Naundorf et al., 130. Würzburg: Königshausen & Neumann, 1985). See also Despeux, "Chuzhen jielü."

[23] *Chuzhen jielü* (DZJY 24 *zhangji* 7: 58a-b and ZWDS 12:29). For a translation see

(2) The Intermediate Precepts (*zhongji jie* 中極戒) which consist of three hundred precepts given to Daoist priests since the Six Dynasties and compiled according to the precepts for Buddhist monks.[24]

(3) The Great Precepts of the Celestial Immortals (*tianxian dajie* 天仙大戒) which often reformulate the content of the preceding precepts from a more doctrinal point of view.[25] Only those who observe all of these precepts are in a position to ordain others.

According to Wang, the Initial Precepts of Perfection "teach one how to control the body of form (*seshen* 色身) without letting it erroneously move and rashly act;" the Intermediate Precepts "teach to subdue the illusory mind (*huanxin* 幻心) without allowing delusions and wild thoughts to arise;" and the Great Precepts of the Celestial Immortals "teach freeing the True Intention (*zhenyi* 真意) without being bound by attachments."[26]

ALLUSION TO CHAN BUDDHISM IN WANG'S SOTERIOLOGICAL DOCTRINE

Wang compares this three-stage ordination with the teachings of the Sixth Chan Patriarch in the *Platform Sūtra* concerning *śīla* (*jie* 戒, discipline), *dhyāna* (*ding* 定, concentration) and *prajñā* (*hui* 慧, wisdom): "The Initial Precepts of Perfection are *śīla*, the Intermediate Precepts are *dhyāna*,

---

Catherine Despeux, *Immortelles de la Chine ancienne*, 147–155. Puiseaux: Pardès, 1990.

[24] The list of 300 precepts is given in the *Zhongji jie* 中極戒 under the title "Zhongji Shangqing dongzhen zhihui guanshen dajie jing" 中極上清洞真智慧觀身大戒經 (DZJY 24 *zhangji* 7: 62a-79b and ZWDS 12: 31–40), whose content brings to mind the *Shangqing dongzhen zhihui guanshen dajie wen* 上清洞真智慧觀身大戒文 (DZ 1364, fac. 1039). See also Schipper, "Taoist Ordination Ranks," 131; and Toshiaki Yamada, "The Lingbao school," in *Daoism Handbook*, ed. by Livia Kohn, 248. Leiden: Brill, 2000.

[25] A list of these precepts does not appear in Wang's works. However, one is included in the *Santan yuanman tianxian dajie lüeshuo* 三壇圓滿天仙大戒略說 by Liu Shouyuan 柳守元 (DZJY 24, *zhangji* 7; ZWDS 12). See also Min Zhiting 閔智亭, *Daojiao yifan* 道教儀範, 86–116. Beijing: Zhongguo daojiao xueyuan, 1990.

[26] *Biyuan tanjing* 碧苑壇經, ZWDS 10:180. I follow here the substitution of *wanxin* 頑心 (vain mind) by *huanxin* 幻心 (illusory mind), as in *Longmen xinfa* 龍門心法, ZWDS 6: 750.

and the Precepts of the Celestial Immortals are *prajñā*."[27] All of these precepts represent "the practice of subduing and taming the body, mind and Intention; they are the marvellous jewel of the Golden Elixir (*jindan* 金丹) which transcends the worldly and goes beyond the ordinary."[28]

"*Dhyāna* is the house, *sīla* is the way to go home, *prajñā* is the host, and all beings, affairs and circumstances are the guests."[29] Discipline is thus fundamental in Wang's teachings. It implies a strong respect for precepts since *sīla* forms the basis for the spiritual development brought about by *dhyāna* and *prajñā*. All the different alchemical techniques and arts of immortality are encompassed by *dhyāna* and *prajñā* since they concern one's innate Nature or genuine mind.[30]

As a consequence, Wang regarded the cultivation of innate Nature as the fundamental practice of the Incomparable and Supreme Great Vehicle (*zuishang wushang dacheng* 最上無上大乘) and saw this vehicle as congruent with the original meaning of Quanzhen, an orthodox meditative path that regards "purity, tranquillity and non-action" (*qingjing wuwei* 清淨無為) to be the key to self-cultivation.[31] Compared to this, various alchemical techniques are seen as belonging to the "small vehicle" (*xiaocheng* 小乘) or the "small path" (*xiaodao* 小道) as they fail to provide insight into one's own Nature.[32] Wang criticized alchemical methods and their language because they are prone to be misunderstood by masters and adepts who take their symbols as reality.[33] Rather, before devoting oneself to a practice, one must let go of the deluded mind, and before sitting in meditation one must

---

[27] *Biyuan tanjing* 碧苑壇經, ZWDS 10:181. As can be seen, the precepts substitute the original meaning of the Golden Elixir (i.e., the inner alchemical path).

[28] *Biyuan tanjing* 碧苑壇經, ZWDS 10:180.

[29] *Biyuan tanjing* 碧苑壇經, ZWDS 10:183.

[30] *Biyuan tanjing* 碧苑壇經, ZWDS 10:181.

[31] *Biyuan tanjing* 碧苑壇經, ZWDS 10:176, 194–195. On the importance of purity and tranquillity in the Quanzhen meditative path see Yao Tao-chung, "Chuanchen: A New Taoist Sect in North China during the 12th and 13th centuries." Ph. D. diss., University of Arizona, 1980.

[32] *Biyuan tanjing* 碧苑壇經, ZWDS 10:194.

[33] Wang explains his teaching in a way similar to the Quanzhen recorded sayings (*yulu* 語錄). He quotes many anecdotes and parables and refuses esoteric interpretations; see Vincent Goossaert, "Yulu Recorded Sayings," in *The Encyclopedia of Taoism*, ed. by Fabrizio Pregadio, vol. 2, 1200–1202. London: Routledge, 2008.

reflect on one's affective attachments (*aiyuan* 愛緣); otherwise, one will persist in "cultivating without insight and engaging in blind sitting."[34]

Confucian Self-education and Buddhist Soteriology: the "Path of Men" and the "Path of Immortals" in a Daoist Perspective

For Wang, the fact that man has an impermanent body forms the basis of the necessity to follow a well-regulated path starting with respect for the Initial Precepts of Perfection. The "body of form" (*seshen* 色身) is the source of the contamination of original purity. As it is formed by the aggregation of the four elements and arises from the union of the father's semen and the mother's blood, it obscures the True Nature (*zhenxing* 真性) or Absolute Body (*fashen* 法身, *dharmakāya*). Conversely, since according to Wang the Absolute Body is inside the body of form, it can through constant training become master of the external body of form and employ it for good actions.[35] This constant training can be ensured by a genuine education. Mixing Confucian and Buddhist theories, Wang stresses the power of *sīla* for regaining the original status of men through the so-called "path of men" (*rendao* 人道). Following Confucius and Mencius, he affirms the importance of true education, which consists of a self-education and a "self-illuminative sincerity."[36] If Mencius wrote that "there is no greater joy than examining oneself and being sincere,"[37] Wang proclaims that "this sincerity is *sīla*."[38] Because "the Dao exists in the heart, not in books,"[39] it can be revealed through true respect of Confucian ethics (summarized by the three rules and five social relationships, *sangang wuchang* 三綱五常, which

---

[34] *Longmen xinfa* 龍門心法, ZWDS 6:746.
[35] *Biyuan tanjing* 碧苑壇經, ZWDS 10:180–81, 199.
[36] *Mencius*, 6A:15, *The Doctrine of the Mean*, 21, cited by Hsueh-li Cheng, "Psychology, ontology and soteriology in the Platform Sūtra," in *The Sixth Patriarch Platform Sūtra in Religious and Cultural Perspective*, ed by Fo Kuang shan, 105–106. Taichong: Fo Kuang shan, 1989.
[37] *Mencius*, 7A: 4, see Cheng, "Psychology, ontology and soteriology," 106.
[38] *Biyuan tanjing* 碧苑壇經, ZWDS 10: 206.
[39] *Longmen xinfa* 龍門心法, ZWDS 6: 747.

thus form a fundamental prerequisite for realizing the "path of immortals" (*xiandao* 仙道). To quote Wang:

> If one desires to cultivate the path of immortals, one must at first cultivate the path of men. As long as the path of men has not yet been cultivated, the path of immortals will be remote. The Confucians say that only after having harmonized one's family can one pacify the country. Harmonizing the family corresponds to the path of men, and pacifying the country to the path of immortals.
>
> 慾修仙道。先修人道。人道未修。仙道遠矣。儒門曰先齊其家。而后可以治國。齊家猶人道。治國猶仙道。⁴⁰

In his *Chuzhen jielü* 初真戒律, Wang proclaims: "For the visible, there is the royal method (Confucianism), and for the hidden, the Daoist method. Daoist precepts govern the individual, royal precepts the multitude. Both are complementary for supporting the world."[41]

Such promotion of lay ethics was designed to receive support from the ruling class, which wanted both lay people and monks to follow social rules. In fact, Wang further tried to harmonize lay and monastic status through explanations such as: "Secular and religious teachings both are of the same spirit."[42] According to Wang, "the saints who wanted to transcend the secular teachings purified the mind according to them,"[43] and "the path for transcending the world (Daoism as religious path) becomes the royal path (Confucianism as secular path) for those who have the will."[44] In this perspective, differences between Confucianism and Daoism vanished; both the "path of men" and the "path of immortals" focus on the same original nature or genuine mind and are both vehicles for restoring its original purity.

Wang's doctrine may thus be regarded as a real effort to reform Daoism by attempting a strong conciliation with Neo-Confucian "orthodoxy." Ac-

---

[40] *Biyuan tanjing* 碧苑壇經, ZWDS 10: 193. While Wang Changyue attributed this sentence to a generic immortal master or masters (*xianshi* 仙師), Min Yide clearly links it to Patriarch Lü (Lüzu 呂祖); see also note 98 below.

[41] *Chuzhen jielü* 初真戒律, DZJY 24, zhangji 7: 30a and ZWDS 12:15.

[42] *Biyuan tanjing* 碧苑壇經, ZWDS 10: 174. See also the version in *Longmen xinfa* (ZWDS 6: 741) which is slightly different.

[43] *Biyuan tanjing* 碧苑壇經, ZWDS 10: 191.

[44] *Longmen xinfa* 龍門心法, ZWDS 6: 766. In *Biyuan tanjing* 碧苑壇經 (ZWDS 10: 194), the Royal Path (*wangdao* 王道) is substituted by the Orthodox Path (*zhengdao* 正道).

cording to the pragmatic tendency of his time,⁴⁵ Wang stressed religious cultivation and offered a practical method of salvation through the three-stage ordination, described above, with discipline as its fundamental prerequisite. It reaffirms the ideal Quanzhen path which, modeled on Chan Buddhism, emphasizes the importance of ascetic training (the search for a right master, the necessity of engaging in physically demanding pilgrimage, etc.) while rejecting alchemical practices and healing techniques that vainly seek to prolong life. For Wang, the body of form (*seshen* 色身) must die by nature, and the only thing that is permanent is the inner Absolute Body (*fashen* 法身). Once this is understood one can, through concentration and wisdom, ultimately realize the highest path of Celestial Immortals. Free of all exterior and interior marks, the Celestial Immortal is a fully ordained Daoist priest who, like the Bodhisattva, or the Confucian saint, is in a position to save the world.

The Creation of Longmen Branches after Wang Changyue

Due to the effort of Wang Changyue, an official Longmen lineage was established at Beijing's Baiyun guan, and Longmen became the main school in charge of public ordinations for all Daoist priests in North and South China. Wang ordained thousands of disciples in Beijing, Nanjing, Hangzhou, and elsewhere, and thanks to him Longmen has remained the dominant lineage to this day.⁴⁶

---

⁴⁵ The late sixteenth and the early seventeenth centuries were the "period that witnessed the beginning of a new emphasis on empiricism—the pursuit of 'practical learning.'" Late Ming thinkers were interested in practical methods of spiritual cultivation and regarded theoretical discourse unrelated to practice as useless (de Bary, "Individualism and Humanitarism," "Neo-Confucian Cultivation," and *The Trouble with Confucianism*). The work of Wang Changyue inserts itself in this context and has its counterpart in the contemporaneous Buddhist revival of monastic discipline by the reformer Zhuhong (1535–1615); see Yü Chun-fang. *The Renewal of Buddhism in China: Chu-hung and the Late Ming Synthesis*, 2–8. New York: Columbia University Press, 1981. See also note 119 below.

⁴⁶ Preface (1674) by Long Qiqian 龍起潛 to the *Chuzhen jielü* 初真戒律 (DZJY 24 zhangji 7: 37b, and BYGZ 白雲觀志 31–57, 163). Wang Changyue obtained from the court the title of Guoshi 國師 (Preceptor of State) and after his death the posthumous title of Baoyi gaoshi 抱一高師 (Eminent Master Embracing the One). On

In Wang's wake, various Longmen branches were founded. While some were affiliated with temples belonging to famous schools, such as Shangqing 上清, Jingming 淨明, Lingbao 靈寶, others flourished at less noted centers. In Hangzhou, for example, there were branches of the Tianzhu guan 天柱觀, Jin'gu dong 金鼓洞, and Dade guan 大德觀; on Mt. Tongbai 桐柏山 in Tiantai 天台 (Zhejiang) a branch of Tongbai gong 桐柏宮; and on Mt. Jingai 金蓋 (Huzhou 湖州, Zhejiang) a branch of Yunchao 雲巢. Longmen branches were also present in Southwest China, for example the Longmen Tantric branch of Xizhu xinzong 西竺心宗 on Mt. Jizu 雞足 (Yunnan), or in the Northeast, for instance, the Gansu 甘肅 branch of the eleventh patriarch Liu Yiming 劉一明 (1734–1821).[47]

Today, the different Longmen branches are barely known. Their study will be of utmost importance not only for deepening our understanding of the formation of the Longmen official school, but also for its different doctrines and practices that appear to reflect the variety of its branches and the originality of its founding patriarchs. Here, I limit myself to presenting the Longmen branch of Mount Jingai 金蓋山 and its most influential figure: the author of the fundamental history of the Longmen lineage and most important compiler of Longmen texts, Min Yide 閔一得 (1758–1836).

The Local Jingaishan Tradition and its Founding Patriarchs

According to Min Yide's *Jingai xindeng* 金蓋心燈, Mt. Jingai 金蓋山 (Huzhou 湖州, Zhejiang) was affiliated with Longmen around the end of the Ming dynasty via Tao Jing'an 陶靜菴 (d. 1673) and Huang Chiyang 黃赤陽 (1595–1673).[48] Tao and Huang are said to be the direct disciples of the seventh Longmen patriarch Wang Changyue. Tao Jing'an allegedly visited

---

the question of historical reality of such an establishment of the Longmen lineage by Wang Changyue see Esposito, "The Longmen School" {here above, Chapter 2; and in addition Part One of Esposito, *Creative Daoism*}.

[47] Qing Xitai 卿希泰 (ed.), *Zhongguo daojiao shi* 中國道教史, vol. 4: 100–181, Chengdu: Sichuan Renmin, 1996.

[48] See respectively the biographies of Zhao Xujing and Wang Changyue in *Jingai xindeng* 金蓋心燈. For a more detailed analysis of these two biographies, as well their sources, and their contradictions see Esposito, "The Longmen School," 625–631 and 647–654 {here above, Chapter 2, pp. 62–66 and 90–100}.

Baiyun guan in 1658 and met patriarch Wang. Wang promptly recognized Tao as Longmen heir and transmitted to him the precepts and lineage name Shouzhen (守貞). Via this Vinaya investiture, Tao inherited the orthodox Longmen ancestry and came to be recognized as founding patriarch of the Longmen tradition at Jingaishan. In order to legitimize this event, *Jingai xindeng* tells us that Wang Changyue had transmitted to Tao in 1658 the Daoist regalia and manuscripts, thus enabling him to celebrate proper abbot's services at his local temple on Mt. Jingai.[49] Strengthened by such prestige, Tao one year later (1659) brought his fellow Daoist Huang Chiyang to Baiyuan guan so that he could also have the privilege to meet Wang and obtain directly from him the precepts and lineage name.[50] Thus, Huang was recognized as founder of the Longmen line at Hangzhou's Dade guan 大德觀. As for Huang's line, the transmission of the regalia proper to the office of abbot was only conferred via Tao Jing'an. On his deathbed, Tao allegedly ordered to transfer the regalia inherited from Wang Changyue to Huang's disciple, Zhou Mingyang 周明陽 (1628–1711), the future founding patriarch of Hangzhou's Jingu dong 金鼓洞.[51]

By recording these meetings at Baiyun guan and the legendary transmission of regalia to Tao, Min Yide's *Jingai xindeng* creates not only a direct connection between Jingaishan and Baiyun guan in form of this link between Wang and the two future Longmen patriarchs of Mt. Jingai, but in addition empowers Mt. Jingai as the radiating center of Longmen ordination in Jiangnan. Thanks to the mediation of the Founding Patriarch Tao Jing'an, Jingaishan's authority thus soon extended to related Jiangnan temples such as Hangzhou's Dadeguan 大德觀 and Jingu dong 金鼓洞.

In parallel with this myth of Vinaya investiture at Baiyun guan, the two local figures, Tao and Huang, are also presented in *Jingai xindeng* as the two managers of Mt. Jingai's Patriarch-Lü altar 呂祖宗壇 that had allegedly been established around the end of the Song era in honor of Lü Dongbin 呂洞賓. As the center of revelation of Lü Dongbin's texts via spirit writing in Jiangnan, this altar is central to the scriptural tradition of Mt. Jingai. In their role of managers of Lü Dongbin's altar, Tao and Huang are said to have met

---

[49] *Jingai xindeng* 金蓋心燈 j. 2, 21b; ZWDS 31:195. It is worthy of note that the *Daotong yuanliu zhi* 道統源流志 (xia 3–4), though it makes no mention of any direct meeting between Tao and Wang at Baiyun guan, also reports the transmission of regalia from Wang to Tao.

[50] *Jingai xindeng* 金蓋心燈 j. 2, 23a–26a; DTYL xia 4.

[51] *Jingai xindeng* 金蓋心燈 j. 2, 18b–19a; ZWDS 31:194.

Wang Changyue one more time. This encounter is staged at Hangzhou's Zongyang gong 宗陽宮 where the Vinaya Patriarch Wang recognizes Tao and Huang as orthodox recipients of the quintessential doctrine revealed by Lü Dongbin in form of the *Golden Flower*. As remembered by Tao Taiding 陶太定 (alias: Shi'an 石菴, ?-1692), the successor of Tao and Huang's Jingaishan altar, this encounter took place as follows:

> It was in the autumn of the *wuchen* year of the Kangxi era (1688) that the Patriarch of Vinaya [Wang Changyue] came down from North to South and stayed at Hangzhou's Zongyang gong. [Tao] Jing'an and [Huang] Yinzhen went to visit him and presented him this scripture. The Patriarch of Vinaya solemnly bowed, and after having read it he said: "The mind-to-mind transmission of the Supreme Lord (Laozi) is fully expressed in this scripture. This is the method for the perfect practice in this world ... So I order you, my fellows, to remember this, and for this purpose I transmit the printing blocks [of the *Golden Flower*] to posterity." May the disciples of the younger generation make efforts! Sincerely stated by Taiding (Tao Shi'an ?-1692).
>
> 時為康熙戊辰秋、律祖自北南來、館於杭城宗陽宮。靖庵、隱真往謁、呈上此書。律師鄭重其儀、拜而閱之曰："太上心傳、備於此矣。是乃即世圓行之功法 … 二三子毋自欺、亦毋自恃、大行正有待也。" 乃命小子識之。今故附梓於後、後學者勉之、太定謹白。[52]

In this legendary encounter with Tao Jing'an and Huang Chiyang, Patriarch Wang Changyue is thus adduced as a witness for the claim that the fundamental Lü Dongbin scripture known as *Golden Flower* embodies the direct transmission of the Highest Lord Laozi for saving the world. At the end of this passage, Tao Taiding 陶太定 (better known as Tao Shi'an 陶石菴), the successor of Tao and Huang at Mt. Jingai's Lüzu altar, is said to have commemorated this event on the occasion of the publication of the *Golden Flower* for the benefit of future generations. Because this is an event of memory rather than a historical event, one can easily understand why it had to happen in 1688. In fact, all three protagonists of this legendary encounter—the Vinaya Patriarch Wang and his two Longmen heirs at Jingaishan, Tao and Huang—were (at least according to their biographies included in the *Jingai xindeng*) already dead at that time. Rather than being a macabre

---

[52] *Jinhua zongzhi* 金華宗旨, ZWDS 10: 338.

encounter of the living dead, this invented meeting commemorates the date of the *Golden Flower*'s revelation at Patriarch Lü's altar on Mt. Jingai and creates the memory of its legitimization by Wang Changyue, the legendary promoter of Longmen orthodoxy.[53] Through this ideal act of legitimization by Wang Changyue, Jingaishan's Lüzu altar and its revelation (as embodied in the *Golden Flower*) are recognized as heirs of the Daoist orthodox mind-to-mind transmission in Jiangnan. Closely associated with Lü Dongbin's cult and its lore, the Jingaishan local tradition thus came to be integrated into a more universal perspective of orthodoxy symbolically incarnated as the Longmen Vinaya tradition of Baiyunguan. The double identity of Jingaishan's Lüzu altar is also well illustrated by the following words recorded in *Jingai xindeng*'s biography of Tao Shi'an 陶石菴:

> The above-mentioned [Jingaishan altar] inherits the tradition of Lü [Dongbin] and Wei [Zhengjie], without replacing the Vinaya school of Qiu [Chuji] and Wang [Changyue].
> 上承呂衛之宗、不替邱王律派.[54]

This is a good indication that the local tradition of Mount Jingai was seen as associated both with the worship of Lü Dongbin and the Confucian academic tradition of Wei Zhengjie 衛正節. Wei was a renowned local figure connected with Mt. Jingai, a virtuous Confucian who, after having left his post and founded the private academy Baishe shuyuan 白社書院 at Shijintang 石涇塘 (Zhejiang), had withdrawn at the end of the Song dynasty to Mt. Jingai and founded its Shuyinlou 書隱樓 library.[55] Renamed Gu Shuyinlou 古書隱樓, this collection was inherited by Min Yide and represented the scriptural sanctuary of Jingaishan at which Min's scriptures were later to be published under the title of *Gu Shuyinlou cangshu* 古書隱樓藏書. In this way, the Jingaishan local community could pledge allegiance to both its local identity flag and the Longmen universal flag. This means that it agreed to put its local cults, embodied in its Patriarch Lü altar, under the symbolical and universal Longmen authority of Baiyun guan represented by Qiu Chuji, the legendary Jin-Yuan era Daoist leader and mythical found-

---

[53] See the biographies of these three masters in JGXD. Min Yide could have also chosen another date such as 1664 when, according to a JGXD gloss (j. 2, p. 4a/line 3–4), Wang Changyue visited Hangzhou's Zongyang gong and when Tao and Huang should still have been alive. {See here below, pp. 167–168}

[54] JGXD 金蓋心燈 3, 10a, ZWDS 31:213.

[55] JGXD 金蓋心燈 7, 15-6a, ZWDS 31:303–4.

er of the Longmen, and Wang Changyue, the celebrated promoter of Longmen Vinaya transmission 律宗 at the capital.

Min Yide, the Main Compiler of Longmen Texts

Min Yide 閔一得 (1758–1836) hailed from a distinguished family of Wuxing 吳興, today's town of Huzhou 湖州, in Zhejiang.[56] His father, Min Genfu 閔艮甫, was a provincial graduate (*juren* 舉人) in Henan who, worrying about the weak constitution of his son, took Min Yide to Mount Tongbai 桐柏山 in Tiantai 天台 (Zhejiang).[57] Here, Gao Dongli 高東籬 (?-1768), the tenth Longmen patriarch of the Tongbai branch,[58] transmitted Daoist gymnastics (*daoyin* 導引) to the young man. Min also met Gao's disciple Shen Yibing 沈一炳 (1708–1786), who became his main master and taught him the basic Longmen principles.[59] Interestingly, the Longmen

---

[56] For Min Yide's biographies see his *Jingai xindeng* 金蓋心燈 (henceforth abbreviated as JGXD) 1 and 10 ; Esposito, "La Porte du Dragon," 127–134; and Esposito, "Daoism in the Qing," 630–631 {here above, Chapter 1, 15–17}.

[57] Despite his classical education, Min Genfu did not dislike to send his son to Daoists for curing him. Daoists were regarded as expert healers and principal holders of life-prolonging techniques that were well appreciated by the lettered classes (see for example Farzeen Baldrian-Hussein, "Taoist Beliefs in Literary Circles of the Song Dynasty—Su Shi (1037–1101) and his Technique of Survival," *Cahiers d'Extrême-Asie* 9 (1996–97): 15–53; Liu Ts'un-yan, "Taoist Self-Cultivation in Ming Thought," in *Self and Society in Ming Thought*, ed. by Wm Theodore de Bary, 291–326. New York: Columbia University Press, 1970; and Liu Ts'un-yan, "The Penetration of Taoism into the Ming Neo-Confucian Elite," *T'oung Pao* 57 (1971): 31–103. As we will see, these techniques constituted a very important facet of Longmen teachings.

[58] Gao Dongli was the abbot of the Chongdao guan 崇道觀, the temple originally affiliated with the Southern Patriarch Zhang Boduan 張佰端 (984–1082). For the biography of Gao Dongli see JGXD 4: 4.11a-14a; and Esposito, "La Porte du Dragon," 118–119.

[59] These principles are: (1) enduring dishonor (*ren ru* 忍辱); (2) being benevolent and supple (*ren rou* 仁柔); (3) being calm and respectful (*zhi jing* 止敬); (4) being of superior intelligence (*gaoming* 高明); (5) making concessions (*tui rang* 退讓); (6) being firm and centered (*gang zhong* 剛中); (7) being wise and discerning (*hui bian* 慧辨); (8) being diligent (*qin* 勤); (9) being loyal (*xin* 信); and (10) being honest (*lian* 廉). See JGXD 4: 4: 37a. These principles are reminiscent of the teachings of Wang Changyue; see *Biyuan tanjing* 碧苑壇經, ZWDS 10, esp. 202–204. For the biography of Shen Yibing see JGXD 4: 4. 31a-44b; and Esposito, "La Porte du

teaching that Min received included both precepts and healing techniques, the latter of which are credited with restoring Min's health. After recovering his health, Min followed his father's wishes and finished his studies to become a Departmental Vice Magistrate (*zhou sima* 州司馬) in Yunnan. In 1790 he allegedly met Yedaposhe 野怛婆闍,[60] a semi-legendary figure whose origins have been traced back to the Yuezhi 月支 tribe of Central Asia (in outer Persia). However, as he was said to have been living in China since the Yuan dynasty, Yedaposhe was known in Yunnan as Jizu daozhe 雞足道者, "A Man of the Way of Mount Jizu." Yedaposhe reputedly was a direct disciple of Wang Changyue, recipient in 1659 of the three-stage Longmen ordination. Based on this official investiture, Wang Changyue recognized Yedaposhe as Chinese and gave him both a Chinese name (Huang 黃) and a lineage name (Shouzhong 守中, "Guardian of the Center"). Yedaposhe was thus integrated into the Longmen order as the eighth Longmen patriarch and founder of the Mount Jizu branch in Yunnan: the Xizhu xinzong 西竺心宗 (Heart Lineage of West India). Min Yide repeatedly claims that Yedaposhe transmitted Tantric methods to him, methods that belong to Yedaposhe's tradition under the name of *doufa* 斗法.[61] As we will see, Yedaposhe also played an important role in the development of Min's alchemical theories.

Dragon," 119–122. Shen Yibing was a master who also received the Zhengyi transmission (Qing, *Zhongguo daojiao shi*, vol. 4: 114).

[60] For his biography see JGXD 6: 6 *shang* 1a-2b; Esposito, "La Porte du Dragon," 390–391. As Min Yide points out, the Chinese translation of his nickname is "Master who aspires to the Way" (*qiudao shi* 求道士); see *Lü zushi sanni yishi shuoshu xu* 呂祖師三尼醫世說述序, DZXB 2: 1a-b. I follow here the Chinese *pinyin* phonetics since the appellation of Yedaposhe can be pronounced in different ways according to the Chinese-Sanskrit pronunciation. This appellation has some link with Tibeto-Birman languages, and may be derived from Tibetan titles such as *Ye bdag-po rje* or *Ye btang-pa'i rje*; but this requires further study. See Esposito "La Porte du Dragon," 250, n. 212.

[61] This tradition consists for the most part of liturgical texts based on mantra recitations, transcribed from the Sanskrit. It focuses on the magical power of *dhāraṇī* and underlines the value of rituals (see also notes 77 and 78), such as that in honor of Doumu 斗母 (Mother of Dipper) or Mārīcī. Min Yide included all these texts in his compilation, the *Gu shuyinlou cangshu* (abbr. YLCS) vol. 9 and 11; Esposito, "La Porte du Dragon," 132–133. {See also here below, Chapter 5}.

Min Yide's Works at Mt. Jingai, Sanctuary of the Longmen Yunchao Branch

Before dedicating himself to the compilation of Longmen works, Min left his official charge after his father's death and visited different temples. Having finally withdrawn to Mt. Jingai 金蓋山, he wrote the *Jingai xindeng* 金蓋心燈 (The Transmission of the Mind-Lamp from Mt. Jingai), a fundamental text for the Longmen lineage. In its ten fascicles, Min presents the history of Longmen patriarchs and the Longmen lineages, paying particular attention to the Longmen branch of Mt. Jingai. This branch was established by the eighth Longmen patriarch Tao Jing'an 陶靖庵 (1612–1673), who was ordained by Wang Changyue in 1658. Tao was thus officially recognized as founder of the Longmen Yunchao 雲巢 branch of Mount Jingai 金蓋.[62] Eight Vinaya Master (*lüshi*) Tao was also regarded as representative of the transmission of Lü Dongbin's doctrine and supervised the Lü Dongbin altar at Mt. Jingai, the Lüzu *zongtan* 呂祖宗壇.[63] Through Tao, close

---

[62] Tao Jing'an's lineage name is Shouzhen 守貞. He was ordained by Wang Changyue at the same time as another important master, Huang Chiyang 黃赤陽 (1595–1673), founder of the Dade 大德 branch of Hangzhou. However, Tao Jing'an was the only one who allegedly received the transmission of the *Secret of the Golden Flower* (JGXD 2: 2.9a-22a and 25a; Esposito, "La Porte du Dragon," 114–116 and 139–143). Conversely, Huang Chiyang, helped by Tao Jing'an's disciple and nephew Tao Shi'an 陶石庵 (?-1692), later compiled the main text for the transmission of the Longmen soteriological doctrine.

[63] He was in charge of this altar with Huang Chiyang; see JGXD 2: 2. 9a-22a and Esposito, "La Porte du Dragon," 138 and 139–143. The term *zong* 宗 in *zongtan* 宗壇 has different meanings. It has the meaning of "Ancestral Temple" (*zongmiao* 宗廟), ancestor or forefather (*zuxian* 祖先), clan (*zongzu* 宗祖), lineage (*zongpai* 宗派), etc. It also evokes the distinction between a "hereditary" and a "public" temple (see Welch, *Practice of Chinese Buddhism*, 129–141). At the same time, in the Longmen lineage, it is also connected to the distinction of two lines of patriarchal transmission: the Vinaya Line (*lüshi* 律師) and the Doctrinal or Founding Line (*zongshi* 宗師). In explanation of this distinction, the *Daotong yuanliu* 道統源流 (Fanlie 凡例) says: "Lüshi 律師 are those who, after having received the precepts, are firmly able to respect the regulations of the Vinaya," whereas "Zongshi" 宗師 are those who excel in morality and learning and are in charge of the lineage and the transmission of the dharma" (see Esposito, "Longmen School" {here above, pp. 84–85}). As we will see, the term *zong* 宗 refers to a juxtaposition of the temples of the different Longmen branches (Doctrinal or Founding Lines) and the Longmen public abbeys (Vinaya Lines), and more particularly to the juxtaposition between the Longmen temple of Mount Jingai and the Longmen public abbey Baiyun guan. Only the public abbeys

contacts were established with other Longmen branches and, in particular, with the Tantric Xizhu xinzong branch. The Xizhu xinzong's patriarchs often came to Mt. Jingai to receive Tao's teachings and take part in his activities.

Min Yide was thus not only attracted to Mt. Jingai because of its vicinity to his home and his master Shen Yibing 沈一炳 (1708–1786),[64] but also through its association with the Tantric Xizhu xinzong branch. While the avid text collector Min Yide was in charge of the Jingai library, he edited many texts and published them in his *Gu Shuyinlou cangshu* 古書隱樓藏書 (Collection from the Ancient Hidden Pavilion of Books).[65] This corpus contains Wang Changyue's *Biyuan tanjing* 碧苑壇經 as well as a wealth of methods belonging to different traditions with which Min came into contact.[66] Min Yide's close and personal interest in inner alchemical practices appears to be behind their privileged place within the *Daozang xubian* 道藏續編 (Supplementary Collection of the Daoist Canon) edited by him.

---

were allowed to have a public ordination altar where the ordination ceremony was performed by a Vinaya master (*lüshi* 律師). By contrast, the term *zongtan* 宗壇, in this context, authorizes the *Zongshi* 宗師 and his founding temple to have an ordination altar where the ordination ceremony can now also be performed. As heir of the transmission of Lü Dongbin included in the *Doctrine of the Golden Flower* (*Jinhua zongzhi* 金華宗旨, where *zong* stands also for *zongzhi*), the *Zongshi-Lüshi* in charge of Lü Dongbin's lineage is able to transmit a kind of ordination that is different from that of an ordinary Vinaya master. Lü Dongbin's "Doctrinal ordination" (which occurs in the Longmen Temple of Mount Jingai thanks to the transmission of the *Doctrine of the Golden Flower*) marks the foundation of Lü Dongbin's Doctrinal Line through the establishment of Lü Dongbin's spirit writing altar.

[64] Shen Yibing and another disciple, Chen Qiaoyun 陳樵雲 (1730–1785), were in fact responsible for the construction of temple halls at Mt. Jingai; both of them were also in charge of Lü Dongbin's altar.

[65] The name of this collection is based on the original name of the library: Shuyin lou 書隱樓. It was built by Wei Fuyi 衛富益 at the beginning of the Yuan dynasty (1279–1367); see JGXD 7: 7.15a-16a.

[66] The *Gu Shuyinlou cangshu* 古書隱樓藏書 (henceforth abbreviated as YLCS) was first published in 1834 from the wooden printing blocks stored at the Chunyang gong 純陽宮 of Mount Jingai (Huzhou, Zhejiang). Originally it contained more than twenty texts (see Esposito, "La Porte du Dragon," 133, n. 28). The 1904 edition, which I consulted at the Shanghai Library, consists of 14 volumes and 35 texts. Qing Xitai mentions two printed editions of 1894 and 1916 (*Zhongguo daojiao shi*, vol. 4:116). The 1904 edition has been recently published by Guangling guji (1993) and in ZWDS 10. It requires further study since it contains liturgical texts as well as Tantric methods related to the Xizhu xinzong branch.

The *Daozang xubian* 道藏續編, edited by Min Yide, consists of twenty-three texts that originally formed the core of the *Gu Shuyinlou cangshu*.[67] Characteristically, it contains only those texts that may be connected to a kind of "canonization" of Longmen teachings. Since, according to Min Yide, "the transmission by Wang Changyue no longer existed after three generations,"[68] the Longmen founder of the Mt. Jingai branch (Tao Jing'an 陶靖菴, 1612–1673) and his disciples serve as stopgaps. Min Yide thus compiled this anthology (which was significantly named "Canon") in order to guarantee the continuity and orthodoxy of Longmen. It was the altar of Lü Dongbin at Mount Jingai that formed a link with the lost transmission. It is there that the immortal Lü Dongbin, one of the five founding patriarchs of Quanzhen Daoism could transmit his teachings via spirit writing.[69]

Min Yide thus forged a new kind of Longmen doctrine that superseded Wang Changyue's teaching. Beyond the ideal and purist vision of Longmen which had been developed by Wang Changyue and his followers,[70] this

---

[67] The first xylographic edition was printed on Mt. Jingai 金蓋 in 1834 (Esposito, "La Porte du Dragon," 453–459). In 1952 it was reprinted by Ding Fubao 丁福保 (Shouyi zi 守一子, 1874–1952), Shanghai: Yixue shuju. Recent reprints have been published in 1989 (Beijing: Haiyang) and in 1993 (Beijing: Shumu wenxian). For its content see the Appendix below.

[68] *Huangji hepi xianjing* 皇極闔闢仙經, chap. 10 (DZXB 1: 5b). See also Yuria Mori, "Identity and Lineage: The Taiyi jinhua zongzhi and the Spirit writing Cult to Patriarch Lü in Qing China," in *Daoist Identity: History, Lineage, and Ritual*, ed. by Livia Kohn & Harold D. Roth, 181. Honolulu: Univ. of Hawai'i Press, 2002.

[69] Spirit writing or planchette writing (*fuji* 扶乩) is a practice that began in Tang times and was structurally organized in Song times. It centers on receiving written messages that are supposed to be directly transmitted by gods, immortals, or culture heroes who "take possession of a writing implement to compose what they will" (David K. Jordan and Daniel Overmyer, *The Flying Phoenix: Aspects of Chinese Sectarianism in Taiwan*, 38. Princeton: Princeton University Press, 1986). It was highly popular in late Imperial China and was practiced by some very illustrious scholars and literati (see Esposito, "Daoism in the Qing," 648–650) {here above, Chapter 1, pp. 39–41. See also M. Esposito, *Creative Daoism*, pp. 211–215.}

[70] In the preface of his *Changchun daojiao yuanliu* 長春道教源流 (j. 1.1b; ZWDS 31:1), Chen Minggui 陳銘珪 (1824–1881) confirms Wang Changyue's words by saying that the Longmen was founded by Qiu Chuji (1148–1227), one of the Seven Perfected of the Quanzhen school. According to Chen, the Longmen school distinguishes itself from other Daoist schools by its moral and doctrinal interests, and neither deals with alchemical and life-prolonging techniques nor with rituals and talismans. As we know, this point of view corresponds neither to the reality of the Longmen school nor to that of the Quanzhen school (see Yao, "Chuan-chen"; and Stephen Eskildsen, "The Beliefs and Practices of Early Ch'üan-chen Taoism." M.A.

doctrine drew its strength from the cult of Lü Dongbin and its associated spirit writing practice. Additionally, it drew from inner alchemical theories and self-cultivation techniques as well as the belief in universal salvation revealed by Patriarch Lü Dongbin. It is thus not a coincidence that the text on Longmen's precepts by Wang Changyue, the *Biyuan tanjing*, was not included in Min Yide's new elaboration. Rather, another text, attributed to Patriarch Lü Dongbin takes its place as the central doctrinal scripture of the Longmen Canon : the *Jinhua zongzhi* 金華宗旨, or *Secret of the Golden Flower*.

A new Vessel of Min Yide's Longmen Doctrine: the Secret of the Golden Flower

Thanks to the translation of Richard Wilhelm and commentary by C.G. Jung, the *Jinhua zongzhi* 金華宗旨 became widely known in the West as *The Secret of the Golden Flower*.[71] During the Qing dynasty this was a fundamental text for various Daoist lineages. As far as I know, there are six extant different editions of this text. All of these were connected to specific Daoist lineages or spirit writing groups.[72] The earliest edition of the text is found in

---

Thesis, University of British Columbia, 1989). Regarding my use of "perfected" (instead of "authentic") for *zhenren* 真人, it is important to note that the term *zhen* in *zhenren* implies the idea of someone who has realized the vision of Reality beyond the duality of subject and object. Going back to the source which precedes this distinction, the so-called Before-Heaven or *xiantian* 先天, he sees Reality as it is. This constitutes the distinction between a *zhenren* and an ordinary person. The *zhenren* is someone who embodies the primordial perfection of Reality as the expression of his own state beyond duality..

[71] Richard Wilhelm, *Das Geheimnis der Goldenen Blüte: Ein chinesisches Lebensbuch*, München 1929 [trl. *The Secret of the Golden Flower, A Chinese Book of Life*, London: Kegan Paul, Trench and Trübner 1931]. For the different translations see Needham & Lu, *Science and Civilisation*, V-5, 244. {On this text and its history see Part Four of M. Esposito, *Creative Daoism*.}

[72] For a list of these six editions and comments on their association with different Daoist lineages or spirit writing groups see Monica Esposito, "The different versions of the *Secret of the Golden Flower* and their relationship with the Longmen school," *Transactions of the International Conference of Eastern Studies* XLIII (1998), 90–109; and "Longmen pai yu Jinhua zongzhi banben laiyuan" 龍門派與「金華宗旨」版本來源. Paper presented at the Research Meeting on Daoist Culture, Tokyo, Waseda University, March 1998.

the *Lüzu quanshu* 呂祖全書 (1775) by Shao Zhilin 邵志林 (1748–1810). It was revealed via spirit writing for the first time in 1665 to members belonging to the Jingming 淨明 lineage. Later, other Daoist lineages claimed to hold the transmission of this text. The Longmen branch of Mount Jingai declared to have received the transmission of this text from 1668 onward by means of spirit writing sessions in honor of the immortal Lü Dongbin. The printing blocks of this text were said to have been preserved by the ninth Longmen Vinaya Master Tao Shi'an 陶石菴 (d. 1692)[73] at the Longqiao 窿蹻 hermitage of Mount Jingai and were later used by Min Yide for his *Daozang xubian* 道藏續編 edition of 1834. As in the other editions, Min Yide's *Jinhua zongzhi* 金華宗旨 consists of thirteen chapters. However, instead of the various prefaces, postfaces, and appendixes of the other editions, Min Yide's text features a single preface dated 1831 and his introductory note. The particularity of the *Golden Flower* as revised by Min Yide lies in the content of its first chapter. This chapter, entitled "Tianxin" 天心 (Celestial Heart), is almost entirely different from the first chapter of the other editions.[74] Furthermore, each chapter in Min Yide's edition is followed by short notes or commentaries which stem from the oral transmission of Longmen masters of Mount Jingai. These commentaries are very important since they add specific elements of Mount Jingai tradition as well as practical advice on Daoist inner alchemical techniques.[75]

It is important to note that in all different editions, the text of the *Golden Flower* is attributed to the immortal Lü Dongbin and portrayed as the fruit of his teaching transmitted via spirit writing. The fact of having received this text via spirit writing—that is, in a direct way—thus opened for many groups the possibility to become direct disciples of the immortal Lü Dongbin and establish a lineage.[76] This also happened with the Longmen branch of Mount Jingai that was reputed to be the privileged sanctuary for

---

[73] For a biography of Tao Shi'an 陶石菴 see JGXD 3: 3.7a-11a. See also note 54 above.

[74] For a list of some common sentences that Min Yide's text shares with other editions, see Esposito, "La Porte du Dragon," 164 n. 20.

[75] See, for example, , DZXB 1: 5b for the commentary to chapter 3 of *Jinhua zongzhi*.

[76] The appropriation of this text by different Daoist lineages and spirit writing groups in Southern and Northern China shows the presence of a widespread cult in honor of this immortal; see Yuria Mori, "Taiitsu kinka sōshi no seiritsu to hensen" 太乙金華宗旨の成立と變遷. *Tōyō no shisō to shūkyō* 東洋の思想と宗教 15 (1998): 43–64.

the veneration of the immortal Lü because of the altar dedicated to him.[77] The major part of the Longmen texts of Mount Jingai that are included in Min Yide's *Daozang xubian* are in fact spirit writing revelations of the immortal from this altar. Moreover, in Min Yide's eyes, the *Golden Flower* had become the basis of the Longmen doctrine not only because it was the fruit of the direct teaching of the immortal Lü Dongbin but even more because this direct teaching was said to have been recognized by Wang Changyue, the reformer of the Longmen school. In fact, Min Yide relates the following anecdote :

> It was in the autumn of the *wuchen* year of the Kangxi reign [1688], that the Vinaya Master [Wang Changyue] came down from North to South and stayed in Hangzhou at the Zongyang gong. The Perfect hermit [Tao] Jing'an went to meet him. When he offered this text to him, the Vinaya Master showed all his respects, bowed, and read it. He said : "The heart-to heart transmission of the Most High is fully expressed here."
>
> 時為康熙戊辰秋。律祖自北南來。館於杭城宗陽宮。靖庵隱真往謁。呈上此書。律師鄭重其儀。拜而閱之。曰。太上心傳。備於此矣。[78]

Although this meeting between Wang Changyue 王常月 (d. 1680), major leader of the Longmen at the Baiyun guan, and Tao Jing'an 陶靖庵 (1612-1673), founder of the Longmen branch of Mount Jingai, must be fictitious since in 1688 both men had already passed away, one remarks that through this anecdote Min Yide wants to affirm the legitimacy of the Longmen branch of Mount Jingai as holder of the transmission of Laozi. This transmission, conveyed via spirit writing by the immortal Lü Dongbin, was finally recognized as orthodox by Wang Changyue. Min Yide could have also chosen to mention another date, 1664, when, according to a gloss of the *Jingai xindeng*, Wang Changyue came to the Zongyang gong 宗陽宮 in Hangzhou. At that time, a meeting with Tao Jing'an could indeed have

---

[77] See notes 55 and 56. According to JGXD (10: 8.2a, 6a-8b), Mount Jingai was regarded as a holy site of Lü Dongbin where a bronze statue of the immortal stood since the Song dynasty. Many scholars and Daoists came to Mt. Jingai in order to take part in spirit writing sessions. See Esposito "La Porte du Dragon,"135-138; Esposito, "The different versions," 100; Esposito, "Longmen pai yu *Jinhua zongzhi* banben laiyuan"; Mori, "Taiitsu kinka sōshi no seiritsu to hensen," 59-60; and Mori, "Identity and Lineage."

[78] *Jinhua zongzhi* 金華宗旨, chap.8 (DZXB 1: 10b).

taken place.[79] However, for Min Yide the date 1688 is more important than the historical fact since it marks the year when the text of the *Golden Flower* was allegedly revealed at the doctrinal altar of Lü Dongbin in the Longqiao 窿蹻 hermitage of Mount Jingai.[80] What is important for Min Yide is to show that, as soon as this text was revealed at Mount Jingai, it was immediately recognized as a Longmen scripture by the official representative of the Longmen school. By virtue of this official recognition, this text could have have been used by the Longmen patriarchs as a kind of substitute for the transmission of the precepts—those precepts whose transmission had allegedly ceased "three generations after Wang Changyue."

But why did the Longmen patriarchs of Mount Jingai seem to prefer the *Secret of the Golden Flower* 金華宗旨 to Wang Changyue's *Platform Sūtra of the Jade Garden* 碧苑壇經, both of which were included in Min Yide's *Collection from the Ancient Hidden Pavilion of Books* 古書隱樓藏書? Beyond the sense of identity and lineage that the *Golden Flower* symbolized for many groups devoted to its purported author Lü Dongbin,[81] this scripture was also regarded by the Longmen patriarchs of Mount Jingai as the basis of a new Longmen soteriological doctrine and thus came to be known as a "blueprint for healing the world" (*yishi zhangben* 醫世張本). Although the term *yishi* 醫世 ("healing the world"), which will characterize the core of Longmen Jingai's soteriological doctrine, is not yet present in this text, Min Yide nevertheless identifies it as a key element. According to Min, it is exactly for the purpose of healing the world that the Patriarch Lü Dongbin composed the text and transmitted it to the Longmen patriarchs of Mount Jingai.[82] Its content focuses above all on a contemplative training "for men of great talent and capacity" (*dagen daqi* 大根大器) so that they may discover the genuine mind and heal the world.[83]

---

[79] JGXD 2: 2.4a/3–4. This may also indicate a possible mix-up between the year *wuchen* (1688) and the year *shenchen* (1664), but I think that Min Yide chose the date 1668 on purpose. See also Mori, "Identity and Lineage."

[80] Min Yide's preface and introductory gloss to the *Jinhua zongzhi* 金華宗旨, DZXB 1: 1a.

[81] Mori, "Identity and Lineage."

[82] Preface (1831) by Min Yide to the *Jinhua zongzhi* 金華宗旨, DZXB 1: 1a-b.

[83] *Jinhua zongzhi* 金華宗旨, chap. 6, DZXB 1: 8b and 9b.

The Esoteric Ordination in the Longmen Branch of Mount Jingai

To the ethico-spiritual path proposed by Wang Changyue in his three-tiered precepts program, Min Yide thus joins the inner alchemical path which he conceives as a powerful receptacle of skillful means for healing the world. It is important to note that in the first chapter of the *Golden Flower*—the chapter that was almost entirely rewritten by the Longmen patriarchs of Mount Jingai—the Longmen mind-to-mind transmission (*xinchuan* 心傳) is summed up by the two words *cun-cheng* 存誠 (actualizing sincerity). If at first sight this expression seems to hark back to the "self-illuminative sincerity" stressed by Confucians or to the reinterpretation by Wang Changyue of "sincerity as *sīla*," here it is in reality closely related to the transmission of an alchemical formula. This formula consists of visualizing the three-dot symbol ∴ that designates Brahmā (*fantian* 梵天)[84] and is also associated with the three eyes of Shiva.[85] In Daoist exegesis it symbolizes, at the macrocosmic level, the sun, the moon, and the polar star; and at the microcosmic level the left eye, the right eye, and the middle eye.

> Once all obstacles have been let go of, use the three-dot character for Brahmā. By visualizing the central dot of this character in the middle of the eyebrows (*meixin* 眉心), the left dot in the left eye, and the right dot in the right eye, the spiritual light of the two human eyes will spontaneously converge in the middle of the eyebrows. This is the Celestial Eye (*tianmu* 天目), the main gate of exit and entry where the three luminous ones [sun, moon and polar star] converge. If one is able to use the three eyes "as" in the Sanskrit character of Brahmā, and if one can subtly use one's Intention to move "as if" polishing a mirror, then at once the three lights gather in the middle of the eyebrows, and their light shines forth "as if" the sun was appearing in front of you.

---

[84] On the different meanings of Brahmā, see Paul Demiéville et al., *Hōbōgirin*, fasc. 1–2, 113–121.

[85] Soothill and Hodous, *A Dictionary of Chinese Buddhist Terms*, 200, London: Kegan Paul, Trench, Trubner and Co, 1937. As is explained in the gloss (*Jinhua zongzhi* chap. 1, DZXB 1: 2a/3), this corresponds to a Sanskrit sign (*yizi sandian* 伊字三點). To quote Soothill and Hodous, this sign of triangular shape indicates "neither unity nor difference, before nor after." In the *Nirvāna Sūtra* it is applied to "*fashen* 法身 dharmakāya, *banruo* 般若 prajñā, and *jietuo* 解脫 vimokṣa, all three necessary to complete nirvāna."

Then, by your Intention guide [the spiritual light] to the region behind the heart and in front of the Pass. It is this point which is regarded as the Gate of the Mysterious Female. If you use your Intention to guide it, the light at once follows. But if you do not forget the mysterious significance of the two characters *ruo-ru* 若如 ("as-if"), the Celestial Heart (*tianxin* 天心) will without fail open up by itself.

乃於萬緣放下之時。惟用梵天、字。以字中點存諸眉心。以左點存左目。右點存右目。則人兩目神光。自得會眉心。眉心即天目。乃為三光會歸出入之總戶。人能用三目如梵伊字然。微以意運如磨鏡。三光立聚眉心。光耀如日現前。既即以意引臨心後關前。此一處也。按即玄牝之門。以意引之。光立隨臨。而毋忘若如二字玄義。天心必自洞啟。[86]

The Celestial Eye (*tianmu* 天目) is here a synonym of the Celestial Heart (*tianxin* 天心), a term which also forms the title of the first chapter of the *Secret of the Golden Flower*. It symbolizes the Longmen mind-to-mind transmission (*xinchuan* 心傳) that is capable of pointing at the genuine mind, the Center of the Self. Once reality is contemplated from that perspective, one achieves a non-dual view, as in binoculars where the fields of vision of the left and the right eyes merge.

Although the common aim is to perceive one's own nature inwardly, Min Yide proposes an esoteric technique that contrasts with the three-tiered teaching of precepts by Wang Changyue. It allows the adept to embody the non-duality in the trinitarian abyss of the Celestial Eye through the visualization of the three-dot character.[87] The Celestial Eye or Celestial Heart represents for the Longmen branch of Mount Jingai the direct mind-to-mind transmission of the Great Precepts of Celestial Immortals symbolized by an esoteric formula and destined for the Longmen disciples of "great talent and

---

[86] *Jinhua zongzhi*, chap. 1 (DZXB 1: 2b/3–6). My thanks go to Professor Chen Yaoting 陳耀庭 for his help in translating this passage.

[87] This method of visualization of a character is reminiscent of the important role that Tantrism played in the transmission of Chan discipline and of the influence of the "contemplation of the letter A" (*azi guan* 阿字觀); see Bernard Faure, "La volonté d'orthodoxie," 3 vols. Thèse d'Etat. Paris, École Pratique des Hautes Études, Section des Sciences Religieuses, 1984, vol. 1: 230 & 246. Another example of Tantric transmission inside the Longmen branch of Mount Jingai is the text entitled *Erlan xinhua* (DZXB 3: 1a-7a; French translation in Esposito, "La Porte du Dragon," 390–440; and Italian translation in Esposito, *L'alchimia del soffio*. Roma: Ubaldini, 1997).

capacity" who can realize it at once. This formula stems from a method of visualization which was transmitted inside the Longmen branch of Mount Jingai and related to Tantric transmission of precepts harking back to the Xizhu xinzong branch of Yedaposhe.[88]

However, for inferior and intermediate disciples who cannot immediately understand the Great Precepts of Celestial Immortality condensed in the central formula of the *Secret of the Golden Flower*, the branch of Mount Jingai proposes another method of initiation. Instead of the preliminary transmission of the Initial Precepts of Perfection and the Intermediate Precepts, the Longmen branch of Mount Jingai puts forward alchemical methods mainly based on psycho-physiological techniques. In order to justify the presence of such techniques (which belong in Wang Changyue's view to the "small path"), the Longmen branch of Mount Jingai elaborated its own theory.

The Joint Cultivation of Nature and Vital Force

Through its spokesman Min Yide, the Longmen branch of Mount Jingai points out that the highest teaching of the *Golden Flower* must be put in correspondence with a manuscript found at the Qingyang gong 青羊宮 (Palace of Black Sheep) of Chengdu: the *Yin zhenren Donghua zhengmai huangji hepi zhengdao xianjing* 尹真人東華正脈皇極闔闢證道仙經 (Immortals' Scripture of the Perfected Yin Testifying to the Path of Opening and Closing the Sovereign Ultimate according to the Orthodox Lineage of the Eastern Efflorescence). As "blueprints for healing the world" (*yishi zhangben* 醫世張本), these two texts constitute "the fruit of the mind-to-mind transmission of the Most High" (Taishang *xinchuan* 太上心傳),[89] and are simply "the two sides of the same coin" that aim at "the joint culti-

---

[88] Yedaposhe was recognized by Wang Changyue as Vinaya Master of *dhāraṇī* (*tuduo lüshi* 圖哆律師) since he had condensed the transmission of the Great Precepts of the Celestial Immortals into a simple *dhāraṇī*. It is also said that Min Yide received the simplified transmission (*jieyi fa* 戒易法) and for that reason called himself Vinaya Master (*lüshi* 律師). See JGXD 6: 6.34a-b; and Esposito, "La Porte du Dragon," 132.

[89] Preface (1831) by Min Yide to the *Huangji hepi xianjing* 尹真人東華正脈皇極闔闢證道仙經, DZXB 1: 1a/5.

vation of Nature and Vital Force" (*xingming shuangxiu* 性命雙修).⁹⁰ If the *Golden Flower* focuses on the cultivation of Nature (meditative methods) and is more akin to Chan as well as the Quanzhen Northern lineage, the *Immortals' Scripture of the Perfected Yin* puts more weight on the cultivation of Vital Force (psycho-physiological techniques) and the Southern lineage of the Golden Elixir.⁹¹ Whereas in the *Golden Flower* the practitioner starts with visualizing the Celestial Heart, the center of the Self and at the same time the sanctuary of the genuine mind, in *Immortals' Scripture of the Perfected Yin* the practitioner concentrates on the navel, the original receptacle of the Vital Force, which is also named Celestial Heart.⁹² This means that although the starting point of practice appears to be different and indicates a priority of meditative or psycho-physiological techniques, in the end both of them have only a temporary value that must be transcended in order to realize the non-duality of the Celestial Heart. All different methods can thus be used according to practitioners' affinities, but they are only skillful means for understanding the true meaning of the joint cultivation of Nature and Vital Force, that is the encompassing non duality of mind and body.

Through the *Golden Flower*, the Longmen branch of Mount Jingai thus affirms the importance of meditative exercises for the spiritual training of Longmen practitioners. Following Wang Changyue's stress on concentration and wisdom, it proposes different methods for their development

---

⁹⁰ Preface (1831) by Min Yide to the *Jinhua zongzhi* 金華宗旨, DZXB 1: 1b/3. This syncretic tendency inside the different Daoist schools of alchemy also has its Buddhist counterpart in the advocacy of the joint practice of Chan and Pure Land (*chanjing shuangxiu* 禪淨雙修); see Yü, *The Renewal of Buddhism*, 3 and 29–63.

⁹¹ From the doctrinal point of view, both the Northern and Southern lineages claimed the joint cultivation of Nature and Vital Force, but from the point of view of its application there were some differences; see Chen Bing 陳兵, "Jindan pai Nanzong qiantan" 金丹派南宗淺探, *Shijie zongjiao yanjiu* 世界宗教研究 4 (1985): 35–49; Robinet, *Introduction à l'alchimie intérieure*, 179–191; Pregadio & Skar, "Inner Alchemy"; and Yutaka Yokote 横手裕, "Zenshinkyō to nanshū hokushū" 全眞教と南宗北宗, in *Dōkyō no seimeikan to shintai ron* 道教の生命観と身体論, edited by Tetsurō Noguro 鉄郎野口 et al., 180–196. Tokyo: Yuyama kaku, 2000.

⁹² The alchemical work starts from the Lower Field of the Elixir (*xia dantian* 下丹田) which is called Celestial Heart (*tianxin* 天心) and located in the navel. It is also named "Navel Wheel" (*jilun* 臍輪); see *Huangji hepi xianjing* 尹真人東華正脈皇極闔闢證道仙經, DZXB 1: 1a, and Esposito, "La Porte du Dragon," 190–191. In the *Golden Flower*, the term Celestial Heart refers to another location in the body: the heart, that is, *zhong dantian* 中丹田.

without excluding alchemical and visualization techniques. For the Longmen branch of Mount Jingai, body and mind are intrinsically related, which is why a complete training must also include psycho-physiological techniques. This is the reason why it joined *Secret of the Golden Flower* and *Immortals' Scripture*. Furthermore, through *Immortals' Scripture*, the Longmen branch of Mount Jingai shows its will to integrate in the Longmen doctrine the various psycho-physiological techniques that seem to have been rejected in the official teachings of Wang Changyue.

THE AMBIGUOUS FIGURE OF PERFECTED YIN: THE SAINT OF MOUNT JINGAI AND HIS DOCTRINE OF THE CENTRAL PATH

The integration of different Daoist traditions in the Longmen branch of Mount Jingai is well illustrated by the example of Perfected Yin (Yin zhenren 尹真人), the legendary figure to whom the *Immortals' Scripture* is attributed. He was regarded as the local Saint of Mount Jingai who had first engraved the name of this mountain on a rock.[93] He is said to have lived in different epochs: during the Eastern Han (25–220) he was known in the Zhejiang region under the name of Qu Zhen 屈禎, and during the Yuan and Ming dynasties as Yin Pengtou 尹蓬頭.[94] Yin represents the ideal of recluse (*yinshi* 隱士) who lived in the world without being noticed by ordinary mortals.[95] This calls to mind Yin Xi 尹喜, the Guardian of the Pass, who "kept secret his virtues and organized his daily activities with care in such a way that nobody noticed him."[96] Conversely, under the name of Qu Zhen 屈禎 (Daoist name: Wuwo 無我), he was closer to the figure of a

---

[93] See his hagiography under the title "Penglai changshi" 蓬萊長史, JGXD 9: 8, *xia* 37a-37b). See also Esposito, "La Porte du Dragon," 154–155.

[94] *Huangji hepi xianjing* 尹真人東華正脈皇極闔闢證道仙經, j. *xia* (DZXB 1: 7b).

[95] It is to Yin Pengtou that two texts in the DZXB are attributed (see Appendix, Texts 3 and 4). One of these, *Immortals' Scripture* 尹真人東華正脈皇極闔闢證道仙經, is clearly inspired by another compilation which was also allegedly written by an eminent disciple of Yin zhenren and entitled *Xingming guizhi* 性命圭旨. For a translation, see Martina Darga, *Das alchemistische Buch von innerem Wesen und Lebensenergie Xingming guizhi*. München: Eugen Diederichs, 1999; see also Esposito, "La Porte du Dragon," 184–226.

[96] *Liexian zhuan* 列仙傳, translated by Max Kaltenmark, *Le Lie-sien tchouan*, 66. Paris: Collège de France, 1987.

fangshi 方士 or "master of recipes." As expert in breathing techniques (*tuna* 吐呐) and divining arts, he was also reputed for performing, through the power of talismans, rainmaking and flood-control rites.[97]

The figure of Perfected Yin can thus be seen as a symbol of the integration of different traditions inside the Longmen branch of Mount Jingai. Ritualistic, magic, and healing traditions of the ancient "masters of recipes" that were officially said to have been monopolized by the Celestial Masters are here combined with more elitist and meditative methods used by retired scholars and Daoist hermits.[98] This integration finds its full expression not only in the double identity of Perfected Yin but also in his teaching. In fact, Perfected Yin is also credited with having transmitted a specific doctrine under the name of "Yellow Path" (*huangdao* 黃道), or simply "Yellow Center" (*huangzhong* 黃中).[99] This term — which harks back to the famous "communicative principle of the Yellow Center" (*huangzhong tong li* 黃中通理) in the *Yijing* — points to a supplementary channel inside the body as a superior tract for a sudden alchemical transformation.[100] Located between the Control Channel (*dumai* 督脈) or Black Path (*heidao* 黑道) and the

---

[97] According to JGXD, his powers were so strong that when he was invited to Mount Jingai he could stop the trajectory of the sun with his staff (JGXD 9: 8, *xia* 37a).

[98] On the progressive monopoly of the Celestial Masters in ritual and liturgical procedures, see Lowell Skar, "Ritual Movement, Deity Cults and the Transformation of Daoism in Song and Yuan times," in *Daoism Handbook*, ed. by Livia Kohn, 413–463. Leiden: Brill, 2000; de Bruyn, "Daoism in the Ming"; and Esposito, "Daoism in the Qing" {here above, Chapter 1}. By contrast, at the Baiyun guan, the official headquarters of the Longmen, admission was not granted to applicants "who expressed heterodox opinions or were suspected of acting as healers, soothsayers, astrologers, or diviners" (see Yoshioka, "Taoist Monastic Life," 238).

[99] *Xie tianji* 泄天機, DZXB 1: 2b/8; see Esposito, "La Porte du Dragon," 230.

[100] Commentary "Wenyan" 文言 to the fifth line of the hexagram Kun 坤; see *Yin zhenren Donghua zhengmai huangji hepi zhengdao xianjing* 尹真人東華正脈皇極闔闢證道仙經, j. *shang*, chap. 1 (DZXB 1: 2b). Conversely, the term *huangdao* 黃道 is found in the astronomical treatise of the *Hanshu* 漢書 as "the ecliptic of the sun." In the Shangqing texts one finds the expression *huangchi zhi dao* 黃赤之道 (the red and yellow paths) for designating the essence of moon and sun absorbed by the adept during meditation, or the trajectory of sun and moon in the sky (Isabelle Robinet, *La révélation du Shangqing dans l'histoire du taoïsme*, 2 vols., vol. 1:175–76, Paris: École Française d'Extrême-Orient., 1984). Its first alchemical occurrence as *huangdao* is probably the *Wuzhen pian* 悟真篇. For a detailed explanation of this term and its interpretations see Esposito, "Il 'ritorno alle fonti', costituzione di un dizionario di alchimia interiore dell'epoca Ming e Qing." In *Le fonti per lo studio della civiltà cinese*, ed. by Maurizio Scarpari, 110–111. Venezia: Ca'Foscarina, 1995.

Function Channel (*renmai* 任脈) or Red Path (*chidao* 赤道), this Yellow Path becomes a key-word of the Longmen branch of Mount Jingai. Thanks to it, one can in one flash realize the genuine principle of inner alchemy. Through the formulation of the "three paths" revealed by Perfected Yin, the Longmen branch of Mount Jingai proposed a method for transcending all contradictions due to the different ways of practicing in various Daoist and Buddhist traditions and for opening the Central Channel—the symbol of this unification—by means of breathing and visualization exercises.[101] This method again advances, although in a more psycho-physiological context, the esoteric formula of the Celestial Eye or Celestial Heart of the *Secret of the Golden Flower*. In the elaboration of this method, it is clear that the Tantric yoga of the three channels plays a central role, but they are well integrated with Daoist and medical theories of the eight extraordinary channels (*qijing bamai* 奇經八脈) as well as with the orthodoxy of the *Yijing* and its "communicative principle of the Yellow Center."[102] Min Yide explains the meaning of this practice as follows:

> In the alchemical tradition there are basically three paths for mastering the pneuma (*qi* 氣): the red, the black and the yellow. The red is the function channel whose path is located in the front [of the body]. It is the course traveled by the pneuma of the heart (*xinqi* 心氣). As the color of the heart is red, it is called the red path. Since red by nature

---

[101] *Xie tianji* 泄天機, DZXB 1: 2a. These exercises start from the *yinqiao* 陰蹻. This term refers both to an acupoint, localized at the perineum, and to one of the eight extraordinary channels (*qijing bamai*) that links all the yin channels of the body.

[102] In the more recent Daoist psycho-physiological techniques, the alchemical work is mainly done on three channels: the control channel [*dumai*], the function channel [*renmai*], and the central channel [*zhongmai*; *chongmai*]. These three channels belong to the system of the eight extraordinary channels. See Despeux, *Traité d'alchimie*. This practice was probably influenced by the Indian Tantric yoga of three channels: *iḍā* (right, sun, red), *piṅgalā* (left, moon, white), and *suṣumṇā* (center, sky, blue); see Nan Huai-chin, *Tao and Longevity*, London: Element Books, 1984; and Arthur Avalon, *The Serpent Power*. Madras: Ganeshan & Co., 1958. A variety of Tantric exercises was in fact imported to China during the Tang period. See Yi-liang Chou, "Tantric Buddhism in China," *Harvard Journal of Asian Studies* 8 (1944–45): 241–332; Michel Strickmann, *Mantras et mandarins—Le bouddhisme tantrique en Chine*. Paris: Gallimard, 1986; and Yoshinobu Sakade 坂出祥伸, "Shoki mikkyō to dōkyō to no kōshō" 初期密教と道教との交渉, in *Chūgoku mikkyō* 中国密教, ed. by Musashi Tachikawa 武藏立川 & Motohiro Yoritomi 本宏頼富, 153–169. Tokyo: Shunkasha, 1999.

blazes up, the method consists in controlling it without fail by making it descend. Then the heart will be refreshed and the kidneys warm.

The black is the control channel whose path is located in the back. It is the course traveled by the pneuma of the kidneys (*shenqi* 腎氣). As the color of the kidney is black, it is called the black path. Since black by nature drips down, the method consists in controlling it without fail by making it rise. Then, the marrow (*sui* 髓) will circulate and the Spirit (*shen* 神) will be pacified. As these two paths originally generate the seminal essence (*jing* 精) and the pneuma for the survival of mankind and other beings, they are officially labelled "the path of men" (*rendao* 人道). This is what the alchemical and medical traditions have minutely reported.

The yellow is the Yellow Center whose path lies in a middle fissure between the red and the black [paths]. It is located behind the heart and in front of the spine. If virtue governs the two pneumas [of the heart and of the kidneys], it becomes the central master of the opening and closing. That which follows this trajectory [i.e., *jing* and *qi*] temporarily stops in the state of utter emptiness and tranquillity because it belongs to the state before Heaven (*xiantian* 先天). The realization of an immortal or an ordinary embryo is dependent on that state. Although one speaks of three different [channels], in reality they are One. For that reason it is officially labeled "the path of the immortals" (*xiandao* 仙道).

丹家理氣。原有三道。曰赤。曰黑。曰黃。赤乃任脈。道在前。心氣所由之路。心色赤。故曰赤道。而赤性炎上。法必制之使降。則心涼而腎煖。黑乃督脈。道在後。腎氣所由之路。腎色黑。故曰黑道。而黑性潤下。法必制之使升。則髓運而神安。原斯二道。精氣所由出。人物類以生存者。法故標曰人道。丹家醫家詳述如此。黃乃黃中。道介赤黑中縫。位在脊前心後。而德統二氣。為闔闢中主。境則極虛而寂。故所經駐。只容先天。凡夫仙胎之結之圓皆在斯境。雖有三田之別。實則一貫。法故標曰仙道。[103]

---

[103] *Xie tianji* 洩天機, DZXB 1: 2b/1–6. See Esposito, "La Porte du Dragon," 229–231, and "Il 'ritorno alle fonti'," 111. See also the explanation given in the commentary by Min Yide to the *Shangpin danfa jieci* 上品丹法節次 (DZXB 2: 6b) where it is said that the Yellow Path gets its name from the color of earth to which the Intention (*yi* 意) belongs. Min Yide's elaboration of a central doctrine from this Yellow Path must also be put in correspondence with Wang Changyue's teachings, for example

Min Yide's "Path of Men" and "Path of Immortals"

In Wang Changyue's teachings, the "path of men" (*rendao* 人道) corresponds to the practice of Confucian ethical principles, and the "path of immortals" (*xiandao* 仙道) to the full ordination of Celestial Immortals. By contrast, Min Yide interprets these two paths as referring to specific alchemical practices. The "path of men" corresponds to psycho-physiological techniques that were well known under the alchemical terms of "microcosmic orbit" (*xiao zhoutian* 小周天) and were used for the sublimation of *jing* 精 (essence) and *qi* 氣 (pneuma). The "path of immortals," on the other hand, refers to the "macrocosmic orbit" (*da zhoutian* 大周天) and to the sublimation of *shen* 神 (spirit).[104]

In the practice of the "microcosmic orbit" or "path of men," the adept works on places in the body that play the role of "physical markers." These physical markers are like "fingers pointing at the moon" and are used for supporting the practice at the outset. Once their function has been fulfilled, they must be abandoned. The Longmen adept can thus enter the gate without any attachment.[105] This means that he has left behind the cosmological dimension of the "microcosmic orbit" or "state after Heaven" (*houtian* 後天) where it was important to observe the guidelines—the "path of men"—in favor of forgetting and letting be in the metaphysical dimension which is symbolized by the "macrocosmic orbit." This dimension or state before Heaven (*xiantian* 先天) can only be realized without any effort, in the wonder of non-action. This is the genuine meaning of the "path of immortals" as explained by Min Yide; it refers to the discovering of the omnipresent Center beyond space and time. This Center must nonetheless be concretely experienced in one's body through the incorporation of the "path of men."[106]

Wang's explanation of the character *zhong* (Center) in the Intermediate Precepts (*zhongji jie* 中極戒); see *Biyuan tanjing* 碧苑壇經, ZWDS 10:181.

[104] For a description of these orbits and their link with the alchemical stages of sublimation see Despeux, *Traité d'alchimie*; Wile, *Arts of the Bedchamber*, 41–43; and Esposito, "La Porte du Dragon," 73–82.

[105] See for example the commentary to the *Jinhua zongzhi* 金華宗旨, chap. 3, DZXB 1:5a-b.

[106] The commentary by Min Yide to the *Shangpin danfa jieci* 上品丹法節次 (DZXB 2: 7a) contains the following sentence: "If you desire to cultivate the path of immortals you must at first cultivate the path of men. As long as the path of men has not been cultivated, the path of immortals will be remote." This sentence had already been

The Center is thus embodied in different ways depending on the individuality and the qualifications of the adept; it can be found in the Joint Pass of the Spinal Handle (*jiaji shuangguan* 夾脊雙關), the center of the twenty-four dorsal vertebrae,[107] in the Yellow Path through which the Three Passes are suddenly transcended at the crown of the head (*niwan* 泥丸)[108] or, in more alchemical language, in the crossing of the intercourse between Kan 坎 (water) and Li 離 (fire).[109]

Nevertheless, the alchemical interpretations by the Longmen branch of Mount Jingai do not exclude the traditional understanding of Wang Changyue concerning the "path of men" as the moral and ethical path inspired by Confucianism.[110] In fact, the Longmen branch of Mount Jingai found a way to integrate the official teaching of Wang Changyue while affirming its own identity. Whereas Wang Changyue preached the three-stage ordination inspired by the Buddhist threefold training of discipline (*jie* 戒), concentration (*ding* 定) and wisdom (*hui* 慧), Min Yide and his branch of Mount Jingai appear to match the three stages of practitioners— inferior, intermediate and superior—with their corresponding alchemical methods. These methods are divided into gradual and sudden ones.[111] The gradual methods are reserved for inferior and intermediate practitioners and consist of psycho-physiological techniques focusing on *qi* 氣 (e.g. breath-circulation exercises which lead to the progressive opening of the Control and

---

quoted by the reformer Wang Changyue (see note 40 above), but here it is clearly attributed to Patriarch Lü (Lüzu 呂祖). Even though Wang Changyue and Min Yide use the same sentence, their explanations manifest different levels of interpretation.

[107] Commentary to the *Huangji hepi xianjing* 尹真人東華正脈皇極闔闢證道仙經, j. *shang*, chap. 1 (DZXB 1: 2b).

[108] *Shangpin danfa jieci* 上品丹法節次, DZXB 2: 6a-b.

[109] *Jinhua zongzhi* 金華宗旨, chap. 11 (DZXB 1: 13b-14a), and *Shangpin danfa jieci* 上品丹法節次 (DZXB 2: 6b-7b).

[110] This is the central topic of two texts strongly inspired by Neo-Confucianism: *Jiuzheng lu* 就正錄 [Record of the Realization of Rectitude, 1678], and *Yu Lin Fenqian xiansheng shu* 與林奮千先生書 [Letter to Master Lin Fenqian, 1697]. Both are included in vol. 2 of DZXB; see Esposito, "La Porte du Dragon," 241–245.

[111] This can be related to the three stages of realization according to the Southern tradition: the Earthly Immortals (*dixian* 地仙), the Human (*renxian* 人仙) or Aquatic Immortals (*shuixian* 水仙), and the Celestial Immortals (*tianxian* 天仙); see *Xiuxian bianhuo lun* 修仙辨惑論 attributed to Bai Yuchan 白玉蟾 (1194-ca.1227) in *Daozang jinghua lu* 道藏精華錄 *xia* 3a; Esposito, "La Porte du Dragon," 36–38.

Function Channels—the black and red paths of the microcosmic orbit).[112] They also involve harmonization with a constant concentration on the space between the eyes.[113] Conversely, the sudden methods for the superior practitioners are limited to a natural contemplation of the Center of Self symbolized by the "Joint Pass of the Spinal Handle" (*jiaji shuangguan* 夾脊雙關) along with the spontaneous realization of inherent non-duality (i.e., the sudden opening of the Central Channel or Yellow Path of the macrocosmic orbit). This leads, in a flash of vision, to the realization that one can save the world through self-cultivation, and to the actualization of the incomparable path of the Celestial Immortals. This is the ultimate fruit to which the teaching of the *Secret of the Golden Flower* and the *Immortals' Scripture* point. Although the way of practicing in these two texts may show some differences, it represents the common goal of Longmen practitioners.

Wang Changyue had held that this supreme path could only be achieved through the three-stage ordination and had regarded psycho-physiological techniques as belonging to the "small vehicle" or the "small path." By contrast, Min Yide and the Longmen patriarchs of Mount Jingai reaffirmed the importance of such methods for realizing Celestial Immortality.

THE DOCTRINE OF HEALING THE WORLD AND ITS CORPUS OF TEXTS

As in Wang Changyue's teachings, for the Longmen branch of Mount Jingai becoming a Celestial Immortal means to devote oneself to saving the world. However, instead of the threefold teaching of precepts, the branch of Mount Jingai elaborated a specific doctrine for the future Celestial Immortals which goes by the name of "doctrine of the Three Sages for healing the world" (*sanni yishi* 三尼醫世). This teaching lies at the core of the

---

[112] For a detailed explanation of these practices in the Longmen branch of Mount Jingai, see Esposito, "La Porte du Dragon."

[113] *Huangji hepi xianjing* 尹真人東華正脈皇極闔闢證道仙經, j. *shang*, chap. 4 (DZXB 1: 6a); see Esposito, "La Porte du Dragon," 200–201. The intermediate space is named "Root of the Mountain" (*shangen* 山根). As explained in the first chapter of the same text (j. *shang*, chap. 1; DZXB 1: 1b), this method of concentration must be carried out without losing the "Spinal Handle" (*jiaji* 夾脊); see Esposito, "La Porte du Dragon," 190–193.

Longmen tradition of Mount Jingai and finds its preliminary application in the *Secret of the Golden Flower* and the *Immortals' Scripture of the Perfect Yin*. In its developed form, this doctrine appears in a corpus of texts that was also allegedly transmitted by Patriarch Lü Dongbin 呂洞賓 via spirit writing. All of these texts feature in their titles the expression "*sanni yishi.*" This signifies that what "heals the world" (*yishi* 醫世) was originally revealed to Patriarch Lü in heaven by the Three Sages (*sanni* 三尼):[114] Confucius (Zhongni 仲尼), Laozi (Qingni 青尼), and Shakyamuni Buddha (Moni 年尼). Subsequently, Patriarch Lü descended to the altar of Mt. Jingai to transmit this healing doctrine to the Longmen masters by means of spirit writing.[115]

In his 1828 preface to the *Lüzu sanni yishi shuoshu* 呂祖師三尼醫世說述 (Explanations of the Three Sages' Doctrine of Healing the World by Patriarch Lü),[116] Min Yide relates that his master Gao Dongli 高東籬 (?-1768), the tenth Longmen patriarch, discovered in a bamboo casket belonging to Wang Yangming 王陽明 (1472–1529) a text linked to this soteriological doctrine that had been originally transmitted by Fu Xi 伏羲 and the Yellow Emperor Huangdi 黃帝.[117] This discovery and the entire transmission shows through the presence of Wang Yangming the important role that Neo-Confucianism played in the purported transmission of this doctrine. Furthermore, the evocation of the legendary figures of Fu Xi and the Yellow Emperor highlights not only the great age and orthodoxy of this teaching but also the seamless continuity of a lineage of masters. This facilitates a possible return to a Golden Age, which in China corresponds to the historical period starting with Fu Xi and Huangdi and traditionally ending

---

[114] This expression also occurs in the *Xinyin ji jing* 心印集經 (DZJY jiji 10:5b-6a), where it is said: " Qingni reaches the Center, Zhongni takes hold of it, and Moni empties it."

[115] Preface (dated 1604) by Tao Shi'an to the *Lü zushi sannin yishi shuoshu* 呂祖師三尼醫世說述, DZXB 2:1b.

[116] DZXB 2: 1a-7b. This text is followed by a commentary by Min Yide entitled *Du Lü zushi sanni yishi shuoshu guankui* 讀呂祖師三尼醫世說述管窺. On the content of these texts see Esposito, "La Porte du Dragon," 259–267; Qing, *Zhongguo daojiao*, vol. 2: 184–186; and Qing, *Zhongguo daojiao shi*, vol. 4: 117–119.

[117] The discovery of this text evokes that of the revelation of the apocryphal scrolls that were sealed in jade caskets; see Anna Seidel, "Imperial Treasures and Taoist Sacraments: Taoist Roots in the Apocrypha," in *Tantric and Taoist Studies in Honour of R.A. Stein*, ed. by Michel Strickmann, 316–318. Bruxelles: Institut Belge des Hautes Études Chinoises, 1983.

with the Han dynasty. Thanks to the intercession of the immortal Patriarch Lü and the explanations of the Three Sages, this age of cosmic peace could now be recreated. No lesser figures that the Three Sages are in charge of doctrinal content and its transmission:

> This doctrine was transmitted from Fu Xi and the Yellow Emperor onward. The Three Great Sages, Qingni (Laozi), Moni (Shakyamuni), and Zhongni (Confucius) elucidated it in order to establish its teaching. The followers of these Three Teachings all reported how to enter this way. This was collected in a compilation that some called "explanations" (*shuoshu* 說述) and others "mind-to-mind transmission" (*xinchuan* 心傳), "practices and formulae" (*gongjue* 功訣), or "practical uses" (*gongyong* 功用). At present, it is scattered or lost.
>
> 此道傳自義黃。仲尼牟尼青尼三大聖人。闡以立教。三家之徒。各述其入門之徑。彙成一編。或曰說述。或曰心傳。或曰功訣。或曰丂用。今散軼矣。[118]

As is to be expected, the Longmen branch of Mt. Jingai possesses all the crucial texts on this healing doctrine. The main scripture is the *Lü zushi sanni yishi shuoshu* 呂祖師三尼醫世說述 (Explanations of the Three Sages' Doctrine of Healing the World by Patriarch Lü). It was edited by the ninth Longmen Vinaya Master Tao Shi'an 陶石庵 (?-1692). The other texts were mostly transmitted with the help of extraordinary figures such as Li Niwan 李泥丸 and Min Yide's own master Shen Yibing 沈一炳 (1708-1786).[119] They are the *Lü zushi sanni yishi gongjue* 呂祖師三尼醫世功訣 (Practices and Formulae on the Three Sages' Doctrine of Healing the World by Patriarch Lü) and the *Tianxian xinchuan* 天仙心傳 (Mind-to-Mind Transmission of Celestial Immortality). One notes the presence in the citation above of three of the four titles of scriptures mentioned: *shuoshu* stands for *Lü zushi sanni yishi shuoshu* 呂祖師三尼醫世說述 (Explanations of the

---

[118] Preface to *Lü zushi sannin yishi shuoshu* 呂祖師三尼醫世說述, DZXB 2: 1a.

[119] JGXD 10: 8 *xia* 48a-49b. Li Niwan was another extraordinary figure attached to the local tradition of Mount Jingai; (Esposito, "La Porte du Dragon," 144–154). He often appeared to masters such as Shen Yibing and Wu Shouyang (1563-1644) in order to transmit secret methods. See Esposito, "La Porte du Dragon," 119–120 and "The Longmen School" {here above, Chapter 2, pp. 111–115}). Li Niwan was in fact also regarded as a master of the five thunder rites. See Esposito, "La Porte du Dragon," 119–120, 144–154, and "The Longmen School" {here above, Chapter 2, p. 106}; and Boltz, *Survey of Taoist Literature*, 198.

Three Sages' Doctrine of Healing the World by Patriarch Lü), *xinchuan* for *Tianxian xinchuan*, and *gongjue* for *Lü zushi sanni yishi gongjue*.

Lü zushi sanni yishi shuoshu 呂祖師三尼醫世說述 (Explanations of the Three Sages' Doctrine of Healing the World by Patriarch Lü) can be regarded as the most alchemical scripture of the *Daozang xubian*. According to the model of inner-alchemical classics, it presents the practice in close relation with the Twelve-stage Ebb and Flow hexagrams.[120]

Lü zushi sanni yishi gongjue 呂祖師三尼醫世功訣 (Practices and Formulae on the Three Sages' Doctrine of Healing the World by Patriarch Lü) is a commentary to the practice (*gong* 功) of the *Dadong zhenjing* 大洞真經 (Perfect Scripture of the Great Harmony), a fundamental Shangqing scripture that was regarded as belonging to the highest degree in the official ordinations controlled by the Celestial Masters.[121] The term *jue* (訣) mentioned in the title refers to the *Xuanyun zhou* 玄蘊咒 (Spell of the Arcane Aggregates), one of the formulae which open the liturgical recitation.[122]

Tianxian xinchuan 天仙心傳 (Mind-to-Mind Transmission of Celestial Immortality) is a kind of final investiture for the Celestial Immortals which also includes a specific liturgical text (*Xuanke* 玄科) and ends with the excellent advice of two extraordinary Longmen masters.[123] According

---

[120] Fabrizio Pregadio, "The Representation of Time in the Zhouyi Cantong qi." *Cahiers d'Extrême-Asie* 8 (1995):163–164. For a summary description on the content of this alchemical practice in the *Lüzu sanni yishi shuoshu* see Esposito, "La Porte du Dragon," 259–260.

[121] Michael Saso, *The Teachings of the Taoist Master Chuang*, 58–59. New Haven: Yale University Press, 1978. For a study of this text in the Shangqing tradition see Isabelle Robinet, "Le Ta-t'ung chen-ching—son authenticité et sa place dans les textes du Shang-ching ching," in *Tantric and Taoist Studies in Honour of R. A. Stein*, ed. by Michel Strickmann, vol. 2: 394–433. Bruxelles: Institut Belge des Hautes Études Chinoises, 1983. The Longmen branch of Mount Jingai focused on the explanation of the *Dadong yuzhang* 大洞玉章 found in the *Yuanshi taidong yujing* 元始大洞玉經 (1583, DZJY 3 *diji* 3: 12a-18b) attributed to Wenchang dijun 文昌帝君. It is also found in the *Dadong yujing tanyi* 大洞玉經壇儀 (DZJY 3 *diji* 4: 18a-19a) which is one of the commentaries attributed to Wei Huacun 魏華存 (252–334). See also the commentary by Min Yide under the title *Yuxiang tianjing zhou zhu* 雨香天經咒注 in *Gu Shuyinlou cangshu* 古書隱樓藏書 9 (ZWDS 10: 474–497).

[122] This spell is found in the *Taishang xuanmen zaotan gongke jing* 太上玄門早壇功課經 (DZJY 23 *zhangji* 1:4b-5a), a Qing text on the Quanzhen liturgy which includes the morning service (Yoshitoyo Yoshioka 吉岡義豊, *Eisei e no negai: Dōkyō* 永生への願い: 道教, 220. Kyoto: Tankōsha, 1970). A part of it is also found in the *Daomen gongke* 道門功課, DZJY 23 *zhangji* 1:3b-4a.

[123] On its content see the appendix. See also Esposito, "La Porte du Dragon," 268–275.

to the *Tianxian xinchuan,* the realization of Celestial Immortality as the original aim of the Golden Elixir path (*jindan* 金丹)[124] necessitates also, in conformity with Wang Changyue's teaching, a strict ethical discipline. This is well illustrated in two supplementary texts of the *Daozang xubian*: the *Tianxian dao jieji xuzhi* 天仙道戒忌須知 (Required Knowledge on Precepts and Prohibitions for the Path to Celestial Immortality) and the *Tianxian daocheng baoze* 天仙道程寶則 (Precious Principles for the Path to Celestial Immortality). If this kind of "Celestial immortality program" consisting of moral and practical precepts clearly shows the link between the Longmen branch of Mt. Jingai and the Longmen official school (which is the product of the Longmen standardized ordination system and its pure rules), the Jingai branch also added its own interpretations. Beyond the official salvation guaranteed by Longmen Vinaya Masters (*lüshi* 律師) who convey the supreme ordination—the *tianxian jie* 天仙戒 or Great Precepts of Celestial Immortals—, Min Yide's soteriological texts also attest to the survival of individual salvation through alchemical training.

The Efficacy of the Celestial Immortals in the World

Min Yide and his branch of Mount Jingai not only accept the original meaning of "Celestial Immortal" as related to mystical experience,[125] but also felt the need to adapt it to the exigencies of their time and to the Longmen official teachings of Wang Changyue: genuine realization must manifest itself in the world and display its efficacy. It should not restrict itself to the mystical experience of emptiness and individual union with the Dao but must also be able to return to the world and lead an increasing number of people to enlightenment. For this purpose, the Longmen texts in Min Yide's collection add a supplementary step to the three traditional stages of inner alchemy. After having sublimated the essence (*jing* 精), the pneuma (*qi* 氣),

---

[124] It refers to the classical locus found in *Wuzhen pian*: "If you are studying Immortality, you should study Celestial Immortality; only the Golden Elixir is worthwhile" (Thomas Cleary, *Understanding Reality*, 28. Honolulu: University of Hawa'i Press, 1987).

[125] This mystical experience is akin to the elitist Southern tradition, as illustrated by Baopuzi's 抱朴子 words that "the destiny is in one's own hand"; see Robinet, "Notes préliminaires," 232–233.

and the spirit (*shen* 神), the Longmen practitioner who has already unified his spirit with Dao and experienced true emptiness must come back to the world and devote him- or herself to saving people.[126] Indeed, this return to the secular world advocated by the Longmen branch of Mount Jingai shows the integration of Confucian teachings of Wang Changyue (his harmonization of lay and monastic status) and reflects tendencies of the beginning of the Qing dynasty which were characterized by "the primacy of action and the importance of people as source of all wealth."[127] Furthermore, according to the Longmen branch of Mount Jingai, the Celestial Immortal is thus no longer solely one who receives the necessary ordination, as in the system of Wang Changyue, but becomes also a figure who, through alchemical training, masters all kinds of techniques—Daoist or Buddhist, foreign or Chinese—in order to save the greatest number of people in the world.

Instead of the usual terms such as *zhishi* (治世), *jishi* (濟世) or *dushi* (度世), the appellation of this comprehensive method of salvation is thus *yishi* 醫世 (to heal the world). If this medicinal understanding of "salvation" is related to Daoism and to its messianic tradition, it also applies to Buddhism and alchemy in general.[128] In fact, through the term *yishi* alchemical

---

[126] See for example *Huangji hepi xianjing* 尹真人東華正脈皇極闔闢證道仙經, j. *xia*, chap. 10 (DZXB 1: 5a-7b); and Esposito, "La Porte du Dragon," 217–221. The *Daozang xubian* also contains alchemical methods reserved to female adepts because, in the Longmen's universal salvation program, women too can obtain enlightenment; see the *Xiwangmu nüxiu zhengtu shize* 西王母女修正途十則 and the *Niwan Li zushi nüzong shuangxiu baofa* 泥丸李祖師女宗雙修寶筏. These two works have been translated into English by Wile, *The Arts of Bedchamber*, 192–201 and 204–212; and into French by Esposito, "La Porte du Dragon" 280–374. For a study on feminine alchemy see Despeux, *Immortelles de la Chine*.

[127] As Jacques Gernet ("Quelques thèmes de la pensée chinoise au XVIe et XVIIe siècles," *Annuaire du Collège de France (1992–93)*: 675–676) points out: "Les thèmes de la primauté de l'action et de l'importance du peuple comme source de toute richesse apparaissent chez presque tous les penseurs du XVIIème siècle. À un XVIème siècle introverti, s'oppose un XVIIème extroverti" (The themes of the primacy of action and of the importance of the people as source of all wealth appear in almost all thinkers of the 17th century. The introverted 16th century stands in contrast with an extroverted 17th century). This return to practical knowledge well characterizes the beginning of the Qing dynasty and was certainly also stimulated by the scientific and technical contributions of Jesuits. See de Bary, "Individualism and Humanitarism" and "Neo-Confucian Cultivation"; and Weiping Chen 陳衛平, "Lun Mingqing jian xifang chuanjiaoshi dui zhongxi zhexue bijiao" 論明清間西方傳教士對中西哲學比較, *Shijie zongjiao yanjiu* 世界宗教研究 1 (1989):12–18.

[128] Norman J. Girardot, *Myth and Meaning in Early Taoism: The Theme of Chaos (hun-*

techniques are rehabilitated and enriched with specific methods such as the visualization of Brahmā or the practice of the Yellow Path. By the use of this term, Min Yide raises both the *Golden Flower* and the *Immortals' Scripture* to the highest rank. Like a magic wand, the term *yishi* sanctifies a wealth of techniques of different origins that immediately transform themselves into skillful means for saving the world. [129] Moreover, *yishi* is for the Longmen branch of Mount Jingai the foundation stone for the direct lineage which, through worship of Lü Dongbin and spirit writing practice, encompasses the three teachings and ensures the connection of the Longmen patriarchs of Mt. Jingai with the Quanzhen Northern and Southern Lineages, as well as with the Most High Laozi and even Fu Xi and the Yellow Emperor. It revives the lost transmission of Wang Changyue through the *Golden Flower* which constitutes "the blueprint for healing the world," and secures the mind-to-mind transmission of the Supreme Vehicle (*wushang shangcheng* 無上上乘) of the Celestial Immortals.

Having received official "investiture" on the public ordination platform (*jietan* 戒壇) of Wang Changyue, the Celestial Immortal became, in the eyes of the Longmen followers of Mount Jingai, the "Healer of the World" and potential restorer of the lost cosmic unity of the Han. The spiritual function of the Celestial Immortal is now put forward from the highest doctrinal altar (*zongtan* 宗壇) of Patriarch Lü Dongbin. It is conceived on the model of the ancient sages who can, like Confucian masters, instruct a new emperor.

From this perspective, the choice of the term *yishi* 醫世 for designating this new soteriological doctrine of the Longmen branch of Mount Jingai can be easily understood. "Healing" is in fact a key term of millenarian movements; it is linked to the ancient cosmo-political theory of universal salvation. This theory is connected to the eschatological visions of the realm of Great Peace preached not only by utopian seekers but also by literati as

---

tun), 298. Berkeley: University of California Press, 1983. For the important role of medicine in Buddhism see the entry "Byō 病" in Demiéville et al., *Hōbōgirin*, fasc. 3, 224–270.

[129] It is thus not without reason that Min Yide later came to be honored as the founder of a Longmen branch called Fangbian pai 方便派 (Lineage of Skillful Means); see *Longmen zhengzong Jueyun daotong xinchuan* 龍門正宗覺雲本支道統薪傳, 24, by Lu Yongming 陸永銘, the eighteenth patriarch of the Shanghai Longmen branch of Jueyun. This branch was founded by Fei Boyun 費撥雲, a Min Yide's disciple. I am grateful to Professor Chen Yaoting 陳耀庭 for procuring a copy of this text before its 1994 printed publication in ZWDS (31: 419–473).

representations of the old Chinese ideal of the Golden Age.[130] Through the instructions by the major representatives of the Three Teachings, the Longmen masters—"ordained" by the immortal Lü Dongbin at his "doctrinal altar" of Mount Jingai—could now undertake their psycho-physiological and ethical training for the creation of a new world actualized via a heaven-supported ruler.

It appears to be significant that Min Yide claims to have received explanations about the cosmo-political origins of the healing doctrine of universal salvation directly from Yedaposhe.[131] In his preface to the *Lü zushi sanni yishi shuoshu*, Min Yide presents Yedaposhe as an advocate of the ancient doctrine of the interrelation between natural phenomena and social activity. This doctrine was mainly known through the Confucian scholar Dong Zhongshu 董仲舒 (ca. 179–104 BCE) and was traditionally used for supporting the advent of new dynasties. This support was given only under the condition that a new dynasty was regarded as being in harmony with the rhythm of the universe. By quoting Confucian classics and their prophetic interpretations as well as a famous chapter of the *Daodejing* ("The Dao is great, the Heaven is great, the Earth is great, and the Sovereign is also great"), Yedaposhe showed a clear intention of promoting the emperor as the genuine teacher of the people.[132] As the prototype of a foreigner who had been completely integrated into Han culture and received a bombastic Chinese name (Yellow Guardian of the Center),[133] he appears to have been the perfect transmitter of the healing doctrine of universal salvation to the

---

[130] Anna Seidel, "The Image of the Perfect Ruler in Early Taoist Messianism: Lao-tzu and Li Hung." *History of Religions* 9 (1969–70): 216–247; Anna Seidel, "Imperial Treasures and Taoist Sacraments: Taoist Roots in the Apocrypha," in *Tantric and Taoist Studies in Honour of R.A. Stein*, ed. by Michel Strickmann, 291–371. Bruxelles: Institut Belge des Hautes Études Chinoises, 1983; Livia Kohn, "The Beginnings and Cultural Characteristics of East Asian Millenarianism." *Japanese Religions* 23, 1–2 (1998): 29–51.

[131] According to the Preface (1828) by Min Yide to the *Lü zushi sanni yishi shuoshu* 呂祖師三尼醫世說述 (DZXB 2:1b), Yedaposhe, the founder of the Longmen Tantric branch, had an active role in the transmission of the healing doctrine: Yedaposhe is regarded as the recipient of the original text of the *Lü zushi sanni yishi shuoshu* and as a master of *dhāraṇī* recitations capable of healing every disease.

[132] Preface by Min Yide (1828) to the *Lü zushi sanni yishi shuoshu* 呂祖師三尼醫世說述 (DZXB 2:1a-2b). For its content, see Esposito, "La Porte du Dragon," 247–254.

[133] Huang Shouzhong 黃守中; see above, p. 161.

Manchu rulers by reminding them of the importance of adapting to Chinese ways.

In fact, when elaborating the healing doctrine of universal salvation, as well as other specific doctrines such as that of the Yellow Path, the Longmen branch of Mt. Jingai was careful to choose a vocabulary strictly linked to its Chinese cultural heritage. For example, even if it was certainly influenced by Tantrism, the choice of colors is characteristic of the Longmen practice of the three channels. The colors of the three channels (red, black, and yellow) of course occupy a key position in the traditional Chinese theory of correspondences where Yellow is the symbol of the Center and of China itself. In fact, the Yellow Path and the healing doctrine represent for the Longmen branch the means for a twofold return: (1) a return to the alchemical Daoist soteriological path (instead of the Buddhism-inspired three-tiered training of Wang Changyue) through the rehabilitation of all kinds of techniques,[134] and (2) a return to the Golden Age of Fu Xi and the Yellow Emperor. It is this "orthodoxy" that is again celebrated in a time of crisis when the Longmen patriarchs were living under a foreign dynasty.

Conclusion

In parallel with the "official vision" of Longmen encapsulated in the seventeenth-century ideal teachings of Wang Changyue, another Longmen tradition takes shape in the nineteenth-century scriptures of Min Yide and his local branch of Mount Jingai. What I have called the "official vision" refers to the Longmen school of Wang Changyue. It is presented as a monastic tradition centered on discipline and the application of moral precepts. It neither performs magic rituals nor practices alchemical and life-prolonging techniques. It focuses only on meditative exercises by cultivating calmness, purity, and non-action. The spiritual development of priests is ensured by the three-stage ordination that is interpreted in the perspective of the Buddhist threefold training of discipline, concentration and wisdom. On the Chan model, the precepts are in the Longmen ordination program

---

[134] On this revenge of Daoism on Buddhism and Confucianism in the elaboration of the soteriological doctrine of healing the world, see for example the 1664 preface of Tao Shi'an 陶石庵 to the *Lü zushi sanni yishi shuoshu* 呂祖師三尼醫世說述 (DZXB 2: 1b/5–10). See the translation of this preface in Esposito, "La Porte du Dragon," 255–256.

the means for achieving enlightenment through the realization of Celestial Immortality. However, in this vision, the concept of "Celestial Immortal" seems to have lost its connection with the alchemical path and appears mainly as the Daoist counterpart of a Bodhisattva who devotes himself to saving the world. The soteriological aspiration of the Celestial Immortal is incorporated in an ethical program inspired by Confucianism that includes the respect of Confucian rules.

By contrast, the Longmen branch of Mount Jingai puts forward the ideal of the Celestial Immortal as the fruit of extensive alchemical training which includes all kinds of esoteric techniques coming from Daoist and other traditions. Even though this local branch, in order to realize the goal of Celestial Immortality, does not exclude the practice of discipline and the respect of Confucian values, it also rehabilitates life-prolonging techniques and the performance of magic rituals and specific liturgies. Although the study of its rituals and liturgies necessitates further research, in the local branch of Mount Jingai and the elaboration of its own soteriological program one can already detect the signs of a proclamation of independence from the standardized and ideal Longmen teaching of Wang Changyue. Concerning the local branch of Mount Jingai, this program can be summed up in three main points:

(1) Restoration of Private Ordinations

According to the Longmen branch of Mount Jingai, one can be ordained Celestial Immortal not only on the ordination platform (*jietan* 戒壇) of Longmen Vinaya Masters at public monasteries but also at the private doctrinal altar (*zongtan* 宗壇) of Lü Dongbin in the hermitage of Mount Jingai. The latter ordination may not imply a gradual transmission of the threefold precepts (Initial Precepts of Perfection, Intermediate Precepts, and Great Precepts of the Celestial Immortals) but rather a simple esoteric formula. This formula contains the highest ordination—the Great Precepts of the Celestial Immortals—along with the incomparable teaching of the *Golden Flower* by the immortal Lü Dongbin. This recalls the Tantric transmission of precepts by an incantation or *dhāraṇī*; it was allegedly integrated in the Longmen branch of Mount Jingai from the Longmen Tantric master Yedaposhe. Furthermore, in the Longmen branch of Mount Jingai, this private ordination is set in a Daoist context and takes its strength from the cult of Lü Dongbin via spirit writing. The Longmen branch of Mount

Jingai received a corpus of texts directly from the immortal Lü Dongbin and established a specific soteriological program that pretends to supersede that of Wang Changyue. However, without Wang Changyue's teachings and his strong inspiration by Chan formless precepts, the Longmen branch of Mount Jingai would probably not have been able to formulate its own views.

(2) Affirmation of a Threefold Daoist Training

The three-stage ordination with its three Buddhist ideals of *sīla*, *dhyāna* and *prajñā* is thus set in a Daoist context and finds a further development in the Longmen branch of Mount Jingai. In this branch, the "control of the body of form"—ensured in the Initial Precepts of Perfection through the strong respect of discipline—comes to signify the application of all kinds of Daoist psycho-physiological techniques for controlling the body and its functions. In the second stage, the "control of the illusory mind" (*huanxin* 幻心), ensured in the Intermediate Precepts through *dhyāna*, comes to mean in the Longmen branch of Mount Jingai the progressive understanding of the inherent non-duality of mind and body. This is well illustrated by the joint cultivation of Nature and Vital Force as explained in the "blueprints for healing the world," i.e., the *Secret of the Golden Flower* and the *Immortals' Scripture of the Perfected Yin*. In the Longmen branch of Mount Jingai, these first two stages—the control of body and mind— from a gradual perspective constitute the "path of men." They are reserved for the inferior and intermediate Longmen practitioners who are not yet capable of the immediate realization of inherent non-duality.

Finally, the supreme stage of the Great Precepts of the Celestial Immortal or "path of immortals" represents for the Longmen branch of Mount Jingai "the Sudden Highest Vehicle of the Celestial Immortality." In Wang's teaching, this had been brought about by *prajñā* in order "to free the genuine Intention" and occurred only after having received all the precepts of the previous two ordination stages. By contrast, the Longmen branch of Mount Jingai advanced the possibility for superior practitioners to actualize the supreme stage at once through the *Secret of the Golden Flower*'s formula. This kind of "Sudden Celestial Immortal" represents a Perfected Being who realizes in a snap the esoteric formula of the *Secret of the Golden Flower* and simultaneously undergoes a complete alchemical transformation through the opening of the Yellow Path, thus becoming a Healer of the World.

(3) The Longmen Celestial Immortal "Healer of the World"

In this figure of the "Celestial Immortal who heals the world" one can finally detect the fruit of a long integration of different traditions. The ideal priesthood of Daoism which was originally represented by the Celestial Masters, after having absorbed the alchemical Southern tradition of the Golden Elixir and being purified by the strict Northern Quanzhen monastic discipline revitalized by Wang Changyue, appears in a new garb in the Longmen branch of Mount Jingai. Its figure of the Healer of the World represents the originality of this local branch. It reaffirms the messianic aspirations of a Great Peace realm ruled by an enlightened king who can reactualize the Han orthodoxy, although this time it happens with the help of Longmen Celestial Immortals.[135]

The final elaboration of such a soteriological and messianic doctrine by the Longmen branch of Mount Jingai was indeed the fruit of a long integration of earlier Daoist traditions inside and outside the Longmen official school. It shows a revival of Jiangnan traditions that found their spokesman in Min Yide and his branch of Mount Jingai in Zhejiang. This branch is also characterized by Tantric-influenced teachings that were crystallized in the semi-legendary figure of Yedaposhe, as well as by its absorption of local cults and saints as in the case of Perfected Yin. All of this finds full expression in the establishment of Longmen Jingai's identity and lineage driven by its will to establish a genuine doctrine and a specific liturgy capable of perfecting the Longmen teaching of Wang Changyue and his ordination system. Claiming independence from Wang Changyue's official teaching of Beijing's Baiyun guan, this local community clearly harbored the hope that Mount Jingai would become the center for the creation of a new Longmen doctrine and a new world.

---

[135] Esposito, "La Porte du Dragon," 144–154; and "The Longmen School" {here above, Chapter 2}.

APPENDIX

Annotated List of Texts in *Daozang Xubian* 道藏續編[136] (Supplementary Collection to the Daoist Canon) by Min Yide 閔一得, 1834, Four Volumes

Volume I

1. *Lü zushi xiantian xuwu Taiyi jinhua zongzhi* 呂祖師先天虛無太一金華宗旨 [Patriarch Lü's Quintessential Doctrine of the Golden Flower of the Great One of the Emptiness Before Heaven]

    Abbreviated title: *Taiyi jinhua zongzhi* 太一金華宗旨
    13 chapters, pp. 1a-15b
    Revealed via spirit writing by Lü Dongbin 呂洞賓
    Edited by Jiang Yuanting 蔣元庭 (1755–1819)
    Revised by Min Yide 閔一得 (1758–1836)
    Preface (1831) and Introductory note by Min Yide 閔一得

This text concerns primarily what is called *xing* 性 (inner nature), a synonym of *xin* 心 or nature of the mind, and the methods connected with its discovery and cultivation. The first chapter can be seen as a kind of Esoteric Transmission of Precepts concerning the Nature of Mind. The basic practice is *fanguang* 返光 or *huiguang* 回光. This text is full of Buddhist Tiantai 天台 and Chan 禪 terminology reinterpreted in a Daoist context. It belongs to the texts for universal salvation (*yishi* 醫世) of the Longmen lineage. Different editions of this text exist, and some of them have been translated.[137] The *Daozang xubian* version differs from other editions mainly with regard to the prefaces, the first chapter, and the commentaries.

---

[136] *Daozang xubian* 道藏續編 [Supplementary Collection of the Daoist Canon], 4 vols., by Min Yide 閔一得 (1758–1836). Wuxing: Jingai cangban, 1834. Photolithographic edition by Ding Fubao 丁福保 (1874–1952), Shanghai: Yixue shuju. The edition used here is the reprint of 1989 (Beijing: Haiyang 海洋). Information about the attribution, etc., of these texts is culled from their colophons and does of course not necessarily reflect historical reality.

[137] {For information on the history of this text, its various editions, and translations see Part 4 of Monica Esposito, *Creative Daoism*. Wil / Paris, UniversityMedia, 2013.}

2. *Yin zhenren Donghua zhengmai huangji hepi zhengdao xianjing*
尹真人東華正脈皇極闔闢證道仙經 [Immortals' Scripture of the Perfected Yin Testifying to the Path of Opening and Closing the Sovereign Ultimate according to the Orthodox Lineage of the Eastern Efflorescence]

> Abbreviated title *Huangji hepi xianjing* 皇極闔闢仙經
> 3 *juan*, 10 chapters:
> (1) j. *shang*, chap. 1–4, pp.1a-6a
> (2) j. *zhong*, chap. 5–6, pp. 1a-3a
> (3) j. *xia*, chap. 7–10, pp. 1a-7a
> Manuscript of the Qingyang gong 青羊宮 (Chengdu)
> Revealed by Yin Pengtou 尹蓬頭
> Corrected by Min Yide 閔一得 (1758–1836)
> Preface (1831) and Postface by Min Yide 閔一得

This text is primarily devoted to the so-called practices on *ming* 命 and aims at identifying and classifying various alchemical stages by establishing physical markers in the body. Its overall purpose is to incorporate meditative practices and to assist in understanding the role of physiological techniques for mastering the discursive mind. The content is similar to the Ming classic *Xingming guizhi* 性命圭旨.[138] Both texts are said to be revealed by the perfected Yin Pengtou 尹蓬頭.[139] The adepts are divided into three classes: inferior and intermediate adepts need to practice progressively and according to psycho-physiological techniques expressed in alchemical terms, whereas superior adepts are capable of sudden realization. The superior adepts can see all practices from the point view of the fruit and are able to devote themselves to the salvation of the world (*yishi* 醫世).

The first *juan* includes the following chapters:

> (1) "Adding Oil for welcoming the Vital Force" (*tianyou jieming* 添油接命). This chapter deals with the moment of being born through cutting the umbilical cord. This is illustrated by the primordial cry or sound of individuation (*huo di yisheng* 囫地一聲) which marks the path toward human alienation, the egotic-self. The Vital Force is represented by a spark of original

---

[138] Translated into German by Martina Darga, *Das alchemistische Buch von innerem Wesen und Lebensenergie Xingming guizhi*. München: Eugen Diederichs, 1999.

[139] See above, pp. 173–174.

Yang which takes part in this process of creation and is stored in the navel (*jilun* 臍輪). Instead of being forgotten, this luminous spark, if cultivated by adding the oil of the spirit, can bring about the "opening of the Celestial Heart-Mind." This method of "adding oil" consists in fixing the attention on the Mountain Root (*shangen*), i.e. the space between the eyebrows. In this chapter two points are emphasized:

(a) The role of the Spinal Handle (*jiaji* 夾脊), the second Pass localized in the shoulder blades;

(b) The establishment of the Yellow Path (*huangdao* 黃道), a central channel seen as the path for overcoming duality.

(2) "Crystallizing the Spirit into the Cavity" (*ningshen ruqiao* 凝神入竅). This chapter is devoted to the presentation of the method of the supreme contemplation of heart-mind (*taishang guanxin* 太上觀心) consisting of inner, outer, and remote contemplation. The Inner contemplation or introspection (*neiguan* 內觀) serves to realize the discursive mind or *renxin* 人心, the source of our constant grasping of things. The External contemplation (*waiguan* 外觀) brings the discovery of the Dao-Mind (*daoxin* 道心) or luminous mind (i.e., the non discursive mind). The Remote contemplation (*yuanguan* 遠觀) concerns the Celestial Heart-Mind (*tianxin* 天心) which appears here as synonym of Cavity of Breath (*qixue* 氣穴). It represents the discovery of the link between breathing and thinking.

(3) "The Interdependency of Spirit and Breathing" (*shenxi xiangyi* 神息相依) concerns the control of the so-called embryo-breathing which is expressed in physiological terms through the experience of a blazing fire at the level of the kidneys. This marks the opening of the first pass. This opening is, at the same time, described through the Chan metaphor of "seeing one's original face" thanks to *zhao* 照 (radiance). The peculiarity of this text consists in regarding the incorporation of physical markers and the corresponding physiological experiences in a spiritual perspective. This signifies understanding the mechanism of the discursive and grasping mind, which is the source of the world of desire, thus allowing the sublimation of the essence into breath and the discovery of the pre-natal essence that can be sublimated into breath, the subject of the subsequent chapter.

(4) "Reassembling the Fire for Opening the Pass" (*juhuo kaiguan* 聚火開關) describes the practice of the so-called *xiao zhoutian* 小周天 or microcosmic orbit. This is summarized by four concepts: *xi* 吸 (inhalation of breath); *shi* 舐 (rolling the tongue up to the palate); *cuo* 措 (pressing the anus), and *bi* 閉 (closing mouth and eyes). The result is the birth of the pre-natal medicine (*xiantian yao* 先天樂).

These techniques are said to be for the disciples of average or inferior capacities who must apply them in conjunction with the practice of fixation of mind as explained in the first chapter.

The second *juan* contains chapters 5–6, pp. 1a–3a:

(5) "Gathering the Medicine and Returning it in the Gourd" (*caoyao guihu* 採藥歸壺). The theme of this chapter is the so-called "gathering." The return to the prenatal state—the great pre-natal medicine or *xiantian dayao* 先天大藥— involves knowing how to catch the right moment for practice in order to experience an ecstatic state of mind that must be cultivated in every moment of one's life.

(6) "The Celestial Circulation Maoyou" (*maoyou zhoutian* 卯酉週天). This chapter deals with a practice of absorption (*shougong* 收功) from left to right its integration in daily practice and life. It marks the second stage of alchemical practice, i.e., sublimating breath into spirit, expressed through the metaphor of the Union of Qian 乾 (heaven) and Kun 坤 (earth).

The third *juan* deals with the third and fourth stage of alchemical practice and includes chapters 7–10, pp. 1a–7a:

(7) "Feeding the Holy Embryo for a long time" (*changyang shengtai* 長養聖胎). This is one of several expressions used for describing the Third Stage. Other expressions are "the five breaths pay homage to the Supreme Yang" (*wuqi ju chao yu shangyang* 五氣俱朝於上陽), or "the three flowers gather at the Qian crown" (*sanhua jie ju yu qianding* 三花皆聚於乾頂). They refer to the progressive development of Pure Yang and the elimination of Yin, expressed in metaphors such as "cinnabar is ripe and the pearl numinous" (*danshu zhuling* 丹熟珠靈). Like a woman who, conscious of her pregnancy, pays constant attention to the embryo in her own womb, the Daoist adept must constantly maintain a state of concentrated awareness.

(8) "Giving the Breast to the Baby" (*rufu ying'er* 乳哺嬰兒). This is a metaphor for describing the culmination of the state of pregnancy and the appearance of the newborn. The state of awareness of the Daoist adept is compared with a baby who still needs to be fed by the Holy Mother and helped by the Numinous Father to be able one day to freely move by itself.

(9) "Shifting the Spirit to the Inner Court (*yishen neiyuan* 移神內院). This refers to the practice of Non-action, Non-being (*wuzuo, wuwei* 無作無為) consisting in "embracing the One and darkening the heart-mind in order to realize one's Inner Nature" (*baoyi mingxin yi liaoxing* 抱一冥心以了性). At this stage, the text discusses the development of the six divine or magical powers (*liutong* 六通).

(10) "Sublimating the Void and Uniting with Dao" (*lianxu hedao* 煉虛合道). This is the fourth and last stage in the alchemical process of sublimation. After having accomplished the normal three alchemical stages, the Longmen school emphasizes the necessity of applying the fruit of personal cultivation in the world. This implies returning to the mundane sphere to save human beings. Like a Bodhisattva or a Confucian saint, accomplished Longmen Daoists must go back to the world and apply their full enlightenment in society. The stress on universal salvation is a core element of Longmen's *yishi* 醫世 (curing the world) doctrine.

3. *Yin zhenren Liaoyang dian wenda bian* 尹真人廖陽殿問答編
[Questions and Answers of the Perfected Yin from the Liaoyang Hall]

> Abbreviated title: *Liaoyang dian wenda bian* 廖陽殿問答編
> 6 chapters, pp. 1a-12b
> Manuscript of the Qingyang gong (Chengdu)
> Revealed by Yin Pengtou 尹蓬頭
> Corrected by Min Yide 閔一得 (1758–1836)

This text is very similar to the precedent one. It is also said to have been revealed by the Perfected Yin (Yin Pengtou 尹蓬頭). It presents a similar but more concise process of sublimation according to the different alchemical stages. It is in "Question and Answer" format and is said to document discussions among Daoist disciples gathered at the Liaoyang hall on Mt. Qingcheng (Sichuan, near Chengdu). The six chapters are:

(1) "Taking the Seat" (*shengzuo pian* 升座篇). This chapter opens with the gathering of disciples at the Liaoyang hall, after having completed the purification in the Baiyun tang of Mt. Qingcheng. The questions and answers turn around topics like "the principle of life-and-death (*saṃsāra*) and Yin and Yang" (*shengsi yinyang zhi li* 生死陰陽之理), the "three frontal fields," (*qian santian* 前三田) the "three rear passes," (*hou sanguan* 後三關) "principle of the Great Ultimate" (*taiji zhi li* 太極之理) and so on.

(2) The second chapter has no subtitle; it deals with alchemical formulae for preserving the Vital Force under the name of "Sixteen Ingots of Gold" (*shiliu dingjin* 十六錠金). It focuses on the method for unblocking the three passes (*sanguan* 三關).

(3) "Initial Foundations" (*shiji pian* 始基篇) discusses laying the foundations for true practice. It is a metaphor for seeing one's true original nature (*jianxing* 見性). This signifies realizing the nature of mind through the practice of introspection (*neiguan* 內觀).

(4) "The Divine Chamber" (*shenshi pian* 神室篇) refers to the Original Spirit (*yuanshen* 元神) or Original nature (*yuanxing* 元性).

(5) "The River Chariot" (*heche pian* 河車篇) is another name for the practice of unblocking the three passes, the path along the Governor Channel (*dumai* 都脈).

(6) "Secret Transmission" (*mishou pian* 秘授篇). It is divided into seven sections: 1. Governing the mind; 2. Going back to inner contemplation; 3. Navel inner vision; 4. Gathering the fire for opening the Passes; 5. Maoyou Celestial circulation; 6. Feeding the Holy Embryo for long time; 7. Shifting of the Embryo and return to Wuji or Great Dao (*dadao* 大道).

4. *Xie tianji* 泄天機 [Disclosing the Celestial Mechanism]

> pp. 1a–6b
> Orally transmitted by the Divine Li Niwan 李泥丸
> Recorded by Anonymous
> Recompiled by Min Yide 閔一得 (1758–1836)
> Postface (1833) by Min Yide 閔一得

The description of alchemical practice (whose principles and techniques are very similar to those of the preceding two texts) is here divided into six sections:

(1) "Direct Indications on the Great Return of Metal Fluid (*jinye dahuan zhizhi* 金液大還直指). This anticipates the fruit of the practice, i.e, the Great return to Dao.
(2) "Laying the Foundations and Fully Relying upon the Bellows (*zhuji quanping tuoye* 築基全憑橐籥). This chapter contains the doctrine of the Three Paths (red, yellow and black).
(3) "Sublimating *ji* 己 by using Genuine Lead and Casting the Sword with Water-metal to Gather the Before-Heaven (*lianji-xuyong zhenqian, jinshui taojian cao xiantian* 煉己須用真鉛。金水鑄劍採先天). *Ji* refers to the sixth celestial branch associated with earth and center, and is a symbol for *zhenyi* 真意 or True Intention. The sword is a metaphor for discursive thoughts, for the heart-mind and its emotional activities that are not yet mastered. This section focuses on the so-called *Jiji* 即濟 method, whose name is derived from hexagram 63 of the *Yijing* and indicates the dynamic balance between Water and Fire.
(4) "By obtaining the medicine through boiling and sublimating it, adding and taking away Fire Time without mistake, one can become a Divine Immortal of this earthly world (*deyao fang shi penglian, choutian huohou bute, fang wei ludi shenxian* 得藥方施烹煉。抽添火候不忒。方為陸地神仙). One has to distinguish between the Small Medicine that leads merely to the stage of Earthly Immortals, and the Great Medicine by virtue of which one attains the Celestial or Golden Immortality.
(5) "Searching again for the Great Medicine in order to testify the Golden Immortality and regulating the Fire Time into nine cycles (*zaiqiu dayao zheng jinxian, huohou xiuchi jiuzhuan* 再求大藥證金仙。火候修持九轉). This explains the practice that is better known as "Feeding the Holy Embryo for ten months" (also referred to as "nine-month practice"; see above Text 2, section "Feeding the Holy Embryo for a long time").
(6) "Original vow of cutting off the chains of the dusty world by facing the wall for nine years and joining with divine immortals" (*jiunian mianbi jue chenyuan, shihe shenxian benyuan* 九年面壁絕塵緣。始合神仙本願). This is the last stage which indicates leaving the world of transmigration and reaching the state of Divine Immortals who, like Buddhist Bodhisattvas, have made the vow of saving all beings.

5. *Gufa yangsheng shisan ze chanwei* 古法養生十三則闡微 [Uncovering the Subtleties of the Thirteen Principles Concerning the Ancient Methods of Nourishing Life]

>   Abbreviated title: *Shisan ze chanwei* 十三則闡微
>   pp. 1a-5b
>   By Min Yide 閔一得 (1758–1836)
>   Postface (1818) by Min Yide 閔一得

This is the only text in the collection that is entirely devoted to the exposition of *daoyin* 導引 methods. It emphasizes the hidden meaning of their functions as part of the alchemical quest for enlightenment.

>   (1) "Clenching one's fists, closing the eyes and darkening the heart-mind" (*liangshou wogu, bimu mingxin* 兩手握固。閉目冥心).
>
>   (2) "Pressing the tongue upward on the palate, and harmonizing the heart-mind thanks to One Intention" (*shidi shang'e, yiyi tiaoxin* 舌抵上腭。一意調心).
>
>   (3) "Rubbing the waist while the spirit roams in the water-abode (*shenyou shuifu, shuang ca yaoshen* 神遊水府。雙擦腰腎).
>
>   (4) "Shrugging repeatedly one's shoulders, while the mind focuses on the *weilü*" (*xin zhu weilü, pin song liangjian* 心注尾閭。頻聳兩肩).
>
>   (5) "Clacking one's teeth and moving one's mouth while looking at the peak-door (*mushi dingmen, kouchi jiaokou* 目視頂門。叩齒攪口).
>
>   (6) "Swallowing frequently one's breath while quietly rolling the eyes (*jingyun liangmu, pinpin yanqi* 靜運兩目。頻頻嚥氣).
>
>   (7) "Rubbing the abdomen to clarify the spirit, and stretching both-feet with one's hands (*chengshen mofu, shoupan liangzu* 澄神摩腹。手攀兩足).
>
>   (8) "Bending forward and beating the drum [by crossing one's legs behind the ears] while counting the breathing to crystallize the spirit" (*fushen minggu, shuxi ningshen* 俯身鳴鼓。數息凝神).
>
>   (9) "Swinging one's waist [while sitting], pushing out the legs [while standing], and supporting the sky with one's hands (*baiyao satui, liangshou tuotian* 擺腰洒腿。兩手托天).
>
>   (10) "Drawing the bow left and right to equilibrate the heart-mind and calming the breath" (*zuoyou kaigong, pingxin jingqi* 左右開弓。平心靜氣).
>
>   (11) "Without 'I' and 'other,' the heart-mind is as tranquil as still

water (*wuwo wuren, xin ru zhishui* 無我無人。心如止水).
(12) "The entire body is constantly warm, and day and night are in full harmony (*bianti changnuan, zhuye chonghe* 遍體常煖。晝夜充和).
(13) "Movement and stillness being not-two, concealing one's brilliance and being as humble as dust" (*dongjing buer, heguang tongchen* 動靜不二。和光同塵).

Volume II

6. *Shangpin danfa jieci* 上品丹法節次 [Alchemical Process of Superior Degree]

   pp. 1a-2b
   Originally recorded by Li Dexia 李德洽
   Recompiled by Min Yide 閔一得 (1758–1836)
   Corrected by Min Yide's disciple Min Yanglin 閔陽林

Through Li Dexia 李德洽, this text belongs to the Hengyang lineage which claims its central position by emphasizing the union of Northern and Southern Lineages under the common lineage of patriarch Lü Dongbin. The content of its sections is very close to the alchemical stages as presented in the *Yin zhenren Huangji*; see above Text 5.

(1) "Sublimating Ji-Thought and Actualizing Sincerity (*lianji cuncheng* 鍊己存誠).
(2) "Laying the Foundations and Nourishing the Medicine" (*zhuji peiyang* 築基培藥).
(3) "The Marriage of Kan and Li" (*kanli jiaogou* 坎離交媾);
(4) "Gathering the Medicine and Taking it Back to the Vessel" (*caoyao guiding* 採藥歸鼎).
(5) "Time Fire of the Celestial Circulation" (*zhoutian huohou* 周天火候).
(6) "The Marriage of Qian and Kun" (*qiankun jiaogou* 乾坤交媾).
(7) "Nourishing the Embryo for 10 Months" (*shiyue yangtai* 十月養胎).
(8) "Shifting the Spirit to the Changed Vessel" (*yishen huanding* 移神換鼎).

(9) "Nourishing Wisdom in the Mud Ball" (*niwan yanghui* 泥丸養慧).

(10) "Sublimating the Spirit and Returning to Void" (*lianshen huanxu* 鍊神還虛).

(11) "Sublimating Void and Uniting with Dao" (*lianxu hedao* 鍊虛合道).

(12) "Unified with Dao joining the Truth" (*yudao hezhen* 與道合真).

7. ***Guankui bian*** 管窺編 [A Personal View]

>pp. 1a-2b
>By Min Yide 閔一得 (1758–1836)

This is A Personal View by Min Yide on the *Xiuxian bianhuo lun* 修仙辨惑論 (Discussion on resolving doubts concerning immortality cultivation) by Bai Yuchan 白玉蟾 (1194 ?-ca. 1227). As Patriarch of the Southern lineage, Bai Yuchan is one of the masters to whom the texts of the *Daozang xubian* often refer.

The alchemical method is here divided into three levels: the superior level is represented by the Celestial Immortals (*tianxian* 天仙) who can fully sublimate their self and ascend to heaven; this method can be transmitted only from mind to mind. The intermediate level is represented by Watery Immortals (*shuixian* 水仙) or Human Immortals (*renxian* 人仙) who, being visible or invisible, can enter and leave the physical dimension. Their methods can only be transmitted orally. The inferior level is that of Earthly Immortals (*dixian* 地仙) who leave their bodies on earth and whose methods are transmitted via writing. In this level, the essence, breath, secretions constitute the matter which must be sublimated. Breathing techniques, retention of breath, saliva, gymnastic practices, massages, etc. are the so called Fire Time. This inferior method can be summed up into the concentration of spirit and breath circulation or Small Celestial Circulation.

8. ***Jiuzheng lu*** 就正錄 [Record of the Realization of Rectitude]

>pp. 1a-5a
>By Lu Shichen 陸世忱
>Preface (1678) by Lu Shichen & Preface (1697) by Yuan Ting 袁綎

In this text there are different quotations of great figures of Confucians and idealist Neo-Confucians, from Mencius 孟子 (ca 372–289) to Wang Yangming 王陽明 (1472–1529), via Shao Yong 邵雍 (1011–1077), Lu Jiuyuan 陸九淵 (1139–1192), and Yang Cihu 養雌虎 (1141–1226). The central practice consists in the discovery of the so called "lost heart" (*fangxin* 放心), an expression from *Mengzi* (chap. 4.A.45/11). This can only be experienced by oneself by following the examples of the great masters quoted above. The accent is on the cultivation of the calmness of heart-mind and the inner rules of moral behavior (*jiyi* 集義 accumulation of righteousness; *Mengzi*, 2A.11/2).

9. *Yu Lin Fenqian xiansheng shu* 與林奮千先生書 [Letter to Master Lin Fenqian]

   pp. 1a–6b
   By Lu Shichen 陸世忱
   Postface (1697) by Huang Ting 黃廷.

On the same line of appreciation of the inner virtues of the Mean 中庸, this text focuses on the term *jue* 覺, discernment or inner perception. Thanks to it one can distinguish between enlightenment and the mundane existence resembling a dream, between life and death, and between man and beast. Along with the study of Confucian virtues the cultivation of the heart-mind is an indispensable requirement for the Longmen alchemical path.

10. *Lü zushi sanni yishi shuoshu* 呂祖師三尼醫世說述 [Explanations of the Three Sages' Doctrine of Healing the World (revealed via spirit writing) by Patriarch Lü]

    pp. 1a–7b
    Entitled by Huang Chiyang 黃赤陽 (1595–1673)
    Edited by Tao Shi'an 陶石庵 (?–1692)
    Commented on by Min Yide 閔一得 (1758–1836)
    Corrected by Shen Yangyi 沈陽一
    Preface (1664) by Tao Shi'an and Preface (1828) by Min Yide.

The alchemical practice is here divided into six stages explained through the use of the Twelve-stage Ebb and Flow hexagrams (*shier xiaoxi* 十二消息). By contrast with the ordinary alchemical process which begins with the hexagram *fu* 復 (the beginning of the Yang, image of the

Winter Solstice and of the body location of the Weilü Pass), the practice here starts with *Dazhuang* 大壯 (the development of Yang, image of the Spring equinox and of the body location of the Jiaji Pass). After a progressive practice marked by different hexagrams, the fruit is achieved with Tai 泰 (Peace).

(1) The first stage is represented by Dazhuang 大壯
(2) The second stage is represented by Kuai 夬 and Qian 乾
(3) The third stage by Gou 姤, Dun 遯, Pi 否, Guan 觀, Bo 剝 and Kun 坤
(4) The fourth stage by Fu 復
(5) The fifth by Lin 臨
(6) The sixth by Tai 泰

11. *Du Lü zushi sanni yishi shuoshu guankui* 讀呂祖師三尼醫世說述管窺 [A Personal Reading of the Explanations of the Three Sages' Doctrine of Healing the World by Patriarch Lü]

   pp.1a-5b
   By Min Yide 閔一得 (1758–1836)
   Postface (1828) by Min Yide

This is presented as a more cosmological reading to the text above. It is divided into seven parts but there are no hexagrams. The text includes cosmological theories on the formation of Heaven and Earth from the distinction between pure and coarse breaths based on *Huainanzi* 淮南子. Previous alchemical techniques are then summarized again from the other texts on *xing* 性 and *ming* 命 in this collection. Specific literature is mentioned, for example "the alchemical classics of *Cantongqi* 參同契 and *Wuzhen pian* 悟真篇 for fulfilling the Vital Force or Ming 命; the *Dadong zhenjing* 大洞真經 for sublimating the ordinary, the *Changdao zhenyan* 常道真言 for sublimating the heart-mind and the cycle of Yishi 醫世 for realizing the fruit."

12. *Lü zushi sanni yishi gongjue* 呂祖師三尼醫世功訣 [Practices and Formulae on the Three Sages' Doctrine of Healing the World by Patriarch Lü]

   pp. 1a-5b
   Transmitted by Shen Yibing 沈一炳 (1708–1786)
   Newly recorded and annotated by Min Yide 閔一得 (1758–1836)

This is a commentary to the practice (*gong* 功) of *Dadong zhenjing* 大洞真經, the fundamental Shangqing scripture which was regarded as belonging to the highest degree in the official ordinations controlled by the Celestial masters. The term *jue* 訣 in the title refers to the Xuanyunzhou 玄蘊咒 (Spell of the Arcane Aggregates), one of the opening formulae of the Quanzhen liturgical recitation for the morning service.

13. *Tianxian xinchuan* 天仙心傳 [Mind-to-Mind Transmission of Celestial Immortality] with two Prefaces (1832, 1834)

    By Min Yide 閔一得 (1758–1836)

The text in five parts opens the *Daozang xubian*'s Tianxian 天仙 cycle. It sums up the doctrine of healing the world and its fruit using four-character verses followed by their exegesis (1–2), a liturgical text (3), and two prose essays (4–5).

   (1) Text pp. 1a-4a; transmitted by Shen Yibing and compiled by Min Yide, including (i) *Neipian* 內篇 [Internal Treatise]; (ii) *Waipian* 外篇 [External Treatise]; (iii) *Yuanjue* 圓訣 [Formulae of achievement]; (iv) *Xupian* 續篇 [Appendix] with a Postface (1833) by Min Yide; (v) *Dadi dong yin* 大滌洞音 [The Sound in the Grotto of Mt. Dadi] with a Postface (1833) by Min Yide; (vi) *Zijing pian* 自警篇 [Treatise on Warnings to Oneself] with a Postface (1834) by Min Yide;

   (2) Commentary pp. 1a-7a including: (i) Commentary to the *Neipian* transmitted by Shen Yibing, recorded and annotated by Min Yide; (ii) Commentary to the *Waipian* transmitted by Shen Yibing and recorded and annotated by Min Yide; (iii) Commentary to the *Yuanjue* recorded by Min Yide and annotated by Xue Yanggui 薛陽桂;

   (3) *Xuanke* 玄科 [Mysterious Liturgy] pp. 7b-12b, transmitted by Shen Yibing and recorded by Min Yide with his Postface (1833);

   (4) *Shenren Li Pengtou fayan yize* 沈人李蓬頭法言一則 [Excellent Advice in a Single Precept by the Divine Li Pengtou], pp. 13a-b, recorded by Dingfan shi 定梵氏 (Min Yide) with his postface (1834);

   (5) *Zhenshi Taixu shi fayan yize* 真師太虛氏法言一則 [Excellent Advice in a Single Precept by Perfected Master of the Supreme Vacuity (Shen Yibing)], pp. 14a-15b, recorded by Dingfan shi 定梵氏 (Min Yide).

Volume III

14. *Tianxian dao jieji xuzhi* 天仙道戒忌須知 [Required Knowledge on Precepts and Prohibitions for the Path to Celestial Immortality]

    pp. 1a-10a
    Transmitted by Li Niwan 李泥丸
    Recorded by Shen Yibing 沈一炳
    Compiled by Lanyun shi 懶雲氏 (Min Yide)
    Revised by Fanzhen zi 返真子

This text is devoted to the description of the Way of Celestial Immortals, as distinct from less lofty earthly immortals, and their practice of the mind (*xinxue* 心學) which leads to perfect awakening (*yuanjue* 圓覺). It lists a total of sixteen prohibitions and precepts, each of which is first listed and then explained by Li Niwan 李泥丸.

15. *Tianxian daocheng baoze* 天仙道程寶則 [Precious Principles for the Path to Celestial Immortality]

    pp. 1a-7a
    Transmitted by Li Niwan 李泥丸
    Recorded by Shen Yibing 沈一炳
    Compiled by Lanyun shi 懶雲氏 (Min Yide)
    Revised by Fanzhen zi 返真子

This text presents a total of nine "precious principles" explained by Li Niwan 李泥丸 concerning (1) perfect clarity (*yuanming* 圓明), (2) perfect purity (*yuanjing* 圓淨), (3) perfect essence (*yuanjing* 圓精), (4) perfect channeling (*yuanyong* 圓庸), (5) perfect oneness (*yuanyi* 圓一), (6) perfect quietude (*yuanji* 圓寂), (7) perfect reflection (*yuanzhao* 圓照), (8) perfect awakening (*yuanjue* 圓覺), and (9) perfect melting (*yuanrong* 圓鎔).

16. *Erlan xinhua* 二懶心話 [Heart-to-Heart Dialogue Between the Two Leisurely (Masters)]

    pp. 1a-7a
    By Min Yide 閔一得 (1758–1836)?
    Postface (1818) by Min Yide.

This text belongs to a Longmen branch called Xizhu xinzong 西竺心宗 (The Heart School of Western India) from Yunnan, a Daoist-Tantric branch of Longmen. Although this text does not mention the name of its author, one can suppose that it was compiled by Min Yide. It is presented in the form of a dialogue between two masters who both have the surname of Lan: Venerable Lan (Lanweng 懶翁) and Old Lan (Dalan 大懶). Min Yide claimed to have received Xizhu xinzong teachings when he was in Yunnan, and one of his surnames was Lanyun 懶雲. The central theme is the practice of the inner vision or *neizhao* 內照 and its alchemical stages. This method has many points of convergence with Kundalini Yoga techniques or Tibetan techniques focused on developing inner heat (*gtum mo*). The text is divided into three chapters:

(1) "Fortuitous Encounter" (*pingfeng* 萍逢). This opens with a meeting between the two masters Lan and the presentation of their common lineage, i.e. Xizhu xinzong.

(2) "Opportune Questions (*shanwen* 善問). In this part, the *neizhao* 內照 method is explained as divided into nine stages:

(i) Washing the marrow;

(ii) Washing the heart-mind;

(iii) Calming the Earth, i.e the Yellow Center (spleen and stomach);

(iv) Calming the Ocean i.e. *dantian* 丹田;

(v) Dragon Rising from the Bottom of the Ocean (*haidi* 海底 i.e. perineum, the activation of the essence which, in Tantric terminology, corresponds with awakening of the Kundalini);

(vi) Tiger Diverting from the Bottom of the Water (the sublimation of the essence into breath which begins its ascent along the vertebral column);

(vii) The Water of the Yellow River Flowing against the Current (i.e., the reverse movement in which Fire goes down while Water goes up)

(viii) Returning the Essence for Repairing the Brain (an ancient *yangsheng* 養生 technique associated with sexual practices and known also as *coitus reservatus*; it describes the circulation of the essence going up to the crown of the head);

(ix) Illuminating the Entire Body from Top to Bottom. This is the fruit of this method described through the metaphors of "the formula of the holy sun and moon illuminating the

Golden Court," and "the water in the Yangzi River and the moon in the sky." The experience is a light enveloping a no-more-perceived body in which subject and object are transcended (the text underlines that "one loses the sensation of having a body").

(3) Beneficial Doubts (*shanyi* 善疑). This last part focuses on problems related to the circulation of *qi* 氣 in the body. It describes physiological reactions by pointing out possible adversities that can occur on the way. Medical advice and explanations related to the circulation of *qi* in the body are designed to help in mastering it.

17. *Sanfeng zhenren xuantan quanji* 三丰真人玄潭全集 [Complete Collection of the Mysterious Words by the Perfected (Zhang) Sanfeng]

> pp. 1a-10a
> Compiled and corrected by Min Yide 閔一得 (1758–1836)
> Preface attributed to Zhang Sanfeng 張三丰.

This text focuses on the ancient method of the "White and Yellow" and on the representation of reality in the form of diagrams. It is attributed to the immortal Zhang Sanfeng who played a fundamental role in the relationship between the Ming court and Daoism. It probably was because of this that Min Yide and Longmen decided to include this important figure in this collection. It is worthy of note that this is the only text in this collection that uses the term *neidan* 內丹 (which usually is translated as "inner alchemy"). All other texts of this collection use the term *jindan* 金丹 or Golden Elixir.

The text opens with a diagram of the "Buddhist exterior landscape," the image of emptiness represented by a circle symbolizing Inner Nature before heaven. Juxtaposed is the "Daoist inner landscape" represented as the image of a body enveloping a breathing embryo. This is explained as the trace of the human will through which consciousness of one's own Vital Force appears. Min Yide comments that it is only through the union of these two landscapes that the doctrine of the universal salvation emerges. Unlike other works in this collection, this text uses symbols for the "representation of the Center" as conceived by Buddhists, Daoists and Confucianists and explains their different conceptions. For example: "With regard to the Center of Dao: Confucianists call it

'Reaching the Center' (*zhizhong* 至中), Daoists 'Guarding the Center' (*shouzhong* 守中), and Buddhists 'Emptying the Center' (*kongzhong* 空中). What is called Center in Inner alchemy is the Opening within the Opening. This is the True Center."

18. *Rushi wo wen* 如是我聞 [Thus I Have Heard]

> pp. 1a-5a
> Transmitted by anonymous
> Recorded by Tianshui zi 天水子 (?)
> Newly revised by Min Yide 閔一得 (1758–1836).

This text of the Southern Lineage proclaims its central position through the practice of the Yellow path, a practice also found in the *Xie tianji* 泄天機 (Text 4) and *Guankui bian* 管窺編 (Text 7). Although its title represents the usual opening phrase of Buddhist sutras, the preface states that *rushi* 如是 ("thus") refers to the oral transmission of a practical formula, *wo* 我 ("I") to the anonymous master who transmitted it, and *wen* 聞 ("heard") to the comprehension obtained thanks to this oral transmission. The text consists of three chapters:

(1) "On the Golden Elixir"(*jindan shuo* 金丹說). This teaching is included in the key term *jingding* 靜定 (absorption); it indicates that its method consists in calming the mind.

(2) "On the method of opening the Pass" (*kaguan fa shuo* 開關法說). This refers to the localization of the Three Passes along the back and the Three Elixir or Cinnabar Fields.

(3) "Essential instructions on the Golden Elixir" (*jindan yaozhi* 金丹要旨). This refers to the manifestation of the Central or Yellow path which is regarded as the general rule for Celestial Immortality. The path transcends duality and is thus symbolized in the alchemic *opus* by binary terms such as Dragon and Tiger, Lead and Mercury, etc., which are summed up by the term *xingming* 性命 on which the adept works.

19. *Xiwang mu nüxiu zhengtu shize* 西王母女修正途十則 [Ten Rules of the Queen Mother of the West on the Correct Path of Female Cultivation]

    pp. 1a-6b
    Revealed by the Queen Mother of the West 西王母
    Expounded, corrected and newly entitled by Lü Dongbin 呂洞賓
    Modified by Sun Bu'er 孫不二 (1119–1182)
    Transmitted by Shen Yibing 沈一炳
    Annotated by Min Yide 閔一得 (1758–1836)
    Corrected by Shen Yangyi 沈陽一

This text, whose original title was *Nü jindan jue* 女金丹訣 (Women's Golden Elixir Formula), is the result of a spirit writing séance from the year 1799. Before explaining its ten rules for women's correct practice, it presents a brief outline of the nine basic precepts from one of the main Longmen ordination texts, the *Chuzhen jielü* 初真戒律 (Regulation of the Initial Precepts of Perfection) by Wang Changyue 王常月 (1656, DZJY 24, zhangji 7, and ZWDS 12: 13–31). This is followed by the ten rules stemming from the "golden mouth" of the Queen Mother of the West whose objective is the realization of the source of woman's nature (*xingyuan* 性原) and the understanding of woman's destiny (*nüming* 女命). Practices leading to such realization and understanding are then explained; they include "cultivation of pathways" (*xiujing* 修經), "slaying of the red dragon" (*zhan chilong* 斬赤龍),[140] "embryo respiration" (*taixi* 胎息), breast massage, breathing exercises, seated meditation, etc. The supreme goal of such efforts is, as the text explains toward its end, not just individual transformation and the achievement of quietude and peace of mind, but the lofty ideal of healing the world (*yishi* 醫世).

20. *Niwan Li zushi nüzong shuangxiu baofa* 泥丸李祖師女宗雙修寶筏 [Precious Raft of Joint Cultivation in Feminine Alchemy by Patriarch Li Niwan]

    pp. 7a-12b
    Revealed by Li Niwan 李泥丸
    Recorded and annotated by Shen Yibing 沈一炳
    Received and revised by Min Yide 閔一得 (1758–1836)
    Postface (1830) by Min Yide 閔一得

---

[140] {About this practice and other issues of female inner alchemy, see Chapter 4 below.}

As the subtitle of this text—*Nügong zhinan* 女功指南 (Direct Instructions on Female Practices)—suggests, this text offers instructions for female practice. Its nine rules, presented as the utterances of the immortal wonder-worker Li Niwan, begin with the stopping of thought (*zhinian* 止念) and regulation of mind (*tiaoxin* 調心) and advocate various physical and mental practices that are said to produce peace of mind, wisdom, and the formation of an enlightened body within.

21. *Jindan sibai zi zhushi* 金丹四百字注釋 [Commentary and Explanations on the *Four Hundred Words on the Golden Elixir*]

    (1) Preface by Zhang Boduan 張佰端 (?-1082) and Commentary (1835) to this Preface by Min Yide 閔一得 (1758–1836)
    (2) Text of *Jindan sibaizi* 金丹四百字 (pp. 1a-b) by Zhang Boduan 張伯端 (?-1082?)
    (3) Notes and explanations (註解, pp. 1a-7a) by Peng Haogu 彭好古 (fl. 1599) and commentary by Min Yanglin 閔陽林; Postface (1832) by Min Yanglin

22. *Suoyan xu* 瑣言續 [Sequel to an Ignored Transmission]

    Orally transmitted by Shen Yibing 沈一炳
    Recorded by Min Yide 閔一得
    Published by Lu Liuxi 陸柳溪
    Revised by Xue Xinxiang 薛心香
    Preface (1826) by Min Yide 閔一得

The transmission to which this text's title refers is that of the Southern lineage which, according to this text, started with the noted *fangshi* Li Shaojun 李少君 and, after having passed through Liezi 列子, Huainan zi 淮南子 (180–122 B.C), Wei Boyang 魏伯陽 (Han era), Ge Hong 葛洪 (ca. 283–343), and Xu Sun 許遜 (III-IV centuries), it was transmitted to Longmen masters via Li Niwan 李泥丸. This text presents the methods of the four seasons and their priority according to specific circumstances, and it ends with the method of the Twelve daily periods.

    (1) *Practice of Winter-Spring*. It deals with the discovery of *qiji* 氣機 (the right moment and perception of the movement of *qi*) by discerning the two phases of the Time Fire: the Yang (winter, the moment of the solstice when the yang begins rising) and the

Yin (spring, the moment of the equinox when, after the balance between yin and yang, yang reaches its climax before declining again).

(2) *Practice of Summer-Fall.* This deals with the Civil Fire phase (*wenhuo* 文火) represented by Summer and Fall. The adept focuses on *qi* going down through the chest. This is the symbol of the "before-heaven" but containing a spark of "after-heaven." This phase is characterized by non-action, no efforts (Fall-Metal) permitting action and efforts (Summer-Fire).

(3) Although the two precedent practices corresponding to the four seasons have been explained one after the other, the adept must practice them in a *joint manner*. If one focuses only on the practice Summer-Fall, there is the risk of accumulating cold inside, while focusing only on the Practice Winter-Spring carries the risk of accumulating excessive heat. The priority given to one or to the other depends on the characteristics of the practitioner.

(4) The method of the four seasons is then restricted to the *twelve periods of a day*. This fixes the images of *qi* (the physiological experiences perceived by the adept). It is connected with the circulation of *qi* in which every two hours are put in correspondence with a specific physiological experience.

Volume IV

23. *Xiuzhen biannan qianhou bian canzheng* 修真辯難前後編參証
    [Annotations to the *Debate on the Cultivation of Perfection* in Two Sections]

    By Liu Yiming 劉一明 (1734–1821)
    Commented and verified by Min Yide 閔一得 (1758–1836)
    First Section, pp. 1a-39a;
    Second Section, pp. 1a-29a
    Postface (1829) by Min Yide and Postface by Liu Yiming.

This is a voluminous work that occupies the entire last volume of the *Daozang xubian*. It is authorized by the 11th-generation Longmen Patriarch Liu Yiming 劉一明, author of many commentaries on alchemical classics such as the *Yijing* 易經, the *Cantongqi* 參同契, the *Wuzhen pian* 悟真篇, the *Yinfujing* 陰符經, etc. In this work Liu

Yiming divides the Golden Elixir (*jindan* 金丹) into three levels:
 (1) The superior level for adepts with excellent capacities. It consists of methods based on the sudden understanding of the self-so (*ziran* 自然) nature of things.
 (2) The intermediate level for adepts with average capacities. It consists of gradual methods of cultivation of Vital Force (*ming* 命), starting from the Inner or Original Nature (*xing* 性) and vice-versa.
 (3) The inferior level is reserved to adepts with modest capacities. It requires severe training including ascetic practices of body and mind in order to realize the nature of mind, i.e., one's original face.

The gradual methods are devoted to the joint culture of Inner Nature and Vital Force (*xingming shuangxiu* 性命雙修). The explanation of these methods forms the most voluminous part of this text. It begins with the "laying of foundations," which consists in reining in the passions and the discursive mind. This is followed by the sublimation of the essence in breath (according to the teachings described in the *Wuzhen pian* 悟真篇 and inventoried in Bai Yuchan's 白玉蟾 methods), leading to the final stage of sublimation of the spirit and return to emptiness. In his exegesis, Min Yide emphasizes the unique character of Liu Yiming's work which focuses on clarifying doubts regarding practice and pointing to the essence of alchemical teaching free from any superstitious veneer.

ABBREVIATIONS

BYGZ   *Baiyun guan zhi (Hakuunkan shi)* 白雲觀志 [Gazetteer of the Abbey of White Clouds] by Oyanagi Shigeta 小柳司氣太. Tokyo: Tōhō bunka gakuin Tōkyō kenkyūjo, 1934.

DJYL   *Changchun daojiao yuanliu* 長春道教源流 [Origins and Development of the Daoist Teachings of (Qiu) Changchun], 1879, by Chen Minggui 陳銘珪 (1824–1881) in ZWDS (31:1-157).

DTYL   *Daotong yuanliu* 道統源流 [Origins and development of the Orthodox Daoism] by Yan Liuqian 嚴六謙 (*hao*: Zhuangyan jushi 莊嚴居士), Wuxi: Zhonghua yinshuju, 1929.

DZJHL   *Daozang jinghua lu* 道藏精華錄 [Record of Essential Blossoms of the Daoist Canon] by Ding Fubao 丁福保 (*zi*: Shouyi zi 守一子, 1874–1952). Reprint in 2 vols. (*shang* / *xia*), Zhejiang guji chubanshe, 1989.

DZJY   *Chongkan Daozang jiyao* 重刊道藏輯要 [Reedited Epitome of the Daoist Canon] by Yan Yonghe 閻永和, Peng Hanran 彭瀚然 and He Longxiang 賀龍驤 Chengdu: Erxian an 二仙庵, 1906; repr. 25 vols. Taipei: Xinwenfeng, 1977.

DZXB   *Daozang xubian* 道藏續編 [Supplementary Collection of the Daoist Canon] 4 vols., by Min Yide 閔一得 (1758–1836), Wuxing: Jingai cangban 1834. Photolithographic edition by Ding Fubao 丁福保 (*zi*: Shou yi zi 守一子, 1874–1952), Shanghai: Yixue shuju. Reprint Beijing: Haiyang, 1989.

YLCS   *Gu Shuyinlou cangshu* 古書隱樓藏書 [Collection from the Ancient Hidden Pavilion of Books], 14 vols., by Min Yide (1758–1836), Wuxing: Jingai Chunyang gong cangban, 1904. Reedition of 1904 in ZWDS (10:150–721).

JGXD   (*Chongkan*) *Jingai xindeng* 金蓋心燈 [Re-edition of the *Transmission of the Lamp of Mind* from Mt. Jingai], 10 vols., by Min Yide (1758–1836), Wuxing: Yunchao, Gu Shuyinlou cangban, 1876.

ZWDS   *Zangwai daoshu* 藏外道書 [Daoist Books Outside the Canon] by Hu Daojing 胡道靜 et al., Chengdu : Bashu shushe, 1992 (vol: 1–20); 1994 (vol. 21–36).

BIBLIOGRAPHY

PRIMARY SOURCES

Biyuan tanjing 碧苑壇經 [Platform Sūtra of the Jade Garden]. Transmitted by Wang Changyue 王常月 (Kunyang 崑陽, ?-1680), compiled by Shi Shouping 施守平 and revised by Min Yide 閔一得(1758–1836). YLCS 1904 reedition (reprinted in ZWDS 10).

Chuzhen jielü 初真戒律 [Rules for the Precepts of Initial Perfection]. 1656. By Wang Changyue 王常月 (?-1680). DZJY 24 *zhangji* 張集 7 (reprinted in ZWDS 12).

Dadong yujing tanyi 大洞玉經壇儀 [Liturgy of the Jade Scripture of Great Profundity]. Attributed to Wei Huacun 魏華存(252–334). DZJY 3 *diji* 氐集 4.

Daomen gongke 道門功課 [Liturgy for Daoists]. Compiled by Liu Shouyuan 柳守元 (fl. 1798). DZJY 23 *zhangji* 張集 1.

Du Lü zushi sanni yishi shuoshu guankui 讀呂祖師三尼醫世說述管窺, DZXB (see the Appendix).

Erlan xinhua 二嬾心話, DZXB (see the Appendix).

Huangji hepi xianjing 皇極闔闢仙經 abbr. for *Yin zhenren Donghua zhengmai huangji hepi zhengdao xianjing*. DZXB (see the Appendix).

Jinhua zongzhi 金華宗旨. DZXB (see the Appendix).

Jiuzheng lu 就正錄. DZXB (see the Appendix).

Longmen xinfa 龍門心法 [Core Teachings of the Longmen]. 1663. Transmitted by Wang Changyue 王常月 (?-1680) and compiled by Zhan Tailin 詹太林 and Tang Qingshan 唐清善. ZWDS 6.

Longmen zhengzong jueyun benzhi daotong xinchuan 龍門正宗覺雲本支道統薪傳 (Uninterrupted Transmission of Daoist Orthodoxy in the Correct Lineage of the Longmen Jueyun Branch). 1927. Lu Yongming 陸永銘. ZWDS 31.

Lü zushi sanni yishi gongjue 呂祖師三尼醫世功訣. DZXB (see the Appendix).

Lü zushi sannin yishi shuoshu 呂祖師三尼醫世說述. DZXB (see the Appendix).

Niwan Li zushi nüzong shuangxiu baofa 泥丸李祖師女宗雙修寶筏. DZXB (see the Appendix).

Santan yuanman tianxian dajie lüeshuo 三壇圓滿天仙大戒略說 [Abstract of the Great Precepts of the Celestial Immortals for achieving the threefold altar ordination]/ [Abstract on the Celestial Immortals' complete ordination of the threefold altars]. Compiled by Liu Shouyuan 柳守元 (fl. 1798). DZJY 24 *zhangji* 張集 7 (reprinted in ZWDS 12)

Shangpin danfa jieci 上品丹法節次. DZXB (see the Appendix).

Shangqing dongzhen zhihui guanshen dajie wen 上清洞真智慧觀身大戒文 [Great Precepts of the Cavern-Perfected of Highest Clarity for Contemplating the Body by Wisdom]. DZ 1364, fac. 1039.

Taishang Laojun jiejing 太上老君戒經 [Precepts of the Highest Lord Lao]. ca 500. DZ 784, fasc. 562.

Taishang xuanmen zaotan gongke jing 太上玄門早壇功課經 [Morning Liturgy of the Mysterious Teachings of the Most High]. DZJY 23 *zhangji* 張集 1.

Tianxian dao jieji xuzhi 天仙道戒忌須知. DZXB (see the Appendix).

Tianxian daocheng baoze 天仙道程寶則. DZXB (see the Appendix).

Tianxian xinchuan 天仙心傳. DZXB (see the Appendix).

Xie tianji 泄天機. DZXB (see the Appendix).

Xinyin ji jing 心印集經 [Summa of the Heart-Seal]. DZJY (edition Jiaqing era 1796–1820), *jiji* 箕集 10.

Xiuxian bianhuo lun 修仙辨惑論 [Treatise on Resolving Doubts concerning the Cultivation of Immortality]. Attributed to Bai Yuchan 白玉蟾 (1194-ca. 1227). DZJHL *xia*.

Xiwangmu nüxiu zhengtu shize 西王母女修正途十則. DZXB (see the Appendix).

Xuhuang tianzun shijie wen 虛皇天尊十戒文 [Ten Precepts of the Heavenly Worthy Sovereign of Emptiness]. DZ 180 fasc. 77.

Yin zhenren Donghua zhengmai huangji hepi zhengdao xianjing 尹真人東華正脈皇極闔闢證道仙經 abbr. *Huangji hepi xianjing*. DZXB (see the Appendix).

Yu Lin Fenqian xiansheng shu 與林奮千先生書. DZXB (see the Appendix).

Yuanshi dadong yujing 元始大洞玉經 [Jade Scripture of Great Profondity of the Primordial Beginning]. 1583. Attributed to Wenchang dijun 文昌帝君. DZJY 3 *diji* 氐集 3.

Yuxiang tianjing zhou zhu 雨香天經咒注 [Commentary on the Spell of the *Yuxiang tianjing*]. By Min Yide. YLCS 9 (reprinted in ZWDS 10).

Zhongji jie 中極戒 [Intermediary Precepts]. DZJY 24 *zhangji* 張集 7 (reprinted in ZWDS 12)

SECONDARY SOURCES

Avalon, Arthur. 1958. *The Serpent Power*. Madras: Ganeshan & Co.

Baldrian-Hussein, Farzeen. 1984. *Procédés secrets du joyau magique—Traité d'alchimie taoïste du XIe siècle*. Paris: Les Deux Océans.

———. 1996–97. "Taoist Beliefs in Literary Circles of the Song Dynasty—Su Shi (1037–1101) and his Technique of Survival." *Cahiers d'Extrême-Asie* 9 (1996–97): 15–53.

Bianchi, Ester. 2001. *The Iron Statue Monastery*. Firenze: Leo S. Olschki editore.

Boltz, Judith M. 1987. *A Survey of Taoist Literature Tenth to Seventeenth Centuries*. Berkeley: University of California, Institute of East Asian Studies & Center for Chinese Studies.

Chen, Bing 陳兵. 1985. "Jindan pai Nanzong qiantan" 金丹派南宗淺探 [A Brief Study of the Southern lineage of the Golden Elixir school]. *Shijie zongjiao yanjiu* 世界宗教研究 4 (1985): 35–49.

———. 1988. "Qingdai Quanzhen Longmen pai de zhongxing" 清代全真龍門派的中興 [The Qing dynasty's renewal of the Quanzhen Longmen school]. *Shijie zongjiao yanjiu* 世界宗教研究 2 (1988): 84–96.

Chen, Weiping 陳衛平. 1989. "Lun Mingqing jian xifang chuanjiaoshi dui zhongxi zhexue bijiao 論明清間西方傳教士對中西哲學比較" [A Comparison of Chinese and Western Philosophy by Jesuits during Ming-Qing period]. *Shijie zongjiao yanjiu* 世界宗教研究 1 (1989):12–18.

Cheng, Hsueh-li. 1989. "Psychology, ontology and soteriology in the Platform Sūtra." In *The Sixth Patriarch Platform Sūtra in Religious and Cultural Perspective*, edited by Fo Kuang shan, 99–113. Taichong: Fo Kuang shan.

Chou, Yi-liang. 1944–45. "Tantric Buddhism in China." *Harvard Journal of Asian Studies* 8 (1944–45): 241–332.

Cleary, Thomas. 1987. *Understanding Reality*. Honolulu: University of Hawaii.

Darga, Martina. 1999. *Das alchemistische Buch von innerem Wesen und Lebensenergie Xingming guizhi*. München: Eugen Diederichs.

De Bary, Wm Theodore. 1970. "Individualism and Humanitarism in Late Ming Thought." In *Self and Society in Ming Thought*, edited by Wm Theodore de Bary, 145–225. New York: Columbia University Press.

———. 1975. "Neo-Confucian Cultivation and the Seventeenth-Century 'Enlightenment.'" In *The Unfolding of Neo-Confucianism*, edited by Wm Theodore de Bary, 141–216. New York: Columbia University Press.

———. 1991. *The Trouble with Confucianism*. Cambridge, Massachussets: Harvard University Press.

De Bruyn, Pierre-Henry. 2000. "Daoism in the Ming (1368–1644)." In *Daoism Handbook*, edited by Livia Kohn, 594–622. Leiden: Brill.

Demiéville, Paul et al., ed. 1929–30. *Hōbōgirin*, fasc. 1–2. Tokyo: Maison Franco-Japonaise.

———. 1974. *Hōbōgirin*. fasc. 3. Tokyo: Maison Franco-Japonaise.

Despeux, Catherine. 1979. *Traité d'alchimie et de physiologie taoïste*. Paris: Les Deux Océans.

———. 1990. *Immortelles de la Chine ancienne*. Puiseaux: Pardès.

———. 2008. In *The Encyclopedia of Taoism*, ed. by Fabrizio Pregadio, vol. 1:284–85. London: Routledge.

Eskildsen, Stephen. 1989. "The Beliefs and Practices of Early Ch'üan-chen Taoism." M. A. Thesis, University of British Columbia.

Esposito, Monica. 1993. "La Porte du Dragon—L'école Longmen du Mont Jin'gai et ses pratiques alchimiques d'après le *Daozang xubian* (Suite au canon taoïste)." Ph.D diss., Université de Paris VII.

———. 1995. " Il 'ritorno alle fonti', costituzione di un dizionario di alchimia interiore dell'epoca Ming e Qing." In *Le fonti per lo studio della civiltà cinese*, edited by Maurizio Scarpari, 101–117. Venezia: Ca'Foscarina.

———. 1996. "Il Segreto del Fiore d'Oro e la tradizione Longmen del Monte Jingai." In *Conoscenza e interpretazione della civiltà cinese*, edited by Piero Corradini, 151–169. Venezia: Ca' Foscarina.

———. 1997. *L'alchimia del soffio*. Roma: Ubaldini.

———. 1998a. " Longmen pai yu *Jinhua zongzhi* banben laiyuan" 龍門派與「金華宗旨」版本來源 [The Longmen school and the origin of the different editions of the *Secret of the Golden Flower*]. Paper presented at the Research Meeting on Daoist Culture, Tokyo, Waseda University, March 1998.

———. 1998b. "The different versions of the *Secret of the Golden Flower* and their relationship with the Longmen school." *Transactions of the International Conference of Eastern Studies* XLIII 1998: 90–109.

———. 2000. "Daoism in the Qing (1644–1911)." In *Daoism Handbook*, ed. by Livia Kohn, 623–657. Leiden: Brill. {Revised edition here above, Chapter 1}

———. 2004. "The Longmen School and its Controversial History during the Qing Dynasty." In *Religion and Chinese Society: The Transformation of a Field*, edited by John Lagerwey. 2 vols. Vol. 2: 621–698. Hong Kong: École française d'Extrême-Orient & Chinese University of Hong Kong. {Revised edition here above, Chapter 2}

Faure, Bernard. 1984. "La volonté d'orthodoxie." 3 vols. Thèse d'État. Paris, École Pratique des Hautes Études, Section des Sciences Religieuses.

Fo Kuang Shan, ed. 1989.*The Sixth Patriarch Platform Sūtra in Religious and Cultural Perspective* (Report of the International Conference on Ch'an Buddhism). Taichong: Fo Kuang shan.

Gernet, Jacques. 1992–93 "Quelques thèmes de la pensée chinoise au XVIe et XVIIe siècles." *Annuaire du Collège de France* (1992–93): 673–677.

Girardot, Norman J. 1983. *Myth and Meaning in Early Taoism: The Theme of Chaos (hun-tun)*. Berkeley: University of California Press.

Groner, Paul. 1989. "The Ordination Ritual in the Platform Sūtra within the context of the East Asian Buddhist Vinaya Tradition." In *The Sixth Patriarch Platform Sūtra in Religious and Cultural Perspective*, edited by Fo-kuang shan, 220–250. Taichong: Fo kuang shan.

Goossaert, Vincent. "*Yulu* Recorded Sayings." In *The Encyclopedia of Taoism*, ed. by Fabrizio Pregadio, vol. 2:1200–1202. London: Routledge.

Jordan, David K. & Overmyer, Daniel. 1986. *The Flying Phoenix: Aspects of Chinese Sectarianism in Taiwan*. Princeton: Princeton University Press.

Kaltenmark, Max. 1987. *Le Lie-sien tchouan*. Paris: Collège de France.

Kohn, Livia. 1994. "The Five Precepts of the Venerable Lord." *Monumenta Serica* 42 (1994): 171–215.

———. 1998. "The Beginnings and Cultural Characteristics of East Asian Millenarianism." *Japanese Religions* 23, 1–2 (1998): 29–51.

Liu, Ts'un-yan. 1970. "Taoist Self-Cultivation in Ming Thought." In *Self and Society in Ming Thought*, edited by Wm. Theodore de Bary, 291–326. New York: Columbia University Press.

———. 1971. "The Penetration of Taoism into the Ming Neo-Confucian Elite." *T'oung Pao* 57 (1971): 31–103.

Min, Zhiting 閔智亭. 1990. *Daojiao yifan* 道教儀範 (Patterns of Daoist rites). Beijing: Zhongguo daojiao xueyuan.

Mori, Yuria 森由利亞. 1994. "Zenshinkyō ryūmonha keifu kō" 全真教龍門派系譜考"[A study on the Lineage of Longmen school of the Complete Perfection heritage]. In *Dōkyō bunka e no tenbō* 道教文化への展望 [A view of Chinese Culture], edited by Dōkyō bunka kenkyūkai, 181–211. Tokyo: Hirakawa, 1994.

———. 1998. "Taiitsu kinka sōshi no seiritsu to hensen—Sho hanpon no jo, chū no kijutsu wo te ga karini 太乙金華宗旨の成立と変遷—諸版本の序・注の記述を手がかりに—" (The Formation and Transformations of *Taiyi jinhua zongzhi*, based on the prefaces and notes of different versions). *Tōyō no shisō to shūkyō* 東洋の思想と宗教, 15:43–64.

———. 2002. "Identity and Lineage: The *Taiyi jinhua zongzhi* and the Spirit writing Cult to Patriarch Lü in Qing China." In *Daoist Identity: History, Lineage, and Ritual,,* ed. by Livia Kohn & Harold D. Roth, 168–187. Honolulu: Univ. of Hawai'i Press.

Nan, Huai-chin. 1984. *Tao and Longevity*, London: Element Books.

Needham, Joseph & Lu Gui-djen. 1983. *Science and Civilisation in China*, vol. V-5. Cambridge: Cambridge University Press.

Pregadio, Fabrizio. 1995. "The Representation of Time in the *Zhouyi Cantong qi*." *Cahiers d'Extrême-Asie* 8 (1995): 155–173.

———. 2008. *The Encyclopedia of Taoism*. London: Routledge.

Pregadio, Fabrizio & Skar, Lowell. 2000. "Inner Alchemy (Neidan)." In *Daoism Handbook*, ed. by Livia Kohn, 464–497. Leiden: Brill.

Qing, Xitai 卿希泰, ed. 1994. *Zhongguo daojiao* 中國道教 [Chinese Daoism]. 4 Vols. Shanghai: Zhishi 知識.

Qing, Xitai 卿希泰, ed. 1996. *Zhongguo daojiao shi* 中國道教史 [History of Chinese Daoism], 4 vols. Chengdu: Sichuan Renmin.

Reichelt, Karl Ludwig. 1990. *Truth and Tradition in Chinese Buddhism*. Taipei: SMC. Publishing Inc. (first ed. 1927).

Robinet, Isabelle. 1983. "Le Ta-t'ung chen-ching—son authenticité et sa place dans les textes du Shang-ching ching." In *Tantric and Taoist Studies in Honour of R. A. Stein*, edited by Michel Strickmann, II: 394–433. Bruxelles: Institut Belge des Hautes Études Chinoises.

———. 1984. *La révélation du Shangqing dans l'histoire du taoïsme*, 2 vols., Paris: École Française d'Extrême-Orient.

———. 1984. "Notes préliminaires sur quelques antinomies fondamentales entre le bouddhisme et le taoïsme." In *Incontro di Religioni in Asia tra il III e il IV secolo d. C.*, ed. by Lionello Lanciotti, 217–242. Firenze: Leo S. Olschki.

———. 1989. "Original Contributions of *Neidan* to Taoism and Chinese Thought." In *Taoist Meditation and Longevity Techniques*, ed. by Livia Kohn and Yoshinobu Sakade, 297–330. Ann Arbor: The University of Michigan.

———. 1989–90. "Recherche sur l'alchimie intérieure (*neidan*): l'école Zhenyuan," *Cahiers d'Extrême-Asie* 5 (1989–90): 141–162.

———. 1995. *Introduction à l'alchimie intérieure taoïste*. Paris: Le Cerf.

Sakade, Yoshinobu 坂出祥伸. 1999. "Shoki mikkyō to dōkyō to no kōshō" 初期密教と道教との交渉 (The early relation between Tantrism and Daoism). In *Chūgoku mikkyō* 中国密教 (Chinese Tantrism), ed. by Musashi Tachikawa 武藏立川 and Motohiro Yoritomi 本宏頼富, 153–169. Tokyo: Shunkasha.

Saso, Michael. 1978. *The Teachings of the Taoist Master Chuang*. New Haven: Yale University Press.

Schipper, Kristofer. 1985. "Taoist Ordination Ranks in the Tunhuang Manuscripts." In *Religion und Philosophie in Ostasien. Festschrift für Hans Steininger*, edited by Gert Naundorf et al., 127–148. Würzburg: Königshausen & Neumann.

Seidel, Anna. 1969–70. "The Image of the Perfect Ruler in Early Taoist Messianism: Lao-tzu and Li Hung." *History of Religions* 9 (1969–70): 216-247.

———. 1983. "Imperial Treasures and Taoist Sacraments: Taoist Roots in the Apocrypha." In *Tantric and Taoist Studies in Honour of R.A. Stein*, edited by Michel Strickmann, 291–371. Bruxelles: Institut Belge des Hautes Études Chinoises.

———. 1984. "Taoist Messianism," *Numen* XXXI, 2 (1984): 161-174.

Skar, Lowell. 2000. "Ritual Movement, Deity Cults and the Transformation of Daoism in Song and Yuan times." In *Daoism Handbook*, edited by Livia Kohn, 413–463. Leiden: Brill.

Soothill, W. Eduard & Lewis, Hodous. 1937. *A Dictionary of Chinese Buddhist Terms*. London: Kegan Paul, Trench, Trubner and Co.

Strickmann, Michel. 1986. *Mantras et mandarins —Le bouddhisme tantrique en Chine*. Paris: Gallimard.

Wang, Zhizhong 王志忠. 1995. "Quanzhen jiao Longmen pai qiyuan lunkao" 全真教龍門派起源論考 [A study on the origin of the Longmen lineage of the Quanzhen school]." *Zongjiao xue yanjiu* 宗教學研究 4 (1995): 9–13.

Welch, Holmes. 1967. *The Practice of Chinese Buddhism 1900–1950*. Cambridge, Massachusetts: Harvard University Press.

Wile, Douglas. 1992. *Arts of the Bedchamber: The Chinese Sexual Yoga Classics Including Women's Solo Meditation Texts*. Albany: State University of New York Press.

Wilhelm, Richard. 1929. *Das Geheimnis der Goldenen Blüte: Ein chinesisches Lebensbuch*. Munich (English translation by Cary F. Baynes, *The*

Secret of the Golden Flower, A Chinese Book of Life. London: Kegan Paul, Trench and Trübner 1931].

Yamada, Toshiaki, 2000. "The Lingbao school." In *Daoism Handbook*, ed. by Livia Kohn, 225–255. Leiden: Brill.

Yao, Tao-chung. 1980. "Chuan-chen: A New Taoist Sect in North China During the 12 and 13th centuries." Ph. D. diss., University of Arizona.

———. 2000. "Quanzhen: Complete Perfection." In *Daoism Handbook*, edited by Livia Kohn, 567–93. Leiden: Brill.

Yokote, Yutaka 横手裕. 2000. "Zenshinkyō to nanshū hokushū" 全眞教と南宗北宗 [The Complete Perfection school and the Northern and Southern lineages]. In *Dōkyō no seimeikan to shintai ron* 道教の生命観と身体論 [The Daoist View of Life and Body], ed. by Tetsurō Noguro 鉄郎野口 et al., 180–196. Tokyo: Yuyama kaku.

Yoshioka, Yoshitoyo 吉岡義豊. 1970. *Eisei e no negai: Dōkyō* 永生への願い：道教 [Daoism: The quest for eternal life]. Kyoto: Tankōsha.

———. 1979. "Taoist Monastic Life." In *Facets of Taoism*, ed. by Holmes Welch & Anna Seidel, 229–252. New Haven and London: Yale University Press.

Yü, Chun-fang. 1981. *The Renewal of Buddhism in China: Chu-hung and the Late Ming Synthesis*. New York: Columbia University Press.

BEHEADING THE RED DRAGON: THE HEART OF FEMININE ALCHEMY

Around the beginning of the Qing Dynasty (1644–1911) a new kind of alchemical literature appeared in China. Called *nüdan* 女丹 or Feminine Alchemy, it explains alchemical practices and psycho-physiological techniques reserved for women.[1] Although its fundamental principles remain the same as those of Inner Alchemy (*neidan* 內丹), there are nonetheless a number of important differences[2] that are due to the different constitutions of woman and man. The inner alchemical texts for women commonly emphasize the similarities between woman and the moon; this is illustrated by the magic consumption and constant revivifying of the "pale lantern of the night" which symbolizes feminine inner practice. The loss and recovery in woman's menstrual cycle constitutes her life and death, her liberation and imprisonment. "Cultivating the Menses" (*xiujing* 修經)[3] is

---

[1] An initial list of feminine inner alchemy literature is found in Catherine Despeux, *Immortelles de la Chine* (Puiseaux: Pardès, 1990): 291–302. According to Despeux (p. 163) the earliest text stems from 1743; but references to inner alchemical practices for women occur much earlier (see for example Despeux, ibid., p. 79).

[2] On *nüdan* 女丹 methods see Despeux, *Immortelles de la Chine*; Douglas Wile, *The Chinese Sexual Yoga Classics Including Women's Solo Meditation Texts* (New York: State University of New York Press, 1992), in particular pp. 192–219; Monica Esposito, *La Porte du Dragon, l'école Longmen du Mont Jin'gai et ses pratiques alchimiques d'après le Daozang xubian (Suite au canon taoïste)*, 2 vols, (Ph.D. thesis, University of Paris VII, 1993), in particular vol. 1, 280–374; and Monica Esposito, "L'alchimie féminine" in J. Servier (ed.), *Dictionnaire critique de l'ésotérisme* (Paris: Presses Universitaires de France, 1998): 51–52.

[3] The term *jing* 經 has different meanings in Chinese, as is well illustrated by the explanations given in Morohashi Tetsuji 諸橋轍次 (ed.), *Dai Kanwa jiten* 大漢和辭典 (Tokyo: Taishūkan 大修館, 1976, vol. 8, 1072a). According to Morohashi, *jing* 經 stands for *yuejing* 月經 and in the given context refers to the regularity with which women have their monthly cycle ("めぐり。婦人の月經。〔本草、婦人月水〕釋名、時珍曰、經者、常也、有常軌也、云云、女人之經、一月一行、其常也"). This regularity (*zhang* 常) is related to the idea of a constant Way (*zhangdao* 常道), principle or rule (「指常行義理、准則、法制」); see *Hanyu dacidian* 漢語大辭典 (Shanghai: Shanghai shudian, 1986): vol. 9, 859. This indicates what

woman's preliminary practice which is crowned with the emblematic technique of "Beheading the Red Dragon" (*zhan chilong* 斬赤龍). This is the topic I will focus on. It constitutes the heart of Feminine Alchemy or *nüdan* 女丹 and forms its primary difference from male inner practice.[4]

My argument here is primarily based on the only two feminine alchemy texts that are included in the *Daozang xubian* 道藏續編 (1834, 4 vols., reprint Beijing: Haiyang chuban 海洋出版, 1989):

1. *Xiwang mu nüxiu zhengtu shize* 西王母女修正途十則 (Ten Rules of the Queen Mother of the West on the Correct Path of Female Cultivation)[5]

2. *Niwan Li zushi nüzong shuangxiu baofa* 泥丸李祖師女宗雙修寶筏 (Precious Raft of Joint Cultivation in Feminine Alchemy by Patriarch Li Niwan).[6]

---

woman has to cultivate (*xiu* 修). As we are going to see, the notion of *zhang* 常 / *zhangdao* 常道 is indicative of the meaning of menstruation in feminine practice. It is related to the cultivation of specific rules and to the "regularization" of woman's cyclic circulation. Thanks to such rules, woman can experience (*tixian* 體顯) the regularity of the lunar waxing and waning because this lunar cycle directly points to her own monthly experience. Finally, the regular occurrence of menstruation can make her understand the true meaning of the cyclic time which is the fluctuating movement of yin and yang (*yinyang xiaoxi* 陰陽消息) in the world, as reflected in her own body.

[4] These two texts have been translated into English by D. Wile, *The Chinese Sexual Yoga Classics*, 193–201 and 204–212, and into French in my doctoral dissertation *La Porte du Dragon*, vol. 1, 318–374. In addition to the two texts mentioned above, see also the *Nüdan jicui* 女丹集萃 (Beijing: Beijing Shifan daxue chubanshe 北京師範大學出版社, 1989). Many of the ideas presented here were already elaborated in my dissertation to which I refer for some notions that seem central for understanding feminine alchemy.

[5] *Daozang xubian* 道藏續編 vol. 3, 1a-6b. See the concise description of this text in the Appendix to Chapter 3, Text number 19 (here above, p. 208).

[6] *Daozang xubian* 道藏續編 vol. 3, 7a-12b. This text has the subtitle *Nügong zhinan* 女功指南 (Direct Instructions on Female Practices). See my description of this text's overall content here above in the Appendix to Chapter 3, Text number 20 (pp. 208–9). On the role of precepts in feminine inner alchemy see Despeux, *Immortelles de la Chine*, 147–152.

Woman, the Moon, and Menstrual Blood

In the body of texts devoted to feminine alchemy, woman is presented as having a Yin 陰 nature very close to that of the moon.[7] This is not only due to her tendency to become full (pregnant) and her ever-changing character but also to her monthly rhythm which corresponds to the lunar cycle.[8] In many languages, words referring to menstruation are closely related to the moon (for example, "menses" from lat. "mensis" = month; and "menstruation" from lat. "menstrua/menstruus," which means "monthly").[9] In Chinese, common terms for designating this phenomena are *yuejing* 月經 (literally, monthly/lunar regularity) and *yueshi* 月事 (monthly/lunar affair). The latter word is more closely associated with agriculture and its calendar cycle in which welfare is linked to the good auspices of the moon, as when determining the right time for planting seeds. In France, for example, the menses were called "le moment de la lune" [the moment of the moon], and European peasants "are reported to believe that the moon menstruates and that she is 'sickening' during the period of waning, while the red rain or heavenly blood, which old folklore asserts often falls from the skies, is 'moon-blood.'"[10] During menstruation, women are almost universally subject to certain restrictions. Indeed, the word "menses" refers both to the regularity of women's lunar cycles during which they lose their menstrual blood—a symbol of potential fertility as well as of failed production—and to a set of rules and restrictions for women. Because of the great potential of pollution that characterizes women during menstruation, women are re-

---

[7] The *Xiwangmu nüxiu zhengtu shize* 西王母女修正途十則, *Daozang xubian* 道藏續編, vol. 3, 1b/1 states: "Woman is of Yin nature, and the Moon is her symbol" (女子、陰質也、月象也).

[8] "The period of a lunation, the cycle of the moon as it moves in its orbit about the earth, is close to the period of the human menstrual cycle. Evocations of rebirth and fecundity, and the provision of light invest the moon with a deep emotional significance." See E. G. Richards, *Mapping Time* (New York: Oxford University Press, 1998): 7.

[9] See Robert Briffault, *The Mothers* (New York and London, 1927): 2.430–32, quoted in M. Esther Harding, *Woman's Mysteries Ancient and Modern* (Boston & Shaftesbury: Shambhala, 1990): 55.

[10] M. Esther Harding, *Woman's Mysteries Ancient and Modern*, 55. Nowadays, the most common word for menstruation in French is 'règles,' a term which emphasizes the regularity of women's lunar cycles.

garded as impure and thus have to limit contacts with people and things.[11] The object of the taboo is the menstrual blood as carrier of pollution, regarded as a kind of infection and the result of possession by an evil spirit. Seen in this light, the seclusion of women was a necessity, and a system of prohibitions appropriate.[12] Fasting, seclusion, and castigation were the most usual penances prescribed for purification.[13]

Rules and prohibitions are also stressed in Chinese alchemical texts for women. Both of the above-mentioned texts in the *Daozang xubian* 道藏續編 (Supplementary Collection to the Daoist Canon, 1834) that deal with feminine alchemy are based on a system of rules and prohibitions which determines their structure and content. Although women are seen as able to devote themselves to inner alchemy, they are admonished to not neglect their role as mistress of the house, their loyalty toward the husband, their responsibilities in society, etc. They are instructed to be subservient to the voice of family authority and must, prior to engaging in any alchemical practice, undergo acts of ritual purification as codified in precepts reserved for women.[14] Rules and prohibitions that refer to the idea of "cultivating menses" (*xiujing* 修經) play an important role for women, emphasizing as they do the preeminent significance of menstrual blood in their practice.[15]

---

[11] Women were for example forbidden to touch butter, wine or meat since these were believed to turn bad; see for example Emily Martin, *The Women in the Body* (Milton Keynes: Open University Press, 1989): 97–99. On the elaboration of the pollution theory related to menstrual taboos see Mary Douglas, *Purity and Danger* (London: Ark, 1984). On interdictions and taboos still current in different civilizations see for example Karin Kapadia, *Śiva and Her Sisters: Gender, Caste, and Class in Rural South India* (Boulder, Oxford: Westview Press, 1995); and Ruth-Inge Heinze (ed.), *The Nature and Function of Rituals: Fire from Heaven* (Connecticut & London: Bergin & Garvey Westport, 2000).

[12] Deema de Silva, "Sinhalese Puberty Rites for Girls" (in Ruth-Inge Heinze [ed.], *The Nature and Function of Rituals: Fire from Heaven*, 84) reports that the reason for secluding girls during their first menstrual occurrence is to protect them against evil spirits that can enter their body and cause illnesses or affect their mental faculties.

[13] See M. Esther Harding, *Woman's Mysteries Ancient and Modern*, 57–59.

[14] *Xiwangmu nüxiu zhengtu shize* 西王母女修正途十則 opens with the list of nine precepts (*Daozang xubian* 道藏續編 vol. 3, 1a; trl. Wile, *The Chinese Sexual Yoga Classics*, 193). Despeux (*Immortelles de la Chine*, 149–152) remarks that these precepts emphasizing feminine virtues are still applied today by Quanzhen nuns in China.

[15] See in particular the fourth rule in the *Xiwangmu nüxiu zhengtu shize* 西王母女修正途十則, *Daozang xubian* 道藏續編, vol. 3, 2a.

Chapter Four: Beheading the Red Dragon—Feminine Alchemy 227

Fig. 4: Three-faced and six-armed Vajravārāhī, Ch. Jingang haimu 金剛亥母 (image 52 from *Midali bai fazhuzun xiang* 密答喇百法主尊像).

Although many studies have stressed the role of woman's inferiority in relation with the conception of impurity and pollution of her menstrual cycle, the varying contexts of menstrual symbolism have often been ignored. In ancient traditions menstrual blood was also regarded as holy. In particular, in the inverted logic of Tantra, the dangerous and polluting menstrual blood is transformed into a bliss-giving and liberating essence. This stands at the center of the Tantric view of the sacredness of the female body, the image of the Goddess.[16] In India, it is at the time of the Goddess's menses, in August-September that Assamese Tantric practitioners perform their annual gatherings.[17]

If in India the time of the Goddess's menses is regarded as an auspicious time for powerful gatherings and practices, in Chinese feminine alchemical practices the moment of woman's menses also has a special significance. In concomitance with the respect of rules, an inversion logic similar to Tantra came to play an important role also in Chinese feminine alchemy to the point that one wonders about the relationships between these two traditions. This is certainly a topic that needs further investigation, situated as it is in the vast unexplored domain of the relationship between Daoism and Tantrism during the Qing Dynasty. Now, with regard to Feminine Alchemy practice, I will limit myself to the bliss-giving and potentially liberating role played by the moment preceding the menses.

---

[16] In ancient traditions one also finds the idea of blood as a powerful substance without any notion of pollution; see J. L. Brockington, *The Sacred Thread: Hinduism in its Continuity and Diversity* (Edinburgh: Edinburgh University Press, 1981): 147–148; Sarah B. Pomeroy, *Women's History and Ancient History* (Chapel Hill: University of North Carolina Press, 1991): 287; and K. Kapadia, *Śiva and Her Sisters*, 70 & 76). Different examples of blood as empowered subtle body-energy are found in Śākta-Tantras; see for example Madhu Khanna, "The Goddess-Women, Equation in Śākta Tantras," in Mandakranta Bose (ed.), *Faces of the Feminine in Ancient, Medieval, and Modern India* (New York: Oxford University Press, 2000: 116–119), and traditions generally related with Indian Tantric Alchemy (see David White, *The Alchemical Body* [Chicago: Chicago University Press]: 191–202). In the Tibetan Vajrayāna tradition, an example is also provided by the well-known Dakīnī Dorje Pagmo whose menstrual blood is said to form the lake waters of Phodrang Kyomotso, a renowned place of pilgrimage for Tantric practitioners; see Toni Huber, *The Cult of Pure Crystal Mountain* (New York: Oxford University Press 1999: 96). The visualization of this Dakīnī (in Chinese known as *Jin'gang haimu* 金剛亥母, i.e., Vajrayoginī/Vajravārāhī; see Fig. 4) is also practiced in China by young nuns who can thus sublimate their sexual desires; see Monica Esposito, "Una tradizione di rDzogs-chen in Cina, una nota sul Monastero delle Montagne dell'Occhio Celeste," *Asiatica Venetiana* 3, 1998, 221–224 (in particular 222); Monica Esposito, "A Sino-Tibetan Tradition in China at the Southern Celestial Eye Mountains: A First Comparison between Great Perfection (rDzogs chen) and Taoist Techniques of Light." Paper presented at the Conference on "Tantra and Daoism, the Globalization of Religion and its Experience," Boston University, April 19–21, 2002; {and now also Monica Esposito, *The Zen of Tantra*. Wil/Paris: UniversityMedia, 2013.}

[17] David White, *The Alchemical Body*, 195, and 451 note 67.

Chujing 初經, the "Primal Instant" of Realization in Feminine Alchemy and the Role of Celestial Water (Tiangui 天癸)

In Chinese feminine alchemical texts, the most propitious moment for practice is named *chujing* 初經, the period preceding the menstrual flow, emblem of the first appearance of the menses in a young girl.[18] This term indicates, on the physiological level, the beginning of a process related to ovarian activity. Still far from such knowledge, the authors of alchemical texts imagined that in the uterus there existed something like a pearl or star (如星如珠) which gets converted into "red" or is transformed into menses every month if it was not properly cultivated. In order to avoid the degradation of that "most precious treasure before heaven" (*xiantian zhibao* 先天至寶) woman is asked to cultivate what is called *tiangui* 天癸 or Celestial Water (a metaphor for the first menses).[19] Instead of making menstrual blood flow outside, she has to sublimate her creative energy to engender an immortal embryo. Before giving birth to it, however, she has to pass through periods of "apparent cessation" of menses that symbolically mark her "ontological gestations." This means that woman has to pass through a gestation period in which, as in ordinary pregnancy, she experiences "menses cessa-

---

[18] See *Xiwangmu nüxiu zhengtu shize* 西王母女修正途十則, *Daozang xubian* 道藏續編 vol. 3, 1b/11–13 (自有一點初經。含於內牝。如星如珠。乃是先天至寶。藏於坤腹之上。位在中黃之中。....則此一物。得附性天。便成元一。不變赤珠。不化天癸) and 2a/3–4 (按初經命寶。不失知修。則附性天而化元一). The occurrence of the first menses was regarded in many cultures as an important moment of transition marking woman's sexuality and fertility, and rites of "first menstruation" are still celebrated today; see Karin Kapadia, *Siva and Her Sisters*, 70, 95; Victoria J. Baker, *Ritual Practice in a Sinhalese Village* (Forth Worth: Harcourt Brace College Publishers, 1998): 63; and Deema de Silva, "Sinhalese Puberty Rites for Girls," 84–85. In Chinese feminine alchemical texts it is important to note how this moment, regarded as both "dangerous and auspicious," was transposed into the sphere of feminine inner alchemical practice. The term *chujing* 初經 can be seen as the counterpart of the notion of *chuji* 初機 (also referred as *qiji* 氣機 or *chuqi* 初氣) in inner alchemy: the instant preceding the manifestation of *qi* before its division into Yin and Yang (see Esposito, *La Porte du Dragon*, 286–291, 315–316, and 377). For the cosmological significance of these terms see Isabelle Robinet, "Primus movens et création récurrente," *Taoist Resources*, 5.2 (1994): 29–70.

[19] See *Xiwangmu nüxiu zhengtu shize, Daozang xubian* 道藏續編 vol. 3, 1b (trl. Wile, *The Chinese Sexual Yoga Classics*, 194), and note 18 above.

tion." However, in this case, instead of delivering a child she gives birth to her True Self (*zhenwo* 真我).

In inner alchemy, a man must understand how to stop the discursive mind and its flow of thoughts through retention and sublimation of his seminal flow. Similarly, a woman must understand her emotive and ever-changing "lunar nature," subject to menstrual flow, in order to control it. The Celestial Water (*tiangui* 天癸) is her reservoir of energies that must be extracted from the depth of her being. This "extraction" can only be performed through her sincere desire for an inner realization free from pollution. As long as woman depends on longing for external acquisitions, she will see her blood flow outward.

In the first chapter of the *Huangdi neijing suwen* 黃帝內經素問 one finds the term *tiangui* 天癸 associated both with women and men's reproductive systems and their respective powers.[20] *Tiangui* points to the beginning of fecundity (the moment when energy is at its apex) and is closely related to the accumulation of *qi* in the kidneys. This accumulation is associated with sexual functions which, being the basis of other forms of vital energies, serve for attaining long life once they are mastered. This shows why the term *tiangui* 天癸, a synonym in this case of the Original *qi* (*yuanqi* 元氣), plays such an important role in feminine practice.[21] In this light one can understand why the *Ten Rules of the Queen Mother of the West on the Correct Path of Female Cultivation* 西王母女修正途十則 links woman's destiny to *tiangui* 天癸.[22] This term has, however, an ambivalent meaning: while it marks the moment of creative energy at its climax, it simultaneously indicates the point when the genetic inheritance of "Before heaven" (先天) starts dete-

---

[20] See the quotation of this passage by Despeux, *Immortelles de la Chine*, 218.

[21] A clear explanation of the meaning of *tiangui* 天癸 in relation with the above passage of the *Huangdi neijing* is provided by the physician Zhang Jiebin 張介賓 (1563–1640) in his *Zhiyi lu* 質疑錄 (Beijing: Jiangsu kexue jishu 江蘇科學技術, 1989): 28. In contrast with the explanations of all medical schools, he associates this term with Original *qi* (*yuanqi* 元氣) rather than blood or essence (天癸者、天一所生之真水、在人身是謂元陰、即日元氣。... 則知天癸非精血矣); see Esposito, *La Porte du Dragon*, vol, 1, 288 note 285. Zhang Jiebin's explanation of the term *tiangui* applies to the texts of feminine alchemy and general inner alchemy in the *Daozang xubian* (see *Xiwangmu nüxiu zhengtu shize*, *Daozang xubian* 道藏續編 vol. 3, 1b/2, 5 and 13; 2a/2, 6, and 3b/8; *Xietian ji* 3b/14 and *Zhang Sanfeng quanji* 5a/14).

[22] *Xiwangmu nüxiu zhengtu shize* 西王母女修正途十則, *Daozang xubian* 道藏續編 vol. 3, 1b/4–5 (蓋以女命還在天癸。天癸不化。命何能保).

riorating. This term can also be understood by dividing it into two parts where *tian* 天 refers to the celestial inheritance and *gui* 癸, the tenth Celestial Stem traditionally designating puberty, refers to water and its flow. The term *tiangui* also calls to mind another term used for women's menstrual blood and its process: *rengui* 壬癸.[23] In feminine alchemical texts, *rengui* indicates two phases in the menstrual process.

1. A first phase called *ren* 壬 (or *tian* 天, following Liu Yiming's explanations of note 23) that precedes (and follows) the menses and characterizes "true energy." It coincides with the right moment for practicing (extracting Yang within Yin or Yin within Yang) and is associated with the ideas of potential conception and fecundity.
2. The second phase called *gui* 癸 is characterized by ordinary Yin and indicates the menstrual flow.

Feminine practice must focus on the first phase as the reservoir of the original *qi* (*yuanqi* 元氣), the potential source ready to be sublimated. By contrast, the practice must be "interrupted" during the period of menstruation, the time of impure and sterile blood flow, since it is a dead matter incapable of procreation. This menstrual flow is normally designated with terms such as *yueshui* 月水 (monthly water), *yuejing* 月經 (menses), *jingshui* 經水 (menses-water), or *guishui* 癸水 (*gui* water). But the "interruption" of this second phase must also be regarded as bliss-giving and liberating. Thanks to it, the woman perceives the need of practicing since she becomes progressively conscious of the loss of her energy that occurs with convenient regularity every month. As feminine alchemical texts underline, woman has once every month the possibility of either gaining emancipation or failing to do so. The propitious moment is two days before menstruating when Yang is just about to transform into Yin blood. The texts call this moment *xinshui* 信水 (Messenger Water) or *yuexin* 月信 (Monthly Messenger). In both of these terms, the character *xin* 信 points to the arrival of a "message" or a "messenger" announcing the impending menstruation through well-known

---

[23] Liu Yiming 劉一明 (1734–1821), in his *Xiangyan poyi* 象言破疑 [Clarification on Symbolic Words] (j. *xia* 42a in *Daoshu shier zhong* 道書十二種, Zhongguo Zhongyiyao chubanshe 中國中醫藥出版社, 1990, vol. 2, 205), states: "Water-ren is Yang, water-gui is Yin" 壬水陽兮癸水陰. Commenting on the method of Feminine Alchemy by Beheading the Dragon, Liu explains : "Celestial-*ren* and terrestrial-*gui* will meet each other" 天壬地癸相見面 (*Nü jindan*, in *Nüdan jicui*, 304) This is a good illustration of the relationship between dwellers of heaven (*tian-ren* 天人) and earthbound demons (*di-gui* 地鬼) and the necessity of transcending their apparent duality.

symptoms such as leg and waist heaviness, headache, etc.[24] This "message" delivered to the woman is the *qi*, or more specifically, the presence of true Yin within the Yang (or true Yang within the Yin). This is the right moment for practicing, since as soon as the periodic flow ebbs, the Yin essence of blood can no more be gathered. The texts also indicate that one can resume practice two and a half days after the cessation of the menstrual flow.[25]

The texts treat of feminine alchemical practice under the label of "Beheading the Red Dragon" (*zhan chilong* 斬赤龍). What is symbolically called *chilong* 赤龍 or Red Dragon must be understood in connection with the energetic basis of woman before or after her menstrual flow. Although one talks of menstrual blood, it is important to distinguish it from *guishui* 癸水 or *jingshui* 經水, that is, from the ordinary menstrual blood of the second phase. Only after cutting off the head of the Red Dragon can the essence reveal itself as the "true energy" of the first phase connected with the state "Before heaven" (先天). This can be expressed by the inversion from *gui* to *ren* 任←癸 or from *gui* to *tian* 天←癸: "Water-*gui* [inverting its flow to] Heaven."[26] The Red Dragon is the emblem of the reservoir of breath, the inner power which can be transformed into pure energy. It is in this sense that one may understand the symbolic meaning of "Red Dragon" and "its

---

[24] On these terms see Despeux, *Immortelles de la Chine*, 253–256.

[25] See *Nü jindan* 女金丹 (in *Nüdan jicui* 女丹集萃, 302) and *Nüdan hebian* 女丹合編 (in *Nüdan jicui*, 96). In the *Upanishads*, auspicious time (which is also connected with the end of woman's first menses) is besung as follows: "Surely, a woman who has changed her clothes at the end of her menstrual period is the most auspicious of women. When she has changed her clothes at the end of her menstrual period, one should therefore approach that splendid woman and invite her to have sex." (trl. by Patrick Olivelle, *Upanishads*. New York: Oxford University Press, 1996: 88).

[26] This shows the "mutual encounter between the Celestial-*ren* and the Terrestrial-*gui*" (天壬地癸相見面) evoked in the passage by Liu Yiming (see note 23). It also refers to the explanation: "Heaven (*tian*) is reverted (*dian*); this means that the crown of the head has fallen" (天、顛也。謂頭頂顛). See *Sheming* 釋名 (in Hao Yixing 郝懿行 et al. [eds.], *Erya, Guanya, Fangyan, Sheming* 爾雅、廣雅、方言、釋名. Shanghai: Shanghai guji chubanshe 上海古籍出版社, 1989; and He Xin 何新, *Zhushen de qiyuan* 諸神的起源, Taipei: Muduo chubanshe 木鐸出版社, 1989, 269). This is the image of the "upside-down world" of inner alchemy and refers to its inverted logic where water, instead of flowing downward as it does by nature, rises up to heaven. It corresponds to the shift from the "world after heaven" (*houtian* 後天) to the "world before heaven" (*xiantian* 先天). On the concept of the upside-down world in alchemy see Isabelle Robinet, "Le monde à l'envers dans l'alchimie intérieure taoïste [The upside-down world in Daoist inner alchemy]." *Revue de l'Histoire des Religions* 209, 3 (1992): 239–257.

Chapter Four: Beheading the Red Dragon—Feminine Alchemy   233

beheading."²⁷ In order to realize its mystery, one has to go back to the notion of "upside-down" (*dian* 顛, *diandao* 顛到), that is, to the logic of inversion which is one of the fundamental principles of inner alchemy. This is well exemplified by the "inverted image" of man and woman's bodies and their related practice.

---

27 The concept of upside-down world as the image of the reverted or fallen head (*tian* 天 as *dian* 顛; see note above) may also call to mind the myth of the decapitation of the warrior hero Xingtian 刑天 (see He Xin 何新, *Zhushen de qiyuan* 諸神的起源, Taipei: Muduo chubanshe 木鐸出版社 1989, 268–69). As Anne Birrell (*Chinese Mythology*, Baltimore and London: John Hopkins University Press, 1993: 216–217) remarks, this myth of the headless hero "Punished by Heaven (Xingtian 刑天) or "Shaped by Heaven (Xingtian 形天) who uses his nipples and navel to serve as replacement of eyes and mouth, anticipates the concept in medical science of transplants. It may be seen as symbol for the physical modification announced by the practice of Beheading the Dragon: woman will first be transplanted into a body similar to that of a man (see for example *Qiaoyang jing* 樵陽經 in *Nüdan jicui*, 136: 乳頭縮而赤龍斬。變成男體), and finally her body will become like an androgynous one (see here below). Furthermore, the act of decapitation includes the idea of rebirth. Among the wonders that the Ten Islands conceal in the *Shizhou ji* (十州記, DZ 598, fasc. 330, 2b), there is a fantastic animal that is not harmed by fire and, when his head is cut off, returns to life (quoted by Isabelle Robinet, *Méditation taoïste*, Paris: Albin Michel, 1995, 276). Reports of heroes slaying dragons or other fearsome creatures abound in Chinese literature and point to their capacities as powerful healers and exorcists. In India, quite interestingly, one finds a story of the decapitation of a dragon-like demon in relation with the onset of menstruation in women. The legend begins with hero Indra's slaying of a dragon-like demon called Vrtra (demon of drought), a withholder of the waters of heavens. By contrast with Chinese legends, in a later version of the myth, Indra the supreme victor is punished for the killing of Vrtra who has assumed the form of a learned Brahmin. Indra runs to the women for protection and asks them to take upon themselves the third part of this guilt of Brahminicide, a guilt which will then show itself as women's monthly menstrual flow (see Madhu Khanna, "The Goddess-Women, Equation in Sākta Tantras," in Mandakranta Bose [eds.], *Faces of the Feminine in Ancient, Medieval and Modern India*, 117–118). Conversely, in the inverted logic of Tantra, an Indian Goddess beheads demons, as in the well-known story of Durgā killing the Buffalo Demon. Breaking the brahminical image, she becomes the weapon-wielding Goddess whose blood is sacred and no more polluted; see Kim Knott, *Hinduism: A Very Short Introduction*, New York: Oxford University Press, 2000, 45; and D. White, *The Alchemical Body*, 190 and 191–202. See also note 16 here above. Finally, it is worthwhile to mention the metaphor of "killing the Dragon," common to the alchemical world, which refers to the formation of quicklime or metal sulfides; see Needham et al., *Science and Civilisation* vol. 5, Part. 2, Cambridge: Cambridge University Press, 1976, p. 8.

Woman as Inverted Mirror of Man

Woman is characterized by her specific nature and constitution. As we have seen, her energetic basis is blood and her alchemical work must start by sublimating this substance. Before starting with the first stage of sublimation of essence into breath (*lianjing huaqi* 煉精化氣), she has to sublimate the blood into essence (*lianxue huajing* 煉血化精). She must "stop" her physiological hemorrhage that afflicts her every month by causing her to lose her true creative energy. The feminine alchemical practice of "Beheading the Red Dragon" (*zhan chilong* 斬赤龍) constitutes the initial alchemical stage. It is the counterpart of the sublimation of the seminal essence for man. In a text of feminine alchemy, the *Nü jindan* 女金丹, the differences between woman and man are described in the following manner:

> Man regards the nascent Yang as Fire: when Fire returns, Water accomplishes itself.
> Woman regards the nascent Yin as Water: when Water returns, Fire accomplishes itself.
> What does "nascent Yin" mean? It is *chaoxin* 潮信, the signal of the tide.
> Man sublimates *qi* 氣.
> Woman sublimates shape (*xing* 形).
> Man leads the White Tiger.
> Woman decapitates the Red Dragon.
> The White Tiger is the spirit (*shen* 神) and qi (*qi* 氣).
> The Red Dragon is essence (*jing* 精) and blood (*xue* 血).
> In man the nascent Yang is in Zi 子.
> In woman the nascent Yin is in Wu 午.
> Zi 子 indicates the Kidney channel (*shenjing* 腎經).
> Wu 午 indicates the Heart channel (*xinjing* 心經).
> Wu 午 is the root of Yin.
> Zi 子 is the sprout of Yang.
> Man is Yang outside and Yin inside.
> Woman is Yin outside and Yang inside.
> Man seizes the Yang outside in order to add it to Yin.
> Woman seizes the Yin outside in order to add it to Yang.
> This is the path of cultivation of immortality for woman.[28]

---

[28] In *Nüdan jicui* 女丹集萃, p. 301 (男子以陽生為火。火回就水成功。女人以陰

Woman is thus the perfect inverted mirror of man: her blood or Red Dragon, once beheaded, is the synonym of Original *qi* (*yuanqi* 元氣). It is the emblem of her fertilizing power ready to engender.[29] Woman's Red Dragon corresponds to the White Tiger for man. Taking the form of a fluid or female Fire, the Red Dragon hides within the breasts of woman, while the White Tiger, in the form of an ignited or male Water, hides in the testicles of man. The centers on which woman and man focus at the outset of their alchemical work are exactly in opposition. Woman concentrates on the Brook of Milk (*ruxi* 乳溪, the point between the breasts) and lightly massages her breasts to activate the circulation of blood and *qi*.[30] Once purified, the blood descends to the Lower Cinnabar Field (*xia dantian* 下丹田) at the navel level) and transforms into essence (*jing* 精). Conversely, man focuses his attention on his reproductive system (kidneys/testicles). He starts his work by concentrating on the Lower Cinnabar Field in which he progressively accumulates his seminal essence. Once purified, this essence (rather than the semen or sperm) transforms into *qi* 氣 and rises to the Superior Cinnabar Field (*shang dantian* 上丹田, at the level of the brain).

This difference in the location of the energetic fields between woman and man finds its expression in the theories concerning reproduction. These theories are at the basis of the physical, cosmic, and metaphysical procreation to which the alchemical texts refer, since the menstrual blood and the seminal essence are seen as the fundamental ingredients for procreation. However, in the "upside-down world" of the Alchemical Opus, these ingredients must be inverted in their nature in order to generate an Embryo of immortality.

生為水。水回就火成功。何為陰生。陰生者、潮信是也。男子煉氣。女人煉形。男牽白虎。女斬赤龍。白虎者、神與氣。赤龍者、精與血也。男子陽生在子。女人陰生在午。子乃腎經。午乃心經。午是陰之根。子係陽之苗。男子外陽而內陰。女人外陰而內陽。男子奪外陽以點陰。女人奪外陰以點陽。此乃女人修仙之道). A similar passage starting from "Wu is the root of Yin..." (午是陰之根..) is also found in *Nügong lianji huandan tushuo* 女功煉己還丹圖說 (in *Nüdan jicui* 女丹集萃, 132).

[29] As essential blood (*jingxue*), the Red Dragon, once it is beheaded (i.e., sublimated by inverting its nature), returns to the source, the *tiangui*'s 天癸 reservoir; see Zhang Jiebin 張介賓 in his *Zhiyi lu* 質疑錄 (Beijing: Jiangsu kexue jishu 江蘇科學技術, 1989, 28: ....天癸在先、而後精血之..), and notes 21 above and 30 below.

[30] It is exactly by working on the manifestation of the hitherto concealed female nature (menstruations and breasts, the striking marks of her difference to man) that woman attains her liberation. The same logic is also applied to man and to his marks of masculinity. These marks, which in many cultures figure as the reason of female inferiority, become in the logic of alchemy the very sources of her liberation.

They must go against the normal rules that regulate the ordinary world by returning to the World Before Heaven (*xiantian* 先天). Woman must thus work on blood before it changes into menstruation, and man on the essence before it changes into sperm. These "pure" ingredients are the reservoir of power ready to be used as *materia prima* for the Alchemical Work.

Conclusion

From this point of view, one can easily understand the meaning of "the cessation of the menstrual blood" in female alchemy, which is simply the counterpart of the "cessation of spermatic flow" in man. The "cessation" marks the distinction between those who follow the normal course of things, thus engendering an ordinary being, and those who—mastering this course and inverting it—are capable of engendering their True Self.

The first stage of "Beheading the Red Dragon" in feminine alchemy signifies a full control of time and body that correspond to the control of the seminal essence in man. Both are emblems of the mastery over passions and over discursive and emotive flows. Woman thus has the possibility of experiencing the cyclic character of her life (*yinyang xiaoxi* 陰陽消息) and of understanding the value of her waxing and waning lunar cycle in order to live in harmony with her own Celestial nature. Freed from her sterile blood flow, woman experiences the joy of giving birth to her True Self. This marks the beginning of her return to the "Before heaven" (*xiantian* 先天). From this stage onward she can devote herself to the true Work which is not different from that of man. As described also in the standard texts of inner alchemy, she proceeds to the following stages of sublimation of the essence into *qi* (*lianjing huaqi* 煉精化氣), sublimation of the *qi* into spirit (*lianqi huashen* 煉氣化神), and finally to the sublimation of spirit and return to emptiness (*lianshen huaxu* 煉神化虛). Once she resides in the Center, she obtains access to the sphere in which all duality is transcended and in which all distinctions between man and woman, female and male, completely vanish. This is why the texts describe the accomplished practitioner as devoid of sexual attributes and with an androgynous body characterized by the retraction of breasts, corresponding to the retraction of testicles in man.

Finally, "Beheading the Dragon" refers to a true period of menses suspension just like in pregnancy; but this has only the meaning of a microcosmic orbit (*xiao zhoutian* 小周天) if woman limits herself exclusively to the physiological results of the practice. In inner alchemy, woman needs to progress toward the macrocosmic orbit (*da zhoutian* 大周天) in order to accomplish her Embryo of Immortality. This last alchemical stage will be then crowned with eloquent silence, the symphony of her accomplished Work.[31]

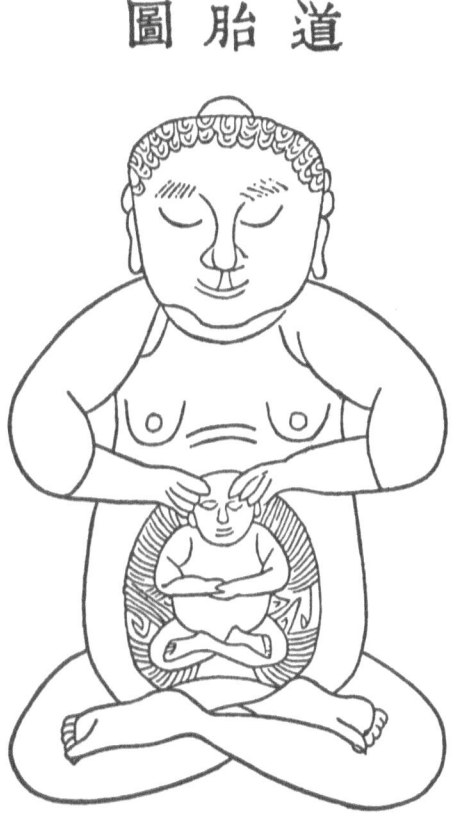

Fig. 5: The immortal foetus. From Lu K'uan Yü (Charles Luk), *Taoist Yoga: Alchemy and Immortality*. New York: Samuel Weiser, 1973, p. 151.

---

[31] See Li Daochun 李道純 (fl. 1288–1306) in *Zhonghe ji* 中和集 [Collection of Central Harmony] (DZ 249, fasc. 118–19, 6.12a): "Silence is eloquent; in speech there is originally silence, and silent speech is precisely the secret of the Golden Elixir" 默即說兮、說處元來有默、只默說便是金丹祕訣.

An Example of Daoist and Tantric Interaction during the Qing Era: The Longmen Xizhu Xinzong

This chapter discusses the relationship between Daoism and Tantrism as well as aspects of inter-religious relationships (Buddhism, Daoism, and Confucianism) during the Qing dynasty. What was the situation of Daoism in the Qing era? What was its role? What kind of Daoist works were produced during this dynasty?

In various manuals on the History of Daoism in China and even in recent works on Qing Daoism, the Daoism of the Qing era (1644–1914) is often thrown into one pot with that of the Ming (1368–1644). Their reader notes with surprise that, according to the common view, Daoism seems to have been in decline or even on the verge of disappearing for over half a millennium. Usual topics of discussion include the secondary role of Daoism at the imperial court, the policy of religious control common to both the Ming and Qing dynasties, and the progressive vulgarization of Daoist beliefs. By being mixed up with or contaminated by so-called "popular," "common," or "folk" religion—so it is argued—Daoism progressively lost its identity. Though such discussions in recent publications address some important features of late imperial Daoism, they are still far from providing a picture of the actual situation of Daoism during that period. It needs to be underlined that the majority of adduced sources for such scenarios are based on official documents propagated by the court or by its supporters. For instance, the accounts by Jesuits who visited China during the Ming and Qing dynasties are naturally biased and reflect their relationship with the court, their missionary strategy, and their particular view of Confucianism. By consequence, Jesuits conveyed a more or less Confucian vision of Daoism and Buddhism when they presented these two religions as marginalized movements full of superstitious beliefs that stand in stark contrast with the rational, moral, and dominant Confucian teaching. There is a clear need for the close study of other sources that also reflect what Daoists or people outside the court had to say. Such study is imperative for enhancing our knowledge in a domain that still remains largely unexplored.

Here I will look at some materials that show how Daoism presented *itself* during the Qing dynasty and explore its links with other religions, in particular with Tantrism. Before introducing such sources, however, a few words need to be said about the so-called Tantrism of the Qing dynasty and the special attention paid to it by the Qing emperors.[1]

ESOTERIC TEACHINGS (*MIJIAO*) DURING THE QING

During the Qing, the term "Esoteric Teaching" (*mijiao* 密教) referred not only to esoteric practices of earlier periods including the Tang era (618–907) but also to Tibetan Buddhism and forms of Buddhism practiced by Tibetans and other monks from the regions to the West and North of China since the Yuan era (1260–1368). The well-known pilgrimage site of Mt. Wutai 五臺山 in Shanxi 山西 shows that Tibetan and Tibet-influenced Buddhism continued to flourish and never disappeared in China even during the Ming dynasty (1368–1644).[2] The support for Tibetan Bud-

---

[1] Most studies emphasize that the Manchus, who were thought to be non-believers in Tibetan Buddhism, patronized the faith only to win the allegiance of the Mongols. However, according to Kam Tak Sing ("Manchu-Tibetan Relations In The Early Seventeenth Century: A Reappraisal," Ph.D. dissertation, Harvard University, 1994), Manchus were syncretistic: in addition to Tibetan Buddhism, they also followed shamanism, Daoism, and Chinese Buddhism. Their belief in Buddhism appears to have been sincere, as evidenced by their translations of Mahayana sutras into the Manchu language, their frequent quotes from Buddhist scriptures such as the *Subhasitaratnanidhi* of Sa Skya Pandita in their discourses, and their receiving the empowerment (*abhiṣeka*), a Tantric ritual, from their gurus. Had the Manchus wanted to exploit Tibetan Buddhism to impinge upon Mongolian politics through the Dalai Lama, it would not have happened before 1643, when the dGe lugs pa emerged victorious from the sectarian struggle that had long divided the lamaist community. For a study and translation of the *Subhasitaratnanidhi* see James E. Bosson, *A Treasury of Aphoristic Jewels: The Subhasitaratnanidhi of Sa Skya Pandita in Tibetan and Mongolian* (Bloomington: Indiana University, 1969).

[2] We know that Tibetan Buddhism began to influence the court from the Yuan onward. See for example Herbert Franke, *China under Mongol Rule* (Aldershot: Brookfield, 1994); Herbert Franke, *Chinesischer und tibetischer Buddhismus im China der Yuanzeit: drei Studien* (München: Kommission für Zentralasiatische Studien, Bayerische Akademie der Wissenschaften, 1996); and Luciano Petech, *Central Tibet and the Mongols: The Yuan–Sa-skya period of Tibetan History* (Roma: Istituto

dhism reached its climax during the reign of Emperor Qianlong 乾隆 (r. 1736–1795). Among Tibetan schools, Qianlong lent his great support to the dGe lugs pa—in China commonly known as Huangjiao 黃教 or Yellow school—and invited the Dalai Lama to Beijing. Qianlong's State Preceptor (*guoshi* 國師) was a lama from A mdo (i.e., Qinghai and Gansu provinces) known as Rol pa'i rdo rje (1717–1786) under whose tutelage the emperor studied Tibetan Buddhism and Sanskrit.[3] Since I will not further discuss the important role of Tibetan Buddhism at the Qing court, I include a selection of references to studies on this topic in this chapter's bibliography. However, as we go along I will highlight some important aspects of Qing religious politics related to the support of Tibetan Buddhism in order to better understand Qing Daoism and its relationship with Tibetan Buddhism.

Did Daoism interact with *mijiao* 密教 (Esoteric Teaching or Esoteric Buddhism)? If so, what stance did it assume toward it? One way to find answers to such questions is by analysing Longmen history as presented by its eleventh patriarch, Min Yide 閔一得 (1758–1836), in his *Jingai xindeng* 金蓋心燈 or *Mind-Lamp of Mount Jingai*. I will focus on several biographies of Min Yide and translate some passages from his *Mind-Lamp* collection. They show not only that he was influenced by the Three Teachings but also how he came in contact with Esoteric Buddhism. But first I will briefly furnish some information about Daoism's Longmen branch (*Longmen pai* 龍門派) and what it represented at the beginning of the Qing, because it is within Longmen that the Daoist encounter with "Esoteric Teaching" took place in form of the so-called Longmen xizhu xinzong 龍門西竺心宗, the "Longmen Mind-Tradition of Western India."

---

italiano per il Medio ed Estremo Oriente, 1990). On the image of Tibetan monks during the Yuan see Shen Weirong 沈衛榮, "Magic Power, Sorcery and Evil Spirits: The Image of Tibetan Monks in Chinese Literature during the Yuan Dynasty," in *The Relationship between Religion and State (chos srid zung 'brel) in Traditional Tibet*, ed. Christoph Cuppers (Bhairahawa: Lumbini International Research Institute, 2004):189–228 ; Chinese version in *Hanxue yanjiu* 漢學研究 (Chinese Studies) 21/2 (2003):219–247. On the presence of Tibetan Buddhism at Wutai shan see Gray Tuttle, "Tibetan Buddhism at Ri bo rtse lnga / Wutai shan in Modern Times," *Journal of the International Association of Tibetan Studies* 2 (August 2006):1–35.

[3] Lcang skya Rol pa'i rdo rje was the second historical figure in the Lcang skya reincarnation lineage which originates in A mdo; see Wang Xiangyun, *Tibetan Buddhism at the Court of Qing: The Life and Work of lCang skya Rol pa'i rdo rje*. Ph.D. dissertation, Harvard University 1995; and Wang Xiangyun, "The Qing court's Tibet Connection: Lcang skya Rol pa'i rdo rje and the Qianlong Emperor," *Harvard Journal of Asiatic Studies* 60.1 (2000):125–163.

Daoism during the Qing: Longmen—The Gate of Daoist Ordinations

The Quanzhen Daoist Chen Minggui 陳銘珪 (1824–1881) stated in his *Origins and Development of the Daoist Teachings of [Qiu] Changchun* (*Changchun daojiao yuanliu* 長春道教源流) of 1879:[4]

> It is commonly said that Longmen 龍門 and Linji 臨濟 share the empire. Those called *shi* 釋 [i.e., Buddhist clergy] are of the Linji Tradition, and [those called] *dao* 道 [i.e., Daoist clergy] are of the Longmen Branch.
>
> 世稱龍門、臨濟半天下。謂釋之臨濟宗、道之龍門派也。

Linji 臨濟 (Jap. Rinzai), a major branch of Chan 禪 (Jap. Zen) Buddhism, is named after Master Linji Yixuan 臨濟義玄 (d. 866). Holmes Welch has shown that Buddhist monks in late imperial and Republican China were commonly ordained according to the procedures of the Linji tradition (*Linji zong* 臨濟宗) and thus referred to themselves, irrespective of their practices, as members of the Linji branch of Chan Buddhism.[5] Similarly, from the Qing era to the present day, "Longmen 龍門" (Dragon Gate) is used as a generic label for Daoist clergy because the Longmen branch of Daoism held the monopoly of the ordination procedure.[6] How

---

[4] See *Daotong yuanliu* 道統源流 6.28b, in *Zangwai daoshu* 藏外道書 vol. 31, p. 113. Chen Mingui was the Quanzhen abbot of the Sulao dong 酥醪洞主 at Mount Luofu 羅浮山 in Guangdong province.

[5] According to Holmes Welch (*The Practice of Chinese Buddhism 1900–1950* [Cambridge, Mass.: Harvard University Press, 1967]), the Linji or Lin-chi sect (*Linji zong* 臨濟宗) "had become a pure institution and no longer involved any doctrine at all. That is, if a monk's sect was Lin-chi, it meant simply that the sect of his master was Lin-chi, not that he accepted the doctrines or employed the methods of the original founder of the sect ... who lived at Mt. Lin-chi during the T'ang dynasty" (p. 396). Thus belonging to a sect did not necessarily have any doctrinal significance and could be purely a matter of lineage, which is why "almost all Chinese Buddhist monks" belonged one of the two dominant factions of Chan Buddhism, Linji 臨濟 or Caodong 曹洞 (Ts'ao-tung, Jap. Sōtō) (p. 281).

[6] The ordination procedure refers to a collective ceremony of "taking the vows" or "accepting the precepts" (*shoujie* 受戒) which takes place in an authorized and public monastery on whose ordination platform the cleric is fully recognized as such. See Yoshioka Yoshitoyo 吉岡義豐, "Taoist Monastic Life." In *Facets of Taoism*, ed. Holmes Welch & Anna Seidel (New Haven and London: Yale University Press,

Chapter Five: Daoism and Tantrism in the Qing 243

did this come about? In the case of Daoism this trend can be traced back to the end of the Ming dynasty (1368–1644). Under the strong domination of the Zhengyi 正一 Daoists at the court, the Quanzhen 全真 movement began to be reevaluated. The basis of this reevaluation was established from the beginning of the Qing. Given that the Qing was a foreign dynasty that declared its inheritance of the right to rule established by Chinggis Khan, it was probably not by accident that the Qing rulers, inspired by their Yuan-era predecessors, again favored the Quanzhen order of Daoism. Among the Seven Perfected (*qizhen* 七真) of this order, Qiu Chuji 邱處機 (1148–1227) was most famous. He was celebrated for his long journey to Central Asia to meet Chinggis Khan.[7] Following this meeting, the Quanzhen order entered its Golden Age by obtaining an edict granting exemption from taxes and labor. Thus Qiu Chuji became the leader of all native religions in North China in charge of "all those who leave their families."[8] It is to him that the foundation of the Longmen tradition was attributed[9] even though

---

1979): 235–236; and Welch, *The Practice of Chinese Buddhism*, 285–296.

[7] This journey is reported in the *Changchun zhenren xiyouji* 長春真人西遊記 (DZ 1429 fasc. 1056) by Li Zhichang 李志常, one of the eighteen disciples who took part in it; tr. Arthur Waley, *Travels of an Alchemist: The Journey of the Taoist Ch'ang-ch'un to the Hindukush at the Summons of Chingiz Khan* (London: George Routledge & Sons, Ltd, 1931); see also J. Boltz, *A Survey of Taoist Literature* (Berkeley: Institute of East Asian Studies & Center for Chinese Studies, University of California, 1987): 66–68 and 157–59. Because of his important relationship with the ruler, Qiu Chuji was even granted a biography in the official history of the Yuan dynasty (*Yuanshi* 元史 j. 202).

[8] Yao Tao-chung, "Quanzhen: Complete Perfection," in Livia Kohn (ed.), *Daoism Handbook* (Leiden: Brill, 2000): 572.

[9] The name of Longmen traditionally refers to Mt. Longmen 龍門山 situated in the Longzhou 隴州 district of Western Shaanxi 陝西 where Qiu Chuji retreated and underwent seven years of ascetic training; see *Ganshui xian yuanlu* 甘水仙源錄 (DZ 973 fasc. 611–613, DZ vol. 19: 734). According to other hypotheses, the name of Longmen may be traced to a place in Huashan 華山 (Shaanxi 陝西) or even to a grotto (*dong* 洞) located in Sichuan. See Wang Zhizhong 王志忠, "Quanzhen jiao Longmen pai qiyuan lunkao" 全真教龍門派起源論考, *Zongjiao xue yanjiu* 宗教學研究 4 (1995): 9–13; Monica Esposito, "La Porte du Dragon—L'école Longmen du Mont Jin'gai et ses pratiques alchimiques d'après le *Daozang xubian*" (Suite au canon taoïste)" (Ph.D. dissertation, Université de Paris VII, 1993): 144–154; and Monica Esposito "The Longmen School and its Controversial History during the Qing Dynasty," in John Lagerwey (ed.), *Religion and Chinese Society: The Transformation of a Field* (Hong Kong: École Française d'Extrême-Orient & Chinese University of Hong Kong, 2004): 621–698 {included as Chapter 2 here above}.

the official promoter of Longmen at the court, and its *de facto* founder, was a man who lived about four centuries later: Wang Changyue 王常月 (also called Wang Kunyang 王崑陽, ?-1680).

According to nineteenth-century Longmen historiography spearheaded by Min Yide 閔一得 (1748/58–1836), Wang was recognized by the Qing court as the reformer of strict Quanzhen discipline and moral rules. Regardless of this claim, he obtained official permission to perform public ordinations, and—as abbot of the Baiyun guan 白雲觀 public monastery in the Beijing capital—began in 1656 to perform ordinations and supervise the religious training of the Daoist clergy. The content of these ordinations was established by Wang Changyue in his work entitled *Chuzhen jielü* 初真戒律 (Code of Initial Precepts for Perfection, 1656)[10] and also in a later compilation by Wang's disciples known as *Biyuan tanjing* 碧苑壇經 (Platform Sūtra of the Emerald Garden).[11] The ordination program "re-established" by Wang Changyue under the Longmen label is said to have consisted of the so-called "great precepts of the triple ordination platform" (*santan dajie* 三壇大戒), a term that in Wang's times was in use for Buddhist ordination procedures. It refers to an ordination in three stages or acts:

1. the novice ordination (*shami jiefa* 沙彌戒法)
2. the *bhikhsu /bhikshuni* or complete ordination (*biku jiefa* 比丘戒法)
3. the Bodhisattva ordination (*pusa jiefa* 菩薩戒法).[12]

---

[10] This text is found in DZJY vol. 24 (*zhangji* 張集 7: 25a-61b) and in the *Zangwai daoshu* 藏外道書 vol. 12, pp. 13–31. For a brief survey of its content see Catherine Despeux, "Chuzhen jielü," in Fabrizio Pregadio (ed.), *The Encyclopedia of Taoism* (London & New York: Routledge, 2008): 284–286.

[11] This text is found in the *Gu Shuyinlou cangshu* 古書隱樓藏書, vol. 1. I use here the edition of 1904 reprinted in *Zangwai daoshu* 藏外道書 10:158–217). Another version of this text is known under the title *Longmen xinfa* 龍門心法 (Core Teachings of the Longmen), *Zangwai daoshu* 藏外道書 6:727–785. It shows some differences with the *Biyuan tanjing* which would be worthy of further study. This text consists of discourses held during an ordination ceremony allegedly held by Wang Changyue in 1663 at the Biyuan abbey in Nanjing. The title clearly alludes to the famous *Platform Sūtra* of the Sixth Patriarch Huineng 六組慧能 of Chan Buddhism. For different perspectives on the influence of the *Platform Sūtra* of Huineng see Fo Kuang shan, *The Sixth Patriarch Platform Sūtra*. On the meaning of the term platform (*tan* 壇) referring to a precepts or ordination platform (*jietan* 戒壇) see Paul Groner's contribution in the same book entitled "The Ordination Ritual in the Platform Sūtra within the context of the East Asian Buddhist Vinaya Tradition," pp. 220–222.

[12] See Karl Ludwig Reichelt, *Truth and Tradition in Chinese Buddhism* (Taipei: SMC

Chapter Five: Daoism and Tantrism in the Qing 245

Fig. 6: Three-tiered altar (*Shishi yuanliu yinghua shiji* 釋氏源流應化事蹟, 1486)

It is difficult to know exactly when this kind of ordination ceremony began to be performed in a single session; but there are traces of a combined use of noviciate precepts, complete ordination, and Bodhisattva precepts in works by Buddhist Chan reformers of the late Ming and early Qing eras who had emigrated to Japan. Called *Sandan kaie* 三檀戒會 (Triple-Platform Ordination Ceremony) in Japan, it was around the end of the Ming

---

Publishing, 1990 [¹1927]): 229–240; and Holmes Welch, *The Practice of Chinese Buddhism*, pp. 285–296.

era also performed by Chinese Zen masters of the Huangbo 黃檗 (Jap. Ōbaku) lineage who founded the Manpukuji 萬福寺 Zen monastery in the city of Uji 宇治 near Kyoto. It may have been introduced in Japan by Chan master Yinyuan Longji 隱元隆琦 (Jap. Ingen Ryūki, 1592–1673).[13]

It is likely that Daoism adopted this kind of Buddhist ordination ceremony around the same period. Wang's Longmen Daoist variant of the "threefold altar" ordination took place in three stages:

(1) The Precepts of Initial Perfection (*chuzhen jie* 初真戒) which are intended for male and female novices. They consist of:

    a) The three refuges (Dao, sacred scriptures, and master);[14]
    b) Five cardinal lay precepts;[15]
    c) Ten precepts for novices;[16]

---

[13] See Hasebe Yūkei 長谷幽蹊, *Minshin bukkyō kyōdanshi kenkyū* 明清佛教團史研究 (Kyoto: Dōhōsha 同朋舍, 1993): 155–173; and Helen Baroni, *Obaku Zen* (Honolulu: University of Hawai'i Press, 2000): 94–98.

[14] *Sangui yijie* 三皈依戒. *Biyuan tanjing* 碧苑壇經 (*Zangwai daoshu* 藏外道書 10:159–162); *Chuzhen jielü* (DZJY 24 zhangji 7: 34a-b & *Zangwai daoshu* 12:17). This reproduces the refuge portion in the early eighth-century Zhengyi ordination text by Zhang Wanfu 張萬福 (fl. 713), the *Sandong zhongjie wen* 三洞眾戒文 (DZ 178, 2a–b), with the addition of short annotations.

[15] For the Five Precepts (*wujie* 五戒) that are quoted in the *Chuzhen jielü* (DZJY 24 zhangji 7:34b-35a and *Zangwai daoshu* 藏外道書 12:18) under the section "Taishang Laojun suoming zhigong guigen wujie" 太上老君所命扻功歸根五戒, see the *Taishang Laojun jiejing* 太上老君戒經 (DZ 784, fasc. 562; trl. Livia Kohn, "The Five Precepts of the Venerable Lord," *Monumenta Serica* 42 [1994]: 171–215). They derive from the five precepts of Buddhism: to abstain from killing, intoxication, lying, sexual misconduct, and stealing: "1. Do not kill any living being; 2. Do not partake of impure food or wine; 3. Do not say "yes" and think 'no;' 4. Do not rob and steal; 5. Do not fornicate." 一者、不得殺生。二者、不得葷酒。三者、不得口是心非。四者、不得偷盜。五者、不得邪淫。

[16] These ten precepts are derived from the Lingbao scripture *Xuhuang tianzun Chuzhen shijie wen* 皇天尊初真十戒文 (DZ 180) stripped of its commentaries. They are found in the *Chuzhen jielü* 初真戒律 (DZJY 24 zhangji 7: 35a-35b and *Zangwai daoshu* 藏外道書 12:17) under the section "Xuhuang tianzun suoming chuzhen shijie" 虛皇天尊所命初真十戒 (*Xuhuang tianzun shijie wen* DZ 180 fasc. 77). See Mori Yuria 森由利亞, "Zenshinkyō ryūmonha keifu kō" 全真教龍門派系譜考, in *Dōkyō bunka e no tenbō* 道教文化への展望 (Tokyo: Hirakawa, 1994): 197–198. During the Tang, they formed the Precepts of Initial Perfection intended for those who "leave the family" (Schipper, "Taoist Ordination Ranks," 130). For English translations see Livia Kohn, *Cosmos and Community. The Ethical Dimension of Daoism* (Cambridge, MA: Three Pines Press, 2004): 255–256 {and Monica Esposito, *Creative Daoism* (Wil/Paris: UniversityMedia, 2013): 124–125.}

(d) Nine precepts for women.[17]

(2) The Intermediate Ultimate Precepts (*zhongji jie* 中極戒) which consist of three hundred precepts given to Daoist priests since the Six Dynasties and are modeled on the precepts for Buddhist monks.[18]

(3) The Great Precepts of Celestial Immortals (*tianxian dajie* 天仙大戒) which often reformulate the content of the preceding precepts from a more doctrinal and spiritual point of view.[19] Only those who observe all of these precepts are in a position to ordain others.[20]

Beginning with Wang Changyue, the abbotship of the Baiyun guan in Beijing was purportedly transmitted to Longmen-ordained masters. Long-

---

[17] *Chuzhen jielü* 初真戒律 (DZJY 24 zhangji 7: 58a-b and *Zangwai daoshu* 藏外道書 12:29). For a translation see Catherine Despeux, *Immortelles de la Chine ancienne* (Puiseaux: Pardès, 1990): 147–155.

[18] The list of three hundred precepts is given in the *Zhongji jie* 中極戒 (DZJY 24 zhangji 7: 62a-79b and *Zangwai daoshu* 藏外道書 12: 31–40) under the title "Zhongji Shangqing dongzhen zhihui guanshen dajie jing" 中極上清洞真智慧觀身大戒經, whose content calls to mind the *Shangqing dongzhen zhihui guanshen dajie wen* 上清洞真智慧觀身大戒文 (DZ 1364, fasc. 1039); see Kristofer Schipper, "Taoist Ordination Ranks in the Tunhuang Manuscripts," in *Religion und Philosophie in Ostasien*, eds. Gert Naudorf, Karl-Heinz Pohl and Hans-Hermann Schmidt (Würzburg: Königshausen & Neumann, 1985): 131.

[19] A list of these precepts does not appear in Wang's works. However, it is included in the *Santan yuanman tianxian dajie lüeshuo* 三壇圓滿天仙大戒略說 by Liu Shouyuan 劉守元 (DZJY 24, zhangji 7; *Zangwai daoshu* 藏外道書 12); see also Min Zhiting 閔智亭, *Daojiao yifan* 道教儀範 (Beijing: Zhongguo daojiao xueyuan, 1990): 86–116.

[20] Oyanagi Shigeta 小柳司氣太, *Hakuunkan shi* 白雲觀志 (Tokyo: Tōhō bunka gakuin Tōkyō kenkyūjo, 1934): 70–73 and Yoshioka Yoshitoyo 吉岡義豊, *Dōkyō jittai* 道教の實態 (Kyoto: Hōyū shoten 朋友書店, 1975): 402–405 describe three-staged ordinations at the Republican-era Baiyun guan whose relationship to Wang Changyue's procedure necessitates further study. Oyanagi explains: "With regard to taking the precepts and ordination, one commonly distinguishes three phases. The first takes place in front of the main hall and consists in taking the indispensable vows. The second is a secret one, and vows are taken at a quiet time at night. Outsiders must not know about it. Having received this ordination, the new precepts make one a full-fledged Daoist priest and one obtains the ordination robe, the ordination certificate, staff and bowl, and the four kinds of rules. The third consists in taking the great precepts of Quanzhen consisting of more than one hundred items." 凡分戒壇為三期。第一壇在大殿之前。宣示要目。第二壇為密壇。夜間人靜時宣示之。不令外人知。過此壇後。新戒方為真正道士。發給戒衣・戒牒・錫鉢・規之四種。第三壇宣示全真大戒。約一百餘條。

men influence under the Qing thus became widespread—a fact that proved crucial for the creation of Longmen and its own lineage.[21]

Fundamental Sources for the History and Doctrine of the Longmen Lineage: Min Yide's *Jingai xindeng* and *Gu Shuyinlou cangshu*

The fundamental source for the early history and lineage of Longmen is the *Bojian* 缽鑑 (Examination of the Bowl), a lost—or possibly fictitious—work attributed to Wang Changyue.[22] It is interesting to note that the content of the *Bojian*, which can be regarded as "the foundation stone of the Longmen lineage," is only known through a few quotations in the *Jingai xindeng* 金蓋心燈 (Transmission of the Mind-Lamp from Mount Jingai, abbr. JGXD). This *Mind-Lamp*, compiled by eleventh-generation Longmen master Min Yide 閔一得 (1748/58–1836),[23] contains detailed biographies of Longmen masters of South-eastern China which are a remarkable tool for shedding more light on Ming-Qing Daoism. The majority of the *Jingai xindeng*'s biographies include commentaries by the well-known

---

[21] See for example Yoshioka Yoshitoyo 吉岡義豊, *Eisei e no negai: Dōkyō* 永生への願い: 道教 (Kyoto: Tankōsha, 1970): 199.

[22] Though the *Bojian* has been copiously mentioned in recent scholarly studies, it seems that nobody has ever actually held this text in hand. See for example Chen Bing 陳兵, "Qingdai Quanzhen dao Longmen pai de zhongxing 清代全真道龍門派的中興," *Shijie zongjiao yanjiu* 世界宗教研究 2, 1988, pp. 84–96; Mori Yuria 森由利亞, "Zenshinkyō ryūmonha keifu kō" 全真教龍門派系譜考, in Dōkyō bunka kenkyūkai (ed.), *Dōkyō bunka e no tenbō* 道教文化への展望 (Tokyo: Hirakawa, 1994): 189; Qing Xitai 卿希泰 (ed.), *Zhongguo daojiao* 中國道教, 4 Vols. (Shanghai: Zhishi 知識, 1994): vol. 3: 393; and Qing Xitai 卿希泰 (ed.), *Zhongguo daojiao shi* 中國道教史 (Chengdu: Sichuan Renmin, 1996): vol. 4: 81. Chen Yaoting 陳耀庭, "Quanzhen pai jielü" 全真派戒律, *Daojiao wenhua ziliaoku* 道教文化資料庫 http://www.taoism.org.hk/religious-activites&rituals/religious-discipline/pg5-2-3.htm. According to a personal communication from Professor Chen Yaoting, this *Bojian* text is stored at Beijing's Baiyun guan but its consultation is still off limits for scholars.

[23] On the life of Min Yide see Monica Esposito, "Daoism in the Qing (1644–1911)," in Livia Kohn (ed.), *Daoism Handbook*, 630–31, Leiden: Brill, 2000 (here above, Chapter 1, pp. 15–16) and "Longmen Taoism in Qing China: Doctrinal Ideal and Local Reality," *Journal of Chinese Religions* 29 (2001): 199–203 (here above, Chapter 3, pp. 160–165)

scholar Bao Tingbo 鮑廷博 (1728–1814)[24] and revisions by Bao Kun 鮑
錕 (fl. 1814).[25] The *Jingai xindeng* was published for the first time in 1821 at the library of the Ancient Hidden Pavilion of Books (Gu Shuyinlou cangshu 古書隱樓藏書) in the Yunchao 雲巢 ("Cloud's nest") temple on Mount Jingai 金蓋山. It was reprinted with newly carved printing blocks in 1876 (in eight *juan* and with an appendix) because the original printing blocks had been destroyed in a fire. A copy of the 1876 edition is stored at the Library of the Collège de France in Paris. The 1876 text has also been published in volumes 10 and 11 of the *Daojiao wenxian* 道教文獻, edited by Tu Jiexiang 杜潔祥 (Taipei: Danqing tushu 丹青圖書, 1983) and in vol. 31 of the *Zangwai daoshu* 藏外道書.

The Yunchao temple, where the original printing blocks of Min Yide's *Jingai xindeng* 金蓋心燈 had been stored and later destroyed, still exists today.

---

[24] A native of Xin'an 新安 (Anhui), style name Yiwen 以文 and Tongchun 通純, Bao was known as the Zhejiang erudite (*boshi* 博士). He passed the provincial examination during the Jiaqing era (1796–1820). He was the editor of the *Zhibuzu zhai congshu* 知不足齋叢書 in 30 volumes (1776); see Nancy Lee Swan "Pao T'ing-bo," in Arthur Hummel, ed. *Eminent Chinese of the Ch'ing Period*, Taipei: Ch'eng Wen Publishing Company, 1975: 612–13. In 1792, Bao Tingbo 鮑廷博 came to Mount Jingai to take charge of the *Jingai xindeng's* 金蓋心燈 compilation, and in 1811 he revised it with Min Yide and other Longmen disciples; see the "Zhibuzu zhai zhuren zhuan" 知不足齋主人專 (JGXD 7. 31a-32a in *Zangwai daoshu* 藏外道書 31:311–312). According to the commentator Bao Tingbo, these biographies of the *Jingai xindeng* 金蓋心燈 are based on the following works: (1) *Bojian* 缽鑑 by Wang Changye (?-1680); (2) *Daopu yuanliu tu* 道譜源流圖 (Map of the Origins and Development of Daoist Genealogical Registers) compiled by the Eighth Longmen Vinaya Master Lü Yunyin 呂雲隱 (fl. 1710); (3) *Yangshi yilin* 揚氏逸林 (Circle of Recluses) by Yang Shen'an 揚慎菴, a compilation that is said to be mostly based on Wang Changyue's *Bojian*; (4) *Bojian xu* 缽鑑續 (Supplement to the Examination of the Bowl) by the Ninth Longmen Doctrinal Master (*zongshi* 宗師) Fan Qingyun 范清雲 (Taiqing 太清, 1606–1748?) who allegedly received the *Bojian* in 5 *juan* from Wang Changyue in 1667 and later expanded it to nine juan; (5) *Dongyuan yulu* 東原語錄 (Recorded Sayings of Dongyuan) by Lü Quanyang 呂全陽. However, except for the *Daopu yuanliu tu*, all above-mentioned works seem to have survived only in the quotations of Min Yide's *Jingai xindeng* 金蓋心燈. See for example the "Longmen zhengzong liuchuan zhipai tu" 龍門正宗流傳支派圖 (JGXD 1.1a-7b in *Zangwai daoshu* 藏外道書 31:166–168); *Longmen zhengzong jueyun benzhi daotong xinchuan* 龍門正宗覺雲本支道統薪傳 (*Zangwai daoshu* 藏外道書 31: 427–446); *Jingudong zhi* 金鼓洞志 (*Zangwai daoshu* 藏外道書 20: 189–299); *Daotong yuanliu zhi* 道統源流志; and Yoshioka Yoshitoyo 吉岡義豊, *Dōkyō no jittai* 道教の實態 (Kyoto: Hōyū shoten, 1975): 231–32.

[25] Bao Kun 鮑錕 was native of Yuhang 餘杭 (today Hangzhou); see his 1814 preface (JGXD 1a-2b, in *Zangwai daoshu* 藏外道書 31: 159–60).

It is located near the town of Huzhou 湖州 in Zhejiang 浙江. Two reproductions included in the *Daotong yuanliu* 道統源流志 (1929) show the Jingai mountains 金蓋山 and its central temple complex called Gu Meihua guan 古梅花觀 (Old Plum Blossom Abbey).[26] Today's villagers still call this temple Yunchao miao 雲巢廟 or "Cloud-Nest Temple."

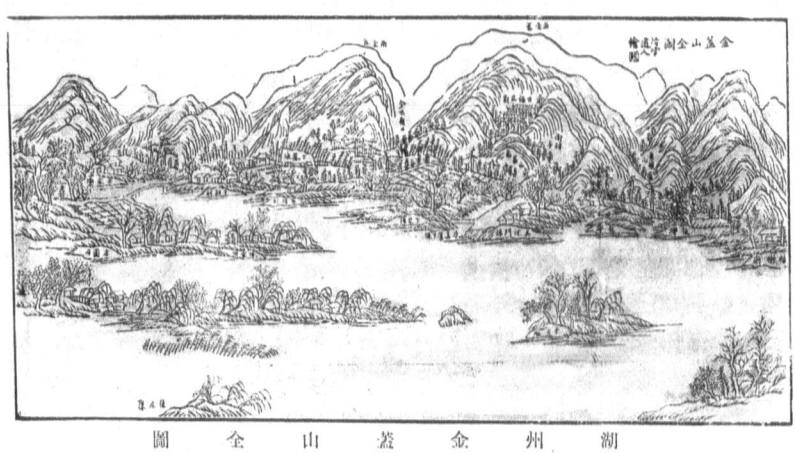

Fig. 7: Overall view of Mt. Jingai (*Daotong yuanliu zhi* 道統源流志, 1929)

Fig. 8: Old Plum Blossom Abbey (Gu Meihua Guan) on Mt. Jingai (*Daotong yuanliu zhi* 道統源流志, 1929)

---

[26] The *Daotong yuanliu zhi* 道統源流志 was compiled by Yan Liuqian 嚴六謙 (Huzhou 湖州: Wuxi Zhonghua yinshuaju 無錫中華印刷局, 1929).

When I first visited Mt. Jingai and the Old Plum Blossom Abbey in 1988, the sanctuary had reopened less than a year ago and was staffed by Daoist priests, some of whom were of fairly advanced age (see Fig. 9). Although many buildings had suffered damage, the overall layout of the buildings corresponded roughly to that of Fig. 8.

Fig. 9: Mt. Jingai Abbey & Daoist priests (Photo M. Esposito, 1991)

Fig. 10: Lü Dongbin, in *Jindan dayao* 金丹大要 2.52a

On the walls of the abbey's central hall (Chunyang gong 純陽宮), which is dedicated to Lü Dongbin 呂洞賓, I found remains of a stone inscription whose full text we know from an appendix to the *Jingai xindeng* that narrates the history of this hall.[27] The other walls were nicely decorated with hymns to Chairman Mao. A striking difference from the images of Mt. Jingai in Figs. 7 and 8 was the huge TV broadcasting antenna on the mountain top which had me wonder whether this attracts or interferes with visits by wandering Daoist immortals who are said to frolic in the mountain's lush bamboo forests. The most celebrated immortal linked to Mt. Jingai is Lü Dongbin 呂洞賓 (Fig. 10). Indeed, this Daoist saint was instrumental in

---

[27] "Jingai shan Chunyang gong gujin jilüe" 金蓋山純陽宮古今蹟略, in *Jingai xindeng* 金蓋心燈, appendix entitled *Shanlüe fu* 山略附 (found after *juan* 8).

bringing Min Yide to this site. The preface (1873) by Shen Bingcheng 沈秉成 to the reprint of the *Jingai xindeng* explains:

> [Min Yide] withdrew to Mt. Jingai because he had learned that it is a site frequented since ancient times by the Returning Immortal [Lü Dongbin]. Because of this he [chose this site to] write the book called *Mind-Lamp*, modeling it after the "Transmission of the Lamp" [texts] of the [Chan] Buddhists. [Hence] his book begins with a genealogical table of Dao transmission and continues with the history of the Longmen tradition.
>
> (閔一得)所居金蓋山側、習開山為回仙舊遊地。因著為《心燈》一書、取釋氏傳燈之義。其書首列道譜。繼敍龍門宗派。²⁸

Min Yide thus withdrew to Mt. Jingai to write the *Jingai xindeng* 金蓋心燈 because of the site's connection with the Returning Immortal 回仙 Lü Dongbin. Chan Buddhist *Lamp Histories* 傳燈 tracing the "mind to mind transmission" (*yixin chuanxin* 以心傳心) from founder Buddha to a succession of patriarchs had been a smashing success in China and had been instrumental in catapulting a relatively small movement of meditators to its dominating position in Chinese Buddhism. Taking this approach as model, Min Yide in his *Mind-Lamp* presented the origin and development of the Longmen lineage in explicit genealogical terms by mapping out a Daoist "family tree" (*daopu* 道譜).²⁹ Tracing Longmen's tradition back to the Ancestor of the Dao (Daozu 道祖, i.e., Laozi 老子) and to its Lineage Master (Daozong 道宗, i.e., Lü Dongbin 呂洞賓), this genealogy was designed to equip Longmen with an unsurpassable Daoist pedigree and identity, which is exactly what it does until the present day. Analogous to its Chan Buddhist models, Min Yide's *Jingai xindeng* also includes an intricate genealogical chart, the "Longmen zhengzong liuchuan zhipai tu" 龍門正宗流傳支派圖, which records the uninterrupted transmission of the orthodox Longmen tradition from its first seven patriarchs to the diffusion in Jiangnan 江南 in the wake of Wang Changyue.³⁰

---

28 "Chongkan Jingai xindeng xu" 重刊金蓋心燈序 (1873) by Shen Bingcheng in JGXD, 1.1b/5–7.

29 See the "Daopu yuanliu tu" 道譜源流圖 in *Jingai xindeng* 金蓋心燈 1.1a-7b.

30 The first seven generations of patriarchs are recognized as the holders of the Longmen orthodox lineage (*Longmen zhengzong* 龍門正宗) at the Baiyun guan, at its affiliated monasteries, and in subsequent Longmen branches and sub-branches. In

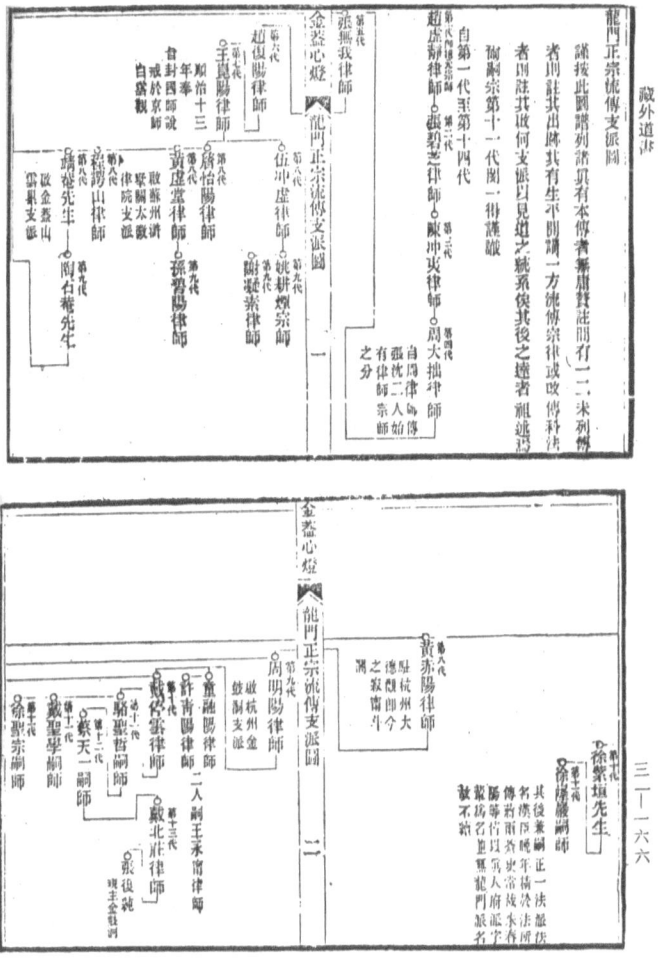

Fig. 11: Longmen genealogical chart in Min Yide's *Jingai xindeng* 金蓋心燈: "Longmen zhengzong liuchuan zhipai tu" 龍門正宗流傳支派圖

fact, this lineage also appears in Oyanagi's *Hakuunkan shi* 白雲觀志 (abbr. BYGZ) and in Igarashi Kenryū's 五十嵐賢隆 work on the *Taiqing gong* 太清宮 (another important Longmen monastery, situated in Shenyang 沈陽, Liaoning). See BYGZ pp. 32–35 and Igarashi Kenryū, *Taiseikyū shi* 太清宮志 (Tokyo: Kokushō kankōkai, 1938): 64–65. From the Qing dynasty, the list of the first seven Longmen patriarchs came to represent for all ordained Daoist clergy the orthodox lineage of Longmen abbots of the Baiyun guan, a lineage that was gradually adopted also by other Longmen public monasteries. Moreover, this list was also accepted by Longmen sub-branches which, after the advent of Wang Changyue, had allegedly spread throughout China. {See Part One of M. Esposito, *Creative Daoism*, 2013.}

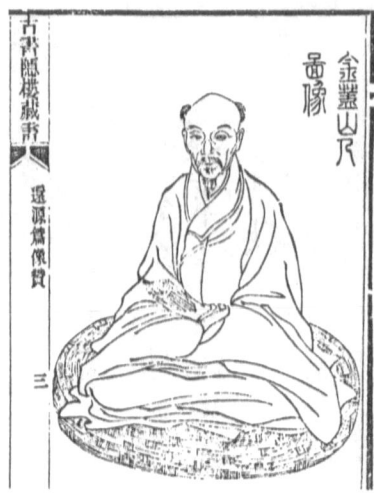

Fig. 12: Min Yide, from *Gu Shuyinlou cangshu* 古書隱樓藏書

Readers familiar with the background of Chan 禪 Buddhist *Lamp Histories* might wonder whether Min Yide, in authoring the *Jingai xindeng* 金蓋心燈, also embraced an additional purpose, namely, the promotion of the Longmen Daoist tradition "for the protection of the state."[31] At any rate, an ideal pedigree and transmission scenario of Longmen was created and transmitted to posterity through the efforts of scholars and Longmen disciples under the guidance of Min Yide. A retired scholar, Min Yide is thus a key figure in the promotion of the self-image of the "orthodox" Longmen in Southern China. As we are going to see, he portrayed the Longmen not only as a firmly established Daoist institution at the capital equipped with a standardized ordination system, monastic rules, codes of behavior, and liturgy, but also as an intellectual and doctrinal tradition capable of producing specific rituals and inner-alchemical perspectives on cosmology, self-culti-

---

[31] For this role of the Chan "Lamp Histories" see Yanagida Seizan 柳田聖山 "Tōshi no keifu" 燈史の系譜 (The genealogy of the Lamp histories), *Nihon bukkyō gakkai nenpō* 日本仏教学会年報 19.1 (1954): 1–46, and "Shinzoku tōshi no keifu" 新続燈史の系譜 [The genealogy of the Lamp histories, continued], *Zengaku kenkyū* 禅学研究 59 (1978): 1–39. See also Helwig Schmidt-Glintzer, *Die Identität der Buddhistischen Schulen und die Kompilation Buddhistischer Universalgeschichten in China* (Wiesbaden: Steiner, 1982): 26–63; Theodore Griffith Foulk, "The Chan school and its place in the Buddhist Monastic Tradition" (Ph. D. dissertation, University of Michigan, 1987): 42–44 and 50–52; Dale S. Wright, "Les récits de transmission du bouddhisme Ch'an et l'historiographie moderne," *Cahiers d'Extrême-Asie* 7 (1993–94): 105–114; and Albert Welter, "Lineage and Context in the *Patriarch's Hall Collection* and the *Transmission of the Lamp*," in Steven Heine & Dale S. Wright (eds.), *The Zen Canon* (Oxford: Oxford University Press, 2004): 137–179. However, it is also worthy of mention that towards the end of the Ming and the beginning of the Qing, members of the various Chan Buddhist lines began compiling continuations of the biographical "transmissions of the lamp" 傳燈 with the aim of claiming privilege for their respective schools; see Hasebe Yūkei 長谷部幽蹊, *Meishin bukkyōdanshi kenkyū* 明清佛教團史研究 (Kyoto: Dōmeisha, 1993): 435–534. It is thus also in this context that the Daoist "transmission of the lamp" (i.e., the *Jingai xindeng*) must be seen.

vation, and ethics. This is well documented in a second text compilation authorized by Min Yide: the *Gu Shuyinlou cangshu* 古書隱樓藏書 (Collection from the Ancient Hidden Pavilion of Books).³² It is in these two collections—the *Jingai xindeng* and the *Gu Shuyinlou cangshu*—that works related to Tantrism are found, and what interests us here are in particular those texts that are connected with the Longmen Tantric branch called *Longmen xizhu xinzong* 龍門西竺心宗 or Longmen's Mind-Tradition of Western India.

According to Qing Xitai 卿希泰 there are at least four editions of the *Gu Shuyinlou cangshu* 古書隱樓藏書: 1834, 1894, 1904 and 1916.³³ The 1904 edition containing thirty-seven texts is best known because it forms part of the *Zangwai daoshu* 藏外道書 collection.³⁴ The 1834 edition mentioned by Qing Xitai probably consisted of twenty-three texts printed from the wooden printing blocks stored at Mt. Jingai. Rather than appearing under the title of *Gu Shuyinlou cangshu*, this collection of twenty-three alchemical texts from the *Gu Shuyinlou cangshu* was called *Daozang xubian* 道藏續編 (Supplement to the Daoist Canon). It remained little known and rare, but during the Minguo period 民國 (1912–1949), the scholar and bibliophile Ding Fubao 丁福保 (alias Shouyi zi 守一子, 1874–1952) got hold of a copy and had it printed in moveable type.³⁵ This version appeared in four volumes in 1952 under the title *Daozang xubian chuji* 道藏續編初集 (Original Collection of the *Daozang xubian*).³⁶ The comparison of this

---

³² The core of the Gu Shuyinlou collection is formed by twenty-three texts of inner alchemy known as *Daozang xubian* 道藏續編 (Supplement to the Daoist Canon) that were compiled by Min Yide and printed in 1834 on Mt. Jingai. See Qing Xitai 卿希泰 (ed.), *Zhongguo daojiao shi* 中國道教史, 4 vols. (Chengdu: Sichuan renmin 四川人民, 1996): vol. 2: 184–86) {and Chapter 3 here above}. The bibliophile Ding Fubao 丁福保 (1874–1952) had the *Daozang xubian* reprinted in 1952.

³³ See Qing Xitai 卿希泰 (ed.), *Zhongguo daojiao shi* 中國道教史, vol. 4, p. 116; and "Gu Shuyinlou cangshu" in Qing Xitai (ed.), *Zhongguo daojiao* 中國道教, 4 vols. (Shanghai: Zhishi 知識, 1994): vol. 2, p.184.

³⁴ The *Zangwai daoshu* 藏外道書 reproduces a copy of the Shanghai library in 14 volumes. A list of the texts included in the 1904 edition is given in vol. 1 of *Zhongguo congshu zonglu* 中國叢書綜錄 (Shanghai: Guji chubanshe 古籍出版社, 1986, 3 vols.): 1.818 & 1.1092. This list does not include the three texts in the Appendix. A comparison of the various editions of the *Gu Shuyinlou cangshu* is a desideratum.

³⁵ See "Bianji shuoming" 編輯說明 as well as the explanation given by Ding Fubao (Shou Yizi) in the *Daozang xubian* (1989).

³⁶ Shanghai Yixue shuju 上海醫學書局, 1952. Reprints appeared in 1989 (Beijing: Haiyang chubanshe) and 1993 (Beijing: Shumu wenxian chubanshe).

1952 publication with the *Gu Shuyinlou cangshu* 古書隱樓藏書 of 1904 shows that Ding Fubao's 1952 version contains only texts related to inner alchemy. It is also noteworthy that in the biographies of Min Yide there is not a single mention of the *Daozang xubian* 道藏續編. As we are going to see, the only two works that are constantly mentioned in these biographies are the *Jingai xindeng* 金蓋心燈 (1821) and the *Gu Shuyinlou cangshu* 古書隱樓藏書 (1834). It is from passages in these two works that we will learn more about the connection between the Longmen tradition of Mt. Jingai and the Tantric Longmen xizhu xinzong. Let us thus begin by looking at the biographies of Min Yide in the *Jingai xindeng*.

BIOGRAPHIES OF MIN YIDE

The main biographies of Min Yide 閔一得 (1758–1836) are found in the Appendix to the *Jingai xindeng* 金蓋心燈 (1821, reprinted in 1876) entitled "Min zhuan fu" 閔傳附 which follow *juan* 8. They are also included with some slight modifications in the first volume of *Gu Shuyinlou cangshu* 古書隱樓藏書.[37] There is also an autobiography attributed to Min Yide in one of the relatively recent editions of the *Gu Shuyinlou cangshu* 古書隱樓藏書, but this needs to be studied in more detail while taking into account information contained in prefaces by Min Yide in the *Jingai xindeng* and his introductions to texts of the *Gu Shuyinlou cangshu*. Finally, among other materials on this master, a biography of Min Yide compiled on the basis of all these biographies is found in the *Longmen zhengzong Jueyun benzhi daotong xinchuan* 龍門正宗覺雲本支道統薪傳.[38] Let us now have a look at the three basic biographies of Min Yide in the Appendix to the *Jingai xindeng* 金蓋心燈.

---

[37] See the 1904 edition in the *Zangwai daoshu* 藏外道書 vol. 10, pp. 153–155. The differences between the version of *Jingai xindeng* 金蓋心燈 and that of *Gu Shuyinlou cangshu* 古書隱樓藏書 will be pointed out in the translations. This autobiography (*zizhuan* 自傳) with the title *zishu* 自述 is included in Xiao Tianshi 蕭天石 (ed.), *Longmen pai danfa jueyao* 龍門派丹法訣要, in *Daozang jinghua* 道藏精華 1.8 (Taipei: Ziyou chuban 自由出版, 1982): 235–240. It features some excerpts and texts from an edition of the *Gu Shuyinlou cangshu* that seems to have been published in 1917 rather than 1916 (as Qing Xitai 卿希泰 states), provided that there is no mistake in the date 1917 given in the postface to *Qinggui yuanmiao* 清規元妙 (*Longmen pai danfa jueyao* 龍門派丹法訣要 p. 271). See also below, note 54.

[38] *Zangwai daoshu* 藏外道書 vol. 31. pp. 469–471.

1. *Min Lanyun xiansheng zhuan* 閔懶雲先生傳 by Yan Duanshu 晏端書[39] (Appendix to the *Jingai xindeng* 金蓋心燈, 1a-3a).

The first biography was written by Yan Duanshu 晏端書, a member of the Hanlin academy 翰林院. It states that Min's name was Tiaofu 笤甫, that he had the two style names (*hao* 號) Buzhi 補之 and Xiaogen 小艮, and that his Daoist appellation (*daohao* 道號) was Lanyunzi 懶雲子. He came from a respected family 望族 of Wuxing 吳興, which corresponds to the actual town of Huzhou 湖州 in Zhejiang 浙江 province. Min Yide's father Daxia 大夏[40] had passed the official examinations and accepted the charge of District Magistrate of the Xi district in Henan 河南息縣. Later he had requested to be transferred as Instructor to Hangzhou.

Min Yide was of such weak constitution that at the age of nine he still appeared to have difficulties to walk. It was for that reason that, according to this biography, he went to visit Tongbai shan 桐柏山 (near the actual town of Tiantai 天台 in Zhejiang 浙江) where he studied the art of *daoyin* 導引 under the guidance of Gao Dongli 高東籬 (?-1768).

According to the Longmen lineage poem 龍門派字譜, Min Yide's first teacher Gao Dongli (lineage name 派名: Qingyu 清昱) belonged to the tenth Longmen generation 龍門第十代.[41] He was the abbot (*zhuchi* 住持) of the Tongbai gong 桐柏宮.[42] As we can see from the short biographical note in the *Daotong yuanliu zhi* 道統源流志 (*xia* 下, pp. 9-10), in 1692 Min Yide's teacher Gao had visited the ninth-generation Longmen Vinaya Master 龍門第九代律師 Zhou Mingyang 周明陽 (1628-1711) at Hangzhou's Jingu dong 杭州金鼓洞 and had received ordination from him 受戒律.[43] Later on, Gao had inherited the Tongbai gong 桐柏宮 from

---

[39] Yan Duanshu, member of the Hanlin academy 翰林院, was also the compiler, together with Ying Jiexiu 英傑修, of the *Yangzhou fuzhi* 揚州府志 (1874) in 24 *juan*.

[40] Daxia 大夏 was a name (*wei* 諱) of Min Yide's father; see the Biographical note of Vinaya Master Chen Qiaoyun 陳樵雲律師 (*Daotong yuanliu zhi* 道統源流志 *xia* 下 p. 13) where Chen is said to have met Min Yide's father in Hangzhou in 1785.

[41] See Oyanagi Shigeta 小柳司氣太, *Hakuunkan shi* 白雲觀志 p. 97, and "Longmen zhengzong liuchuan zhipai tu" 龍門正宗流傳支派圖 in JGXD 1.3a.

[42] On Gao Dongli 高東籬 (?-1768) see his biography in JGXD 2.13a.

[43] The *Daotong yuanliu zhi* 道統源流志 [Origins and Development of Orthodox Daoism] was compiled by by Yan Liuqian 嚴六謙, *hao*: Zhuangyan jushi 莊嚴居士 (Huzhou 湖州: Wuxi Zhonghua yinshuaju 無錫中華印刷局, 1929). See also the "Longmen zhengzong liuchuan zhipai tu" 龍門正宗流傳支派圖 in JGXD 1.3a and 7b. For the biography of Zhou Mingyang (lineage name Tailang 太朗) see

Fan Qingyun 范青雲, the founder of the Longmen branch at Tiantai (開天台崇道觀龍門宗派) and first abbot of this temple.[44] As we can gather from the biography of Gao Dongli's master Fan Qingyun, Tongbai gong was rebuilt by imperial order during the Yongzheng era 雍正 (1723–1735) under the name of Chongdao guan 崇道觀.[45] In 1733 Zhang Boduan 張伯端, the well-known Patriarch of the Southern lineage 南宗 and author of the *Wuzhen pian* 悟真篇 who was linked with this sanctuary, received the official title of Chanxian 禪仙 ("Chan immortal").[46] This title was conferred upon him due to his fame as a practitioner of inner alchemy (*neidan* 內丹) and Chan 禪. The link of this sanctuary with Daoism as well as Buddhism is probably due to its geographical location: Tongbai shan 桐柏山 is a gentle peak of the Tiantai mountains that are famous for their Buddhist monasteries.

Fig. 13: Tongbai gong 桐柏宮 in the Tiantai 天台 mountain range, Zhejiang province (Photo M. Esposito, 1986)

JGXD 3.12b-15b.

[44] See the biography of Fan Qingyun in JGXD 3.45a-47b, and "Longmen zhengzong liuchuan zhipai tu" 龍門正宗流傳支派圖 in JGXD 1.7b.

[45] See JGXD 3.46a, line 7, and the "Longmen zhengzong liuchuan zhipai tu" 龍門正宗流傳支派圖 in JGXD 1.7b.

[46] See the "Daopu yuanliu tu" 道譜源流圖, JGXD 1.3b.

The temple on Mt. Tongbai which young Min Yide visited is still extant today, though its location has slightly changed due to the construction of a water reservoir in the early 1980s. During my first visit to this site in 1986, I found a small and poor hermitage that was still named Tongbai gong 桐柏宮 (Fig. 13). It was inhabited by a female Daoist 道姑 named Ye Gaoxing 葉高行 (Fig. 14).

Fig. 14: Tongbai gong's abbess Ye Gaoxing 葉高行 and the author near the stele of 26th-generation Longmen master Xie Chonggen 謝崇根 (2001)

According to the Longmen lineage poem, the character Gao 高 in her Daoist name shows that the abbess belonged to the 27th generation of Longmen.[47] She told me that in 1958 the ancient Chongdao guan 崇道觀 was submerged in a water reservoir built by the government for the Tiantai region, and she accompanied me to the vicinity of the original site of the temple on the other side of the water reservoir where she had erected a stela for her own master Xie Chonggen 謝崇根 (?-1984).[48] She tried to keep, to the best of her abilities, the ancient tradition of Tongbai gong alive. As the

---

[47] See Oyanagi, *Hakuunkan shi* 白雲觀志, p. 97.

[48] The character Chong 崇 in his lineage name shows that he belongs to the 26th generation of Longmen; see Oyanagi, *Hakuunkan shi* 白雲觀志, p. 97

biography of Min Yide also testifies, Tongbai gong had been a renowned place where *daoyin* 導引 and *neidan* methods were transmitted. Ye Gaoxing herself taught such methods to a small group of young villagers. These methods formed part of the so-called Longmen Wuxi gong 五息功 that master Xie Chonggen had transmitted to her. They mainly consisted in *qigong* 氣功 techniques of harmonisation of body postures (調身), mind (調心), and breathing (調息). She showed me some photographs of her master Xie performing the supreme stage of these practices in the lotus position. The aim of such practice was to hold one's breath as long as possible in order to realize the so-called *yuanxi* 原息 or original breathing in which the heart is said to cease beating and one enters a kind of hibernation state.

Fig. 15: *Daoyin* 導引 postures from a Mawangdui manuscript, 2nd century BCE (Pregadio [ed.], *The Encyclopedia of Taoism* vol. 1: 335)

Naturally, from the photographs it was hard to imagine the effects of such practice. It was also difficult to verify whether these methods were indeed original and ancient. However, she was proud to tell me that the ancient tradition by Zhang Boduan was still preserved because such Longmen

Chapter Five: Daoism and Tantrism in the Qing

methods combined Daoist techniques of the circulation of *qi* 氣 with Chan meditation techniques (*zuochan* 坐禪, Jap. *zazen*). The abbess also emphasized that Tongbai gong continued to maintain a good relationship with the famous Tiantai Buddhist monastery of Guoqing si 國清寺. We walked for some hours over the hills to visit the said monastery, and its monks indeed told me that they were very grateful to Ye Gaoxing since she often visited them to offer her medical advice. In fact Ye Gaoxing, who had originally worked as a doctor of traditional medicine, supported her small hermitage thanks to her skill in Chinese traditional medicine and acupuncture. She served the villagers as well as the Buddhist monks on Mt. Tiantai and thus supported her modest life style. I had the opportunity to record with my video camera a session of what she called the ancient method of *ling feizhen* 靈飛針 or magic flying needles. She launched from a short distance rather thick needles toward the naked lower leg of a person who was leaning face to a wall. What for her seemed magic was, to my uninitiated eyes, a rather bloody affair. The treasures of her small hermitage were limited to a few paintings received from her master, a beautiful scroll of the Daoist Three Pure Ones (Sanqing 三清), and the Chart-Talisman of the True Form of the Five Peaks (*wuyue zhenxing tu* 五岳真形圖).

She did not know anything about the history of the Longmen lineage written in the early 19th century by Min Yide. When I presented her with a photocopy of the *Jingai xindeng*, she was thus very happy to discover in it the story of her own lineage. In the year 2001, when I visited her for the last time, she had managed to raise some funds for the restoration and enlargement of Tongbai gong. The donors were mostly disciples residing in the United States. I was surprised to see that a road was now under construction, making it possible to reach the remote Tongbai shan by car. She explained to me her plans to reconstruct the temple and informed me that she had just received a visa to visit her students in the United States. One year after that last visit, in 2002, I learned from one of her students that the day after her arrival in the U.S.A. she had suddenly passed away.

After this detour into modern times, let us now return to the biography of Min Yide. It was in the ancient Tongbai gong, now submerged in the water reservoir, that Min was ordained in the Longmen tradition with the lineage name (*paiming* 派名) of Yide 一得. After a while he recovered thanks to his practice of *daoyin*. He returned to reading texts and studying Neo-Confucianism (*xingli* 性理, i.e., *xingli xue* 性理學) but, as is stressed by all biographies of Min Yide, his research was due to his personal interest and not driven by the aim of passing the official examinations. It was only later, around the age of twenty-five, that on the order of his father he entered an official career and served in Yunnan as Departmental Vice Magistrate 州司馬. Some time after his father's death he abandoned his pursuit of a career in government service and went to visit prestigious men of outstanding talent. Among the extraordinary men he met and impressed was Shen Qingyun 沈輕雲 (1708–1786), the main disciple of his first Daoist teacher Gao Dongli 高東籬 (?–1768).[49] Subsequently, Min Yide studied and combined the Three Teachings and obtained Gao Dongli's genuine transmission. When Gao Dongli was about to pass away, Min Yide rendered him a last visit. After that, in accordance with the last will of his teacher, Min regarded Shen Qingyun as his master.

Although Shen Qingyun belonged to the same Longmen generation as Min Yide (the eleventh), he thus became the main master of Min Yide. He transmitted to him various texts now found in Min Yide's *Gu Shuyinlou cangshu*.[50] To show the special relationship between Shen and Min, this biography states:

> Although the disciples of Shen Qingyun were all excellent, Min Yide alone attained what made him great, and he constantly maintained the ten principles taught by Qingyun. For several decades he did not dare to diverge the slightest bit from them.
>
> 其及門諸子、皆桌举一時、先生獨得其大、常守輕雲十義訓、數十年不敢不懈。[51]

---

[49] Shen Yibing 沈輕雲 (1708–1786) was the 11th Longmen patriarch; he also received the Zhengyi 正一 transmission and was the main master of Min Yide. See his biography in JGXD 4.31a-44b. See also the "Longmen zhengzong liuchuan zhipai tu" 龍門正宗流傳支派圖 (JGXD 1.3b-4a).

[50] The main texts connected with Shen Yibing are: the *Suoyan xu* 瑣言續 [Sequel to an Ignored Transmission]; the *Lü zushi sanni yishi gongjue* 呂祖師三尼醫世功訣 [Practices and Formulae on the Three Sages' Doctrine of Healing the World by Patriarch Lü]; the *Tianxian xinchuan* 天仙心傳 [Mind-to-Mind Transmission of Celestial Immortality]; the *Tianxian dao jieji xuzhi* 天仙道戒忌須知 [Required Knowledge on Precepts and Prohibitions for the Path to Celestial Immortality]; the *Tianxian daocheng baoze* 天仙道程寶則 [Precious Principles for the Path to Celestial Immortality]; the *Xiwang mu nüxiu zhengtu shize* 西王母女修正途十則 [Ten Rules of the Queen Mother of the West on the Correct Path of Female Cultivation]; and the *Niwan Li zushi nüzong shuangxiu baofa* 泥丸李祖師女宗雙修寶筏 [Precious Raft of Joint Cultivation in Feminine Alchemy by Patriarch Li Niwan].

[51] Yan Duan 晏端, *Min Lanyun xiansheng zhuan* 閔懶雲先生傳, JGXD 補遺, 1b2-3.

The biography of Shen Qingyun explains that these ten principles are: (1) being ready to endure humiliation (*renru* 忍辱); (2) being benevolent and supple (*ren rou* 仁柔); (3) being calm and respectful (*zhi jing* 止敬); (4) being perspicacious (*gaoming* 高明); (5) being accommodative (*tuirang* 退讓); (6) being firm and centered (*gang zhong* 剛中); (7) being wise and discerning (*hui bian* 慧辨); (8) being diligent (*qin* 勤); (9) being trustworthy (*xin* 信); (10) being honest (*lian* 廉).[52] These teachings seem in perfect agreement with the official vision of Longmen as a Daoist school focusing on transmitting precepts and supervising the ordination of Daoist priests.

Finally, Min Yide went back to Wuxing, the modern town of Huzhou, which was his place of origin. There he settled at Southern Jingai shan 南金蓋山, the place where Tao Jing'an 陶靖菴 (1612–1673) had previously practiced (修真, lit. "cultivated truth").[53] From the biography of Tao Jing'an we learn that Tao was the eighth Longmen patriarch 龍門第八代 and founder of the Longmen Yunchao branch of Mount Jingai 龍門金蓋山雲巢支派. After the death of his master Shen in 1786, Min Yide continued to live on Mount Jingai and to perpetuate the tradition of its Longmen branch. From the age of twenty-nine he stayed there in seclusion in order to cultivate the Dao.

The biography goes on to furnish information about Jingai shan during the time of Min Yide's stay. The place had been abandoned and its Daoist edifices were in ruins. Confronted with this situation and concerned about the decline of his own tradition, Min Yide resolved to restore the place, to return it to its former splendor, and to enlarge its land holdings. It was at this temple on Mt. Jingai that he devoted himself to compiling books and authoring the *Jingai xindeng* 金蓋心燈 in eight *juan*, as the text explains:

> In authoring the eight-*juan Jingai xindeng*, he followed [the Longmen tradition] back to the source while elucidating its hidden and unfathomable sense. He also wrote the *Gu Shuyinlou cangshu* 古書隱樓藏書 in 28 titles[54] along with the *Huanyuan pian chanwei*

---

[52] See JGXD 4.37a/4–5.
[53] For the biography of Tao Jing'an see JGXD 2.9a-22a. It is under the guidance of this master that a strict relationship was first established between the two Longmen branches: that of Mt. Jingai and that of Mt. Jizu 雞足山 (Yunnan 雲南), i.e., the Longmen xizhu xinzong 龍門西竺心宗. See also "Longmen zhengzong liuchuan zhipai tu" 龍門正宗流傳支派圖 (JGXD 1.2b-7a) and "Longmen fenpai xizhu zhu xinzong liuchuan tu" 龍門分派西竺心宗流傳圖 (JGXD 1.1a).
[54] In the version of the same bibliography found in the YLCS (*Zangwai daoshu* 藏

還源篇闡微 in which, through the Confucian and Buddhist quintessence, he illustrated the original secret of Daoism. Every word of his is an essential instruction, and every character a mind-to-mind transmission; so that those who have the will can follow them in the right sequence and make gradual progress from action (*youwei* 有為) toward non-action (*wuwei* 無為), without falling into confusion about what its meaning comes down to.[55]

所著《金蓋心燈》八卷、沿流溯源、發潛闡幽、又書《隱樓藏書》二十八種、及《還源篇闡微》、以儒釋之精華、詮道家之元妙、言言口訣、字字心傳、俾有志者循序漸進、自有為以造無為、不至昧厥旨歸。

These last sentences point to the content of the Longmen teachings transmitted by Min Yide: a mixture of the Three Teachings combined with explanations on a gradual way of practicing the alchemical path by starting from *youwei* 有為. The expression *youwei* refers to the practice on *ming* 命 (*minggong* 命功) that focuses on *qi* 氣 (i.e., breath-circulation exercises, methods of controlling psycho-physiological functions, etc). These practices, which involve some action or effort, must be combined and eventually lead to the cultivation of *xing* 性 (*xinggong* 性功) or *wuwei* 無為, that is, practices focusing on *shen* 神 (spiritual activities such as the contemplation of the pure mind, the realization of its nature, etc). The sequence of these practices is explained in Min Yide's work as *xianming houxing* 先命後性: first *ming* 命 and subsequently *xing* 性. This refers to the alchemical method of cultivation characterizing the Southern Lineage (*nanzong* 南宗) which forms the theme of a specific group of texts.[56] It is interesting to note that the same sequence from *youwei* to *wuwei* was pointed out in the trans-

---

外道書 10–154) the *Gu Shuyinlou cangshu* is said to include more than thirty titles 書隱樓藏書三十餘種. It is interesting to note that at the end of the *Tianxian xinchuan* (*Zangwai daoshu* 藏外道書 10: 449), Min Yide in his colophon dated 1834 writes of planning the publication of the *Gu Shuyinlou cangshu* as including 20 titles. This part is not included in the version of the *Tianxian xinchuan* published in the DZXB.

[55] JGXD 補遺, 2b1-4.

[56] See for instance the list of Min Yide's works included in the *Daozang xubian* 道藏續編 (as well as in the *Gu Shuyinlou cangshu*, in *Zangwai daoshu* 藏外道書 vol. 10) such as *Yin zhenren Donghua zhengmai huangji hepi zhengdao xianjing* 尹真人東華正脈皇極闔闢證道仙經; *Yin zhenren Liaoyang dian wenda bian* 尹真人廖陽殿問答編; *Xie tianji* 泄天機; *Shangpin danfa jieci* 上品丹法節次; *Rushi wo wen* 如是我聞; *Suoyan xu* 瑣言續; and *Gufa yangsheng shisan ze chanwei* 古法養生十三則。

mission that abbess Ye Gaoxing of the Tongbai gong had received from her master, Xie Chonggen, under the label of Longmen wuxigong 龍門五息功. The present biography of Min Yide ends by stating:

> 先生生於乾隆戊寅十二月初二日。卒於道光丙申十一月初十日。住世七十有九年。

> Min Yide was born on the second day of the 12th month of 1758 and died on the 10th day of the 11th month of 1836 at the age of 78 years.[57]

Additional information about the life and activities of Min Yide at Jingai shan is found in two more biographies included in the appendix of the *Jingai xindeng*.

2. *Min Lanyun xiansheng zhuan* 閔懶雲先生傳 by Yang Weikun 揚維崑[58] (Appendix 4a-5a to the *Jingai xindeng* 金蓋心燈, and in the *Gu Shuyinlou cangshu* 古書隱樓藏書, vol. 1, 6a-b in *Zangwai daoshu* 藏外道書 vol. 10, p. 154).

This biography, written by a disciple of one of Min Yide's successors, furnishes some additional information about Min Yide and his physical constitution:

> When Min Yide was born, his father Sir Genfu (艮甫公) dreamed of the arrival of a man dressed in feathers (i.e., an immortal) who presented himself as Bei Lanyun 貝懶雲. Because of this he [Min Yide] was also called Lanyun zi 懶雲子.[59] In his childhood he

---

[57] JGXD 補遺, 3a1-3.

[58] Yang Weikun 揚維崑 belongs to the 13th Longmen generation. He was a disciple of Fei Boyun 費撥雲, one of Min Yide's disciples. See *Daotong yuanliu zhi* 道統源流志, *xia*, pp. 18 and 15.

[59] It is interesting to compare this information with the more detailed dream of Min Yide's father recorded in the autobiography of Min Yide found in a later edition of the *Gu Shuyinlou cangshu* (1906). This autobiography has been published in the *Longmen pai danfa jueyao* 龍門派丹法訣要 in *Daozang jinghua* 8-1 道藏精華第一集之八, edited by Xiao Tianshi 蕭天石 (Taipei: Ziyou 自由, 1982): 235-36. According to his father's dream, Min Yide is seen as the new manifestation of the Daoist Bei Daqin 貝大欽 (*hao*: Lanyun 懶雲) who is reputed to have been abbot of Hangzhou's Dongxiao gong 洞宵宮 during the Southern Song 南宋. As Min Yide was associated with the old Daoist Bei Lanyun, he exhibited signs characteristic of

exhibited extraordinary talent. While playing with a group of children he fell into a well, but it was as if someone had helped him out. Being thin and weak, he visited Gao Dongli at Tongbai shan and stayed there for a number of years until he recovered.

生時其父艮甫公夢羽服者至、自稱貝懶雲、故又自號懶雲子。幼穎異。從群兒戲、墮井中、若有扳之出者。素羸弱、謁東離高子於桐柏山、留數載、體始充。[60]

After similar information about Min Yide's official career and devotion to his master Shen Qingyun, this biography states that Min Yide decided after the death of Shen to visit renowned places. "He traversed all regions from south to north, leaving his traces in half the empire." By contrast with the first biographer, Yang Weikun 楊維崑 tells us that Min Yide had the opportunity to meet the patriarchs of the 10th and 11th generation of a Longmen branch called Longmen xizhu xinzong 龍門西竺心宗.[61] They are Jin Huaihuai 金懷懷,[62] Baima Li 白馬李,[63] Li Pengtou 李擎頭 (?-1784)[64] and Longmen daoshi 龍門道士.[65] The affinity between these two Longmen branches, the Longmen branch of Min Yide and the Longmen xizhu xinzong branch, is emphasized through the mention of the frequent discussions he had with them in which they were "for the most part in agreement."[66] Through such fruitful exchanges Min Yide acquired a good reputation among prestigious officials and sages who held debates with him in mutual respect. After that, this second biographer states that Min Yide withdrew to Mt. Jingai where, as we already know, he devoted himself to restoring and enlarging its land holdings and Daoist temples. Also, Min Yide

---

old men like having weak legs. This may allude to the legend of Laozi who is said to have been born as an octogenarian infant.

[60] JGXD 補遺, 4a1-4.

[61] See "Longmen fenpai xizhu zhu xinzong liuchuan tu" 龍門分派西竺心宗流傳圖 (JGXD 1.1a).

[62] On this lineage see "Longmen fenpai xizhu zhu xinzong liuchuan tu" 龍門分派西竺心宗流傳圖 (JGXD 1.1a). For the Biography of Jin Huaihai, see JGXD 6.91-11b.

[63] See the biography of Baima Li in JGXD 6.12a-14a.

[64] See the biography of Li Pengtou in JGXD 6. 23a-b.

[65] See the biography of Longmen daoshi in JGXD 6.24a-55a.

[66] This is also underlined in the introduction to the *Erlan xinhua* 二懶心話 (Heart-to-Heart Dialogue between the Two Leisurely [Masters]) in *Gu Shuyinlou cangshu* vol. 8, 35a (*Zangwai daoshu* 藏外道書 vol. 10, p. 467).

is here portrayed as a good teacher whose students increased in number day by day and whom he guided and fostered, encouraged and rewarded without respite. He is also described as vital and generous:

> When he was more than 70 years old his vitality was not in decline and he was like a man of 40 to 50 years of age. Once during the winter he met an old man. As he was very cold, he dressed him with his fur coat.

年七十餘、精力不衰、如四五十人。嘗冬月遇一故人寒甚、即解身上裘衣之。

If this second biography started out with a dream of Min Yide's father announcing Min Yide's birth and with his appellation Lanyun zi in memory of the manifestation of a Daoist immortal, it ends with another dream of Min Yide's father, this time related to his own burial:

> Min was so poor that the relatives had to interrupt the burial of his father many times because he could not afford it. When [his father] Sir Liangfu still occupied his official post, Min Yide dreamed of a tomb containing a hat and clothes to which many generations came to pay respect. Min Yide did not know what to make of this dream. But later he understood that it was a premonition of the evening of the burial [of his own father] (葬柩之夕).

族中停柩十數、貧不能舉、為經理葬焉。時艮甫公在任所、夢衣冠者數輩來謝、疑之、後始知其故。蓋即葬柩之夕也。其慷慨任事類如此。

Finally, as in the first biography, the two main works by Min Yide are mentioned: the *Jingai xindeng* in 8 *juan* and the *Yinlou cangshu* containing more than 20 titles.[67]

3. ***Min Lanyun xiansheng zhuan*** 閔懶雲先生傳 by Shen Bingcheng 沈秉成 (1821–1894),[68] (Appendix to the *Jingai xindeng* 金蓋心燈, 6a–7a and YLCS, vol. 1, 7a–8a in *Zangwai daoshu* 藏外道書 vol. 10, p. 155).

---

[67] In the version of the same bibliography found in the *Gu Shuyinlou cangshu* (*Zangwai daoshu* 藏外道書 10–154), the *Gu Shuyinlou cangshu* is said to include more than thirty titles.

[68] Shen belongs to the 13th Longmen generation and was a disciple of Fei Boyun 費撥雲; see his biographical note in *Daotong yuanliu zhi* 道統源流志, *xia*, pp. 17–18.

Similar information is given in the third biography which can be regarded as a copy of the biography written by Yang Weikun. It is clear that biographies two and three made use of the same sources. The only variations worth pointing out are found at the end of this biography. After having mentioned Min Yide's main works, i.e., "the *Yinlou* collection of more than 20 titles[69] and the *Jingai xindeng* in 8 *juan*, written to expound the quintessence of his masters' doctrine (發明本師宗旨) and to get rid of the unorthodox theories inside the alchemical schools (於丹家邪說闢之)," biographer Shen Bingcheng portrays Min Yide as an ideal Confucian:

> Min Yide was honest and sincere, pure and serene, modest and easy of approach; and his discussions had the allure of a Confucian. He died in the year 16 of Daoguang (1836) at the age of 79 years.
>
> 篤實純靜、平易近人、論者以為有儒者氣象。道光十六年卒、年七十九。[70]

To summarize, from these three biographies we learn that Min Yide came from a renowned family of officials in Wuxing (Huzhou, Zhejiang). He was well educated in the Confucian mold and, despite his chosen poverty, maintained high moral values and was widely appreciated by people. His first contacts with Daoism and in particular with the Longmen were due to his weak constitution as an infant. In his youth he received *daoyin* instruction from the Longmen master Gao Dongli at Tongbai gong. After a short official career, Min Yide choose to consecrate himself to the Daoist path of cultivation and eventually withdrew to Mt. Jingai. In his time, the previously prosperous Longmen tradition was in decline, but thanks to his activities Mt. Jingai became once more a renowned sanctuary of Longmen Daoism. Furthermore, biographies two and three state that Min Yide had a close relationship with a Tantric-Daoist branch called Longmen xizhu xinzong 龍門西竺心宗. He is said to have met its important patriarchs and shared with them common doctrinal views. According to Min Yide's preface to the *Lü zushi sanni yishi shuoshu* 呂祖師三尼醫世說, he even met the founder of the Tantric-Daoist branch, Jizu daozhe 雞足道者. Who was this man, and what was Min Yide's—and Longmen Daoism's—connection with him and his teachings?

---

[69] In the *Gu Shuyinlou cangshu* version of the same bibliography (*Zangwai daoshu* 藏外道書 vol. 10, p. 154–5), the *Shuyinlou cangshu* is said to include more than thirty titles 書隱樓藏書三十餘種.

[70] JGXD 補遺, 6b8-7a1-2.

BIOGRAPHIES OF JIZU DAOZHE

Regarding Min Yide's connection with Longmen's Mind-Tradition of West-India (Longmen xizhu xinzong 龍門西竺心宗) and with Jizu daozhe 雞足道者 there are two important sources:

1. the preface by Min Yide to the *Lü zushi sanni yishi shuoshu* 呂祖師三尼醫世說述 (Explanations of the Three Sages' Doctrine of Healing the World [revealed] by Patriarch Lü); and

2. the biography of Jizu daozhe in Min Yide's *Jingai xindeng* 金蓋心燈. An additional short biography of Jizu daozhe is found in the *Chishi tuoluoni jing fa* 持世陀羅尼經法 under the title *Dushi Yedaposhe zhuan* 度師野怛婆闍傳 (*Zangwai daoshu* 藏外道書 10: 553).

Jizu daozhe is also mentioned in a number of texts of the *Gu Shuyinlou cangshu*, some of which will be adduced in the notes below.

1. Preface by Min Yide to the *Lü zushi sanni yishi shuoshu* 呂祖師三尼醫世說述[71] (1828)

This preface, which is found in the *Gu Shuyinlou cangshu* 古書隱樓藏書,[72] is very interesting because Min Yide here emphasizes the union of the Three Teachings in an original way using the term *sanni yishi* 三尼醫世, i.e., "the Three Sages' [Doctrine of] Healing the World." The Three Sages (*sanni* 三尼) are Confucius (Zhongni 仲尼), Laozi (Qingni 青尼), and Shakyamuni Buddha (Mouni 牟尼).[73] In this preface, Min describes his visit in 1792 of Mt. Jizu 雞足, a mountain close to Dali 大理 in Yunnan 雲南 that is widely known for its Buddhist monasteries.[74]

---

[71] The *Lü zushi sanni yishi shuoshu* 呂祖師三尼醫世說述 includes two prefaces: The first was written by Tao Shi'an 陶石庵 (?-1692) in 1664, and the second was written by Min Yide in 1828.

[72] *Zangwai daoshu* 藏外道書 vol. 10, p. 344.

[73] In the *Lü zushi sanni yishi shuoshu* 呂祖師三尼醫世說述 (*Daozang xubian* 道藏續編 1a/5-6; *Gu Shuyinlou cangshu* 9a/7-8, in *Zangwai daoshu* 藏外道書 vol. 10, p. 348) it is said that the *Xinyin ji jing* 心印集經 states: "Qingni [Laozi] reaches the Center, Zhongni [Confucius] takes hold of it, and Mouni [Buddha] empties it." 心印集經曰。青尼致中。仲尼時中。牟尼空中。See also *Daozang jiyao* 道藏輯要, 箕集 10, 6a-b.

[74] For a study of Jizu shan and its monasteries in the context of Yunnan as an important region for the transmission of Indian and Tibetan Buddhism see Yang Xuezheng 楊

Fig. 16: The Three Sages (Confucius, Buddha, and Laozi) (Brinker & Kanazawa 1996: 16)

學政 et al. (eds.), *Yunnan zongjiao shi* 雲南宗教史 (Kunming: Yunnan Renmin, 1999), and Shigeo Kamata 鎌田茂雄, "*Unnan・Keisokusan no bukkyō* 雲南・雞足山の仏教", *Kokusai bukkyō daigakuin daigaku kiyō* 国際仏教大学院大学紀要 1 (1998): 1–34. See also *Jizushan zhi* 雞足山志 vol. 13 (Yunnan renmin chubanshe, 雲南人民出版, 2003).

It is in the Nāgārjuna hermitage (Longshu shanfang 龍樹山房)⁷⁵ of Mt. Jizu 雞足 that Min Yide claims to have encountered Jizu daozhe 雞足道者, a divine immortal residing on earth 住世神仙. He describes this man and event as follows:

> The family name of the immortal was Huang 黃 and his given name Shouzhong 守中. He was a man from the Yuezhi 月支 (= 月氏) tribe⁷⁶ of the Western regions of China (西域月支人).⁷⁷ During the Yuan era he entered China and became during his long residence on Mt. Jizu known as Jizu daozhe 雞足道者. In 1659 he entered the Capital in search of the transmission of the Three Great Precepts of Taishang from the Vinaya Master 律師 Wang Changyue 王常月. Originally he had no name or style names 字, only the appellation Yedaposhe 野闒婆闍 which in Chinese means "Seeker of the Dao (lit. Gentleman Searcher of the Dao 求道士).⁷⁸ After residing in China for years, the

---

⁷⁵ Unfortunately the name of Longshu shanfang 龍樹山房 is not mentioned in the *Jizushan zhi* 雞足山志. As is well known, Nāgārjuna (Longshu pusa 龍樹菩薩) was the famous Doctor of the Mādhyamika who lived around the 3rd century and was later confounded with a namesake of the 7th century. The latter was a Tantric master recognized by the Sino-Japanese esoteric (*mijiao / mikkyō* 密教) tradition as the Third Patriarch, the first human patriarch after Mahāvairocana and Vajrapāṇi.

⁷⁶ The term Yuezhi 月支, which stands for 月氏, generally refers to Tokharestan and to the Bactrian region of Central Asia. It is important to distinguish between Da Yueshi 大月氏, whose major branch was called the Tocharioi and reigning in Tokharestan, and Yuezhi or Xiao Yuezhi 小月氏, a term referring to the Tibetan minority Qiang 羌 and in general to Tibetans of the Gansu.

⁷⁷ In the Han dynasty, the term "western regions" (西域) was used for areas west of the Jade Gate (Yumenguan 玉門關), for Yangguan 陽關 including present Xinjiang, and for parts of Central Asia and even India, the eastern part of Europe, and the northern part of the Philippines. It can also stand for "the West" in general. In mythology it also refers to the country of the Queen Mother of the West, Xiwangmu. From the Yuan, the tern Xiyu often stands for Tibet.

⁷⁸ Regarding the name Yetapozhe 野闒婆闍, one finds more frequently the Chinese characters Yedapozhe/she 野恒婆闍 (see the biography below). If one follows the Chinese translation *qiudao shi* 求道士 (in which *qiudao* also implies the meaning of leaving home in search of Dao [*chujia qiudao* 出家求道]), one can think of some Sanskrit compounds used in Chinese transliteration. Here are some speculations: *yeda* 野恒 may stand for *ayedana* 阿耶恒那 (skr. *āyatana*, seat, abode), in the sense of *ru* 入 (to enter; entry; Skt. *Pravesa*?). *Po* 婆 may stand for *poluomen* 婆羅門教 (Brāhman teaching) and *she* for *asheli* 阿闍梨 (skr. *ācārya*; tib. *slob dpon*). This may refer to the idea of "*ācārya* who enters the sacred teachings." But I miss the verb *qiu* 求 here and this might be farfetched. Furthermore, this may call to mind Sanskrit sounds such as *Yātrābhāja*, but also Tibetan sounds such as **ye bdag-po rje* or Lord

Vinaya Master (Wang Changyue) conferred upon him the Chinese name of Huang Shouzhong 黃守中. Until today, all the people of Yunnan call him Huang the Perfected 黃真人. Though he was already over 500 years old, he appeared like a man of about sixty. He had a pair of penetrating eyes and a voice booming like a large bell. On his desk there were not many books: besides the *Foshuo chishi tuoluoni jing* 佛說持世陀羅尼經 there was only the *Sanni yishi shuoshu* 三尼醫世說述.

仙姓黃名守中、西域月支人、元時進中國、久休雞足、故有是號。順治十六年入京師、求授太上三大戒於崑陽王律師。初無名字、自號野闉婆闍、華言求道士也。律師以其身休中國有年、因命以華人姓名曰黃守中。迄今滇人咸以黃真人呼之。年已五百有餘歲、而貌若六十許人、雙眸炯炯、聲若洪鐘、案頭無多書、《佛說持世陀羅尼經》外、惟《三尼醫世說述》。

With regard to this preface it is important to underline that, in Min Yide's portrayal, the teachings of the Tantric-Daoist branch of Jizu daozhe are mainly based on two texts, namely the *Foshuo chishi tuoluoni jing* 佛說持世陀羅尼經 and the *Sanni yishi shuoshu* 三尼醫世說述. To get a more precise idea of Jizudaozhe as alleged founder figure of the Longmen Tantric-Daoist branch, a closer look at his biography is needed.

2. "Jizu daozhe Huang lüshi zhuan" 雞足道者黃律師 (Biography of the Vinaya Master Huang, Man of the Way from Mt. Jizu), *Jingai xindeng* 金蓋心燈 (j. 6 shang.1a-2b)[79]

> Jizu daozhe 雞足道者 came from Yuezhi 月支 (Jizu 雞足 is the name of a mountain in Diannan 滇南 [today's Yunnan]. Yuezhi 月支 is the name of the country in the West formerly called Diguo 氐國.[80] According to Lanyun, the governor of

---

Sovereign of the Origin (*rje* =君 Lord; *bdag-po* 主宰 Sovereign; *ye* Origin) or **yang-dag-pa'i rje* Authentic/Most Pure Lord. However these two expressions are not attested in Tibetan titles. A more plausible counterpart to the Chinese translation *qiudao shi* 求道士 might be **ye bstan-pa'i rje*, "Lord who teaches (*bstan-pa* 教) the Path" (although such form is not attested in Tibetan either).

[79] In the following translations, commentary originally printed between the lines in smaller Chinese characters is set in small type within parentheses.

[80] *Diren* 氐人 indicates the name of a tribe as well as Diren guo 氐人國, the mythical country of the descendants of Yandi 炎帝 with a human head and a fish body (see

Diannan 滇南 stated that at the beginning of the Yuan [Jizu] was already living there but nobody knew when he had arrived.⁸¹) He withdrew to Mt. Jizu and called himself Yedaposhe 野怛婆闍.⁸² He had neither a family name 姓, name 名 nor style name 字 but only the appellation 號 Yedaposhe which in Chinese means "Gentleman in Search of the Dao" 求道士. He was an expert of the *doufa* 斗法 (Dipper rite). In 1660, when he first came to the capital [Beijing], he observed the ordination ceremony 演鉢,⁸³ and Patriarch Wang Changyue bestowed upon him the family name Huang 黄 and the name Shouzhong 守中.

雞足道者來自月支。(雞足、滇南山名。月支、西方國名、即古之氐國。懶雲子謂滇南士人相傳：元初已有此道者、不知其來自何代也。) 休於雞足、自稱野怛婆闍、而無姓、名、字、號、華言求道士。所精惟斗法。順治庚子(十六年)始至京師、觀光演鉢、王崑陽祖贈姓曰黄、命名守中。⁸⁴

Furthermore, Wang told him: "As your stay in the world will last over 130 years, you will spontaneously obtain the Great Precepts." He then urged him to return [to Yunnan] and preserve the secret of the Dipper. (In the *Bojian* 鉢鑑, Jizu daozhe is also mentioned as having the appelation Yedaposhe and this is quite similar to what is reported above.) He was conscentious, diligent, and untiring. Having heard about his exploits,

---

"Hainei nanjing" 海內南經 in *Shanhaijing* 山海經: 氏人國在建木西。其為人、人面而魚身、無足); quoted in *Hanyu dacidian* 漢語大詞典 vol. 6, p. 1420. It also stands for the mythical western country of Yeni 野尼 described in the *Waiguo fangpin* 外國方品 where the mythical country of Niweiluoluna 尼維羅綠那 is located in which the Di 氏 and Yuezhi 月支 people live. See Isabelle Robinet, "Randonnées extatiques des taoïstes dans les astres," *Monumenta Serica* 32 (1976): 159–273; here 215.

81 In the *Xiuzhen biannan canzheng* 修真辨難參證 (YLCS 46a/5 in *Zangwai daoshu* 藏外道書 vol. 10, p. 243). Jizu daozhe is said to have been born in the Song era.
82 On this appellation see note 78 (pp. 271–2) above and p. 282 below.
83 Literally, "performing the bowl." On this term see below, p. 287 ff.
84 Here a long inserted comment explains: "[Jizu] daozhe came from a foreign country to China. He was capable of establishing 創開 the teachings 法門 and widely transmitting its traditions 宗派. He had all the time predestined relationships. Wang Changyue had already met him in the distant past. Thus, in that year [i.e., 1660] he gave him the injunction 囑 to stay in the world for 130 years because in these 130 years he would transmit numerous rituals 法科. [Jizu] daozhe was from the outset an extraordinary man and [Wang] Changyue had the premonition 有意 that after 130 years [i.e., in 1790], the Great Precepts would be naturally conveyed to him."

Guan Tianxian 管天仙 revered him as Master and received the name Taiqing 太清. (Guan Tianxian's biography follows here below.)

且曰： 汝但住世越百三十秋、大戒自得。遂促返、仍持斗秘。(按《缽鑑》亦載有難足道者自稱野怛婆闍、與上文所記、大略相同。) 精勤不息、管天仙聞蹟而師之、命名太清。(管天仙傳列次篇。)

In the year *gengxu* 庚戌 (the 55th year of the Qianlong era [i.e., 1790], just 130 years after the year *gengzi* of the Shunzhi era [i.e., 1660]), I [Min Yide] went to visit him, bringing with me the book of the Great Precepts. When Daozhe saw me he joyfully said to me: "Let's exchange this" (This means that he transmitted his *xizhu doufa* 西竺斗法, the Western Indian Dipper Rite, to Lanyun zi [Min Yide] in exchange for Min's book of the Great Precepts), so we will both gain profit."

歲庚戌 (乾隆五十五年、距順治庚子正一百三十年) 余往謁攜有大戒書。道者見而喜曰:交易之、(謂以其西竺斗法傳懶雲子、以易大戒書也) 則兩得也。

While staying there for three months, [Min] learned the Sanskrit pronunciation, and [Jizu] daozhe transcribed the Book of the Great Precepts; and after having displayed the portrait of Wang Changyue, he tearfully prostrated and prayed. Turning to me he then said: "You have obtained in exchange the supreme treasure of West India. Kindly safeguard the orthodox lineage. If the [observation of] precepts is deficient, its strength will diminish. Since the soul of Patriarch Wang is present, he knows and sees everything." (Changyue whose soul was in Heaven simply had to descend from on high in order to legitimate this.) [Min Yide] tearfully prostrated and received the transmission. (This is why [Jixu] daozhe is called Vinaya Master Huang 黃律師. According to Lanyun, he [Lanyun=Min Yide] obtained Huang's Dipper Ritual 斗法, in conformity with the Heart Lineage of the Western India. At last he compiled the *Dafan xiantian fanyin douzhou* 大梵先天梵音斗咒 in ten sections amounting to twelve *juan* in order to publish and transmit it to the world. In the Dipper Ritual 斗法 the person who is called Tuduo lüshi is the Vinaya Master Huang 黃律師). When I [Min] rose, he [Jizu daozhe] urged me to return. (At that time Lanyun [Min Yide] served as official in Yunnan and then he returned to his post in Yunnan). Half way on my journey back, the Regulator-general Mr. Fu 富 (name: Gang 綱) dispatched an envoy to meet (Jizu daozhe). When on his return he reported that he [Jizu daozhe] had passed away, I said: "That is not so."

Chapter Five: Daoism and Tantrism in the Qing   275

Had he not practiced the five excellent methods? In the year *wuwu* 戊午 (the third year of the Jiaqing era [i.e., 1798]) there was someone who saw him [Jizu daozhe] in Sichuan at the Qingyang gong.

遂止宿三月、梵音得。道者則手錄大戒書、懸崑陽王祖像、泣拜而祝、轉顧余曰：《西竺至寶、汝已易得、善護正宗、戒勵則力薄、王祖靈在、悉知悉見也。》余亦泣拜而受之。(此道者之所以稱黃律師也。愚按懶雲得其斗法、奉為西竺心宗、歸纂大梵先天梵音斗咒、凡十部、計十二卷、刊傳於世。按斗法所稱囗圖哆律師、即黃律師也) 起、促余返。(時懶雲子服官滇南。蓋仍返至滇省也。) 至半途總制富公(名綱)、遣使往迎、及使返、述子已逝。余曰：《不然。》子蓋行五假法耳。歲戊午(嘉慶三年)果有見子於四川青羊宮者。

Fig. 17: Pavilion in the precincts of Qingyang gong 青羊宮 in Chengdu, Sichuan province (Photo M. Esposito, 2006)

Fig. 18: Taizi 太子 Hermitage on the steep slopes of Mount Jizu 雞足山 (Photo M. Esposito, 1990)

THE FIGURE OF JIZU DAOZHE AND HIS ROLE

After having presented the biographical sources on Jizu daozhe, I would like to comment on some important issues related to this figure and summarize the content of the two texts linked with the transmission of the Longmen xizhu xinzong: the *Foshuo chishi tuoluoni jing* 佛說持世陀羅尼經 and the *Sanni yishi shuoshu* 三尼醫世說述). The main points from these sources can be summed up as follows:

THE FOREIGN ORIGIN OF JIZU DAOZHE

Jizu daozhe is portrayed as a legendary figure from Western countries 西方國. He is a Yuezhi 月支 from Gansu 甘肅 and Qinghai 青海 (the Tibetan A mdo), provided that one attributes to Yuezhi its original meaning of "homeland located in the Qilian mountains south of the Gansu corridor (Gansu-Qinghai border)." This biography mentions the former Diguo 氐國, which might indicate that Jizu daozhe was of Tibetan origin.[85] However, one should not forget that Yuezhi was also used, at least until the Tang era, to designate Indo-European tribes of Central Asia and North-West India.[86] For the Chinese, the Yuezhi were probably archetypal foreigners from Western regions linked by the Silk Road, one of the most important roads of transmission of Buddhism from India to China. Dharmarakṣa 竺法護 (d. after 313 CE), one of the first translators of Tantric works and in particular of *dhāraṇī*, is an example of an apparently sinicized Yuezhi from Dunhuang.[87]

---

[85] As is well-known, Yuezhi were a major nomadic power at the beginning of the second century BCE. As a result of their defeat by the Xiongnu 匈奴, part of their tribe, thenceforth known as Da Yuezhi 大月支／氏, moved west. They occupied first Sogdiana (present Uzbekistan) and then crossed the Oxus into Bactria (northern Afghanistan). Another part of the tribe, the Xiao Yuezhi 小月支／氏, remained in Gansu. However, since Diguo is mentioned here, one should remember that in the *Shijing* the names Qiang 羌 and Di 氐 occur in association. The Di are in fact linked to the Qiang in Han times but are seldom mentioned in earlier texts. See E.G. Pulleyblank, "The Chinese and Their Neighbors in Prehistoric and Early Historic Times," in David K. Keightley (ed.), *The Origins of Chinese Civilization*, pp. 411–466. Berkeley: University of California Press, 1983, p 419.

[86] E.G. Pulleyblank, "The Chinese and Their Neighbors," pp. 456–459.

[87] "It is characteristic of Dharmaraksa to translate the meaning of *dhāraṇī* instead of

Furthermore, as the name Jizu daozhe shows, he is also associated with Yunnan and in particular with Mt. Jizu near the town of Dali (Fig. 18). As is well known, Mt. Jizu 雞足山 (Kukkutpāda) was an important center of Indian Buddhist teachings where Buddha's disciple Mahākāśyapa 摩訶迦葉, claimed by Chan Buddhism as its first Indian patriarch, was thought to be waiting for the manifestation in the world of the Buddha of the Future, Maitreya 彌勒. According to tradition, it is on Mt. Jizu that Mahākāśyapa will eventually bestow the symbol of direct transmission, the monastic robe he had received from the Buddha, on Maitreya.[88] This points to the importance of this place as an archetypal "ordination sanctuary" whose core function lies in the regeneration of unadulterated, original Buddhist teaching for future generations in an age when the Buddha dharma has vanished (mofa 末法, Jap. mappō, lit. "end of Dharma"). We are going to see that

---

transcribing the sound." See Chou Yi-liang, "Tantric Buddhism in China," *Harvard Journal of Asian Studies* 8 (1944–45), p. 242. As Chou Yiliang remarks (p. 243), it was also around the time of Dharmaraksa's activity that the earliest mention of a Buddhist monk praying for rain in China occurs. The monk in question was Shegong from Central Asia. From that time on, Tantric masters were all supposed to be able to produce rain. Jizu daozhe is also said to be a transmitter of *dhāraṇīs* for making rain. On the relationship between Tantrism and Daoism, see Yoshinobu Sakade 坂出祥伸, "Shoki mikkyo to dōkyō to no kōshō" 初期密教と道教との交渉 [The Early Relation between Esoteric Buddhism and Daoism], in *Chūgoku mikkyō* 中国密教 [Chinese Esoteric Buddhism], ed. Tachikawa Musashi 立川武蔵 (Tokyo: Shunkasha, 1999): 153–169. On Dharmaraksa see also the article by Antonello Palumbo, "Dharmaraksa and Kanthaka—White Horse Monasteries in Early Medieval China," in Giovanni Verardi & Silvio Vita (eds.), *Buddhist Asia 1* (Kyoto: Italian Institute of East Asian Studies, 2003):167–216. My thanks to Antonello Palumbo for his explanations on the meaning of Yuezhi and for his information about important studies on this topic. On the Chinese view of India, see Michel Strickmann, "India in the Chinese Looking-glass," in *The Silk Route and the Diamond Path*, ed. D. E. Klimburg-Salter (Los Angeles: UCLA Art Council, 1982).

[88] It is of interest that among the monasteries and temples of Mt. Jizu in Yunnan there is a temple named Chuanyi si 傳衣寺 ("Temple of the Robe Transmission") which was established at the beginning of the Jiaqing 嘉靖 era (1522–1566) by Li Yuanyang 李元陽; see *Jizushan zhi* 雞足山志 230. As Shigeo Kamata 鎌田茂雄 ("*Unnan・Keisokusan no bukkyō* 雲南・雞足山の仏教," p. 14) explains, the custom in Chan Buddhism of conferring robe and bowl as symbols of dharma transmission accounts for the origin of this temple name which is also connected to the transmission from Mahākāśyapa to Maitreya and from Maitreya onward. For the relationship between the transmission of the robe and Chan ordination see Anna Seidel, "Den'e" (*Hōbōgirin* vol. 8, 2003): 1171–78, especially 1177; and H. Welch, *The Practice of Chinese Buddhism*, pp. 156–157, 290.

in the Daoist context, too, Mt. Jizu as archetypal *locus* of transmission and the figure named after it, Jizu daozhe, seem related to the regeneration of original teachings and of their certified transmission to future generations of Daoists.[89]

Moreover, Mt. Jizu is connected with India and the so-called Acāryā Tantrism 阿吒力密教;[90] and due to its geographical proximity with today's Tibet it is also related to Tibetan Buddhism.[91] Min Yide probably had the

---

[89] Buddhist sources have long held that in Magadha 摩伽陀國, the homeland of Buddhism in India, there was a montain called Kukkutapada-giri (translated into Chinese as Jizu shan 雞足山 or "Cock-foot mountain"). This mountain was visited by the famous 7th-century Chinese pilgrim Xuanzang 玄奘 who, in the ninth fascicle of his *Datang xiyuji* 大唐西域記, mentioned this mountain's link with Mahākāśyapa; see Shigeo Kamata 鎌田茂雄, "*Unnan・Keisokusan no bukkyō* 雲南・雞足山の仏教," and Kin Bunkyō 金文京, "Tonkō shutsudo bunsho kara mita tōdai no Bindora shinkō" 敦煌出土文書からみた唐代の賓頭盧信仰, in Tadao Yoshikawa 吉川忠夫 (ed.), *Tōdai no shūkyō* 唐代の宗教 (Kyoto: Hōyū shoten 朋友書店, 2000): 195–219, especially 203–5. For the relationship between Kukkutapada and Mahākāśyapa see also the Biography of Mahākāśyapa in *Jizushan zhi* 雞足山志, p. 16. On this mountain Mahākāśyapa is said to remain in samādhi while waiting for the manifestation of Buddha Maitreya; see Étienne Lamotte, *Le Traité de la Grande Vertu de Sagesse* (Louvain: Université de Louvain, 198): 192, note 1; and Anna Seidel, "Den'e" (*Hōbōgirin* vol. 8, 2003): 1172. For the link of Kukkutapada Mountain and the cult of Maitreya see Chūsei Suzuki 鈴木中正, "Seichō chūki ni okeru minkan shūkyō kessha to sono sennen ōkoku undō e no keisha" 清朝中期における民間宗教結社とその千年王国運動への傾斜, in Chūsei Suzuki 鈴木中正 (ed.), *Sennen ōkokuteki minshū undō no kenkyū* (Tokyo: Tōkyō daigaku shuppankai, 1982): 247–256. My thanks for this last reference to Professor Kin. For a study on how this Indian mountain of Kukuttapada was transplanted to China's Yunnan region around the 15th century, see Wang Bangwei 王邦維, "Mahākasyāpa and Kukuttapāda-giri: From Magadha to Yunnan," Paper presented at the Conference "Crossing the Borders of China: A Conference on Cross-Cultural Interactions in Honor of Professor Victor H. Mair," December 5–7, 2003, University of Pennsylvania, Philadelphia. My thanks to Professor Tōru Funayama for this reference and to Professor Wang Bangwei for allowing me to quote his conference paper.

[90] See Yang Xuezheng 楊學政 et al. (ed.), *Yunnan zongjiao shi* 雲南宗教史 (Kunming: Yunnan renmin, 1999): 3–25 & 243–328. The transmission of Tantric/Esoteric Buddhism in this south-western region of China was also associated with the transmission of Sanskrit and its uses. Walter Liebenthal has published inscriptions in Sanskrit which are mainly *dhāranī* that show the penetration of Tantrism during the 9th and 10th centuries CE in these regions of southwestern China. See Walter Liebenthal, "Sanskrit Inscriptions from Yunnan I (and the Dates of Foundation of the Main Pagodas in that Province)," *Monumenta Serica* 12 (1947): 1–40, and "Sanskrit Inscriptions from Yünnan II," *Sino-Indian Studies* 5 (1955): 1–23.

[91] What we today call Tibet is the result of the differentiation of two broad geopoliti-

opportunity of becoming familiar with this tradition while serving in Yunnan as provincial administrator. Beside this, I wonder if the possible Tibetan origin of Jizu daozhe and his entering China during the Yuan dynasty may also have some connections with the Qing government and its politics. In their aspiration of conquering the Mongols, earlier Qing emperors made special efforts to favor them by patronizing Tibetan Buddhism. They expressed their support to lamas by hosting them and having them perform rites. Above all, they presented themselves as the successors of Genghis Khan, i.e., the Yuan dynasty. Such political aspiration reached its climax during the long reign of emperor Qianlong 乾隆 (r. 1736–1795) during which Min Yide was born and when the mythical meeting with Jizu daozhe purportedly took place.

Emperor Qianlong intended to turn the imperial capital Beijing into the spiritual capital of the lamaist realm (Fig. 19). Tibetan Buddhism prospered in various temples linked to the imperial family. The most famous among them is the Yonghe gong 雍和宮 which represents the birthplace of Qianlong. Qianlong also sponsored massive projects dedicated to the translation and publication of the Tibetan Tripitaka in Mongolian and Manchu. Furthermore, due to his close relationship with Rol pa'i rdo rje (1717–1786) whose Lcang skya lineage came from A mdo (roughly the Gansu-Qinghai area with which Jizu daozhe appears to be associated), Qianlong and the Qing court in general attached great importance to A mdo lamas. These lamas comprised the majority among Beijing's resident "living Buddhas" *khutuktus* (*huofo* 活佛).

One may thus wonder whether the integration of Jizu daozhe in the Daoist Longmen lineage by Min Yide was also politically motivated. Was one of its purposes the promotion of the Longmen lineage at the court? Could Jizu daozhe, in the cloak of a Tibetan lama from A mdo, an expert in esoteric teachings, be related to Qianlong's State Preceptor Rol pa'i rdo rje who, like Jizu daozhe, came from A mdo? Was he a reminder of A mdo lamas, those "living Buddhas" so highly esteemed by the Qing court?

---

cal categories known as "political" and "ethnographic" Tibet. Political Tibet refers to the polity of the Dalai Lamas and is equivalent to today's Tibet Autonomous Region (TAR). Ethnographic Tibet refers to the ethnic Tibetan areas of of A mdo and Kham that the Chinese today consider to be part of the Qinghai, Sichuan, and Yunnan provinces. See Melvyn C. Goldstein, "Introduction," in M. C. Goldstein & M. Kapstein (eds.), *Buddhism in Contemporary Tibet* (Berkeley: University of California Press, 1998): 4.

Chapter Five: Daoism and Tantrism in the Qing 281

Fig. 19: Emperor Qianlong as the bodhisattva Mañjuśrī in Tibetan Thangka style (Ho & Bronson 2004: 120)

Jizu daozhe's original appellation Yedaposhe 野怛婆闍 also deserves further attention. Although it is said to correspond to the Chinese *qiudao shi* 求道士 or "seeker of the Dao," it is difficult to trace this name to Sanskrit, Tibetan, or other Central Asian languages. It might remind us of Sanskrit sounds such as *Yātāpāca* or *Yātāpāja*, but compounds with the Chinese meaning of 求道士 are elusive.[92] For Tibetan, one might think of sounds such as *ye bdag-po rje, Lord Sovereign of the Origin (rje =君 Lord; bdag-po 主宰 Sovereign; ye Origin), or *yang-dag-pa'i rje, Authentic Lord; but such expressions are not at all attested in Tibetan sources. Following the Chinese translation *qiudao shi* 求道士, a more plausible counterpart might be *ye bstan-pa'i rje, "Lord who teaches (*bstan-pa* 教) the Path/Origin." But neither of these forms are attested in Tibetan. One might also speculate that the name Yedaposhe 野怛婆闍 represents a symbolic interpretation of Chinese characters. For instance *ye* 野 might be an allusion to Yeni 野尼, the mythical country described in the *Waiguo fangpin* 外國方品 where Di 氐 and Yuezhi 月支 people were said to live. Po 婆 may allude to *poluomen jiao* 婆羅門教 (Brāhman teaching) and *she* for *asheli* 阿闍梨 (skr. *ācārya*; tib. *slob dpon*, Jap. *ajari*). Though regarding Jizu daozhe as *ācārya* would fit his role of *dushi* 度師 or Master of Initiation and also his transmission of an Indian esoteric *dhāraṇī* text, I was unable to find proof for this interpretation.[93]

What can be said with assurance is that the figure of Jizu daozhe and his name Yedaposhe 野怛婆闍 both emphasize his foreign origin. This origin points to Jizu daozhe as original recipient of the Sanskrit esoterica (*fanmi* 梵密) which was traditionally imported from the West to China by "West-

---

[92] My thanks to Professor Funayama for his help and suggestions for Sanskrit derivations.

[93] In Indian Buddhism, *ācārya* 阿闍梨 means teacher, master, or preceptor. This is said to be an eminent monk who guides his students in conduct and sets an example. There are several types of *ācārya*: 1. A monk-*ācārya* 出家阿闍梨, who performs ordination ceremonies; 2. A master *ācārya* 教師阿闍梨, who serves as an exemplar of practice and behavior; 3. A karma-*ācārya* 羯磨阿闍梨, who gives instruction in ritual to novices; 4. A scripture-*ācārya* 受經阿闍梨, who teaches scriptures In the case of Jizu daozhe, he is presented as master of initiation (*dushi* 度師; see below), and his role would correspond to a karma-*ācārya* 羯磨阿闍梨. For the role of the *ācārya* in Buddhist ordination (Hīnāyana and Māhāyana precepts), see for instance Paul Groner, *Saichō, The Establishment of the Japanese Tendai School* (Honolulu: University of Hawai'i Press, 2000): 138–144. The connection between Jizu daozhe and the so called Acāryā Tantrism 阿吒力密教 is also worthy of mention, see above note 90.

ern monks" (*fanseng* 番僧). From the Yuan era, such "Western monks" include not only Indian but also Tibetan and Tangut monks who were called *fanseng*, *xifan seng* or *xiyu huseng*. Furthermore, as is well known, Sanskrit esoterica were in the Chinese mind linked with the Tang dynasty. It is not surprising that we find the revival of such a Tang tradition via Jizu daozhe. This figure is in fact not only related to the transfer of Indian Mt. Kukkutapada to China's Mt. Jizu but also to the transmission of Indian teachings going back to great Tang patriarchs such as Xuanzang and Amoghavajra. As we are going to see, these two patriarchs are at the center of Jizu daozhe's transmission of the *Chishi tuoluoni jing* 持世陀羅尼經. The legendary figure of Jizu daozhe and his foreign origins are symptomatic for the revival of Tang esoteric tradition and its integration in Qing Longmen Daoism. In this revival, Tibet appears to play an important role as it comes to be equated with the original source of Buddhist traditions, India. It is probably in this sense that one can interpret the reference of Jizu daozhe as Xiyu Yuezhi (a Yuezhi from the Western regions) and of his special teachings.

Jizu daozhe as Specialist of *Doufa* and Recipient of the *Chishi Tuoluoni Jing*

Regarding his special teachings, Jizu daozhe is said to be a specialist of *doufa* 斗法.[94] Although the nature of what is here called *doufa* 斗法 is not clearly explained, from various works found in the *Gu Shuyinlou cangshu* 古書隱樓藏書 one can gather that it is associated with the recitation of *dhāranī* within the so-called Jiatuo zhengzong 伽陀正宗, i.e., the Orthodox Lineage of *Gātha*.[95] According to the biography of Jizu daozhe it is linked to the compilation of the "*Dafan xiantian fanyin douzhou* 大梵先天梵音斗咒 in 10 sections amounting to 12 juan." This compilation was undertak-

---

[94] This tradition consists for the most part of liturgical texts based on mantra recitations, transcribed from the Sanskrit language. It focuses on the magical power of *dhāranī* and underlines the value of rituals. Among them is the ritual in honor of Doumu 斗母 (Mother of Dipper) or Mārīcī.

[95] See *Chishi tuoluoni jing fa, Gu Shuyinlou cangshu* 古書隱樓藏書, in *Zangwai daoshu* 藏外道書 10: 552. *Jiatuo* 伽陀 has three meanings (1) *gātha*, i.e., song; *gāthā*, i.e., metrical narrative or hymn with moral purport; (2) *agada* as adjective meaning "healthy," or as noun "antidote" (3) *gata*, arrived at, fallen into, or "in a state"; see Soothill and Hodous, *A Dictionary of Chinese Buddhist Terms* (London: Kegan Paul, Trench, Trubner and Co, 1937).

en by Min Yide after having received the transmission from Jizu daozhe. Unfortunately, in the *Gu Shuyinlou cangshu* one does not find a title such as *Dafan xiantian fanyin douzhou* but rather a series of texts that may correspond to the meaning of what is called *Dafan xiantian fanyin douzhou* 大梵先天梵音斗咒, i.e., *dhāraṇī* to the Dipper according to the Sanskrit pronunciation of the Anterior Heaven of Brahma. We know that the recitation of *dhāraṇī* or magical formulas was highly appreciated by Qianlong and his imperial family. In fact, Qianlong not only sponsored the publication of a huge amount of literary works (such as the gigantic *Siku quanshu* 四庫全書) but also supported the translation and publication of religious texts such as the Tibetan canon and commentaries on Tibetan scriptures. He also promoted the publication of an anthology of all *dhāraṇī* and *mantra* in Sanskrit from the Tibetan canon. Carefully set in Tibetan, Mongolian, Chinese and Manchu scripts, this anthology was published in 1773 in eighty volumes under the title *Yuzhi Man Han Mengu Xifan hebi dazang quanzhou* 禦製滿漢蒙古西番合璧大藏全咒. It was surely one of the most complex typographical undertakings ever attempted up to that time.[96] Beside this support for *dhāraṇī* collections, it is worthwhile to stress that texts focusing on the recitation of *dhāraṇī* were among the first scriptures to be translated in Chinese.[97] They were closely associated with Dhāraṇī Tantrism 陀羅尼密教 whose teachings were highly appreciated at the Tang court.[98] The text transmitted by Jizu daozhe is in fact attributed to the great translator Xuanzang 玄奘 (600–664) and to one of the great patriarchs of

---

[96] See David M. Farquhar, "Emperor as Bodhisattva in the Governance of the Ch'ing Empire," *Harvard Journal of Asiatic Studies* 38.1 (1978), pp. 23–24, and the photographic reproduction of this collection in Lokesh Chandra ed. *Sanskrit Texts from the Imperial Palace at Peking in the Manchurian, Chinese, Mongolian and Tibetan scripts*, Satapitaka Series, vol. 71 (New Delhi: International Academy of Indian Culture, 1966).

[97] See Chou Yi-liang, "Tantric Buddhism in China," pp.. 242–243; Yoshinobu Sakade 坂出祥伸, "Shoki mikkyō to dōkyō to no kōshō" 初期密教と道教との交渉, pp. 153–169; and Michel Strickmann, *Mantra et mandarins* (Paris: Gallimard, 1996).

[98] See Yoritomi Motohiro 頼富本宏, "Chūgoku mikkyō no nagare" 中国密教の流れ, in 中国密教, eds. Tachikawa Musashi and Yoritomi Motohiro (Tokyo: Shunkasha, 1999), pp. 15–39; in the same volume Yoritomi Motohiro, "Chūgoku mikkyō no shisōteki tokushitsu" 中国密教の思想的特質, pp. 113–140, esp. 137–139; Yoshinobu Sakade 坂出祥伸, "Shoki mikkyō to dōkyō to no kōshō" 初期密教と道教との交渉, pp. 153–169; and Hisao Inagaki, *Kūkai's Principle of Attaining Buddhahood with the Present Body* (Kyoto: Ryūkoku University, 1975).

Tang Esoteric Buddhism: Amoghavajra (Bukong 不空, 705–774).[99] It is found in the Buddhist Canon (Taishō vol. 20, Esoteric section 密教, No. 1162 [1163–1165]) under the title *Chishi Tuoluoni jing* 持世陀羅尼經 (Vasu[n]dhārādhāranī). Its original Sanskrit is still extant. There is also a Tibetan version under the title title *'phags pa nor gyi rgyun shes bya ba'i gzung* (To. 662/1007, P.341/632), but this requires further study. Because this text was associated with such important Tang figures, it was naturally also esteemed within Longmen Daoism; Min Yide published it in his YLCS along with his own Daoist commentary.

The story of the transmission of the *Chishi Tuoluoni jing* 持世陀羅尼經 (Vasu[n]dhārādhāranī) starts with the Bhagavat 薄伽梵 who conveyed such teaching to Miaoyue 妙月 (Suchandra, Tib. Dawa Sangpo). In the *Dharanijing fa* the so-called Miaoyue Changzhe figures, for instance, as a Patriarch belonging to the lineage of the Gatha Tradition which was inherited by Jizu daozhe. The figure of Suchandra, however, seems to be of little importance in Indian Buddhism. By contrast, in the Tibetan Buddhist tradition, Suchandra is none other than the King of Shambhala, the fabulous country purportedly located north of the Himalayan range. As is well known, Shambhala was a symbol of Tibetan utopia. This mythical kingdom was associated with the practice of the *Kālachakra tantra*. Suchandra is in fact the main interlocutor of the Buddha in this important *tantra* linked with one of the highest Tantric rites of initiation within the dGe lugs pa tradition.[100] Could this again have some connection with the fact that Emperor Qianlong sponsored among all Tibetan schools the dGe lugs pa and was initiated (*abhiṣeka* 灌頂) to this tradition by his State Preceptor?[101]

---

[99] See the biography of Bukong (Amoghavajra, 705–774) in Chou Yi-liang, "Tantric Buddhism in China," *Harvard Journal of Asian Studies* 8 (1944–45): 284–307.

[100] See Hopkins Jeffrey, *The Kalachakra Tantra: Rite of Initiation for the Stage of Generation* (London: Wisdom Publications, 1985); Tanaka Kimiaki 田中公明, *Chō mikkyō jirin tantora* 超密教時輪タントラ (Osaka: Tōhō, 1994); Edwin Bernbaum, *The Way to Shambhala* (Boston & London: Shambhala, 2001); and Leonard van der Kuijp, "The Mongol Imperial Family in Yuan China and Mongolia as Patrons of the Printing of Tibetan *Kālacakra* Texts." *The Central Eurasian Studies Lectures*, no. 4. Bloomington: Research Institute for Inner Asian Studies, 2004.

[101] Emperor Qianlong studied Tibetan and received the initiation by Rol pa'i rdo rje while aspiring to be recognized as the universal ruler according to the Buddhist ideal of the "wheel-turning king" (*cakravartin*); see David M. Farquhar, "Emperor as Bodhisattva in the Governance of the Ch'ing Empire," *Harvard Journal of Asiatic Studies* 38.1 (1978): 5–34; and Wang Xiangyun, "The Qing Court's Tibet Connec-

Although the association with such a renowned Tantric esoteric ordination is very unlikely, what is interesting is that both texts in possession of the so-called Master of Initiation or Tuduo Lushi Jizu daozhe were also linked with a kind of esoteric ordination or initiation. As we are going to see, within Daoist Longmen this kind of ordination came to be called *tianxian dajie* 天仙大戒. However, the role of this esoteric ordination inside the Longmen Daoism needs to be further studied, particularly with regard to the *Chishi Tuoluoni jing* (Vasu[n]dhārādhāraṇī) ritual and its liturgical transmission of Sanskrit *dhāraṇī*.[102]

---

tion: Lcang skya Rol pa'i rdo rje and the Qianlong Emperor." (Ph.D.dissertation, Harvard University, 1995).

[102] In the *Chishi tuoluoni jing* there is no mention of the link of Suchandra with Shambhala. It is interesting that when the ninth Panchen Lama (1883–1937) gave the Kalacakra initiation to Chinese and Tibetans in 1924, the Chinese term for Suchandra was Yueshan and not Miaoyue. It is also worthy of mention that in the Chinese accounts from the 1930s the name of the Suchandra related to Shambhala is Yueshan, a very literal translation from the Tibetan Zla ba bzang po; see Gray Tuttle, "Tibet as the Source of Messianic Teachings to Save Republican China," in Monica Esposito (ed.), *Images of Tibet in the 19th and 20th Centuries* (Paris: École Française d'Extrême-Orient, 2008): 303–327. The important fact, however, is that the *Chishi tuoluoni jing* 持世陀羅尼經 and the *Sanni yishi shuoshu* 三尼醫世說述序 are connected and that this link is often emphasized (see for instance the *Chishi tuoluoni jing fa guize xiaoxu* by Min Yide, *Gu Shuyinlou cangshu* 古書隱樓藏書 8b, *Zangwai daoshu* 藏外道書 10: 550; *Sanni yishi shuoshu xu* by Min Yide, *Zangwai daoshu* 藏外道書 10: 344–346). At the end of Min Yide's commentary to the *Chishi tuoluoni jing* it is stressed that both of these texts are the fruit of uninterrupted mind-to-mind transmission (*xinzong* 心宗) and are devoted to saving the world. In fact it is explained that in the great path of the *Yishi shuoshu*, "supporting the world has the same meaning as curing the world" (*Chishi tuoluoni jing zhu, Zangwai daoshu* 藏外道書 10: 557). The link between the *Chishi tuoluoni jing* and the *Sanni yishi shuoshu* is apparent in various passages; see for instance the *Chishi tuoluoni jing fa guize xiaoxu* 持世陀羅尼經法規則小序 by Min Zhenxian 閔真仙 (i.e., Min Yide 閔一得) in *Zangwai daoshu* 藏外道書 vol. 10, p. 550; and *Lü zushi sanni yishi shuoshu xu* 『呂祖師三尼醫世說述序 by Min Yide in *Zangwai daoshu* 藏外道書 vol. 10, pp. 344–346. At the end of the commentary by Min Yide on the *Chishi tuoluoni jing* (*Zangwai daoshu* 藏外道書 vol. 10, p. 577) it is stressed that these two texts are testimony for the orthodox tradition 正宗 and are devoted to supporting the world 持世. Thus, the text ends by saying "in the Great Way of healing the world, supporting the world is healing the world" 醫世之大道, 醫世即持世也. For the link between the Indian rite of the Abhiṣeka, the transmission of the Buddhist law, and the transmission of Daoist registers, see Anna Seidel, "Den'e" (*Hōbōgirin* vol. 8, 2003): 1176–77. Sanskrit *abhiṣeka* ("sprinkling" or "anointment"), in esoteric Buddhism, is a purificatory or initiatory rite in which a candidate is sprinkled with water or some other liquid, signifying a change in status. Originally, *abhiṣeka* was

Jizu daozhe as a direct disciple of Wang Changyue and recipient of the *Yishi Shuoshu*

A third and last point is that Yedaposhe alias Jizu daozhe is here presented as a direct disciple of Wang Changyue, the reformer and official promoter of Longmen's Great Precepts of the Triple Altar ordination (龍門三壇大戒) at Beijing's Baiyun guan. Jizu daozhe is said to have come to Beijing in 1660, just at the moment when Wang Changyue was performing the ordination ceremony. As we have seen above, the text states:

> In 1660 when he [Jizu daozhe] first came to the capital, he observed the *yanbo* 演缽.
>
> 順治庚子始至京師、觀光演缽。

The special term *yanbo* 演缽 may literally indicate "to perform the bowl [rite]" or "to transmit the teaching (演教) at the Bowl [Hall]." In the stone inscription attributed to Wang Changyue but dated 1706 it is mentioned, for instance, that a "bowl-hall" was built in 1440 at the Baiyun guan. It was rebuilt in 1706.[103] The expression *yanbo* 演缽 in the *Santan dajie* 三壇大戒[104] designates the teachings given by the Vinaya Master Wang Changyue during the 100 days of the ordination (開壇傳戒、戒後行持、演缽一百日). In this case, the term seems to refer to ordination training referred to as "Hall of Performing the Bowl" (*yanbotang* 演缽堂, which can be seen as the counterpart of the Buddhist "ordinands' hall")[105] that lasted one hundred days. During this period of collective seclusion the ordinands attended lectures, were trained in liturgy, and underwent severe ascetic practice. We have seen above that Wang Changyue's Daoist ordina-

---

an integral part of the ancient Indian royal consecration rite. Water from the four oceans was poured from golden jars onto the head of the seated monarch during his accession ceremony. On the relationship between the Buddhist *abhiṣeka* rite and the Daoist initiation involving transmission of the registers, see Anna Seidel, "Den'e" (*Hōbōgirin* vol. 8, 2003): 1176–77.

[103] See Oyanagi Shigeta, *Hakuunkan shi* 白雲觀志, pp. 141–142.

[104] *Daozang jiyao* 道藏輯要 vol. 24, 40b-41a.

[105] Holmes Welch, *The Practice of Chinese Buddhism*, p. 287 explains that the ordination training begins with the division of classes collectively known as "the hall of ordinands" (*xin jietang* 新戒堂). "As a period of time it lasted through the final day of ordination. As a place, it meant each of the halls in which classes 堂口 met. (...) Each hall—each class—had sixty to seventy persons. It was arranged like a meditation hall 禪堂, with sleeping platforms along the sides."

tion, modeled on Buddhist models, is known as "the Great Precepts of the Threefold Altar" (*santan dajie* 三壇大戒) or "The Great Precepts of the Triple Halls" (*santang dajie* 三堂大戒). As in the case of the Buddhist "hall of the ordinands," the term *yanbo* 演缽 may refer both to the time and place of ordination training. Furthermore, the expression *yanbo* (where *bo* 缽 means "bowl") appears connected with the idea of transmitting robe and bowl in Chan Buddhism.[106]

Returning now to our text, the passage continues:

> The Patriarch Wang Kunyang [i.e., Wang Changyue] bestowed on him [Yedaposhe] the family name Huang 黃 and the name Shouzhong 守中.
>
> 王崑陽祖贈姓曰黃、命名守中。

In the case of Jizu daozhe (Yedaposhe), it seems that he only observed Wang Changyue's ordination ceremony without receiving the transmission of the Great Precepts of Celestial Immortals (*tianxian dajie* 天仙大戒). However, Wang Changyue recognized Yedaposhe as a sinicized figure and gave him both a Chinese name (Huang 黃) and a lineage name 派名 (Shouzhong 守中 or "Guardian of the Center"). Finally, Yedaposhe alias Jizu daozhe was integrated into the Longmen lineage (*zongpai* 宗派) as the eighth Long-

---

[106] On the meaning of transmitting the robe (and the bowl) in Chan / Zen Buddhism see Anna Seidel, "Den'e" (*Hōbōgirin* vol. 8, 2003): 1171–78. For Daoism, see for instance the article Chen Yaoting 陳耀庭, "Quanzhen pai jielü" 全真派戒律, *Daojiao wenhua ziliaoku* 道教文化資料庫 (http://www.taoism.org.hk/religious-activites&rituals/religious-discipline/pg5-2-3.htm) where the ordinands are portrayed as having received the bowl (*jiezi shou bo* 戒子受缽). Finally, one finds also another expression related to the bowl: *zuobo* 坐缽 or "sitting around the bowl-clepsydra." This is connected with the the Quanzhen collective meditation in which the bowl was used as clepsydra timer. This was a particularity of Quanzhen communities; see *Tianhuang zhidao taiqing yuce* 天皇至道太清玉冊 (DZ1483, fasc. 1109–1111, chap. 5). On this meditation see J. Boltz, *A Survey of Taoist Literature*, 239 & note 679; Vincent Goossaert, "La création du taoïsme moderne. L'ordre Quanzhen," Ph. D. diss. (Paris: École Pratique des Hautes Études, 1997): 220–258; and Mori Yuria 森由理亞, "Mingdai Quanzhendao yu zuobo – yi zuobo he neidan de guanxi wei zhongxin" 明代全真道與坐缽 – 以坐缽和內丹的關係為中心, in Lu Guolong 盧國龍 (ed.), *Quanzhen hongdao ji* 全真弘道集 (Hong Kong: Qingsong chubanshe 青松出版社, 2004): 126–142. Various documents mention the existence of Quanzhen halls in which this meditation was performed under the name of Zuobo tang 坐缽堂 (Hall of Sitting around the Bowl-clepsydra). However, as Mori emphasizes, the bowl in Daoism is also a symbol of the alchemical measure of time.

men patriarch 龍門祖師 and founder 開祖 of the Mount Jizu branch in Yunnan, the Xizhu xinzong 西竺心宗 (Heart Lineage of West India). It was only later, after 130 years that, according to Wang Changyue's prediction, he received the ultimate ordination. This happened thanks to the transmission of the Great Precepts text 大戒書 which Min Yide brought to him. In exchange, Min Yide obtained from Jizu daozhe the Longmen xizhu xinzong's esoteric ordination.

An interesting mention of *Yishi shuoshu* 醫世說述 and its connection with the Beijing Baiyun guan's ordination ceremony is found in the *Huangji xianjing* 皇極仙經:[107]

> It was between the Shunzhi 順治 [1644–1661] and Kangxi 康熙 [1662–1722] eras that the Vinaya Ancestor [Wang Changyue] opened five times the Hall for Transmitting the Bowl 五開演缽堂 and conveyed the Three Great Precepts of the Supreme Lord (Taishang sandajie 太上三大戒). The disciples numbered more than 3,000. The transmission of the precepts, robe and bowl 傳戒衣缽[108] included the *Lüzu yishi shuoshu* 呂祖醫世說述, more than 3,000 copies of which were obtained by the ordinands 戒子. How could this fail to be a great enaction of the true Dao? Furthermore, the Hall of Precepts of the Vinaya Ancestor 律祖戒堂 was opened at the capital's Baiyun guan. At that time Buddhist and Daoist ordinations needed to be authorized by imperial edict and could not take place in private. What was transmitted included the code 律, scriptures 書 and manuscript scrolls 手卷.

> (王崑陽) 律祖於順治康熙間五開演缽堂、付授太上三大戒。弟子三千餘人。傳戒衣缽、有呂祖醫世說述、則得受者有三千餘部。豈非真道之大行乎。況律祖戒堂、開在京邸白雲觀。爾時佛道兩宗傳戒、非奉旨不得私開。其所傳、有律有書有手卷。

---

[107] *Gu Shuyinlou cangshu* 古書隱樓藏書, in *Zangwai daoshu* 藏外道書 10:381.

[108] The full one-hundred day ordination of the triple platform 百日圓滿三壇大戒. In Chan Buddhism, one finds the expression *chuan yibo* 傳衣缽, "transmitting robe and bowl," or simply *chuanyi* 傳衣, "transmitting the robe"; see Anna Seidel, "Den'e" (*Hōbōgirin* vol. 8, 2003): 1171–78. On the transmission of precepts at Beijing's Baiyunguan, see also Yoshioka, *Hakuunkan shi* 白雲觀志, pp. 70–73.

The text continues:

> Three generations after the Vinaya patriarch [Wang Changyue], this way [of transmission of precepts] was extinct. In the ordination class (lit., the class of transmitting the bowl) that was opened during the present Jiaqing era 嘉慶 (1796–1820), the precept text by Patriarch Qiu [Chuji] 邱祖戒本 is no longer transmitted. What is transmitted in recent times can be found in the *Jingming zongjiao lu* 淨明宗教錄,[109] but this is quite different from what Patriarch Qiu transmitted. The previous generations of masters from my own mountain [Mt. Jingai], though observing the precepts, had burned them [the texts transmitted by Patriarch Qiu].[110] Though transcribed copies of scriptures survived, the scrolls and code 卷律 were lost.
>
> 律祖三傳而道遂絕。今嘉慶間所開演缽、邱祖戒本失傳。近所傳訪諸淨明宗教錄、與邱祖所傳、小同而大異也。我山先輩、亦守戒焚之。書則錄本倖存、而卷律亡矣。

The text thus claims that the ordination ceremonies, which in the past had taken place under the guidance of Wang Changyue, were no more performed in their true form because the precept code 律 and manuscript scrolls 手卷 had been lost. Fortunately, the memory of such genuine ordination survived in the Longmen tradition of Mount Jingai. Thanks to the *Yishi shuoshu*—the Great Precept scripture 大戒書 transmitted in Wang's time during the official ordination ceremony at Beijing's Baiyun guan—the Longmen Jingai branch found itself uniquely qualified to continue the tradition of orthodox ordinations.

---

[109] This text is found in DZJY weiji 4, vol. 12.

[110] The text explained that Vinaya's heirs burned the texts if they failed to find qualified successors to transmit them to.

CONCLUSION

As the biography of Jizu daozhe shows, the performance of the ordination procedure is very simple: it consists of displaying the image of the patriarch Wang Changyue and prostrating sincerely in front of it. Thanks to the possession of the *Yishi shuoshu* 醫世說述, the direct transmission of precepts restablished by Wang Changyue could continue. However, this transmission seems newly to take place in private and not in the Hall of Performing the Bowl 演缽堂. This kind of ordination appears to be similar to the conferral of the Bodhisattva precepts in Buddhism. Such precepts in fact could be administered not only by a qualified teacher during an ordination ceremony but also by the candidate himself through a simple vow in front of an image of the Buddha. Could this kind of ordination, a Daoist counterpart of the Bodhisattva precepts in Buddhism, indicate how the Longmen tradition of Mt. Jingai transmitted its own ordinations? Or does it express the will of Longmen Jingai patriarchs to restore private ordinations, or to legitimize such private ordinations in opposition to the standardized ordination based on texts like the *Jingming zongjiao lu* 淨明宗教錄? In contrast with public ordinations that are said to have been held during the Jiaqing era, the Longmen branch of Mount Jingai claims to have maintained the genuine transmission of the supreme ordination 無上大戒 —the Great Precepts of the Celestial Immortals 天仙大戒—based on the transmission of the *Yishi shuoshu*. It is thanks to this text that Jizu daozhe received the Longmen ordination; and in exchange Min Yide received the Tantric transmission of *doufa* based on *dhāraṇī*. It is just in this reciprocal exchange between Min Yide and the legendary figure of Jizu daozhe that one may find an explanation for the establishment of the so-called Longmen xizhu xinzong as a symbol of the "Interaction of Daoism and Tantrism during the Qing Dynasty." In the eyes of Min Yide, the Longmen tradition was uniquely capable of restoring the genuine transmission of the Dao linked to Qiu Chuji. The legitimacy of Longmen and its transmission scenario forms the background of Min's purported encounter—at the archetypal Mt. Jizu site loaded with transmission symbolism—with a mythical figure connected both to age-old "West Indian" Tantric traditions and to Qiu Chuji, Wang Changyue, the Baiyun guan, resulting in an impressive display of Longmen's will to orthodoxy.

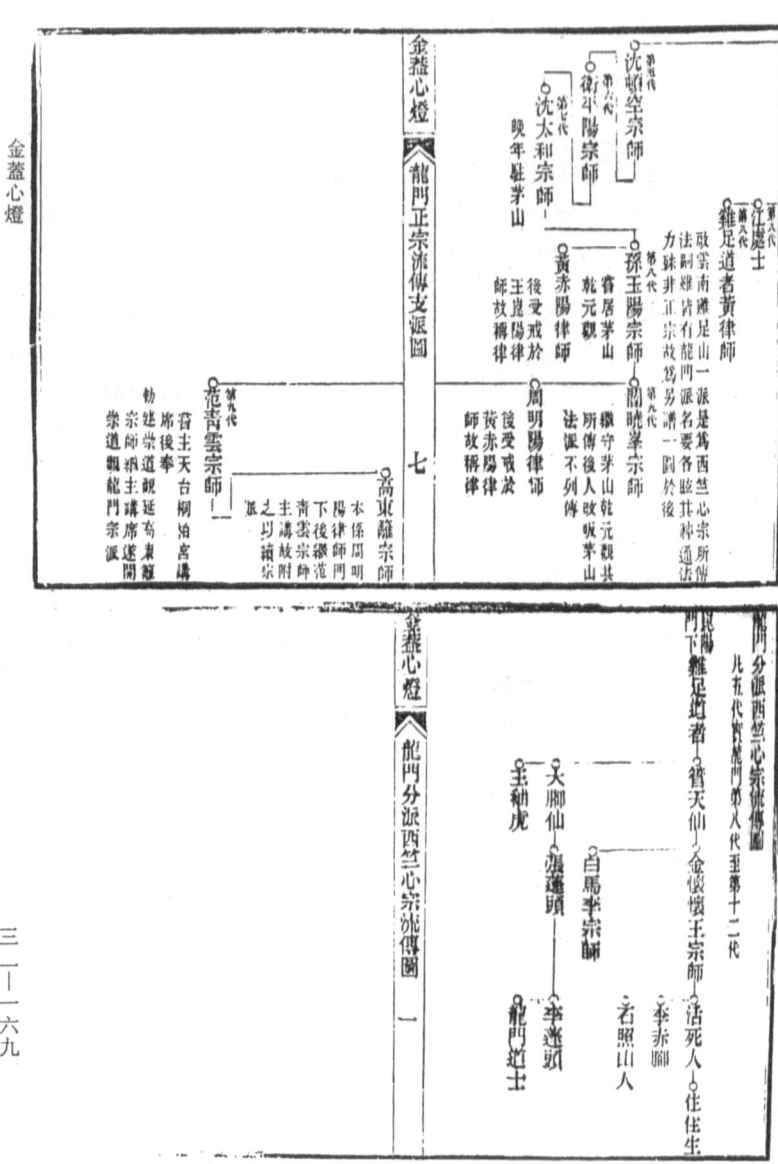

Fig. 20: Genealogical chart of Longmen; Jizu daozhe and his special Longmen lineage 龍門分派西竺心宗 in Min Yide's *Jingai xindeng* 金蓋心燈

REFERENCES

Abbrevations

BYGZ   *Baiyun guan zhi (Hakuunkan shi)* 白雲觀志 [A Monograph on the White Clouds Abbey], by Oyanagi Shigeta 小柳司氣太. Tokyo: Tōhō bunka gakuin Tōkyō kenkyūjo, 1934.

DJYL   *Changchun daojiao yuanliu* 長春道教源流 [Origins and Development of the Daoist Teachings of (Qiu) Changchun 1879], by Chen Minggui 陳銘珪 (1824–1881). In *Zangwai daoshu* 藏外道書 31:1–157.

DTYL   *Daotong yuanliu* 道統源流 [Origins and Development of Orthodox Daoism] by Yan Liuqian 嚴六謙 (*hao*: Zhuangyan jushi 莊嚴居士). Wuxi: Zhonghua yinshuju, 1929.

DZJY   *Chongkan Daozang jiyao* 重刊道藏輯要 [Reedited Epitome of the Daoist Canon] by Yan Yonghe 閻永和, Peng Hanran 彭瀚然 and He Longxiang 賀龍驤. Chengdu: Erxian an 二仙庵, 1906. Reprint in 25 vols. Taipei: Xinwenfeng, 1977.

DZXB   *Daozang xubian* 道藏續編 [Supplementary Collection of the Daoist Canon] 4 vols., by Min Yide 閔一得(1758–1836). Wuxing 吳興: Jingai shan cangban 金蓋山藏板, 1834. Typeset and printed by Ding Fubao 丁福保 (*zi*: Shou yi zi 守一子 1874–1952) as *Daozang xubian chuji* 道藏續編初集. Shanghai: Yixue shuju. Repr. Beijing: Haiyang 1989.

JGXD   *(Chongkan) Jingai xindeng* 金蓋心燈 (Re-edition of the Transmission of the Lamp of Mind from Mt. Jingai), 10 vols., by Min Yide (1758–1836). Wuxing: Yunchao, Gu Shuyinlou cangban, 1876 (1st ed. 1821). Repr. in

	Zangwai daoshu 藏外道書 31 and *Daojiao wenxian* 道教文獻, ed. by Tu Jiexiang 杜潔祥 (Taipei: Danqing tushu) 1983, vols. 10- 11.
T	*Taishō shinshū daizōkyō* 大正新修大藏經 [Buddhist Canon of the Taishō Era], 100 vols. Tokyo: Taishō shinshū daizōkyō kankōkai, 1975.
YLCS	*Gu Shuyinlou cangshu* 古書隱樓藏書 [Collection from the Ancient Hidden Pavilion of Books], 14 vols., by Min Yide (1758–1836). Wuxing: Jingai Chunyang gong cangban, 1904. Repr. in *Zangwai daoshu* 藏外道書 10:150–721.
ZWDS	*Zangwai daoshu* 藏外道書 [Daoist Books Outside the Canon] edited by Hu Daojing 胡道靜 et al. Chengdu: Bashu shushe, 1992 (vol: 1–20); 1994 (vol. 21–36).

Primary sources

Biyuan tanjing 碧苑壇經 [Platform Sūtra of the Jade Garden]. Transmitted by Wang Changyue 王常月 (Kunyang 崑陽, ?-1680), compiled by Shi Shouping 施守平 and revised by Min Yide 閔一得 (1758–1836). In YLCS (reprinted in *Zangwai daoshu* 藏外道書 10).

Changchun zhenren xiyouji 長春真人西遊記 [Report on the Journey of the Adept Changchun to the West]. 1228. DZ 1429, fasc. 1056. By Li Zhichang 李志常.

Chuzhen jielü 初真戒律 [Code of Initial Precepts for Perfection]. 1656. By Wang Changyue 王常月 (?-1680). DZJY 24 *zhangji* 張集 7 (reprinted in *Zangwai daoshu* 藏外道書 vol. 12: 13–31).

Chishi tuoluonijing 持世陀羅尼經 [Vasu(n)dhārādhāranī]. T. vol. 20, no. 1162 (Nos. 1163–1165). Translated by Xuanzang 玄奘 (600–664).

Chishi tuoluonijing fa 持世陀羅尼經法 [Vasu(n)dhārādhāranī ritual] . It includes the *Foshuo chishi tuoluonijing* 佛說持世陀羅尼經 based on T. vol. 20, no.1162, and the ritual connected to it. Attributed to Tuluo lüshi 圖多律師 (i.e., Jizu daozhe 雞足道者) and transcribed by Min Zhenxian 閔真仙 (i.e., Min Yide 閔一得). Postface by Min

Yide (1834). In YLCS (reprinted in *Zangwai daoshu* 藏外道書 10: 547–558).

Chishi tuoluonijing zhu 持世陀羅尼經注 [Commentary on the Vasu(n) dhārādhāraṇī]. Translated by Xuanzang 玄奘. Commented by Faseng Jilian 髮僧際連 (i.e., Min Yide 閔一得). In YLCS (reprinted in *Zangwai daoshu* 藏外道書 10: 559–578).

Daojiao wenxian 道教文獻 [Daoist Literature], ed. by Tu Jiexiang 杜潔祥. Taipei: Danqing tushu 丹青圖書, 1983.

Du Lü zushi sanni yishi shuoshu guankui 讀呂祖師三尼醫世說述管窺 [A Personal Reading of the Explanations of the Three Sages' Doctrine of Healing the World by Patriarch Lü]. By Min Yide 閔一得 (1758–1836). Postface (1828) by Min Yide. In DZXB and YLCS (reprinted in *Zangwai daoshu* 藏外道書 10).

Daomen gongke 道門功課 [Liturgy for Daoists]. Compiled by Liu Shouyuan 柳守元 (fl. 1798). DZJY 23 *zhangji* 張集 1.

Daotong yuanliu zhi 道統源流志 [Origins and Development of Orthodox Daoism]. Compiled by by Yan Liuqian 嚴六謙, *hao*: Zhuangyan jushi 莊嚴居士. Huzhou 湖州: Wuxi Zhonghua yinshuaju 無錫中華印刷局, 1929.

Erlan xinhua 二懶心話 [Heart-to-Heart Dialogue Between the Two Leisurely (Masters)]. By Min Yide 閔一得. Postface (1818) by Min Yide. In DZXB and YLCS (reprinted in *Zangwai daoshu* 藏外道書 10).

Ganshui xian yuanlu 甘水仙源錄 [Record of the Immortals from the Sweet Water (River)]. By Li Daoqian 李道謙. 1289. DZ 973, fasc. 611–613.

Longmen xinfa 龍門心法 [Core Teachings of the Longmen]. 1663. Transmitted by Wang Changyue 王常月 (?-1680) and compiled by Zhan Tailin 詹太林 and Tang Qingshan 唐清善. *Zangwai daoshu* 藏外道書 6: 727–785.

Longmen zhengzong jueyun benzhi daotong xinchuan 龍門正宗覺雲本支道統薪傳 [Uninterrupted Transmission of the Orthodox Teaching in the Right Lineage of the Longmen Jueyun Branch]. 1927. Lu Yongming 陸永銘. *Zangwai daoshu* 藏外道書 31: 427–446.

Lü zushi sanni yishi shuoshu 呂祖師三尼醫世說述 [Explanations of the Three Sages' Doctrine of Healing the World (revealed via spirit writing) by Patriarch Lü]. Entitled by Huang Chiyang 黃赤陽 (1595–1673), edited by Tao Shi'an 陶石庵 (?-1692), commented by Min Yide and corrected by Shen Yangyi 沈陽一. Preface (1664) by Tao Shi'an and Preface (1828) by Min Yide. In DZXB and YLCS (reprinted in *Zangwai daoshu* 藏外道書 10).

Lü zushi sanni yishi gongjue 呂祖師三尼醫世功訣 [Practices and Formulae on the Three Sages' Doctrine of Healing the World by Patriarch Lü]. Transmitted by Shen Yibing 沈一炳 (1708–1786), newly recorded and annotated by Min Yide. In DZXB and YLCS (reprinted in *Zangwai daoshu* 藏外道書 10).

Min Lanyun xiansheng zhuan 閔懶雲先生傳 [Biography of Master Min Lanyun (Yide)]. By Yan Duanshu 晏端書. In *Jingai xindeng's* 金蓋心燈 Min zhuan fu 閔傳附.

Min Lanyun xiansheng zhuan 閔懶雲先生傳 [Biography of Master Min Lanyun (Yide)]. By Yang Weikun 揚維崑. In *Jingai xindeng's* 金蓋心燈 Min zhuan fu 閔傳附.

Min Lanyun xiansheng zhuan 閔懶雲先生傳 [Biography of Master Min Lanyun (Yide)]. By Shen Bingcheng 沈秉成 (1821–1824). In *Jingai xindeng's* 金蓋心燈 Min zhuan fu 閔傳附.

Sandong zhongjie wen 三洞眾戒文 [Comprehensive Prescriptions of the Three Caverns]. By Zhang Wanfu 張萬福 (fl. 713). DZ 178, fasc. 77.

Santan yuanman tianxian dajie lüeshuo 三壇圓滿天仙大戒略說 [Abstract of the Great Precepts of the Celestial Immortals for Achieving the Threefold Altar Ordination]. Compiled by Liu Shouyuan 柳守元 (fl. 1798). DZJY 24 zhangji 張集 7 (reprinted in *Zangwai daoshu* 藏外道書 12).

Shangqing dongzhen zhihui guanshen dajie wen 上清洞真智慧觀身大戒文 [Great Rules of Wisdom in Self-Examination]. Six Dynasties. DZ 1364, fasc. 1039.

Taishang Laojun jiejing 太上老君戒經 [Commandments of the Most High Lord Lao]. Early Tang. DZ 784, fasc. 562.

Xiuzhen biannan qianhou bian canzheng 修真辯難前後編參証 [Annotations to the *Debate on the Cultivation of Perfection* in Two Sections]. By Liu Yiming 劉一明 (1734–1821). Commented and verified by Min Yide. Postface (1829) by Min Yide and Postface by Liu Yiming.

Xuhuang tianzun Chuzhen shijie wen 皇天尊初真十戒文 [Text of the Ten Rules for the Initial Stage of Perfection, (Spoken) by the Heavenly Worthy Xuhuang]. DZ 180, fasc. 77.

Yin zhenren Donghua zhengmai huangji hepi zhengdao xianjing 尹真人東華正脈皇極闔闢證道仙經 [Immortals' Scripture of the Perfected Yin Testifying to the Path of Opening and Closing the Sovereign Ultimate according to the Orthodox Lineage of the Eastern Efflorescence], abbr. *Huangji hepi xianjing* 皇極闔闢仙經, in 3 *juan* and 10 chapters. Manuscript of the Qingyang gong 青羊宮 (Black Sheep Palace), Chengdu; corrected by Min Yide; Preface (1831) and Postface by Min Yide. In DZXB and YLCS (reprinted in *Zangwai daoshu* 藏外道書 10).

Zhongji jie 中極戒 [Intermediary Precepts]. DZJY 24 *zhangji* 張集 7 (reprinted in *Zangwai daoshu* 藏外道書 12).

Selective Thematic Bibliography

Tibetan Buddhism and the Qing Court

Berger, Patricia. 1994. "Preserving the Nation: The Political Uses of Tantric Art in China." In Marsha Weidner (ed.), *Latter Days of the Law: Images of Chinese Buddhism, 850–1850*: 89–123. Honolulu: University of Hawai'i Press.

———. 2003. *Empire of Emptiness: Buddhist Art and Political Authority in Qing China*. Honolulu: University of Hawaii Press, 2003.

Bosson, James E. 1969. *A Treasury of Aphoristic Jewels: The Subhasitaratnanidhi of Sa Skya Pandita in Tibetan and Mongolian*. Bloomington: Indiana University.

Chandra, Lokesh, ed. 1966. *Sanskrit Texts from the Imperial Palace at Peking in the Manchurian, Chinese, Mongolian and Tibetan Scripts*, Satapitaka Series, vol. 71. New Delhi: International Academy of Indian Culture.

Charleux, Isabelle. 2002. "Les 'lamas' vus de Chine: fascination et répulsion." *Extrême-Orient Extrême-Occident* 24 (October 2002):133–151

Chayet Anne. 1985. *Les Temples de Jehol et leurs modèles tibétains*. Paris: Editions Recherche sur les civilisations.

Farquhar, David. 1978. "Emperor as Bodhisattva in the Governance of the Ch'ing Empire." *Harvard Journal of Asiatic Studies* 38.1 (1978): 5–34.

Franke, Herbert. 1994. *China under Mongol Rule*. Aldershot: Brookfield.

———. 1996. *Chinesischer und tibetischer Buddhismus im China der Yuanzeit: drei Studien*. München: Kommission für Zentralasiatische Studien, Bayerische Akademie der Wissenschaften.

Hasebe, Yūkei 長谷幽蹊. 1993. *Minshin bukkyō kyōdanshi kenkyū* 明清佛教團史研究, 155–173. Kyoto: Dōhōsha 同朋舍.

Henss, Michael. 2001. "The Bodhisattva-Emperor: Tibeto-Chinese Portraits of Sacred and Secular Rule in the Qing Dynasty, Part 1." *Oriental Art* 47.3 (2001): 2–16.

———. 2001. "The Bodhisattva-Emperor: Tibeto-Chinese Portraits of Sacred and Secular Rule in the Qing Dynasty, Part 2." *Oriental Art* 47.5 (2001): 71–83.

Ho, Chuimei, and Bennet Bronson. 2004. *Splendors of China's Forbidden City. The Glorious Reign of Emperor Qianlong*. London: Merrell.

Hong, Dichen 洪滌塵. 1979. "Qingshi dui Xizang de zhengjiao ce lüe" 清時對西藏的政教策略 [Religious politics of the Qing toward Tibet]. In Zhang Matao 張曼濤 (ed.), *Hanzang fojiao guanxi yanjiu* 漢藏佛教關係研究 [Studies on the relationship between Chinese and Tibetan Buddhism], 146–172. Taipei: Dacheng wenhua.

Kam, Tak Sing. 1994. "Manchu-Tibetan Relations In The Early Seventeenth Century: A Reappraisal." Ph.D. diss., Harvard University.

Kolmas, Josef. 1967. *Tibet and Imperial China. A Survey of Sino-Tibetan Relations up to the End of the Manchu Dynasty in 1912*. Canberra: Australian National University.

Lessing, Ferdinand (in collaboration with Gosta Montell). 1942. *Yung-ho-kung: An Iconography of the Lamaist Cathedral in Peking with Notes on Lamaist Mythology and Cult*. Stockholm.

Petech, Luciano. 1972. *China and Tibet in the Early 18th Century*. Leiden: Brill, 1972 (1st ed. 1950).

———. 1990. *Central Tibet and the Mongols: The Yuan–Sa-skya period of Tibetan History*. Rome: Istituto italiano per il Medio ed Estremo Oriente.

Rockhill, W. W. 1910. "The Dalai Lamas of Lhasa and their Relations with the Manchu Emperors of China 1644–1908," *T'oung Pao* 2.11(1910): 1–104.

Schulemann, Günther. 1958. *Die Geschichte der Dalai-Lamas*. Leipzig: Otto Harrassowitz, 1958.

Shen, Weirong 沈衛榮. 2004. "Magic Power, Sorcery and Evil Spirits: The Image of Tibetan Monks in Chinese Literature during the Yuan Dynasty," in *The Relationship between Religion and State (chos srid zung 'brel) in Traditional Tibet*, ed. Christoph Cuppers. Bhairahawa: Lumbini International Research Institute, 2004):189–228. Chinese version in *Hanxue yanjiu* 漢學研究 [Chinese Studies] 21/2 (2003):219–247.

Tucci, Giuseppe. 1980. *Tibetan Painted Scrolls*. Roma: Libreria dello stato, 1949. Reprint Kyoto: Rinsen.

Tuttle, Gray. 2006. "Tibetan Buddhsim at Ri bo rtse lnga / Wutai shan in Modern Times." *Journal of the International Association of Tibetan Studies* 2 (August 2006):1–35.

Wang, Xiangyun. 1995. *Tibetan Buddhism at the Court of Qing: The Life and Work of lCang skya Rol pa'i rdo rje*. Ph.D.dissertation, Harvard University.

Wang, Xiangyun. 2000. "The Qing Court's Tibet Connection: Lcang skya Rol pa'i rdo rje and the Qianlong Emperor." *Harvard Journal of Asiatic Studies* 60, no. 1 (June 2000): 125–63.

Welch, Holmes. 1967. *The Practice of Chinese Buddhism 1900–1950*. Cambridge, MA: Harvard University Press.

Yu, Benyuan 於本源. 1999. *Qingwangchao de zongjiao zhengce* 清王朝的宗教政策 [Religious politics of the Qing court]. Beijing: Shehui kexueyuan (especially pp. 117–148).

Zahiruddin, Ahmad. 1970. *Sino-Tibetan Relations in the Seventeenth Century*. Roma: Istituto italiano per il Medio ed Estremo Oriente.

Zhou, Shujia 周叔迦. 2000. *Qingdai fojiao shiliao jigao* 清代佛教史料輯稿 [Collected articles on historical sources of Buddhism during the Qing dynasty]. Taipei : Xinwenfeng (especially pp. 91–104 and 303–380).

Tantrism in China and its Relationship with Daoism

Bernbaum, Edwin. 2001. *The Way to Shambhala*. Boston & London: Shambhala.

Chou Yi-liang. 1944–45. "Tantric Buddhism in China." *Harvard Journal of Asian Studies* 8 (1944–45): 241–332.

Eliade, Mircea. 1954. *Le Yoga, Immortalité et liberté*. Paris: Payot.

Hopkins Jeffrey. 1985. *The Kalachakra tantra: rite of initiation for the stage of generation*. London: Wisdom publications.

Kapstein, Matthew, ed. 2009. *Buddhism Between Tibet and China*. Somerville: Wisdom Publications.

Needham, Joseph. 1986. "Chinese Physiological Alchemy (*Nei Tan*) and the Indian Yoga, Tantric and Hathayoga Systems." In Needham, Joseph, *Science and Civilisation in China*, vol. V: 5, 257–288. Cambridge: Cambridge University Press.

Sakade, Yoshinobu 坂出祥伸. 1999. "Shoki mikkyō to dōkyō to no kōshō" 初期密教と道教との交渉 (The early relation between Tantrism and Daoism). In *Chūgoku mikkyō* 中国密教 (Chinese Tantrism), ed. by Musashi Tachikawa 武藏立川 and Motohiro Yoritomi 本宏賴富, 153–169. Tokyo: Shunkasha.

Strickmann, Michel. 1986. *Mantras et mandarins — Le bouddhisme tantrique en Chine*. Paris: Gallimard.

Tanaka, Kimiaki 田中公明. 1994. *Chō mikkyō jirin tantora* 超密教時輪タントラ. Osaka: Tōhō.

van der Kuijp, Leonard. 2004. "The Mongol Imperial Family in Yuan China and Mongolia as Patrons of the Printing of Tibetan *Kālacakra* Texts." *The Central Eurasian Studies Lectures*, no. 4. Bloomington: Research Institute for Inner Asian Studies.

Yang Xuezheng 楊學政 et al. (eds.). 1999. *Yunnan zongjiao shi* 雲南宗教史. Kunming: Yunnan renmin.

Yoritomi, Motohiro 賴富本宏. 1999. "Chūgoku mikkyō no nagare" 中国密教の流れ [The current of Tantrsim in China]. In Tachikawa Musashi 立川武藏 and Yoritomi Motohiro (eds.), *Chūgoku mikkyō* 中国密教 [Chinese Tantrism], 15–39. Tokyo: Shunkasha.

———. 1999. "Chūgoku mikkyō no shisōteki tokushitsu" 中国密教の思想的特質 [Ideological Characteristics of Chinese Tantrism]. In Tachikawa Musashi 立川武藏 and Yoritomi Motohiro (eds.), *Chūgoku mikkyō* 中国密教 [Chinese Tantrism], 113–140. Tokyo: Shunkasha.

Xiao Dengfu 蕭登福. 1993. *Daojiao yu mizong* 道教與密宗 [Daoism and Tantrism]. Taipei: Xinwen feng.

Qing Daoism and Longmen

Chen, Bing 陳兵. 1988. "Qingdai Quanzhen Longmen pai de zhongxing" 清代全真龍門派的中興 [The Qing dynasty's renewal of the Quanzhen Longmen]. *Shijie zongjiao yanjiu* 世界宗教研究 2 (1988): 84–96.

———. 1991. "Ming Qing daojiao" 明清道教 [Ming-Qing Daoism]. In Mou Zhongjian 牟鐘鑑 (ed.), *Daojiao tonglun* 道教通論 [A General Discussion of Daoism], 551–579. Jinan: Wenlu,.

Esposito, Monica. 1993. "La Porte du Dragon — L'école Longmen du Mont Jin'gai et ses pratiques alchimiques d'après le *Daozang xubian* (Suite au canon taoïste)." Ph.D. dissertation, Université de Paris VII, 1993.

———. 1997. *L'alchimia del soffio*. Roma: Ubaldini.

———. 2000. "Daoism in the Qing (1644–1911)." In Livia Kohn (ed.), *Daoism Handbook*, 623–658. Leiden: Brill, 2000. {Revised edition here above, Chapter 1}.

———. 2001. "Longmen Taoism in Qing China: Doctrinal Ideal and Local Reality." *Journal of Chinese Religion*. 29 (2001):191–231. {Revised and augmented edition here above, Chapter 3}.

———. 2004. "The Longmen School and its Controversial History during the Qing Dynasty." In John Lagerwey (ed.), *Religion and Chinese Society: The Transformation of a Field*, 621–698. Hong Kong: École française d'Extrême-Orient & Chinese University of Hong Kong. {Revised edition here above, Chapter 2}.

Gai, Jianmin 蓋建民. 2003. "Cong 'jiushi' dao 'yishi'" 從救世到醫世 [From 'rescuing the world' to 'healing the world']. In Guo Wu 郭武 (ed.), *Daojiao jiaoyi yu xiandai shehui* 道教教義與現代社會, 194–209. Shanghai: Shanghai Guji.

Goossaert, Vincent. 2004. "The Quanzhen Clergy, 1700–1950." In John Lagerwey (ed.), *Religion and Chinese Society: The Transformation of a Field*. Hong Kong: École française d'Extrême-Orient & Chinese University of Hong Kong.

Igarashi, Kenryū 五十嵐賢隆. 1938. *Taiseikyū shi* 太清宮志 [Gazetteer of the Palace of Great Purity]. Tokyo: Kokushō kankōkai.

Li, Yangzheng 李養正. 2003. *Xinbian Beijing Baiyuanguan zhi* 新編北京白雲觀志 [Newly compiled Monograph on the White Clouds Abbey in Beijing]. Beijing: Zongjiao wenhua.

Marsone, Pierre. 1999. "Le Baiyun guan de Pékin: épigraphie et histoire." *Sanjiao wenxian* 3 (1999):73–136.

Min, Zhiting 閔智亭. 1990. *Daojiao yifan* 道教儀範 [Patterns of Daoist rites]. Beijing: Zhongguo daojiao xueyuan.

Mori, Yuria 森由利亞. 1994. "Zenshinkyō ryūmonha keifu kō" 全真教龍門派系譜考 [A study on the lineage of the Longmen school of Complete Perfection heritage]. In Dōkyō bunka kenkyūkai 道教文化研究会 (ed.), *Dōkyō bunka e no tenbō* 道教文化への展望 [Observations on Chinese culture], 181–211. Tokyo: Hirakawa 平川.

———. 1999. "Ryo Dōhin to Zenshin kyō: Shinchō koshū kingai san no jirei o chūshin ni" 呂洞賓と全真教-清朝湖州金蓋山の事例を仲心に [Lü Dongbin and the Quanzhen: An example at Mt. Jingai in Huzhou during the Qing dynasty]. In Noguchi Tetsurō 野口鉄郎

(ed.), *Kōza Dōkyō daiichi kan: Dōkyō no kamigami to kyōten* 講座道教弟一卷:道教の神々と経典 [Daoist Lectures, vol. 1: Daoist gods and sacred scriptures], 242–264. Tokyo: Yūzan kaku.

———. 2002. "Identity and Lineage: The *Taiyi jinhua zongzhi* and the Spirit writing Cult to Patriarch Lü in Qing China." In Livia Kohn & Harold D. Roth (eds.), *Daoist Identity: History, Lineage, and Ritual*, 168–187. Honolulu: University of Hawaii Press.

Mou, Zhongjian 牟鐘鑒 & Zhang Jian 張踐. 2000. *Zhongguo zongjiao tongshi* 中國宗教通史 [General history of Chinese religion]. 2 vols. Beijing: Shehui kexue.

Oyanagi, Shigeta 小柳司氣太. 1934. *Hakuunkan shi* 白雲觀志. Tokyo: Tōhō bunka gakuin Tōkyō kenkyūjo.

Qing, Xitai 卿希泰 (ed.). 1994. *Zhongguo daojiao* 中國道教 [Chinese Daoism], 4 vols. Shanghai: Zhishi.

———. 1996. *Zhongguo daojiao shi* 中國道教史 [History of Chinese Daoism]. 4 vols. Chengdu: Sichuan renmin.

Ren, Jiyu 任繼愈 (ed.). 1990. *Zhongguo daojiao shi* 中國道教史 [History of Chinese Daoism]. Shanghai: Shanghai renmin.

Tang, Dachao 唐大潮. 1985. "Ming-Qing zhi ji daojiao sanjiao heyi sixiang de lilun biaoxian luelun 明清之際道教三教合一思想的理論表現略論" (Brief presentation of the syncretic theory of the three teachings in Ming-Qing Daoism). *Shijie zongjiao yanjiu* 世界宗教研. 3: 87–95.

Wang, Zhizhong 王志忠. 1995. "Quanzhen jiao Longmen pai qiyuan lunkao" 全真教龍門派起源論考 [A Study on the Origin of the Quanzhen's Longmen]. *Zongjiao xue yanjiu* 宗教學研究 4 (1995): 9–13.

———. 1995. "Lun Mingmo Qingchu Quanzhen jiao 'zhongxing' de chengyin" 論明末清初全真教中興的成因 [On contributing factors to the 'revival' of Quanzhen between the end of Ming and the beginning of Qing]. *Zongjiao xue yanjiu* 宗教學研究 3 (1995): 32–38.

———. 2000. *Ming-qing Quanzhen jiao lungao* 明清全真論稿 [Articles on the Quanzhen of the Ming and Qing dynasties]. Chengdu: Basu shushe.

Yoshioka, Yoshitoyo 吉岡義豊. 1970. *Eisei e no negai: Dōkyō* 永生への願い: 道教 [The Quest for Eternal Life: Daoism]. Kyoto: Tankōsha, 1970.

———. 1975. *Dōkyō no jittai* 道教の実態 [Daoism today]. Kyoto: Hōyū shoten.

———. 1979. "Taoist Monastic Life." In Holmes Welch & Anna Seidel (eds.), *Facets of Taoism*, 229–252. New Haven and London: Yale University Press.

Zhang, Tianzhi 張天志 & Sun Tie 孫鐵 (eds.). 1991. *Daojiao shi ziliao* 道教史資料 [Daoist historical sources]. Shanghai: Shanghai Guji.

Comprehensive Bibliography

Primary Sources

Baiyun xianbiao 白雲仙表 [A Chart of the Immortals of Baiyun Abbey]. 1848. Meng Huoyi 孟豁一. *Zangwai daoshu* 藏外道書 31: 373 ff.

Baiyun guan zhi (Hakuunkan shi) 白雲觀志 [Gazetteer of the White Clouds Abbey]. By Oyanagi Shigeta 小柳司氣太. Tokyo: Tōhō bunka gakuin Tōkyō kenkyūjo, 1934.

Beixi ji 杯溪集 [Collection from Bei Mountain Stream]. By Fu Jinquan 傅金銓. *Daoshu shiqi zhong* 道書十七種 [Seventeen Daoist Books], ZWDS 11.

Biyuan tanjing 碧苑壇經 [Platform Sūtra of the Jade Garden]. Transmitted by Wang Changyue 王常月 (Kunyang 崑陽, ?-1680), compiled by Shi Shouping 施守平 and revised by Min Yide 閔一得 (1758-1836). 1904 edition reprinted in *Zangwai daoshu* 藏外道書 10: 158-217.

Bu Han tianshi shijia 補天師世家 [Supplement to the Lineage of the Han Dynasty Celestial Master], in BYGZ 347-356.

Cantongqi zhizhi 參同契直指 [Direct Pointers to "The Triplex Agreement"]. 1799. In *Daoshu shier zhong* 道書十二種 (Twelve Daoist Books).

Changchun daojiao yuanliu 長春道教源流 [Origins and Development of the Daoist Teachings of (Qiu) Changchun]. 1879. By Chen Minggui 陳銘珪 (1824-1881). In *Zangwai daoshu* 藏外道書 31:1-157.

Changchun zhenren xiyouji 長春真人西遊記 [The Journey to the West of the Perfected (Qiu) Changchun]. By Li Zhichang 李志常 (1193-1256). DZ 1429, fasc. 1056.

Chishi tuoluoni jing 持世陀羅尼經 [Vasu(n)dhārādhāranī]. T. vol. 20, no.1162 (Nos. 1163-1165). Translated by Xuanzang 玄奘 (600-664).

Chishi tuoluonijing fa 持世陀羅尼經法 [Vasu(n)dhāradhāraṇī ritual]. Includes the *Foshuo chishi tuoluonijing* 佛說持世陀羅尼經 based on T. vol. 20, no.1162, and the ritual connected to it. Attributed to Tuluo lüshi 圖多律師 (i.e., Jizu daozhe 雞足道者) and transcribed by Min Zhenxian 閔真仙 (i.e., Min Yide 閔一得). Postface by Min Yide (1834). Reprinted in *Zangwai daoshu* 藏外道書 10: 547–558.

Chishi tuoluonijing zhu 持世陀羅尼經注 [Commentary on the Vasu(n)dhāradhāraṇī]. Translated by Xuanzang. Commented by Faseng Jilian 髮僧際連 (i.e., Min Yide 閔一得). Reprinted in *Zangwai daoshu* 藏外道書 10: 559–578.

Chishui yin 赤水音 [Songs on the Red Water]. By Fu Jinquan 傅金銓. *Daoshu shiqi zhong* 道書十七種 [Seventeen Daoist Books], ZWDS 11.

Chongkan Daozang jiyao 重刊道藏輯要 [Reedited Epitome of the Daoist Canon] by Yan Yonghe 閻永和, Peng Hanran 彭瀚然 and He Longxiang 賀龍驤. Chengdu: Erxian an 二仙庵, 1906. Repr. 25 vols. Taipei: Xinwenfeng, 1977.

Chongxiu Longhu shanzhi 重修龍虎山志 [Gazetteer of the Reconstruction of Mount Longhu]. 16 juan. By Lou Jinyuan 婁近垣 (1689–1776). In ZWDS 19: 419–636; *Zhonghua xu daozang* 中華續道藏 [Supplement to the Daoist Canon], vol. 3 (Taipei: Shinwenfeng, 1999). *Daojiao wenxian* 道教文獻 2 (Taipei: Danqing tushu, 1983); Taipei: Guangwen shuju yinxing, 1989.

Chuzhen jielü 初真戒律 [Code of Initial Precepts for Perfection]. 1656. Attributed to Wang Changyue 王常月 (?-1680). DZJY 24 *zhangji* 張集 7 (reprinted in *Zangwai daoshu* 藏外道書 vol. 12: 13–31).

Dadong yujing tanyi 大洞玉經壇儀 [Liturgy of the Jade Scripture of Great Profundity]. Attributed to Wei Huacun 魏華存 (252–334). DZJY 3 *diji* 氐集 4.

Daode zhenjing sanjie 道德真經三解 [A Threefold Explication of the *Daodejing*]. 1298. Deng Qi 鄧錡. DZ 687, fasc. 370–71.

Daofa huiyuan, 道法會元 [Collected Sources on Daoist Ritual]. 1356. DZ 1220, fasc. 884–941.

Daohai jinliang 道海津梁 [Bridge of the Sea of the Path]. By Fu Jinquan 傅金銓. *Daoshu shiqi zhong* 道書十七種 [Seventeen Daoist Books], ZWDS 11.

Daojiao wenxian 道教文獻 [Daoist Literature], ed. by Tu Jiexiang 杜潔祥. Taipei: Danqing tushu 丹青圖書, 1983.

Daomen gongke 道門功課 [Liturgy for Daoists]. Compiled by Liu Shouyuan 柳守元 (fl. 1798). DZJY 23 *zhangji* 張集 1.

Daoqiao tan 道竅談 [Discussion of the Opening of the Path). By Li Xiyue 李西月 (fl. 1796-1850). DZJH 2-2.

Daoshu shi'er zhong 道書十二種 [Twelve Daoist Texts]. Compiled by Liu Yiming 劉一明 (1734-1821). Beijing: Zhongguo zhongyiyao chubanshe 中國中醫藥出版社, 1990. ZWDS 8.

Daoshu shiqi zhong 道書十七種 [Seventeen Daoist Books]. 17 texts. By Fu Jinquan 傅金銓 of the Daoguang era (1796-1850). Shudong shancheng tang, 1825 (see Needham et al. 1983, 5:5, 231, 240-43). Guangling guji, 1993. ZWDS 11.

Daotong yuanliu 道統源流 [Origins and Development of Orthodox Daoism] by Yan Liuqian 嚴六謙 (*hao*: Zhuangyan jushi 莊嚴居士). Wuxi: Zhonghua yinshuju, 1929.

Daotong yuanliu zhi 道統源流志 [Origins and Development of Orthodox Daoism]. Compiled by by Yan Liuqian 嚴六謙, *hao*: Zhuangyan jushi 莊嚴居士. Huzhou 湖州: Wuxi Zhonghua yinshuaju 無錫中華印刷局, 1929.

Daozang jinghua lu 道藏精華錄 [Record of Essential Blossoms of the Daoist Canon] by Ding Fubao 丁福保 (*zi*: Shouyi zi 守一子, 1874-1952). Reprint in 2 vols. (*shang* / *xia*). Zhejiang guji chubanshe, 1989.

(Chongkan) Daozang jiyao 重刊道藏輯要 [Reedited Epitome of the Daoist Canon] by Yan Yonghe 閻永和, Peng Hanran 彭瀚然 and He Longxiang 賀龍驤. Chengdu: Erxian an 二仙庵, 1906. Repr. 25 vols. Taipei: Xinwenfeng, 1977.

Daozang jiyao zongmu 道藏輯要總目 [Table of Contents of the Epitome of the Daoist Canon]. *Daozang jinghua lu* 道藏精華錄 (1989) 1:1a-8a.

Daozang xubian 道藏續編 [Supplementary Collection of the Daoist Canon], 4 vols., by Min Yide 閔一得 (1758-1836). Wuxing: Jingai cangban, 1834. Photolithographic edition by Ding Fubao 丁福保 (*zi*: Shou yi zi 守一子, 1874-1952): *Daozang xubian chuji* 道藏續編初集. Shanghai: Yixue shuju. Reprint Beijing: Haiyang 1989.

Daqing huidian 大清會典 [Collected Statutes of the Great Qing Dynasty]

Du Lü zushi sanni yishi shuoshu guankui 讀呂祖師三尼醫世說述管窺 [A Personal Reading of the Explanations of the Three Sages' Doctrine of Healing the World by Patriarch Lü]. By Min Yide 閔一得. DZXB vol. 2 (see here above, Appendix to Chapter 3, Text 11). Reprinted in *Zangwai daoshu* 藏外道書 10.

Erlan xinhua 二懶心話 [Heart-to-Heart Dialogue Between the Two Leisurely (Masters)]. By Min Yide 閔一得. DZXB vol. 3 (see here above, Appendix to Chapter 3, Text 16). Reprinted in *Zangwai daoshu* 藏外道書 10.

Fahai yizhu 法海遺珠 [Bequeathed Pearls from the Sea of Ritual]. 1344. DZ 1166, fasc. 825–33.

Ganshui xian yuanlu 甘水仙源錄 [Record of the Immortals from the Sweet Water (River)]. By Li Daoqian 李道謙. 1289. DZ 973, fasc. 611–613.

Gu Shuyinlou cangshu 古書隱樓藏書 [Collection from the Ancient Hidden Pavilion of Books], 14 vols., by Min Yide (1758–1836). Wuxing: Jingai Chunyang gong cangban, 1904. Repr. in *Zangwai daoshu* 藏外道書 10:150–721.

Guangcheng yizhi 廣成儀制 [Ritual Systematization of Master Guangcheng]. 270 texts, ed. by Chen Chongyuan 陳仲遠. Chengdu: Erxian'an, 1911, reprinted 1913; ZWDS 13–15.

Guangyang zaji 廣陽雜記 [Miscellaneous Records of Guangyang]. Liu Xianting 劉獻廷. Beijing: Zhonghua shuju, 1957.

Guankui bian 管窺編 [A Personal View]. By Min Yide 閔一得. DZXB vol. 2 (see here above, Appendix to Chapter 3, Text 7).

Gufa yangsheng shisan ze chanwei 古法養生十三則闡微 [Uncovering the Subtleties of the Thirteen Principles Concerning the Ancient Methods of Nourishing Life]. DZXB vol. 1 (see here above, Appendix to Chapter 3, Text 5).

Hakuunkan shi (Baiyun guan zhi) 白雲觀志 [Gazetteer of the White Clouds Abbey]. By Oyanagi Shigeta 小柳司氣太. Tokyo: Tōhō bunka gakuin Tōkyō kenkyūjo, 1934.

Han tianshi shijia 漢天師世家 [Lineage of the Han Dynasty Celestial Master]. 1607. DZ 1463, fasc. 1066.

Huangji hepi xianjing 皇極闔闢仙經, abbreviated title of *Yin zhenren Donghua zhengmai huangji hepi zhengdao xianjing*, q.v.

Huangting jingjie 黃庭經解 [Explanations of the Yellow Court Scripture]. In *Daoshu shier zhong* 道書十二種 (Twelve Daoist Books).

Huayue zhi 華嶽志 [Gazetteer of the Hua Peak]. Compiled by Li Rong 李榕 (fl. 1821). Edited by Yang Xiwu 楊翼武 (fl. 1831). *Zangwai daoshu* 藏外道書 20: 3–185.

Huiming jing 慧命經 [Scripture of Wisdom and Life]. Liu Huayang 柳華陽 (1735–1799). In *Wu-Liu xianzong* 伍柳仙宗. Reprint of 1897 edition: Henan renmin chubanshe, 1988, 379–541.

Huixin ji 會心集 [Collection of Encounters of the Mind]. By Liu Yiming 劉一明. 1801. In *Daoshu shier zhong* 道書十二種 (Twelve Daoist Books).

Huixin waiji 會心外集 [Outer Collection of the Encounters with the Mind]. By Liu Yiming 劉一明 (1734–1821). In *Daoshu shi'er zhong* 道書十二種. Beijing: Zhongguo zhongyiyao chubanshe 中國中醫藥出版社, 1990.

Jindan sibaizi jie 金丹四百字解 [Explanations of the *Four Hundred Words on the Golden Elixir*]. In *Daoshu shier zhong* 道書十二種 (Twelve Daoist Books).

Jindan sibai zi zhushi 金丹四百字注釋 [Commentary and Explanations on the *Four Hundred Words on the Golden Elixir*]. DZXB vol. 3 (see here above, Appendix to Chapter 3, Text 21).

Jingai xindeng 金蓋心燈 [Transmission of the Lamp of Mind from Mt. Jingai], 10 vols., by Min Yide (1758–1836). Wuxing: Yunchao, Gu Shuyinlou cangban, 1876 (1st ed. 1821). Repr. in *Zangwai daoshu* 藏外道書 31.

Jingudong zhi 金鼓洞志 [Gazetteer of the Golden Drum Cavern]. 1807. Zhu Wenzao 朱文藻 (1736–1806). *Zangwai daoshu* 藏外道書 20: 189–299.

Jinhua zongzhi 金華宗旨 [The Secret of the Golden Flower]. Edited by Jiang Yuanting 蔣元庭 (1755–1819) and revised by Min Yide 閔一得 (1758–1836). DZXB I: 1a–15b.

Jinlian zhengzong ji 金蓮正宗記 [Record of the Orthodox Lineage of the Golden Lotus]. 1241. Qin Zhian 秦志安 (1188–1244). DZ 173, fasc. 75–76.

Jinlian zhengzong xianyuan xiangzhuan 金蓮正宗仙源像傳 [Illustrated Hagiographies of the Immortal Origins of the Orthodox Lineage of the Golden Lotus]. 1326. Liu Tiansu 劉天素 and Xie Xichan 謝西蟾. DZ 174 fasc. 76.

Jinxian zhenglun 金仙証論 [A Testimony to Golden Immortality]. 1799. In *Wu-Liu xianzong* 伍柳仙宗. Reprint of 1897 edition: Henan renmin chubanshe, 1988.

Jiuzheng lu 就正錄 [Record of the Realization of Rectitude]. By Lu Shichen 陸世忱. DZXB vol. 2 (see here above, Appendix to Chapter 3, Text 8).

Kongyi chanzhen 孔易闡真 [True Explanation of the Confucian "Changes"]. In *Daoshu shier zhong* 道書十二種.

Lishi zhenxian tidao tongjian 歷世真仙體道通鑒 [Comprehensive Mirror of the Perfected and Immortals who embodied the Dao through the Ages]. Zhao Daoyi 趙道一 (late 13th century). DZ 296, fasc. 138–48.

Longmen xinfa 龍門心法 [Core Teachings of the Longmen]. 1663. Transmitted by Wang Changyue 王常月 (?-1680) and compiled by Zhan Tailin 詹太林 and Tang Qingshan 唐清善. *Zangwai daoshu* 藏外道書 6: 727–785.

Longmen zhengzong jueyun benzhi daotong xinchuan 龍門正宗覺雲本支道統薪傳 [Uninterrupted Transmission of the Orthodox Teaching in the Right Lineage of the Longmen Jueyun Branch]. 1927. Lu Yongming 陸永銘. *Zangwai daoshu* 藏外道書 31: 427–446.

Lü zushi sanni yishi gongjue 呂祖師三尼醫世功訣 [Practices and Formulae on the Three Sages' Doctrine of Healing the World by Patriarch Lü]. Transmitted by Shen Yibing 沈一炳 (1708–1786), newly recorded and annotated by Min Yide. DZXB vol. 2 (see here above, Appendix to Chapter 3, Text 12). Reprinted in *Zangwai daoshu* 藏外道書 10.

Lü zushi sanni yishi shuoshu 呂祖師三尼醫世說述 [Explanations of the Three Sages' Doctrine of Healing the World (revealed via spirit writing) by Patriarch Lü]. Entitled by Huang Chiyang 黃赤陽 (1595–1673), edited by Tao Shi'an 陶石庵 (?-1692), commented by Min Yide and corrected by Shen Yangyi 沈陽一. Preface (1664) by Tao Shi'an and Preface (1828) by Min Yide. In DZXB (see here above, Appendix to Chapter 3, Text 10). Reprinted in *Zangwai daoshu* 藏外道書 10.

Lü zushi xiantian xuwu Taiyi jinhua zongzhi 呂祖師先天虛無太一金華宗旨 [Patriarch Lü's Quintessential Doctrine of the Golden Flower of the Great One of the Emptiness Before Heaven] (Abbreviated title: *Taiyi jinhua zongzhi* 太一金華宗旨). 13 chapters. DZXB vol. 1 (see here above, Appendix to Chapter 3, Text 1).

Maoshan quanji 茅山全志 [Complete Gazetteer of Mount Mao]. 14 *juan*. Ed. by Da Changuang 笪蟾光. Preface dated 1878. ZWDS 20: 697–964.

Min Lanyun xiansheng zhuan 閔懶雲先生傳 [Biography of Master Min Lanyun (Yide)]. By Shen Bingcheng 沈秉成 (1821–1824). In *Jingai xindeng's* 金蓋心燈 Min zhuan fu 閔傳附.

Min Lanyun xiansheng zhuan 閔懶雲先生傳 [Biography of Master Min Lanyun (Yide)]. By Yan Duanshu 晏端書. In *Jingai xindeng's* 金蓋心燈 Min zhuan fu 閔傳附.

Min Lanyun xiansheng zhuan 閔懶雲先生傳 [Biography of Master Min Lanyun (Yide)]. By Yang Weikun 揚維崑. In *Jingai xindeng's* 金蓋心燈 Min zhuan fu 閔傳附.

Niwan Li zushi nüzong shuangxiu baofa 泥丸李祖師女宗雙修寶筏 [Precious Raft of Joint Cultivation in Feminine Alchemy by Patriarch Li Niwan]. DZXB vol. 3 (see here above, Appendix to Chapter 3, Text 20).

Nüdan jicui 女丹集萃 [Anthology on Feminine Alchemy]. Beijing: Beijing shifan daxue chubanshe, 1989.

Qiaoyang jing 樵陽經 [Classic of Qiaoyang]. By Fu Jinquan 傅金銓. *Daoshu shiqi zhong* 道書十七種 [Seventeen Daoist Books], ZWDS 11.

Qingshi gao 情史稿 [Draft History of the Qing Dynasty].

Qiongguan Bai zhenren ji 瓊琯白真人集 [Anthology of Perfected Bai of Haiqiong]. DZJY *louji* 婁集 4, vol. 14.

Qiuzu quanshu 邱祖全書 [Complete Works of the Patriarch Qiu (Chuji)]. *Daoshu shiqi zhong* 道書十七種 [Seventeen Daoist Books], ZWDS 11.

Rixia jiuwen kao 日下舊聞考 [Investigation of Peking's Antiquities]. 1774/1882. SKQS vol. 497–99.

Rushi wo wen 如是我聞 [Thus I Have Heard]. DZXB vol. 3 (see here above, Appendix to Chapter 3, Text 18).

Sandong bizhi 三洞秘旨 [Secret Principles of the Three Vehicles]. By Li Xiyue 李西月 (fl. 1796–1850). DZJH 2-2.

Sandong zhongjie wen 三洞眾戒文 [Comprehensive Prescriptions of the Three Caverns]. By Zhang Wanfu 張萬福 (fl. 713). DZ 178, fasc. 77.

Sanfeng zhenren xuantan quanji 三丰真人玄潭全集 [Complete Collection of the Mysterious Words by the Perfected (Zhang) Sanfeng]. By Min Yide 閔一得. DZXB vol. 3 (see here above, Appendix to Chapter 3, Text 17).

Sanfeng danjue 三丰丹訣 [Sanfeng's Alchemical Formulas]. By Fu Jinquan 傅金銓. *Daoshu shiqi zhong* 道書十七種 [Seventeen Daoist Books], ZWDS 11.

Santan yuanman tianxian dajie lüeshuo 三壇圓滿天仙大戒略說 [Abstract on the Celestial Immortals' complete ordination of the threefold altars]. Compiled by Liu Shouyuan 柳守元 (fl. 1798). DZJY 24 *zhangji* 張集 7 (reprinted in *Zangwai daoshu* 藏外道書 12).

Shangpin danfa jieci 上品丹法節次 [Alchemical Process of Superior Degree]. By Li Dexia 李德洽. DZXB vol. 2 (see here above, Appendix to Chapter 3, Text 6).

Shangqing dongzhen zhihui guanshen dajie wen 上清洞真智慧觀身大戒文 [Great Precepts of the Cavern-Perfected of Highest Clarity for Contemplating the Body by Wisdom]. DZ 1364, fac. 1039

Shangqing dongzhen zhihui guanshen dajie wen 上清洞真智慧觀身大戒文 [Great Rules of Wisdom in Self-Examination]. Six Dynasties. DZ 1364, fasc. 1039.

Shangyang zi jindan dayao 上陽子金丹大要 [Great Essentials on the Golden Elixir of Shangyang zi]. Chen Zhixu 陳致虛 (1298-after 1335). DZ 1067, fasc. 736–38.

Shenshi bafa 神室八法 ([Eight Elements of the Spiritual Abode]. By Liu Yiming 劉一明. 1798. *Daoshu shier zhong* 道書十二種 (Twelve Daoist Books).

Shenxian zhuan 神仙傳 [Biographies of Divine Immortals]. SKQS.

Suoyan xu 瑣言續 [Sequel to an Ignored Transmission]. DZXB vol. 3 (see here above, Appendix to Chapter 3, Text 22).

Taishang ganyin pian 太上感應篇 [Treatise on Retribution of the Most High]. DZ 1167, fasc. 834–839.

Taishang Laojun jiejing 太上老君戒經 [Commandments of the Most High Lord Lao]. Early Tang. DZ 784, fasc. 562.

Taishang xuanmen zaotan gongke jing 太上玄門早壇功課經 [Morning Liturgy of the Mysterious Teachings of the Most High]. DZJY 23 *zhangji* 張集 1.

Tianxian daocheng baoze 天仙道程寶則 [Precious Principles for the Path to Celestial Immortality]. DZXB vol. 3 (see here above, Appendix to Chapter 3, Text 15).

Tianxian dao jieji xuzhi 天仙道戒忌須知 [Required Knowledge on Precepts and Prohibitions for the Path to Celestial Immortality]. DZXB vol. 3 (see here above, Appendix to Chapter 3, Text 14).

Tianxian xinchuan 天仙心傳 [Mind-to-Mind Transmission of Celestial Immortality]. By Min Yide 閔一得. DZXB vol. 2 (see here above, Appendix to Chapter 3, Text 13).

Tianxian zhengli 天仙正理 [Correct Principles of Celestial Immortality]. By Wu Shouyang 伍守陽 (1574–1634). In *Wu-Liu xianzong* 伍柳仙宗 and DZJY *biji* 4–5 (Chongkan ed. 17.7541–95).

Tianxian zhengli qianshuo 天仙正理淺說 [Simple Explanations of the Correct Principles of Celestial Immortality]. Wu Shouyang 伍守陽 (1574–1634). DZJY *biji* 5, vol. 17.

Tianxian zhengli zhilun 天仙正理直論 [Forthright Discourses on the Correct Principles of Celestial Immortality]. 1639. Wu Shouyang. DZJY *biji* 4, vol. 17.

Tianxian zhengli 天仙正理 [Correct Principles of Celestial Immortality]. Wu Shouyang 伍守陽 (1574–1634). DZJY *biji* 4, vol. 17.

Tianxian zhilun 天仙值論 [Forthright Discourses on Celestial Immortality]. By Wu Shouyang 伍守陽 (1574–1634). *Daoshu shiqi zhong* 道書十七種 [Seventeen Daoist Books], ZWDS 11.

Tongguan wen 通關文 [Treatise on Going through the Passes]. By Liu Yiming 劉一明. 1812. In *Daoshu shier zhong* 道書十二種 (Twelve Daoist Books).

Wenyuan ge Siku quanshu 文淵閣四庫全書 [Complete Texts in Four Repositories]. 1773–1782. 1500 vols. By Yong Rong 永瑢 et al. Edited by Zhu Jianmin 朱建民. Taiwan: Shangwu yinshuguan, 1986.

Wudang fudi zongzhen ji 武當富地總真集 [Collection of the Assembled Perfected of Mount Wudang]. 1291. Compiled by Liu Daoming 劉道明. DZ 962, fasc. 609.

Wudao lu 悟道錄 [Record of Awakening to the Path]. By Liu Yiming 劉一明 (1734–1821). 1810. In *Daoshu shier zhong* 道書十二種 (Twelve Daoist Books).

Wu-Liu xianzong 伍柳仙宗 [The Immortals' Tradition of Wu-Liu]. By Wu Chongxu 伍沖虛 (1552–1641) and Liu Huayang 柳華陽 (1735–1799). Edited by Deng Huiji 鄧徽績. 1897. Reprint: Henan renmin chubanshe, 1988.

Wugen shu 無根樹 [Tree Without Roots]. Poems attr. to Zhang Sanfeng; commented by Li Xiyue 李西月 (fl. 1796–1850). In *Daoshu qizhong* 道書七種 (Seventeen Daoist Books); DZJH 8.

Wuzhen zhizhi 悟真直指 [Direct Pointers to "Awakening to Perfection"]. In *Daoshu shier zhong* 道書十二種 (Twelve Daoist Books).

Xianfo hezong yulu 仙佛合宗語錄 [Recorded Sayings on the Merged Tradition of Buddhism and Daoism]. By Wu Shouyang 伍守陽 (1574–1634); annotated by Wu Shouxu 伍守虛. DZJY *biji* 6; 1; 2.1a-25a; 3.31b-39b (Chongkan ed. 17.7403–7540).

Xiangyan poyi 象言破疑 [Clarification of Symbolic Words]. By Liu Yiming 劉一明 (1734–1821). 1811. In *Daoshu shier zhong* 道書十二種, Zhongguo Zhongyiyao chubanshe 中國中醫藥出版社, 1990.

Xiaoyao shan wanshou gong zhi 逍遙山萬壽宮志 [Gazetteer of the Palace of Longevity on Mount Xiaoyao]. Jin Guixin 金桂馨 and Qi Fengyuan 漆逢源. 1878. ZWDS 20: 653–977.

Xie tianji 泄天機 [Disclosing the Celestial Mechanism]. DZXB vol. 1 (see here above, Appendix to Chapter 3, Text 4).

Xingtian zhenggu 性天正鵠 [Striking the Center of Celestial Nature's Target]. By Fu Jinquan 傅金銓. *Daoshu shiqi zhong* 道書十七種 [Seventeen Daoist Books], ZWDS 11.

Xinxue 心學 [Study of the Heart-Mind]. By Fu Jinquan 傅金銓. *Daoshu shiqi zhong* 道書十七種 [Seventeen Daoist Books], ZWDS 11.

Xinyin ji jing 心印集經 [Summa of the Heart-Seal]. DZJY (edition Jiaqing era 1796–1820), *jiji* 箕集 10.

Xiuxian bianhuo lun 修仙辨惑論 [Treatise on Resolving Doubts concerning the Cultivation of Immortality]. Attributed to Bai Yuchan 白玉蟾 (1194-ca. 1227). *Daozang jinghua lu* 道藏精華錄 *xia*.

Xiuzhen biannan 修真辯難 [Debate on the Cultivation of Perfection]. By Liu Yiming 劉一明. 1798. In *Daoshu shier zhong* 道書十二種 (Twelve Daoist Books).

Xiuzhen biannan qianhou bian canzheng 修真辯難前後編參証 [Annotations to the *Debate on the Cultivation of Perfection* in Two Sections]. By Liu Yiming 劉一明. Commented and verified by Min Yide. Postface (1829) by Min Yide and Postface by Liu Yiming. DZXB vol. 4 (see here above, Appendix to Chapter 3, Text 23).

Xiuzhen jiuyao 修真九要 [Nine Principles in the Cultivation of Perfection]. By Liu Yiming 劉一明. 1798. In *Daoshu shier zhong* 道書十二種 (Twelve Daoist Books).

Xiwang mu nüxiu zhengtu shize 西王母女修正途十則 [Ten Rules of the Queen Mother of the West on the Correct Path of Female Cultivation]. DZXB vol. 3 (see here above, Appendix to Chapter 3, Text 19).

Xiyou yuanzhi 西遊原旨 [The Original Meaning of the "Journey to the West"]. By Liu Yiming 劉一明. 1778. In *Daoshu shier zhong* 道書十二種 (Twelve Daoist Books).

Xuanjiao da gong'an 玄教大公案 [The Great Case of the Teachings of the Mysteries]. 1324. Wang Zhidao 王志道. DZ 1065, fasc. 734.

Xuhuang tianzun Chuzhen shijie wen 虛皇天尊初真十戒文 [Text of the Ten Rules for the Initial Stage of Perfection, (Spoken) by the Heavenly Worthy Xuhuang]. DZ 180, fasc. 77.

Xuhuang tianzun shijie wen 虛皇天尊十戒文 [Ten Precepts of the Heavenly Worthy Sovereign of Emptiness]. DZ 180, fasc. 77.

Yiguan zhenji yijian lu 一貫真機易簡錄 [Simple Notes on the Mechanism that Unifies All]. By Fu Jinquan 傅金銓. *Daoshu shiqi zhong* 道書十七種 [Seventeen Daoist Books], ZWDS 11.

Yin zhenren Donghua zhengmai huangji hepi zhengdao xianjing 尹真人東華正脈皇極闔闢證道仙經 [Immortals' Scripture of the Perfected Yin Testifying to the Path of Opening and Closing the Sovereign Ultimate according to the Orthodox Lineage of the Eastern Efflorescence], abbr. *Huangji hepi xianjing* 皇極闔闢仙經, in 3 *juan* and 10 chapters. Manuscript of the Qingyang gong 青羊宮 (Black Sheep Palace), Chengdu. Attributed to Yin Pengtou 尹蓬頭; corrected by Min Yide; Preface (1831) and Postface by Min Yide. In DZXB (see here above, Appendix to Chapter 3, Text 2) and *Zangwai daoshu* 藏外道書 10.

Yin zhenren Liaoyang dian wenda bian 尹真人廖陽殿問答編 [Questions and Answers of the Perfected Yin from the Liaoyang Hall]. 6 chapters. DZXB (see here above, Appendix to Chapter 3, Text 3).

Yuanshi dadong yujing 元始大洞玉經 [Jade Scripture of Great Profondity of the Primordial Beginning]. 1583. Attributed to Wenchang dijun 文昌帝君. DZJY 3 *diji* 氐集 3.

Yinfujing zhu 陰符經註 [Commentary on the Scripture on Joining with the Hidden]. In *Daoshu shier zhong* 道書十二種 (Twelve Daoist Books).

Yu Lin Fenqian xiansheng shu 與林奮千先生書 [Letter to Master Lin Fenqian]. By Lu Shichen 陸世忱. DZXB vol. 2 (see here above, Appendix to Chapter 3, Text 9).

Yuxiang tianjing zhou zhu 雨香天經咒注 [Commentary on the Spell of the *Yuxiang tianjing*]. By Min Yide. YLCS 9 (reprinted in *Zangwai daoshu* 藏外道書 10).

Yuxuan miaozheng zhenren yulu 御選妙正真人語錄 [Imperially Selected Recorded Sayings of the Perfected of Mysterious Orthodoxy]. By Lou Jinyuan 婁近垣 (1689–1776). In *Chongxiu longhu shanzhi*, j. 11, and *Yuxuan yulu* 御選語錄.

Yuxuan yulu 御選語錄 [Imperially Selected Recorded Sayings], ed. by emperor Yongzheng. 1733. ZZ no. 1319, vol. 68; *Wanzi xu zangjing* 卍字續藏經 (Taiwan reprint of ZZ), Taipei 1976, vol. 119.

Zangwai daoshu 藏外道書 [Daoist Texts Outside the Daoist Canon] edited by Hu Daojing 胡道靜 et al. Chengdu: Bashu shushe, 1992 (vol: 1–20); 1994 (vol. 21–36).

Zhang Sanfeng quanji 張三丰全集 [Complete Works of Zhang Sanfeng], compiled by Li Xiyue 李西月 (fl. 1796–1850). Hangzhou: Zhejiang guji chubanshe, 1990.

Zhonghe ji 中和集 [Collection of Central Harmony]. By Li Daochun 李道純 (fl. 1288–1306). DZ 249, fasc. 118.

Zhongji jie 中極戒 [Intermediate Ultimate Precepts]. DZJY 24 *zhangji* 張集 7 (reprinted in *Zangwai daoshu* 藏外道書 12).

Zhongnan shan zuting xianzhen neizhuan 終南山祖庭仙真內傳 [Inner Biographies of the Immortals and Perfected at (Wang Chongyang's) Ancestral Hall in Zhongnan Mountains]. Li Daoqian 李道謙 (1219–1296). DZ 955 fasc. 604.

Zhouyi chanzhen 周易闡真 [True Explanation of the "Changes"]. 1798. In *Daoshu shier zhong* 道書十二種 (Twelve Daoist Books).

Zhuzhen zongpai zongbu 諸真宗派總簿 [Comprehensive Register of all Genuine Lineages]. In BYGZ 1934:91 ff.

Ziti suohua 自題所畫 [Painting Inscriptions]. By Fu Jinquan 傅金銓. *Daoshu shiqi zhong* 道書十七種 [Seventeen Daoist Books], ZWDS 11.

Secondary Sources

Akioka, Hideyuki 秋岡英行. 1994. "Chō Sanhō to Shindai Dōkyō seiha 張三峰と清代道教西派" [Zhang Sanfeng and the Western School of Daoism in the Qing period]. *Tōhō Shūkyō* 東方宗教 83: 1–15.

Akizuki, Kan'ei 秋月観. 1978. *Chūgoku kinsei dōkyō no keisei: Jōmyōdō no kisoteki kenkyū* 中国近世道教の形成：浄明道の基楚的研究 [The Structure of Recent Chinese Daoism: Basic Research on the Jingmingdao]. Tokyo: Sōbunsha 創文社.

Ang, Isabelle. 1993. "Le culte de Lü Dongbin des origines jusqu'au début du XIVème siècle. Caractéristiques et transformations d'un Saint Immortel dans la Chine pré-moderne." Ph. D. diss., Université de Paris VII.

———. 1997. "Le culte de Lü Dongbin sous les Song du Sud." *Journal Asiatique* 285/2 (1997): 473–507.

Avalon, Arthur. 1958. *The Serpent Power*. Madras: Ganeshan & Co.

Baker, Victoria J. 1998. *Ritual Practice in a Sinhalese Village*. Forth Worth: Harcourt Brace College Publishers.

Baldrian-Hussein, Farzeen. 1984. *Procédés secrets du joyau magique—Traité d'alchimie taoïste du XIe siècle*. Paris: Les Deux Océans.

———. 1986. "Lü Tung-pin in Northern Sung Literature." *Cahiers d'Extrême-Asie* 2 (1986): 133–169.

———. 1996–97. "Taoist Beliefs in Literary Circles of the Song Dynasty—Su Shi (1037–1101) and his Technique of Survival." *Cahiers d'Extrême-Asie* 9 (1996–97): 15–53.

Bardol, Philippe. 1992. "Le bouddhisme Chan sous la dynastie des Qing, à l'époque du *Xindeng Lu*." M.A. thesis. Paris: Institut Nationale des Langues et Civilisations Orientales.

Barrett, Thomas. 1978. "Chinese Sectarian Religion." *Modern Asian Studies* 12: 333–352.

Bell, Catherine. 1996. "Stories from an Illustrated Explanation of the *Tract of the Most Exalted on Action and Response*." In *Religion of China in Practice*, edited by Donald S. Lopez Jr., 437–445. Princeton: Princeton University Press.

Berger, Patricia. 1994. "Preserving the Nation: The Political uses of Tantric Art in China." In Marsha Weidner (ed.), *Latter Days of the Law: Images of Chinese Buddhism, 850–1850*: 89–123. Honolulu: University of Hawai'i Press.

———. 2003. *Empire of Emptiness: Buddhist Art and Political Authority in Qing China*. Honolulu: University of Hawaii Press, 2003.

Berling, Judith. 1980. *The Syncretic Religion of Lin Chao-en*. New York: Columbia University Press.

———. 1985. "Religion and Popular Culture: The Management of Moral Capital in *The Romance of the Three Teachings*. In *Popular Culture in Late Imperial China*, edited by David Johnson, Andrew J. Nathan and Evelyn S. Rawski, 188–218. Berkeley: University of California Press.

Bernbaum, Edwin. 2001. *The Way to Shambhala*. Boston & London: Shambhala.

Bertuccioli, Giuliano. 1953. "Note taoiste II. A proposito di un recente caso di applicazione del rogo nel convento taoista del Pai-yun Kuan." *Rivista degli studi orientali* XXVIII, 1953: 185–186.

———. 1957. "Il Taoismo nella Cina contemporanea." *Cina* 2, 1957: 67–77.

Bianchi, Ester. 2001. *The Iron Statue Monastery*. Firenze: Leo S. Olschki editore.

Birrell, Anne. 1993. *Chinese Mythology*. Baltimore and London: John Hopkins University Press.

Bokenkamp, R. Stephen. 1997. *Early Daoist Scriptures*. Berkeley: University of California Press.

Boltz, Judith M. 1987. *A Survey of Taoist Literature. Tenth to Seventeenth Centuries*. Berkeley: University of California, Institute of East Asian Studies & Center for Chinese Studies.

———. 1993. "Not by the Seal of Office alone: New Weapons in Battles with the Supernatural." In *Religion and Society in T'ang and Sung China*, edited by Patricia Buckley Ebrey and Peter Gregory, 241–305. Honolulu:University of Hawai'i Press.

Bose, Mandakranta, ed. 2000. *Faces of the Feminine in Ancient, Medieval, and Modern India*. New York: Oxford University Press.

Bosson, James E. 1969. *A Treasury of Aphoristic Jewels: The Subhasitaratnanidhi of Sa Skya Pandita in Tibetan and Mongolian*. Bloomington: Indiana University.

Briffault, Robert. 1927. *The Mothers*. New York and London.

Brockington, J. L. 1981. *The Sacred Thread: Hinduism in its Continuity and Diversity*. Edinburgh: Edinburgh University Press.

Brokaw, Cynthia. 1991. *The Ledgers of Merit and Demerit: Social Change and Moral Order in Late Imperial China*. Princeton: Princeton University Press.

Burkhardt, V. Rodolphe. 1919. *Chinese Creeds and Customs*. Hong Kong: South China Morning Post.

Chandra, Lokesh (ed.). 1966. *Sanskrit Texts from the Imperial Palace at Peking in the Manchurian, Chinese, Mongolian and Tibetan Scripts*, Satapitaka Series, vol. 71. New Delhi: International Academy of Indian Culture.

Chang, Chung-li. 1967. *The Chinese Gentry: Studies on Their Role in nineteenth-Century Chinese Society*. Seattle: University of Washington Press.

Charleux, Isabelle. 2002. "Les 'lamas' vus de Chine: fascination et répulsion." *Extrême-Orient Extrême-Occident* 24 (October 2002):133–151

Chayet, Anne. 1985. *Les Temples de Jehol et leurs modèles tibétains*. Paris: Editions Recherche sur les civilisations.

Chen, Bing 陳兵. 1985. "Jindan pai Nanzong qiantan" 金丹派南宗淺探 [A Brief Study of the Southern Lineage of the Golden Elixir School]. *Shijie zongjiao yanjiu* 世界宗教研究 4, 1985: 35–49.

———. 1988. "Qingdai quanzhen longmen pai zhongxing 清代全真龍門派的中興神" [The Renewal of the Quanzhen Longmen School during the Qing Dynasty]. *Shijie zongjiao yanjiu* 世界宗教研究. 1988/2:84–96.

———. 1990. "Ming-Qing daojiao liang dapai 明清道教兩大派" [The Two Great Schools of Ming-Qing Daoism]. In *Zhongguo daojiao shi* 中國道教史, edited by Ren Jiyu 任繼愈, 672–82. Shanghai: Shanghai wenwu.

———. 1991. "Ming Qing daojiao" 明清道教 [Ming-Qing Daoism]. In Mou Zhongjian 牟鐘鑑 (ed.), *Daojiao tonglun* 道教通論 [A General Discussion of Daoism], 551–579. Jinan: Wenlu.

———. 1992a. "Ming-Qing Quanzhen dao 明清道教 [The Quanzhen of the Ming and Qing dynasties]. *Shijie zongjiao shi* 世界宗教研究 1: 40–51.

———. 1992b. "Mingdai Quanzhen dao" 明代全真道[Quanzhen in Ming Times]. *Shijie zongjiao yanjiu* 世界宗教研究 1, 1992:40–51.

Chen, Weiping 陳衛平. 1989. "Lun Mingqing jian xifang chuanjiaoshi dui zhongxi zhexue bijiao 論明清間西方傳教士對中西哲學比較" [A Comparison of Chinese and Western Philosophy by Jesuits during Ming-Qing Period]. *Shijie zongjiao yanjiu* 世界宗教研究 1 (1989):12–18.

Chen, Wenyi 陳免宜. 1993. "Tan Miaozheng zhenren Lou Jinyuan you Qing Shizong de zhiyu zhi Gaozong de youli." *Daojiao xue tansuo* 7:295–313.

Chen, William. 1987. *A Guide to Tao-tsang chi yao*. New York: Stony Brook.

Cheng, Anne. 1997. *Histoire de la pensée chinoise*. Paris: Seuil.

Cheng, Hsueh-li. 1989. "Psychology, Ontology and Soteriology in the Platform Sūtra." In *The Sixth Patriarch Platform Sūtra in Religious and Cultural Perspective*, edited by Fo Kuang shan, 99–113. Taichong: Fo Kuang shan.

Chou, Yi-liang. 1944–45. "Tantric Buddhism in China." *Harvard Journal of Asian Studies* 8 (1944–45): 241–332.

Cleary, Thomas. 1986a. *The Taoist I Ching*, Boston and London: Shambhala.

———. 1986b. *The Inner Teachings of Taoism*. Boston and London: Shambhala.

———. 1987. *Understanding Reality*. Honolulu: University of Hawaii Press.

———. 1988. *Awakening to the Tao*. Boston and Shaftesbury: Shambhala.

———. 1991. *Vitality, Energy, Spirit: A Taoist Sourcebook*. Boston and London: Shambhala.

———. 1992. *The Secret of the Golden Flower. The Classic Chinese Book of Life*. San Francisco: Harper.

Darga, Martina. 1999. *Das alchemistische Buch von innerem Wesen und Lebensenergie Xingming guizhi*. München: Eugen Diederichs.

Davis, Edward L. 2001. *Society and the Supernatural in Song China*. Honolulu: University of Hawai'i Press.

Dean, Kenneth. 1993. *Taoist Rituals and Popular Cults of Southeast China*. Princeton: Princeton University Press.

de Bary, William Theodore. 1970. "Individualism and Humanitarianism in Late Ming Thought." In *Self and Society in Ming Thought*, edited by Wm Theodore de Bary, 145–225. New York: Columbia University Press.

———— (ed.). 1975. *The Unfolding of Neo-Confucianism*. New York: Columbia University Press.

————. 1975. "Neo-Confucian Cultivation and the Seventeenth-Century 'Enlightenment.' " In *The Unfolding of Neo-Confucianism*, edited by Wm Theodore de Bary, 141–216. New York: Columbia University Press.

————. 1981. *Neo-Confucian Orthodoxy and the Learning of the Mind and Heart*. New York: Columbia University Press.

————. 1991. *The Trouble with Confucianism*. Cambridge, Massachussets: Harvard University Press.

de Bruyn, Pierre-Henry. 1997. "Le Wudang shan: Histoire des récits fondateurs." Ph.D. diss., Université de Paris VII.

————. 2000. "Daoism in the Ming (1368–1644)." In *Daoism Handbook*, edited by Livia Kohn, 594–622. Leiden: Brill.

de Groot, J. J. M. 1892–1910. *The Religious System of China*. 6 vols. Leiden: E. Brill.

————. 1903–4. *Sectarianism and Religious Persecution in China*. Amsterdam.

de Silva, Deema. 2000. "Sinhalese Puberty Rites for Girls." In Heinze, Ruth-Inge, ed. *The Nature and Function of Rituals: Fire from Heaven*. Connecticut & London: Bergin & Garvey Westport.

Demiéville, Paul et al. (eds.). 1929–30. *Hōbōgirin*, fasc. 1–2. Tokyo: Maison Franco-Japonaise.

————. 1974. *Hōbōgirin*. fasc. 3. Tokyo: Maison Franco-Japonaise.

Despeux, Catherine. 1979. *Traité d'Alchimie et de Physiologie taoïste*. Paris: Les Deux Océans.

————. 1981. *Taiji quan, art martial de longue vie*. Paris: Guy Trédaniel.

————. 1985. "Les lectures alchimiques du *Hsi-yu chi*." In Gert Naundorf et al. (eds.). *Religion und Philosophie in Ostasien: Festschrift für Hans Steininger*, 61–72. Würzburg: Könighausen und Neumann.

————. 1988. *La moelle du phénix rouge: santé et longue vie dans la Chine du XVI siècle*. Paris: Guy Trédaniel.

————. 1990. *Immortelles de la Chine Ancienne*. Puiseaux: Pardès.

————. 1994. *Taoïsme et corps humain*. Paris: Trédaniel.

————. 2008. "Chuzhen jielü." In *The Encyclopedia of Taoism*, ed. by Fabrizio Pregadio, vol. 1: 284–86. London: Routledge.

Ding, Peiren 丁培仁. 1996. *Daojiao dianji baiwen* 道教典籍百問 [One Hundred Questions about Daoist Sciptures]. Beijing: Jinri Zhongguo 今日中國.

Dong, Zhongji 董中基. 1987. *Daojiao Quanzhen zuting Beijing Baiyun guan* 道教全真祖庭北京白雲觀 [The Abbey of the White Clouds, Ancestral Seat of Quanzhen Daoism]. Beijing: Zhongguo daojiao xiehui.

Douglas, Mary. 1984. *Purity and Danger*. London: Ark.

Duara, Prasenjit. 1988. "Superscribing Symbols: The Myth of Guandi, Chinese God of War." *Journal of Asian Studies* 47, 4: 778–95.

Eliade, Mircea. 1954. *Le Yoga, Immortalité et liberté*. Paris: Payot.

———. 1983. *Le chamanisme et les techniques archaïques de l'extase*. Paris: Payot.

Engelhardt, Ute. 1981. *Theorie und Technik des Taijiquan*. Schorndorf: WBV Biologisch-medizinische Verlagshandlung.

———. 1987. *Die klassische Tradition der Qi-Übungen: Eine Darstellung anhand des Tang-zeitilichen Textes Fuqi jingyi lun von Sima Chengzhen*. Wiesbaden: Franz Steiner.

Erdberg-Consten, Eleanor. 1942. "A Statue of Lao-tzu in the Pö-yun-kuan." *Monumenta Serica* VII, 1942: 235–241.

Eskildsen, Stephen. 1989. "The Beliefs and Practices of Early Ch'üan-chen Taoism." M. A. Thesis, University of British Columbia.

———. 1990. "Asceticism in Ch'üan-chen Taoism." *British Columbia Asian Review* 3/4, 1990:153–91.

Esposito, Monica. 1992. "Il *Daozang xubian*, raccolta di testi alchemici della scuola Longmen." *Annali dell'Istituto Universitario Orientale* 4: 429–49.

———. 1993. *La Porte du Dragon—L'école Longmen du Mont Jin'gai et ses pratiques alchimiques d'après le Daozang xubian (Suite au canon taoïste)*. 2 vols. Ph. D. Université Paris VII. PDF version with emendations by the author: Rorschach / Kyoto: UniversityMedia, 2012.

———. 1995. *Il qigong—La nuova scuola taoista delle cinque respirazioni*. Padova: Muzzio.

———. 1995. " Il 'ritorno alle fonti', costituzione di un dizionario di alchimia interiore dell'epoca Ming e Qing." In *Le fonti per lo studio della civiltà cinese*, edited by Maurizio Scarpari, 101–117. Venezia: Ca'Foscarina.

———. 1996. "Il Segreto del Fiore d'Oro e la tradizione Longmen del Monte Jingai." In *Conoscenza e interpretazione della civiltà cinese*, edited by Piero Corradini, 151–169. Venezia: Ca' Foscarina.

———. 1997. *L'alchimia del soffio*. Roma: Ubaldini.

———. 1998a. "Una tradizione di rDzogs-chen in Cina, una nota sul Monastero delle Montagne dell'Occhio Celeste. *Asiatica Venetiana* 3 (1998): 221–224.

———. 1998b. " Longmen pai yu *Jinhua zongzhi* banben laiyuan" 龍門派與金華宗旨版本來源 [The Longmen School and the Origin of the Different Editions of the *Secret of the Golden Flower*]. Paper presented at the Dōkyō bunka kenkyūkai 道教文化研究会 at Waseda University, Tokyo (March 1998).

———. 1998c. "The different versions of *The Secret of the Golden Flower* and their relationship with the Longmen school." *Transactions of the International Conference of Eastern Studies* 43: 90–109.

———. 1998d. "L'alchimie féminine" in J. Servier (ed.), *Dictionnaire critique de l'ésotérisme* (Paris: Presses Universitaires de France, 1998): 51–52.

———. 2000. "Daoism in the Qing (1644–1911)." In *Daoism Handbook*, ed. by Livia Kohn, 623–657. Leiden: Brill. (Revised edition: Chapter 1 of *Facets of Qing Daoism*. Wil / Paris: UniversityMedia, 2014).

———. 2001. "Longmen Taoism in Qing China: Doctrinal Ideal and Local Reality." *Journal of Chinese Religion*. 29 (2001): 191–231. (Revised and augmented edition: Chapter 3 of *Facets of Qing Daoism*. Wil / Paris: UniversityMedia, 2014).

———. 2002. "A Sino-Tibetan Tradition in China at the Southern Celestial Eye Mountains: A First Comparison between Great Perfection (rDzogs chen) and Taoist Techniques of Light. Paper presented at the Conference on "Tantra and Daoism, the Globalization of Religion and its Experience." Boston University, April 19–21, 2002.

———. 2004. "The Longmen School and its Controversial History during the Qing Dynasty." In John Lagerwey (ed.), *Religion and Chinese Society: The Transformation of a Field*, 621–698. Hong Kong: École française d'Extrême-Orient & Chinese University of Hong Kong. (Revised edition: Chapter 2 of *Facets of Qing Daoism*. Wil / Paris: UniversityMedia, 2014).

———. 2013a. *Creative Daoism*. Wil / Paris: UniversityMedia.

———. 2013b. *The Zen of Tantra*. Wil / Paris: UniversityMedia.

———. 2014a. "The Invention of a Quanzhen Canon: The Wondrous Fate of the *Daozang jiyao*." In Xun Liu and Vincent Goossaert (eds.), *Quanzhen Daoism in Modern Chinese History and Society*, 44–77. Berkeley: Institute of East Asia Studies.

———. 2014b. *Facets of Qing Daoism*. Wil / Paris: UniversityMedia.

Farquhar, David. 1978. "Emperor as Bodhisattva in the Governance of the Ch'ing Empire." *Harvard Journal of Asiatic Studies* 38.1 (1978): 5–34.

Faure, Bernard. 1984. "La volonté d'orthodoxie." 3 vols. Thèse d'état. Paris: École Pratique des Hautes Études, Section des Sciences Religieuses.

———. 1989. *Le Bouddhisme Ch'an en mal d'histoire: Genèse d'une tradition religieuse dans la Chine des T'ang*. Paris: École Française d'Extrême-Orient.

Feng, Youzhi 馮佑哲 and Li Fuhua 李富華. 1994. *Zhongguo minjian zongjiao shi* 中國民間宗教史 [History of China's Popular Religions]. Taipei: Wenjin 文津.

Fo Kuang Shan (ed.). 1989. *The Sixth Patriarch Platform Sūtra in Religious and Cultural Perspective* (Report of the International Conference on Ch'an Buddhism). Taichong: Fo Kuang shan.

Foulk, Theodore Griffith. 1987. "The Chan school and its Place in the Buddhist Monastic Tradition." Ph. D. diss., University of Michigan.

Franke, Herbert. 1994. *China under Mongol Rule*. Aldershot: Brookfield.

———. 1996. *Chinesischer und tibetischer Buddhismus im China der Yuanzeit: drei Studien*. München: Kommission für Zentralasiatische Studien, Bayerische Akademie der Wissenschaften.

Gai, Jianmin 蓋建民. 2003. "Cong 'jiushi' dao 'yishi'" 從救世到醫世 [From 'rescuing the world' to 'healing the world']. In Guo Wu 郭武 (ed.), *Daojiao jiaoyi yu xiandai shehui* 道教教義與現代社會, 194–209. Shanghai: Shanghai Guji.

Gernet, Jacques. 1992–93. "Quelques thèmes de la pensée chinoise au XVIe et XVIIe siècles." *Annuaire du Collège de France* (1992–93): 673–677.

Girardot, Norman J. 1983. *Myth and Meaning in Early Taoism: The Theme of Chaos (hun-tun)*. Berkeley: University of California Press.

Goossaert, Vincent. 2001. "The Invention of an Order: Collective Identity in 13th Century Quanzhen." *Journal of Chinese Religion* 29, 2001: 111–138.

———. 2004. "The Quanzhen Clergy, 1700–1950." In John Lagerwey (ed.), *Religion and Chinese Society: The Transformation of a Field*. Hong Kong: École française d'Extrême-Orient & Chinese University of Hong Kong.

———. 2008. "*Yulu* Recorded Sayings." In *The Encyclopedia of Taoism*, ed. by Fabrizio Pregadio, vol. 2:1200–1202. London: Routledge.

Goossaert, Vincent, and Xun Liu (eds.). 2014. *Quanzhen Daoism in Modern Chinese History and Society*. Berkeley: Institute of East Asia Studies.

Groner, Paul. 1989. "The Ordination Ritual in the Platform Sūtra within the context of the East Asian Buddhist Vinaya Tradition." In *The Sixth Patriarch Platform Sūtra in Religious and Cultural Perspective*, edited by Fo-kuang shan, 220–250. Taichong: Fo kuang shan.

Gu, Zhizhong (trans.). 1992. *Creation of the Gods*. 2 vols. Beijing: New World Press.

Gyatso, Geshe Kelzang. 1982. *Clear Light of Bliss*. London: Wisdom.

Güntsch, Gertrud. 1988. *Das Shen-hsien chuan und das Erscheinungsbild eines Hsien*. Frankfurt: Peter Lang.

Gōyama, Kiwamu 合山究. 1994. "Min Shin no bunjin to okaruto shumi 明清の文人とオカルト趣味 [The Occult Predilection of Ming and Qing Literati]." In *Chūka bunjin no seikatsu* 中華文人生活, edited by Arai Ken 荒井建, 469–502.Kyoto: Heibonsha 平凡社.

Hachiya, Kunio 蜂屋邦夫. 1998. *Kingen jidai no dōkyō—shichi shin kenkyū* 金元時代の道教―七眞研究 [The Daoism of the Jin and Yuan Dynasties—Research on the Seven Perfected]. Tokyo: Tōkyō daigaku Tōyō bunka kenkyūjo hōkoku, Kyūko shoin.

Hanyu dacidian 漢語大辭典. 1986. Shanghai: Shanghai shudian.

Hao, Yixing 郝懿行 et al. (eds.). 1989. *Erya, Guanya, Fangyan, Sheming* 爾雅, 廣雅, 方言, 釋名. Shanghai: Shanghai guji chubanshe 上海古籍出版社.

Harding, M. Esther. 1990. *Woman's Mysteries Ancient and Modern*. Boston & Shaftesbury: Shambhala.

Hasebe, Yūkei 長谷幽蹊. 1993. *Minshin bukkyō kyōdanshi kenkyū* 明清佛教團史研究 [Research on the Institutional History of Ming and Qing Buddhism], 155–173. Kyoto: Dōhōsha 同朋舎.

Hawkes, David. 1981. "Quanzhen Plays and Quanzhen Masters." *Bulletin de l'Ecole Française d'Extrême Orient* 69, 1981: 153–170.

Hayes, James. 1985. "Specialists and Written Materials in the Village World." In *Popular Culture in Late Imperial China*, edited by David Johnson, Andrew J. Nathan and Evelyn S. Rawski, 75–111. Berkeley: University of California Press.

He, Xin 何新. 1989. *Zhushen de qiyuan* 諸神的起源 [The Origin of Divinities]. Taipei: Muduo chubanshe 木鐸出版社.

Heinze, Ruth-Inge (ed.). 2000. *The Nature and Function of Rituals: Fire from Heaven*. Connecticut & London: Bergin & Garvey Westport.

Henss, Michael. 2001. "The Bodhisattva-Emperor: Tibeto-Chinese Portraits of Sacred and Secular Rule in the Qing Dynasty, Part 1." *Oriental Art* 47.3 (2001): 2–16.

———. 2001. "The Bodhisattva-Emperor: Tibeto-Chinese Portraits of Sacred and Secular Rule in the Qing Dynasty, Part 2." *Oriental Art* 47.5 (2001): 71–83.

Ho, Chuimei, and Bennet Bronson. 2004. *Splendors of China's Forbidden City. The Glorious Reign of Emperor Qianlong*. London: Merrell.

Hong, Dichen 洪滌塵. 1979. "Qingshi dui Xizang de zhengjiao ce lüe" 清時對西藏的政教策略 [Religious Politics of the Qing toward Tibet]. In Zhang Matao 張曼濤 (ed.), *Hanzang fojiao guanxi yanjiu* 漢藏佛教關係研究 [Studies on the Relationship between Chinese and Tibetan Buddhism], 146–172. Taipei, Dacheng wenhua.

Hopkins, Jeffrey. 1985. *The Kalachakra Tantra: Rite of Initiation for the Stage of Generation*. London: Wisdom publications.

Huber, Toni. 1999. *The Cult of Pure Crystal Mountain*. New York: Oxford University Press.

Hucker, Charles. 1985. *A Dictionary of Official Titles in Imperial China*. Stanford: Standford University Press.

Hummel, Arthur W. 1943–44. *Eminent Chinese of the Ch'ing Period (1644–1912)*. Washington: Library of Congress.

Huters, Theodore et al. 1997. *Culture and State in Chinese History*. Stanford: Stanford University Press.

Igarashi, Kenryū 五十嵐賢隆. 1938. *Taiseikyū shi* 太清宮志 [Gazetteer of the Palace of Great Purity]. Tokyo: Kokushō kankōkai.

Ishida, Kenji 石田憲司. 1992. "Mingdai Dōkyō shijō no Zenshin to Seii" 明代道教史上の全真と正一 [The Quanzhen and Zhengyi in Ming Daoism]. In Sakai Tadao 酒井忠夫 (ed.), *Taiwan no shūkyō to Chūgoku bunka* 台湾の宗教と中国文化 [Taiwanese Religion and Chinese Culture], 145–185. Tokyo: Fukyūsha.

Isobe, Akira 磯部彰. 1980. "Chūgoku ni okeru 'Saiyūki' no juyō to ryūkō 中国における西遊記に受容と流行 [The Reception and Spread of *The Journey to the West* in China]. *Tōhō shūkyō* 東方宗教 55: 26–50.

James E. Bosson. 1969. *A Treasury of Aphoristic Jewels: The Subhasitaratnanidhi of Sa Skya Pandita in Tibetan and Mongolian.* Bloomington: Indiana University.

Johnson, David. 1997. "Confucian Elements in the Great Temple Festivals of Southeastern Shansi in Late Imperial Times." *T'oung-pao* 83, 1–3: 126–161.

Jordan, David K. & Overmyer, Daniel. 1986. *The Flying Phoenix: Aspects of Chinese Sectarianism in Taiwan.* Princeton: Princeton University Press.

Kaltenmark, Max. 1987. *Le Lie-sien tchouan.* Paris: Collège de France.

Kam, Tak Sing. 1994. "Manchu-Tibetan Relations In The Early Seventeenth Century: A Reappraisal." Ph.D. diss., Harvard University.

Kamitsuka, Yoshiko 神塚淑子. 1990. "Hōsho Seidō kun o megutte 方諸青童君をめぐって" [On Fangzhu Qingtong jun]. *Tōhō shūkyō* 東方宗教 76, 1990: 1–23.

Kapadia, Karin. 1995. *Śiva and Her Sisters: Gender, Caste, and Class in Rural South India.* Boulder, Oxford: Westview Press.

Kapstein, Matthew (ed.). 2009. *Buddhism Between Tibet and China.* Somerville: Wisdom Publications.

Katz, Paul. 1996. "Enlightened Alchemist or Immoral Immortal? The Growth of Lü Dongbin's Cult in Late Imperial China. In *Unruly Gods: Divinity and Society in China* edited by Meir Shahar and Robert P. Weller, 70–104. Honolulu: University of Hawai'i Press.

Kelley, David E. 1982. "Temples and Tribute Fleets: The Luo Sects and Boatmen's Associations in the Eighteenth Century." *Modern China* 8: 361–91.

Khanna, Madhu. 2000. "The Goddess-Women, Equation in Sākta Tantras," in Mandakranta Bose (ed.), *Faces of the Feminine in Ancient, Medieval, and Modern India.* New York: Oxford University Press.

Kieschnick, John. 1997. *The Eminent Monk Buddhist Ideals in Medieval Chinese Hagiography.* Honolulu: University of Hawaii.

Kleeman, Terry F. 1994. *A God's Own Tale: The Book of Transformations of Wenchang, the Divine Lord of Zitong.* Albany: State University Press.

Knott, Kim. 2000. *Hinduism: A Very Short Introduction.* New York: Oxford University Press.

Kohn, Livia.1994. "The Five Precepts of the Venerable Lord." *Monumenta Serica* 42 (1994): 171–215.

———. 1997. "Yin Xi: The Master at the Beginning of the Scripture." *Journal of Chinese Religion*, 25, 1997:83–139.

———. 1998. "The Beginnings and Cultural Characteristics of East Asian Millerianism." *Japanese Religions* 23, 1–2 (1998): 29–51.

——— (ed.). 2000. *Daoism Handbook*. Leiden: Brill.

Kolmas, Josef. 1967. *Tibet and Imperial China. A Survey of Sino-Tibetan Relations up to the End of the Manchu Dynasty in 1912*. Canberra, Australian National University.

Kroll, W. Paul. 1985. "In the Halls of the Azure Lad." *Journal of the American Oriental Society* 105/1, 1985: 75–94.

Kuijp, Leonard van der. 2004. "The Mongol Imperial Family in Yuan China and Mongolia as Patrons of the Printing of Tibetan *Kālacakra* Texts." *The Central Eurasian Studies Lectures*, no. 4. Bloomington: Research Institute for Inner Asian Studies.

Lagerwey, John. 1987. *Taoist Ritual in Chinese Society and History*. New York: Macmillan Publishing Company.

Lai, T.C. 1974. *The Eight Immortals*. Hong Kong: Swindon Book Co.

Lessing, Ferdinand (in collaboration with Gosta Montell). 1942. *Yung-ho-kung: An Iconography of the Lamaist Cathedral in Peking with Notes on Lamaist Mythology and Cult*. Stockholm.

Li, San-pao. 1993. "Ch'ing Cosmology and Popular Precepts." In *Cosmology, Ontology and Human Efficacy*, edited by R. Smith and D.W.Y. Kwok, 113–139. Honolulu: University of Hawai'i Press.

Li, Yangzheng 李養正. 1989. *Daojiao gaishuo* 道教概說 [An Outline of Daoism]. Beijing: Zhonghua shuju.

———. 2003. *Xinbian Beijing Baiyuanguan zhi* 新編北京白雲觀志 [Newly compiled Monograph on the White Clouds Abbey in Beijing]. Beijing: Zongjiao wenhua.

Li, Yuanguo 李遠國. 1985. "Daojiao qigong yu neidan shu yanjiu 道教與氣功與內丹術研究" [A Study on Inner Alchemy and Daoist Qigong]. In *Daojiao yanjiu wenji*, edited by Li Yuanguo. Chengdu: Bashu shushe.

———. 1987. *Qigong jinghua ji* 氣功精華集. [An Anthology of Qigong]. Chengdu: Bashu shushe.

———. 1988. *Daojiao qigong yangsheng xue* 道教氣功養生學 [A Study on Daoist Nurturing Principle and Qigong]. Chengdu: Sichuan sheng shehui kexue yuan 四川省社會科學院.

Liu, Guoliang 劉國梁. 1991. *Daojiao jingcui* 道教精萃 [The Essence of Daoism]. Changchun: Jilin wenshi 吉林文.

Liu, Jingcheng 劉精誠. 1993. *Zhongguo daojiao shi* 中國道教史 [History of Chinese Daoism]. Taipei:Wenjin 文津.

Liu, Kwang-Ching. 1990. "Orthodoxy in Chinese Society." In *Orthodoxy in Late Imperial China*, edited by Liu Kwang-Ching, 1–24. Berkeley: University of California Press.

Liu, Ts'un-yan 劉存仁. 1962. *Buddhist and Taoist Influences on Chinese Novels*. Wiesbaden: Harrassowitz.

———. 1967. "Yanjiu Mingdai Daojiao sixiang zhongriwen shumu juyao 研究明代道教思想中日文書目舉要." *Chongji xuebao* 崇基學報 6:2:107–130.

———. 1970. "Taoist Self-Cultivation in Ming Thought." In *Self and Society in Ming Thought*, edited by Wm Theodore de Bary, 291–326. New York: Columbia University Press.

———. 1971. "The Penetration of Taoism into the Ming Neo-Confucian Elite." *T'oung Pao* 57 (1971): 31–103.

———. 1973. "The Compilation and Historical Value of the *Tao-tsang*." In *Essays on the Sources for Chinese History*, edited by Donald Leslie, 104–20. Canberra: Australian National University Press.

———. 1984. "Wu Shou-yang: The Return to the Pure Essence." In *New Excursions from the Hall of Harmonious Wind,* ed. by Liu Ts'un- yan, 184–208. Leiden: Brill.

——— (ed.). 1984. *New Excursions from the Hall of Harmonious Wind*. Leiden: Brill, 1984.

Liu, Xun and Vincent Goossaert (eds.). 2014. *Quanzhen Daoism in Modern Chinese History and Society*. Berkeley: Institute of East Asia Studies.

Ma, Shutian 馬書田. 1991. *Huaxia zhushen* 華夏諸神 [Chinese Divinities]. Beijing: Yanshan CBS.

Ma, Xiaohong 馬曉宏. 1986. "Lü Dongbin shenxian xinyang suyuan" 呂洞賓神仙信仰溯源 [Tracing the Source of the Cult of the Divine Immortal Lü Dongbin]. *Shijie zongjiao yanjiu* 世界宗教研究 XXV, 3, 1986: 79–95.

Ma, Xisha 馬西沙 and Han Bingfang 韓秉方. 1992. *Zhongguo minjian zongjiao shi* 中國民間宗教史 [History of Chinese Popular Religion]. Shanghai: Renmin.

Mair, Victor. 1985. "Language and Ideology in the Written Popularizations of the *Sacred Edict*." In *Popular Culture in Late Imperial China*, edited by David Johnson, Andrew J. Nathan and Evelyn S. Rawski, 325–359. Berkeley: University of California Press.

Marsone, Pierre. 1999. "Le Baiyun guan de Pékin: épigraphie et histoire." *Sanjiao wenxian* 3 (1999):73–136.

———. 2001. "Wang Chongyang (1113–1170) et la fondation du Quanzhen." Ph.D. diss. Paris: École Pratique des Hautes Études, section des Sciences Religieuses.

Martin, Emily. 1989. *The Women in the Body*. Milton Keynes: Open University Press.

McRae, John R. 1993. "Yanagida Seizan's Landmark Works on Chinese Ch'an." *Cahiers d'Extrême-Asie* 7, 1993–94: 51–103.

Mesnil, Evelyne. 1996–97. "Zhang Suqing et la peinture taoïste à Shu." *Cahiers d'Extrême-Asie* 9, 1996–97: 131–158.

Min, Zhiting 閔智亭. 1990. *Daojiao yifan* 道教儀範 [Patterns of Daoist Rites]. Beijing: Zhongguo daojiao xueyuan.

Miura, Kunio. 1989. "The Revival of *Qi*: Qigong in Contemporary China." In *Taoist Meditation and Longevity Techniques*, edited by L. Kohn, 331–362. Ann Arbor: The University of Michigan, Center for Chinese Studies.

Miyakawa, Hisayuki 宮川尚志. 1954. "Ryū Ichimei no *Goshin chokushi* ni tsuite 劉一明の悟眞直指について "[A Study on the *Wuzhen zhizhi* by Liu Yiming]. *Okayama Daigaku Hōbungakubu gakujutsu kiyō* 岡山大学法文学部学術機要 3: 49–59.

Mollier, Christine. 1990. *Une apocalypse taoïste du Ve siècle: Le Livre des Incantations Divines des Grottes Abyssales*. Paris: Collège de France, Institut des Hautes Études Chinoises.

———. 2008. "Messianism and millenarianism." In *The Encyclopedia of Taoism*, edited by Fabrizio Pregadio, vol. 1, 94–96. London: Routledge.

Mori, Yuria 森由利亞. 1990. "Sōdai ni okeru Ryo Dōhin setsuwa ni kansuru ichi shiron" 宋代における呂洞賓説話にかんする一試論 [A Preliminary Study on Lü Dongbin-related Stories of the Song Dynasty]. *Bungaku kenkyūka kiyō, bessatsu* 文學研究科紀要, 別冊 17, 1990: 55–65.

———. 1994. "Zenshinkyō ryūmonha keifu kō" 全真教龍門派系譜考 [A Study on the Lineage of the Longmen School of Complete Perfection Heritage]. In *Dōkyō bunka e no tenbō* 道教文化への展望 [Observations on Chinese Culture], edited by Dōkyō bunka kenkyūkai, 181–211. Tokyo, Hirakawa.

———. 1998a. "Taiitsu kinka sōshi no seiritsu to hensen—Sho hanpon no jo, chū no kijutsu wo tegakari ni 太乙金華宗旨の成立と変遷—諸版本の序・注の記述を手がかりに—" [The Formation and Transformations of *Taiyi jinhua zongzhi*, Based on the Prefaces and Notes of Different Versions]. *Tōyō no shisō to shūkyō* 東洋の思想と宗教, 15:43–64.

———. 1998b. "Taiyi jinhua zongzhi and the Spirit Writing Cult to the Patriarch Lü (Lü Dongbin) in Qing China." Paper presented at the Seminar for Research in Religion, Komazawa University, Tokyo.

———. 1998c. "Kyuso goroku ni tsuite 邱祖語錄について" [About the Records of Patriarch Qiu]. In: *Dōkyō no rekishi to bunka* 道教の歴史と文化 [History and Culture of Daoism], edited by Yamada Toshiaki 山田利明 & Tanaka Fumio 田中文雄 257–273. Tokyo: Yūzan kaku 雄山閣.

———. 1999. "Ryo Dōhin to Zenshin kyō: Shinchō koshū kingai san no jirei o chūshin ni" 呂洞賓と全真教-清朝湖州金蓋山の事例を仲心に [Lü Dongbin and the Quanzhen: The Example of Mt. Jingai in Huzhou during the Qing Dynasty]. In Noguchi Tetsurō 野口鉄郎 (ed.), *Kōza Dōkyō daiichi kan: Dōkyō no kamigami to kyōten* 講座道教弟一巻:道教の神々と経典 [Daoist Lectures, vol. 1: Daoist Gods and Sacred Scriptures], 242–264. Tokyo: Yūzan kaku.

———. 2002. "Identity and Lineage: The *Taiyi jinhua zongzhi* and the Spirit writing Cult to Patriarch Lü in Qing China." In *Daoist Identity: History, Lineage, and Ritual,*, ed. by Livia Kohn & Harold D. Roth, 168–187. Honolulu: Univ. of Hawai'i Press.

Morohashi, Tetsuji 諸橋轍次, ed. 1976. *Dai Kanwa jiten* 大漢和辭典 [Large Chinese-Japanese Dictionary]. Tokyo: Taishūkan 大修館, 1976.

Mou, Zhongjian 牟鍾鑒 et al. (eds.). 1991. *Daojiao tonglun* 道教通論 [A General Survey of Daoism]. Jinan: Wenlu.

Mou, Zhongjian 牟鍾鑒 & Zhang, Jian 張踐. 2000. *Zhongguo zongjiao tongshi* 中國宗教通史 [General History of Chinese Religions]. 2 vols. Beijing: Shehui kexue.

Nan, Huai-chin. 1984. *Tao and Longevity*, London: Element Books.

Naquin, Susan. 1976. *Millenarian Rebellion in China: The Eight Trigrams Uprising of 1813*. New Haven: Yale University Press.

———. 1981. *Shantung Rebellion: The Wang Lun Uprising of 1774*. New Haven: Yale University Press.

———. 1982. "Connections Between Rebellions: Sect Family Networks in North China in Qing China." *Modern China* 8: 337–360.

———. 1985. "The Transmission of White Lotus Sectarianism in Late Imperial China." In *Popular Culture in Late Imperial China*, edited by David Johnson, Andrew J. Nathan and Evelyn S. Rawski, 255–291. University of California Press.

Needham, Joseph & Lu Gui-djen. 1983. *Science and Civilisation in China*, vol. V-5. Cambridge: Cambridge University Press.

Needham, Joseph. 1986. "Chinese Physiological Alchemy (*Nei Tan*) and the Indian Yoga, Tantric and Hathayoga Systems." In Needham, Joseph, *Science and Civilisation in China*, vol. V: 5, 257–288. Cambridge: Cambridge University Press.

Ōfuchi, Ninji 大淵忍爾. 1964. *Dōkyō shi no kenkyū* 道教史の研究 [Research on the History of Daoism]. Okayama: Okayama Daigaku Kyōsaikai Shosekibu.

———. 1998. "The Beginnings and Cultural Characteristics of East Asian Millenarianism." *Japanese Religions* 23, 1–2, 1998: 29–51.

Olivelle, Patrick. 1996. *Upanishads*. New York: Oxford University Press.

Overmyer, Daniel L. 1976. *Folk Buddhist Religion: Dissenting Sects in Late Traditional China*. Cambridge, Mass:Harvard University Press.

———. 1978. "Boatmen and Buddhas: The Lo chiao in Ming Dynasty China." *History of Religion* 17.3–4:284–288.

———. 1981. "Alternatives:Popular Religious Sects in Chinese Society." *Modern China* 7.2:153–90.

———. 1985. " Values in Chinese Sectarian Literature: Ming and Ch'ing *pao-chüan*. " In *Popular Culture in Late Imperial China*, edited by David Johnson, Andrew J. Nathan and Evelyn S. Rawsky, 219–254. Berkeley:University of California Press.

Oyanagi, Shigeta 小柳司氣太. 1934. *Hakuunkan shi* 白雲觀志 [Gazetteer of the Abbey of the White Clouds]. Tokyo: Tōhō bunka gakuin Tōkyō kenkyūjo 東方文化學院東京研究所.

Petech, Luciano. 1972. *China and Tibet in the Early 18th Century*. Leiden: Brill, 1972 (1st ed. 1950).

———. 1990. *Central Tibet and the Mongols: The Yuan–Sa-skya period of Tibetan History*. Rome: Istituto italiano per il Medio ed Estremo Oriente.

Plaks, Andrew. 1987. *The Four Masterworks of the Ming Novel*. Princeton: Princeton University Press.

Pomeroy, Sarah B. 1991. *Women's History and Ancient History*. Chapel Hill: University of North Carolina Press.

Pregadio, Fabrizio & Skar, Lowell. 2000. "Inner alchemy (*Neidan*)." In *Daoism Handbook*, edited by Livia Kohn, 464–497. Leiden: Brill.

Pregadio, Fabrizio. 1995. "The Representation of Time in the *Zhouyi Cantong qi*." *Cahiers d'Extrême-Asie* 8 (1995): 155–173.

———. 1996. *Zhouyi Cantong Qi: Dal Libro dei Mutamenti all'elisir d'oro*. Venezia: Ca' Foscarina.

——— (ed.). 2008. *The Encyclopedia of Taoism*. London: Routledge.

———. 2008. "Daoshu shi'er zhong." In *Encyclopedia of Taoism*, edited by Fabrizio Pregadio. Vol. 1:331–333. London: Routledge.

Pu, Jiangqing 浦江清. 1931. "Baxian kao" 八仙考 [A Study on the Eight Immortals]. *Qinghua xuebao* 1, 1931: 89–136.

Qing, Xitai 卿希泰 (ed.). 1994. *Zhongguo daojiao shi* 中國道教史 [History of Chinese Daoism]. 4 vols. Shanghai: Zhishi 知識. 1996 edition: Chengdu: Sichuan Renmin 四川人民.

——— (ed.). 1994. *Zhongguo daojiao* 中國道教 [Chinese Daoism]. 4 vols. Shanghai: Zhishi. Revised 1996 edition: Chengdu: Sichuan Renmin 四川人民.

Rawski, Evelyn S. 1979. *Education and Popular Literacy in Ch'ing China*. Ann Arbor: University of Michigan, Center for Chinese Studies.

———. 1985. "Economic and Social Foundations of Late Imperial Culture." In *Popular Culture in Late Imperial China*, edited by David Johnson, Andrew J. Nathan and Evelyn S. Rawsky, 3–33. Berkeley: University of California Press.

Reichelt, Karl Ludwig. 1990. *Truth and Tradition in Chinese Buddhism*. Taipei: SMC. Publishing Inc. (first ed. 1927).

Reiter, Florian. 1983. "Some Observations concerning Taoist Foundations in Traditional China." *Zeitschrift der Deutschen Morgenländischen Gesellschaft* 133, 1983: 363–376.

———. 1985. "Der Name Tung-hua ti-chün und sein Umfeld in der taoistischen Tradition." In *Religion und Philosophie in Ostasien. Festschrift für Hans Steininger*, edited by Gert Naundorf et al., 87–101. Würzburg: Königshausen & Neumann.

———. 1988. *Grundelemente und Tendenzen des religiösen Taoismus*. Stuttgart: Franz Steiner.

Ren, Jiyu 任繼愈 (ed.). 1990. *Zhongguo daojiao shi* 中國道教史 [History of Chinese Daoism]. Shanghai: Shanghai renmin.

Robinet, Isabelle. 1983. "Le Ta-t'ung chen-ching—son authenticité et sa place dans les textes du Shang-ching ching." In *Tantric and Taoist Studies in Honour of R. A. Stein*, edited by Michel Strickmann, II: 394–433. Bruxelles: Institut Belge des Hautes Études Chinoises.

———. 1984. *La révélation du Shangqing dans l'histoire du taoïsme*, 2 vols., Paris: École Française d'Extrême-Orient.

———. 1984. "Notes préliminaires sur quelques antinomies fondamentales entre le bouddhisme et le taoïsme." In *Incontro di Religioni in Asia tra il III e il IV secolo d. C.*, edited by Lionello Lanciotti, 217–242. Firenze: Leo S. Olschki.

———. 1989–90. "Recherche sur l'alchimie intérieure (*neidan*): l'école Zhenyuan," *Cahiers d'Extrême-Asie* 5 (1989–90): 141–162.

———. 1989. "Original Contributions of *Neidan* to Taoism and Chinese Thought." In *Taoist Meditation and Longevity Techniques*, ed. by Livia Kohn and Yoshinobu Sakade, 297–330. Ann Arbor: The University of Michigan.

———. 1992. "Le monde à l'envers dans l'alchimie intérieure taoïste [The upside-down world in Daoist inner alchemy]." *Revue de l'Histoire des Religions* 209, 3 (1992): 239–257.

———. 1994. "Primus movens et création récurrente" *Taoist Resources* 5.2 (1994) 29–70.

———. 1995. *Introduction à l'alchimie intérieure taoïste*. Paris: Le Cerf.

———. 1995. *Méditation taoïste*. Paris: Albin Michel.

Rockhill, W. W. 1910. "The Dalai Lamas of Lhasa and their Relations with the Manchu Emperors of China 1644–1908," *T'oung Pao* 2.11(1910): 1–104.

Sakade, Yoshinobu 坂出祥伸. 1999. "Shoki mikkyō to dōkyō to no kōshō" 初期密教と道教との交渉 [The Early Interaction between Tantrism and Daoism]. In *Chūgoku mikkyō* 中国密教 [Chinese Tantrism], ed. by Musashi Tachikawa 武藏立川 and Motohiro Yoritomi 本宏頼富, 153–169. Tokyo: Shunkasha.

Sakai, Tadao 酒井忠夫. 1960. *Chūgoku zensho no kenkyū* 中国善書の研究 [Researches on Chinese Morality Books]. Tokyo:Kokusho kankōkai 国書刊行会.

———. 1970. "Confucianism and Popular Educational Works." In *Self and Society in Ming Thought*, edited by Wm. Th. de Bary, 331–66. New York: Columbia University Press.

Saso, Michael. 1978. *The Teachings of the Taoist Master Chuang*. New Haven: Yale University Press.

Sawada, Mizuho 沢田瑞穂. 1957. "Kōyōkyō shitan 弘陽教試探 [Preliminary Investigation of the Hung-yang Sect]. *Tenri daigaku gakuhō* 天理大学年宗報 24: 63–85.

———. 1981. "Ishū Hakuunkan jinbōki 維修白雲觀尋訪記 [Report of a Visit to the Restored Abbey of White Clouds]." *Tōhō shūkyō* 東方宗教 57, 1981: 71–77.

Schafer, Edward H. 1980. *Mao Shan in T'ang Times*. Society for the Study of Chinese Religions Monograph no. 1. Boulder, Col: Society for the Study of Chinese Religions.

Schipper, Kristofer. 1985. "Taoist Ordination Ranks in the Tunhuang Manuscripts." In *Religion und Philosophie in Ostasien. Festschrift für Hans Steininger*, edited by Gert Naundorf et al., 127–148. Würzburg: Königshausen & Neumann.

———. 1987. "Master Chao I-chen and the Ch'ing-wei School of Taoism." In *Dōkyō to shūkyō bunka*, edited by Akizuki Kan'ei, 715–734. Tokyo: Hirakawa.

———. 1991. "Temples et liturgie de Pékin." *Annuaire de l'EPHE* (Vème Section) 100, 1991–92: 91–96.

Schulemann, Günther. 1958. *Die Geschichte der Dalai-Lamas*. Leipzig: Otto Harrassowitz, 1958.

Seaman Gary. 1987. *Journey to the North: An Ethnohistorical Analysis and Annotated Translation of the Chinese Folk Novel "Pei-you chi."* Berkeley: University of California Press.

Seidel, Anna. 1969–70. "The Image of the Perfect Ruler in Early Taoist Messianism: Lao-tzu and Li Hung." *History of Religions* 9 (1969–70): 216–247.

———. 1983. "Imperial Treasures and Taoist Sacraments: Taoist Roots in the Apocrypha." In *Tantric and Taoist Studies in Honour of R.A. Stein*, edited by Michel Strickmann, 291–371. Bruxelles: Institut Belge des Hautes Études Chinoises.

———. 1984. "Taoist Messianism," *Numen* XXXI, 2 (1984): 161–174.

Shahar, Meir. 1996. "Vernacular Fiction and the Transmission of Gods' Cults in Late Imperial China." In *Unruly Gods: Divinity and Society in China* edited by Meir Shahar and Robert P. Weller, 184–211. Hawaii: University of Hawai'i Press.

Shek, Richard. 1980. *Religion and Society in Late Ming: Sectarianism and Popular Thought in Sixteenth and Seventeenth Century China*. Ph. D. diss. University of California, Berkeley.

———. 1982. "Millenarianism Without Rebellion: The Huangtian Dao in North China." *Modern China*, 8: 305–336.

Shen, Weirong 沈衛榮. 2004. "Magic Power, Sorcery and Evil Spirits: The Image of Tibetan Monks in Chinese Literature during the Yuan Dynasty," in *The Relationship between Religion and State (chos srid zung 'brel) in Traditional Tibet*, ed. Christoph Cuppers. Bhairahawa: Lumbini International Research Institute, 2004):189–228. Chinese version in *Hanxue yanjiu* 漢學研究 [Chinese Studies] 21/2 (2003):219–247.

Shiga, Ichiko 志賀市子. 1995. "Hong Kong no dōtan 香港の道壇" [Daoist Institutions in Hong Kong]. *Tōhō shūkyō* 東方宗教 85: 1–13.

Shinohara, Kōichi. 1994. "Passages and Transmission in Tianhuang Daowu's Biographies." In *Other Selves Autobiography & Biography in Cross-Cultural Perspective*, edited by Phyllis Granoff and Shinohara Kōichi, 132–149. Oakville, Buffalo: Mosaic Press.

Skar, Lowell. 1996–97. "Administering Thunder: A Thirteenth-Century Memorial Deliberating the Thunder Rites." *Cahiers d'Extrême-Asie* 9, 1996–97: 159–202.

———. 2000a. "Alchemy, Local Cults, and Daoism: A Perspective on the Formation of the Southern Lineage from Tang to Ming." Paper presented at the Conference "Religion and Chinese Society: The Transformation of a Field," Hong Kong, May 29–June 2, 2000.

———. 2000b. "Ritual Movement, Deity Cults and the Transformation of Daoism in Song and Yuan times." In *Daoism Handbook*, edited by Livia Kohn, 413–463. Leiden: Brill.

Smith, Richard. 1983. *China's Cultural Heritage: The Ch'ing Dynasty, 1644–1912*. Boulder: Westview Press.

———. 1990. "Ritual in Ch'ing Culture." In *Orthodoxy in Late Imperial China*, edited by Liu Kwang-Ching, 281–310. Berkeley: University of California Press.

———. 1991. *Fortune-Tellers and Philosophers*. Boulder: Westview Press.

Soothill, W. Eduard & Lewis, Hodous. 1937. *A Dictionary of Chinese Buddhist Terms*. London: Kegan Paul, Trench, Trubner and Co.

Strickmann, Michel. 1978. "The Longest Taoist Scripture." *History of Religion*, 17, 3–4, 1978:331–354.

———. 1986. *Mantras et mandarins —Le bouddhisme tantrique en Chine*. Paris: Gallimard.

Swan, Nancy Lee. 1975. "Pao T'ing-bo." In *Eminent Chinese of the Ch'ing Period*, edited by Arthur Hummel, 612–13. Taipei: Ch'eng Wen Publishing Company.

Tanaka, Kimiaki 田中公明. 1994. *Chō mikkyō jirin tantora* 超密教時輪タントラ. Osaka: Tōhō.

Tang, Dachao 唐大潮. 1985. "Ming-Qing zhi ji daojiao sanjiao heyi sixiang de lilun biaoxian luelun 明清之際道教三教合一思想的理論表現略論" [Brief presentation of the syncretic theory of the three teachings in Ming-Qing Daoism]. *Shijie zongjiao yanjiu* 世界宗教研. 3: 87–95.

Taylor, Romeyn. 1995. "Some Changes and Continuities in the Official Religion During Ming and Qing: A Survey of Gazetteers." (Paper presented at the Paris conference on State and Ritual in East Asia. Paris: Collège de France, June 1995).

———. 1997. "Official Altars, Temples and Shrines Mandated for All Counties in Ming and Qing." *T'oung pao*, 88, 1–3: 93–125.

ter Haar, Barend. 1992. *The White Lotus Teachings in Chinese Religious History*. Leiden: Brill.

Tsui, Bartholomew P. M. 1991. *Taoist Tradition and Change. The Story of the Complete Perfection Sect in Hong Kong*. Hong Kong: Christian Study Centre on Chinese Religion and Culture.

Tucci, Giuseppe. 1980. *Tibetan Painted Scrolls*. Roma: Libreria dello stato, 1949. Reprint Kyoto: Rinsen.

Tuttle, Gray. 2006. "Tibetan Buddhsim at Ri bo rtse lnga / Wutai shan in Modern Times." *Journal of the International Association of Tibetan Studies* 2 (August 2006):1–35.

Vercammen, Dany. 1989. *Neijia wushu —The Internal School of Chinese Martial Arts: Its Written and Oral Tradition, History, and the Connection with Qigong* (3 vols). Ph.D. thesis, Ghent University, Belgium.

———. 1991. *The History of Taijiquan*. Antwerp: Belgian Taoist Association (Dao Association).

Waley, Arthur. 1931. *Travels of an Alchemist: The Journey of the Taoist Ch'ang-ch'un to the Hindukush at the Summons of Chingiz Khan.* London: George Routledge & Sons, Ltd..

Wang, Zhizhong 王志忠. 1995. "Quanzhen jiao Longmen pai qiyuan lunkao" 全真教龍門派起源論考 [A study on the Origin of the Longmen lineage of the Quanzhen School]." *Zongjiao xue yanjiu* 宗教學研究 4(1995): 9–13.

Wang Xiangyun. 1995. *Tibetan Buddhism at the Court of Qing: The Life and Work of lCang skya Rol pa'i rdo rje.* Ph.D.dissertation, Harvard University.

———. 2000. "The Qing Court's Tibet Connection: Lcang skya Rol pa'i rdo rje and the Qianlong Emperor." *Harvard Journal of Asiatic Studies* 60, no. 1 (June 2000): 125–63.

Wang Zhizhong 王志忠. 1995. "Lun Mingmo Qingchu Quanzhen jiao 'zhongxing' de chengyin" 論明末清初全真教中興的成因 [On Contributing Factors to the 'Revival' of Quanzhen between the End of Ming and the Beginning of Qing]. *Zongjiao xue yanjiu* 宗教學研究 3, 1995: 32–38.

———. 1995. "Quanzhen jiao Longmen pai qiyuan lunkao" 全真教龍門派起源論" [A Study on the Origin of the Longmen Branch of Quanzhen]. *Zongjiao xue yanjiu* 宗教學研, 1995/4: 9–13.

———. 2000. *Ming-qing Quanzhen jiao lungao* 明清全真論稿 [Articles on the Quanzhen of the Ming and Qing Dynasties]. Chengdu: Basu shushe.

Ware, James. 1966. *Alchemy, Medicine and Religion in the China of A.D. 320: The Nei P'ien of Ko Hung (Pao-pu-tzu).* Cambridge (Mass.): M.I.T. Press.

Watson, L. James.1985. "Standardizing the Gods: The Promotion of T'ien Hou ("Empress of Heaven") Along the South China Coast, 960–1960." In *Popular Culture in Late Imperial China*, edited by David Johnson, Andrew J. Nathan and Evelyn S. Rawski, 292–324. Berkeley: University of California Press.

Welch, Holmes. 1967. *The Practice of Chinese Buddhism 1900–1950*. Cambridge, Massachusetts: Harvard University Press.

Welch, Holmes, and Anna Seidel (eds.). 1979. *Facets of Taoism*. New Haven: Yale University Press.

Welter, Albert. 1988. "The Contextual Study of Chinese Buddhist Biographies: the Example of Yung-Ming Yen-Shou (904–975)." In *Monks and Magicians Religious Biographies in Asia*, edited by Phyllis Granoff and Shinohara Koichi, 247–268. Oakville: Mosaic Press.

White, David. 1998. *The Alchemical Body*. Chicago: Chicago University Press.

Wile, Douglas. 1992. *Arts of the Bedchamber: The Chinese Sexual Yoga Classics Including Women's Solo Meditation Texts*. Albany: State University of New York Press.

Wilhelm, Richard. 1929. *Das Geheimnis der Goldenen Blüte: Ein chinesisches Lebensbuch*. Munich (English translation by Cary F. Baynes, *The Secret of the Golden Flower, A Chinese Book of Life*. London: Kegan Paul, Trench and Trübner 1931].

Wong, Eva. 1998. *Cultivating the Energy of Life, A Translation of the Hui-ming ching and its Commentaries*. Boston: Shambhala.

Wong, Shiu Hon. 1982. *Investigation into the Authenticity of the Chang San-feng Ch'uan-chi*. Canberra: Australian National University Press.

———. 1988a. *Daojiao yanjiu lunwen ji* 道教研究論文集 (A Collection of Daoist studies]. Hong Kong: Zhongwen wenxue.

———. 1988b. *Mingdai daoshi Zhang Sanfeng kao* 明代道士張三丰. Taiwan, Xuesheng.

Wright, Dale S. 1993-94. "Les récits de transmission du bouddhisme Ch'an et l'historiographie moderne." *Cahiers d'Extrême-Asie* 7, 1993-94: 105–114.

Wädow, Gerd. 1992. *Tien-fei hsien-sheng lu: Die Aufzeichnungen von der manifestierten Heiligkeit der Himmelsprinzessin. Einleitung, Übersetzung, Kommentar*. St. Augustin/Nettetal: Steyler Verlag, Monumenta Serica Monograph 29.

Xiao, Dengfu 蕭登福. 1993. *Daojiao yu mizong* 道教與密宗 [Daoism and Tantrism], Taipei: Xinwen feng.

Xu, Dishan 許地山. 1941. *Fuji mixin di yanjiu* 扶箕迷信底研究 [A Study on the Foundation of the Superstition of Planchette-writing]. Shanghai. Shangwu yinshuguan.

Yamada, Toshiaki 山田利明. 1977. "Shinsen Ri Happyaku den kō" 神仙李八百伝考 [Observations on the Biography of Li Babai]. In Yoshioka Yoshitoyo hakase kanreki kinen kenkyū ronshū kankōkai 吉岡義豊博士還暦記念研究論集刊行会, edited by *Yoshioka Yoshitoyo hakase kanreki kinen dōkyō kenkyū ronshū* 吉岡義豊博士還暦記念道教研究論集 [Collected Studies on Daoism Offered to Dr. Yoshioka Yoshitoyo on his Sixtieth Birthday], 145–163. Tokyo, Kokusho Kankōkai.

———. 2000. "The Lingbao school." In *Daoism Handbook*, ed. by Livia Kohn, 225–255. Leiden: Brill.

Yanagida, Seizan 柳田聖山. 1967. *Shoki zenshū shisho no kenkyū* 初期禪宗史書の研究 [Studies in the Historical Sources of Early Chan]. Kyoto: Hōzōkan 法藏館.

Yang, C.K. 1961. *Religion in Chinese Society*. Berkeley:University of California Press.

Yang, Richard F. S. 1958. "A Study in the Origin of the Eight Immortals." *Oriens Extremus* 5, 1958: 1–22.

Yang Xuezheng 楊學政 et al. ed. 1999. *Yunnan zongjiao shi* 雲南宗教史 [History of Yunnan Religion]. Kunming: Yunnan renmin.

Yao, Tao-chung. 1980. "Chuan-chen: A New Taoist Sect in North China During the 12 and 13th centuries." Ph. D. diss., University of Arizona.

———. 2000. "Quanzhen: Complete Perfection." In *Daoism Handbook*, edited by Livia Kohn, 567–93. Leiden: Brill.

Yao, Chi-on 遊子安. 1999. *Quanhua jinzhen—Qingdai shanshu yanjiu* 勸化金箴—清代善書研究 [Quanhua jinzhen—Research on Qing-Era Morality Books]. Tianjin: Tianjin renmin.

Yao, Tao-chung. 1980. "Chuan-chen: A New Taoist Sect in North China During the 12th and 13th centuries." Ph. D. diss., University of Arizona.

———. 2000. "Quanzhen: Complete Perfection." In *Daoism Handbook*, edited by Livia Kohn, 567–593. Leiden: Brill.

Yetts, Perceval W. 1916. "The Eight Immortals." *Journal of the Royal Asiatic Society* (1916): 773–807.

———. 1922. "More Notes on the Eight Immortals." *Journal of the Royal Asiatic Society* (1922): 397–426.

Yokote, Hiroshi 横手裕. 1994. "Ri Kankyo shotan—Aru dōkyōteki shugyōhō to chōetsu no michi 李涵虚初探 — ある道教的修行法と超越の道" [Preliminary Studies on Li Hanxu—A Particular Daoist Practice and the Way of Transcendence]. Kamata Shigeru 鎌田繁 and Mori Hideki 森秀樹. *Chōetsu to shinpi—Chūgoku, Indo, Isurāmu no shisō sekai* 超越と神秘 — 中国・インド・イスラームの思想世界" [The Transcendence and the Mystics—The Worldview of Islam, India and China]. Tokyo: Daimeidō 大明堂.

Yokote, Yutaka 横手裕. 2000. "Zenshinkyō to nanshū hokushū" 全眞教と南宗北宗 [The Quanzhen School and the Northern and Southern Lineages], in Tetsurō Noguro 鉄郎野口 et al., *Dōkyō no seimeikan to shintai ron* 道教の生命観身体論 [The Daoist View of Life and Body], 180–196. Tokyo: Yūyama kaku.

Yoritomi, Motohiro 頼富本宏. 1999. "Chūgoku mikkyō no nagare" 中国密教の流れ [The Current of Tantrism in China]. In Tachikawa Musashi 立川武藏 and Yoritomi Motohiro (eds.), *Chūgoku mikkyō* 中国密教 [Chinese Tantrism], 15–39. Tokyo: Shunkasha.

———. 1999. "Chūgoku mikkyō no shisōteki tokushitsu" 中国密教の思想的特質 [Ideological Characteristics of Chinese Tantrism]. In Tachikawa Musashi 立川武藏 and Yoritomi Motohiro (eds.), *Chūgoku mikkyō* 中国密教 [Chinese Tantrism], 113–140. Tokyo: Shunkasha.

Yoshioka, Yoshitoyo 吉岡義豊. 1955. *Dōkyō kyōten shiron* 道教経典史論" [On the History of Daoist Scriptures]. Tokyo: Dōkyō kankōkai 道教刊行会.

———. 1970. *Eisei e no negai: Dōkyō* 永生への願い：道教 [Daoism: The Quest for Eternal Life]. Kyoto: Tankōsha 淡交社.

———. 1975. *Dōkyō no jittai* 道教の実体 [Daoism today]. Kyoto: Hōyū shoten.

———. 1979. "Taoist Monastic Life." In Holmes Welch & Anna Seidel (eds.), *Facets of Taoism*, 229–252. New Haven and London: Yale University Press.

Yu, Anthony C. 1991. "How to read *The Original Intent of the Journey to the West*." In *How to Read the Chinese Novel*, edited by David L. Rolston, 299–315. Princeton: Princeton University Press.

Yu, Benyuan 於本源. 1999. *Qingwangchao de zongjiao zhengce* 清王朝的宗教政策 [Religious Politics of the Qing Court]. Beijing: Shehui kexueyuan (especially pp. 117–148).

Yü, Chun-fang. 1981. *The Renewal of Buddhism in China: Chu-hung and the Late Ming Synthesis.* New York: Columbia University Press.

Zahiruddin, Ahmad. 1970. *Sino-Tibetan Relations in the Seventeenth Century.* Roma: Istituto italiano per il Medio ed Estremo Oriente.

Zeng, Zhaonan 曾召南. 1995. "Longmen pai" 龍門派. In *Zhongguo daojiao dacidian* 中國道教大辭典, edited by Hu Fuchen 胡孚琛, 66–67. Beijing: Zhongguo shehui kexue.

Zhang, Jiebin 張介賓. 1989. *Zhiyi lu* 質疑錄. Beijing: Jiangsu kexue jishu 江蘇科學技術.

Zhang, Tianzhi 張天志 & Sun Tie 孫鐵 (eds.). 1991. *Daojiao shi ziliao* 道教史資料 [Sources on the History of Daoism]. Shanghai: Shanghai Guji.

Zhou, Shujia 周叔迦. 2000. *Qingdai fojiao shiliao jigao* 清代佛教史料輯稿 [Collected Articles on Sources on the History of Buddhism during the Qing Era]. Taipei: Xinwenfeng (especially pp. 91–104 and 303–380).

Zito, Angela. 1977. *Of Body and Brush: Grand Sacrifices as Text / Performance in Eighteenth-Century China.* Chicago: University of Chicago Press.

Zong, Li 宗力 and Liu Qun 劉群. 1987. *Zhongguo minjian zhushen* 中國民間諸神 [China's Popular Pantheon]. Shijiazhuang: Hebei renmin.

Index

A

abhiseka (guanding 灌頂) 240, 285–287
ācārya (ch. asheli 阿闍梨; tib. slob dpon; jap. ajari) 271, 282
Acāryā Tantrism 阿吒力密教 279, 282
aiyuan 愛緣 (affective attachments) 153
Akioka, Hideyuki 秋岡英行 42
Akizuki, Kan'ei 秋月観 19, 32, 65
alchemy 7, 11, 12, 16, 18–20, 22–29, 41, 42, 60, 63, 72, 76, 78, 79, 86, 97, 100, 101, 105, 106, 107, 111, 112, 115, 116, 118–122, 145, 150, 152, 155, 161, 163–166, 169, 171–178, 182–184, 187, 188–190, 192, 194–196, 198–202, 205–211, 223–237, 254–256, 258, 264, 268, 288
    alchemical process, practice 19, 23, 105, 116, 182, 194–196, 201, 226, 229, 232, 234
    cauldron 23
    elixir 25, 26, 28, 65, 72, 100–102, 104, 152, 172, 183, 190, 206–209, 211, 237
    feminine inner alchemy 26, 29, 223, 224
    firing process 29
    inner alchemy (neidan 內丹) 7, 11, 12, 16, 18, 20, 22–29, 41–42, 79, 145, 150, 175, 183, 206, 208, 223, 224, 226, 229, 230, 232, 233, 236, 237, 255, 256, 258, 260, 264, 288
    inner alchemy collections 22–29
    inner alchemical ideas and practices 16
    opus of alchemy 235
    Wu-Liu 伍柳 School, inner alchemy 7, 17, 18, 25
Ang, Isabelle 95, 100, 122
App, Urs 4, 55, 143
asceticism 12, 56, 63, 68, 70, 77, 78, 80, 83, 84, 89, 95, 98, 101, 104, 113–115, 125, 128, 144, 155, 211, 243, 287
astrology 39
azi guan 阿字觀 (contemplation of the letter A) 170

B

Babai sui gong 八百歲公 (Sir Eight-Hundred-Years; Li Babai, q.v.) 119
Bai Xuanfu 白玄福 (fl. 1656) 99
Bai Yuchan 白玉蟾 (1194-ca.1227) 26, 116, 117, 119, 178, 200, 211

bailuan 拜鸞 (spirit writing cults) 41
Baima Li 白馬李 266
Baiyun Guan 白雲觀 (White Cloud Abbey, Beijing) 12, 13, 56, 58, 59, 61, 63–67, 69, 70–73, 81, 82, 85, 90, 91, 93, 95–99, 106, 110, 124–129, 144, 147, 148, 155, 157, 162, 167, 174, 190, 244, 247, 248, 252, 253, 287, 289, 290, 291
    abbotship and Longmen 247–248
    and Qiu Chuji's grave 12
    and standardization of religious rules 13
    association with Longmen 65–66
    Citang 祠堂 (Hall of Ancestral Worship) 96
    Daoist Association at Baiyun guan 61, 128
    dual role as public monastery and headquarters of the Longmen school 12–13
    emergence as training center for all Daoist schools under Wang Changyue 13
    headquarters of the orthodox Longmen lineage 61
    history 63–65
    in Yuan, Ming and Qing eras 64–66
    legendary transmission of regalia to Tao Jing'an 157
    Longmen abbots starting with Wang Changyue 56
Baiyun guan zhi 白雲觀志 (*See* Hakuunkan shi, Oyanagi)
Baiyun xianbiao 白雲仙表 (Chart of Immortals at Baiyun Abbey) 91, 109
Baker, Victoria J. 229
Baldrian-Hussein, Farzeen 100, 145, 160
Bao Kun 鮑錕 (fl. 1814) 58, 249
Bao Tingbo 鮑廷博 (1728–1814) 58–60, 69, 249
baojuan 寶卷 (precious scrolls) 37, 38
Baopuzi 抱朴子 120, 183
baoyi 抱一 (embracing the One) 195
Bardol, Philippe 6, 14
Baroni, Helen 246
Baxian chuchu dongyouji 八仙出處東遊記 115
Bei Daqin 貝大欽 265
Bei Lanyun 貝懶雲 265
Beixi ji 杯溪集 (Collection from Bei Mountain Stream) 24
Beixi lu 杯溪錄 (Records from Bei Mountain Stream) 20
Beizhen miao 北鎮廟 (Liaoning) 73
Bell, Catherine 36
Berling, Judith 6, 33, 36, 41
Bianchi, Ester 149
Birrell, Anne 233
Biyang dong 碧陽洞 (Sichuan) 103
Biyuan guan 碧苑觀 (Nanjing) 14

Biyuan tanjing 碧苑壇經 (Platform Sūtra of the Jade Garden) 14, 27, 97, 145, 147–154, 160, 163, 165, 177, 244, 246
    versions, background of text 244
Board of Rites 9
Bodhisattva 149, 155, 188, 195, 244, 245, 285, 291
    Bodhisattva precepts 149, 245, 291
Bojian 缽鑑 (Examination of the Bowl; attr. to Wang Changyue) 14, 56, 57, 59, 91, 248, 249, 273
    as source for early Longmen history 56, 57
    known only through quotations by Min Yide in Jingai xindeng (1821) 57, 248
Bokenkamp, R. Stephen 109
Boltz, Judith 17, 18, 23, 30–32, 63, 64, 80, 81, 103, 108, 110, 118, 181, 243, 288
Bose, Mandakranta 228, 233
Bosson, James E. 240
Brahmā (fantian 梵天) 169, 185
breast massage 208, 235, 236
breathing 23, 174, 175, 193, 198, 206, 208, 260
Briffault, Robert 225
Brockington, J. L. 228
Brokaw, Cynthia 36
Brook, Timothy 235
Bu Han tianshi shijia 補漢天師世家 (Supplement to the Lineage of the Han Celestial Master) 9–11
Buddha, Buddhahood 23, 150, 180, 252, 269, 270, 278, 279, 284, 285, 291
Buddhism, Buddhist (*see also* Chan, Daoism of Qing era) 5, 6, 7, 10, 11, 14, 18, 19, 23, 27, 31–42, 55, 57, 69, 76, 88, 89, 96, 101, 128, 143, 144, 148–151, 155, 162, 169, 172, 175, 178, 184, 185, 187, 191, 197, 206, 207, 239–247, 252, 254, 258, 261, 264, 269, 277–279, 280, 282–289, 291
    Buddhism and Daoism as seen by Jesuit missionaries 239
    Buddhism translated into Daoist context at Mt. Jingai 189–190
    Buddhist doctrines rejected by Qing scholars 34
    Buddhist ideals
    Buddhist lay groups 36–37
    Buddhist lineages, standardization 55
    Buddhist ordination, influence on Longmen ordination 244–246
    Buddhist sūtras 10
    Chan *See* Chan Buddhism
    five precepts of Buddhism (wujie 五戒) 150, 246
    Huayan 華嚴 Buddhism 7, 18
    Linji 臨濟 (jap. Rinzai) lineage 55, 143, 242
    Pure Land Buddhism 172
    Wu-Liu school mixing inner alchemy with Huayan Buddhism 7

C

Cai Yongqing 蔡永清 71
Cantongqi 參同契 28, 202, 210
Cantongqi zhizhi 參同契直指 28
Cao Changhua 曹常化 (1562–1622) 17, 18, 23, 62, 100, 101, 102, 107
Cao Guanmiao 曹觀妙 (?-1236) 105
Cao Huanyang 曹還陽 104
Celestial Immortal
   as healer of the world in Longmen Mt. Jingai branch 188–190
Celestial Masters (see also Zhengyi 正一) 9–13, 30, 31, 64, 73, 74, 78, 79, 117, 122, 123, 125–127, 174, 182, 190, 203
   lost supreme authority in Jiangnan 11
   and Qing rulers 12
Central Asia 63, 70, 161, 243, 271, 277, 278
Central Daoist Registry (Daolu si 道錄司) 5, 9, 65
Chan 禪 (Chinese Zen) Buddhism 14, 18, 57, 69, 76, 84, 88, 128, 144, 148–149, 151, 155, 172, 187, 191, 193, 242, 244–246, 252–254, 258, 278
   curious intermingling of "Northern" and "Southern" schools 128
   Huangbo 黃檗 (Jap. Ōbaku) lineage 246
   Huineng 慧能 (6th patriarch of Chan Buddhism) 14, 148, 244
   influence on Longmen ordination system 244–246
   Lamp Histories as model for Min Yide's *Jingai xindeng* 57, 252–254
   Linji Yixuan 臨濟義玄 (jap. Rinzai) lineage 55, 143, 242
   metaphor of seeing one's original face 193
   Platform Sūtra of Sixth Chan Patriarch Huineng 14, 148, 151, 244
   Platform Sūtra of Huineng and Longmen's *Biyuan tanjing* 148–149
   transmission of bowl and Longmen bowl 288
Chang Chung-li 34
Chang Guang 常光 (Huashan line) 62
Changchun daojiao yuanliu 長春道教源流 (Origins and Development of the Daoist Teachings of [Qiu] Changchun) 72, 80, 91, 97, 147, 164, 242
Changchun gong 長春宮 (Palace of Perennial Spring) 64
Changchun zhenren xiyouji 長春真人西遊記 63, 70, 243
changluan 唱鸞 (reading and reciting characters in spirit writing) 40
channels in inner alchemy and Tantric Yoga 174–176
Chaoyuan guan 朝元觀 (Abbey of Worshiping the Prime) on Mt. Qiyun (Gansu) 17
charms 39
Chen Bing 陳兵 12, 19, 42, 56, 57, 60, 84, 172, 248
Chen Chongyuan 陳仲遠 30

Chen Tongwei 陳通微 (fl. 1387; second generation Longmen Vinaya line) 62, 76–83, 127, 146
   biography 76–79
Chen Minggui 陳銘珪 (1824–1881) 72, 73, 74, 78, 97, 164, 242
Chen Nan 陳楠 (d. 1175/91) 116
Chen Qiaoyun 陳樵雲 (1730–1785) 163, 257
Chen Tuan 陳摶 (ca. 906–989) 27, 95, 105, 147
Chen Wenyi 10
Chen Yaoting 陳耀庭 55, 170, 185, 248, 288
Chen Yingning 陳攖寧 19
Chen, William 21
Cheng, Hsueh-li 153
Cheng, Anne 34
Chengdu 21, 26, 71, 113, 171, 192, 195, 275
chidao 赤道 (Red Path) 175
Chinggis Khan 28, 63, 70, 243
Chishi Tuoluoni jing 持世陀羅尼經 (Vasu[n]dhāradhāraṇī) 269, 283, 285, 286
Chishui yin 赤水音 (Songs on the Red Water) 24
Chongdao guan 崇道觀 160, 258, 259
Chongkan daozang jiyao 重刊道藏輯要 *See* Daozang jiyao
Chongxiu Longhu shanzhi 重修龍虎山志 (Gazetteer of the Reconstructions of Mt. Longhu) 10, 11, 30
Chou, Yi-liang 175, 278, 284, 285
Chuandeng lu 傳燈錄 (Transmission of the Lamp Records) 57
chuanjie lüshi 傳戒律師 (ordination master) 13
chujing 初經 (period preceding the menstrual flow) 229
Chuzhen jielü 初真戒律 (Precepts of Initial Perfection, attr. Wang Changyue) 14, 67, 95, 97, 148, 150, 154, 155, 208, 244, 246, 247
Cinnabar Fields (dantian 丹田) 207
Cleary, Thomas 19, 27–29, 183
clepsydra 81, 288
clergy 5, 6, 14, 56, 58, 68, 110, 126, 143, 242, 244, 253
compassion 36
Confucianism, Confucian 5–7, 11–14, 16, 18, 20, 27, 33, 34, 36, 38, 40–42, 55, 76, 84, 86, 87, 90, 122, 144, 153–155, 159, 160, 169, 177, 178, 180, 184–188, 195, 201, 239, 264, 268
   Confucian ethics 13, 14, 20, 36, 144, 153
   Confucian propaganda 34
   Confucian vision of Jesuits of Daoism and Buddhism 239
   ruzong shenjiao 儒宗神教 (Confucian spirit religions) 41

Confucius 35, 37, 95, 153, 180, 181, 269, 270
    worship by late Qing emperors 35
cosmology 60, 254
cun-cheng 存誠 (actualizing sincerity) 169

D

Da Changuang 笪蟾光 31
Da guangming dian 大光明殿 (Palace of the Great Light) 10
Da Jiaoxian 大腳仙 (teacher of Zhang Pengtou) 81
da zhoutian 大周天 (macrocosmic orbit) 19, 105, 177, 237
Dafan xiantian fanyin douzhou 大梵先天梵音斗咒 (Dhāraṇī to the Dipper according to the Sanskrit pronunciation of the Anterior Heaven of Brahma) 274, 283, 284
Dalai Lama 280
Dali 大理 (Yunnan) 269
dantian 丹田 (elixir field below navel) 172, 205, 235
Daodejing 道德經 77, 92, 186
Daoguang 道光 (emperor / reign 1820–1850) 8, 11, 24, 268
Daohai jinliang 道海津梁 (Bridge of the Sea of the Path) 24
Daoism of the Qing era (1644–1911)
    and Confucian cultural norms 33
    and Daoism of Ming era 239
    and government control 33
    and modern Chinese Daoism 6
    and Neo-Confucianism 5
    and Tibetan Buddhism 5
    Buddhism translated into Daoist context at Mt. Jingai 189–190
    Buddhist ordination, influence on Longmen ordination 244–246
    Canons 21–22
    clergy recruited for civil service 6
    Daoist doctrines rejected by Qing scholars 34
    Daoist Longmen and Buddhist Linji lineages dominant 242
    Daozang jiyao 道藏輯要, value as source for Ming and Qing Daoism 22
    declining influence 11–12
    decreasing clergy, low status 5, 6
    difference between official portrayal and events 7
    Gazetteers 30–33
    growth of lay groups and practices 6
    Huashan 華山 line 62
    inadequate financial support, weakened position 5–6
    increased lay practice 6
    inner alchemy collections 22–29
    inner alchemical ideas and practices 16

Jesuit accounts of Qing Daoism and Buddhism 239–240
  Jingming 淨明 (Pure Brightness) school 7, 9–20
  lack of strong religious structure, charitable works 5
  lineage verses and transmission 13
  local Daoist schools and associations 5, 6
  Longmen as key Daoist school, branch of Quanzhen 7, 15
  Longmen standardization 7, 13, 55
  main characteristics 5–7
  major schools 9–20
  morality books 6
  movement toward unity 6–7
  new forms of popular and lay Daoism 6
  official versus other sources 239–240
  ordination procedures 242–248
  Qingwei 清微 30, 64, 65, 79, 105–107, 125, 128
  Quanzhen "renaissance" 12
  revelation of precious scrolls 6
  ritual texts 30
  spirit-writing cults and groups, role and importance 6, 39–41
  state ritual and standardization of local cults 34–35
  supposed decline, vulgarization, loss of identity 239
  texts on feminine inner alchemy 223
  tight state control 5–6
  two major official schools, Zhengyi and Quanzhen 7
  uniformity versus plurality 6–7
  unity and integration 33–36
  well-defined and controlled schools 33
  Western School, also known as Yinxian pai 隱仙派 (Hidden Immortal School)
     or Youlong pai 猶龍派 (Like Unto a Dragon School) 18–19
  worldview 33–38
  Wu-Liu 伍柳 School, inner alchemy 7, 17, 18, 25
  Wulong (Five Dragons) school of Daoism 105
  Zhengyi Tradition (Celestial Masters) 9–12
Daoist Association at Baiyun guan, Beijing 61, 128
Daoist gymnastics 15, 160
Daojiao wenxian 道教文獻 30, 249
Daolu si 道錄司 (Central Daoist Registry) 5, 9, 65
Daopu yuanliu tu 道譜源流圖 (Map of the Origins and Development of Daoist
   Genealogical Registers) 59, 108, 109, 111, 114, 115, 123, 249, 252, 258
daoqi 道器 (vessel of the Dao) 75
Daoqiao tan 道竅談 (Discussion of the Opening of the Path) by Li Xiyue 19
Daoshu shier zhong 道書十二種 (Twelve Daoist Books) 17, 27, 231
Daoshu shiqi zhong 道書十七種 (Seventeen Daoist Books) 20, 24, 25, 94
daotan 道壇 (Daoist altar; Hong Kong spirit writing groups) 41

daotang 道堂 (Daoist hall; Hong Kong spirit writing groups) 41
Daotong yuanliu 道統源流 (Origins and Development of Orthodox Daoism) 59, 78, 79, 80, 81, 84, 91, 97, 147, 148, 157, 162, 242, 249, 250, 257, 265, 267
daoyin 導引 (Daoist gymnastics) 160, 198, 257, 260, 261, 268
Daozang jinghua lu 道藏精華錄 (Record of Essential Blossoms of the Daoist Canon) 19, 21, 22, 59, 178, 256, 265
Daozang jiyao 道藏輯要 (Essence of the Daoist Canon) 14, 21, 22, 40, 148, 269, 287
    as fundamental source on cults, schools, doctrines, practices of Ming and Qing Daoism 22
Daozang jiyao zongmu 道藏輯要總目 (Comprehensive Repertory of the Daozang jiyao) 21
Daozang xubian 道藏續編 (Supplementary Collection of the Daoist Canon) 25, 26, 60, 81, 94, 97, 144, 145, 147, 161, 163, 164, 166–184, 186, 187, 191–211, 223–226, 229, 230, 243, 255, 256, 264, 269
    aim of Min Yide's compilation of *Daozang xubian* 164–165
    Daozang xubian and *Gu Shuyinlou cangshu* 255
    list of *Daozang xubian* texts and their contents 191–211
    not mentioned in Min Yide's biographies 256
Daozang xubian chuji 道藏續編初集 (Original Collection of the Daozang xubian) 255
Daozong 道宗 (Lineage Master of the Dao; i.e., Lü Dongbin 呂洞賓) 57, 252
Daozu 道祖 (Ancestor of the Dao, i.e. Laozi) 57, 252
Daqing huidian 大清會典 5, 7, 10
Darga, Martina 173, 192
Daxiang zhuan 大象傳 (Commentary of General Images) 27
de Bary, William Theodore 155, 160, 184
de Bruyn, Pierre-Henry 76, 105, 106, 174
De Groot, J. J. M. 39
de Silva, Deema 226, 229
Demiéville, Paul 185
Deng Huiji 鄧徽績 22
Despeux, Catherine 14, 20, 26, 28, 42, 106, 145, 148, 150, 151, 175, 177, 184, 223, 224, 226, 230, 232, 244, 247
dhāraṇī 15, 27, 161, 171, 186, 188, 277, 278, 279, 282, 283, 284, 286, 291
Dhāraṇī Tantrism (dharani mijiao 陀羅尼密教) 284
Dharmarakṣa 竺法護 (d. after 313 CE) 277, 278
Diao Ziran 刁自然 71, 74
ding 定 (concentration) 151, 152, 178, 189
Ding Bing 丁丙 32
Ding Fubao 丁福保 (1874–1952) 22, 164, 191, 255, 256

Ding Peiren 21, 22
Dipper method (doufa 斗法) 15, 161, 273, 274, 283, 291
discursive mind 149, 192, 193, 211, 230
disease (see also illness) 16, 147, 186
dissidence 34, 36
diversity 13, 34
divination 36, 39, 40, 174
Dong Zhongshu 董仲舒 (ca. 179–104 BCE) 113, 186
Donghua dijun 東華帝君 108, 108–120, 109–120, 122, 123, 126, 127
Donglao yishu 東老遺書 (Testament of Shen Donglao) 100
Dongwang gong 東王公 (Royal Sire of the East) 109
Dongyou ji 東遊記 (Journey to the North; novel) 42
Dongyuan yulu 東原語錄 (Recorded Sayings of Dongyuan) 59, 249
Dongyue miao 東嶽廟 (Temple of the Eastern Peak) 10
Douglas, Mary 226
Doumu 斗母 (Mother of Dipper; Mārīcī) 96, 117, 161, 283
dream interpretation 39
duality 165, 170, 172, 179, 189, 193, 207, 231, 236
Duara, Prasenjit 40
Du Lü zushi sanni yishi shuoshu guankui 讀呂祖師三尼醫世說述管窺 [A Personal Reading of the Explanations of the Three Sages' Doctrine of Healing the World by Patriarch Lü] 26, 202
dumai 督脈 (Control Channel) 174, 175, 196
Duren haijing 度人頦經 (The Path of Universal Salvation) 24
Durgā 233
Dushi Yedaposhe zhuan 度師野怛婆闍傳 (Biography of Vinaya master Yedaposhe) 269
dhyāna (ding 定, concentration) 151, 152, 189

E

Eight Immortals 109, 113, 114, 120, 121
elite 33–38, 40, 90
elixir 25, 26, 28, 65, 72, 100–102, 104, 152, 172, 183, 190, 206–209, 211, 237
embracing the One (baoyi 抱一) 195
embryo 23, 104, 176, 193, 194, 196, 197, 199, 206, 208, 229, 235, 237
embryo respiration 23, 208
Emei shan 峨眉山 (mountain in Sichuan province) 19
Engelhardt, Ute 42
Erlan xinhua 二懶心話 (Heart-to-Heart Dialogue Between the Two Leisurely [Masters]) 26, 170, 204–206, 266

Erxian'an 二仙庵 (Hermitage of the Two Immortals) 21, 30
Eskildsen, Stephen 68, 164
ethics 13, 14, 20, 34, 36, 60, 144, 153, 154, 255
eunuchs 37
examinations, examination system 5, 15, 36, 38–40, 58, 60, 86, 145, 249, 257, 262
exorcism 10, 36, 76, 115, 120, 122, 233

F

Fahai yizhu 法海遺珠 119
Fan Qingyun 范清雲 (1606–1748?; ninth-generation Longmen doctrinal master) 59, 249, 258
Fan Taiqing 范太清 91
Fangbian pai 方便派 (Skillful Means), group founded by Min Yide 15, 185
fangshi 方士 (Masters of Recipes) 117, 174, 209
fanguang 返光 191
fanseng 番僧 (Western monks) 283
Farquhar, David M. 284, 285
fashen 法身 (dharmakāya, absolute body) 153, 155, 169
fasting 226
Fei Boyun 費撥雲 (disciple of Min Yide) 185, 265, 267
feiluan 飛鸞 (the flying phoenix [in spirit writing]) 40
feminine alchemy *See* alchemy
Fengshen yanyi 封神演義 (Creation of the Gods; novel) 42
festivals 35
filial piety 20, 34, 89, 90, 112, 115, 122
Five Dragons 104–106
five precepts of Buddhism (wujie 五戒) 150, 246
Five Thunder rites (wulei fa 五雷法) 10, 18, 100, 106, 117–120, 122, 181
fly-whisk 87, 88
Foshuo chishi tuoluoni jing 佛說持世陀羅尼經 (Vasu[n]dhārā-dhāraṇī) 15, 27, 272, 277
Foulk, Theodore Griffith 57, 254
Franke, Herbert 240
Fu Jinquan 傅金銓 (b. 1765) 20, 24, 25, 94
Fu Xi 伏羲 180, 181, 185, 187
fuji 扶乩 (spirit writing or planchette writing) 39, 164
fuluan 扶鸞 (supporting the phoenix [in spirit writing]) 40
Funayama, Tōru 船山徹 279, 282
Fuyang de daoji 復陽得道記 91

G

Ganshui xian yuanlu 甘水仙源錄 243
Gansu province 16, 17, 156, 241, 271, 277, 280
Gao Dongli 高東籬 (?-1768), tenth Longmen patriarch 15, 160, 180, 257, 258, 262, 266, 268
Gao Xuanli 高玄禮 97
Gaozong 高宗 (emperor, re. 1735–1796) 8, 11
    proclaimed Gelugpa as state religion 11
    lack of interest in Daoism 11
Ge Hong 葛洪 (283–343) 121, 209
Ge Xuan 葛玄 25
genealogical chart 252, 253
genealogy 13, 61, 252, 254
geomancy 39
Gezao shan 閤皂山 (mountain in Jiangxi) 79
Golden Age 63, 180, 186, 187
Golden Elixir *See* jindan
Golden Flower *See* Jinhua zongzhi
gongguo ge 功過格 (Ledgers of Merit and Demerit) 36
Goossaert, Vincent 68, 69, 76, 77, 79, 109, 152, 288
government 5, 9, 12, 33, 34, 36, 37, 41, 65, 84, 85, 122, 144, 259, 262, 280
Gōyama, Kiwamu 39, 40
gradual and sudden 178
Granoff, Phyllis 90
Groner, Paul 149, 244, 282
Gu shuyinlou cangshu 古書隱樓藏書 (Collection from the Ancient Hidden Pavilion of Books) 14, 15, 16, 25, 29, 58, 148, 159, 161, 164, 182, 244, 248, 249, 254, 255, 256, 262–269, 283, 284, 286, 289
    and the *Daozang xubian* 255
Gu Zhizhong 42
Guan Tianxian 管天仙 274
Guandi 關帝 40
Guangcheng yizhi 廣成儀制 (Ritual Systematization of Master Guangcheng) 30
Guangchengzi 廣成子 25
Guangxu 光緒 (emperor / reign 1875–1908) 8
Guangyang zaji 廣陽雜記 (Miscellaneous Records of Guangyang) 71
Guankui bian 管窺編 (A Personal View) 26, 200, 207
Guanyin 觀音 37
Gufa yangsheng shisan ze chanwei 古法養生十三則闡微 (Uncovering the Subtleties of the Thirteen Principles Concerning the Ancient Methods of Nourishing Life) 198–199

Guoshi 國師 (State Instructor) 96, 101, 124, 125, 155, 241

H

Hachiya, Kunio 蜂屋邦夫 110, 115
Hakuunkan shi 白雲觀志 (Gazetter of the Abbey of the White Clouds, ch. *Baiyun guan zhi*, 1934, by Oyanagi Shigeta) 9, 58, 64, 65, 66, 70, 71, 74, 91, 95, 96, 147, 148, 155, 247, 252, 253, 257, 259, 287, 289
Han dynasty 112, 120, 181, 271
Han Tianshi shijia 漢天師世家 123
Hangzhou 10, 15, 32, 58, 86, 101, 155, 156–159, 162, 167, 249, 257, 265
    Dongxiao gong 洞宵宮 265
Hanlin academy 翰林院 257
Hao Dadong 郝大通 (1140–1212; one of the Seven Perfected of Quanzhen) 80
Harding, M. Esther 225, 226
Hasebe Yūkei 長谷幽蹊 246, 254
Hayes, James 35
He Longxiang 賀龍驤 21
He mountain 何山 (Zhejiang province) 100
He Xin 何新 232, 233
healing 26, 36, 38, 91, 115, 120, 121, 147, 155, 161, 168, 169, 171, 174, 179, 180, 181, 185–187, 189, 203, 208, 286
health 15, 16, 112, 161
heidao 黑道 (Black Path) 174
Heinze, Ruth-Inge 226
Helin Gong 鶴林宮 (Crane Forest Temple) 32
Henan province 15, 73, 75, 89, 90, 98, 147, 160, 257
heterodoxy, heterodox paths 10, 24, 33, 93, 121, 122, 174
heterogeneity 34
Holy Embryo (shengtai 聖胎) 194, 196, 197
Hong Kong 41, 79, 85, 114, 143, 243, 288
    spirit writing groups engendering Daoist sects 41
Hongyang jiao 紅楊教 (Religion of Expansive Yang) 38
houtian 後天 (after heaven) 177, 232
Hu Ying Stele (of 1444) 12, 64
Huainan zi 淮南子 (180–122 B.C) 202, 209
Huang Chiyang 黃赤陽 (1595–1673) 156, 157, 158, 162, 201
Huang Shouyuan 黃守元 (1585–1673; Longmen Doctrinal line, eighth generation) 62, 146
Huang Shouzhong 黃守中 (*see* Yedaposhe)
Huang Ting 黃廷 201

huangdao 黃道 (Yellow Path) 174, 193
Huangdi 黃帝 (Yellow Emperor) 108, 180, 230
huangguan jia yushi 黃冠家羽士 (Daoists of the Yellow Hats) 86
Huangji hepi zhengdao xianjing 皇極闔闢證道仙經 (Immortals' Scripture Testifying to the Path of Opening and Closing the Sovereign Ultimate) 26, 147, 171–174, 179, 180, 184, 185, 189, 192–195, 264, 289
Huanglu keyi 黃籙科儀 (Yellow Register Liturgies) 11
Huangshi gong 黃石宮 80
Huangting jingjie 黃庭經解 (Explanations of the Yellow Court Scripture) 28
huangzhong 黃中 (Yellow Center) 174
huanxin 幻心 (mind of illusion) 151, 189
Huashan 華山 (Mt. Hua, Shaanxi province) 31, 62, 71–74, 76, 77, 90, 96–99, 113, 114, 127, 129, 144, 243
    Wangdiao dong 王刁洞 72, 74
Huashan zhi 華山志 (Gazetteer of Mount Hua) 31
Huayan 華嚴 Buddhism 7, 18
Huayang dongtian 華陽洞天 (Huayang celestial grotto) 110
Huayue quanji 華嶽全集 (Complete Collection on Mount Hua) 32
Huayue zhi 華嶽志 (Gazetteer of Sacred Mount Hua) 31, 32, 72, 73
Hubei 湖北 province 13, 89, 93, 98, 99, 107, 148
Huber, Toni 228
Hucker, Charles 5
huiguang 回光 191
Huiming jing 慧命經 (Book of Wisdom and Life) by Liu Huayang 18, 23
Huineng 慧能 (6th patriarch of Chan Buddhism) 14, 148, 244
Huixin ji 會心集 (Collection of Encounters of the Mind) 29
Huixin waiji 會心外集 (Outer Collection of the Encounters with the Mind) by Liu Yiming 16
Hummel, Arthur W. 58, 249
Hunan province 20, 27, 101

I

Igarashi, Kenryū 五十嵐賢隆 58, 252, 253
illness and quest for immortality 16, 39, 91
immortality, immortal 7, 14, 16, 18–20, 22, 23, 25, 26, 36, 42, 76, 94, 95, 100–104, 111, 112, 114–117, 122, 128, 147, 149, 150, 152, 154, 164, 166, 167, 171, 176, 179, 181–183, 186, 188, 189, 200, 203, 204, 206, 207, 209, 229, 234, 235, 237, 251, 258, 262, 265, 267, 271

Immortals' Scripture (Yin zhenren Donghua zhengmai huangji hepi zhengdao xianjing 尹真人東華正脈皇極闔闢證道仙經) 26, 147, 171–174, 179, 180, 184, 185, 189, 192–195, 264, 289
imperial patronage 35
imperial ritual (li 禮) 34, 35
Inagaki, Hisao 284
Indra 233
Initial Precepts of Perfection (chuzhen jie 初真戒) 67, 68, 95, 150, 151, 153, 171, 188, 189, 208, 244
inner alchemy (neidan 內丹; *see also* alchemy) 7, 11, 12, 16, 18, 20, 22–29, 41–42, 79, 145, 150, 175, 183, 206, 208, 223, 224, 226, 229, 230, 232, 233, 236, 237, 255, 256, 258, 260, 264, 288
    inner alchemy collections 22–29
    of Southern lineage 264
    simplified forms in Qing era 41–42
integration 33, 34, 35, 40, 69, 78, 79, 106, 107, 117, 120, 123, 126, 128, 129, 173, 174, 184, 190, 194, 280, 283
Intermediate Precepts (zhongji jie 中極戒) 14, 68, 151, 171, 177, 188, 189
Ishida, Kenji 石田憲司 64–66, 106

J

jade liquid (yuye 玉液) 19
Jesuits 184, 239
Prince Ji 吉王 101, 102
Ji'an 吉安 (Jiangxi) 100
jiaji 夾脊 (Spinal Handle) 178, 179, 193
jiaji shuangguan 夾脊雙關 (Joint Pass of the Spinal Handle) 178, 179
Jiajing 嘉靖 emperor (re. 1522–1566) 93, 103
Jiang Shanxin 姜善信 (fl. 1260–1283; Huashan line) 62, 73, 74
Jiang Yuanting 蔣元庭 (=Jiang Yupu 蔣予蒲, 1755–1819) 21, 191
Jiang Yupu 蔣予蒲 (1755–1819) 21, 22, 40
jiangluan 降鸞 (descent of the phoenix [in spirit writing]) 39
Jiangnan 江南 11, 74, 114, 120, 126, 157, 159, 190, 252
Jiangsu province 20, 79, 85, 89, 97–99, 103, 119, 121, 230, 235
Jiangxi province 9, 18, 20, 32, 79, 94, 99–101, 104, 107, 117
Jiaqing 嘉慶 (emperor / reign 1796–1820) 8, 21, 22, 58, 124, 249, 275, 278, 290, 291
Jiatuo zhengzong 伽陀正宗 (Orthodox Lineage of Gāthā) 283
jibi 乩筆 (writing point of spirit writing instrument) 39
jie 戒 (precepts) 149, 151, 178

jiefa 戒法 (method of precepts) 67, 83
jietan 戒壇 (ordination platform) 149, 185, 188, 244
jietuo 解脫 (vimoksha) 169
jilun 臍輪 (navel) 172, 193
Jin dynasty 12
Jin Guixin 金桂馨 32
Jin Huaihuai 金懷懷 266
Jin Zhenchang 靳貞常 (Huashan line) 62, 73
jindan 金丹 (Golden Elixir) 25, 104, 118, 152, 183, 206–208, 211, 231, 232, 234
Jindan sibaizi 金丹四百字 (400 Words on the Golden Elixir) 26, 28, 209
Jindan sibaizi jie 金丹四百字解 (Explanations of the Four Hundred Words on the Golden Elixir) 28
Jindan sibai zi zhushi 金丹四百字注釋 (Commentary and Explanations on the Four Hundred Words on the Golden Elixir)
　description and content 209
jing 精 (essence) 19, 23, 150, 176, 177, 183, 234, 235
Jingai shan 金蓋山 (Huzhou, Zhejiang province) 15, 16, 18, 25, 26, 57, 58, 100, 128, 145, 147, 156–159, 162–164, 166–175, 178–190, 241, 248–252, 255, 256, 263, 266, 268, 290, 291
　Gu Meihua guan 古梅花觀 (Old Plum Blossom Abbey) 250
　importance of Jingai shan's branch of Longmen 145
　Longqiao 窿蹺 hermitage 166, 168
　Patriarch-Lü altar, scriptural tradition 呂祖宗壇 157–159
　Shuyinlou 書隱樓 library 159, 163
　soteriological program of Mt. Jingai's Longmen branch 188–190
　Yunchao 雲巢 ("Cloud's nest") temple 58, 156, 162, 249, 250, 263
Jingai xindeng 金蓋心燈 (Mind-Lamp of Mount Jingai) 12, 14–17, 55, 57–61, 63, 65, 67–69, 71, 75, 76, 79–82, 85, 86, 88, 91, 94, 95–98, 100, 101, 106, 107, 108, 111–113, 118–120, 122, 124, 125, 127, 128, 147, 148, 156–163, 166–168, 173, 174, 181, 241, 248–258, 261–269, 272, 292
　and creation of Longmen self-image 59–60
　and promotion Longmen "for the protection of the state" 57
　as fundamental source for first seven Longmen generations 58
　as link of Mt. Jingai tradition to Baiyun guan 157
　as source for Ming and Qing Daoism 57–58
　history of text and role 57–58, 248–256
　textual history and role
Jingai xindeng zhengkao wenxian lu 金蓋心燈徵考文獻錄 (Index of Works used for the Compilation of the Transmission of the Mind-Lamp from Mount Jingai) 58
Jingai yunjian 金蓋雲笈 (Cloudy Satchel of Jingai) 91

Jingang haimu 金剛亥母 (Vajravārāhī) 227, 228
jingding 靜定 (absorption) 207
Jingming 淨明 (Pure Brightness) School 7, 19, 20, 24, 25, 32, 65, 94, 156, 166, 290, 291
Jingming zhongxiao dao 淨明忠孝道 65, 94
Jingu dong 金鼓洞 (Hangzhou) 32, 157, 257
Jingu dong zhi 金鼓洞志 (Gazetteer of the Golden Drum Cavern) 32
Jinhua zongzhi 金華宗旨 (Secret of the Golden Flower; also called *aiyi jinhua zongzhi* 太一金華宗旨) 19, 26, 81, 145, 158, 159, 162–175, 177–180, 185, 188, 189, 191
    as substitute for precept transmission 168
    as vessel of Min Yide's doctrine 165–168
Jinlian zhengzong ji 金蓮正宗記 (Account of the Orthodox Lineage of the Golden Lotus) 108, 109, 116
Jinlian zhengzong xianyuan xiangzhuan 金蓮正宗仙源像傳 (Illustrated Biographies of the Immortal Origins of the Orthodox Lineage of the Golden Lotus) 108, 109, 111, 115, 116
Jinque dijun 金闕帝君 108, 118, 123, 127
Jinshan 金山 80, 81
jinshi 進士 degree 36
Jinxian zhenglun 金仙証論 (A Testimony to Golden Immortality) 23
jipan 乩盤 (spirit writing tray; planchette) 39
jitan 乩壇 (spirit writing altar) 39
Jiugong shan 九宮山 (mountain in Hubei) 13, 93, 98, 148
Jiuzheng lu 就正錄 (Record of the Realization of Rectitude) 27, 178, 200, 201
    description and content 200–201
Jiyi zi Daoshu shiqi zhong 濟一子道書十七種 (Seventeen Books by Master Who Saves the One) 25
Jizu daozhe 雞足道者 (Daoist of Chicken Foot Mountain;=Yedaposhe 野怛婆闍; = Huang Shouzhong 黃守中) 15, 26, 161, 171, 186, 188, 190, 268, 269, 271–289, 291, 292
    as Dipper rite specialist and text transmitter 283–286
    as disciple of Wang Changyue, recipient of Yishi Shuoshu 287–290
    biographies 269–275
    Chuanyi si 傳衣寺 (Temple of the Robe Transmission) 278
    Dushi Yedaposhe zhuan 度師野怛婆闍傳 (Biography of Vinaya master Yedaposhe) 269
    foreign origin 277–283
    hypotheses about origin of name 282
    integration in Longmen lineage as eighth patriarch 288–289
    name Yedaposhe 野怛婆闍 etymology 271–272

Jizu daozhe Huang lüshi zhuan 雞足道者黃律師 (Biography of the Vinaya Master Huang, Man of the Way from Mt. Jizu) 272
Jizu shan 雞足山 (mountain in Yunnan province) 156, 263, 269, 271, 272, 273, 278, 279, 283, 291
    Longshu shanfang 龍樹山房 (Nāgārjuna hermitage) 271
    Taizi hermitage 276
Jizushan zhi 雞足山志 (Gazetteer of Mt. Jizu) 270, 271, 278, 279
Jordan, David K. 39, 40, 164
juetan 覺壇 (Altar of Awakening; spirit writing altar) 21, 40
jueyuan 覺源 (Source of Awakening; spirit writing altar) 40

K

Kālachakra tantra 285
Kaltenmark, Max 173
Kamata Shigeo 鎌田茂雄 270, 278, 279
Kamitsuka, Yoshiko 神塚淑子 109, 110, 113, 123
Kangu laoren 龕谷老人 (Old Man of the Recessed Cavern) 16
Kangxi 康熙 (emperor / reign 1662–1722) 8, 9, 14, 21, 34, 68, 96, 99, 124, 158, 167, 289
Kapadia, Karin 226, 228, 229
karma 36, 282
Katz, Paul 22, 40
Ke Daochong 柯道沖 118
Kelley, David E. 38
Khanna, Madhu 228, 233
khutuktus (huofo 活佛; living Buddhas) 280
Kin Bunkyō 金文京 279
Kleeman, Terry F. 40
Knott, Kim 233
Kohn, Livia 121, 123, 186
Kong Changgui 孔常圭 99
Kongyi chanzhen 孔易闡真 (True Explanation of the Confucian "Changes") 27
Kroll, W. Paul 109, 113, 123
Kukkutpāda mountain. *See* Jizu shan
Kundalini 205
Kunyang Wang zhenren daoxing bei 崑陽王真人道行碑 (Stele on the Virtuous Behavior of the Perfected Wang Kunyang) 91

L

Lagerwey, John 79, 90, 143, 243
Lamotte, Étienne 279
Lamp Histories 57, 59, 252, 254
Laoshan 嶗山 (Mt. Lao) 62, 80–82, 90, 97, 98, 129
Laozi (Lao-tse) 老子 37, 57, 94, 96, 108, 114–116, 121–124, 147, 158, 167, 180, 181, 185, 252, 266, 269, 270
lay associations 33, 34
lay precepts 150, 246
leifa 雷法 (thunder rites) 10, 18
Leng Tiejiao 冷鐵腳 97
Leshan 樂山 district (Sichuan) 18
li 禮 34
Li A 李阿 119, 120, 121, 122, 127
Li Babai 李八百 111, 112, 113, 114, 115, 117, 119, 120, 121, 122, 127
Li Daochun 李道純 (fl. 1288–90) 118, 119, 237
Li Daoqian 李道謙 (1219–1296) 70
Li Dexia 李德洽 199
Li Hong 李弘 121, 123, 124, 125, 127
Li Jie 李楷 72, 73
Li Liang 李良 (Tang immortal; Li Babai) 117
Li Lingyang 李靈陽 115
Li Ningyang 李凝陽 114–116, 119, 120
Li Niwan 李泥丸 18, 100, 106, 107, 111–115, 120, 122, 181, 184, 196, 204, 208, 209, 224, 262
Li Pengtou 李鑿頭 (?–1784) 203, 266
Li Quan 李筌 26
Li Rong 李榮 31
Li Shaojun 李少君 209
Li Shifang 李時芳 32
Li Shizhong 李時中 65
Li Tieguai 李鐵拐 (Iron Crutch Li; one of the eight immortals) 114–116, 119, 120, 122
Li Xiantuo 李顯陀 (master of Sun Xuanqing) 80
Li Xiyue 李西月 (fl. 1796–1850) 18
Li Xu'an 李虛庵 104, 106, 107, 112
Li Ya 李亞 109, 110, 114, 116, 117, 118, 119, 120, 122, 127
Li Yuanguo 28, 29
Li Zhenyuan 李眞元 (1525–1573?; Wudangshan line) 17, 62, 102, 120

Li Zhichang 李志常 (disciple of Qiu Chuji) 19, 243
Liaoyang dian wenda bian 廖陽殿問答編 (Questions and Answers from the Liaoyang Hall) 26, 195, 264
libu 禮部 (Ministry of Rites) 5
Lidai shenxian tongjian 歷代神仙通鑑 115
Liebenthal, Walter 279
Liexian quanzhuan 列仙全傳 115
Liexian zhuan 列仙傳 173
Liezi 列子 209
Lijia dao 李家道 (the Way of the Li family) 120–122
Lin Lingsu 林靈素 117
Lin Zhaoen 林兆恩 33, 41
lineage name (paiming 派名 or ming 名) 69, 148, 261
lineage verse (paishi 派詩) 13, 68, 69, 99, 257, 259
ling feizhen 靈飛針 (magic flying needles) 261
Lingbao 靈寶 30, 78, 79, 151, 246
Lingyou gong 靈右宮 (Numinous Palace to the Right) 9, 13
Linji Yixuan 臨濟義玄 (d. 866) (jap. Rinzai) 55, 143, 242
literati 12, 35, 38, 39, 40, 41, 55, 74, 123, 124, 126, 164, 185
liturgy 60, 86, 87, 182, 190, 254, 287
Liu An 劉安 25
Liu Bozi 劉跛子 (Limping Liu) 116
Liu Chuxuan 劉處玄 (1147–1203) 81
Liu Haichan 劉海蟾 108, 116, 118
Liu Huayang 柳華陽 (1735–1799; Chan monk) 18, 23
Liu Shouyuan 柳守元 151, 247
Liu, Guoliang 28
Liu, Jingcheng 5, 11, 12
Liu, Ts'un-yan 劉存仁 21, 42, 103, 160
Liu Yiming 劉一明 (1734–1821; 11th Longmen generation) 16–17, 26, 27, 156, 210, 211, 231, 232
    biography, writings 16–17
Liu Yu 劉玉 (founder of Jingming school) 20, 24, 25, 94, 124
    Qiaoyang zi yulu 樵陽子語錄 (Records of Master Qiaoyang [=Liu Yu 劉玉]) 24
    Qiaoyang jing 樵陽經 (Classic of Qiaoyang) 24, 94, 233
Liu Yuanran 劉淵然 (1351–1432; Qingwei master) 65, 106, 128
liutong 六通 (six divine or magical powers) 195
local cults 34, 35, 120, 159, 190
    standardization in Qing 34–35

Long Qiqian 龍起潛 (disciple of Wang Changyue) 97, 155
Longhu mountain 龍虎山 in Jiangxi 9, 10, 11, 30, 31, 79, 117
Longmen 龍門 (Dragon Gate) tradition of Daoism *passim*
    affirmation of meditative practices 172
    allegedly founded by Qiu Chuji 邱處機 (1148–1227) 63–64, 243
    aim of Mt. Jingai movement's identity and lineage 190
    and older local traditions 144
    and ordination monopoly 56
    and public ordinations 88
    and purported link to Yuan-era Quanzhen 61
    and Quanzhen ancestors 61, 108–110, 243
    and Quanzhen "renaissance" in the Qing era 56
    and role of Baiyun guan abbotship 56, 65–66
    and the unification of Southern and Northern traditions 126–129
    and Wang Changyue 王常月 (?-1680) 12–15, 155–156
    as "Quanzhen Northern lineage" 127, 172
    as relatively recent tradition of inner alchemy 12
    cannot be traced to Quanzhen alone 12
    beginnings of more systematic tradition 104–105
    Chan-like curious intermingling of "Northern" and "Southern" schools 128–129
    chart of Vinaya and Doctrinal line patriarchs 146
    creation of "orthodox" patriarchal lineage and institutionalization 126–129
    doctrinal and vinaya lines 85, 129
    early history 60–142
    emergence in Qing era 12–18
    established by Wang Changyue 14
    establishment at Baiyun guan 71
    historical origin and lineage full of contradictions 12
    history by Min Yide 16
    history, Bojian 缽鑑 (Examination of the Bowl) as source 56
    history, first critical studies 60
    Huashan lineage foundation 73–74
    in charge of public ordinations 143
    "incubation" period linked with Zhengyi 56
    influence of Confucianism and Chan Buddhism 14
    integration of psycho-physiological techniques 173
    integration of various traditions in its lineage 114–120
    key Daoist school of the Qing period (1644–1911) 143
    links with Zhengyi and Quanzhen 56
    location in Shaanxi province 12
    Longmen and Lingbao registers 78–79
    Longmen branches established after Wang Changyue 155–156
    Longmen epicenters (map) 66
    Longmen hagiography, intentions of authors 98–99
    Longmen lineage as product of southern legacies, literati 123
    Longmen lineage established in organized form by Wang Changyue 147–149

Longmen lineage grafted on earlier historical figures 106–107
Longmen lineage officially established at Baiyun guan 155–156
Longmen lineage poem (paishi 派詩) 13, 68, 69, 71, 73, 81, 97, 99, 102, 148, 257, 259
Longmen local lineages and Wang Changyue 98–100
Longmen masters and the Baiyun guan 65–66
Longmen Northern lineage (Beizong Longmen 北宗龍門) 103
Longmen ordination program established by Wang Changyue 244–247
Min Yide as key figure in establishment of self-image 60, 254
monopoly of Daoist ordination 144
most common lineage of Daoist priests from Qing to present 143
Mt. Jingai branch and the *Secret of the Golden Flower* 145
Mt. Jingai branch, importance 145
Mt. Jingai branch's soteriological program 188–190
Mt. Jingai branch's claim of genuine supreme ordination transmission 291
Mt. Jingai, Perfected Yin as symbol of integration of different traditions 174
official teachings and Mt. Jingai 145, 187–190
opening to wider public 107
most influential vehicle of inner alchemy transmission 12
most of China's Daoist sanctuaries claim association with 12
roots in local Daoist movements, spread throughout China 12, 14–15
soteriological program 188–190
Taishang zhengzong 太上正宗 (orthodox lineage of the Most High) 76
unification of Southern and Northern traditions 118–120
variety of views about origin of name "Longmen" 243
Vinaya master line 律師 62, 66, 85, 129, 147, 148
will to orthodoxy 127, 129, 291
Wuxi gong 五息功 260
Yunchao 雲巢 branch at Mt. Jingai, founded by Tao Jing'an 162, 263
Zhengyi, Quanzhen legacy connections 126–129
Longmen daoshi 龍門道士 266
Longmen dong 龍門洞 (grotto in the Xindu 新都 district of Chengdu) 113, 121, 127
Longmen orthodox lineage 龍門正宗 (Longmen zhengzong)
    a posteriori creation 98–99
    and Baiyun guan; epigraphic sources 63–65
    and its Chan Buddhist model 57, 128–129
    fundamental textual sources 58–59
    orthodox line, Sichuan connection 126–127
    orthodox transmission (zhengzong liuchuan 正宗流傳) 59, 63, 249, 252, 253, 257, 258, 262, 263
    patriarchal tradition as late Ming concoction 56
    pseudo-historical construction, similar to Chan 14, 128–129
Longmen shan 龍門山 (mountain) 67, 70, 73, 74, 103, 107
    Jianji gong 建極宮 (Palace of Ascending the Throne) 73, 74

Longmen xinfa 龍門心法 (Core Teachings of the Longmen) 14, 96, 147, 148, 151, 153, 154, 244

Longmen xizhu xinzong 龍門西竺心宗 (Longmen Mind-Tradition of Western India) 241, 255, 256, 263, 266, 268, 269, 277, 289, 291

Longzhou 隴州 prefecture (Shaanxi province) 12, 63, 144, 243

Lotus Sūtra, parable of the three carts 19

Lou Jinyuan 婁近垣 (1689–1776) 10, 30

loyalty 10, 12, 20, 34, 56, 226

Lu mountain 廬山 (Jiangxi) 18, 100

Lu Jiuyuan 陸九淵 (1139–1192) 201

Lu Shichen 陸世忱 27, 200, 201

Lü Dongbin 呂洞賓 7, 15, 18, 20–22, 24, 25, 32, 40, 41, 57, 95, 96, 100, 108, 116, 118, 122, 147, 154, 157, 158, 159, 162, 163, 164, 165, 166, 167, 168, 178, 180, 181, 182, 185, 186, 188, 189, 191, 199, 201, 202, 208, 251, 252, 262, 269

    Lüzu zongtan 呂祖宗壇 altar at Mt. Jingai 162

    ordinations at his altar in Mt. Jingai 188–189

Lü Quanyang 呂全陽 59, 249

Lü Yunyin 呂雲隱 (fl. 1710; eighth-generation Longmen Vinaya master) 59, 91, 249

Lu'an 潞安 (Shanxi) 13, 90, 147

luantang 鸞堂 (spirit writing hall) 39

luluan 錄鸞 (recording characters in spirit writing) 40

Luo Menghong 羅蒙紅 37

Luojiao 羅教 (Teaching of Luo), also Wuwei jiao 無為教 (Nonaction Religion) 37, 38

lüshi 律師 (Vinaya masters / line) 13, 63, 67–69, 75, 76, 82, 84–86, 88, 91, 100, 124, 148, 162, 163, 171, 183, 272, 274

Lüzu quanshu 呂祖全書 (Patriarch Lü [Dongbin]'s Collected Works) 40, 166

Lüzu wupian 呂祖五篇 (Five Compositions of Patriarch Lü) 24

Lüzushi sanni yishi gongjue 呂祖師三尼醫世功訣 [Practices and Formulae on the Three Sages' Doctrine of Healing the World by Patriarch Lü] 181, 182, 187, 202, 262

Lüzushi sanni yishi shuoshu 呂祖師三尼醫世說述 [Explanations of the Three Sages' Doctrine of Healing the World (revealed via spirit writing) by Patriarch Lü] 15, 161, 180–182, 186, 187, 201, 202, 268, 269, 286

Lüzushi xiantian xuwu Taiyi jinhua zongzhi 呂祖師先天虛無太一金華宗旨 [Patriarch Lü's Quintessential Doctrine of the Golden Flower of the Great One of Emptiness Before Heaven] (*see also* Jinhua zongzhi) 191

M

Ma Danyang 馬丹陽 (1123–1183; one of the Seven Perfected of Quanzhen) 70
Ma Mingqing 馬明卿 32
Ma Shutian 馬書田 115, 116
Ma Zhenyi 馬眞一 (Huashan line) 62, 71, 72, 73, 74, 97
macrocosmic orbit (da zhoutian 大周天) 19, 177, 179
Mādhyamika 271
magic 174, 185, 187, 188, 223, 261
Mahākāśyapa 摩訶迦葉 (Buddha's disciple) 278, 279
Mair, Victor 34, 279
Maitreya 37, 38, 278, 279
Manchu 6, 12, 56, 187, 240, 280, 284
Manchu syncretism 240
Mañjuśrī 281
Manpukuji 萬福寺 Zen monastery (Uji 宇治 near Kyoto) 246
mantras 15
Mao Zedong 毛澤東 251
Maoshan 茅山 (mountain in Jiangsu province) 31, 79, 89, 90, 99
Maoshan quanji 茅山全志 (Complete Gazetteer of Mount Mao) 31
Maoshan zhi 茅山志 (Record of Maoshan) 31
Mārīcī. *See* Doumu
Marsone, Pierre 64, 65, 66, 71, 109, 110, 116, 119
martial arts 38, 42
Martin, Emily 226
Mayi daozhe 麻衣道者 (nickname for Lü Dongbin, q.v.) 95, 147
Mazu 媽祖 35
medicine 16, 18, 23, 29, 39, 42, 72, 104–106, 113, 120, 175, 176, 185, 194, 197, 199, 206, 230, 233, 261
meditation 37, 38, 41, 42, 77, 81, 82, 89, 103, 104, 152, 168, 172, 174, 187, 192, 208, 261, 287, 288
meditation hall 287
mediums 37, 39, 40
Mei Zichun 梅子春 100
Mencius 孟子 153, 201
menstrual blood 225, 226, 227, 228, 229, 231, 232, 235, 236
menstrual symbolism 227–228
menstruation, menstrual cycle 223–237
    xiujing 修經 (cultivating the menses) 223
Mesnil, Evelyne 113, 120
messianism 121, 121–127, 184, 190, 286
    messianic aspiration of Mt. Jingai Longmen 190

Miao Shanshi 苗善時 (fl. 1288–1324) 122
Miaoyue 妙月 (Suchandra, Tib. Dawa Sangpo) 285, 286
microcosmic orbit (xiao zhoutian 小周天) 19, 23, 177, 179
mijiao 密教 (Esoteric Teaching or Esoteric Buddhism) 240, 241
millenarianism 37, 38, 125, 185
Min Lanyun xiansheng zhuan 閔懶雲先生傳 257, 262, 265, 267
Min Yanglin 閔陽林 26, 199, 209
Min Yide 閔一得 (1748/58–1836) 14–18, 25, 26, 29, 58, 60, 63, 127, 145, 147, 148, 154, 156, 157, 159–172, 175–183, 185–187, 190–192, 195, 196, 198–211, 241, 244, 248, 249, 252–257, 259–269, 271, 272, 274, 279, 280, 284–286, 289, 291
    activities at Mt. Jingai 162–165
    and importance of Lü Dongbin 165
    as creator of link between Jingai tradition and Baiyun guan 157
    as key figure in the creation of Longmen self-image 60
    as Longmen historiographer 16
    biographies 15–16, 256–268
    forged new kind of Longmen doctrine 164–165
    literary works 162–168
    purported meeting with Yedaposhe 160–161
Min Zhiting 閔智亭 151, 247
Ming dynasty 34, 55, 56, 65, 79, 80, 81, 90, 93, 99, 100, 104, 106, 107, 115, 125, 128, 129, 143, 156, 240, 243
Ming era Daoism 55–56
Mingxia dong 明霞洞 (Laoshan 嶗山, Shandong) 80
Ministry of Rites (libu 禮部) 5
Miura, Kunio 42
Miyakawa, Hisayuki 28
mofa 末法 (Jap. mappō; end of Dharma) 278
Mollier, Christine 121
monastic rules 60, 129, 254
monasticism 37, 38, 60, 64, 83, 110, 129, 149, 154, 155, 184, 187, 190, 254, 278
Mongolia 85, 240, 280, 284
moon 169, 174, 175, 177, 205, 206, 223, 225
morality 5, 12, 20, 26, 35, 36, 41, 42, 56, 94, 164, 178, 183, 187, 201, 239, 244, 268, 283
morality books (shanshu 善書) 6, 34, 36, 38, 40, 41
Mori, Yuria 森由利亞 12, 14, 17, 18, 20, 22, 25, 26, 40, 57, 60, 70, 100–103, 105, 106, 150, 164, 166–168, 246, 248, 288
Mou, Zhongjian 牟鐘鑑 60
Mugitani, Kunio 麥谷邦夫 4, 55
Music Master (Taichang leyuan 太常樂員) 11

N

Nāgārjuna 271
Nan Huai-chin 175
Nan'an 南安 (Gansu province) 16
Nanchang 17, 104
Nanjing 15, 149, 155, 244
Naquin, Susan 33, 37, 38, 42
nature of the mind 29, 191
Needham, Joseph 24, 145, 165, 233
neidan 內丹 (inner alchemy) *See* alchemy
neiguan 內觀 (introspection) 193, 196
Neo-Confucianism 5, 11, 33, 34, 178, 180, 261
    Cheng-Zhu school 5
Ni Zhengdao 倪正道 65
Ningxia 17
Niwan Li zushi nüzong shuangxiu baofa 泥丸李祖師女宗雙修寶筏 [Precious Raft of Joint Cultivation in Feminine Alchemy by Patriarch Li Niwan] 184, 208–209, 224, 262
non-duality 170, 172, 179, 189
nourishing life 22
nüdan 女丹 (feminine alchemy) 223, 224
Nüzhen jiujie 女眞九戒 (Nine Precepts for Women Perfected; Wang Changyue) 14

O

officials 9, 11, 14, 34, 35, 37, 40, 86, 101, 266, 268
Olivelle, Patrick 232
oral traditions 37
orbits 24, 177
ordination 13–15, 56, 60, 64, 68, 69, 77, 84, 88, 95, 99, 124, 126, 129, 143, 144, 148–151, 155, 157, 161, 163, 177–179, 182–190, 203, 208, 242, 244–247, 254, 257, 263, 273, 278, 282, 286, 287, 288, 289, 290, 291
ordination of the threefold altar *See santan dajie* 三壇大戒
original face 193, 211
orthodoxy 33, 60, 65, 69, 85, 122, 127, 128, 129, 154, 159, 164, 175, 180, 187, 190, 291
Overmyer, Daniel L. 36, 37, 38, 39, 40, 164
Oyanagi Shigeta 小柳司氣太 9–13, 58, 147, 247, 252, 257, 259, 287

P

paishi 派詩 (lineage verse) 13, 68, 69, 99, 257, 259
Pan Jingguan 潘靜觀 25
path of immortals 154, 177, 189
path of men 153, 154, 176, 177, 178, 189
Peng Dingqiu 彭定求 (1645–1719) 21
Peng Hanran 彭瀚然 21
Peng Haogu 彭好古 26, 209
Pengtou laoweng 蓬頭老翁 (Old Man of the Tousled Head) 16
Petech, Luciano 240
physiognomy 39
piety 20, 34, 36, 89, 90, 112, 115, 122
planchette 39, 40, 164
Platform Sūtra of Huineng, Sixth Patriarch of Chan 14, 148, 151, 244
pollution 225, 226, 227, 228, 230
Pomeroy, Sarah B. 228
possession 39, 145, 164, 226, 286, 291
prajñā (hui 慧, wisdom) 151, 152, 169, 189
precepts 13, 14, 26, 42, 67–69, 77, 83, 84, 92, 93, 95, 99, 101, 107, 143, 144, 148–154, 157, 161, 162, 165, 168–171, 177, 179, 183, 187, 188, 189, 191, 204, 208, 224, 226, 242, 244–247, 262, 263, 271, 273, 274, 282, 287–289, 290, 291
    five Buddhist precepts 150
    great precepts of celestial immortality (tianxian dajie 天仙大戒) 14, 68, 69, 93, 151, 183, 247, 288
    intermediate precepts (zhongji jie) 中極戒 14, 68, 151, 177, 247
    precepts for novices 150, 246
    precepts for women 150, 247
    precepts of initial perfection (chuzhen jie 初真戒) 14
precious scrolls 6, 36, 37
Pregadio, Fabrizio 28, 78, 79, 118, 119, 143, 145, 172, 182
prohibitions 204, 226
propaganda 34
protection of the state 57, 254
psycho-physiological techniques 171–173, 175, 177–179, 189, 192, 223
Pulleyblank, E.G. 277
Pure Land Buddhism 172
purification 40, 72, 196, 226

Q

qi 氣 (vital energy) 19, 23, 150, 175, 177, 178, 183, 206, 234, 235, 261, 264

Qi Fengyuan 漆逢源 32
Qianlong 乾隆 (emperor, re. 1736–1795) 5, 8, 10, 11, 241, 274, 280, 281, 284–286
Qianque leishu 潛確類書 115
Qiao Xiu 譙秀 113
Qiaoyang jing 樵陽經 (Classic of Qiaoyang) 24, 94, 233
Qiaoyang zi yulu 樵陽子語錄 (Records of Master Qiaoyang [=Liu Yu 劉玉]) 24
qigong 氣功 42, 260
qijing bamai 奇經八脈 (eight extraordinary channels) 175
Qin'an dian 欽安殿 (in imperial palace) 10
Qingcheng shan 青城山 (mountain in Sichuan) 77, 78, 83, 87, 88, 90, 120, 121, 123, 127, 129, 195, 196
    fundamental role in Longmen transmission 88
Qing Daoism (*see* Daoism of the Qing era)
Qing dynasty (1644–1911) 5, 6, 8, 12, 34, 55, 58, 61, 99, 110, 127, 128, 165, 184, 239, 240, 253
    list of emperors and reigns 8
    Qing Daoism *See* Daoism of the Qing era
    Qing era rulers and Zhengyi / Quanzhen 12
    Qing vs. Ming religious policy 33–34
Qing Xitai 卿希泰 19, 20, 25, 30, 42, 57, 60, 72–74, 79, 80, 81, 84, 99, 102, 115, 117–120, 147, 156, 163, 248, 255, 256
Qinghai 青海 241, 277, 280
Qingshi gao 情史稿 (Draft History of the Qing) 9, 10, 11
Qingtong jun 青童君 (Lord Azure Lad; Donghua dijun), also called Qinghua Xiaotong jun 青華小童君 (Lord Little Lad of Azure Florescence) 109, 110–112, 115, 123
Qingwei 清微 30, 64, 65, 79, 105–107, 125, 128
    and Baiyun guan 64–65
Qingyang gong 青羊宮 (Black Sheep Temple), Chengdu 26, 171, 192, 195, 275
Qiu Chuji 邱處機 (1148–1227) 12, 25, 28, 61–65, 67, 69–71, 73, 74, 77, 79, 81, 84, 93, 96, 98–100, 102, 103, 106, 107, 110, 113, 124–128, 144, 146, 147, 160, 164, 243, 290, 291
    as origin of xindeng 心燈 (mind lamp [transmission]) 63
    biography 63–64
Qiuzu quanshu 邱祖全書 (Complete Works of the Patriarch Qiu [Chuji]) 25
qixue 氣穴 (Cavity of Breath) 193
Qiyun shan 栖雲山 (mountain in Gansu province) 16, 17
Qu Shisi 瞿式耜 81
Qu Zhen 屈禎 (Han era appearance of Perfected Yin) 173

Quanzhen 全真 (Complete Perfection) tradition 7, 12–18, 30, 55–57, 59–61, 63, 64–70, 73, 76–82, 84, 85, 90, 95, 98, 105–113, 116, 119, 120, 122, 123, 125–128, 143, 144, 148, 152, 155, 164, 172, 182, 185, 190, 203, 226, 242, 243, 244, 247, 248, 288
    and roots of Longmen tradition 56
    and Wang Changyue 77
    Five Ancestors (wuzu 五祖) 61, 108
    generational names 69
    golden age in Yuan era 63, 243
    integrated many aspects of Zhengyi 7
    link of Longmen patriarchal line to Quanzhen's Northern lineage 61
    northern and southern lineages 172
    northern tradition 61, 65, 85, 95, 110, 119, 120, 123, 125–128, 172, 185, 190
    original meaning of term Quanzhen 152
    Qing era "renaissance" 56
    Quanzhen identity and Wang Changyue 77–78
    Quanzhen ritual text collection 30
    Quanzhen teachings and Zhengyi 77–78
    reevaluation from end of Ming era 55–56, 243–244
    Seven Perfected (qizhen 七真) 63, 70, 82, 113, 119, 164, 243
    Wang Changyue presented as unique heir 98
Qubilai Khan (Emperor Shizu, r. 1260–1293) 69, 74
Queen Mother of the West (西王母 Xiwangmu) 114, 208, 224, 230, 262
quietude 204, 208

R

rainmaking 9, 39, 81, 106, 174, 278
Rawski, Evelyn S. 34
recipe 16
Red Dragon 223, 224, 232, 234–236
Reichelt, Karl Ludwig 149, 244
Reiter, Florian 78, 109, 110, 111, 115, 116, 117, 119
religious organizations / associations 5, 33, 40, 41
rendao 人道 (path of men) 153, 176, 177
renmai 任脈 (Function Channel) 175
Renshousi 仁壽寺 (Temple of Humane Life), Beijing 23
revelation 36, 40, 112, 113, 153, 158, 165, 166, 168, 175, 180, 192, 195, 201, 269
ritual 5, 9–12, 18, 22, 30, 34, 35, 41, 72, 74, 78, 79, 81, 82, 88, 90, 106, 111, 117–122, 149, 161, 164, 174, 181, 187, 188, 226, 229, 240, 244, 248, 254, 273, 274, 280, 282, 283, 285, 286, 288
robe and bowl transmission 68, 69, 75, 87, 93, 99, 278, 288, 289
Robinet, Isabelle 4, 106, 109, 145, 150, 172, 174, 182, 183, 229, 232, 233, 273

Rol pa'i rdo rje (1717–1786) 241, 280, 285, 286
Rushi wo wen 如是我聞 [Thus I Have Heard] 207
ruzong shenjiao 儒宗神教 (Confucian spirit religions) 41

S

Sacred Edicts 34
Sakade, Yoshinobu 坂出祥伸 4, 55, 175, 278, 284
samādhi 104, 279
Sandan kaie 三檀戒會 (jap.; Triple-Platform Ordination Ceremony) 245
Sandong bizhi 三洞秘旨 (Secret Principles of the Three Vehicles) by Li Xiyue 19
Sanfeng danjue 三丰丹訣 (Sanfeng's Alchemical Formulas) 25
Sanfeng zhenren xuantan quanji 三丰真人玄譚全集 (Complete Collection of the Mysterious Words by the Perfected [Zhang] Sanfeng) 27, 206, 207
sangang wuchang 三綱五常 (three rules and five social relationships) 153
sangui yijie 三皈依戒 (three refuges: Dao, scriptures, master) 246
sanjiao heyi 三教合一 (unity of the three teachings) 6
sanni 三尼 (Three Sages: Confucius, Laozi, Buddha) 15, 161, 179, 180–182, 186, 201, 202, 262, 268, 269, 286
sanni yishi 三尼醫世 (the Three Sages' [Doctrine of] Healing the World) 15, 161, 179–183, 186, 187, 201, 202, 262, 268, 269, 286
Sanni yishi shuoshu 三尼醫世說述 272, 277, 286
Sanqing 三清 (Three Pure Ones) 71, 261
santan dajie 三壇大戒 (great precepts of the triple ordination platform) 149–153, 244–246, 287, 288
  and three-stage ordination in Buddhism 149
  in Buddhist and Daoist contexts 149–153
  in Wang Changyue's time used in Buddhist ordinations 244–246
  Wang Changyue's three-stage ordination 150–151
santang dajie 三堂大戒 (Great Precepts of the Triple Halls) 288
Santan yuanman tianxian dajie lüeshuo 三壇圓滿天仙大戒略說 151, 247
Sa Skya Pandita 240
Sawada, Mizuho 澤田瑞穗 37, 38
Schafer, Edward H. 31
Schipper, Kristofer 65, 150, 151, 246, 247
Schmidt-Glintzer, Helwig 254
Secret of the Golden Flower (*See Jinhua zongzhi* 金華宗旨)
sectarian groups and activities 6, 33, 36, 37, 40, 41, 42, 240
Seidel, Anna 69, 120–125, 127, 143, 180, 186, 242, 278, 279, 286–289
self-cultivation 17, 33, 60, 77, 78, 87, 128, 152, 165, 179, 254
semen 153, 235

seshen 色身 (body of form / passions) 151, 153, 155
sexual practices 205
Shaanxi province 12, 17, 63, 70, 71, 74, 76, 77, 78, 82, 83, 98, 127, 144, 243
shamanism 39, 40
Shambhala 285, 286
Shandong province 76, 80, 88, 98, 113, 116
Shangpin danfa jieci 上品丹法節次 [Alchemical Process of Superior Degree] 176–178, 199–200, 264
Shangqing 上清 10, 30, 31, 79, 109, 110, 111, 112, 113, 115, 119, 123, 124, 151, 156, 174, 182, 203, 247
Shangyang zi jindan dayao 上陽子金丹大要 118
Shanhaijing 山海經 (Book of Mountains and Seas) 273
shanshu 善書 (morality books) 36
Shanxi province 13, 16, 17, 77, 78, 90, 147, 240
Shao Shoushan 邵守善 96, 147
Shao Yizheng 邵以正 65, 66
Shao Yong 邵雍 (1011–1077) 201
Shao Zhilin 邵志林 (1748–1810) 166
shapan 砂盤 (spirit writing tray; planchette) 39
Shek, Richard 65
Shen Bingcheng 沈秉成 252, 267, 268
Shen Changjing 沈常靜 (1523–1633; Longmen Doctrinal line, seventh generation) 62, 146
Shen Donglao 沈東老 100
Shen Jingyuan 沈靜圓 (fl. 1448; fifth generation Longmen orthodox line; doctrinal line) 62, 78, 84, 85, 146, 148
Shen Qingyun 沈輕雲 (1708–1786) 262, 263, 266
Shen Weirong 沈衛榮 241
Shen Yangyi 沈陽一 201, 208
Shen Yibing 沈一炳 (1708–1786), 11th-generation Longmen patriarch 15, 26, 160, 161, 163, 181, 202, 203, 204, 208, 209, 262
   texts associated with this author 262
Shen Zhaoding 申兆定 (fl. 1764) 17, 102
shengtai 聖胎 (Holy Embryo) 194, 196, 197
Shengyu guangxun 聖語廣訓 (Extensive Explanation of the "Sacred Edict") 34
shenjiao 神教 ("spirit religions") 41
Shenshi bafa 神室八法 (Eight Elements of the Spiritual Abode) 29
Shenxianzhuan 神仙傳 112, 123
Shenxiao 神霄 legacy 117, 120, 122
Shiga, Ichiko 志賀市子 41

Shinohara, Kōichi 90
Shi Shouping 施守平 147
Shi Tai 石泰 (d. 1158) 116
Shishi yuanliu yinghua shiji 釋氏源流應化事蹟 245
Shiva 169
Shizong 世宗 (emperor, re. 1722–1735) 8, 11
Shizu 世祖 (emperor, r. 1260–1293) 8, 69, 73, 74, 93, 111
shoujie 受戒 (taking the precepts) 13, 84, 143, 242
shoujie zhe 受戒者 (ordained priests) 13
shouzhong 守中 (guarding the center) 23, 207
Shunzhi 順治 (emperor, re. 1644–1661) 8, 289
Sichuan province 18, 19, 20, 21, 30, 57, 71, 77, 78, 103, 104, 112, 113, 114, 120, 121, 126, 127, 144, 147, 156, 195, 243, 248, 255, 275, 280
Siku quanshu 四庫全書 (Complete Books in Four Repositories) 11, 284
sīla (jie 戒, discipline) 151, 152, 153, 169, 189
Silk Road 277
Skar, Lowell 74, 78, 79, 85, 117–119, 145, 172, 174
Smith, Richard 5, 35, 39
spirit mediums 37
spirit possession 39
spirit writing, or planchette writing (fuji 扶乩) 6, 7, 20–22, 38–41, 157, 163–167, 180, 185, 188, 191, 201, 208
    by Qing era literati 40–41
    importance of practices and scriptures 39–41
    origins 39
    planchette 39, 40, 164
    technique and instruments 39
    spirit-writing scriptures as basis for new sects 38, 40
standardization 5, 7, 13, 30, 34, 35, 55, 144
state 5, 6, 7, 11, 34, 35, 37, 57, 74, 82, 85, 86, 90, 96, 99, 101, 124, 145, 155, 165, 176, 177, 194, 195, 197, 223, 232, 241, 254, 260, 268, 280, 283, 285
Strickmann, Michel 117, 175, 180, 182, 186, 278, 284
Sun Xuanqing 孫玄清 (1497–1563; Laoshan line) 62, 79, 80–82, 98
Sun Zongwu 孫宗武 (fl. 1651) 71
Suoyan xu 瑣言續 (Sequel to an Ignored Transmission) 26, 209–210, 262, 264
sūtra-recitation 37, 38
Suzuki, Chūsei 鈴木中正 279
Swan, Nancy Lee 58
syncretism 24, 33, 34, 41, 172, 240

T

taboo character 68
Taichang leyuan 太常樂員 (Music master) 11
Taihe zhenren 太和真人 (Perfected Taihe) 80
Taiji tu 太極圖 (Chart of the Great Ultimate) 95, 147
Taiping guangji 太平廣記 112, 119
Taiqing gong 太清宮 (Longmen abbey in Shenyang 沈陽, Liaoning) 58, 252
Taiseikyū shi 太清宮志 (ch. Taiqing gong zhi; Gazetteer of the Taiqing gong) 58, 253
Taishang ganyin pian 太上感應篇 (Treatise on Retribution of the Most High) 36
Taishang Laojun jiejing 太上老君戒經 150, 246
Taiwan 41, 64, 164
Taiyi jinhua zongzhi 太一金華宗旨 (Secret of the Golden Flower) *See* Jinhua zongzhi
talismans 10, 40, 72, 78, 121, 122, 164, 174
tan 壇 (platform; ordination platform) 149, 244
Tanaka, Kimiaki 田中公明 285
Tang Dachao 唐大潮 42
Tang Gongfang 唐公昉 112
Tantric yoga 175
Tantrism 15, 27, 80, 156, 161, 163, 170, 171, 175, 180, 182, 186–188, 190, 205, 227, 228, 233, 239, 240, 255, 256, 268, 271, 272, 277, 278, 279, 282, 284–286, 291
Tao Hongjing 陶宏景 97, 109
Tao Jing'an 陶靖菴 (1612–1673; founder of Mt. Jingai branch of Longmen) 145, 156, 157, 158, 162, 164, 167, 263
Tao Shi'an 陶石庵 91, 158, 159, 162, 166, 180, 181, 187, 201, 269
Taylor, Romeyn 6
ter Haar, Barend J. 37, 38, 69
testicles 235, 236
Three Jewels (Dao, sacred scriptures, and master) 150
three passes (sanguan 三關) 196
three-stage ordination / precepts 77, 99, 149, 151, 178, 179, 187, 189
three teachings (Confucianism, Buddhism, Daoism) 6, 10, 11, 13, 17, 19, 28, 29, 33–34, 90, 92, 95, 181, 185, 186, 241, 262, 264, 269
  and Confucian elite 33–34
thunder rites (leifa 雷法) 10, 18, 100, 106, 117–120, 122, 181
Tianchang guan 天常觀 (Abbey of Celestial Endurance, Beijing) 63

tiangui 天癸 (Celestial Water) 229, 230, 231, 235
Tianhou 天后 (Empress of Heaven = Mazu 媽祖) 35
tianmu 天目 (celestial eye) 169, 170
Tianshang shengmu 天上聖母 (Heavenly Saintly Mother = Mazu 媽祖) 35
Tiantai shan 天台山 (mountain in Zhejiang province) 15, 86, 87, 88, 89, 90, 101, 127, 156, 160, 191, 257–259, 261
tianxian 天仙 (celestial immortal; celestial immortality) 150, 178, 200
tianxian (da)jie 天仙(大)戒 (great precepts of celestial immortals) 14, 68, 69, 93, 151, 183, 247, 288
Tianxian daocheng baoze 天仙道程寶則 [Precious Principles for the Path to Celestial Immortality] 183, 204, 262
Tianxian dao jieji xuzhi 天仙道戒忌須知 [Required Knowledge on Precepts and Prohibitions for the Path to Celestial Immortality] 183, 204, 262
Tianxian xinchuan 天仙心傳 [Mind-to-Mind Transmission of Celestial Immortality] 26, 181, 182, 183, 203, 262, 264
Tianxian zhengli 天仙正理 (Proper Principles of Celestial Immortality) by Wu Shouyang 18, 22, 101, 102, 103, 106
Tianxian zhilun 天仙值論 (Forthright Discourses on Celestial Immortality) 25
tianxin 天心 (celestial heart-mind) 170, 172, 193
Tiaoxi 苕溪 (Zhejiang) 86
tiaoxin 調心 (regulation of mind) 198, 209
Tibet
    A mdo region 241, 277, 280
    Kham region 280
Tibetan Buddhism 5, 240, 241, 269, 279, 280
    at Mt. Wutai (Shanxi) 240–241
    Dalai Lama 240, 241
    dGe lugs pa 5, 11, 240, 241, 285
    dGe lugs pa accepted by emperor Gaozong as state religion 11
    influence on Chinese court from Yuan era 240
    Tibetan Tripitaka 280
Tiecha shan 鐵查山 (mountain in Shandong) 80
    Yunguang dong 雲光洞 80
Tongbai gong 桐柏宮 (Cypress Temple, in Tiantai mountain range, Zhejiang) 15, 156, 257–261, 265, 268
Tongbai shan 桐柏山 (mountain in Tiantai, Zhejiang) 15, 89, 156, 160, 257–261, 265, 266, 268
Tongguan wen 通關文 (Treatise on Going through the Passes) 28
Tongyuan zi 通源子 (master of Sun Xuanqing) 80, 81
Tongzhi 同治 (emperor / reign 1861–1875) 8
transcendence 23

transmission 14, 19, 31, 36, 42, 63, 68–70, 76–79, 83, 84, 87–90, 93, 95, 96, 99, 102–107, 111, 116, 118, 123, 126, 127, 157–159, 161–164, 166–171, 180, 181, 185, 186, 188, 207, 209, 252, 254, 262, 264, 269, 271, 274, 277–279, 282–291
transmission of robe / robe and bowl *See* robe and bowl transmission
transmission of the registers 287
Tsui, Bartholomew P.M. 41
tuna 吐呐 (breathing techniques) 174
Tuttle, Gray 241, 286
Twelve Immortals 120, 121

U

uniformity 6, 34, 35, 144
universal salvation 165, 184–187, 191, 195, 206
uterus 229

V

van der Kuijp, Leonard 285
Vasu[n]dhārā-dhāranī (Foshuo chishi tuoluoni jing 佛說持世陀羅尼經) 15, 27
Vercammen, Dany 42
Verellen, Franciscus 305
vinaya 59, 62, 66, 68, 75, 76, 83–85, 87–89, 94, 96, 99, 100, 104, 124–126, 129, 146–149, 157–160, 162, 163, 166, 167, 171, 181, 183, 188, 244, 249, 257, 271, 272, 274, 287, 289, 290
Vinaya regulations 62, 88, 146
Vinaya transmission 83, 84, 87

W

Wädow, Gerd 35
Waley, Arthur 63, 70, 243
wall-meditation 104
Wang Bangwei 王邦維 279
Wang Changyue
Wang Changyue 王常月 (?-1680) 12–14, 17, 18, 27, 41, 42, 56, 59, 61, 62, 65, 71, 77, 85, 88–92, 94–103, 110, 124–126, 128, 144–150, 154–165, 167–173, 176–179, 183–185, 187–190, 208, 244, 247–249, 252, 253, 271–274, 287–291
  and the establishment of a Longmen official lineage 100
  as guoshi 國師 (National Instructor) 125
  Baoyi gaoshi 抱一高師 (posthumous title) 14, 96, 155

biographical sources 147
  biography 13–15, 90–99, 147–149
  central role in reorganization of Daoist discipline 144–145
  compromise between Quanzhen rigor and Confucian rules 14
  conciliation with Neo-Confucian orthodoxy 154–155
  Confucian self-education and Buddhist soteriology 153–155
  controversial date of birth 147
  division of Daoist precepts into three stages 14
  establishment of Longmen lineage 14–15
  harmonizing lay and monastic status 154–155
  inspired by Chan Buddhism 144–145, 151–153
  jie 戒 (precepts) as key of his teaching 149–151
  Longmen founder/reformer and his teachings 147–155
  Longmen ordination program 244–247
  meeting with Tao Jing'an in 1688, fictitious 167
  reincarnation as Qiaoyang 124–125
  reorganized Daoist religious precepts 14
  spread of Longmen teachings throughout China 14–15
Wang Changyue, attributed works
  Biyuan tanjing 碧苑壇經 (Platform Sūtra of the Jade Garden) 14
  Bojian 缽鑑 (Examination of the Bowl) 14
  Chuzhen jielü 初真戒律 (Precepts of Initial Perfection) 14
  Nüzhen jiujie 女真九戒 (Nine Precepts for Women Perfected) 14
Wang Chuyi 王處一 32, 80
Wang Dingqian 王定乾 11
Wang Kunyang 王崑陽. *See* Wang Changyue 王常月
Wang Kunyang lüshi zhuan (Biography of Vinaya Master Wang Changyue) 王崑陽律師傳 91
Wang Kunyang zhuan 王崑陽傳 (Biography of Wang Changyue) 91
Wang Laiyang 王萊陽 71, 73
Wang Qiaoyang 王樵陽 94
Wang Qingzheng 王清正 (fl. 1651; Huashan line) 62, 71, 72, 97, 99
Wang Shouzhen 王守真 (714–789) 117
Wang Wenqing 王文卿 (1093–1153) 117
Wang, Xiangyun 241, 285
Wang Xuanfu 王玄甫 (Donghua dijun) 109, 110, 111, 113, 116, 117, 119, 120
Wang Yangming 王陽明 33, 180, 201
Wang Yao 王遙 (immortal of Song era) 71, 74
Wang Zhenchang 汪真常 105
Wang Zhizhong 王志忠 60, 70, 73, 84, 144, 243
Wangdiao dong 王刁洞 (Huashan) 73, 74
Wangdiao dong 王刁洞 (Longmen) 73, 74

Wangwu shan 王屋山 (mountain in Henan province) 13, 17, 89, 90, 91, 95, 98, 101, 147
    Celestial Grotto of Pure Emptiness 89
Wanyan Chongshi 完顏崇實 91
Ware, James 120
Watson, L. James 35
Wei Boyang 魏伯陽 209
Wei Fuyi 衛富益 163
Wei Hanjin 魏漢津 117
Wei Huacun 魏華存 31, 182
Wei Zhending 衛眞定 (1441–1645?; Longmen Doctrinal line) 62, 146
Wei Zhengjie 衛正節 159
Welch, Holmes H. 55, 69, 143, 148, 162, 242, 243, 245, 278, 287
Welter, Albert 89, 96, 254
Wenchang 文昌 40, 182
Western School, also known as Yinxian pai 隱仙派 (Hidden Immortal School) or Youlong pai 猶龍派 (Like Unto a Dragon School) 18, 19
White Lotus 白蓮 movement 33, 37, 38, 69
White, David 228, 233
Wile, Douglas 20, 26, 145, 177, 184, 223, 224, 226, 229
Wilhelm, Richard 18, 19, 23, 165
Wong, Eva 18, 23
Wong, Shiu Hon 18, 21, 42
Wright, Dale S. 76, 96, 254
Wu Chongxu lüshi zhuan 伍沖虛律詩傳 (Biography of Vinaya Master Wu) 100
Wu-Liu 伍柳 School 7, 17, 18, 25
Wu Liu xianzong 伍柳仙宗 (Immortality Teachings of Wu and Liu) 18, 22, 22–24, 23
Wu Shouxu 伍守虛 23, 62, 101, 102, 103, 104, 105
Wu Shouyang 伍守陽 (ab. 1552–1641) 17–18, 22, 23, 25, 41, 62, 66, 81, 100–104, 106, 107, 113, 120, 146, 181
    association with Longmen 17–18
    biography 17–18
    biography and lineage 100–104
    works 18
Wu zhenren dandao jiupian 伍真人丹道九篇 (Nine Chapters on the Alchemical Path by the Perfected Wu) by Wu Shouyang 18, 102
Wudang shan 武當山 (Mt. Wudang) 17, 62, 66, 89, 90, 99, 103, 105–107, 129
    Wudang shan line 62, 66
Wudao lu 悟道錄 (Record of Awakening to the Path) by Liu Yiming 16, 29

Wugen shu 無根樹 (Tree Without Roots), attributed to Zhang Sanfeng 19
Wugen shujie 無根樹解 (Explanation of "The Tree Without Roots") by Liu Yiming 16
wulei fa 五雷法 (*See* Five Thunders rite)
Wuling 武陵 (Hangzhou) 101
Wulong (Five Dragons) school of Daoism 105
Wusheng laomu 無生老母 (Eternal Venerable Mother) 37, 38, 41
Wutai shan 五臺山 (mountain in Shanxi province) 240, 241
Wuwei jiao 無為教 (Nonaction Religion), also Luojiao 羅教 (Teaching of Luo) 37
wuwei 無為 (non-action) 264
wuyue zhenxing tu 五岳真形圖 (Chart-Talisman of the True Form of the Five Peaks) 261
Wuzhen pian 悟真篇 174, 183, 202, 210, 211, 258
Wuzhen zhizhi 悟真直指 (Direct Pointers to "Awakening to Perfection") 28

X

xiandao 仙道 (path of immortals) 154, 176, 177
Xianfeng 咸豐 (emperor / reign 1850–1861) 8
Xianfo hezong yulu 仙佛合宗語錄 (Recorded Sayings on the Common Tradition of Daoism and Buddhism) 17, 23, 101–104
Xianfo tongyuan 仙佛同源 (Common Origins of Daoism and Buddhism) 23
xiang'an 香案 (spirit writing table) 39
Xiangyan poyi 象言破疑 (Resolving Symbolic Language) 28, 231
Xianliu zhangren 仙留丈人 (Elder Remaining Immortal) 17
xianshi 仙師 (immortal master) 154
xiantian 先天 (before Heaven) 165, 176, 177, 191, 194, 197, 229, 232, 236, 274, 283, 284
xiaocheng 小乘 (small vehicle) 152
xiaodao 小道 (small path) 152
xiao zhoutian 小周天 (microcosmic orbit) 19, 177, 194, 237
Xiaoyao shan wanshou gong zhi 逍遙山萬壽宮志 (Gazetteer of the Palace of Longevity on Mount Xiaoyao) 20, 32
Xie Chonggen 謝崇根 (?-1984) 259, 260, 265
Xie tianji 泄天機 (Disclosing the Celestial Mechanism) 174, 175, 176, 196, 197, 207, 264
xin jietang 新戒堂 (ordinands' hall) 287
xinchuan 心傳 (mind-to-mind transmission) 59, 169–171, 181–183, 185, 203, 249, 256, 262, 264

Xingming guizhi 性命圭旨 173, 192

xingming shuangxiu 性命雙修 (joint cultivation of nature and vital force) 171–173, 211

Xingtian zhenggu 性天正鵠 (Striking the Center of Celestial Nature's Target) 24

Xinjiang 271

Xinxue 心學 (Study of the Heart-Mind) 24

Xinye 新野 (Hebei) 67

Xinyin ji jing 心印集經 180, 269

Xishan 西山 (mountain in Jiangxi province) 20, 32, 99, 101, 104, 107

Xiuxian bianhuo lun 修仙辨惑論 (On Doubts Concerning the Cultivation of Immortality) by Bai Yuchan 白玉蟾 26, 178, 200

Xiuzhen biannan 修真辯難 (Debate on the Cultivation of Perfection) by Liu Yiming 劉一明 26, 29, 210, 273

Xiuzhen biannan qianhou bian canzheng 修真辯難前後編參証 (Annotations to the Debate on the Cultivation of Perfection in Two Sections) description and content 210–211

Xiuzhen jiuyao 修真九要 (Nine Principles in the Cultivation of Perfection) 28, 29

Xiuzhen shishu 修真十書 (Ten Books on the Cultivation of Perfection) 22

Xiwang mu 西王母 (Queen Mother of the West) 109, 114–116, 184, 225, 226, 229, 230, 271

Xiwang mu nüxiu zhengtu shize 西王母女修正途十則 [Ten Rules of the Queen Mother of the West on the Correct Path of Female Cultivation] 208, 224, 262

Xiyou yuanzhi 西遊原旨 (The Original Meaning of the "Journey to the West") 28

Xiyouji 西遊記 (Journey to the West) 28

Xiyue huashan zhi 西嶽華山志 (Gazetteer of Mount Hua, the Western Peak) 32

Xizhu xinzong 西竺心宗 (Mind School of India) 15, 80, 156, 161, 163, 171, 205, 289

Xu Shouchen 徐守誠 (1632–1692) 20

Xu Sun 許遜 209

Xu Xun 許遜 32

Xu, Dishan 39, 40

Xuanjiao da gong'an 玄教大公案 118

xuanmen 玄門 (mysterious teaching) 67, 182

Xuantong 宣統 (emperor / reign 1908–1911) 8

Xuanyunzhou 玄蘊咒 (Spell of the Arcane Aggregates) 203

Xuanzang 玄奘 (600–664) 279, 283, 284
Xue Xinxiang 薛心香 209

Y

Yamada, Toshiaki 山田利明 112, 119, 151
Yanagida, Seizan 柳田聖山 128, 254
Yan Duanshu 晏端書 (biographer of Min Yide) 257
Yan Xiyan 閻希言 (?-1588) 99
Yan Yanfeng 嚴雁峰 (1855–1918) 21
Yan Yonghe 閻永和 219
yanbo 演缽 287, 288
    and transmission of robe and bowl in Chan Buddhism 288
yanbotang 演缽堂 (Hall of Performing the Bowl) 287, 291
Yang Cihu 養雌虎 (1141–1226) 201
Yang Shen'an 揚慎菴 59, 249
Yang Weikun 揚維崑 265, 266, 268
Yang, C.K. 5, 6
yangsheng 養生 198, 205, 264
Yangshi yilin 揚氏逸林 (Circle of Recluses) 59, 69, 249
Yangzi river 30, 121, 206
Yao Shu 姚樞 73
Yao Tao-chung 63, 108, 152, 243
Yau, Chi-on 36, 40
Ye Gaoxing 葉高行 (abbess of Tongbai gong) 259, 260, 261, 265
Yedaposhe 野怛婆闍 (*See* Jizu daozhe)
Yellow Emperor (Huangdi 黃帝) 180, 181, 185, 187
Yellow Path 174–176, 178, 179, 185, 187, 189, 193
Yijing 易經 27, 39, 174, 175, 197, 210
Yin Pengtou 尹蓬頭 (Yin zhenren 尹真人, Perfected Yin) 26, 97, 171–176, 189, 190, 192, 195
    and Longmen of Mt. Jingai 173–176
    Qu Zhen 屈禛 (Han era appearance of Perfected Yin) 173
Yin Xi 尹喜 (guardian of the pass) 108, 118, 123, 173
Yin zhenren Donghua zhengmai huangji hepi zhengdao xianjing 尹真人東華正脈皇極闔闢證道仙經 (Immortals' Scripture of the Perfected Yin Testifying to the Path of Opening and Closing the Sovereign Ultimate according to the Orthodox Lineage of the Eastern Efflorescence) 26, 147, 164, 171–174, 178–180, 184, 185, 189, 192–195, 264, 289

Yin zhenren Liaoyang dian wenda bian 尹真人廖陽殿問答編 (Questions and Answers of the Perfected Yin from the Liaoyang Hall) 195–196

Yin Zhiping 尹志平 (1169–1251; disciple of Qiu Chuji) 64

Yinfujing 陰符經 (Scripture on Joining with Obscurity) by Li Quan 李筌 26, 28, 210

Yinxian an 隱仙庵 (Hermitage of the Recluse Immortal) 97

Yinxian pai 隱仙派 (Hidden Immortal School); *see also* Western School 18

Yinyuan Longji 隱元隆琦 (Jap. Ingen Ryūki, 1592–1673) 246

yishi 醫世 (healing the world) 15, 26, 161, 168, 171, 179–182, 184–187, 191, 192, 195, 201, 202, 208, 262, 268, 269, 272, 277, 286, 289

Yishi shuoshu 醫世說述 286, 289, 290, 291

yixin chuanxin 以心傳心 (mind-to-mind transmission) 252

yizi sandian 伊字三點 (three-dot symbol) 169

Yoga 145, 205, 223, 224, 226, 229, 237

Yokote, Hiroshi 18, 19

Yokote, Yutaka 横手裕 116, 118, 172

Yongming Yanshou 永明延壽 (904–975) 89

Yongzheng literary inquisition (1772–88) 10–11

Yongzheng 雍正 (emperor, re. 1722–1735) 6, 8, 10, 34, 258

Yoritomi, Motohiro 頼富本宏 175, 284

Yoshioka, Yoshitoyo 吉岡義豊 13, 21, 56, 59, 69, 99, 110, 112, 143, 148, 174, 182, 242, 247–249, 289

Youlong pai 猶龍派 (Like Unto a Dragon School); see also Western School 18

youwei 有為 (action) 264

Yü Chun-fang 155

Yu Lin Fenqian xiansheng shu 與林奮千先生書 (Letter to Master Lin Fenqian) 27, 178, 201

Yu, Anthony C. 28

Yuan dynasty (1281–1367) 12, 19, 61, 63, 64, 77, 80–82, 85, 105, 111, 116, 118, 123, 126, 143, 160, 161, 163, 240, 243, 271, 280, 283

Yuan Mingshan 元明善 (1269–1322) 30

Yuan Ting 袁挺 200

yuanqi 元氣 (original Qi) 230, 231, 235

yuanxi 原息 (original breathing) 260

Yuezhi 月支／月氏 161, 271, 272, 273, 277, 278, 282, 283

Yuhang 餘杭 (modern Hangzhou) 58, 86, 249

yulu 語錄 (Recorded Sayings) 11, 17, 23, 24, 59, 101, 102, 103, 104, 152, 249

Yunji qiqian 雲笈七籤 (Seven Tablets in a Cloudy Satchel) 22

Yunnan 15, 101, 156, 161, 205, 262, 263, 269, 270, 272, 273, 274, 278, 279, 280, 289

Yuxuan miaozheng zhenren yulu 御選妙正真人語錄 (Imperially Selected Recorded Sayings of the Perfected of Mysterious Orthodoxy) 11
yuye 玉液 (jade liquid) 19
Yuzhi Man Han Mengu Xifan hebi dazang quanzhou 禦製滿漢蒙古西番合璧大藏全咒 284
Yuzhong 榆中 (Gansu province) 16, 17

Z

Zagua zhuan 雜卦傳 (Commentary on Miscellaneous Hexagrams) 27
Zangwai daoshu 藏外道書 (Daoist scriptures not contained in the Daoist Canon) 14, 20, 55, 147, 242, 244, 246, 247, 249, 255, 256, 263–269, 273, 283, 286, 289
Zeng Zhaonan 曾召南 60, 84
zhan chilong 斬赤龍 (slaying of the Red Dragon) 208, 224, 232, 234
Zhan Shouchun 詹守椿 96, 147
Zhang Bixu 張碧虛 25
Zhang Bizhi lüshi zhuan 張碧芝律師傳 75
Zhang Boduan 張佰端 (ca. 983-ca. 1082) 26, 116, 119, 160, 209, 258, 260
Zhang Daoling 張道陵 31, 113, 117, 123
Zhang Dechun 張德純 (fl.1312–1367; Longmen Vinaya line, second generation) 62, 67, 75–77, 127, 146
Zhang Fuchun 張復純 32
Zhang Guolao 張果老 (one of the Eight Immortals) 109
Zhang Hongren 張洪仁 (1624–1667; 53rd Celestial Master) 9
Zhang Jiebin 張介賓 (1563–1640) 230, 235
Zhang Jingding 張静定 (fl. 1450; fifth generation Longmen Vinaya line) 62, 84, 86–89, 146, 148
Zhang Jingxu 張静虛 (b. 1432?; Wudangshan line) 17, 62, 102–106
Zhang Jizong 張繼宗 (1666–1715; 54th generation Celestial Master) 9
Zhang Mayi 張麻衣 91, 95, 96, 147
Zhang Pengtou 張蓬頭 80, 81
Zhang Pihu 張皮虎. *See* Zhang Jingxu
Zhang Qilong 張起隆 (58th generation Celestial Master) 11
Zhang Sanfeng 張三丰 16, 19, 25, 27, 42, 206, 230
Zhang Sanfeng quanji 張三丰全集 (Complete Works of Zhang Sanfeng) 19, 230
Zhang Suqing 張素卿 (ca. 845-ca. 957) 113, 120, 121
Zhang Taixu 張太虛 11
Zhang Wuwo lüshi zhuan 張無我律師傳 86

Zhang Xilin 張錫麟 (55th generation Celestial Master) 9, 10, 31
Zhang Yingjing 張應京 (52nd generation Celestial Master) 9
Zhang Yu 張鈺 (59th generation of Celestial Masters) 11
Zhang Yuchu 張宇初 (43rd generation Celestial Master) 30, 65, 78
Zhao Daojian 趙道堅 (1163–1221; Longmen Vinaya line, first generation) 62, 63, 67–70, 75, 79, 99, 103, 146
Zhao Fuyang 趙復陽 13, 17, 88, 91, 93, 95
Zhao Fuyang lüshi zhuan 趙復陽律師傳 88
Zhao Sheng 趙昇 (disciple of Zhang Daoling) 116, 117
Zhao Xujing lüshi zhuan 趙虛靜律師傳 63, 67, 68, 69
Zhao Youqin 趙友欽 (fl. 1329) 23
Zhao Zhensong 趙真嵩 (fl. 1522/1628?; Longmen Vinaya line, sixth generation) 62, 87, 88–91, 95, 96, 101, 146, 147
Zhejiang 15, 22, 58, 85, 86, 88–90, 100, 112, 121, 127, 145, 156, 159, 160, 163, 173, 190, 249, 250, 257, 258, 268
Zhengyi 正一 (Orthodox Unity) 7, 9, 11, 12, 19, 31, 55, 56, 64, 65, 76–79, 82, 90, 105–107, 125–128, 161, 243, 246, 262
  and Baiyun guan 64–65
  and Quanzhen / Longmen 77–79
zhengzong liuchuan 正宗流傳 (orthodox transmission) 63
zhenren 真人 (perfect master; perfected) 65, 165
zhenwo 真我 (True Self) 230
zhenxing 真性 (true nature) 153, 261
zhenyi 真意 (true intention) 23, 151, 197
zhinian 止念 (stopping of thought) 209
Zhiyi lu 質疑錄 230, 235
zhongji jie 中極戒 (intermediate precepts) 14, 68, 151, 177, 247
Zhongli Quan 鍾離權 108, 116, 117, 118
Zhongnan mountains 115
Zhou Dajing 周大經 10
Zhou Mingyang 周明陽 (1628–1711) 32, 157, 257
Zhou Tailang 周太朗 (1628–1711; united Longmen Doctrinal & Vinaya lines) 62, 146
Zhou Xuanpu 周玄朴 (fl. 1450?; fourth generation Longmen Vinaya line) 62, 77, 78, 82–85, 87, 146, 148
Zhouyi chanzhen 周易闡真 (True Explanation of the "Changes") 27
Zhu Changchun 朱常淳 18
Zhu Cikui 朱慈煃 (see also Prince Ji) 18, 101
Zhu Taihe 朱太和 (1562–1622) 62, 146
Zhu Wenzao 朱文藻 32

Zhu Youlian 朱由練 (d. 1635) 18
Zhuangzi 莊子 (Nanhuajing) 11, 92
Zhuangzi commentary
    Nanhua jingzhu 南華經注 (by Lou Jinyuan) 11, 92
Zhuzhen zongpai zongbu 諸真宗派總簿 (Comprehensive Register of All Genuine Lineages) 13
zipu 字譜 (ideogram genealogy) 13
ziran 自然 (self-so) 211
Ziti suohua 自題所畫 (Painting Inscriptions) 24
Zito, Angela 34
Zizai wo 自在窩 (Nest of Freedom) on Mt. Qiyun (Gansu) 17
zongshi 宗師 (doctrinal master) 59, 84, 85, 148, 162, 249
zongtan 宗壇 162, 163, 185, 188
Zongyang gong 宗陽宮 (Hangzhou) 158, 159, 167
zuobo 坐缽 (collective meditation) 82, 288
Zuobo tang 坐缽堂 (Hall of Sitting around the Bowl-clepsydra) 80, 288
zuochan 坐禪 (Jap. zazen; seated meditation) 261

Other Books by Monica Esposito

Creative Daoism
Wil / Paris: UniversityMedia, 2013. 392 p. ISBN 978-3-906000-04-6 (hardcover)
Wil / Paris: UniversityMedia, 2016. 400 p. ISBN 978-3-906000-05-3 (paperback)

Just as Christianity has its Vatican in Rome, modern Daoism boasts of a unique center of religious authority and administration: the Temple of the White Clouds (Baiyun guan) in Beijing, today the seat of the general headquarters of the Chinese Daoist Association. Monica Esposito describes in this book how Daoist masters and historiographers in China, much like their Catholic counterparts in Europe, invented a glorious patriarchal lineage as well as a system of ordination designed to perpetuate orthodox transmission and central control. They also created a kind of New Testament: a new canonical collection of scriptures entitled "The Essence of the Daoist Canon" (*Daozang jiyao*). This book presents the gist of twenty-five years of research on pre-modern and modern Daoism. Its four parts throw new light on the history, historiography, scriptures, and doctrines of Qing Daoism.

The Zen of Tantra
Wil / Paris: UniversityMedia, 2013. 179 p. ISBN 978-3-906000-25-1 (paperback)

Tibetan Buddhism has a long history in China. Various forms of it were practiced and promoted since the Yuan dynasty (1271-1368), and during the Qing dynasty (1644-1911) it was at times even China's state religion. But the teachings and practices of Tibetan Buddhism known as Great Perfection (Dzogs chen) are only now becoming more widely known. On a journey to an old Daoist site on the Celestial Eye mountains (Mt. Tianmu, Zhejiang) in 1988, Dr. Esposito discovered a thriving community of Buddhist nuns in a monastery founded and headed by the Chan (Chinese Zen) and Dzogs chen master Fahai Lama (1920-1991). In documenting this man's life and teachings as well as daily life at his monastery in text and photographs, this book offers a unique glimpse into the reception of Tibetan Buddhist teachings in a nunnery in modern Communist China.

La Porte du Dragon—*L'école Longmen du Mont Jin'gai et ses pratiques alchimiques d'après le Daozang xubian*

Vol. 1: ISBN 978-3-906000-15-2, PDF. Free download at www.universitymedia.org.
Vol. 2: ISBN 978-3-906000-16-9, PDF. Free download at www.universitymedia.org.

Monica Esposito's hitherto unpublished two-volume Ph.D. thesis (University Paris VII, 1993). Searchable PDF format with embedded index and English bookmarks. Includes the original text as well as the author's handwritten corrections and notes.

www.ingramcontent.com/pod-product-compliance
Lightning Source LLC
Chambersburg PA
CBHW021148230426
43667CB00006B/302